THE BLACKWELL ENCYCLOPEDIA OF SOCIOLOGY

The Blackwell Encyclopedia of Sociology

Volume I

A–B

Edited by

George Ritzer

Blackwell
Publishing

© 2007 by Blackwell Publishing Ltd

BLACKWELL PUBLISHING
350 Main Street, Malden, MA 02148-5020, USA
9600 Garsington Road, Oxford OX4 2DQ, UK
550 Swanston Street, Carlton, Victoria 3053, Australia

First published 2007 by Blackwell Publishing Ltd

1   2007

Library of Congress Cataloging-in-Publication Data

Blackwell encyclopedia of sociology, the / edited by George Ritzer.
   p. cm.
Includes bibliographical references and index.
ISBN 1-4051-2433-4 (hardback : alk. paper) 1. Sociology—Encyclopedias. I. Ritzer, George.

HM425.B53 2007
301.03—dc22

                                                        2006004167

ISBN-13: 978-1-4051-2433-1 (hardback : alk. paper)

A catalogue record for this title is available from the British Library.

Set in 9.5/11pt Ehrhardt
by Spi Publisher Services, Pondicherry, India
Printed in Singapore
by COS Printers Pte Ltd

The publisher's policy is to use permanent paper from mills that operate a sustainable forestry policy, and which has been manufactured from pulp processed using acid-free and elementary chlorine-free practices. Furthermore, the publisher ensures that the text paper and cover board used have met acceptable environmental accreditation standards.

For further information on
Blackwell Publishing, visit our website:
www.blackwellpublishing.com

Contents

About the Editor and Managing Editors

EDITOR

George Ritzer is Distinguished University Professor at the University of Maryland. Among his awards: Honorary Doctorate from La Trobe University, Melbourne, Australia; Honorary Patron, University Philosophical Society, Trinity College, Dublin; American Sociological Association's Distinguished Contribution to Teaching Award. He has chaired the American Sociological Association's Section on Theoretical Sociology, as well as the Section on Organizations and Occupations. Among his books in metatheory are *Sociology: A Multiple Paradigm Science* and *Metatheorizing in Sociology*. In the application of social theory to the social world, his books include *The McDonaldization of Society*, *Enchanting a Disenchanted World*, and *The Globalization of Nothing*. He has published two volumes of his collected works, one in theory and the other in the application of theory to the social world, especially consumption. In the latter area, he is founding editor of the *Journal of Consumer Culture*. He has edited the *Blackwell Companion to Major Social Theorists* and co-edited the *Handbook of Social Theory*. In addition to the *Encyclopedia of Sociology*, he has edited the two-volume *Encyclopedia of Social Theory*. His books have been translated into over 20 languages, with over a dozen translations of *The McDonaldization of Society* alone.

SENIOR MANAGING EDITOR

J. Michael Ryan is a PhD candidate in sociology at the University of Maryland. His dissertation will focus on the fusion of emerging new urban and consumer landscapes. He has contributed to two other encyclopedias, *The Encyclopedia of Social Theory* and *Great Events in History: The LGBT Series*. He currently serves as Managing Editor of the *Journal of Consumer Culture* as well as listserv manager for the Consumer Studies Research Network. His awards include the UMD 2004 LGBT Award for Outstanding Leadership and Community Advocacy as well as a C. Wright Mills fellowship. His other publications with George Ritzer include "Toward a Richer Understanding of Global Commodification: Glocalization and Grobalization," *Hedgehog Review* 5 (2) and "Transformations in Consumer Settings: Landscapes and Beyond" (also with Jeff Stepnisky) in *Inside Consumption*, edited by R. Ratneshwar and David Mick.

ASSISTANT MANAGING EDITOR

Betsy Thorn is a doctoral student in Sociology at the University of Maryland. Her interests include social theory and the sociology of the family. Her recent work includes a master's thesis that applies Pierre Bourdieu's theory to a qualitative analysis of women's roles as consumers and in the labor force in the post-war era, as well as quantitative analyses of time-use patterns within the family. Her awards include a C. Wright Mills fellowship.

Advisory Editors

Rebecca G. Adams is Professor of Sociology at the University of North Carolina at Greensboro. Her publications include: *Deadhead Social Science* (2000), *Placing Friendship in Context* (1998), *Adult Friendship* (1992), and *Older Adult Friendship: Structure and Process* (1989). A Past President of the Southern Sociological Society and Fellow of the Gerontological Society of America and of the Association for Gerontology in Higher Education, she serves as Editor of *Personal Relationships* and as a Member-at-Large of the Council of the American Sociological Association.

Syed Farid Alatas is an Associate Professor at the National University of Singapore specializing in sociological theory and historical sociology. His publications include *Alternative Discourse in Asian Social Science: Responses to Eurocentrism* (2006) and *Democracy and Authoritarianism in Indonesia and Malaysia: The Rise of the Post-Colonial State* (1997).

Graham Allan is Professor of Sociology at the University of Keele, UK, and Visiting Professor in Family Studies at the University of British Columbia, Vancouver. His recent books include *Placing Friendship in Context* (1998, with Rebecca Adams); *Families, Households, and Society* (2001, with Graham Crow); and *The State of Affairs* (2004, with Jean Duncombe, Kaeren Harrison, and Dennis Marsden).

Peter Beilharz is Professor of Sociology and Director of the Thesis Eleven Center for Critical Theory at La Trobe University, Australia. He is author or editor of 22 books, including *Imagining the Antipodes* (1997) and *Zygmunt Bauman* (2000). He was Professor of Australian Studies at Harvard, 1999–2000, and is Fellow of the Center for Cultural Sociology at Yale. He is collaborating on an intellectual biography of the founding mother of Australian sociology, Jean Martin.

Suzanne M. Bianchi is Professor and Chair of the Department of Sociology at the University of Maryland. She is a Past President of the Population Association of America and co-editor of the journal *Demography*. She is author of *Changing Rhythms of American Family Life* (with John Robinson and Melissa Milkie, 2006).

Chris Carter is a Professor of Management at the University of St. Andrews in Scotland. He is a Visiting ICAN Fellow at the University of Technology, Sydney. He has published in journals such as *Accounting, Organizations and Society*, *Critical Perspectives on Accounting*, *Human Relations, Industrial Relations Journal*, and *Organization and Organization Studies*.

Roberto Cipriani is Professor of Sociology and Chair of the Department of Sciences of Education at the University of Rome 3. He has served as a Visiting Professor at the University of São Paulo, at the University of Buenos Aires, and at Laval University, Quebec. He served as editor-in-chief of *International Sociology*, and is currently President of the Italian Sociological Association.

Stewart R. Clegg is a Professor at the University of Technology, Sydney, and Director of ICAN Research, a Key University Research Center. He also holds Chairs at Aston University and is a Visiting Professor at the University of Maastricht and the Vrije Universiteit, Amsterdam. He has published extensively in many journals and has contributed a large number of books to the literature, including the award-winning *Handbook of Organization Studies* (2nd edition 2006, co-edited with Cynthia Hardy, Walter Nord, and Tom Lawrence). His most recent books are *Managing and Organizations: An Introduction to Theory and Practice* (2005, with Martin Kornberger and Tyrone Pitsis) and *Power and Organizations* (2006, with David Courpasson and Nelson Phillips).

Jay Coakley is Professor Emeritus of Sociology at the University of Colorado at Colorado Springs. He is author of *Sports in Society: Issues and Controversies* (2007). He was also founding editor of the *Sociology of Sport Journal* (1984–89) and co-editor of *Handbook of Sport Studies* (2000, with Eric Dunning) and *Inside Sports* (1999, with Peter Donnelly).

William C. Cockerham is Distinguished Professor of Sociology at the University of Alabama at Birmingham and the 2004 recipient of the university's prestigious Ireland Prize for Scholarly Distinction. His recent publications include *Medical Sociology*, 10th edition (2007), *Risk-Taking Society: Living Life on the Edge* (2006), *Sociology of Mental Disorder*, 7th edition (2006), *The Blackwell Companion to Medical Sociology* (2005), and "Health Lifestyle Theory and the Convergence of Agency and Structure" in the *Journal of Health and Social Behavior* (2005).

Miriam Alfie Cohen is a Professor at Autonomous Metropolitan University. Her publications include *Cross-Border Activism and Its Limit: Mexican Environmental Organizations and the United States* (with Barbara Hogenboom and Edit Antal, 2003), *Maquila y Movimientos Ambientalistas: Examen de un Riesgo Compartido Matamoros, Brownsville* (with Luis H. Menendez Berrueta, 2000), *Y el Desierto Se Volvio Verde: Movimentos Ambientalistas Binacionales Ciudad Juarez-El Paso* (1998), and *Democracia y Desafio medioambiental en México* (2005).

Daniel Thomas Cook is Associate Professor of Advertising and Communications at the University of Illinois, Champaign-Urbana. He is the author of *The Commodification of Childhood* (2004) and editor of *Symbolic Childhood* (2002). His articles on children and consumer culture have appeared in academic journals such as the *Sociological Quarterly*, the *Journal of Consumer Culture*, and *Childhood*, and in more popular publications like *Global Agenda* and *LiP Magazine*.

Rutledge M. Dennis is Professor of Sociology and Anthropology at George Mason University. He is editor of *Black Intellectuals* (1997)

and *Marginality, Power, and Social Structure* (2005). He is the co-author of *The Politics of Annexation* (1982), and co-editor of *Race and Ethnicity: Comparative and Theoretical Approaches* (2003), *The Racial Politics of Booker T. Washington* (2006), and *The New Black* (2006). He is the recipient of the Joseph Himes Distinguished Scholarship Award (2002) and the Du Bois-Johnson-Frazier Award for an Outstanding Career in Research, Writing, Teaching, and Social Action, presented by the American Sociological Association.

Erich Goode is Sociology Professor Emeritus at the State University of New York at Stony Brook and Senior Research Scientist in the Department of Criminology and Criminal Justice at the University of Maryland at College Park. He is the author of ten books, mainly on deviance and drug use.

Jeff Goodwin is Professor of Sociology at New York University. He is the author of *No Other Way Out: States and Revolutionary Movements, 1945–1991* (2001), and the co-editor of *Passionate Politics: Emotions and Social Movements* (2001), *The Social Movements Reader: Cases and Concepts* (Blackwell, 2003), and *Rethinking Social Movements: Structure, Culture, and Emotion* (2004). He has published articles on social movements, revolutions, and terrorism in the *American Sociological Review*, the *American Journal of Sociology*, *Social Forces*, *Theory and Society*, *Politics and Society*, *Mobilization*, *Sociological Forum*, and other journals.

Kevin Fox Gotham is an Associate Professor at Tulane University. He is the author of *Race, Real Estate, and Uneven Development: The Kansas City Experience, 1900–2000* (2002). His forthcoming book, *Transforming New Orleans* (2007), examines the intersection of race, culture, and tourism in the historical development of New Orleans. He is on leave from Tulane University from 2006 to 2008, living in Washington, DC, and working as a Program Officer for the Sociology Program of the National Science Foundation (NSF).

Axel Groenemeyer is Professor of Sociology at the University of Applied Sciences, Esslingen, Germany. He has been Professor of

Sociology at the University of Essen; Professor of Social Policy, Social Work, and Social Administration at the University of Siegen; and invited Professor of Sociology at universities in St. Petersburg, Russia, Sofia, Bulgaria, and Lille, France. He is President of the Social Problems and Social Control Section within the German Association of Sociology, editor of *Soziale Probleme*, and a member of the editorial board of *Déviance et Société*.

Eva Illouz was born in Morocco and has lived for extended periods of time in France, the United States, and Israel. She currently holds Israeli and French citizenships. In 1991 she completed her PhD in the United States. She has taught at the University of Pennsylvania, the New School for Social Research, New York University, and at Tel Aviv University. She currently teaches at the Department of Sociology at the Hebrew University of Jerusalem.

Peter Kivisto is the Richard Swanson Professor of Social Thought and Chair of Sociology at Augustana College. Among his recent books are *Multiculturalism in a Global Society* (2002), *Key Ideas in Sociology*, 2nd edition (2004), *Incorporating Diversity: Rethinking Assimilation in a Multicultural Age* (2005), and *Intersecting Inequalities* (2007, with Elizabeth Hartung). With Thomas Faist, he is completing a book on citizenship for Blackwell. He is the current editor of the *Sociological Quarterly*.

Yvonna S. Lincoln is Professor of Higher Education and Human Resource Development at Texas A&M University, and holds the Ruth Harrington Chair of Educational Leadership and University Distinguished Professor of Higher Education. She is the co-author of *Effective Evaluation, Naturalistic Inquiry, and Fourth Generation Evaluation*, the editor of *Organizational Theory and Inquiry*, the co-editor of the newly released *Handbook of Qualitative Research*, 2nd edition, and co-editor of the international journal *Qualitative Inquiry*.

David R. Maines is Professor of Sociology and Chair (2000–6) at Oakland University in Rochester, Michigan. He has contributed to narrative studies and to efforts at developing a symbolic interactionist conception of macrosociology.

Much of his work is found in his recent book, *The Faultline of Consciousness: A View of Interactionism in Sociology* (2001). In the past decade he has conducted research on liturgical change in Catholicism, which will be published in his forthcoming book *Transforming Catholicism: Liturgical Change in the Vatican II Church* (2007, with Michael J. McCallion).

Barry Markovsky is Professor and Chair of Sociology at the University of South Carolina. He has been the editor, with several other sociologists, of *Advances in Group Processes*, Vols. 4–14 (1987–97), and, with Edward J. Lawler, published *Social Psychology of Groups: A Reader* in 1993.

Chandra Muller is Associate Professor of Sociology at the University of Texas at Austin. She has written extensively on the topic of educational achievement, adolescence, parental involvement in education, and educational policy. She is the recipient of grants and fellowships from the National Science Foundation, National Institute of Child Health and Human Development, and the Spencer Foundation.

Nancy A. Naples is Professor of Sociology and Women's Studies at the University of Connecticut. She is author of *Feminism and Method: Ethnography, Discourse Analysis, and Activist Research* (2003) and *Grassroots Warriors: Activist Mothering, Community Work, and the War on Poverty* (1998), and editor of *Community Activism and Feminist Politics: Organizing Across Race, Class, and Gender* (1998). She is also co-editor, with Manisha Desai, of *Women's Activism and Globalization: Linking Local Struggles with Transnational Politics* and, with Karen Bojar, of *Teaching Feminist Activism*, both published in 2002.

Jodi O'Brien is a Professor of Sociology at Seattle University. She is the author of *Social Prisms: Reflections on Everyday Myths and Paradoxes* (1999) and was the editor of *The Production of Reality: Essays and Readings on Social Interaction* (2005).

Nick Perry is Professor in the Department of Film, Television, and Media Studies at the University of Auckland, New Zealand. His publications include *Controlling Interests: Business, the State, and Society in New Zealand* (1992, co-edited with John Deeks); *The Dominion of Signs: Television, Advertising, and Other New Zealand Fictions* (1994); *Hyperreality and Global Culture* (1998); and *Television in New Zealand: Programming the Nation* (2004, co-edited with Roger Horrocks). He was President of the Sociological Association of Australia and New Zealand, 1985–6.

Ken Plummer is Professor of Sociology at the University of Essex, and a Visiting Professor of Sociology at the University of California at Santa Barbara. He is editor of the journal *Sexualities* and his books include *Sexual Stigma* (1975); *Documents of Life* (1983); *Telling Sexual Stories* (1995); and *Inventing Intimate Citizenship* (2003). He has also edited *The Making of the Modern Homosexual* (1981); *Modern Homosexualities* (1992); *Symbolic Interactionism* (1990); *The Chicago School* (1997); and *Sexualities: Critical Assessments* (2002). In addition, he has co-authored two textbooks: *Sociology: A Global Introduction*, 2nd edition (2002) and *Criminology: A Sociological Introduction* (2004).

Chris Rojek is Professor of Sociology and Culture at Brunel University, West London. He is the author of many books, the most recent of which are *Celebrity* (2001), *Stuart Hall* (2003), *Frank Sinatra* (2004), *Leisure Theory* (2005), and *Cultural Studies* (2006). He is currently writing a book on "Brit-Myth."

John Stone is Professor and Chair of the Department of Sociology at Boston University. He has published on race and ethnic conflict, migration and nationalism, and sociological theory. His books include *Colonist or Uitlander?*; *Alexis de Tocqueville on Democracy, Revolution, and Society* (with Stephen Mennell); *Racial Conflict in Contemporary Society*; and *Race and Ethnicity* (Blackwell, with Rutledge M. Dennis). He is the Founder Editor of the journal *Ethnic and Racial Studies* (1978–).

Yoshio Sugimoto is a Professor of Sociology at La Trobe University, Australia. His publications include *An Introduction to Japanese Society* (2003) and *Images of Japanese Society: A Study in the Social Construction of Reality* (1990). He

was, with J. Arnason, the editor for *Japanese Encounters with Postmodernity* (1995).

Edward A. Tiryakian is Emeritus Professor of Sociology at Duke University. He taught at Princeton and Harvard prior to his appointment at Duke, where he has served as Departmental Chair and as Director of International Studies. He is a Past President of the American Society for the Study of Religion (1981–4) and of the International Association of French-Speaking Sociologists (1988–92). He has twice been Chair of the Theory Section of the American Sociological Association and was Chair of the ASA History of Sociology Section (2005–6). He has had visiting appointments at Laval University (Quebec), the Institut d'Études Politiques (Paris), and the Free University of Berlin.

Ruth Triplett is Associate Professor in the Department of Sociology and Criminal Justice at Old Dominion University. She received her PhD in 1990 from the University of Maryland, College Park. Her research interests include social disorganization, labeling theory, and the role of gender and class in criminological theory. Her most recent publications are found in *Theoretical Criminology*, *Journal of Criminal Justice*, and *Journal of Crime and Justice*.

Wout Ultee is a Professor of Sociology at the University of Nijmegen. He has been published in the *Annual Review of Sociology* (1991), *European Sociological Review* (1990), *American Sociological Review* (1998), and *American Journal of Sociology* (2005).

Steve Yearley is Professor of the Sociology of Scientific Knowledge at the University of Edinburgh, Scotland, and Director of the ESRC Genomics Forum. He specializes in the sociology of science and in environmental sociology. His recent books include *Making Sense of Science* (2005) and *Cultures of Environmentalism* (2005).

Milan Zafirovski is Associate Professor in the Department of Sociology at the University of North Texas. He holds doctoral degrees in economics and sociology. His research interests are interdisciplinary, focusing on the relations between economy and society. He is the author of the books *Market and Society*, *The Duality of Structure in Markets*, and *Exchange, Action, and Social Structure*, and of about 50 articles in refereed economics and sociology journals. He is also a co-editor of the *International Encyclopedia of Economic Sociology* (2006).

Contributors

Abbott, Andrew
University of Chicago

Abels, Gabriele
University of Bielefeld

Ablett, Phillip
University of the Sunshine Coast

Ackroyd, Stephen
Lancaster University Management School

Acquaviva, Sabino
University of Padua

Adam, Barry
University of Windsor

Adam, Kanya
University of British Columbia

Adams, Michele
Tulane University

Adams, Rebecca G.
University of North Carolina at Greensboro

Adler, Patricia
University of Colorado

Adler, Peter
University of Denver

Agar, Michael
Professor Emeritus, University of
Maryland, and University of Alberta

Agigian, Amy
Suffolk University

Agnew, Robert
Emory University

Aguirre, Adalberto
University of California, Riverside

Ajrouch, Kristine
Eastern Michigan University

Alasuutari, Pertti
University of Tampere

Alatas, Syed Farid
National University of Singapore

Alba, Richard
SUNY Albany

Albright, Julie M.
University of Southern California

Alexandre, Renata
Middle Tennessee State University

Aliberti, Dawn
Case Western Reserve University

Allam, Khaled Fouad
University of Trieste

Allan, Graham
Keele University

Allan, Stuart
University of the West of England

Allinson, Christopher W.
University of Leeds

Allmendinger, Jutta
Institut für Arbeitsmarkt und
Berufsforschung (IAB)

Alter, Norbert
Université Paris

Altheide, David L.
Arizona State University

Alvesson, Mats
Lund University

Alwin, Duane
Pennsylvania State University

Amenta, Edwin
New York University

Andersen, Peter B.
University of Copenhagen

Anderson, Eric
University of Bath

Anderson, Kevin B.
Purdue University

Andrews, Christopher
University of Maryland

Andrews, David L.
University of Maryland

Angel, Ronald
University of Texas at Austin

Antonio, Robert J.
University of Kansas

Arabandi, Bhavani
George Mason University

Arena, John
Tulane University

Armstrong, Gary
Brunel University

Armstrong, Elizabeth A.
Indiana University

Aronowitz, Stanley
City University of New York Graduate Center

Aronson, Pamela
University of Michigan at Dearborn

Arrigo, Bruce A.
University of North Carolina at Charlotte

Arthur, Mikaila Mariel Lemonik
New York University

Aseltine, Elyshia
University of Texas at Austin

Asquith, Pamela
University of Alberta

Atalay, Zeynep
University of Maryland

Atchley, Robert C.
Naropa Institute, Boulder, CO

Athens, Lonnie
Seton Hall University

Atkinson, Michael
McMaster University

Auf der Heide, Laura
University of Arizona

Austrin, Terry
University of Canterbury

Avison, William R.
University of Western Ontario

Avruch, Kevin
George Mason University

Bachnik, Jane
National Institute of Multimedia Education,
Japan

Badahdah, Abdallah
University of North Dakota

Baer, Hans
University of Melbourne

Bagdikian, Ben H.
University of California at Berkeley

Bahr, Stephen J.
Brigham Young University

Bainbridge, William
National Science Foundation

Bairner, Alan
Loughborough University

Bakker, J. I. (Hans)
University of Guelph

Bale, John
Keele University

Barbalet, Jack
University of Leicester

Barkan, Steven E.
University of Maine

Barker, Chris
University of Wollongong

Barker, Eileen
London School of Economics

Barner, Louise
Universidad Autónoma Metropolitana,
Azcapotzalco

Barone, Tom
College of Education, Arizona State
University

Bartkowski, John
Mississippi State University

Bartley, Tim
Indiana University

Bartolome, Lilia
University of Massachusetts at Boston

Battle, Juan
Hunter College and Graduate Center,
City University of New York

Baubérot, Jean
EPHE-GSRL, Paris

Bauchspies, Wenda K.
Pennsylvania State University

Baur, Nina
Technical University, Berlin

Baxter, Vern
University of New Orleans

Beamish, Rob
Queen's University

Beamish, Thomas D.
University of California at Davis

Bean, Frank D.
University of California, Irvine

Becker, Rolf
University of Bern

Beeghley, Leonard
University of Florida

Befu, Harumi
Stanford University

Beichner, Dawn
Illinois State University

Beilharz, Peter
La Trobe University

Belk, Russell
University of Utah, DESB

Bell, David
University of Leeds

Bengtson, Vern L.
University of Southern California

Bennett, Tony
Open University

Ben-Rafael, Eliezer
Tel-Aviv University

Benson, Michael
University of Cincinnati

Berard, T. J.
Kent State University

Berezin, Mabel
Cornell University

Berends, Mark
Vanderbilt University

Berger, Joseph
Stanford University

Berger, Michele
University of North Carolina-Chapel Hill

Bernard, Miriam
Keele University

Bernard, Paul
Université de Montréal

Bernardi, Fabrizio
UNED

Best, Amy
George Mason University

Bettez, Silvia
University of North Carolina-Chapel Hill

Beyer, Peter
University of Ottawa

Bezdek, William
Oakland University

Bianchi, Alison J.
Kent State University

Biblarz, Timothy J.
University of Southern California

Biddlecom, Ann E.
Alan Guttmacher Institute

Bierman, Alex
University of Maryland

Biernacki, Richard
University of California, San Diego

Biggart, Nicole Woolsey
University of California at Davis

Bills, David B.
University of Iowa

Binkley, Sam
Emerson College, Massachusetts

Binnie, Jon
Manchester Metropolitan University

Blank, Grant
American University

Blatt, Jessica
Graduate Faculty of the New School for
Social Research

Blee, Kathleen M.
University of Pittsburgh

Boatca, Manuela
Catholic University of Eichstätt-Ingolstadt

Bögenhold, Dieter
University of Bremen

Boerema, Albert
Calvin College

Bongaarts, John
Policy Research Division of the Population
Council, New York

Bonstead-Bruns, Melissa
University of Wisconsin-Eau Claire

Boon, Vivienne
University of Liverpool

Booth, Charles
University of the West of England

Bora, Alfons
University of Bielefeld

Boruch, Robert F.
University of Pennsylvania Graduate School
of Education

Bose, Christine E.
SUNY Albany

Bosserman, Phillip
Emeritus Professor, Salisbury University,
Maryland

Boswell, Gracie
University of North Carolina at Chapel Hill

Bottero, Wendy
University of Manchester

Bouffard, Jeff A.
North Dakota State University

Bowker, Geoffrey
Santa Clara University

Bowser, Benjamin
California State University at Hayward

Brady, David
Duke University

Brady, Ivan
SUNY Oswego

Branden, Karen
Minnesota State University at Moorhead

Brannen, Julia
Institute of Education, University of London

Breen, Richard
Nuffield College

Brenner, Neil
New York University

Breslau, Daniel
Virginia Tech

Brewer, Thomas
Kent State University

Brint, Steven
University of California at Riverside

Brito, Myriam
Universidad Autónoma Metropolitana,
Azcapotzalco

Bromley, David G.
Virginia Commonwealth University

Brown, Stephen E.
East Tennessee State University

Brown, Susan K.
University of California, Irvine

Browning, Christopher R.
Ohio State University

Bruce, Steve
University of Aberdeen

Bruce, Toni
University of Waikato

Brunson, Rod K.
University of Missouri at St. Louis

Brustein, William I.
University of Pittsburgh

Bryant, Clifton D.
Virginia Tech

Bryman, Alan
University of Leicester

Buchanan, Ian
Cardiff University

Buchmann, Claudia
Ohio State University

Büchs, Milena
University of Southampton

Buechler, Steven M.
Minnesota State University at Mankato

Bunzel, Dirk
Keele University

Bures, Regina
University of Florida

Burkam, David T.
University of Michigan

Burke, Peter
University of California at Riverside

Burns, Lawton R.
University of Pennsylvania

Burns, Tom
Uppsala University

Burrows, Roger
University of York

Butler, Rex
University of Queensland

Bytheway, Bill
Open University

Cagney, Kathleen A.
University of Chicago

Calasanti, Toni
Virginia Tech

Calder, Ryan
University of California, Berkeley

Calhoun, Thomas
University of Southern Illinois at Carbondale

Callero, Peter L.
Western Oregon University

Campbell, John L.
Dartmouth College

Cannella, Gaile
Arizona State University

Capraro, Robert M.
Texas A&M University

Caputo, Richard K.
Yeshiva University

Cardinale, Matthew
University of California, Irvine

Caren, Neal
New York University

Carey, James
University of California at Davis

Carmines, Edward
Indiana University

Carmody, Dianne Cyr
Old Dominion University

Carmody, Moira
University of Western Sydney

Carpenter, Laura M.
Vanderbilt University

Carr, Deborah
Rutgers University

Carrington, Ben
University of Texas at Austin

Carspecken III, Phil
Indiana University

Carter, Chris
University of St. Andrews

Carter, Mike
University of California at Riverside

Cashmore, Ellis
Staffordshire University

Casper, Lynne M.
University of Southern California

Casper, Monica J.
Vanderbilt University

Catsambis, Sophia
Queens College, CUNY

Chadwick, Jan
George Washington University

Chamard, Sharon
University of Alaska at Anchorage

Chambers, J. K.
University of Toronto

Chan, Andrew
City University of Hong Kong

Chanlat, Jean-François
CREPA, Dauphine

Chaplin, Beverley
University of Essex

Charmaz, Kathy
Sonoma State University

Chase, Susan E.
University of Tulsa

Cheal, David
University of Winnipeg

Chee-Beng, Tan
Chinese University of Hong Kong

Chesher, Chris
University of Sydney

Chilton, Roland
University of Massachusetts at Amherst

Chin, Elizabeth
Occidental College

Chorbajian, Levon
University of Massachusetts at Lowell

Chriss, James J.
Cleveland State University

Christ, O.
Philipps-Universität, Marburg

Christ, William G.
Trinity University

Chu, Doris
Arkansas State University

Chua, Peter
San José State University

Cipriani, Roberto
University of Rome 3

Cisneros-Puebla, Cesar A.
Universidad Autónoma Metropolitana,
Iztapalapa

Clair, Jeffrey Michael
University of Alabama at Birmingham

Clark, D. Anthony Tyeeme
University of Illinois at Urbana-Champaign

Clark, M. Carolyn
Texas A&M University

Clark, Peter
Queen Mary, University of London

Clarke, Adele E.
University of California at San Francisco

Clarke, Peter B.
Professor Emeritus, King's College,
University of London, and University of
Oxford

Clegg, Stewart
University of Technology, Sydney, and
Aston Business School

Coakley, Jay
University of Colorado at Colorado Springs

Coates, Rodney
Miami University

Cochrane, Allan
Open University

Cockerham, William C.
University of Alabama at Birmingham

Cody, Susan
LaGrange College

Cohen, Miriam Alfie
Universidad Autónoma Metropolitana,
Azcapotzalco

Cohen, Robin
University of Warwick

Cohn, Steven F.
University of Maine

Coleman, Marilyn
University of Missouri

Conlon, Bridget
University of Iowa

Connidis, Ingrid Arnet
University of Western Ontario

Connor, Walker
Middlebury College

Conrad, Peter
Brandeis University

Conversi, Daniele
London School of Economics

Cook, Daniel Thomas
University of Illinois

Cook, Karen S.
Stanford University

Cooksey, Elizabeth
Ohio State University

Copelton, Denise A.
SUNY Brockport

Copes, Heith
University of Alabama at Birmingham

Corteen, Karen
Edge Hill

Corwin, Zoë Blumberg
University of Southern California

Coupland, Christine
Nottingham University Business School

Courpasson, David
EM Lyon

Cox, Lloyd
Macquarie University

Crane, Diana
University of Pennsylvania

Crawford, Garry
University of Salford

Crenshaw, Edward M.
Ohio State University

Cronin, Ann
University of Surrey

Crook, Tim
Goldsmiths College, University of London

Crosnoe, Robert
University of Texas at Austin

Cross, Simon
University of Lincoln

Crow, Graham
University of Southampton

Crowder, Kyle
Western Washington University

Crowley, Gregory J.
Coro Center for Civic Leadership

Crump, Jeff
University of Minnesota

Crystal, Stephen
Rutgers University

Cubitt, Sean
University of Waikato

Culver, Leigh
University of Nebraska at Omaha

Cumming, Geoff
La Trobe University

Curra, John
Eastern Kentucky University

Curran, Sara R.
Princeton University

Currie, Graeme
Nottingham University Business School

Curry, Timothy Jon
Ohio State University

Curtis, Bruce
Carleton University

Custer, Lindsay
Bellevue Community College

Cutler, Stephen J.
University of Vermont

Dahlgren, Peter
Lund University

Dandaneau, Steven P.
University of Dayton

Daniel, E. Valentine
Columbia University

Dant, Tim
University of East Anglia

Darby, John
University of Notre Dame

Das Gupta, Prithwis
George Washington University

David, Matthew
University of Liverpool

Davidson, Alastair
University of Wollongong

Davidson, Kate
University of Surrey

Davies, Scott
McMaster University

Dawson, Patrick
University of Aberdeen

de Boer, Connie
University of Amsterdam

de Graaf, Paul M.
Radboud University, Nijmegen

De Knop, Paul
Free University of Belgium

de Peuter, Greig
Simon Fraser University

Dean, Hartley
London School of Economics

Dean, James
SUNY Albany

Debuyst, Christian
Catholic University, Leuven

Decker, Scott H.
University of Missouri at St. Louis

Deegan, Mary Jo
University of Nebraska at Lincoln

Deflem, Mathieu
University of South Carolina

Defrance, Jacques
Institut de Recherche sur les Sociétés
Contemporaines

Deibert, Gini
Texas State University at San Marcos

Deil-Amen, Regina
Pennsylvania State University

DeKeseredy, Walter S.
University of Ontario Institute of
Technology

Delacroix, Jacques
Leavey School of Business, Santa Clara
University

Delanty, Gerard
Santa Clara University

Demo, David H.
University of North Carolina at Greensboro

Dennis, Kimya
North Carolina State University

DeNora, Tia
University of Exeter

Dennis, Rutledge M.
George Mason University

Denton, Nancy
SUNY Albany

Denzin, Norman K.
University of Illinois at Urbana-Champaign

Dermott, Esther
University of Bristol

Derné, Steve
SUNY Geneseo

Desai, Manisha
University of Illinois at Urbana-Champaign

DeVault, Marjorie L.
Syracuse University

Devine, Joel A.
Tulane University

deYoung, Mary
Grand Valley State University

Diani, Mario
University of Trento

Dickinson, James
Rider University

Diekmann, Andreas
Swiss Federal Institute of Technology, Zurich

Dillon, Michele
University of New Hampshire

Dilworth-Anderson, Peggye
University of North Carolina at Chapel Hill

Dingwall, Robert
University of Nottingham

Diotallevi, Luca
University of Rome 3

Doane, Randal
Oberlin College

Dobbelaere, Karel
Katholieke Universiteit Leuven, Belgium

Dodd, Nigel
London School of Economics

Dominelli, Lena
Durham University

Donnelly, Peter
University of Toronto

Dorst, John
University of Wyoming

Douglas, Conor M. W.
University of York

Downes, David
London School of Economics

Downs, Heather
University of Illinois at Urbana-Champaign

Dowty, Rachel
Rensselaer Polytechnic Institute

Doyle, Rosemary
University of Edinburgh

Drentea, Patricia
University of Alabama at Birmingham

Dronkers, Jaap
European University Institute

Drysdale, John
Concordia University

Duleep, Harriet Orcutt
Urban Institute

Dumais, Diana
University of New Hampshire

Duncombe, Stephen
New York University

Dunlap, Riley E.
Oklahoma State University

Dunn, Jennifer
Southern Illinois University at Carbondale

Dunning, Eric
University of Leicester

Dwyer, Rachel
Ohio State University

Dykstra, Pearl
Utrecht University

Earl, Jennifer
University of California at Santa Barbara

Easton, Martha
Elmira College

Edwards, Bob
East Carolina University

Edwards, Jennifer
University of Washington

Edwards, John
Aston University

Edwards, Rosalind
London South Bank University

Efron, Noah
Bar Ilan University

Eisenberg, Anne F.
SUNY Geneseo

Eisendstat, S. N.
Van Leer Jerusalem Institute

Eitzen, D. Stanley
Colorado State University

Ekins, Richard
University of Ulster at Coleraine

Elder, Jr., Glen H.
University of North Carolina at Chapel Hill

Elger, Tony
University of Warwick

Elizabeth, Vivienne
University of Auckland

Eller, Andrea
Middle Tennessee State University

Eller, Jackie
Middle Tennessee State University

Elliott, David L.
University of Missouri at Columbia

Elliott, James
Tulane University

Ellis, Lee
Minot State University

Elo, Irma T.
University of Pennsylvania

El-Ojeili, Chamsy
Victoria University of Wellington

Emanuelson, Pamela
University of South Carolina

Embong, Abdul Rahman
Institute of Malaysian and International
Studies, Universiti Kebangsaan, Malaysia

Epstein, Debbie
Cardiff University

Ericksen, Eugene P.
Temple University

Ericksen, Julia A.
Temple University

Eriksson, Lena
University of York

Essletzbichler, Jürgen
University College, London

Esterchild, Elizabeth
University of North Texas

Etzioni, Amitai
George Washington University

Evans, Geoffrey
Nuffield College

Evans, David T.
University of Glasgow

Eyerman, Ron
Yale University

Falk, Pasi
University of Helsinki

Falk, William W.
University of Maryland

Fan, Xitao
University of Virginia

Fantasia, Rick
Smith College

Fararo, Thomas J.
University of Pittsburgh

Farkas, George
Penn State University

Farley, John E.
Southern Illinois University at Edwardsville

Farnsworth, John
Otago University

Farrar, Margaret E.
Augustana College

Fazio, Elena
University of Maryland

Fearfull, Anne
University of St. Andrews

Feldman, Steven P.
Case Western Reserve University

Fellman, Gordon
Brandeis University

Fenstermaker, Sarah
University of California at Santa Barbara

Fermin, Baranda J.
Michigan State University

Ferrell, Jeff
Texas Christian University

Few, April L.
Virginia Polytechnic Institute and State University

Field, Mark G.
Harvard University

Finch, Emily
University of East Anglia

Fincham, Robin
Stirling University

Fincher, Warren
Augustana College

Fine, Gary Alan
Northwestern University

Fine, Mark
University of Missouri at Columbia

Firebaugh, Glenn
Harvard University

Firestone, Juanita M.
University of Texas at San Antonio

Flacks, Richard
University of California at Santa Barbara

Flannery, Daniel J.
Kent State University

Flood, Robert Louis
Independent scholar

Flores, David
University of Nevada at Reno

Floyd, Steven W.
University of Connecticut

Flynn, Nicole
University of South Alabama

Foner, Anne
Rutgers University

Fontana, Andrea
University of Nevada at Las Vegas

Foran, John
University of California at Santa Barbara

Forbes-Edelen, D.
University of Central Florida

Forrester, John
University of York

Fourcade-Gourinchas, Marion
University of California at Berkeley

Fowler, Bridget
University of Glasgow

Frank, David John
University of California at Irvine

Frank, Gelya
University of Southern California

Frankel, Boris
Independent scholar

Franklin, Adrian
University of Tasmania

Franks, David D.
Virginia Commonwealth University

Freston, Paul
Calvin College

Friedman, Judith J.
Rutgers University

Friedrichs, David O.
University of Scranton

Frieze, Irene Hanson
University of Pittsburgh

Frisbie, Parker
University of Texas at Austin

Frisco, Michelle L.
Penn State University

Fuchs, Stephan
University of Virginia

Fuller, Steve
University of Warwick

Fulton, John
St. Mary's University College

Funabashi, Harutoshi
Hosei University

Fusco, Caroline
University of Toronto

Gabriel, Karl
University of Münster

Gadsden, Gloria
Fairleigh Dickinson University

Gafford, Farrah
Tulane University

Gaines, Larry
California State University

Gallagher, Eugene
University of Kentucky

Gallagher, Sally K.
Oregon State University

Galligan, Brian
University of Melbourne

Gamble, Andrew
University of Sheffield

Gamoran, Adam
University of Wisconsin-Madison

Gangl, Markus
University of Mannheim

Ganong, Lawrence H.
University of Missouri at Columbia

Garner, Larry
DePaul University

Garner, Robert
University of Leicester

Garner, Roberta
DePaul University

Garnham, Nicolas
University of Westminster

Gartner, Rosemary
University of Toronto

Geis, Gilbert
University of California at Irvine

Genosko, Gary
Lakehead University

George, Linda K.
Duke University

Gerami, Shahin
Missouri State University

Germann Molz, Jennie
Lancaster University

Gerteis, Joseph
University of Minnesota

Ghezzi, Simone
Università di Milano-Bicocca

Ghiaroni, Simone
Università di Modena e Reggio Emilia

Gillespie, Wayne
East Tennessee State University

Gimlin, Debra
University of Aberdeen

Giordan, Giuseppe
University of Valle d'Aosta

Girling, Evi
Keele University

Giulianotti, Richard
University of Aberdeen

Glenn, Norval D.
University of Texas at Austin

Go, Julian
Boston University

Goetz, Ernest T.
Texas A&M University

Gold, Sara
University of Michigan at Dearborn

Gold, Steven J.
Michigan State University

Goldscheider, Frances
Brown University

Goldson, Annie
University of Auckland

Gomes, Ralph
Howard University

Gómez Morales, Yuri Jack
Universidad Nacional de Colombia

Gomez-Smith, Zenta
University of Florida

Goode, Erich
University of Maryland

Goode, Luke
University of Auckland

Gordon, Kristin
Emory University

Gordon, Ray
University of Technology, Sydney

Gorman, Lyn
Charles Sturt University

Gotham, Kevin Fox
Tulane University

Gottfredson, Michael R.
University of California at Irvine

Gough, Brendan
University of Leeds

Grady, John
Wheaton College

Grant, Linda
University of Georgia

Green, Nicola
University of Surrey

Greenwood, Royston
University of Alberta

Gregson, Nicky
University of Sheffield

Greil, Arthur L.
Alfred University

Griffin, Sean
Penn State, Abington

Grills, Scott
Brandon University

Groenemeyer, Axel
University of Bielefeld

Gronow, Jukka
University of Uppsala

Grunstein, Arturo
Universidad Autónoma Metropolitana,
Azcapotzalco

Grusky, David B.
Stanford University

Grzywacz, Joseph G.
Wake Forest University School of Medicine

Guba, Egon G.
Indiana University

Gudergan, Siegfried P.
University of Technology, Sydney

Hadfield, Lucy
London South Bank University

Hadjicostandi, Joanna
University of Texas of the Permian Basin

Hafferty, Frederic
University of Minnesota Medical School,
Duluth

Hagedorn, John M.
University of Illinois at Chicago

Haggett, Claire
University of Newcastle

Hakim, Catherine
London School of Economics

Halfon, Saul
Virginia Tech

Hall, Jeffrey E.
University of Alabama at Birmingham

Hall, John R.
University of California Study Center

Hall, Lesley A.
Wellcome Library for the History and
Understanding of Medicine, London

Hall, Matthew
Western Washington University

Hall, Peter M.
University of Missouri

Hall, Thomas D.
University of Kansas

Halle, David
University of California at Los Angeles

Hallett, Tim
Indiana University

Hallinan, Maureen T.
University of Notre Dame

Halnon, Karen Bettez
Pennsylvania State University

Hamilton, Laura
Indiana University

Hammersley, Martyn
Open University

Handelman, Jay M.
Queen's School of Business, Ontario

Haney, Timothy J.
Tulane University

Hannigan, John
University of Toronto at Scarborough

Hardey, Michael
University of Newcastle

Harding, David J.
Harvard University

Hardy, Melissa
Pennsylvania State University

Hardy, Simon
University College, Worcester

Harney, Nicholas De Maria
University of Western Australia

Harrington, Austin
University of Leeds and University of Erfurt

Harris, Brandy D.
Florida State University

Harris, Dave
College of St. Mark and St. John

Harris, Richard J.
University of Texas at San Antonio

Harrison, Kaeren
University College, Chichester

Hartnett, Stephen
University of Illinois

Harvey, David L.
University of Nevada at Reno

Harvey, Jean
University of Ottawa

Hasegawa, Koichi
Tohoku University

Hassrick, Elizabeth McGhee
University of Chicago

Hatch, Amos J.
University of Tennessee

Hawkes, Gail
University of New England

Hayward, Keith
University of Kent

Hayward, Mark
Penn State University

Healey, Dan
Swansea University

Heaphy, Brian
University of Manchester

Hearn, Jeff
Swedish School of Economics

Heath, Sue
University of Southampton

Heckert, Daniel Alex
Indiana University of Pennsylvania

Heckert, Druann
Fayetteville State University

Heeren, John W.
California State University at San Bernardino

Hegtvedt, Karen A.
Emory University

Heinemann, Gloria D.
SUNY Buffalo

Hekma, Gert
University of Amsterdam

Hendricks, Jon
Oregon State University

Henning, Christoph
Zeppelin University

Henricks, Thomas
Elon University

Henry, Stuart
Wayne State University

Henson, Robin K.
University of North Texas

Hering, Sabine
University of Siegen

Hermanowicz, Joseph C.
University of Georgia

Hernandez, Donald J.
SUNY Albany

Hess, Martin
University of Manchester

Heugens, Pursey P. M. A. R.
Rotterdam School of Management, Erasmus
University

Higgins, Matthew
University of Leicester

Hill, Annette
University of Westminster

Hill, Michael R.
Editor, *Sociological Origins*

Hilliard, Betty
University College, Dublin

Hills, Matthew
Cardiff University

Hillyard, Daniel
Southern Illinois University at Carbondale

Hilton-Morrow, Wendy
Augustana College

Hindess, Barry
Australian National University

Hindin, Michelle J.
Johns Hopkins Bloomberg School of Public
Health

Hinote, Brian P.
University of Alabama at Birmingham

Hinze, Susan W.
Case Western Reserve University

Hirschman, Charles
University of Washington

Hodson, Randy
Ohio State University

Hofferth, Sandra L.
University of Maryland

Hogan, John
University of Hertfordshire

Hogan, Trevor
La Trobe University

Holman Jones, Stacy
University of South Florida

Holmes, Mary
University of Aberdeen

Holt, Douglas B.
Said Business School, Oxford University

Holzner, Burkart
University of Pittsburgh

Honea, Joy Crissey
Montana State University at Billings

Hornsby, Anne M.
Centers for Medicare and Medicaid Services

Horrocks, Roger
University of Auckland

Hoskins, Janet
University of Southern California

Houlihan, Barrie
Loughborough University

House, James
University of Michigan

Houser, Jeffrey
University of Northern Colorado

Hudis, Peter
Purdue University

Huffer, David
University of Maryland

Hughes, Jason
University of Leicester

Hummer, Robert A.
University of Texas at Austin

Humphery, Kim
RMIT University

Hunt, Stephen
University of the West of England

Hutchinson, Ray
University of Wisconsin

Hutter, Mark
Rowan University

Hydén, Lars-Christer
Linköping University, Sweden

Iceland, John
University of Maryland

Indergaard, Michael
St. John's University

Inglehart, Ronald
University of Michigan

Ingraham, Chrys
Russell Sage College

Ingram, Paul
Columbia University

Inoue, Keiko
Stanford University

Introvigne, Massimo
CESNUR

Isvan, Nilufer
Robert College, Istanbul

Jackson, Shirley A.
Southern Connecticut State University

Jackson, Steven
University of Otago

Jackson, Stevi
University of York

Jacobs, A. J.
East Carolina University

Jacobs, Mark D.
George Mason University

Jacobsen, Martin M.
West Texas A&M University

Jalali, Rita
Stanford University

Jamieson, Lynn
University of Edinburgh

Janesick, Valerie J.
University of South Florida

Jarmon, Charles
Howard University

Jasper, James M.
Independent scholar

Jasso, Guillermina
New York University

Jehle, Alayna
University of Nevada at Reno

Jekielek, Susan M.
Child Trends

Jenkins, Richard
University of Sheffield

Jenks, Chris
Brunel University

Jenness, Valerie
University of California at Irvine

Jennings, Laura
University of Illinois

Jessop, Bob
Lancaster University

Joffe, Carole
University of California at Davis

Johns, Gary
Concordia University

Johnson, David
University of New Orleans

Johnson, Helen
University of Queensland

Johnson, Phyl
University of Strathclyde

Johnston, Barry V.
Indiana University Northwest

Johnston, Hank
San Diego State University

Jonas, Andrew E. G.
University of Hull

Jones, Paul R.
University of Liverpool

Junisbai, Azamat
Indiana University

Kada, Yukiko
Kyoto Seika University

Kahn, Joan R.
University of Maryland

Kaiser, Susan B.
University of California at Davis

Kane, Nazneen
University of Maryland

Kangas, Olli R.
Danish National Institute for Social Research

Kantzara, Vasiliki
Panteion University

Kardash, Teddy
University of Wisconsin-Madison

Karstedt, Susanne
Keele University

Katz, Fred Emil
Independent scholar

Katz-Fishman, Walda
Howard University

Kaufman, Erin
University of Iowa

Katz-Gerro, Tally
University of Haifa

Kaufmann, Franz-Xaver
Universität Bielefeld

Keating, Norah
University of Alberta

Kellerhals, Jean
University of Geneva

Kellner, Douglas
University of California at Los Angeles

Kelly, Liz
CWASU

Kelly, Russell
University of Central Lancashire

Kemmelmeier, Markus
University of Nevada at Reno

Kerr, Anne
University of York

Kibria, Nazli
Boston University

Kidd, Bruce
University of Toronto

Kim, Ann H.
Brown University

Kim, Chigon
Wright State University

Kim, SangJun
Kyung Hee University

Kimmel, Michael S.
SUNY Stony Brook

King, C. Richard
Washington State University

King, Dave
University of Liverpool

Kinney, William J.
University of St. Thomas

Kippax, Susan
University of New South Wales

Kirk, Roger E.
Baylor University

Kirmeyer, Sharon
National Center for Health Statistics

Kirton, Gill
Queen Mary, University of London

Kishor, Sunita
ORC Macro

Kivisto, Peter
Augustana College

Klein, Lloyd
Bemidji State University

Kleinman, Daniel Lee
University of Wisconsin-Madison

Klesse, Christian
University of Hamburg

Kliman, Andrew
Pace University

Knights, David
Keele University

Knöbl, Wolfgang
University of Göttingen

Knorr Cetina, Karin
University of Chicago

Kohli, Martin
European University Institute

Kokosalakis, Nikos
Panteion University, Athens

Kong, Travis S. K.
Hong Kong Polytechnic University

Konty, Mark
Washington State University

Kornberger, Martin
University of Innsbruck

Kosaka, Kenji
Kwansei Gakuin University

Kotarba, Joseph A.
University of Houston

Kozinets, Robert V.
University of Wisconsin-Madison

Krase, Jerome
Brooklyn College of the City University of
New York

Krasmann, Susanne
University of Hamburg

Krasner, Stephen D.
Stanford University

Kritz, Mary M.
Cornell University

Krohn, Wolfgang
University of Bielefeld

Kroska, Amy
Kent State University

Kulik, Liat
Bar Ilan University

Kurihara, Tomoko
University of Cambridge

Kusow, Abdi M.
Oakland University

Kuwayama, Takami
Hokkaido University

Lackey, Gerald F.
University of North Carolina at Chapel Hill

Lahelma, Eero
University of Helsinki

Lahm, Karen
Capital University

Lair, Craig D.
University of Maryland

Lal, Barbara Ballis
University of California at Los Angeles

Lamb, Julie
University of Surrey

Lamnek, Siegfried
Catholic University of Eichstätt-Ingolstadt

Land, Kenneth C.
Duke University

Lang, Rainhart
Chemnitz University of Technology

Langenkamp, Amy G.
University of Texas at Austin

Langer, Beryl
La Trobe University

Langman, Lauren
Loyola University of Chicago

Lareau, Annette
University of Maryland

Larsen, Ulla
Harvard School of Public Health

Lather, Patti
Ohio State University

Lauderdale, Pat
Arizona State University

Lavender, Abraham D.
Florida International University

Law, Ian
University of Leeds

Layte, Richard
Economic and Social Research Institute

Lealand, Geoff
University of Waikato

Leclerc–Madlala, Suzanne
University of KwaZulu-Natal

Lee, Barrett A.
Penn State University

Lee, Cheuk-Yin
National University of Singapore

Lee, Sooho
Georgia Institute of Technology

Lee, Susan Hagood
Boston University College of General Studies

Lee, Valerie
University of Michigan

Le Galès, Patrick
CNRS/CEVIPOF/Sciences Po, Paris

Lehnerer, Melodye
Missouri State University

Leiter, Valerie
Simmons College

Lemarchand, René
University of Florida at Gainesville

Lemelle, Anthony
University of Wisconsin-Milwaukee

LeMoyne, Terri
University of Tennessee at Chattanooga

Lengermann, Patricia
George Washington University

Leoussi, Athena S.
University of Reading

Leslie, Leigh A.
University of Maryland

Lessenich, Stephan
Friedrich-Schiller-Universität, Jena

Lesthaeghe, Ron J.
Vrije Universiteit, Brussels

Leufgen, Jill
University of California, Irvine

Levin, Jack
Northeastern University

Levy, Donald P.
Wesleyan College

Levy, Judith A.
University of Illinois at Chicago

Lewis, Tyson E.
University of California at Los Angeles

Lezaun, Javier
London School of Economics

Lichter, Daniel T.
Cornell University

Lichter, Michael
SUNY Buffalo

Lidz, Victor
Drexel University College of Medicine

Lie, John
University of California at Berkeley

Light, Donald W.
University of Medicine and Dentistry of
New Jersey

Lin, Jan
Occidental College

Lincoln, Karen D.
University of Washington

Lincoln, Yvonna S.
Texas A&M University

Lind, Amy
Arizona State University

Lind, Ben
Arizona State University

Linstead, Stephen
University of Durham

Lipscomb, Michael
Winthrop University

Lister, Martin
University of the West of England

Little, Craig B.
SUNY Cortland

Livingstone, Sonia
London School of Economics

Lizardo, Omar
University of Arizona

Lloyd, Richard
Vanderbilt University

Loe, Meika
Colgate University

Lofland, Lyn H.
University of California at Davis

Löfström, Jan
University of Helsinki

Long, Elizabeth
Rice University

Long, John F.
US Census Bureau

Longino, Jr., Charles F.
Wake Forest University

Lonsdale, Chris
University of Birmingham

Lovaglia, Michael J.
University of Iowa

Lovell, David W.
University of New South Wales

Loveridge, Ray
University of Oxford

Loy, John W.
University of Rhode Island

Loyal, Steve
University College, Dublin

Lucas, Jeffrey W.
University of Maryland

Luccarelli, Mark
University of Oslo

Lucio, Miguel Martínez
Bradford University School of Management

Lucke, Glenn
Center on Religion and Democracy

Luijkx, Ruud
Tilburg University

Lunneborg, Clifford E. (d. 2005)
Formerly of University of Washington

Lupton, Deborah
Charles Sturt University

Lutz, Amy
Syracuse University

Lyon, David
Queen's University

Lyson, Thomas A.
Cornell University

Maahs, Jeff
University of Minnesota at Duluth

McAdam, Doug
Stanford University

McCallion, Michael J.
Archdiocese of Detroit

McCammon, Holly J.
Vanderbilt University

McCarthy, E. Doyle
Fordham University

McCleary, Rachel M.
Harvard University

McCormick, Charles
SUNY Albany

McCulloch, B. Jan
University of Minnesota

Macdonald, Keith
University of Surrey

McDonald, Peter
Australian National University

McGann, PJ
University of Michigan

McGinty, Patrick J. W.
Western Illinois University

Machalek, Richard
University of Wyoming

MacInnis, Kim
Bridgewater State College

Mackay, Hugh
Open University

McKay, Jim
University of Queensland

McKenzie, Kathryn Bell
Texas A&M University

McKinlay, Alan
University of St. Andrews

McLaughlin, Neil
McMaster University

MacLean, Vicky M.
Middle Tennessee State University

Mcleod, Kembrew
University of Iowa

McNair, Brian
University of Strathclyde

McNamee, Sally
University of Hull

McNeal, Ralph B., Jr
University of Connecticut

McPhail, Clark
University of Illinois at Urbana-Champaign

McQuail, Denis
University of Southampton

McShane, Marilyn D.
University of Houston-Downtown

Macy, Michael W.
Cornell University

Madan, T. N.
Delhi University

Magdalinski, Tara
University of the Sunshine Coast

Maguire, Joseph
Loughborough University

Mahutga, Matthew C.
University of California at Irvine

Main, Regan
Urban Institute

Malcolm, Dominic
University of Leicester

Malinick, Todd E.
University of British Columbia

Mandes, Evans
College of Visual and Performing Arts,
George Mason University

Manning, Peter Kirby
Northeastern University

Mansfield, Louise
Christ Church University College,
Canterbury, UK

Mardin, Serif
Sabanci University, Istanbul

Margolis, Eric
Arizona State University

Markovsky, Barry
University of South Carolina

Markson, Elizabeth W.
Boston University

Markula, Pirkko
University of Exeter

Marlin, Randal
Carleton University

Marsden, Peter
Harvard University

Marshall, Victor W.
University of North Carolina at Chapel Hill

Martin, Dominique
Université Grenoble 2

Martin, Randy
New York University

Martin, Steven
University of Maryland

Martinelli, Alberto
Università Studi Milano

Marx, Gary T.
Massachusetts Institute of Technology

Marza, Manuel M. (d. 2005)
Formerly of Universidad Antonio Ruiz de
Montoya

Mather, Mark
Population Reference Bureau

Matsueda, Ross
University of Washington

Matsumoto, Yasushi
Tokyo Metropolitan University

Mau, Steffen
University Bremen

Mauthner, Melanie
Open University

Mayer, Robert N.
University of Utah

Maynard, Douglas W.
University of Wisconsin

Mazerolle, Lorraine
Griffith University

Meeker, Barbara F.
University of Maryland

Meeks, Chet
Northern Illinois University

Meier, Robert F.
University of Nebraska

Méndez y Berrueta, Luis
Universidad Autónoma Metropolitana,
Azcapotzalco

Menken, Jane
University of Colorado at Boulder

Menzies, Robert
Simon Fraser University

Messerschmidt, James W.
University of Southern Maine

Meyer, David S.
University of California at Irvine

Michel, Patrick
Institute of Political Studies, Paris

Michlic, Joanna
Brandeis University

Mickelson, Roslyn Arlin
University of North Carolina at Charlotte

Miguel Martínez, Lucio
University of Hertfordshire

Mihelj, Sabina
Loughborough University

Milardo, Robert M.
University of Maine

Miller, Dan E.
University of Dayton

Miller, Monica K.
University of Nevada at Reno

Miller, Toby
University of California at Riverside

Millward, Peter
University of Liverpool

Milner, Andrew
Monash University

Milner, Jr., Murray
University of Virginia

Min, Pyong Gap
Queens College

Mingione, Enzo
Università di Milano-Bicocca

Misra, Joya
University of Massachusetts

Modood, Tariq
University of Bristol

Moe, Angela M.
Western Michigan University

Moland Jr., John
Alabama State University

Moller, Stephanie
University of North Carolina at Charlotte

Molm, Linda D.
University of Arizona

Monnier, Christine
College of DuPage

Monsour, Michael
University of Colorado at Denver

Moodley, Kogila
University of British Columbia

Moore, Christopher D.
University of Georgia

Moore, Kelly
University of Cincinnati

Moore, Kristin A.
Child Trends

Moore, Laura
Hood College

Moran, Leslie J.
Birkbeck, University of London

Morgan, David H. J.
Keele University

Morgan, Jamie
University of Lancaster

Morgan, Stephen L.
Cornell University

Morgan, S. Philip
Duke University

Morrione, Thomas
Colby College

Morris, Aldon
Northwestern University

Morrison, Linda
Oakland University

Morrissey, Marietta
University of Toledo

Morrow, Virginia
Institute of Education

Moss, Laurence
Babson College

Mouer, Ross
Monash University

Mouw, Ted
University of North Carolina

Movahedi, Siamak
University of Massachusetts at Boston

Mozetič, Gerald
University of Graz

Mueller, Carol
Arizona State University

Muggleton, David
University College, Chichester

Mukerji, Chandra
University of California at Davis

Mullany, Britta
Johns Hopkins Bloomberg School of Public
Health

Muller, Chandra
University of Texas at Austin

Mumby, Dennis K.
University of North Carolina at Chapel Hill

Muniz, Albert
DePaul University

Munroe, Paul T.
Towson University

Murphy, Peter
Monash University

Musick, Kelly
University of Southern California

Muzzatti, Stephen L.
Ryerson University

Myers, Daniel J.
University of Notre Dame

Nagel, Joane
University of Kansas

Nakamaki, Hirochika
National Museum of Ethnology, Japan

Nakano, Tsuyoshi
Soka University

Naples, Nancy A.
University of Connecticut

Nederveen Pieterse, Jan
University of Illinois at Urbana-Champaign

Nee, Victor
Cornell University

Nettleton, Sarah
University of York

Nevarez, Leonard
Vassar College

Nguyen, Kim
University of Maryland

Nicholls, Brett
University of Otago

Niebrugge, Gillian
American University

Nielsen, Donald A.
University of Wisconsin-Eau Claire

Nielsen, François
University of North Carolina

Nikolova, Natalia
Australian Graduate School of Management

Nixon, Howard L., II
Towson University

Nkomo, Stella
Graduate School of Business Leadership,
UNISA

Nolan, Peter
University of Leeds

Nomi, Takako
Pennsylvania State University

Nordenmark, Mikael
University of Umeå

Null, Crystal
University of Alabama at Birmingham

Nunn, Sam
Indiana University/Purdue University at
Indianapolis

O'Connell Davidson, Julia
University of Nottingham

Oleson, James
Old Dominion University

Oliker, Stacey
University of Wisconsin-Milwaukee

Olson, Josephine E.
University of Pittsburgh

Olvera Serrano, Margarita
Universidad Autónoma Metropolitana

Olzak, Susan
Stanford University

O'Neil, Kathleen M.
Denison University

Onwuegbuzie, Anthony J.
University of South Florida

Onyx, Jenny
University of Technology, Sydney

O'Rand, Angela M.
Duke University

Orbuch, Terri L.
Oakland University

Orcutt, James D.
Florida State University

Orenstein, David
Wright State University

Orser, Edward
University of Maryland, Baltimore County

Ortman, Jennifer M.
University of Illinois at Urbana-Champaign

Orum, Anthony M.
University of Illinois at Chicago

Otnes, Cele
University of Illinois

Ottermann, Ralf
Catholic University of Eichstätt-Ingolstadt

Outhwaite, William
University of Sussex

Oviedo, Lluís
Pont. Ateneo Antonianum

Owens, Ann
Harvard University

Owens, Erica
Marquette University

Owens, Timothy J.
Purdue University

Pace, Enzo
University of Padua

Page, Frank
University of Utah

Pallas, Aaron
Teachers College, Columbia University

Palma, Esperanza
Universidad Autónoma Metropolitana,
Azacapotzalco

Paquin, Jamie
York University

Paradeise, Catherine
University of Marne la Vallée

Pardee, Jessica W.
Tulane University

Parker, Patricia
Middle Tennessee State University

Parrillo, Vincent N.
William Paterson University

Pastrana, Jr., Antonio
City University of New York

Patch, Jason
New York University

Paternoster, Ray
University of Maryland

Patil, Vrushali
University of Maryland

Patton, Michael Quinn
Utilization-Focused Evaluation, St. Paul, MN

Pavlich, George
University of Alberta

Payne, Brian K.
Old Dominion University

Pearson, Jennifer
University of Texas at Austin

Peart, Sandra J.
Baldwin-Wallace College

Pelak, Cynthia Fabrizio
University of Memphis

Pelias, Ronald J.
Southern Illinois University

Peñaloza, Lisa
University of Colorado

Peräkylä, Anssi
University of Helsinki

Perrin, Robin D.
Pepperdine University

Perry, Nick
University of Auckland

Pescosolido, Bernice
Indiana University

Pestello, Frances
University of Dayton

Peterson, Richard A.
Vanderbilt University

Pettigrew, Thomas F.
University of California at Santa Cruz

Phillipson, Chris
Keele University

Pickering, Michael
Loughborough University

Pierce, Clayton
University of California Los Angeles

Pina e Cunha, Miguel
Universidade Nova de Lisboa

Pinna, Tomasino
University of Sassari

Piquero, Alex R.
University of Florida

Pitsis, Tyrone S.
ICAN Research

Pixley, Jocelyn
University of New South Wales

Piya, Bhumika
Saint Anselm's College

Plante, Rebecca F.
Ithaca College

Plass, Peggy S.
James Madison University, Harrisonburg

Platt, Jennifer
University of Sussex

Plummer, Ken
University of Essex and University of
California at Santa Barbara

Poggio, Andrew
University of Kansas

Poggio, John
University of Kansas

Polichetti, Massimiliano A.
National Museum of Oriental Art

Polletta, Francesca
Columbia University

Polonko, Karen
Old Dominion University, Norfolk

Pontell, Henry N.
University of California at Irvine

Posocco, Silvia
London School of Economics and Political Science

Potter, Sharyn
University of New Hampshire

Potter, W. James
University of California at Santa Barbara

Potts, Annie
University of Canterbury

Poulat, Emile
University of Rome 3

Powell, Brian
Indiana University

Powell, Jason L.
University of Liverpool

Powell, Joel
Minnesota State University at Moorhead

Prandi, Carlo
University of Parma

Prechel, Harland
Texas A&M University

Preisendörfer, Peter
University of Mainz

Presdee, Michael
University of Kent

Press, Andrea
University of Illinois

Prior, Lindsay
Cardiff School of Social Sciences

Procter, James
University of Stirling

Pruijt, Hans
Erasmus University, Rotterdam

Pugh, Allison
University of California at Berkeley

Quadagno, Jill
Pepper Institute on Aging

Quah, Stella
National University of Singapore

Raley, Sara
University of Maryland

Ramella, Francesco
University of Urbino

Ramirez, Francisco O.
Stanford University

Ramírez, Ricardo Gamboa
Universidad Autónoma Metropolitana

Ramji, Hasmita
City University, London

Rank, Mark R.
Washington University

Rashotte, Lisa
University of North Carolina at Charlotte

Rauscher, Lauren
Emory University

Rawlins, William
Ohio University

Rawls, Anne
Bentley College

Ray, Larry
University of Kent

Redmon, David
SUNY Albany

Rees, Amanda
University of York

Rees, C. Roger
Adelphi University

Reger, Jo
Oakland University

Reible, Heidi L.
University of Illinois

Reisman, D. A.
Nanyang Technological University

Remennick, Larissa
Bar-Ilan University

Renzulli, Linda
University of Georgia

Rex, John
University of Warwick

Rhodes, Carl
University of Technology, Sydney

Riccardo, Gaetano
Istituto Universitario Orientale, Naples

Rice, Janet C.
Tulane University

Ridgeway, Cecilia L.
Stanford University

Rieger, Jon
University of Louisville

Riegle-Crumb, Catherine
University of Texas at Austin

Rigakos, George S.
Carleton University

Riley, Dylan
University of California at Berkeley

Riordan, Cornelius
Providence College

Riska, Elianne
University of Helsinki

Ritchey, Ferris J.
University of Alabama at Birmingham

Ritchie, Ian
Brock University

Ritzer, George
University of Maryland

Ritzer, Jeremy
Issaquah High School

Rizova, Polly S.
Boston University

Róbert, Péter
TARKI Social Research Center

Robert, Philippe
Centre National de la Recherche Scientifique
(CNRS), Groupe Européen de Recherches
sur les Normativités (GERN)

Roberts, Alison
University of North Carolina at Chapel Hill

Roberts, J. Kyle
Baylor College of Medicine

Robertson, Roland
University of Aberdeen

Robinson, Courtland
Johns Hopkins University

Robinson, Dawn
University of Georgia

Rock, Paul
London School of Economics

Rogalin, Christabel L.
University of Iowa

Rogers, Richard G.
University of Colorado

Rogowski, Ralf
University of Warwick

Rohlinger, Deana A.
Florida State University

Rojek, Chris
Theory, Culture, and Society Center

Roman, Paul
University of Georgia

Romo, Harriett
University of Texas at San Antonio

Rondero López, Norma
Universidad Autónoma Metropolitana

Rootes, Christopher
University of Kent

Rosa, Eugene A.
Washington State University

Rosenbaum, James E.
Northwestern University

Roth, Silke
University of Southampton

Rothchild, Jennifer
University of Minnesota at Morris

Rousseau, Nicole
George Mason University

Rowe, David
University of Newcastle

Rowlingson, Karen
University of Bath

Rucht, Dieter
Social Science Research Center Berlin

Ruef, Martin
Princeton University

Rumbo, Joseph
James Madison University

Rumney, Philip N. S.
Sheffield Hallam University

Rupp, Leila J.
University of California at Santa Barbara

Ryan, Barbara
Widener University

Ryan, J. Michael
University of Maryland

Ryan, Michael T.
Dodge City Community College

Rytina, Steven
McGill University

Sachs, Michael L.
Temple University

Sadovnik, Alan R.
Rutgers University

Sage, George H.
University of Northern Colorado

Saint Onge, Jarron M.
University of Colorado at Boulder

St. Pierre, Elizabeth Adams
University of Georgia

Salkind, Neal J.
University of Kansas

Samele Acquaviva, Sabino
University of Padua

Sammond, Nicholas
Hobart and William Smith Colleges

Samuel, Laurie
Howard University

Sandefur, Melissa
Middle Tennessee State University

Sanders, Clinton
University of Connecticut

Sanders, James R.
Western Michigan University

Sanders, Jimy M.
University of South Carolina

Sanderson, Stephen K.
Indiana University of Pennsylvania

Sanford, Marc M.
University of Chicago

Santana, Rafael
University of Chicago

Sassen, Saskia
University of Chicago

Sassler, Sharon
Ohio State University

Sauceda, Laura
University of Texas at Austin

Sawyer, R. Keith
Washington University

Scambler, Graham
University College, London

Scheff, Thomas J.
University of California at Santa Barbara

Scheid, Teresa L.
University of North Carolina at Charlotte

Schellenbach, Cynthia
Oakland University

Scherschel, Karin
Otto-von-Guericke Universität, Magdeburg

Scheurich, James Joseph
Texas A&M University

Schieman, Scott
University of Toronto

Schijf, Huibert
European University Institute

Schiller, Kathryn S.
SUNY Albany

Schimmel, Kimberly S.
Kent State University

Schlueter, Elmar
University of Marburg

Schmid, A. Allan
Michigan State University

Schmidt, Lucia
University of Bielefeld

Schneider, Barbara
University of Chicago

Schneider, Christopher J.
Arizona State University

Schneider, Jacqueline L.
University of Leicester

Schneider, Mark A.
Southern Illinois University at Carbondale

Schock, Kurt
Rutgers University

Schoen, Bob
Pennsylvania State University

Scholz, Claudia W.
University of Texas at San Antonio

Schor, Juliet
Boston College   ⟩

Schroeder, Jonathan
University of Exeter

Schubert, Hans-Joachim
Erfurt University

Schulz, Jeremy
University of California at Berkeley

Schulz, Markus S.
New York University

Schutt, Russell K.
University of Massachusetts at Boston

Schutte, Gerhard
University of Wisconsin-Parkside

Schwandt, Thomas A.
University of Illinois

Schwartz, Barry
University of Georgia

Schwartz, Jennifer
Washington State University

Schwirian, Kent
Ohio State University

Scimecca, Joseph
George Mason University

Scott, Jerome
Project South

Scraton, Sheila
Leeds Metropolitan University

Segrave, Jeffrey O.
Skidmore College

Seifert, Wolfgang
University of Heidelberg

Seiyama, Kazuo
University of Tokyo

Sekulic, Dusko
Flinders University

Sell, Jane
Texas A&M University   ⌐

Seltzer, Judith
University of California at Los Angeles

Settersten, Richard
Case Western Reserve University

Shahidian, Hammed
University of Illinois at Springfield

Shapiro, Eve
University of California at Santa Barbara

Shavit, Yossi
Tel Aviv University

Shayne, Julie
Emory University

Shehan, Constance
University of Florida

Shepard, Benjamin
Hunter College School of Social Work

Shepherd, Gary
Oakland University

Shepherd, Gordon
University of Central Arkansas

Shinberg, Diane S.
University of Memphis

Shionoya, Yuichi
Hitotsubashi University

Shuval, Judith T.
Hebrew University of Jerusalem

Sica, Alan
Pennsylvania State University

Siegrist, Johannes
University of Düsseldorf

Siemsen, Cynthia
California State University at Chico

Sillince, John
Aston Business School

Silver, Hilary
Brown University

Silverstein, Merril
University of Southern California

Simmons, Laurence
University of Auckland

Simpson, Brent
University of South Carolina

Sims, Barbara
Penn State Harrisburg

Sinclair, John
University of Melbourne

Sinha, Vineeta
National University of Singapore

Sklair, Leslie
London School of Economics

Skrla, Linda
Texas A&M University

Slevin, James
Amsterdam University

Slotkin, Richard
Wesleyan University

Small, Mario L.
Princeton University

Smith, Darren P.
University of Brighton

Smith, Gregory W. H.
University of Salford

Smith, Irving
University of Maryland

Smith, Jackie
SUNY Stony Brook

Smith, Melanie
University of Greenwich

Smith, Michael R.
McGill University

Smith, Paula
University of Cincinnati

Smith, Philip
Yale University

Smyth, Bruce
Australian Institute of Family Studies

Smyth, Michael
University of California, Irvine

Snead, M. Christine
UAB

Snow, David A.
University of California at Irvine

Snyder, Patricia
Center for Child Development, Vanderbilt
University Medical Center

Soeters, Joseph
Royal Netherlands Military Academy/
University of Tilburg

Song, Miri
University of Kent

Soule, Sarah A.
University of Arizona

Southerton, Dale
University of Manchester

Spence, Crawford
University of St. Andrews

Spillman, Lynette
University of Notre Dame

Squires, Gregory D.
George Washington University

Stack, Steven
Wayne State University

Stafford, Mark
University of Texas at Austin

Stanfield, Jacqueline Bloom
University of Northern Colorado

James Ronald, Stanfield
Colorado State University

Stanfield, John H.
Indiana University

Staples, Clifford L.
University of North Dakota

Starks, Brian
Florida State University

Staub-Bernasconi, Sylvia
Zentrum für postgraduale Studien Sozialer
Arbeit, Zurich

Stauth, Georg
University of Bielefeld

Stebbins, Robert A.
University of Calgary

Stehr, Nico
Zeppelin University

Stein, Edward
Cardozo School of Law

Steinmetz, George
University of Michigan

Stepan-Norris, Judith
University of California at Irvine

Sternberg, Yitzhak
Tel Aviv University

Stevens, Fred
University of Maastricht

Stevens, Gillian
University of Illinois

Stevens, Mitchell L.
Steinhardt/New York University

Stevenson, Chris
University of New Brunswick

Stillman, Todd
University of Maryland

Thio, Alex
Ohio University

Thompson, Bruce
Texas A&M University

Thorn, Betsy
University of Maryland

Thornton, Patricia M.
Trinity College, Hartford

Throsby, Karen
Warwick University

Thye, Shane
University of South Carolina

Tierney, William G.
University of Southern California

Timberlake, Michael
University of Utah

Time, Victoria
Old Dominion University

Timmermans, Stefan
Brandeis University

Tindall, D. B.
University of British Columbia

Tiryakian, Edward A.
Duke University

Tittle, Charles R.
North Carolina State University

Tomlinson, Alan
University of Brighton

Tong, Chee Kiong
National University of Singapore

Tonkinson, Robert
University of Western Australia

Torigoe, Hiroyuki
Tsukuba University

Torr, Berna
Brown University

Toscano, Alberto
Goldsmiths College

Townley, Barbara
University of Edinburgh

Trapp, Erin
University of Colorado at Boulder

Travis, Toni-Michelle
George Mason University

Treiman, Donald J.
University of California at Los Angeles

Trencher, Susan R.
George Mason University

Triplett, Ruth
Old Dominion University

Troyer, Lisa
University of Iowa

Tucker, Jr., Kenneth H.
Mount Holyoke College

Tudor, Andrew
University of York

Tunnell, Kenneth D.
Eastern Kentucky University

Turner, Bryan S.
National University of Singapore

Turner, Charles
University of Warwick

Turner, Jonathan H.
University of California at Riverside

Turner, Stephen
University of South Florida

Twaddle, Andrew C.
University of Missouri

Tyson, Will
University of South Florida

Tzanelli, Rodanthi
University of Kent

Ueno, Koji
Florida State University

Ulmer, Gregory L.
University of Florida

Ulmer, Jeffery T.
Penn State University

Ultee, Wout
Radbond University

Usher, Carey L.
Mary Baldwin College

Vacha-Haase, Tammi
Colorado State University

Vail, D. Angus
Willamette University

Valocchi, Stephen
Trinity College, Hartford

van Amersfoort, Hans
University of Amsterdam

van de Rijt, Arnout
Cornell University

van de Walle, Etienne
Population Studies Center

van den Berghe, Pierre L.
University of Washington

van der Zee, Jouke
Netherlands Institute of Health Services
Research

van Eeden-Moorefield, Brad
Central Michigan University

van Krieken, Robert
University of Sydney

van Swaaningen, René
Erasmus University

van Tubergen, Frank
Utrecht University

Vandecar-Burdin, Tancy J.
Old Dominion University

VanLandingham, Mark
Tulane School of Public Health and
Tropical Medicine

Varcoe, Ian
University of Leeds

Vares, Tiina
University of Canterbury

Varul, Matthias Zick
University of Exeter

Venkatesh, Alladi
University of California at Irvine

Vidal-Ortiz, Salvador
American University

Vitt, Lois A.
Institute for Socio-Financial Studies

Volker, Beate
Utrecht University

vom Lehn, Dirk
King's College London

von Otter, Casten
Arbetslivsinstitutet, Stockholm

von Trotha, Trutz
University of Siegen

Voss, Kim
University of California at Berkeley

Vromen, Suzanne
Bard College

Vryan, Kevin
Indiana University at Bloomington

Wachs, Faye
Cal Poly Pomona

Waddington, Ivan
University College, Dublin, University
College, Chester, and Norwegian University
of Sport and Physical Education, Oslo

Wagner, David G.
SUNY Albany

Wagner, Michael W.
Indiana University

Waites, Matthew
Sheffield Hallam University

Waldschmidt, Anne
University of Cologne

Walker, Gordon
Cox School of Business

Walker, Henry A.
University of Arizona

Walker, Jan
Newcastle University

Wall, Karin
Instituto de Ciências Sociais/University of
Lisbon

Wallerstein, Immanuel
Yale University

Walter, James
Monash University

Walzer, Susan
Skidmore College

Warner, Barbara D.
Georgia State University

Wasserman, Jason
University of Alabama at Birmingham

Wasson, Leslie
Chapman University

Way, Sandra
New Mexico State University

Weakliem, David L.
University of Connecticut

Webster Jr., Murray
University of North Carolina at Charlotte

Weeden, Kim
Cornell University

Weeks, Jeffrey
London South Bank University

Weeks, John R.
San Diego State University

Weiler, Bernd (d. 2006)
Formerly of Zeppelin University

Weinberg, Darin
King's College, University of Cambridge

Weininger, Elliot B.
SUNY Brockport

Weinstein, Raymond M.
University of South Carolina

Weiss, Otmar
President European Association for Sociology
of Sport

Weitz, Tracy A.
University of California at San Francisco

Weitzer, Ronald
George Washington University

Weitzman, Eben A.
University of Massachusetts at Boston

Wellman, Barry
NetLab, University of Toronto

Wells, Amy Stuart
Teachers College, Columbia University

Welzel, Christian A.
University of Michigan

Wernet, Christine A.
University of South Carolina at Aiken

West, Michael
Aston Business School

Westover, Jonathan H.
Brigham Young University

White, Michael J.
Brown University

Whitehead, John T.
East Tennessee State University

Whittier, David Knapp
Centers for Disease Control and Prevention

Whittier, Nancy
Smith College

Wholey, Douglas R.
University of Minnesota

Whooley, Owen
New York University

Wiedenhoft, Wendy A.
John Carroll University

Wight, Vanessa R.
University of Maryland

Wilcox, Melissa M.
Whitman College

Willaime, Jean-Paul
EPHE-CNRS, Paris

Willer, David
University of South Carolina

Williams, Brad
National University of Singapore

Williams, Christine
University of Texas at Austin

Williams, Christopher R.
State University of West Georgia

Williams, Frank P., III
University of Houston-Downtown

Williams, Joyce E.
Texas Woman's University

Williams, Matthew
Boston College

Williams, Rhys
University of Cincinnati

Willis, Leigh A.
University of Georgia

Wilmoth, Janet
Syracuse University

Wilson, David C.
Warwick Business School

Wilson, Nicholas Hoover
University of California, Berkeley

Wilterdink, Nico
University of Amsterdam

Wilton, Tamsin
University of the West of England

Wimmer, Andreas
University of California at Los Angeles

Winant, Howard
University of California at Santa Barbara

Wincup, Emma
University of Leeds

Wisely, Nancy
Stephen F. Austin State University

Wolf, Kelly
North Dakota State University

Wolff, Kristina
University of Maine at Farmington

Wood, Helen
University of Manchester

Wood, Stephen
University of Sheffield

Woods, Brian
University of York

Wooldredge, John
University of Cincinnati

Worth, Heather
University of New South Wales

Wortmann, Susan L.
University of Nebraska at Lincoln

Wouters, Cas
Utrecht University

Wrenn, Mary
Colorado State University

Wright, Earl
Fisk University

Wright, J.
University of Central Florida

Wunder, Delores F.
College of DuPage

Yair, Gad
Hebrew University of Jerusalem

Yamane, David
University of Notre Dame

Yang, Guobin
Barnard College

Yeh, Yenli
University of Virginia's College at Wise

York, Richard
University of Oregon

Yoshimura, Mako
Hosei University

Yoshino, Kosaku
Sophia University

Young, Joseph T.
University of Colorado

Young, Kevin
University of Calgary

Youngreen, Reef
University of Iowa

Yu, Jinchun
Pennsylvania State University

Yuill, Richard
University of Glasgow

Zafirovski, Milan
University of North Texas

Zeiss, Ragna
Vrije Universiteit, Amsterdam

Zeni, Jane
University of Missouri at St. Louis

Zerilli, Sal
University of California at Los Angeles

Zinn, Jens
University of Kent

Zippel, Kathrin
Northeastern University

Zukin, Sharon
Brooklyn College and City University
Graduate Center

Zussman, Robert
University of Massachusetts

Acknowledgments

Needless to say, there are many people at the University of Maryland, throughout the world, and within the Blackwell Publishing Company to thank for their invaluable contributions to this *Encyclopedia of Sociology*.

I begin with the graduate students at the University of Maryland, especially Mike Ryan, who served as Senior Managing Editor for this project. The truth is that it is Mike who ran this project and managed the day-to-day details with great diligence and aplomb. It simply could not have been done without him. His skill and commitment allowed me to focus most of my attention on reading and commenting on the submissions (Mike did a good deal of this as well). If it wasn't for the fact that he has such a brilliant future in sociology, Mike could make a career as a manager of projects like this one. I also need to single out the help of another graduate student, Betsy Thorn, who served as Assistant Managing Editor. Betsy went about handling many aspects of the project quietly but with great skill and perseverance. She complemented Mike very well and was not only there on a regular basis, but also could be counted on when one of the project's periodic crises arose. Thanks also to Jeff Stepnisky, who served as Senior Managing Editor on the *Encyclopedia of Social Theory* and stayed on to help get this project started by sharing the expertise he had acquired in that role. Further thanks are due to a number of other graduate students who served as Editorial Assistants and helped in various ways, including Zeynep Atalay, Chris Andrews, Craig Lair, Theo DeJager, and Jon Lemich. Special thanks also to Sara Raley, who was invaluable in reading and commenting on the methods and statistics entries.

Great contributions were made by the encyclopedia's 35 Advisory Editors. They were given preliminary suggestions for topics to be included in their areas, but they were urged to go well beyond this initial selection in formulating a fuller list of topics. They then recruited authors and worked with them in developing drafts of entries. Those drafts eventually were read by the Editor and in many cases went back to authors as well as to Advisory Editors for further work. I am very grateful to the Advisory Editors. These volumes would simply have been impossible without their many contributions. Several scholars were recruited at the end of the process to review this introduction as well as other components of the encyclopedia (including the Lexicon). Thanks to all of these reviewers and, especially, John Scott for last-minute input that helped to improve the final product in various ways.

Then there is a long list of people at Blackwell to thank. I begin with Justin Vaughan (Publisher) in Oxford, England (as well as his boss, Philip Carpenter, Books Director), who worked with me from the beginning in the planning and execution of this project. He has been deeply involved all along the way and his imprint is felt here in innumerable ways. He was particularly good at coming up with additional people and resources as the project developed and exploded to the point that it simply could no longer be handled by the people at the University of Maryland. It was at that juncture that Blackwell's Boston office became more focally involved, especially Ken Provencher (Project Editor), who capably took on more and more responsibilities as the project moved toward completion. He was our key liaison with Blackwell and also managed a staff of people in Boston that included Senior Editorial Assistants Sarah Mann, Jennifer Cove, and Dorian Fox; and Editorial Assistants Jon Dubé, Erikka Adams, Loranah Dimant, Kara Race-Moore, Jessica Rotondi, and Marissa Zanetti. Ken and his team commissioned, contracted, and shepherded several hundred entries to completion, in coordination with Mike and Betsy. Many thanks also go to Blackwell's marketing staff, especially Matt Bennett (Senior Product Manager) in the Boston office, and Jennifer Howell (Marketing Manager) in the Oxford office, for their great publicity efforts; to the UK production staff, including Kelvin Matthews (Editorial Controller), Production Controllers Brian Johnson and Rhonda Pearce, Assistant Production Controller Stephen Erdal, Project Managers Jack Messenger and

Brigitte Lee, and Indexer Marie Lorimer, who handled the enormous task of copyediting, typesetting, and indexing. Tim Beuzeval and Kieran Thomas in Web Services also deserve thanks for building an administrative website that allowed us to manage the project worldwide. Other people at Blackwell who deserve special thanks are Steve Smith (International Editorial Director), Jayne Fargnoli (Executive Editor), Jane Huber (Senior Acquisitions Editor), Chris Cardone (Executive Editor), Rebecca Harkin (Publisher), Nick Bellorini (Commissioning Editor), Paul Millicheap (Marketing Director), Edward Crutchley (Book Sales Director), Jeanne Fryar (Senior Marketing Manager), Jessica Morgan (Product Manager), Louise Cooper (Associate Divisional Marketing Man-ager), Dawn Williams (Online Marketing Specialist), Matt Glidden (Electronic Marketing Coordinator), Ally Dunnett (Senior Production Manager), and Kevin Smith (Systems Architect).

Finally, I should, once again, thank my wife, Sue, for putting up with me throughout this long and arduous process. She generally remained cheerful and supportive even though she tired of seeing me with entries in hand or carting mountains of them wherever in the world we happened to be traveling. I'm not sure I was always so happy having those manuscripts accompany me every-where I went, but it was always good to have Sue along and to be able to look forward to her company after another long day of reading "just one more entry."

Introduction

The origins of sociology are usually traced back to 1839 and the coining of the term by Auguste Comte, one of the important thinkers in the history of the discipline. However, others trace intellectual concern for sociological issues much further back, and it could be argued that scholars (and non-scholars) have been thinking sociologically since the early history of humankind. However, it was not until about a half-century after Comte's creation of the concept that sociology began to develop as a formal and clearly distinct discipline, primarily, at least at first, in Europe and the United States. It was another French thinker, Émile Durkheim, who in the late 1800s was responsible for distinguishing clearly the subject matter of sociology from neighboring fields. Sociology became institutionalized in France (thanks, importantly, to Durkheim's efforts), as well as in Germany, Great Britain, and the United States. While sociology in the United States did not take the early lead in the development of key ideas and theories, it did move strongly in the direction of institutionalization (as did sociology in other nations, especially Great Britain). Sociology has grown enormously in the one hundred-plus years since the work of Durkheim and the early institutionalization of the field and is today a truly globe-straddling discipline. The sociological literature is now huge and highly diverse, and is growing exponentially. Journals, and therefore journal articles, devoted to sociology and its many subfields have proliferated rapidly, as has the number of books devoted to sociological topics. This is part of a broader issue identified by another early leader in sociology, Georg Simmel, who was concerned with the increasing gap between our cultural products and our ability to comprehend them. Sociology is one of those cultural products and this encyclopedia is devoted to the goal of allowing interested readers to gain a better understanding of it.

FRAMING THE *ENCYCLOPEDIA OF SOCIOLOGY*

The magnitude and the diversity of the sociological literature represent a challenge to a wide range of people-scholars and students in sociology and closely related disciplines (some of which were at one time part of sociology) such as criminology, social work, and urban studies; in all of the other social sciences; and in many other disciplines. More generally, many others, including secondary school students and interested laypeople, often need to gain a sense not only of the discipline in general, but also of a wide range of specific topics and issues in the domain of sociology. Journalists and documentary filmmakers are others who frequently seek out ideas and insights from sociology. This encyclopedia gathers together in one place state-of-the-art information on, and analyses of, much of what constitutes contemporary sociology.

While plans are already in place to revise this project in various ways, we have sought to make it as complete as possible at this point. Several approaches have been used to ensure that it is as inclusive as possible in terms of coverage.

First, there is the sheer number of essays — 1,786 in all. We began with the intention of having approximately 1,200 entries, but it quickly became clear that that was a gross underestimate. Rather than artificially set a limit, the number was allowed to grow to its current level. Often the submission of one entry led to the realization of the need to add others that had been omitted initially. Often, advisory editors, staff members, and authors came forth with suggestions, many of which were readily accepted. There were certainly suggestions and topics that we chose not to include for one reason or another, but in the main we usually erred on the side of inclusion rather than exclusion.

Second, an effort was made to cast a very wide net in terms of areas to be included. In the end, we came up with 35 such areas. It turned out that a majority of the entries that were recruited for a given area also fit into one or more – in some cases four or five – other areas. In order to clarify and simplify matters for readers, the original list of 35 areas was reduced to the 22 general categories that now form the organizational base of the Lexicon to be found soon after this introduction. The Lexicon represents the best way to get a quick overview of both sociology today and the contents of the encyclopedia (more on the Lexicon below).

Third, a wide and global search was conducted to find advisory editors to be placed in charge of each of the predefined areas. These are all luminaries in their respective areas and well-known scholars. An effort was also made to make this a truly international board of advisory editors. As a result, there is a strong representation of editors from ten countries – Australia, Germany, Israel, Italy, Mexico, The Netherlands, New Zealand, Singapore, the United Kingdom, and the United States. This, in turn, helped to ensure that the authors of the entries would be from many different parts of the world. The following are among the many countries from which authors have been drawn: Australia, Austria, Belgium, Canada, China, Denmark, Finland, France, Germany, Greece, Hungary, Ireland, Israel, Italy, Japan, The Netherlands, New Zealand, Norway, Portugal, Singapore, South Korea, Spain, Sweden, Switzerland, the United Kingdom, the United States, and Zambia.

Fourth, as a result of the international diversity of editors and authors, the entries themselves are extraordinarily diverse. All, or virtually all, of the expected topics and people are included in these pages, especially given the transcontinental collaboration of an American editor (and editorial team) and a British-based publisher. But the entries go far beyond that to include topics and people that are not typically included in a work like this emanating from the West and the North. This is truly a work that represents *global sociology*. While a major effort was made to be sure that there was representation from all parts of the world, there are certain to be omissions and oversights. One of the goals of both the online version and the next

edition will be to do an even better job of inclusion of authors and topics from throughout the world.

Another useful reference source found in this encyclopedia is the timeline of sociology. While this cannot cover everything that everyone would consider of particular significance, it is a listing of over 700 of the most influential events, figures, and publications to have made an impact on the field. As with the entries themselves, the timeline covers a lot of ground both temporally (stretching back over 2,500 years) and geographically (ranging from the Philippines to Argentina to Poland and many places in between).

Another kind of diversity is reflected in the fact that legendary figures in the field of sociology (S. N. Eisenstadt, Thomas J. Scheff), contemporary leaders (Karin Knorr Cetina, Saskia Sassen, Linda D. Molm, Karen S. Cook, Roland Robertson, Chandra Mukerji, Gary Alan Fine), young scholars (Karen Bettez Halnon, Wendy A. Wiedenhoft, Lloyd Cox), and even some graduate students (Elena Fazio, Kevin D. Vryan) are represented as authors in these pages. This diversity of authorship helped guarantee that the entries in this volume would range all the way from the expected "old chestnuts" to those on hot, new, cutting-edge topics.

I should point out that I personally read, and in many cases re-read (sometimes several times), all of the entries in this volume. Many went through two, three, or more rewrites and I read them all (as, in many cases, did the relevant advisory editors). I say that not because I am by any means an expert in all of the areas and topics covered here, but to make the point that all of the contributions were seriously reviewed, and from a uniform perspective. I tried my best to be sure that all of these entries were accurate, up to date, and of high quality.

As pointed out above, the overall design of this ambitious project can be gleaned from the Lexicon. First, a glance at the 22 broad headings gives the reader a sense of the great sweep of sociology that includes such diverse subfields as crime and deviance, demography/population, education, family, gender, health and medicine, media, politics, popular culture, race/ethnicity, religion, science, sexuality, social psychology, social stratification, sport, and urbanization. Second, a more detailed examination of the topics listed under each of the broad headings in the Lexicon yields a further sense not only of that sweep, but also of the enormous depth of work in sociology. Thus, the coverage of the field in these volumes is both wide and deep. To take just one example, the crime and deviance category includes not only a general entry on crime, but also entries on such specific topics as capital punishment, child abuse, cybercrime, gangs, hate crimes, homicide, police, prisons, rape, victimization, and many more. To take another example, entries on the economy range all the way from major events (Industrial Revolution and the rise of post-industrial society), theories (rational choice), and people (Karl Marx) to a wide array of other topics including money, occupations, poverty, wealth, shopping, super-markets, and credit cards. Similar and often even greater depth is reflected in the lists of terms under most of the other headings in the Lexicon.

Sociology is a highly dynamic discipline that is constantly undergoing changes of various types and magnitudes. This greatly complicates getting a sense of the expanse of sociology. This is traceable to changes both within the field and in the larger social world that it studies.

In terms of changes in sociology, the ency-clopedia includes many traditional concepts, such as primary groups, dyad and triad, norms, values, culture, and so on, but supplements these with a broad assortment of more recently coined and/or popularized concepts, such as distanciation and disembedding, glocalization, simulation, implosion, postsocial, actants, and imagined communities. Similarly, some key figures in the history of the discipline (e.g., Herbert Spencer) have receded in importance, while others have taken on new or renewed significance. For example, feminist theory has led to a rise in interest in the work of Marianne Weber, postmodernism and poststructuralism have led to a revival in interest in Friedrich Nietzsche, and growing interest in spatial issues has led to more attention to the ideas of Henri Lefebvre.

More generally, changes in the relative importance of various subareas in the discipline lead to increases (and decreases) in attention to them. Among the areas that seem to be attract-ing greater interest are globalization (see below) as well as the sociology of consumption and sport. A significant number of entries in the encyclopedia can be included under one (or more) of these headings.

The entries included in the encyclopedia also reflect recent changes in the larger social world. For example, the study of cybercrime above is a relatively recent addition to the area of crime because the cyberspace in which it occurs is itself relatively new. Furthermore, new ways of engaging in criminal behavior on the Inter-net are constantly being invented. For example, a new crime has emerged that involves the sending of emails to large numbers of people around the world claiming that help is needed in transferring money from one country to another. In return, the email recipient is offered a significant share of the money. Those who respond with a willingness to help are eventually lured into transferring considerable sums to the sender of the emails in order, they are told, to help with the transfer by, for exam-ple, bribing officials. People have lost tens and even hundreds of thousands of dollars in such scams. While the perpetrators are hard to find, victims (especially in the US) are not and are subject to prosecution for illegal activities on their part (e.g., deceiving others in order to get needed funds).

A more general recent social change that is profoundly affecting sociology is globalization. This is clearly an emerging and multifaceted process that is dramatically altering the land-scape of the world. Sociology (and many other disciplines including political science, interna-tional relations, and economics) has been com-pelled to deal with the process and its various aspects in many different ways. Thus, we have seen the emergence of various theories and methods devoted to dealing with this topic. Furthermore, the many different aspects and dimensions of the process of globalization have attracted the notice of sociologists (and other scholars). Much consideration has been paid to the economic dimensions of globalization, but there are myriad other aspects – social, cultural, political, and the like – that are also drawing increasing attention from sociologists. Thus, in addition to a general entry on globalization, this encyclopedia includes a number of more specific entries on such issues as world cities, the global justice movement, and the globalization of sport, sexuality, and so on. Further such topics and issues will emerge as globalization as a process continues to evolve and develop. Sociology will respond by devoting attention to them.

By its very nature, sociology is also highly topical and its focus is often drawn to the most recent and publicly visible developments, events, and people. There are, of course, far too many of these to cover completely in these volumes, and in any case the topics covered are constantly changing with current events. However, in order to give a sense of this topicality, some of the most important such issues are covered here. For example, changes in science are dealt with under entries on cloning, genetic engineering, the measurement of risk, and technological innovation. Topical issues in health and medicine include AIDS, aging and health policy, stress and health, and exercise and fitness. A flavor of the many new topics in culture of interest to sociologists is offered here in entries on popular culture icons and forms, postmodern culture, surveillance, and xenophobia.

The dynamic character of sociology makes it extremely interesting, but also very difficult to grasp in some general sense. Thus, it is useful to offer a definition of sociology, although the fact is that the complexity and diversity of the discipline have led to many different definitions and wide disagreement over precisely how to define it. While I recognize that it is one among many definitions, the following is a variant on one that I have employed previously in various contexts and is consistent with the thrust of most definitions in the discipline: *Sociology is the study of individuals, groups, organizations, cultures, societies, and transnational relationships and of the various interrelationships among and between them.*

Unpacking this definition gives us yet another way of gaining an impression of the field of sociology. On the one hand, it is clear that sociology spans the workings of a number of levels of analysis all the way from individuals to groups, organizations, cultures, societies, and transnational processes. On the other, sociology is deeply concerned with the interrelationship among and between all of those levels of analysis. Thus, at the extremes, one might be concerned with the relationship between individuals and the transnational relationships involved in globalization. While globalization is certainly affecting individuals (for example, outsourcing is leading to the loss of jobs in some areas of the world and to the creation of others elsewhere around the globe), it is also the case that globalization is the outcome of the actions of various people (business leaders, politicians, workers). Sociology is attuned to such extreme micro (individual) and macro (global) relationships as well as everything in between. A slightly different way of saying this is that sociology is concerned, at its extremes, with the relationship between individual *agents* and the *structures* (e.g., of global transnational relationships) within which they exist and which they construct and are constantly reconstructing.

USING THE *ENCYCLOPEDIA OF SOCIOLOGY*

One way of gaining an impression of the expanse of sociology is, of course, to read *every* entry in this encyclopedia. Since few (save the editor) are likely to undertake such an enormous task, a first approach would be to scan the entire Lexicon and then select headings and terms of special interest. The reader could then begin building from there to encompass areas and topics of less direct and immediate interest.

However, readers without time to work their way through the entire encyclopedia would be well advised to focus on several rather general Lexicon entries: *Key Concepts*, *Key Figures*, *Theory*, and *Methods*. Let us look at each of these in a bit more detail.

In a sense the vast majority of entries in this encyclopedia are key concepts in sociology, but a large number of the most important and widely used concepts in the discipline have been singled out for inclusion under the heading of *Key Concepts*. An understanding of this range of ideas, as well as of the content of each, will go a long way toward giving the reader an appreciation of the field. For example, one can begin at the level of the individual with the ideas of *mind* and *self,* and then move through such concepts as *agency, interaction, everyday life, groups (primary* and *secondary), organizations, institutions, society,* and *globalization.* This would give the reader a sound grasp of the scope of sociology, at least in terms of the extent of its concerns, all the way from individuals and their thoughts and actions to global relationships and processes. Readers could then work their way through the key concepts in a wide range of other ways and directions, but in the end they would emerge with a pretty good conception of the discipline.

A second way to proceed is through the topics under the heading of *Key Figures.* This is, in some ways, a more accessible way of gaining a broad understanding of the discipline because it ties key ideas to specific people and their biographical and social contexts. One could begin with Auguste Comte and the invention of the concept of sociology. One could then move forward to the development of sociology in France (especially the work of Émile Durkheim and his key role in the institutionalization of sociology in that country). One could then shift to the development of the field in other parts of the world, including Germany (Karl Marx, Max Weber, and Georg Simmel; Weber and Simmel were central to the institutionalization of sociology in Germany), Great Britain (Herbert Spencer), Italy (Vilfredo Pareto), the United States (Thorstein Veblen, George Herbert Mead), and similar developments could be traced in East Asia, Latin America, the Muslim world, as well as other parts of the globe. Another way to go is to move back in time from Comte to even earlier figures such as Ibn Khaldun and then push forward to later key figures such as W. E. B. Du Bois, Talcott Parsons, and Robert Merton (US), Michel Foucault and Pierre Bourdieu (France), Max Horkheimer, Theodor Adorno, and Marianne Weber (Germany), Karl Mannheim and Norbert Elias (Great Britain, although both were born in Germany), and so on. While we have restricted coverage in this encyclopedia to deceased key figures, it *is* also possible to gain a sense of the contributions of living key sociologists, either through entries written by them for these volumes (e.g., Immanuel Wallerstein, Thomas Scheff) or through innumerable topical entries that inevitably deal with their ideas. For example, the entry on structuration theory deals with one of the major

contributions of Anthony Giddens (Great Britain), simulacra and simulation is at the heart of Jean Baudrillard's work (France), glocalization is closely associated with the work of Roland Robertson (also Great Britain), while ethnomethodology was "invented" by Harold Garfinkel (US).

All of those mentioned in the previous paragraph are theorists, but there are many other key figures in or associated with the discipline as well. One can read entries on these people and gain an understanding of specific areas in sociology, including demography (Kingsley Davis), race relations (E. Franklin Frazier), feminism (Charlotte Perkins Gilman), sexuality (Magnus Hirschfeld, Alfred Kinsey), gender (Mirra Komarovsky), media (Marshall McLuhan), urbanization (Lewis Mumford), crime (Edwin H. Sutherland), and many more.

A distinctive quality of sociology is that it has sets of elaborated theories and methods. Even though there is no overall agreement on which theory or method to use, they provide the keys to understanding the discipline as a whole. We have already encountered a number of theorists, but the encyclopedia is also loaded with broad discussions of both general theories and specific theoretical ideas. Among the more classical theories that are covered are structural functionalism, system theory, structuralism, Marxism and neo-Marxism, critical theory, conflict theory, feminism, phenomenology, symbolic interactionism, labeling theory, role theory, dramaturgy, ethnomethodology, existential sociology, semiotics, psychoanalysis, behaviorism, social exchange theory, and rational choice theories. In addition, much attention is given to newer theories such as recent feminist theories, actor-network theory, chaos theory, queer theory, expectation states theory, as well as a variety of the "posts" – postpositivism, poststructuralism, postsocial, and a range of postmodern perspectives.

The methods entries have similarly diverse coverage, which can be divided roughly into qualitative and quantitative methods. All are of varying degrees of utility in studying virtually any topic of concern in sociology. Among the notable qualitative methods covered are ethnography, autoethnography, performance ethnography, feminist methodology, visual methods, *verstehen*, and participant and non-participant observation. More quantitative methods covered include a variety of demographic techniques, experiments, social network analysis, and survey research. Also covered under the heading of methods is a wide range of statistical techniques. Finally, a series of broad methodological issues is dealt with, such as validity, reliability, objectivity, rapport, triangulation, and many others.

All of the above can be brought to bear on the 22 categories in the Lexicon. Thus, for example, another area covered here is the economy, especially consumption, and of relevance to a study of the latter might be the classical work of the theorist Thorstein Veblen, the concept of simulation, postmodern theory, and the use of ethnographic techniques.

Of course, since sociology is constantly expanding, so too are its key concepts, figures, theories, and methods. For example, globalization is, as we have seen, a relatively new issue and sociological concept. It is leading to a reconceptualization of the work of classical theorists (such as Marx and Weber) and of the relevance of their ideas (imperialism, rationalization) to globalization, the generation of a wide range of new concepts (e.g., glocalization, empire, McDonaldization, time-space distanciation) needed to get a handle on it, and theories (transnationalism, network society) and methods (quantitative cross-national studies as well as methods that rely on data not derived from the nation-state) appropriate to the study of global issues and processes. We can expect that in the coming years other new topics will come to the fore, with corresponding implications for how we think about the work of classical theorists as well as leading to the generation of new or revised concepts, theories, and methods.

STATE OF THE ART

It is safe to say that the *Blackwell Encyclopedia of Sociology* represents the largest and most complete, diverse, global, and up-to-date repository of sociological knowledge in the history of the discipline. It stands as a resource for professional sociologists, scholars in other fields, students, and interested laypeople. Given the point made above about the continuing growth and expansion of the field, the bound, 11-volume version in which this introduction appears is just the beginning.

Thus, there will be an online version (www.sociologyencyclopedia.com) of the material represented here. Not only will this constitute another way of accessing the text, it will also make it clear that this encyclopedia is not a sociological "museum" but a living and lively work that will grow and change in the ensuing years. Bound volumes, especially encyclopedias, are not easy to update, but online versions lend themselves readily to change. New substantive topics can be added, as can new biographical sketches. Furthermore, extant entries can be updated and errors, should they have occurred, can be corrected. Thus, the online version of this encyclopedia will begin to grow and change almost as soon as it comes into existence.

In fact, although we were extremely successful in getting virtually all of the entries we recruited into the bound volumes before the publication deadline, there is a handful that, for one reason or another, did not arrive in time. Work continues on them and they will be among the first to be included among the additional entries in the online version.

Another obvious and early set of additions will flow from the decision to include only deceased sociologists (as well as scholars in many cognate fields whose work is closely related to sociology) in the encyclopedia. (This decision was made on the basis of the editor's past experience with his *Encyclopedia of Social Theory* [Sage, 2005], in which the decision to include living theorists created great difficulties since, without the benefit of some history and hindsight, it was sometimes problematic to draw the line between those to be included and excluded.) In the few weeks since the deadline for the bound volumes of this encyclopedia has passed, several notable figures have died (Betty Friedan, John Kenneth Galbraith, Jane Jacobs). Their biographies will appear in the online version, which will be updated in this way regularly since, life being as it is, we can expect other luminaries to pass.

However, the intention of the editor and the publisher is that this hardback version will also be a living document in that it, too, will be revised. That revision will encompass any new additions made to the online version in the interim, but it will also involve other additions based on a full-scale review of the volumes and reactions, solicited and unsolicited, from experts and readers.

Thus this encyclopedia can be seen as both an effort to define the field of sociology as it stands on the cusp of 2007 and a platform for continually refining and expanding that definition as we go forward. Sociology is a living discipline and it requires a living encyclopedia to do it justice.

George Ritzer
Editor, Encyclopedia of Sociology

Distinguished University Professor,
University of Maryland
June 2006

Timeline

This timeline provides a listing of over 700 of the most influential events, figures, and publications to have made an impact on the field of sociology.

551–479 BCE	Confucius theorizes life and society. His work is primarily known through the *Analects of Confucius*, compiled by his disciples posthumously
469–399 BCE	Socrates lays the foundation of western philosophy
384–322 BCE	Aristotle makes further contributions to western science and philosophy
360 BCE	Plato debates the nature of ethics and politics in *Republic*
973–1048 CE	Al-Biruni, Abu Rayhan Muhammad ibn Ahmad
1332–1406	Ibn-Khaldun, Abdel Rahman
1377	Ibn-Khaldun writes *Muqaddimah*, which many consider one of the first important works in sociology
1516	Thomas More's *Utopia*, in which the term "utopia" is coined
1588–1679	Hobbes, Thomas
1637	René Descartes pronounces "cogito, ergo sum" (I think, therefore I am) in his *Discourse on Method*
1651	Thomas Hobbes's *Leviathan* discusses the requirement of surrender of sovereignty to the state needed to prevent a "war of all against all"
1689–1755	Montesquieu, Baron de
1692–3	Edmund Halley publishes the first life table
1712–78	Rousseau, Jean-Jacques
1713	James Waldegrave introduces an early form of game theory
1723–90	Smith, Adam
1724–1804	Kant, Immanuel
1739	David Hume publishes *Treatise on Human Nature* advocating the study of humanity through direct observation rather than abstract philosophy
1748	Baron de Montesquieu argues that society is the source of all laws in *The Spirit of the Laws*
1759–97	Wollstonecraft, Mary
1760–1825	Saint-Simon, Claude-Henri
1762	Jean-Jacques Rousseau publishes *The Social Contract*, which prioritizes contracts between people and the social will over government control
1764	Reverend Thomas Bayes's *Essay Towards Solving a Problem in the Doctrine of Chances*, published posthumously, contains a statement of his Bayes theorem, the foundation of Bayesian statistics
1766–1834	Malthus, Thomas Robert
1767	Adam Ferguson asserts that conflict between nations leads to solidarity and paves the way for civil society in *Essay on the Origin of Civil Society*
1770–1831	Hegel, G. W. F.
1772–1823	Ricardo, David
1775	American Revolution begins
1776	Thomas Paine's pamphlet *Common Sense* presents a commonsense critique of British monarchical rule over America
1776	Adam Smith discusses the invisible hand of capitalism in *An Inquiry into the Nature and Causes of the Wealth of Nations*
1781	Kant argues against the radical empiricism of Hume in *Critique of Pure Reason*

1788	Kant argues for the essence of free will in *Critique of Practical Reason*
1789	Jeremy Bentham develops the greatest happiness principle in *Introduction to the Principles of Morals and Legislation*, introducing a theory of social morals
1789	Condorcet coins the term "social science"
1789	French Revolution begins
1790	First US Census taken
1792	Wollstonecraft's *A Vindication of the Rights of Woman*, an early feminist classic
1798	Malthus theorizes demographics with his *Essay on the Principle of Population*
1798–1857	Comte, Auguste
1801	First British Census taken
1802–76	Martineau, Harriet
1804–72	Feuerbach, Ludwig
1805–59	Tocqueville, Alexis de
1805	The method of least squares presented by Adrien Marie Legendre in *Nouvelles méthodes pour la détermination des orbites des comètes* [*New Methods for Determining the Orbits of Comets*]
1806–73	Mill, John Stuart
1806–82	Le Play, Frédéric
1807	Hegel's *Phenomenology of Mind*, a key source on Hegel's idealism
1809–82	Darwin, Charles
1812–87	Mayhew, Henry
1817	Ricardo's *The Principles of Political Economy and Taxation*, a classic in political economy laying out the advantages of free trade
1818–83	Marx, Karl
1820–95	Engels, Friedrich
1820–1903	Spencer, Herbert
1822–1911	Galton, Francis
1832–1917	Tylor, Sir Edward Burnett
1833–1911	Dilthey, William
1834	Statistical Society of London (later Royal Statistical Society) founded
1835–82	Jevons, William
1835–1909	Lombroso, Cesare
1835	Adolphe Quételet authors *Sur l'homme et le développement de ses facultés, ou Essai de physique sociale* [*On Man and the Development of his Faculties, an Essay on Social Physics*] outlining his ideas of "the average man," a statistical denotation of the mean values of measured variables
1837	Hegel's *Philosophy of History*, a dialectical analysis of the goal of human history
1837	Martineau's *Society in America*, an early sociological classic based on the author's travels through America
1838–1909	Gumplowicz, Ludwig
1839	Comte coins the term "sociology"
1839	American Statistical Association founded
1840	Tocqueville offers early insight into the United States in *Democracy in America*
1840–1902	Krafft-Ebing, Richard von
1840–1910	Sumner, William Graham
1840–1916	Booth, Charles
1841–1913	Ward, Lester Frank
1842	Comte's *Course in Positive Philosophy* lays out a positivistic approach
1842–1904	Ratzenhofer, Gustav
1842–1910	James, William
1843	Mill in *A System of Logic* says that science needs both inductive and deductive reasoning

1843–1904	Tarde, Gabriel
1844	Marx's early humanistic thinking is laid out in *Economic and Philosophic Manuscripts of 1844* (not published until 1932)
1844–1900	Nietzsche, Friedrich
1846	Marx authors *The German Ideology*, proposing a methodology of historical materialism
1848	Marx and Engels inspire the masses and call for revolution with the *Communist Manifesto*
1848	Mill debates the principles of socialism in his *Principles of Political Economy*
1848–1923	Pareto, Vilfredo
1849–1928	Howard, George Elliott
1850	Spencer introduces his ideas of social structure and change in *Social Statics*
1851	Feuerbach's *Lectures on the Essence of Religion*
1851	The Crystal Palace opens during first World's Fair in London
1854–1926	Small, Albion W.
1854–1932	Geddes, Sir Patrick
1854–1941	Frazer, Sir James
1855–1936	Tönnies, Ferdinand
1855	Le Play authors *Les Ouvriers européens*, a series of 36 monographs on the budgets of typical families selected from diverse industries
1856–1939	Freud, Sigmund
1857	In Britain, the Society of the Study of Social Problems is created
1857–1913	Saussure, Ferdinand de
1857–1929	Veblen, Thorstein
1857–61	Marx lays the groundwork for his later work on political economy and capitalism in *Grundrisse: Foundations of the Critique of Political Economy*
1857–84	The National Association for the Promotion of Social Science operates in Britain
1857–1936	Pearson, Karl
1858–1917	Durkheim, Émile
1858–1918	Simmel, Georg
1858–1922	Sarasvati, Pandita Ramabai
1858–1941	Mosca, Gaetano
1858–1942	Boas, Franz
1858–1943	Webb, Beatrice
1858–1916	Kidd, Benjamin
1859	Charles Darwin writes about evolution through natural selection in *The Origin of Species*
1859–1939	Ellis, Havelock
1859–1952	Dewey, John
1859–1938	Husserl, Edmund
1860–1935	Addams, Jane
1860–1935	Gilman, Charlotte Perkins
1861–96	Rizal, José
1863–1931	Mead, George Herbert
1863–1941	Sombart, Werner
1863–1945	Spearman, Charles Edward
1863–1947	Thomas, William I.
1864–1920	Weber, Max
1864–1929	Cooley, Charles Horton
1864–1929	Hobhouse, L. T.
1864–1944	Park, Robert E.
1866–1951	Ross, Edward Alsworth

1867	Marx publishes one of the greatest insights into capitalism with *Capital*, Vol. 1: *A Critique of Political Economy*
1868–1935	Hirschfeld, Magnus
1868–1963	Du Bois, W. E. B.
1869–1940	Goldman, Emma
1870–1954	Weber, Marianne
1870–1964	Pound, Roscoe
1871–1919	Luxemburg, Rosa
1871–1954	Rowntree, Benjamin Seebohm
1873	Spencer's *Study of Sociology* becomes the first book used as a text to teach sociology in the United States, although no formal sociology class yet exists
1875–1962	Yanagita, Kunio
1876–96	Spencer writes his three-volume work on *Principles of Sociology*
1876–1924	Gökalp, Ziya
1876–1936	Michels, Robert
1876–1937	Gosset, William Sealy
1876–1958	Beard, Mary Ritter
1877–1945	Halbwachs, Maurice
1877	Galton introduces the statistical phenomenon of regression and uses this term, although he originally termed it "reversion"
1879–1963	Beveridge, William Henry
1881–1955	Radcliffe-Brown, Alfred R.
1882–1958	Znaniecki, Florian
1882–1970	MacIver, Robert
1883–1950	Schumpeter, Joseph A.
1883–1972	Takata, Yasuma
1884	Engels argues that women are subordinated by society, not biology, in *The Origins of the Family, Private Property, and the State*
1884–1942	Malinowski, Bronislaw K.
1885–1971	Lukács, Georg
1886	Krafft-Ebing publishes *Psychopathia Sexualis*, one of the first systematic studies of sexuality
1886	Sarasvati authors *The High-Caste Hindu Woman*, raising public consciousness about the plight of Hindu women and marking the beginning of family and kinship studies in India
1886–1964	Polanyi, Karl
1886–1966	Burgess, Ernest W.
1887	Tönnies's *Gemeinschaft und Gesellschaft* introduces his concepts of the same name
1887	Rizal publishes his first novel, *Noli Me Tangere* [*Touch Me Not*], describing the problems of Filipino society and blaming Spanish colonial rule
1887–1949	Sarkar, Benoy Kumar
1889	Charles Booth publishes his pioneering study of London poverty as *Life and Labour of the People of London*
1889–1968	Sorokin, Pitirim A.
1889–1976	Heidegger, Martin
1890	William James's *Principles of Psychology* is an early scientific work in psychology noted for its emphasis on the self
1890	Tarde distinguishes between the imitative and inventive in *Laws of Imitation*
1890	The first course in sociology is taught at the University of Kansas in Lawrence
1890	Sir James Frazer authors *The Golden Bough*, a comparative study of mythology and religion
1890–1947	Lewin, Kurt

1890–1962	Fisher, Sir Ronald Aylmer
1891	The first department of sociology and history is founded at the University of Kansas in Lawrence
1891	Walter Francis Wilcox's *The Divorce Problem: A Study in Statistics*
1891–1937	Gramsci, Antonio
1892	Small founds first major Department of Sociology at the University of Chicago
1892–1940	Benjamin, Walter
1893	Durkheim discusses the transition from mechanical to organic solidarity in *The Division of Labor in Society*
1893	New Zealand becomes the first country in the world to grant women the right to vote
1893	The first journal of sociology, *Revue Internationale de Sociologie*, is edited by René Worms in Paris
1893	The first sociological society, the Institut International de Sociologie, is founded in France
1893	Pearson introduces the term "standard deviation"
1893–1947	Mannheim, Karl
1893–1950	Sutherland, Edwin H.
1893–1956	Johnson, Charles Spurgeon
1893–1981	Marshall, Thomas Humphrey
1894	Kidd publishes *Social Evolution*, setting forth his ideas about the constant strife between individual and public interest
1894–1956	Kinsey, Alfred
1894–1962	Frazier, E. Franklin
1894–1966	Suzuki, Eitaro
1895	Durkheim presents a methodological foundation for sociology in *Rules of the Sociological Method*
1895	The first large-scale census of the German Empire is taken
1895	The first Department of Sociology in Europe is founded by Durkheim at the University of Bordeaux
1895	The Fabians found the London School of Economics (LSE)
1895	The *American Journal of Sociology* (*AJS*) is begun by Albion Small
1895	Nietzsche attacks sociology in *Twilight of the Idols*
1895–1973	Horkheimer, Max
1895–1988	Mendieta y Núñez, Lucio
1895–1990	Mumford, Lewis
1896–1988	Kurauchi, Kazuta
1897	Durkheim uses *Suicide* to demonstrate how even the most seemingly individual of acts still has a basis in the social
1897	*Rivista Italiana di Sociologia* appears in Italy
1897–1957	Reich, Wilhelm
1897–1962	Bataille, Georges
1897–1990	Elias, Norbert
1898	Durkheim founds the journal *L'Année Sociologique* (later *Annales de Sociologie*)
1898–1970	Warner, William Lloyd
1898–1979	Marcuse, Herbert
1899	Veblen develops his idea of conspicuous consumption in *The Theory of the Leisure Class*
1899	Du Bois's *The Philadelphia Negro: A Social Study* is one of the first urban ethnographies
1899–1959	Schütz, Alfred
1899–1960	Becker, Howard

1899–1977	Thomas, Dorothy Swain
1900	Freud introduces his early principles of psychoanalysis in *Interpretation of Dreams*
1900	Husserl lays the groundwork of phenomenology in *Logical Investigations*
1900	Simmel discusses the tragedy of culture in *The Philosophy of Money*
1900	Pearson introduces the chi-squared test and the name for it in an article in the *London, Edinburgh, and Dublin Philosophical Magazine and Journal of Science*
1900–80	Fromm, Erich
1900–87	Blumer, Herbert
1901	E. A. Ross authors *Social Control*, in which he analyzes societal stability in terms of sympathy, sociability, and social justice
1901–74	Cox, Oliver Cromwell
1901–76	Lazarsfeld, Paul
1901–78	Mead, Margaret
1901–81	Lacan, Jacques
1901–91	Lefebvre, Henri
1902	Cooley's *Human Nature and Social Order* is an early classic that influenced symbolic interactionism, noted for its emphasis on the "looking-glass self"
1902	Ebenezer Howard inspires urban reform with his *Garden Cities of To-morrow*
1902	Durkheim becomes the first Professor of Sociology in Europe with his appointment to a position at the Sorbonne
1902	The United States Census Bureau is founded
1902–79	Parsons, Talcott
1902–85	Braudel, Fernand
1902–92	Imanishi, Kinji
1903	Du Bois introduces the concepts of the veil and double consciousness in *The Souls of Black Folk*
1903	The LSE houses the first British Department of Sociology
1903	Durkheim and his nephew Marcel Mauss's *Primitive Classification* shows the basis of classification in the social world rather than the mind
1903	Formation of the Sociological Society in London; operates on a UK-wide basis
1903–69	Adorno, Theodor W.
1903–96	Bernard, Jessie
1904	Robert Park's *The Crowd and the Public* is an early contribution to the study of collective behavior
1904	Contingency tables introduced by Pearson in "On the Theory of Contingency and its Relation to Association and Normal Correlation," which appeared in *Drapers' Company Research Memoirs Biometric Series I*
1904	Spearman develops rank correlation
1904–33	*Archiv für Sozialwissenschaft und Sozialpolitik* founded by Max Weber, Werner Sombart, and Edgar Jaffé; it was shut down when the Nazis took power
1904–80	Bateson, Gregory
1904–90	Skinner, Burrhus Frederic
1905	American Sociological Society (ASS) [later ASA] founded at a meeting held at Johns Hopkins University in Baltimore, Maryland
1905	Weber ties the rise of the capitalist spirit to Calvinism in *The Protestant Ethic and the Spirit of Capitalism*
1905–6	Lester Ward serves as the first President of the ASS
1905–80	Sartre, Jean-Paul
1905–83	Aron, Raymond
1905–99	Komarovsky, Mirra
1906	First ASS meeting is held in Providence, Rhode Island
1906	Sombart's *Why Is There No Socialism in the United States?*

1906	Hobhouse publishes *Morals in Evolution: A Study in Comparative Ethics*
1906–75	Arendt, Hannah
1907	Hobhouse becomes the first Professor of Sociology at a British university, the LSE (although Edvard Westermarck had held the position part-time a few weeks before Hobhouse)
1907	James's *Pragmatism* helps set the stage for the rise of symbolic interactionism
1907	Eugenics Society founded in the UK
1908	Simmel publishes *Soziologie*, a wide-ranging set of essays on various social phenomena
1908	*Sociological Review* founded
1908	William Sealy Gosset, who went by the pseudonym "student," introduces the statistic z for testing hypotheses on the mean of the normal distribution in his paper "The Probable Error of a Mean" (*Biometrika*)
1908–86	Beauvoir, Simone de
1908–97	Davis, Kingsley
1908–2006	Galbraith, John Kenneth
1908–	Lévi-Strauss, Claude
1909	German Sociological Association founded with Tönnies serving as the first President
1909	Freud delivers first lectures on psychoanalysis in the US at Clark University
1909–2002	Riesman, David
1910	Addams's *Twenty Years at Hull House* contains recollections and reflections of the social reformer and feminist
1910–89	Homans, George
1910–2003	Merton, Robert K.
1911	Frederick W. Taylor authors *The Principles of Scientific Management*, laying out his ideas of the same name
1911–63	Kuhn, Manford
1911–79	Germani, Gino
1911–80	McLuhan, Marshall
1911–2004	Riley, Matilda White
1912	Durkheim equates religion with the social in *The Elementary Forms of the Religious Life*
1912–96	Lemert, Edwin M.
1913	James Broadus Watson introduces the term "behaviorism"
1913	The first assembly line introduced in a Ford factory
1913–2003	Coser, Lewis
1914–18	World War I
1914–96	Maruyama, Masao
1914–2000	Whyte, William Foote
1915	Pareto's *General Treatise on Sociology* is a major contribution to sociology by a thinker most associated with economics
1915	Sir Patrick Geddes authors *Cities in Evolution*, an essay on the growth of cities
1915–80	Barthes, Roland
1915–2005	Shanas, Ethel
1916	Saussure distinguishes between the signifier and the signified in *Course in General Linguistics*
1916–62	Mills, C. Wright
1916–72	Kent, Donald P.
1916–96	Strauss, Anselm
1916–2006	Jacobs, Jane
1917	Russian Revolution begins
1917	Sociology taught for the first time in India at Calcutta University

1917–	Whyte, William H.
1918	Znaniecki and Thomas use multiple methods in *The Polish Peasant in Europe and America*
1918	Weber's lecture on "Science as Vocation"
1918	The first Chair in Sociology in Germany is established at the University of Frankfurt
1918	The phrase "analysis of variance" appears in Sir Ronald Aylmer Fisher's "The Causes of Human Variability" (*Eugenics Review*)
1918–22	Oswald Spengler's *Decline of the West* argues that the development of civilizations follows a recognizable series of repetitive rises and falls
1918–90	Althusser, Louis
1918–2002	Blau, Peter
1918–	Tsurumi, Kazuko
1919	Sorokin's doctoral dissertation, *System of Sociology*, is published secretly after the Russian Revolution
1919	Hirschfeld opens the Institute for Sexual Research in Berlin
1919	The New School for Social Research is founded
1919	Takata Yasuma writes *Shakaigaku Genri* [*Treatise on Sociology*], in which he attempts a general sociological theory based on methodological individualism
1919	First Sociology Department in India formed at Bombay University
1919–	Bell, Daniel
1920	Znaniecki becomes the first Chair in Sociology in Poland at the University of Poznan
1920–76	Braverman, Harry
1920–80	Gouldner, Alvin
1920–92	Bottomore, Thomas Burton
1921	Park and Burgess author *Introduction to the Science of Sociology*, the first major sociology textbook
1921–88	Williams, Raymond
1921–2002	Rawls, John
1921–2004	Duncan, Otis Dudley
1921–2006	Friedan, Betty
1922	Weber's *Economy and Society* is published in three volumes posthumously, introducing his comparative historical methodology
1922	Malinowski publishes *Argonauts of the Western Pacific*, in which he classifies ethnographic research into three parts based on complexity
1922	Social Science Research Council established in the US
1922–82	Goffman, Erving
1922–92	Rosenberg, Morris
1922–96	Kuhn, Thomas
1922–97	Castoriadis, Cornelius
1922–	Casanova, Pablo González
1923	Lukács's *History and Class Consciousness* anticipates a more humanist interpretation of Marx; it is a key source on the concept of "reification"
1923	The Institute of Social Research, also known as the Frankfurt School, is founded
1923	Weber's *General Economic History* (published posthumously)
1923–2003	Kitsuse, John I.
1923–	Eisenstadt, Shmuel N.
1924	Hisatoshi Tanabe founds Tokyo Shakaigaku Kenkyukai (Tokyo Society of Sociological Study)
1924	Sutherland presents the first systematic textbook study of crime in *Criminology*
1924	Hobhouse publishes *Social Development: Its Nature and Conditions*

1924–33	Elton Mayo conducts the Hawthorne Experiments on worker productivity and concludes that the very act of studying something can change it, a principle that has come to be known as the "Hawthorne effect"
1924–98	Lyotard, Jean-François
1924–	Berger, Joseph
1924–	Pearlin, Leonard
1924–	Stryker, Sheldon
1925	Mauss develops his theory of gift exchange in *The Gift*
1925	Halbwachs helps establish social memory studies with *The Social Frameworks of Memory*
1925	Park and Burgess invigorate urban sociology with *The City*
1925	Fisher's *Statistical Methods for Research Workers* becomes a landmark text in the field of statistics
1925–61	Fanon, Franz
1925–82	Emerson, Richard M.
1925–86	Certeau, Michel de
1925–94	Liebow, Elliot
1925–95	Deleuze, Gilles
1925–95	Gellner, Ernst
1925–	Bauman, Zygmunt
1925–	Rex, John Arderne
1925–	Touraine, Alain
1926–84	Foucault, Michel
1926–95	Coleman, James
1926–2002	Illich, Ivan
1926–	Smith, Dorothy
1927	Heidegger's *Being and Time* is an existentialist analysis of individuals' relationship to modern society
1927	Znaniecki founds the Polish Sociological Institute
1927–40	Benjamin collects notes that later become *The Arcades Project*, an early classic on, among many other things, consumption sites
1927–98	Luhmann, Niklas
1927–	Bellah, Robert
1927–	Ichibangase, Yasuko
1927–	Luckmann, Thomas
1928	William I. Thomas and Dorothy S. Thomas introduce the Thomas theorem – what humans perceive as real will be real in its consequences – in *The Child in America*
1928–2003	Hess, Beth
1928–	Alatas, Syed Hussein
1928–	Becker, Howard S.
1928–	Chomsky, Noam
1928–	Townsend, Peter Brereton
1929	Mannheim's *Ideology and Utopia* elaborates his sociology of knowledge
1929	The Great Depression begins in the US and spreads to the rest of the world
1929	Robert S. Lynd and Helen M. Lynd conduct the Middletown studies
1929	k-statistics are introduced by Sir Ronald Aylmer Fisher
1929–68	King, Jr., Martin Luther
1929–	Baudrillard, Jean
1929–	Berger, Peter
1929–	Dahrendorf, Ralf
1929–	Etzioni, Amitai
1929–	Garfinkel, Harold

1929–	Habermas, Jürgen
1929–	Scheff, Thomas Joel
1929–	Tilly, Charles
1930	J. L. Moreno invents sociometry, the cornerstone of network analysis
1930	Yanagita introduces his theory of *shūkenron* (concentric area theory) in his book *Kagyükö [On Snails]*
1930–89	Spence, Donald L.
1930–92	Guattari, Félix
1930–2002	Bourdieu, Pierre
1930–2004	Derrida, Jacques
1930–	Wallerstein, Immanuel
1931	The Sociology Department at Harvard is established by Sorokin
1931	Population Association of America (PAA) founded
1931	The term "factor analysis" introduced by Louis L. Thurstone in "Multiple Factor Analysis" (*Psychological Review*)
1931–94	Debord, Guy
1931–	Cardozo, Fernando Henrique
1931–	Rorty, Richard
1931–	Tominaga, Ken'ichi
1931–	Yoshida, Tamito
1932	Schütz's *The Phenomenology of the Social World* introduces phenomenology into mainstream social theory
1932–	Hall, Stuart
1932–	Irigaray, Luce
1932–	Stavenhagen, Rodolfo
1932–	Virilio, Paul
1933–77	Shariati, Ali
1933–84	Milgram, Stanley
1934	Mead develops ideas central to symbolic interactionism in *Mind, Self, and Society*
1934	The term "confidence interval" coined by Jerzy Neyman in "On the Two Different Aspects of the Representative Method" (*Journal of the Royal Statistical Society*)
1934	The F distribution tabulated by G. W. Snedecor in *Calculation and Interpretation of Analysis of Variance and Covariance*
1934–92	Lorde, Audre
1934–	Gergen, Kenneth
1934–	Jameson, Fredric
1935	Mannheim suggests a planned society in *Man and Society in an Age of Reconstruction*
1935	*American Sociological Review* (*ASR*) begins with Frank Hankins as editor
1935	The term "null hypothesis" is used by Fisher in *The Design of Experiments*
1935–75	Sacks, Harvey
1935–91	Bonfil Batalla, Guillermo
1935–2002	Sainsaulieu, Renaud
1935–2003	Faletto, Enzo
1935–2003	Said, Edward W.
1935–	Wilson, William Julius
1936	John Maynard Keynes introduces his economic theory in *General Theory of Employment, Interest, and Money*
1936–79	Poulantzas, Nicos
1937	Parsons helps bring European theory to the United States in *The Structure of Social Action*
1937	Mass Observation research unit set up by Tom Harrison, Charles Madge, and Humphrey Jennings

1937–	Lemert, Charles
1937–	Mita, Munesuke
1937–	Willer, David
1938	Skinner's *The Behavior of Organisms* is a major contribution to psychological behaviorism
1938	*Journal of Marriage and the Family* founded
1938–2002	Nozick, Robert
1938–	Giddens, Anthony
1938–	Robertson, Roland
1939	Elias develops his figurational sociology in *The Civilizing Process*
1939–45	World War II
1939–2004	Lechner, Norbert
1939–	Burke, Peter J.
1940–91	Fajnzylber, Fernando
1940–	Ritzer, George
1940–	Komai, Hiroshi
1941	Kinji Imanishi publishes *Seibutsu no Sekai* [*The World of Living Things*], which is a philosophical statement of his views on the origins and interactions of organisms with their environment and development of the biosphere
1941	William Lloyd Warner authors *The Social Life of a Modern Community*, the first volume in the "Yankee City" series
1941–	Collins, Randall
1941–	Kristeva, Julia
1942	Schumpeter's *Capitalism, Socialism, and Democracy*, best known for the idea of "creative destruction" in capitalism
1942	William Henry Beveridge publishes *Social Insurance and Allied Services*, known as the Beveridge Report, establishing the foundations for the welfare state
1942–2004	Anzaldúa, Gloria
1942–	Bartra, Roger
1942–	Castells, Manuel
1942–	Turner, Jonathan
1943	Sartre further develops existentialism in *Being and Nothingness*
1943	William Foote Whyte's *Street Corner Society* is a classic ethnography on street corner life in Boston
1943	The statistical P-value is discussed in *Statistical Adjustment of Data* by W. E. Deming
1943–	Ahmed, Akbar S.
1943–	Hartsock, Nancy
1944	Polanyi's *The Great Transformation* discusses issues of socialism, free trade, and the Industrial Revolution
1944–	Beck, Ulrich
1944–	Brunner, José Joaquín
1944–	Chodorow, Nancy
1944–	Haraway, Donna
1944–	Inagami, Takashi
1945	Kingsley Davis and Wilbert Moore lay the groundwork for stratification in "Some Principles of Stratification" (*ASR*)
1945	United Nations founded
1945–	Turner, Bryan
1946	Parsons establishes the Department of Social Relations at Harvard
1946–	Cook, Karen S.
1946–	Huat, Chua Beng

1946–	Plummer, Kenneth
1946–	Wuthnow, Robert
1947	Kinsey Institute founded at Indiana University at Bloomington
1947	Horkheimer and Adorno criticize the Enlightenment in *The Dialectic of Enlightenment*
1947–	Alexander, Jeffrey
1947–	Latour, Bruno
1947–	Wright, Erik Olin
1948	Alfred Kinsey, Wardell Pomeroy, and Clyde Martin revolutionize the way many think about sexuality with *The Sexual Behavior of the Human Male*
1948	E. Franklin Frazier is elected the first black President of the ASS
1948	Oliver Cromwell Cox authors his famous analysis in *Caste, Class, and Race*
1948–2002	Rosenfeld, Rachel
1948–	Collins, Patricia Hill
1948–	Molm, Linda
1948–	Shimazono, Susumu
1948–	Ueno, Chizuko
1949	Lévi-Strauss helps develop structuralist thinking with his *The Elementary Structures of Kinship*
1949	Merton's *Social Theory and Social Structure* appears, the first edition of a classic collection of essays
1949	Simone de Beauvoir challenges the traditional concept of "woman" in *The Second Sex*
1949	International Sociological Association founded with Louis Wirth serving as the first President
1949	Stoufer et al., *The American Soldier: Adjustment During Army Life*, Vol. 1, is a major empirical study of the American military
1949–	Bhabha, Homi
1949–	Žižek, Slavoj
1950	David Reisman, Nathan Glazer, and Reuel Denney develop inner- and other-directedness in *The Lonely Crowd*
1950–	Fine, Gary Alan
1951	C. Wright Mills offers an analysis of working life in the United States in *White Collar*
1951	Parsons furthers his structural functional theory in *The Social System*
1951	Parsons develops action theory in *Toward a General Theory of Action*
1951	Society for the Study of Social Problems (SSSP) founded in the United States
1951	SSSP begins publishing journal *Social Problems*
1951	British Sociological Association is founded
1951	Asch experiments are published demonstrating the power of group conformity
1951	Arendt's *The Origins of Totalitarianism* is a classic work in political theory, especially totalitarianism
1951	Indian Sociological Society founded at Bombay
1951–	DiMaggio, Paul
1952	International Social Science Council established
1952	*Current Sociology*, an official journal of the International Sociological Association, is launched
1952	American Psychiatric Association publishes first edition of the *Diagnostic and Statistical Manual* (*DSM*)
1952	Dorothy Swain Thomas is elected the first female President of the ASS
1952	*Sociological Bulletin* first published at Bombay University
1952–	Bianchi, Suzanne

1953	Skinner's *Science and Human Behavior* is a further contribution to psychological behaviorism
1953	Ludwig Wittgenstein's ideas of language games are presented in his work *Philosophical Investigations*
1954	Abraham Maslow makes famous his hierarchy of needs in *Motivation and Personality*
1954	Manford Kuhn and Thomas McPartland lay the groundwork for structural symbolic interactionism in "An Empirical Investigation of Self-Attitudes" (*ASR*)
1954	The United States Supreme Court decision in *Brown* v. *Board of Education of Topeka, Kansas* ends officially sanctioned segregation in that country
1955	L. J. Moreno's *Sociometry* is a major contribution to social psychology
1955	Gino Germani's *Estructura Social de la Argentina* [*The Social Structure of Argentina*] uses empirical data from the Argentinian national census of 1947 to analyze contemporary Argentina
1956	Mills argues that there has been a convergence of economic, political, and military power and that members of this elite largely share a common social background in *The Power Elite*
1956	Dahrendorf's *Class and Class Conflict in Industrial Society* becomes a central work in conflict theory
1956	Coser integrates a Simmelian approach with structural functionalism in the *Functions of Social Conflict*
1956–	Butler, Judith
1956–	Markovsky, Barry
1957	Barthes helps develop semiology in *Mythologies*
1957	Chomsky revolutionizes the field of linguistics and helps spark the cognitive revolution with *Syntactic Structures*
1957	Richard Hoggart's *The Uses of Literacy* is an early contribution and exemplification of the Birmingham School
1957	Maruyama Masao writes *Denken in Japan* [*Japanese Thought*], which still serves as a reference point for ongoing debates on the intellectual development of modern Japan
1957	Michael Young and Peter Willmott author *Family and Kinship in East London*, exploring changes in kinship networks and contacts of families in East London as they are affected by urban change
1958	Galbraith challenges the idea of consumer sovereignty in *The Affluent Society*
1958	Homans's article "Social Behavior as Exchange" (*AJS*) develops his notion of exchange theory
1958	Raymond Williams presents his first major analysis of culture in *Culture and Society*
1959	Karl Popper's *The Logic of Scientific Discovery* argues that scientific results can never be proven, merely falsified
1959	Mills critiques structural functionalism in *The Sociological Imagination*, also introducing his concept of the same name
1959	Goffman's early statement on dramaturgy is developed in *The Presentation of Self in Everyday Life*
1959	Thibaut and Kelley's *The Social Psychology of Groups* is an early psychological contribution to exchange theory
1959	ASS changes its name to the American Sociological Association (ASA)
1960	*Journal of Health and Social Behavior* (*JHSB*) founded
1960	Morris Janowitz's *The Professional Soldier: A Social and Political Portrait*
1960	Alvin Gouldner's "The Norm of Reciprocity: A Preliminary Statement" (*ASR*)
1960	Margarey Stacey authors her first major work, *Tradition and Change: A Study of Banbury*
1961	Homans further develops his exchange theory in *Social Behavior: Its Elementary Forms*

1961	Fanon's *The Wretched of the Earth* is a powerful influence on revolutionary movements
1961	Goffman introduces the idea of a total institution in *Asylums: Essays on the Social Situation of Mental Patients and Other Inmates*
1961	Jane Jacobs analyzes urban culture in *The Death and Life of Great American Cities*
1961	*International Journal of Comparative Sociology* founded
1962	Richard Emerson introduces his first major statement on exchange theory in "Power-Dependence Relations" (*ASR*)
1962	Thomas Kuhn in *The Structure of Scientific Revolutions* offers a revolutionary rather than evolutionary theory of scientific change
1962	Habermas's *The Structural Transformation of the Public Sphere* is an important early contribution to current debate on civil society
1962	Herbert Gans's *Urban Villagers* is a classic in urban sociology
1963	Goffman publishes *Stigma*, one of the first major works in labeling theory
1963	Betty Friedan's *The Feminine Mystique* marks the beginning of the second wave of feminism for many
1963	Australian Sociological Association founded (originally known as the Sociological Association of Australia and New Zealand)
1963	Stanley Milgram's experiments are outlined in his article "Behavioral Study of Obedience" (*Journal of Abnormal and Social Psychology*)
1963	*Demography* journal founded by Donald Bogue
1963	S. N. Eisenstadt presents analytic tools helpful for cultural comparison in *The Political Systems of Empires*
1963	European Fertility Project begun by Ansley Coale
1963	First issue of *Sociology of Education* published
1963	Nathan Glazer and Daniel P. Moynihan's *Beyond the Melting Pot* is known for its focus on assimilation
1963	Martin Luther King, Jr. delivers his "I Have a Dream" speech in Washington, DC
1963	Becker's *Outsiders: Studies in the Sociology of Deviance* is a key document in the sociology of deviance, especially labeling theory
1964	Blau's major integrative statement in exchange theory is laid out in *Exchange and Power in Social Life*
1964	McLuhan discusses the global village in *Understanding Media: The Extensions of Man*
1964	Marcuse publishes *One-Dimensional Man: Studies in the Ideology of Advances in Industrial Society*, outlining what he sees as society's destructive impact on individuals
1964	Center for Contemporary Cultural Studies founded under the leadership of Richard Hoggart at the University of Birmingham, UK
1964	Aaron V. Cicourel's *Method and Measurement in Sociology*
1965	Social Science Research Council established in the UK (name changed to Economic and Social Research Council in 1983)
1965	Foucault argues that the madman has taken the place of the leper in *Madness and Civilization*
1965	*Australian and New Zealand Journal of Sociology* founded (later changed to *Journal of Sociology* in 1998)
1966	William Masters and Virginia Johnson further research into human sexuality in *Human Sexual Response*
1966	Berger and Luckmann further develop social constructionism in *The Social Construction of Reality: A Treatise in the Sociology of Knowledge*
1966	Scheff's *Being Mentally Ill: A Sociological Theory* becomes a major work in studies of mental illness, social constructionism, and labeling theory

1966	George McCall and J. L. Simmons help popularize identity theory in *Identities and Interactions*
1967	Derrida's *On Grammatology* becomes a central text in the emerging area of poststructuralism
1967	Debord criticizes both the media and consumption in *Society of the Spectacle*
1967	Garfinkel's *Studies in Ethnomethodology* develops the field of the same name
1967	*Sociology*, the official journal of the British Sociological Association, is founded
1967	Barney Glaser and Anselm Strauss's *The Discovery of Grounded Theory: Strategies for Qualitative Research* introduces their theory of the same name
1967	Liebow's *Tally's Corner: A Study of Negro Streetcorner Men* is an important ethnographic study carried out in Washington, DC
1967	Gans's *The Levittowners* is another classic ethnography, this time in a paradigmatic suburban development
1967	Otis Dudley Duncan authors *The American Occupational Structure*, detailing how parents transmit their societal status to their children
1968	Student revolts begin in Paris and spread throughout Europe
1968	Paul Ehrlich's *The Population Bomb* issues an early, perhaps overheated, warning about the population explosion
1968	John Goldthorpe, David Lockwood, Frank Bechhofer, and Jennifer Platt, in *The Affluent Worker: Industrial Attitudes and Behavior*, argue that the growing affluence of sections of the working class in Britain does not entail the end of class division, but that class remains a central feature of British life even in a prosperous, consumer society
1968	*Chinese Sociology and Anthropology* founded
1969	Blumer gives one of the first systematic statements of symbolic interactionism in *Symbolic Interactionism: Perspectives and Methods*
1969	Althusser lays the groundwork of structural Marxism in *For Marx*
1969	Native Americans take over Alcatraz Island in California, launching their civil rights movement
1969	The gay rights movement is launched during the Stonewall Riots in New York City
1969	Faletto and Cardoso author *Dependencia y Desarrollo en América Latina* [*Dependency and Development in Latin America*], which attempts to systematize an interpretive model of economic development in Latin America
1970	Students protesting the American invasion of Cambodia are shot by National Guardsmen at Kent State University in Kent, Ohio, setting off a wave of student strikes across the United States
1970	Gouldner critiques trends in sociology, especially structural functionalism, in *The Coming Crisis of Western Sociology*
1970	Baudrillard's *Consumer Society: Myths and Structures* becomes a classic text in the study of consumption
1970	Thomas S. Szasz launches a critique of psychiatry in *The Manufacture of Madness: A Comparative Study of the Inquisition and the Mental Health Movement*
1970	The first Women's Studies Program in the United States opens at San Diego State College
1970	Phillip Slater's *The Pursuit of Loneliness* discusses individualism, isolation, loneliness, and hyperconsumption circa the 1960s
1970	Fajnzylber publishes his first important work, *Sistema Industrial y Exportación de Manufacturas: Análisis de la Experiencia Brasileña* [*The Industrial System and Manufactured Goods: An Analysis of the Brazilian Experience*]
1971	Habermas presents a prehistory of modern positivism with the intention of analyzing knowledge-constitutive interests in control, understanding, and emancipation in *Knowledge and Human Interests*

1971	Antonio Gramsci's *Prison Notebooks* are published, making his ideas, including hegemony, better known
1971	Phillip Zimbardo conducts his famous prison experiments at Stanford
1971	Sociologists for Women in Society (SWS) founded
1971	William Ryan's *Blaming the Victim* appears; the title becomes a catchphrase to describe placing blame on victims rather than on perpetrators
1972	The First General Social Survey (GSS) is taken
1972	The destruction of the Pruitt-Igoe housing complex in St. Louis marks the end of the modernist reign for some postmodernists
1972	*Journal on Armed Forces and Society* founded
1972	*Philippine Sociological Review* founded
1973	Baudrillard challenges Marx in *The Mirror of Production*
1973	Clifford Geertz introduces his notion of "thick descriptions" in *The Interpretation of Cultures*
1973	David Rosenhan questions taken-for-granted notions of sanity and insanity in "On Being Sane in Insane Places" (*Science*)
1973	The United States Supreme Court decision in *Roe* v. *Wade* gives women the right to choose in issues of abortion
1973	Mark Granovetter's "The Strength of Weak Ties" (*AJS*) introduces his concept of the same name
1973	Bell's *The Coming of Post-Industrial Society* documents and anticipates dramatic social change
1974	Immanuel Wallerstein develops world-systems theory in the first of his three-volume work, *The Modern World-System*
1974	First issue of *Theory and Society* published
1974	Goffman's *Frame Analysis: An Essay on the Organization of Experience* introduces the influential idea of frames
1974	Glen Elder, Jr.'s *Children of the Great Depression* sets the stage for the development of the life course perspective
1974	The National Commission for the Protection of Human Subjects of Biomedical and Behavioral Research is established
1974	Henri Lefebvre brings spatial concerns to the forefront of social analysis in *The Production of Space*
1975	George Ritzer's *Sociology: A Multiple Paradigm Science* outlines the paradigmatic status of sociology and constitutes a contribution to metatheory
1975	Randall Collins develops a micro perspective on conflict theory in *Conflict Sociology: Toward an Explanatory Science*
1975	E. O. Wilson's *Sociobiology: A New Synthesis* is a key statement in the development of sociobiology
1975	Foucault outlines the history and theory of the carceral system in *Discipline and Punish: The Birth of the Prison*
1975	Foucault employs his idea of an archeology of knowledge in *The Birth of the Clinic: An Archeology of Medical Perception*
1975	Castoriadis's *The Imaginary Institution of Society* presents an interdisciplinary critique of contemporary capitalist societies, in part by formulating an alternative to both foundationalist social science and poststructural relativism
1975	Peter Singer's *Animal Liberation* becomes an important text in the animal rights movement
1975	*Canadian Journal of Sociology* founded
1976	Baudrillard argues that we can no longer engage in symbolic exchange in his *Symbolic Exchange and Death*
1976	Elijah Anderson's *A Place on the Corner* becomes a cornerstone of classical ethnography

1977	Bourdieu introduces habitus, field, and his constructivist structuralism in *Outline of a Theory of Practice*
1977	Albert Bandura's *Social Learning Theory* introduces the perspective of the same name
1977	James House's "The Three Faces of Social Psychology" (*Sociometry*) provides perspective for the field
1977	Joseph Berger, M. Hamit Fisek, Robert Norman, and Morris Zelditch's *Status Characteristics and Social Interaction: An Expectation States Approach* introduces the theory of the same name
1977	Richard Sennett's *The Fall of Public Man* demonstrates the impoverishment of the social world
1977	R. W. Connell's *Ruling Class, Ruling Culture: Studies of Conflict, Power, and Hegemony in Australian Life* deals with Australian class relations and culture
1977	Norbert Lechner urges Latin Americans to use political reflection as a guide to theoretical analysis in *La Crisis del Estado en América Latina*
1978	The publication of Edward Said's *Orientalism* is a foundational historical moment in the rise of postcolonial studies
1978	Derrida's *Writing and Difference* is another key contribution to poststructuralism
1978	Nancy Chodorow expands on Freud in *The Reproduction of Mothering: Psychoanalysis and the Sociology of Gender*
1978	The Society for Applied Sociology founded
1979	Roy Bhaskar authors *The Possibility of Naturalism: A Philosophical Critique of the Contemporary Human Sciences*, a cornerstone of critical realism
1979	Arlie Hochschild introduces the idea of emotional labor in "Emotion Work, Feeling Rules, and Social Structure"
1979	Lyotard's *The Postmodern Condition* declares war on the modern grand narrative and totalizations
1979	Bruno Latour and Steve Woolgar's *Laboratory Life: The Social Construction of Scientific Facts* introduces actor-network theory (ANT)
1979	Rorty argues for a pragmatic philosophy in *Philosophy and the Mirror of Nature*
1979	Theda Skocpol's *States and Social Revolutions* makes the case for the importance of the state in social revolutions
1979	Morris Rosenberg broadens understandings of the self-concept in *Conceiving the Self*
1979	Chinese Sociological Association is founded
1980	Foucault publishes the first of his three-volume *The History of Sexuality*, which becomes a classic in poststructuralist and queer theories
1980	Stuart Hall's "Encoding/Decoding" appears in *Culture, Media, Language* and argues that audiences interpret the same television material in different ways
1980	Adrienne Rich introduces the lesbian continuum in "Compulsory Heterosexuality and the Lesbian Existence"
1980	Sheldon Stryker develops structural identity theory in *Symbolic Interactionism: A Social Structural Version*
1980	Ali Shariati publishes *On the Sociology of Islam*
1980	The Institute of Sociology of the Chinese Academy of Social Sciences founded
1981	Gary Becker authors *A Treatise on the Family*, a key text in the sociology of the family
1981	Alain Touraine outlines the techniques of "sociological intervention" in *The Voice and the Eye*
1981	Leonard Pearlin's "The Stress Process" (*JHSB*) outlines the concept of the same name
1981	Willer and Anderson's *Networks, Exchange and Coercion*
1981	First AIDS case reported in the United States

1982	First issue of *Theory, Culture, and Society* is published
1982	Luhmann's early work on systems theory is presented in *The Differentiation of Society*
1982	Margaret Archer's "Morphogenesis versus Structuration: On Combining Structure and Action" (*BJS*) makes the case for systems theory vs. structuration theory
1982–3	Jeffrey Alexander updates functionalism in his four-volume *Theoretical Logic in Sociology*
1983	Karen Cook, Richard Emerson, Mary Gillmore, and Toshio Yamagishi further develop exchange theory in "The Distribution of Power in Exchange Networks: Theory and Experimental Results" (*AJS*)
1983	Baudrillard's *Simulations* introduces his famous concept of the same name
1983	Nancy Hartsock authors "The Feminist Standpoint: Developing the Ground for a Specifically Feminist Historical Materialism," a key contribution to standpoint theory
1983	Hochschild analyzes the emotional labor of airline attendants and bill collectors in *The Managed Heart: Commercialization of Human Feeling*
1983	First issue of *Sociological Theory* published
1983	Barry Wellman's contribution to network analysis in "Network Analysis: Some Basic Principles" (*Sociological Theory*)
1983	Melvin Kohn and Carmi Schooler's *Work and Personality: An Inquiry into the Impact of Social Stratification* is a key work on the relationship between class and work
1983	Paul DiMaggio and Walter Powell's "The Iron Cage Revisited: Institutional Isomorphism and Collective Rationality in Organizational Fields" will achieve the most cumulative citations in *ASR* history
1984	Anthony Giddens's most developed statement on structuration theory appears in *The Constitution of Society: Outline of the Theory of Structuration*
1984	Habermas develops his ideas of communicative rationality in *The Theory of Communicative Action, Vol. 1: Reason and the Rationalization of Society*
1984	Certeau's *The Practice of Everyday Life* accords great power to the agent
1984	Bourdieu's *Homo Academicus* is a study of academia from the author's distinctive theoretical perspective
1984	Bourdieu's *Distinction: A Social Critique of the Judgment of Taste*
1984	Luhmann develops his systems theory in *Social Systems*
1985	Gayatri Spivak's "Can the Subaltern Speak? Speculations on Widow Sacrifice" (*Wedge* 7/8) becomes a classic in postcolonial studies
1985	Deleuze and Guattari's *Anti-Oedipus: Capitalism and Schizophrenia* makes an important contribution to poststructural/postmodern theory
1985	Jeffrey Alexander and Paul Colomy's "Toward Neo-Functionalism" (*Sociological Theory*) develops the short-lived theory of the same name
1985	Ernesto Laclau and Chantal Mouffe's *Hegemony and Socialist Strategy: Towards a Radical Democratic Politics* marks an important shift in neo-Marxian theory
1985	*European Sociological Review* founded
1986	Ulrich Beck develops the notion of risk in *Risk Society: Towards a New Modernity*
1986	Lacan revises Freudian psychoanalysis in the context of Saussurean linguistics in *Écrits*
1986	Paul Virilio's *Speed and Politics* introduces the idea of speed through his notion of dromology
1986	*International Sociology* founded
1987	Dorothy Smith presents a phenomenological feminist critique in *The Everyday World as Problematic: A Feminist Sociology*
1987	Gilles Lipovetsky develops a post-postmodernism in *The Empire of Fashion: Dressing Modern Democracy*

1987	Candace West and Don Zimmerman differentiate sex, sex category, and gender in "Doing Gender" (*Gender and Society*)
1988	Noam Chomsky and Edward Herman argue that the mass media are a political tool of political propaganda in *Manufacturing Consent: The Political Economy of the Mass Media*
1988	Barry Markovsky, David Willer, and Travis Patton author "Power Relations in Exchange Networks" (*ASR*)
1988	Linda Molm emphasizes rewards in exchange theory in "The Structure and Use of Power: A Comparison of Reward and Punishment Power" (*Social Psychology Quarterly*)
1988	*Journal of Historical Sociology* founded
1989	Žižek develops his ideas of ideology critique and cultural analysis in *The Sublime Object of Ideology*
1989	Bauman's *Modernity and the Holocaust* argues that the Holocaust was an instantiation of modernity and argues for a sociology of morality
1989	David Harvey further develops social geography and the idea of time-space compression in *The Condition of Postmodernity: An Enquiry into the Origins of Cultural Change*
1989	Edward Soja brings spatial concerns to the forefront once again in *Postmodern Geographies: The Reassertion of Space in Critical Social Theory*
1989	Trinh Minh-ha's *Woman, Native, Other: Writing Postcoloniality and Feminism*
1989	Michael Moore's first major documentary, *Roger & Me*, exposes the effects of plant closures on social life in Flint, Michigan
1989	Berlin Wall falls
1990	James S. Coleman develops rational choice theory in *Foundations of Social Theory*
1990	Judith Butler's *Gender Trouble* challenges traditional ideas of sex, gender, and sexuality
1990	Giddens introduces his idea of the juggernaut in *The Consequences of Modernity*
1990	Donna Haraway contributes to postmodern feminism with "A Manifesto for Cyborgs: Science, Technology, and Socialist Feminism"
1990	Patricia Hill Collins develops intersectionality in *Black Feminist Thought: Knowledge, Consciousness, and Empowerment*
1990	Tamito Yoshida publishes *Jyoho to Jiko Soshiki-sei no Riron* [*Theory of Information and Self-Organizing Systems*], outlining his general systems theory
1990	*Sociétés Contemporaines* founded
1990–2	The National Comorbidity Survey administers structured psychiatric exams to respondents to assess levels of disorder
1991	Jameson's *Postmodernism, or the Cultural Logic of Late Capitalism* integrates neo-Marxian and postmodern ideas
1991	Kenneth Gergen brings postmodernity to bear on the self in *The Saturated Self: Dilemmas of Identity in Contemporary Life*
1991	Giddens's *Modernity and Self-Identity: Self and Society in the Late Modern Age* is a discussion of important microsociological issues
1991	Sharon Zukin links power to geography in *Landscapes of Power: From Detroit to Disney World*
1991	The term "new urbanism" is introduced at a meeting of urban reformers in California
1991	Steven Best and Douglas Kellner's *Postmodern Theory: Critical Interrogations* is a useful overview of postmodern theory
1991	Saskia Sassen introduces the term "global city" in her book *The Global City: New York, London, Tokyo*
1991	*Berliner Journal für Soziologie* founded in Berlin

1992	Francis Fukuyama argues in *The End of History and the Last Man* that the progression of human history as a struggle between ideologies is largely at an end, with liberal democracy coming out the winner
1992	Marc Auge's *Non-Places: An Introduction to an Anthropology of Supermodernity* introduces the ideas of non-place and supermodernity
1992	Roland Robertson develops the idea of glocalization in *Globalization: Social Theory and Global Culture*
1992	First European Conference of Sociology is held in Vienna
1992	Bourdieu and Wacquant's *An Invitation to Reflexive Sociology* presents an overview of Bourdieu's ideas
1992	Bauman's *Intimations of Postmodernity* contains contributions to postmodern theory by a modernist
1992	European Sociological Association founded
1992	Mitchell Duneier's *Slim's Table: Race, Respectability, and Masculinity* becomes a classic in ethnographic studies
1992	*International Journal of Japanese Sociology* founded
1993	Bruno Latour establishes actor-network theory (ANT) in *We Have Never Been Modern*
1993	Ritzer's *The McDonaldization of Society: An Investigation into the Changing Character of Contemporary Social Life* brings Weber's thesis of rationalization to bear on contemporary society and consumption
1994	Homi Bhabha contributes to studies of both culture and postcolonialism with *The Location of Culture*
1994	Cornell West's *Race Matters* is an important contribution to multidisciplinary thinking on race
1994	Cairo hosts UN International Conference on Population and Development, which leads to major reforms in population planning
1994	Giddens's *Beyond Left and Right: The Future of Radical Politics* marks a shift in his work to more practical issues
1995	Benjamin Barber's *Jihad vs. McWorld* contrasts a homogenizing and heterogenizing approach to global politics
1995	Michel Maffesoli develops neotribalism in *The Time of Tribes*
1995	*Soziale Systeme* founded
1996	Castells argues the importance of information in *The Rise of the Network Society*
1996	Appadurai's *Modernity at Large: Cultural Dimensions of Globalization* introduces the idea of "scapes"
1996	Samuel Huntington argues the importance of cultural civilizations in *The Clash of Civilizations and the Remaking of World Order*
1996	Asia Pacific Sociological Association founded
1997	Chomsky authors *Media Control: The Spectacular Achievements of Propaganda*, summarizing his views on the media as well as terrorism
1997	Peter Burke outlines his model of a cybernetic identity theory in "An Identity Model of Network Exchange" (*ASR*)
1997	Hochschild's *The Time Bind: When Work Becomes Home and Home Becomes Work* discusses the time bind placed on contemporary families, the importance of the "second shift," and even the "third shift"
1997	Kathryn Edin and Laura Lein demonstrate the inefficiencies of the welfare system in the United States in *Making Ends Meet: How Single Mothers Survive Welfare and Low-Wage Work*
1998	*Interventions: International Journal of Postcolonial Studies* founded
1998	Arts and Humanities Research Board established in the UK (changed to Arts and Humanities Research Council in 2005)

1999	Barry Glassner publishes a critical insight into the role of fear in US culture in *The Culture of Fear: Why Americans are Afraid of the Wrong Things*
2000	Michael Hardt and Antonio Negri's *Empire* argues that imperialism is being replaced by an empire without a national base
2000	Robert Putnam's *Bowling Alone: The Collapse and Revival of American Community*
2000	Bauman's *Liquid Modernity* provides new imagery in a theory of the contemporary world
2001	Edward Lawler advocates the role of emotion in "An Affect Theory of Social Exchange" (*AJS*)
2001	September 11, 2001: terrorists hijack airplanes and destroy the World Trade Center in New York City
2001	Barbara Ehrenreich brings light to the difficulties of living on the minimum wage in *Nickled and Dimed: On Not Getting By in America*
2002	Leslie Sklair argues for alternatives to global capitalism in *Globalization: Capitalism and its Alternatives*
2003	Chandra Mohanty's *Feminism Without Borders: Decolonizing Theory, Practicing Solidarity*
2003	John Urry brings chaos theory to bear on globalization in *Global Complexity*
2003	Annette Lareau argues that class-based childrearing practices perpetuate social inequality in *Unequal Childhoods: Race, Class, and Family Life*
2004	Michael Burawoy, President of the ASA, launches a major debate on public sociology with his presidential address
2004	Hardt and Negri release *Multitude: War and Democracy in the Age of Empire* as a follow-up to their 2000 work on empire
2005	ASA holds Centennial meeting in San Francisco, California

Lexicon

Reputation
Ritual
Science and Culture
Science across Cultures
Semiotics
Sexualities and Culture Wars
Sexuality and Sport
Simulacra and Simulation
Simulation and Virtuality
Smoking
Soccer
Social Theory and Sport
Socialization and Sport
Society and Biology
Sociocultural Relativism
Sport
Sport, Alternative
Sport, Amateur
Sport and the Body
Sport and Capitalism
Sport as Catharsis
Sport and the City
Sport, College
Sport and Culture
Sport Culture and Subcultures
Sport and the Environment
Sport and Ethnicity
Sport, Professional
Sport and Race
Sport and Religion
Sport and Social Capital
Sport and Social Class
Sport and Social Resistance
Sport as Spectacle
Sport and the State
Sport as Work
Sportization
Sports Heroes and Celebrities
Sports Industry
Sports Stadia
Stereotyping and Stereotypes
Subculture
Subcultures, Deviant
Surveillance
Symbolic Classification
Taste, Sociology of
Technology, Science, and Culture
Telephone
Televangelism
Television
Text/Hypertext
Tradition

Transgression
Urbanism/Urban Culture
Urbanism, Subcultural Theory of
Values
Values: Global
Video Games
Violence Among Athletes
Violence Among Fans
Virtual Sports
Williams, Raymond
Xenophobia
Youth Sport

DEMOGRAPHY AND ECOLOGY

Age, Period, and Cohort Effects
Aging, Demography of
Aging, Longitudinal Studies
Benefit and Victimized Zones
Biodemography
Consumption, Green/Sustainable
Daily Life Pollution
Davis, Kingsley
Demographic Data: Censuses, Registers,
    Surveys
Demographic Techniques: Decomposition and
    Standardization
Demographic Techniques: Event History
    Methods
Demographic Techniques: Life-Table
    Methods
Demographic Techniques: Population
    Projections and Estimates
Demographic Techniques: Population
    Pyramids and Age/Sex Structure
Demographic Techniques: Time Use
Demographic Transition Theory
Demography
Demography: Historical
Differential Treatment of Children by Sex
Ecofeminism
Ecological Problems
Ecology
Ecology and Economy
Environment, Sociology of the
Environment and Urbanization
Environmental Criminology
Environmental Movements
Family Demography
Family Migration

ECONOMY AND CONSUMPTION

KEY FIGURES

Emerson, Richard M.
Engels, Friedrich
Fajnzylber, Fernando
Faletto, Enzo
Fanon, Franz
Feuerbach, Ludwig
Foucault, Michel
Frazier, E. Franklin
Freud, Sigmund
Fromm, Erich
Gellner, Ernst
Germani, Gino
Gilman, Charlotte Perkins
Goffman, Erving
Gökalp, Ziya
Goldman, Emma
Gramsci, Antonio
Guattari, Félix
Gumplowicz, Ludwig
Gurvitch, Georges: Social Change
Halbwachs, Maurice
Hegel, G. W. F.
Hirschfeld, Magnus
Hobhouse, L. T.
Homans, George
Horkheimer, Max
Howard, George Elliott
Imanishi, Kinji
James, William
Jevons, William
Johnson, Charles Spurgeon
Khaldun, Ibn
Kinsey, Alfred
Kitsuse, John I.
Komarovsky, Mirra
Krafft-Ebing, Richard von
Kurauchi, Kazuta
Lacan, Jacques
Lazarsfeld, Paul
Lechner, Norbert
Lefebvre, Henri
Lemert, Edwin M.
Lewin, Kurt
Liebow, Elliott
Lombroso, Cesare
Luhmann, Niklas
Lukács, Georg
Luxemburg, Rosa
McLuhan, Marshall
Malinowski, Bronislaw K.
Malthus, Thomas Robert

Mannheim, Karl
Marcuse, Herbert
Marianne Weber on Social Change
Marshall, Thomas Henry
Martineau, Harriet
Maruyama, Masao
Marx, Karl
Mead, George Herbert
Mead, Margaret
Mendieta y Núñez, Lucio
Merton, Robert K.
Michels, Robert
Milgram, Stanley (Experiments)
Mill, John Stuart
Mills, C. Wright
Mosca, Gaetano
Mumford, Lewis
Nietzsche, Friedrich
Nozick, Robert
Pareto, Vilfredo
Park, Robert E. & Burgess, Ernest W.
Parsons, Talcott
Polanyi, Karl
Poulantzas, Nicos
Pound, Roscoe
Radcliffe-Brown, Alfred R.
Ratzenhofer, Gustav
Rawls, John
Reich, Wilhelm
Riesman, David
Rizal, José
Robert E. Park, Ernest W. Burgess, and
    Urban Social Research
Rosenberg, Morris
Rosenfeld, Rachel
Sacks, Harvey
Said, Edward W.
Sainsaulieu, Renaud
Saraswati, Pandita Ramabai
Sarkar, Benoy Kumar
Sartre, Jean-Paul
Saussure, Ferdinand de
Schumpeter, Joseph A.
Schütz, Alfred
Shariati, Ali
Simmel, Georg
Small, Albion W.
Smith, Adam
Sombart, Werner
Sorokin, Pitirim A.
Spencer, Herbert

RACE AND ETHNICITY

Nationalism
Nihonjinron
One Drop Rule
Orientalism
Outsider-Within
Passing
Paternalism
Plural Society
Pogroms
Polyethnicity
Prejudice
Race
Race (Racism)
Race and Crime
Race and the Criminal Justice System
Race and Ethnic Consciousness
Race and Ethnic Etiquette
Race and Ethnic Politics
Race and Schools
Race/Ethnicity and Friendship
Race/Ethnicity, Health, and Mortality
Racial Hierarchy
Racialized Gender
Racism, Structural and Institutional
Racist Movements
Redlining
Refugees
Reparations
Residential Segregation
Scapegoating
School Segregation, Desegregation
Schools, Magnet
Scientific Racism
Segregation
Self-Determination
Separatism
Slavery
Slurs (Racial/Ethnic)
Solidarity
Sport and Ethnicity
Sport and Race
Steering, Racial Real Estate
Stratification, Race/Ethnicity and
Third World and Postcolonial Feminisms/
   Subaltern
Tolerance
Transnationalism
Tribalism
Truth and Reconciliation Commissions
Whiteness
Womanism
Xenophobia

RELIGION

Animism
Anti-Semitism (Religion)
Anti-Semitism (Social Change)
Asceticism
Atheism
Belief
Buddhism
Catholicism
Charisma
Charismatic Movement
Christianity
Church
Civil Religion
Confucianism
Consumption, Religion and
Cults: Social Psychological Aspects
Denomination
Economy, Religion and
Folk Hinduism
Fundamentalism
Globalization, Religion and
Health and Religion
Hinduism
Islam
Jehovah's Witnesses
Judaism
Laicism
Magic
Martyrdom
Millenarianism
Myth
New Age
New Religious Movements
Orthodoxy
Pietism
Popular Religiosity
Primitive Religion
Protestantism
Religion
Religion, Sociology of
Religions, African
Religious Cults
Rite/Ritual
Ritual
Sacred
Sacred, Eclipse of the
Sacred/Profane
Sacrifice
Satanism
Schools, Religious

SOCIAL PROBLEMS

A

abolitionism

René van Swaaningen

When social scientists use the word abolitionism they mostly refer to the criminological perspective that dismisses penal definitions and punitive responses to criminalized problems, and that proposes their replacement by dispute-settlement, redress, and social justice. In more general, historical terms it refers to the abolition of state (supported) institutions that are no longer felt to be legitimate. There have been abolitionist movements against slavery, torture, prostitution, capital punishment, and prison.

The word abolitionism as we currently understand it in criminology is adopted from the North American anti-prison movement of the early 1970s. Herein most notably Quakers take up their historical mission from the anti-slavery movement. They see prison as an institution that today fulfills the same social functions as slavery did till the late nineteenth century: disciplining the (mostly black) under-class. This American abolitionism is mainly grounded in religious inspiration, and less in considerations about the counter-effectiveness of criminal justice, as is the case in Europe. The European abolitionist social movements of that era were prisoners' unions and more intellectual radical penal reform movements (Van Swaaningen 1997). Academic abolitionism has its roots in symbolic interactionism and social constructionism, with a strongly Foucauldian focus on discipline in a carceral society.

Unlike the literal meaning of the verbal phrase "to abolish," abolitionism cannot be conceived in absolute terms. Abolitionists do not argue that the police or courts should be abolished. The point is that crime is not to be set apart from other social problems and that the social exclusion of culprits seldom solves any problems. The penal system itself is seen as a social problem, and penality is rejected as a metaphor of justice. Abolitionists both question the ethical caliber of a state that intentionally and systematically inflicts pain upon other people, and point out that, because generally accepted goals of general and special prevention cannot be supported with empirical data, the credibility of the penal system is at stake.

Abolitionism knows a negative and a positive momentum. It implies a negative critique of the fundamental shortcomings of the penal system to realize social justice, and aims at the prevention and control of criminalized problems by social means. In this negative phase, depenalization (pushing back the punitive character of reactions) and decriminalization (against the labeling of social problems as crimes) are the central topics. Cohen (1988) characterizes abolitionism's destructuring moves as decarceration, diversion (away from the institution), decategorization, delegalization (away from the state), and deprofessionalization (away from the expert). In the positive phase, a distinction is to be made between abolitionism as a way of thinking (an alternative way of understanding crime and punishment) and as a way of acting (a radical approach of penal reform). In the first sense, abolitionism is an example of a replacement discourse (Henry & Milovanovic 1996). In the second sense, it moves between Pepinsky and Quinney's (1991) "peacemaking criminology" and Braithwaite's (1989) theory of reintegrative shaming. It is more modest than the former – for it is oriented at mechanisms of social control rather than at rebuilding community-spirit – and embedded in a more radical, dismissive position toward the penal system than the latter.

Initially, abolitionists shot their arrows at the prison system. Around 1980, the attention shifted to (the pros and cons of) non-custodial alternatives. Warnings against the net-widening effects of such sanctions were contrasted with their potential value in the attrition of the penal system. In this respect, Mathiesen's (1974) penal action theory has been very influential. This Norwegian criminologist argues that alternatives to prison should remain "unfinished" in order not to be absorbed by a penal rationale. He distinguishes between positive reforms, which ultimately strengthen the penal system, and negative reforms, which are of an abolishing kind.

Other abolitionists have focused on the penal procedure. Dutch criminologist Herman Bianchi (1994) proposes an assensus model: a form of dispute settlement that should mandatorily replace penal intervention if the directly involved parties agree on a solution. Both the consensus model of criminal law and the dissensus embedded in conflict models imply a fight over the representation of the facts, whereas assensus is "just" focused on the follow-up. With these contentions Bianchi rejects both functionalist and conflict sociology. Norwegian criminologist Nils Christie (1981) has also advocated a participatory model of justice.

The development of (counter-)criteria for penal intervention is another theme for abolitionists. According to Dutch criminologist Louk Hulsman, we do not need to wait for radical political reform or structural analyses in order to start with decriminalization: coercion needs legitimation, giving up on coercion does not. This pragmatic approach makes Hulsman's perspective an interesting challenge for those intellectual skeptics who advocated radical penal reform but were paralyzed by all the structural configurations it implies – which leads them to the idea that nothing works. According to Hulsman, the main change lies in a transformation from a top-down vision of reform within the limits of a penal rationale to an approach from below, in which the language from the "lifeworld" is adopted (Bianchi & van Swaaningen 1986).

In today's academic debate, abolitionism is mainly discussed as one of the many critical criminologies of the twenty-first century. Many of its visions have been adopted by and integrated into other criminological perspectives. Now, popular perspectives such as constitutive criminology (Henry & Milovanovic 1996) or restorative justice (Braithwaite 1989) are grounded in abolitionist thought. Abolitionism's major merit is that it offers us a fundamentally different vision of crime and justice. Its epistemology offers an excellent basis for creative empirical research into penal and social control.

SEE ALSO: Criminal Justice System; Deconstruction; Deviance, Constructionist Perspectives; Deviance, Crime and; Foucault, Michel

REFERENCES AND SUGGESTED READINGS

Bianchi, H. (1994) *Justice as Sanctuary: Toward a New System of Crime Control.* Indiana University Press, Bloomington.

Bianchi, H. & van Swaaningen, R. (Eds.) (1986) *Abolitionism: Towards a Non-Repressive Approach to Crime.* Free University Press, Amsterdam.

Braithwaite, J. (1989) *Crime, Shame and Reintegration.* Cambridge University Press, Cambridge.

Christie, N. (1981) *Limits to Pain.* Martin Robertson, Oxford.

Cohen, S. (1988) *Against Criminology.* Transaction, New Brunswick, NJ.

Contemporary Crises (1985) Special issue on abolitionism: 4.

Haan, W. de (1990) *The Politics of Redress: Crime, Punishment and Penal Abolition.* Unwin Hyman, London.

Henry, S. & Milovanovic, D. (1996) *Constitutive Criminology: Beyond Postmodernism.* Sage, London.

Mathiesen, T. (1974) *The Politics of Abolition.* Martin Robertson, Oxford.

Pepinsky, H. & Quinney, R (Eds.) (1991) *Criminology as Peacemaking.* Indiana University Press, Bloomington.

Van Swaaningen, R. (1997) *Critical Criminology: Visions from Europe.* Sage, London.

abortion as a social problem

Michele Dillon and Diana Dumais

Abortion has been legal in the US and in almost all Western European countries since the early 1970s, and in Belgium and Ireland since the early 1990s. Although abortion was legal in the Soviet Union for several years prior to its collapse, abortion politics have subsequently come to the fore in some Eastern European countries (e.g., Poland) as a result of government attempts to restrict it. But abortion is most intensely debated in the US, where legal and congressional initiatives to amend the US Supreme Court's recognition (*Roe* v. *Wade*, 1973) of a woman's legal right to an abortion continue unabated. Abortion activism is pursued by several religious and secular organizations, and abortion politics dominate presidential and congressional elections and debates over judicial appointments. Grassroots efforts to restrict abortion have met with some success, as subsequent Supreme Court decisions have imposed various restrictions on what many observers as well as pro-life activists see as America's comparatively permissive law on abortion. Most notably, the imposition of spousal and parental notification requirements seeks to redress the emphasis on abortion as solely being a woman's right to choose and has sought to recognize the relational context of women's lives while not imposing an undue burden on women's freedom. The issue of late-term abortion is currently one of the most intensely debated aspects of abortion law (even though most abortions are performed in the first trimester of pregnancy).

Notwithstanding the intensity of pro-choice and pro-life activism, American public opinion on abortion has remained steadfastly consistent. Since 1975, approximately one-fifth of Americans agree that abortion should be illegal in all circumstances, another one-fifth believe that abortion should be legal in all circumstances, and a broad majority take the moderate position that abortion should be legal but restricted. Whereas large majorities

T(approximately 80–85 percent) agree that abortion should be legally available to women in the case of rape, or when the pregnancy poses a physical threat to the mother or fetus, significantly fewer (approximately 40 percent) believe that it should be available if the woman/family cannot economically afford to have the child, or for other elective reasons (NORC, General Social Survey, various years).

According to the Alan Guttmacher Institute (2005: 5–6), abortion is one of the most common surgical procedures performed in the US: 1.29 million abortions were performed in 2002, and each year 47 percent of all unintended pregnancies in the US end in abortion. The abortion rate has been in decline since its peak of 29.3 (per 1,000 women ages 15 to 44) in the early 1980s, to 20.9 currently, and there has been an especially noticeable drop in its incidence among 15 to 19-year-old girls (from 43.5 in the mid-to-late 1980s to 24.0 currently). By contrast, the overall abortion rate in England and Wales is considerably lower, at 17.0 (for women aged 15–44).

Many Americans argue that the number of abortions alone constitutes a social problem, although other commentators suggest that the aging and declining prevalence of abortion providers is a social problem in ferment. The majority of obstetricians who perform abortion are age 50 or over, and the proportion of US counties without abortion providers increased from 77 percent in the late 1970s to 86 percent in the late 1990s (Finer & Henshaw 2003: 6). Although its incidence might suggest that abortion has become a primary method of birth control, a majority of women who face the dilemma of an unintended pregnancy report using contraception during the month they became pregnant (53 percent), though not always correctly (Finer et al. 2005). Clearly, there are many, frequently overlapping, reasons why women seek abortion, including inadequate finances, relationship problems, concerns over readiness for motherhood, and psychological and physical health problems. Nonetheless, 60 percent of those who get an abortion are already mothers, and 12 percent have previously had an abortion.

The incidence of abortion is greater not only among teenagers, but across all age groups, among women who are single, poor, and non-white (Hispanic, black, or other ethnic minority). Most abortions in the US are obtained by women who have never been married (67 percent); a similar trend is evident elsewhere (e.g., 63 percent in England and Wales). Similarly, white women in both the US (41 percent) and England and Wales (37 percent) are more likely than women from any other single racial or ethnic group to obtain an abortion.

Although women in all economic groups seek abortion, low-income women represent the majority of abortion patients. In 2000, 57 percent of women who obtained an abortion were poor or low income (defined as living at less than twice the poverty level, or earning less than $28,300 for a family of three). However, low-income women are less likely to end a pregnancy by abortion; their over-representation in the abortion statistics is due to the fact that the rate of unintended pregnancy for this group is higher overall than for women with higher incomes. The impoverished economic circumstances of these low-income women are further strained by recent changes in American welfare policy, which prior to the 1996 Welfare Reform Act was already significantly less supportive of maternity, child, and family welfare than European social policy. With low-income pregnant women less likely than others to choose abortion, this means that their living situation and that of their children will further deteriorate, and lead to the inevitable downward spiral of poverty and its associated constellation of social problems.

Given the socio-demographic trends in abortion usage, pro-choice supporters argue that it is not abortion per se that is a social problem but the social and economic circumstances of many women's lives. In particular, they highlight that women's lack of resources, including the absence of health insurance, the lack of access to and effective use of contraception, and the absence of school sexual education programs, contributes to unintended pregnancies. Abortion supporters also point out that restrictions on abortion, such as demanded by spousal and parental notification requirements, do not recognize the high incidence of spousal and family violence in society

and the well-grounded fears that many women and teenagers may have in disclosing their pregnancies.

SEE ALSO: Culture of Poverty; Domestic Violence; Family Planning, Abortion, and Reproductive Health; Pro-Choice and Pro-Life Movements; Public Opinion; Welfare State

REFERENCES AND SUGGESTED READINGS

Alan Guttmacher Institute (2005) *An Overview of Abortion in the United States.* Alan Guttmacher Institute, New York.

Finer, L. B. & Henshaw, S. K. (2003) Abortion Incidence and Services in the United States in 2000. *Perspectives on Sexual and Reproductive Health* 35: 6–15.

Finer, L. B. et al. (2005) Reasons US Women Have Abortions: Quantitative and Qualitative Perspectives. *Perspectives on Sexual and Reproductive Health* 37: 110–18.

absenteeism

Gary Johns

Absenteeism is failing to report for scheduled work. As such, it is the violation of a social obligation to be in a particular place at a particular time (Johns 1997; Harrison & Martocchio 1998). Traditionally, absenteeism was viewed as an indicator of poor individual performance and a breach of an implicit contract between employee and employer. Thus, it was seen as a management problem and framed in economic or quasi-economic terms. Indeed, economists most frequently view absenteeism in labor supply terms. More recently, absenteeism has increasingly been viewed as an indicator of psychological, medical, or social adjustment to work.

The most prominent of the psychological models is the withdrawal model, which assumes that absenteeism represents individual withdrawal from dissatisfying working conditions.

This model finds empirical support in a negative association between absence and job satisfaction, especially satisfaction with regard to the content of the work itself. It also finds support in a "progression" of withdrawal from being late, to being absent, to quitting a job. Psychological approaches have also linked employee disposition to absenteeism. Hence, the conscientious, those high in positive affect, and those who score high on composite tests of integrity are disinclined to be absent. Dispositional explanations find some corroboration in the fact that individual absenteeism is fairly stable over time, even in the face of changed work situations.

Medical models find support in research that links absenteeism to smoking, problem drinking, low back pain, and migraine. However, absence ascribed to medical causes frequently exhibits motivational correlates that suggest voluntariness. The line between psychological and medical causation is surely blurry, as positive links between both work stress and depression and absenteeism illustrate. Although medical mediation is often implied in the stress–absence connection, this has not often been explicitly tested. Correspondingly, depressive tendencies might underpin much absence ascribed to poor physical health, as might the adoption of a culturally approved sick role. Thus, placing the adjective *sickness* before the word absence carries a burden of more proof than is usually offered.

Another stream of scholarship that speaks to the adjustive aspects of absence is decidedly more social in nature, and thus of particular interest to sociologists. Much evidence indicates that absence is generally viewed as mildly deviant workplace behavior. For example, people tend to hold negative stereotypes of absentees, underreport their own absenteeism, and view their own attendance record as superior to that of their peers. In turn, negative attributions about absence give rise to three important consequences: the behavior is open to considerable social control, sensitive to social context, and the potential source of considerable workplace conflict.

One of the most important findings of contemporary absence research is the extent to which the behavior is open to social influence.

This stands as a salient complement to explanations that portray absence as a component of individual employee performance, a personal response to job dissatisfaction, a reflection of disposition, or a consequence of medical misfortune. Absence is open to social influence for two reasons. First, the connotation of *mild* deviance makes people sensitive to but not absolutist concerning its occurrence. Second, it is far from clear what constitutes a fair and reasonable level of absence. Markedly different absence rates across social units (e.g., teams, departments, plants, nations) are suggestive of this ambiguity. For instance, absence rates have been shown to vary by as much as a ratio of 7:1 between developed nations.

It was this observation of distinctive absence levels and patterns across meaningful social groupings that gave rise to the notion of *absence cultures*, which (in their strong form) constitute shared agreement about the appropriate meaning and expression of absenteeism within a social unit. Shared views about the *legitimacy* of the behavior under various circumstances are crucial. Evidence in support of the absence culture concept has been cumulative. At its base is considerable research suggesting that individual absence is influenced by social (often work group) norms, with such norms having been operationalized in a wide variety of ways. Absenteeism is generally negatively related to work group cohesiveness. This said, some research shows cohesive units colluding to take days off. However, absenteeism seems to peak under conditions of very low social integration: when cohesiveness is low, discourse on the legitimacy of the behavior is missing, and deviant overtones lack salience. The most persuasive evidence for the existence of absence cultures derives from formal cross-level studies. In this research, work group absenteeism and beliefs about the behavior (generally aggregated to the group level) have been shown to influence the absenteeism of individual group members.

Most recently, the absence culture concept has been extended to understand how absenteeism is viewed and enacted among various occupations, social classes, and national cultures. Much of this research can also be described as cross-level. In general, more prestigious occupations exhibit lower absence rates. However, the dominant social class of the community in which employees live has been shown to influence absenteeism over and above occupational norms per se (Virtanen et al. 2000). Although there may be differences in the perceived legitimacy of absence across national cultures, the basic connotation of deviance seems to hold. However, indigenous mechanisms can reconcile the tendency to be self-serving about one's own attendance with the need to exhibit collective solidarity. For instance, Johns and Xie (1998) found that both Chinese and Canadians underreported their own actual absenteeism and viewed their own attendance records as superior to those of their work group peers. However, the more collective Chinese reconciled this self-serving by viewing the attendance of their work groups as being much superior to that of the occupational norm.

Given its deviant connotations and economic consequences for employers, absenteeism has often been a source of conflict in organizations. For these same reasons, it has also been a result of conflict, a way to assert control in the workplace. Given their respective organizational roles, managers and workers often hold different expectations about employee attendance, with managers expecting less absence than do their subordinates. As a result of this, excessive absenteeism is one of the most common subjects of labor arbitration. However, contemporary work designs that stress highly interdependent team structures and self-management have also prompted conflict among employees themselves concerning absenteeism, as it is often an impediment to smooth teamwork.

On the other hand, conflict can also prompt absenteeism. At the heart of this are matters of social exchange. Thus, there is substantial research by social and organizational psychologists showing elevated absenteeism when distributive justice (i.e., equity) and support from management are perceived to be low. Hence, the appropriation of valuable time is one way to achieve fairer balance in one's exchange with the organization, especially when paid sick days are available. Sociologists and industrial

relations scholars have been most interested in the more collective manifestations of such exchange problems, seeing absenteeism as a means of asserting control in the work setting and resisting abuse by management. However, absenteeism has most often been viewed as a relatively individualized and less organized form of resistance, at least compared to strikes. Nonetheless, clear cases of collusion in support of absence have been observed, and unionized employees have been repeatedly shown to exhibit higher levels of absenteeism compared to those without representation.

Longitudinal research and research that is sensitive to social context illustrate how the social construction of absenteeism can change over time. For instance, Tansey and Hyman (1992) illustrate how this otherwise innocuous workplace behavior was reframed by employers to be a treasonous menace during the World War II production drive. Turnbull and Sapsford (1992) illustrate how absenteeism on the British docks changed from tolerated self-expression to an entrenched expression of industrial conflict as technology and labor laws changed. In recent years, the increase in dual-career couples and elder-care issues, and the consequent drive for "family friendly" workplaces, has challenged the deviant overtones of absenteeism among some employees and employers.

The foregoing suggests that absenteeism is work behavior with a variety of meanings (socially constructed or not) masquerading as a unitary phenomenon. Also, the behavior can be studied at levels of analysis ranging from individual to national. These factors offer both challenges and opportunities for researchers. Because absenteeism has such a wide variety of causes, it has attracted the attention of a variety of disciplines, including sociology, psychology, economics, management, industrial relations, medicine, rehabilitation, and law. Except for integrative literature reviews (Johns 1997; Harrison & Martocchio 1998), however, there have not been enough synergies among these disciplinary approaches to absence. On the other hand, in part due to this multidisciplinary interest and in part due to the difficulties inherent in studying an infrequent and mildly deviant behavior, absenteeism has been subjected to a great range and variety of research methods, a phenomenon that is very rare in the organizational sciences (Johns 2003). This multimethod approach, much advocated but seldom applied, has led to great advances in understanding the subtlety of absenteeism among those willing to accept the full complexity of this apparently routine work behavior.

SEE ALSO: Conflict Theory; Deviance; Norms; Stress and Work; Work, Sociology of

REFERENCES AND SUGGESTED READINGS

Edwards, P. & Whitston, C. (1993) *Attending to Work: The Management of Attendance and Shopfloor Order*. Blackwell, Oxford.

Harrison, D. A. & Martocchio, J. J. (1998) Time for Absenteeism: A 20-Year Review of Origins, Offshoots, and Outcomes. *Journal of Management* 24: 305–50.

Johns, G. (1997) Contemporary Research on Absence from Work: Correlates, Causes and Consequences. *International Review of Industrial and Organizational Psychology* 12: 115–73.

Johns, G. (2002) Absenteeism and Mental Health. In: Thomas, J. C. & Hersen, M. (Eds.), *Handbook of Mental Health in the Workplace*. Sage, Thousand Oaks, CA.

Johns, G. (2003) How Methodological Diversity has Improved our Understanding of Absenteeism from Work. *Human Resource Management Review* 13: 157–84.

Johns, G. & Xie, J. L. (1998) Perceptions of Absence from Work: People's Republic of China versus Canada. *Journal of Applied Psychology* 83: 515–30.

Roscigno, V. J. & Hodson, R. (2004) The Organizational and Social Foundations of Worker Resistance. *American Sociological Review* 69: 14–39.

Tansey, R. R. & Hyman, M. R. (1992) Public Relations, Advocacy Ads, and the Campaign against Absenteeism during World War II. *Business and Professional Ethics Journal* 11: 129–64.

Turnbull, P. & Sapsford, D. (1992) A Sea of Discontent: The Tides of Organized and "Unorganized" Conflict on the Docks. *Sociology* 26: 291–309.

Virtanen, P., Nakari, R., Ahonen, H., et al. (2000) Locality and Habitus: The Origins of Sickness Absence Practices. *Social Science and Medicine* 50: 27–39.

accommodation

Rutledge M. Dennis

Accommodation was one of the four features of Robert Park and Ernest Burgess's model of social interaction. Though the concept illustrated racial and ethnic social changes taking place in the United States and the rest of the world during the last half of the nineteenth century and the first two or three decades of the twentieth, and for this reason lacks a certain relevance today, there are still aspects of the term, as defined by Park and Burgess, which might provide insights into specific patterns of racial and ethnic interaction and aid in our understanding of the dynamics of social change. Utilizing Simmel's model of dominance and its pivotal role in superordinate and subordinate relations, Park and Burgess describe accommodation as a procedure which limits conflicts and cements relations, in that groups and individuals recognize dominant individuals and groups as well as their positions within these super- and subordinate relations. On the surface, this logic appears to be one of "live and let live," and appears to be grounded in an idea similar to that of social and cultural pluralism.

In the United States, the term has been closely associated with the policies of Booker T. Washington, founder of the Tuskegee Institute and the most influential black leader in the US between the 1890s and 1915. Washington adopted a strategy of racial accommodation because he knew confrontational politics would have resulted in the mass slaughter of Southern blacks, with the national government standing on the sidelines. He thus began a program of literally pacifying and engaging in compromises with Northern and Southern whites, and cajoling Southern blacks, who had the most to lose from confrontational policies, into joining such a strategy. He wanted this strategy to protect blacks from physical harm, while guaranteeing them some role in the economy, albeit at the lower levels for the time being. For whites the accommodative strategy was designed to demonstrate that they had nothing to fear from black

Southerners, who wished only to advance themselves through habits of work, sobriety, morality, and so on.

The situations and circumstances that determine the types of accommodation engaged in by various, and conflicting, racial, ethnic, linguistic, and religious groups vary. Type One accommodation is an accommodation in which there is a great power imbalance between two or more groups, based on population, military and police powers, and the economic and legal controls exerted by dominant groups. Less powerful groups must adjust to this power imbalance. The position of blacks and Native Americans in the US and Indians throughout Latin America adheres to this type, but the accommodation by Indian populations was reached after prolonged warfare against European colonial powers and their representatives. Type One might also include the accommodation by Scotland and Wales to England after the military and/or political arrangements that resulted in their respective incorporation into Great Britain. However, as the contemporary ongoing process of "devolution" demonstrates, neither Scotland nor Wales was satisfied with the hegemonic accommodative arrangement, which they viewed as highly beneficial to England. A similar arrangement may characterize the accommodative relationship between French Canadians and English Canadians and between Catalonians, the Basque region, and the rest of Spain, though a large percentage of those in the Basque region have opted for independence rather than remain a province within Spain.

Type Two accommodation represents an accommodation in which contending groups may be relatively equal in size. Issues may revolve around how and why the groups settled into a territory, and how political and economic division of labor was defined and distributed among groups. Into this class may be placed Guyana, with its division between East Indians and Black Guyanese. Since independence from England, the accommodative strategy had been one of Black Guyanese political power and East Indian economic power. The election of Cheddi Jagan in 1992 threw the country into crisis, overturning the long-existing accommodation strategy and signaling the possibility that East Indians would now have political as well as economic control. Another example of political accommodation, focusing on language, is offered by Belgium, with the dialectics of accommodation and conflict involving Flemish and Walloon. Trinidad and Tobago can also be placed in the Type Two accommodation category, where the accommodating groups are East Indians and Black Trinidadians, the former controlling the economy, the latter retaining political control. As in Guyana, a crisis erupted in the 1990s when an East Indian became prime minister. Lastly, Malaysia offers another perspective on accommodation, this time with a large Malayan population and a much smaller Chinese population. The pattern of accommodation here was that Malayans would hold political power while the Chinese would retain economic control. The threat of the Chinese gaining political power erupted in the 1960s, resulting in the removal of Singapore (predominantly Chinese) from the Malaysian Federation.

The Type Two cases reflect accommodation between groups. The examples given demonstrate that accommodation may clearly constitute a strategy and a theory of how multi-ethnic groups must construct programs and policies to ensure a degree of cooperation and peace and to discourage social disorder. But under strategies of accommodation, groups wage silent political, economic, and social warfare in order to achieve or retain an edge over another group. Whenever one of the groups finds that it has an advantage, it immediately seizes upon an opportunity to secure it. This is clearly seen in attempts by both Flemish and Walloon speakers to extend their language into each other's provinces. Thus accommodation may be a temporary strategy engaged in by groups and nations when they perceive themselves as weak, or when groups are of comparable size and one group cannot have a decisive victory over another group. Unlike the Park and Burgess model, accommodation may not lead to assimilation but may be a stage leading to another form of conflict. What this illustrates is that people and nations may view accommodation as a useful strategy during periods of group weakness; it does not mean that they have accepted accommodation as a final solution in their relationship with other groups.

Finally, to return to Washington, it is a matter of debate whether he saw his accommodationism as a temporary strategy to buy time for blacks, or whether he saw it as a long-term goal. A careful reading of Washington suggests the latter. For all his insight, W. E. B. Du Bois was blinded by a certain ideology and failed to understand that Washington simply could not play the same role in the South that he, Du Bois, played in the North. He also failed to see that the wisest policy would have called for a Northern and a Southern strategy for racial and social justice, and a willingness to understand in reality what Du Bois knew in theory: that different historical situations and circumstances require different approaches and strategies. Those unduly critical of Washington tend to confuse theory and reality.

SEE ALSO: Assimilation; Bilingualism; Conflict (Racial/Ethnic); Double Consciousness; Du Bois: "Talented Tenth"; Du Bois, W. E. B.; Park, Robert E. and Burgess, Ernest W.

REFERENCES AND SUGGESTED READINGS

Dennis, R. M. (1994) *Racial and Ethnic Politics*. JAI Press, Greenwich, CT.
Dennis, R. M. (2005) *Marginality, Power, and Social Structure: Issues in Race, Class, and Gender Analyses*. Elsevier, Oxford.
Stone, J. & Dennis, R. M. (2003) *Race and Ethnicity: Comparative and Theoretical Approaches*. Malden, MA, Blackwell.

accounts

Robert Zussman

An account, as the term is most commonly used in sociology, refers to statements that explain disruptions in the social and moral order. In this sense, accounts are linguistic devices by which actors attempt to reposition themselves as socially acceptable and morally reputable in the face of imputations of deviance or failure. Although the concept of accounts has roots in C. Wright Mills's 1940 article on "Situated Actions and the Vocabularies of Motives," in Gresham Sykes and David Matza's 1957 article on "Techniques of Neutralization," and more generally in the work of Erving Goffman, the term itself was introduced in its distinctive sociological sense by Marvin Scott and Sanford Lyman in their 1968 article, entitled simply "Accounts."

Since roughly the middle 1980s, the concept of accounts has given ground to the closely related concept of narrative. In certain respects, accounts and narratives refer to similar phenomena. Both accounts and narratives are (primarily) forms of talk. Both accounts and narratives call attention to the importance to the social production of meanings in addition to (or, in some instances, instead of) behavior. Both accounts and narratives are key tools in the negotiation of social identities. While no hard and fast distinction can or should be drawn between accounts and narratives, the two terms have, however, typically been used in somewhat different ways. Narrative, with strong resonance in literary theory, is a more general term than accounts and one with a more complex and varied history. Sociologists almost always treat accounts as an object of analysis; narratives, in contrast, are treated both as an object of analysis and, in some formulations, as a mode of analysis. As the terms are used in sociology, accounts typically refer to statements produced in tightly bounded situations, while narrative more often refers to longer statements, to full-blown stories, deployed across situations. Similarly, accounts refer to responses to disruptions of a particular social order and by calls to accounts by an identifiable other. In contrast, narrative more often refers to storytelling produced under a wide variety of circumstances, including putatively spontaneous efforts to find, create, or express meaning, even in the absence of an identifiable other demanding such storytelling. For this reason, the analysis of accounts is typically focused tightly on strategies of social interaction, particularly on efforts to avoid blame. The analysis of narrative more frequently focuses on the expressive aspects of culture or on the effects of such cultural forms as the structure of plots. Finally, accounts most often refer to efforts to repair a moral order, while narratives are more often understood as involving resistance as well as restoration.

The analysis of accounts has generated a lively research tradition, but it is a research tradition of a very particular sort. With the exception of some research conducted by scholars affiliated more with communication studies than with sociology, the analysis of accounts has generated few testable propositions and little quantitative research. Rather, accounts have served as a sensitizing concept, alerting researchers to a type of analysis that can be applied across a wide variety of sociological subfields and substantive areas, including, most prominently, deviance but also law, marriage, therapeutic communities, welfare, illness, and employment. Although these applications of account analysis could be classified in any number of ways, two useful ways of thinking about them are (1) in terms of the circumstances that provoke accounts and (2) what accounts accomplish in social interaction.

Because rule breaking, virtually by definition, represents a breach of the moral order, instances of rule breaking (crime, delinquency, and less explicit varieties of deviance), when observed, almost invariably involve calls for accounts from putative rule breakers. The density of accounts will vary, however, depending on the power of those agents of control (including, among many others, police, judges, social service workers, and, in some instances, physicians) who demand accounts and on the degree of control exercised by those agents over resources, symbolic and material, desired by rule breakers. Similarly, the likelihood that a rule breaker's account is honored, in the sense of granting forgiveness, will depend on the rule breaker's ability to generate a credible account consonant with the expectations of the agents of control.

While rule breaking involves an offense to a social and moral order upheld by someone other than the rule breaker, other forms of disruption unsettle the social and moral order of actors themselves, even in the absence of sanctions by others. Probably the most frequent account-producing situations of this sort involves disruptions of an expected life course, as is the case in divorce and in unexpected

illness. Other account-producing occasions emerge not from changes in the actor's life, but from changes in an environment which generate changed expectations about unchanged behavior. Changes in the gender order or the economic order or changes across generations, each as they alter, in their concrete manifestations, the expectations of individual actors, also generate accounts. Unlike accounts generated by rule breaking, accounts generated by unanticipated individual and social changes often lack a specific audience and clear standards by which they are honored or dishonored, and are as often directed inward (to the actor) as outward.

A third class of account-producing situations consists not so much of disruptions of routine but of routinely generated demands for accounts. Many organizations expect their members routinely to produce accounts of their activities, both retrospectively and prospectively. The employee self-evaluation is perhaps the most familiar form of such accounts, but similar phenomena may be found in student self-evaluations and in a wide variety of therapeutic settings. Similarly, various events marking stages in the life course – anniversaries, retirements, school and military reunions – all encourage account giving at highly predictable intervals. Accounts produced under such circumstances combine elements of the accounts produced by rule breaking and by disruptions of other sorts. Although routine accounts typically involve distinct audiences, they may be directed inward as well as outward and involve a great deal of ambiguity and variation as to the circumstances under which they will be honored.

Accounts may also be classified by what they accomplish, by their functions and consequences, both for individual actors and for the social and moral order.

First, accounts may restore breaches in the social order. Scott and Lyman (1968) proposed that restorative accounts could be classified as excuses or justifications. Excuses, including appeals to accident and the absence of intention, acknowledge that a breach has taken place, but deny responsibility for it. Justifications, in contrast, involve techniques of neutralization, including either a denial of injury or a claim that a victim of an act was deserving of injury. Unlike excuses, justifications involve an acceptance of responsibility but a denial that an act is incongruent with established standards of behavior. Both excuses and justifications, then, entail an acceptance of agreed upon general standards of behavior, even while recasting interpretations of particular behaviors. In this sense, accounts may be what Stokes and Hewitt (1976) call aligning actions: statements that create a congruity between conduct and cultural expectations for conduct in the face of actions that appear to depart from those expectations. Because both excuses and justifications involve an acceptance of agreed upon standards, accounts are a central contributor to the maintenance of a consensual moral order.

Second, accounts, even taken narrowly as explanations of disruptions of an ongoing moral order, are deeply implicated in processes of social control. In some instances, however, accounts may be understood as forms of resistance to the inclusion of an individual (or collectivity) in a discredited category. In yet other instances, as McLaughlin et al. (1983) have shown, individuals may refuse to produce accounts, even when reproached directly, denying not only the grounds of the reproach but also the reproacher's right to evaluate. Taken more broadly, accounts, understood as stories, may contribute not only to resistance but also to social change. Here used in a sense closer to that of narratives, accounts of injustice and protest have proven particularly powerful tools for mobilization in, for example, both the civil rights and labor movements.

Third, and more generally, accounts are a form of making meaning. Whether, as some suggest, this meaning making emerges from a deep-felt human urge or, as is more demonstrable, from specific social situations that challenge existing understandings, accounts provide interpretations of behavior and its motives. Understood narrowly, accounts are efforts to give socially acceptable meanings to particular and otherwise discredited behaviors. Understood more broadly, as plotted narratives, accounts are efforts to connect a series of events and behaviors into a coherent story, with a beginning, a middle, and an end, causally related and with a more or less explicit moral content.

Fourth, and more specifically, accounts create identities. Because accounts involve the imputation of motives, and the selective avowal and disavowal of behaviors as motivated, they also involve claims as to what is and is not a part of the self. When offered with deep-felt belief on the part of the speaker, as is often the case in response to illness, divorce, or other disruptions of a previous routine, accounts contribute to the formation of both personal (internally held) and social (publicly enacted) identities. When offered cynically, as self-conscious efforts to manipulate impressions, whether for the enhancement of status or to avoid sanctions, accounts may not contribute to the formation of personal identities but nonetheless still contribute to the formation of social identities.

SEE ALSO: Accounts, Deviant; Identity Theory; Mills, C. Wright; Narrative; Social Order

REFERENCES AND SUGGESTED READINGS

Davis, J. E. (2000) Accounts of False Memory Syndrome: Parents, "Retractors," and the Role of Institutions in Account Making. *Qualitative Sociology* 23: 29–56.

Goffman, E. (1959) *The Presentation of Self in Everyday Life*. Doubleday-Anchor, Garden City, NY.

McLaughlin, M., Cody, M., & Rosenstein, N. (1983) Account Sequences in Conversations between Strangers. *Communication Monographs* 50: 102–25.

Mills, C. W. (1940) Situated Actions and Vocabularies of Motives. *American Sociological Review* 5: 904–13.

Orbuch, T. L. (1997) People's Accounts Count: The Sociology of Accounts. *Annual Review of Sociology* 23: 455–78.

Polkinghorne, D. (1988) *Narrative Knowing and the Human Sciences*. State University of New York Press, Albany.

Scott, M. B. & Lyman, S. (1968) Accounts. *American Sociological Review* 33: 46–62.

Stokes, R. & Hewitt, J. P. (1976) Aligning Actions. *American Sociological Review* 41: 838–49.

Sykes, G. M. & Matza, D. (1957) Techniques of Neutralization: A Theory of Delinquency. *American Sociological Review* 22: 664–70.

Vinitzky-Seroussi, V. (1998) *After Pomp and Circumstance: High School Reunion as an Autobiographical Occasion*. University of Chicago Press, Chicago.

accounts, deviant

Michael L. Benson

An account is a statement made by someone to explain unexpected or untoward behavior (Scott & Lyman 1968). For example, Scully and Marolla (1984) interviewed convicted rapists and found that they had a variety of explanations for their behavior. Some men blamed the victim by stating that she had seduced them. Others denied that the woman had not consented. They claimed that she really did want to have sex. Still others contended that the whole episode had been blown out of proportion and was not really very serious. All of these explanations are designed to put the offender in a less unfavorable light, which is the major purpose that accounts are intended to serve. Although accounts are usually developed in reference to a person's own behavior, the behavior in question can be someone else's. Accounts are a universal feature of ordinary interaction, used by most people on a regular basis. Deviant accounts are those developed specifically to account for acts that are widely regarded as deviant and unacceptable to members of a particular social and cultural setting as opposed to acts that are simply unusual or unexpected.

Deviant accounts often apply to specific instances of behavior, such as in the example of the rapists given above. However, they also can apply to broader aspects of a person's life, indeed to an entire lifestyle or to a physical characteristic, such as obesity, which is stigmatized within a particular cultural setting (Goode 2002). For example, a woman who works as a prostitute might seek to account for her lifestyle by claiming it is a reaction to sexual abuse she experienced as a child. Similarly, drug dealers sometimes account for their involvement in dealing by claiming that it enables them to support their children better and to spend more time with them (Adler 1993). Whether accounts are focused on discrete instances of behavior or on entire lifestyles, their purpose is always to remove or at least reduce the stigma and negative connotations that would ordinarily accompany the actor's deviant-appearing behavior.

Typically, accounts are conceived as being given by and applying to the behavior of individuals. However, they can also be used by organizations to defend or restore organizational reputations. For example, consider a situation in which it comes to light that some members of a large organization have committed an illegal act while occupying their organizational positions. As an illustration, we can use individual brokers in a large stock brokerage firm who individually defraud their clients. Other members of the organization may respond by expelling the wrongdoers and publicly claiming that their behavior is not representative of the organization as a whole and was not endorsed by the organization's leaders. Compared to individuals, organizations have some advantages in accounting for deviance in that they can at times disassociate themselves from the behavior of some of their members. Organizational leaders also can claim or feign ignorance of the deviant activities of subordinates and thus maintain their own personal integrity as well as that of the organization as a whole. It is more difficult for individuals to disassociate themselves from their own behavior.

Accounts are part of the subject matter of the sociology of talk, which is based on the premise that talk is the fundamental material of human relations. Accounts also have been considered by philosophers of language who study speech acts (Searle 1969). Even though accounts are in a sense nothing more than talk, it is recognized that they play an important role in the maintenance of social relationships and ultimately of society as a whole. They are techniques by which actors can repair relationships that have been damaged or threatened by the actors' unacceptable or unexpected behavior. Accounts help maintain social order by reducing or preventing conflicts that may arise whenever one person's behavior does not meet the expectations of another. Thus, if a rapist, for example, can convince his friends and family that his accuser was the one who was really at fault, then his relationships are to some extent repaired and conflict reduced. More generally, accounts are part of the inventory of impression management techniques that people call upon to present themselves to others.

Accounts are closely related to a group of other linguistic devices called techniques of neutralization. Techniques of neutralization are reasons that actors use to free themselves from normative restraints that ordinarily would prevent them from engaging in particular deviant acts (Sykes & Matza 1957). If the normative restraints can be neutralized, then individuals can feel free to commit deviant acts. For example, a student may cheat on a test by thinking to herself before the exam that everyone else is going to cheat so I might as well do so, too. In this case, the student's reasoning that everyone else is breaking the rules frees her from responsibility to follow the rules against cheating. Accounts differ from neutralizations in several ways. In theory, neutralizations occur before a deviant act takes place and have a causal role in its occurrence. An account, on the other hand, comes after the act in question and serves to explain the behavior in question to someone else. Accounts do not play a causal role in behavior, though they may describe the reasons that the actor had in mind before committing the act.

How accounts are related to neutralizations is an open question. In some cases, accounts probably reflect neutralizations that occurred to the actor prior to the deviant act. In other cases, accounts may not be preceded by neutralizations. Rather, they may simply be made up by actors after their deviance has come to light.

Research on accounts has focused on classifying the different types. Two major types have been identified – excuses and justifications (Scott & Lyman 1968). In offering an excuse, an account giver admits the act in question was wrong or somehow inappropriate but denies having full responsibility for it. There are various ways of denying full responsibility, such as claiming that the act was an accident or claiming that the actor was not himself. For example, a rapist may attempt to excuse his actions by claiming that he was under the influence of alcohol or drugs at the time (Scully & Marolla 1984). A justification is an account in which the giver accepts responsibility for the act but then denies the negative quality associated with it.

As with excuses, there are a number of different ways in which actors can deny the pejorative content of their acts. For example, a teenage boy may justify assaulting another boy by claiming that the victim had insulted his sister and deserved to be beaten up.

In addition to developing typologies of accounts, researchers have also been concerned with how accounts are culturally situated. Culture influences the structure of accounts, because the account giver assumes that his or her audience shares certain background assumptions about how the world works. For example, in interviews with convicted white-collar offenders, Benson (1985) found that they often justified their offenses by claiming that their actions were necessary in order for them to stay in business and make a profit. For a business person to justify rule-breaking by saying that he or she needed to make a profit to stay in business makes a certain sense in capitalistic economies. It is a rationale that most members of such a society can at least understand, even though they may not agree with its application in any particular instance. However, the same rationale would make much less sense and probably would not serve as an adequate justification for rule-breaking in a communist society, where the idea of individual profit is not recognized or accepted. Thus, accounts often are based in and derive their plausibility from a larger social and cultural context. As this context changes, accounts also change.

Other important questions concern the conditions under which accounts are successful. A successful account normalizes social relations, reduces conflict, and restores the integrity of the account giver's personal and social identity. Researchers have investigated whether and how the social and personal characteristics of individuals influence the types of accounts they develop and their success.

Over the past few decades, the study of accounts has changed in that researchers have turned away from a concern with the empirical validity of accounts and toward the view that accounts must be conceived as tools used by people to accomplish certain ends. Thus, what matters about an account is not so much its empirical validity as a description of reality or what really happened (Goode 2002). Whether any given account accurately portrays what really happened is now seen as a less important question. The more important question is how accounts work. What makes an account successful? How are they generated by social and cultural contexts? To what extent do the personal and social characteristics of the account giver influence the type and success of accounts?

The study of accounts raises a number of methodological problems. Typically, studies have been conducted through the use of qualitative in-depth interviews. Qualitative interviews require a great deal of skill from the investigator to be used successfully. This technique is necessary because accounts can be complex and multifaceted. Further, they must be understood from the account giver's perspective. Research subjects must be permitted to tell their own stories in their own words. Thus, research results in this area depend on the interviewing and interpretive skills of individual researchers and are difficult to replicate. Studies of accounts tend to be based on small samples of respondents and to be very time consuming for investigators. They also tend to generate large amounts of textual data, which can be difficult to organize systematically. Because the samples are small and because the data generated by in-depth interviews are difficult to summarize, only the most rudimentary quantitative analyses are possible. Questions can be raised about the validity and generalizability of the present knowledge base about accounts. Recent advances in computer-based qualitative data analysis software have made it easier for researchers to manage the large amount of textual data that interviews produce and to conduct analyses that can be replicated by others. Nevertheless, it is likely that the knowledge base in this area will grow slowly and not in a cumulative fashion.

SEE ALSO: Accounts; Crime; Crime, White-Collar; Deviance; Deviance, Crime and; Deviance, Explanatory Theories of; Deviance, Theories of; Deviant Beliefs/Cognitive Deviance; Juvenile Delinquency

REFERENCES AND SUGGESTED READINGS

Adler, P. A. (1993) *Wheeling and Dealing: An Ethnography of an Upper-Level Drug Dealing and Smuggling Community*. Columbia University Press, New York.

Benson, M. L. (1985) Denying the Guilty Mind: Accounting for Involvement in a White-Collar Crime. *Criminology* 23: 589–99.

Goode, E. (2002) *Deviance in Everyday Life: Personal Accounts of Unconventional Lives*. Waveland Press, Prospect Heights, IL.

Scott, M. B. & Lyman, S. M. (1968) Accounts. *American Sociological Review* 33: 46–62.

Scully, D. & Marolla, J. (1984) Convicted Rapists' Vocabulary of Motive: Excuses and Justifications. *Social Problems* 31: 530–44.

Searle, J. R. (1969) *Speech Acts: An Essay in the Philosophy of Language*. Cambridge University Press, Cambridge.

Sykes, G. M. & Matza, D. (1957) Techniques of Neutralization: A Theory of Delinquency. *American Sociological Review* 22: 664–70.

acculturation

Kimya N. Dennis

Foster (1962) defines acculturation as the process of bringing previously separated and disconnected cultures into contact with one another. This contact must be substantial enough such that "cultural transmission" takes place (Herskovits 1950). Cultural transmission is a key concept that distinguishes acculturation from other terms that are used interchangeably, including assimilation, enculturation, and diffusion. Both Foster and Herskovits highlight the theme of cultural borrowing. The process through which cultural borrowing occurs is of central concern to sociologists and involves between-group power differentials, cultural artifacts, and group norms and values.

Acculturation is not the absorption of different cultures as a result of a mere physical contact or superficial exposure. The processes of cultural transmission and cultural borrowing are the result of conscious decision-making on the part of an individual or a group that is approaching a culturally distinct group. If no force or coercion is involved, the individual or group must decide whether and to what extent the new culture will be accepted or rejected. There are instances where the new culture will be imposed upon an individual or a group through force or coercion. In such forced circumstances, the individual or group retains the ability to consciously accept or reject certain aspects of the new culture. An example of conscious decision-making under forced circumstances is the refusal of blacks to accept their "inherent inferiority" during Jim Crow. This refusal to accept this aspect of the Jim Crow subculture translated to the struggles of blacks for economic· and political inclusion in American society. This selective acceptance and rejection of the Jim Crow subculture, within the American culture, illustrates the distinction E. Franklin Frazier (1957) made between "material acculturation" and "ideational acculturation." Material acculturation involves the conveying of language and other cultural tools whereas ideational acculturation involves the conveying of morals and norms. Individuals and groups can consciously decide to accept the language and cultural tools of a new culture without accepting and internalizing the morals and norms of the new culture.

The process of acculturation is complex and is not a simple matter of the cultural majority forcing its culture upon the cultural minority. The experiences of racial and ethnic minorities and immigrant populations in the United States highlight this complex process of inclusion or exclusion (Myrdal 1944). The "melting pot" is inclusion as a result of a merging of cultures and assimilation. The "salad bowl," also known as cultural pluralism, is another metaphor to denote inclusion. The cultures within the "salad bowl" do not assimilate but instead maintain their cultural traits and group identities. Both "melting pot" and "salad bowl" are in contrast to cultural exclusion, which fosters segregation by race, ethnicity, and religion. Segregation under cultural exclusion has been rationalized by redefining cultural pluralism. Attempting to include racial, ethnic, and religious segregation under the umbrella of cultural pluralism ignores the antagonism of black–white and native born–immigrant relations. While cultural

transmission is reciprocal, it is most salient from white to black and from native born to immigrant. There has been a degree of acculturation in which white Americans have borrowed aspects of the cultural expression of blacks and immigrant populations. These cultural aspects include music, dance, art, dialect, sports, clothing, foods, and religion.

George Spindler (1963) created a typology of individual and group responses to the process of acculturation. This typology is Passive Withdrawal, Reactive, Compensatory, Adaptive, and Culture Revisionist and was designed to assess college student responses to change. Spindler's (1963) typology can be generalized to individuals and groups beyond the original research design because there are patterns of responses to change and the process of acculturation across contexts. These response patterns are illustrated in various historical accounts, including Frederick Douglass's (1845) acculturation experience as a former slave and other blacks' experiences with acculturation (Andrew 1988; David 1992), as chronicled by Du Bois (1903), Ralph Ellison (1964), and Booker T. Washington (1901). Thomas and Znaniecki's (1956) study of Polish peasants and studies of "new ethnics" by Santoli (1988), Dublin (1996), and Myers (2005) also highlight individual and group responses to acculturation.

Some individuals and groups respond favorably and with relative ease to the possibility of acculturation whereas others respond unfavorably and with unease. In the former, the incoming group views its acculturation in a positive light and in the latter the incoming group views its acculturation in a negative light. Therefore, how the individual or group perceives the process of acculturation and how the larger society perceives this process are both significant. If the larger society views the possibility of an incoming group's acculturation as favorable and with ease, there will be less hostility and discomfort throughout the process. If the acculturation of an incoming group is viewed unfavorably and with unease by the larger society, there will be greater hostility, discomfort, and the process will require more effort on the part of this incoming group. Examples of favorable responses to acculturation include European immigrants such as Poles, Italians, and Germans. The process of acculturation was performed with relative ease and it transitioned into a process of assimilation. In contrast, the process of acculturation for Jewish Americans and blacks has been met with greater hostility and discomfort such that there is a difficult yet enduring process of acculturation and assimilation. Both blacks and Jewish Americans' efforts to acculturate were resisted by whites. However, this hostility and discomfort is not only on the part of the larger society. Jewish Americans, for example, consciously accepted and rejected aspects of the dominant culture in order to maintain a Jewish identity and distinct religious and cultural practices. Therefore, the processes of acculturation and assimilation are gradual and continual for blacks, Jewish Americans, and other old and new racial and ethnic groups.

Because there are patterns of individual and group responses to acculturation which have unique geographical nation-state differences, the political and economic climate of Europe and the European Union is a final illustration of the acculturation process. The acculturation of immigrant populations has particularly been an issue with the Muslim population in France, the Turkish population in Germany, and Caribbean and Asian populations in England. These societies are religiously and ethnically different from the Muslim, Turkish, Caribbean, and Asian populations being introduced into those countries.

SEE ALSO: Accommodation; Assimilation; Culture; Du Bois, W. E. B.; Melting Pot; Racial Hierarchy; Separatism

REFERENCES AND SUGGESTED READINGS

Andrew, W. (1988) *To Tell a Free Story*. University of Illinois Press, Urbana.

David, J. (1992) *Growing Up Black*. Avon Books, New York.

Douglass, F. (1845) *Narrative of the Life of Frederick Douglass*. American Anti-Slavery Society, Boston.

Dublin, T. (Ed.) (1996) *Becoming American, Becoming Ethnic*. Temple University Press, Philadelphia.

Du Bois, W. E. B. (1903) *The Souls of Black Folk*. A. C. McClurg, New York.

Ellison, R. (1964) *Shadow and Act*. Vintage Books, New York.

Foster, G. (1962) *Traditional Cultures and the Impact of Technological Change*. Harper & Row, New York.

Frazier, E. F. (1957) *Race and Cultural Contact in the Modern World*. Beacon Press, Boston.

Herskovits, M. (1950) *Man and His Works*. Alfred A. Knopf, New York.

Myers, J. (2005) *Minority Voices*. Allyn & Bacon, Boston.

Myrdal, G. (1944) *An American Dilemma*. Harper & Row, New York.

Santoli, A. (1988) *New Americans*. Ballantine Books, New York.

Spindler, G. D. (1963) *Education and Culture: Anthropological Approaches*. Holt, Rinehart, & Winston, New York.

Thomas, W. I. & Znaniecki, F. (1956) *The Polish Peasant in Europe and America*. Dover, New York.

Washington, B. T. (1901) *Up From Slavery*. Doubleday, Page, & Co., New York.

action research

Robert Louis Flood

Action research refers to participatory processes that are democratic in nature, in which action is undertaken in a social context that leads to improvements, having accommodated for the needs of all stakeholders, while, at the same time, the process facilitates social research about action for improvement through participation and aids social research in general.

The kinds of actions that constitute action research are unbounded. Action may focus on improving basic conditions in communities in developing countries, performance in a commercial organization, understanding and influencing the impact of humans on the environment, education systems for adults, conservation of diminishing natural resources such as fish stocks or oil, and so on *ad infinitum*. Wherever there is a social issue there is a need for action.

Research in action research is both formative (what might we do?) and summative (what have we learned?). Formative research involves stakeholders in defining key issues, identifying possible kinds of improvement, choosing what to improve and how to make the improvements, and developing ways of evaluating whether improvement has been achieved or not. Summative research involves consolidation of learning from the process of action yielding experiential knowledge about tools and methods employed, concepts and models generated, and indeed the methodology utilized or developed to drive the action process. This is reflective praxis. Summative research provides experiential knowledge that may be drawn upon by future action researchers as well as the research society at large. In most social contexts like organizations, action is ongoing and so are the formative and summative cycles. Figure 1 represents research in action research showing that formative and summative processes in principle constitute interwoven never-ending learning cycles.

One of the main principles of action research is meaningful participation in both action for improvement and the research process involving all stakeholders, insofar as that is reasonably achievable. Stakeholders here are defined as all those people involved in and affected by the process itself and the process outcomes, such as decisions on what constitutes improvement and thus what action to take. Action research thus may lay claim to democratizing social action and social research processes. Further, some action researchers promote their action research as a means to emancipatory social practices and emancipatory social research.

Knowledge acquisition in action research undertaken in social contexts is different from knowledge acquisition in the natural sciences. Natural scientists emphasize repeatability of results in experiments in the belief that the natural world is regular over time and that it is possible to reach a consensus about natural phenomena. However, action researchers emphasize the ever-changing and subjective character of social reality and that intersubjective discourse is the only means by which we may facilitate knowledge acquisition.

"Valid social knowledge [in action research] is derived from practical reasoning engaged in through action" (Greenwood & Levin 1998). Validity of social knowledge generated through action research therefore refers to the

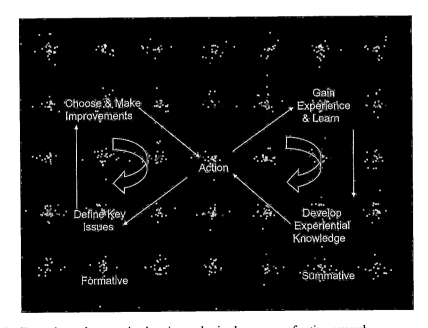

Figure 1 Formative and summative learning cycles in the process of action research.

context from which knowledge is derived. It is context dependent. Thus, while knowledge derived from an action research process may hold utility in other social contexts, knowledge is not perceived to be concrete so that it holds true for all social contexts.

Checkland and Holwell (1998) recognize that outcomes from action research are not repeatable in the manner of the natural sciences, but state that outcomes can be and should be recoverable by interested outsiders. Recoverability means that the formative process and summative outcomes of the process are made transparent and thus more robust. Accordingly, it is essential to state the set of ideas and the process in which they are used methodologically (the epistemology) by means of which action researchers will make sense of their work, and so define what counts for them as acquired knowledge. "This yields a 'truth claim' less strong than that of laboratory experimentation, but one much stronger than that of mere 'plausibility'" (Checkland & Holwell 1998). "Plausibility," Checkland and Holwell state, is all that action research can claim without a process of "recoverability" built into the methodology.

Methods and techniques that may be drawn upon in the process of action research are wide ranging. They include many kinds of qualitative and quantitative approaches drawn from all areas of the social sciences. It is not techniques employed in a process of improvement that define whether the process is action research or not, but the methodology by which the process is driven and the outcomes interpreted. The key driver in methodologies for action research is "dialogue" rather than mere "discussion." Discussion may be thought of as the presentation and defense of ideas where there are winners and losers. This does not sit well within action research. Dialogue requires action researchers to suspend their views and explore the mental models of other participants and stakeholders. Learning and understanding begins only when you start to "see through the eyes of others" (Churchman 1979) in a search for authentic understanding of a multitude of beliefs and values that pervade all social contexts. In this way, dialogue promotes meaningful participation, facilitates deeper mutual understanding between participants,

and generates outcomes such as improvements that accommodate the needs of all participants.

A healthy debate in action research surrounds the question of what constitutes suitable dialogical processes for improvement and learning in social contexts. Numerous methodological approaches have been advocated and the claims of a few of these are summarized below (see the section on "Practices" in Reason & Bradbury 2001).

- *Action inquiry* offers person, second-person, and third-person types of research that each of us can conduct in the midst of our own ongoing practices at home or at work (Torbert 2001).
- *Action science* is an approach to action research that attempts to bridge the gap between social research and social practice by building theories that explain social phenomena, inform practice, and adhere to the fundamental criteria of science (see the seminal publication by Argyris et al. 1985).
- *Appreciative inquiry* is a positive mode of action research that liberates the creative and constructive potential of organizations and human communities (Cooperrider & Srivastva 1987).
- *Clinical inquiry* leads researchers to base their inquiry on needs of the client system and work on developing a healthy relationship with that system in the belief that such a process will obtain deeper and more valid information (Schein 1987).
- *Community action research* offers an approach to cooperation based on an underlying theory of learning communities that integrate research, capacity building, and practice, and on shared understanding of why such integration is both important and difficult (Senge & Scharmer 2001).
- *Cooperative inquiry* is a way of doing cooperative research with people on matters of practical concern to them utilizing a well-considered way of closing the gap between research and the way we live and work together (Heron & Reason 2001).
- *Participatory research* is a way of life, a philosophical or political choice that works in support of groups who are most often excluded or marginalized from dominant knowledge discourses (Hall 2001).

That there is a multitude of methodologies presented under the banner of action research is at least in part explained by the wide-ranging origins and groundings that constitute action research. The origin of action research is often traced to the social research of Kurt Lewin in the 1940s (e.g., Lewin 1943, 1948). In the 1943 publication, Lewin reported on training of housewives in cooking and the effects on their daily cooking habits in their own families. The important step Lewin made was to research in a real-life social setting as opposed to "laboratory science" that hitherto dominated the research process. Lewin's approach involved a deliberate methodical effort to create participative change in organizations. Lewin's work also influenced research on group dynamics and experiential learning about interpersonal interaction in personal development (Schein & Bennis 1965).

Progress in this tradition of social research continued through the Tavistock Institute of Human Relations that employed Lewin's idea of research in real-life social contexts. Psychoanalytic research coupled with an action orientation characterized their socio-technical thinking. The most famous of the Tavistock studies was undertaken in the British coal mining industry (Trist & Bamforth 1951). This was not an action research study as such, but the first real socio-technical study that paved the way for action research. The problem was that new technology did not lead to greater efficiency and the industry wanted to know why. Trist and Bamforth found that production technology and work organization are inextricably linked. Inefficiency arose because of incongruity between demands created by new technology and what is of assistance to miners as a group of interacting human beings. Progress of the industrial democracy movement was influenced by Trist and Bamforth's findings that swayed research away from Tayloristic reductionist approaches that advocate specialization through bounded work groups, towards more holistic real-life social research.

The subsequent rise of industrial democracy promoting semi-autonomous work groups shaped production systems and work practices of many large organizations, including Volvo, Saab-Scania, and Alfa Laval (Greenwood & Levin 1998). Socio-technical thinking soon surfaced in North America (Davis & Taylor 1972) and then in Japan in the quality management movement (Juran 1980; Deming 1983). By the 1980s the idea of holistic research in real-life social settings had pervaded industrial practices across the globe.

Reason and Bradbury (2001) acknowledge that action research is indebted to the Lewin and Tavistock tradition, but also identify crucial intellectual developments that gave rise to a fundamental theoretical framework within which action research would find its grounding. They identify the critique of positivist science and scientism that gave rise to new epistemologies of practice. They recognize a Marxist dictum that the important thing is not to understand the world, but to change it for the better. In this regard, Reason and Bradbury cite for example the educational work of Freire (Shor & Freire 1987), the participatory research practice of people working for the liberation of oppressed and underprivileged people (Fals Borda 2001; Hall 2001), and practices like participatory rural appraisal (Chambers 1997).

Perhaps the most fundamental grounding of action research lies in its systemic, or holistic, awareness (Flood 1999, 2001). Action researchers appreciate that human thought is not capable of knowing the whole, but is capable of "knowing that we don't know." This is an important step forward in human understanding. Such awareness highlights the futility, let alone the hostility, of traditional forms of practice based on science's prediction and control, which dominate today's social organizational arrangements. Such approaches are futile because social dynamics always will remain beyond control. Such approaches are hostile because they attack people's spiritual well-being by isolating us and treating us as separate objects, rather than appreciating patterns of relationship that join us together in one dynamic. Systemic thinking broadens action and deepens research. That is, action research carried out with a systemic perspective in mind promises to construct meaning that resonates strongly with our experiences within a profoundly systemic world.

SEE ALSO: Epistemology; Methods; Praxis

REFERENCES AND SUGGESTED READINGS

Argyris, C., Putnam, R., & Smith, D. (1985) *Action Science: Concepts, Methods, and Skills for Research and Intervention.* Jossey-Bass, San Francisco.

Chambers, R. (1997) *Whose Reality Counts? Putting the First Last.* Intermediate Technology Publications, London.

Checkland, P. & Holwell, S. (1998) Action Research: Its Nature and Validity. *Systemic Practice and Action Research* 11: 9–21.

Churchman, C. W. (1979) *The Systems Approach and Its Enemies.* Basic Books, New York.

Cooperrider, D. L. & Srivastva, S. (1987) Appreciative Inquiry in Organizational Life. In: Pasmore, W. A. & Woodman, R. W. (Eds.), *Research in Organizational Change and Development,* Vol. 1. JAI Press, Greenwich, CT, pp. 129–69.

Davis, L. E. & Taylor, J. C. (1972) *Design of Jobs.* Penguin, London.

Deming, W. E. (1983) *Out of the Crisis: Quality, Productivity, and Competitive Position.* MIT Press, Cambridge, MA.

Fals Borda, O. (2001) Participatory (Action) Research in Social Theory: Origins and Challenges. In: Reason, P. & Bradbury, H. (Eds.), *Handbook of Action Research.* Sage, Thousand Oaks, CA.

Flood, R. L. (1999) *Rethinking the Fifth Discipline.* Sage, London.

Flood, R. L. (2001) The Relationship of "Systems Thinking" to Action Research. In: Reason, P. & Bradbury, H. (Eds.), *Handbook of Action Research.* Sage, Thousand Oaks, CA.

Greenwood, D. J. & Levin, M. (1998) *Introduction to Action Research.* Sage, Thousand Oaks, CA.

Hall, B. L. (2001) I Wish This Were a Poem of Practices of Participatory Research. In: Reason, P. & Bradbury, H. (Eds.), *Handbook of Action Research.* Sage, Thousand Oaks, CA.

Heron, J. & Reason, P. (2001) The Practice of Cooperative Inquiry: Research "With" Rather Than "On" People. In: Reason, P. & Bradbury, H. (Eds.), *Handbook of Action Research.* Sage, Thousand Oaks, CA.

Juran, J. M. (1980) *Quality Planning and Analysis.* McGraw-Hill, New York.

Lewin, K. (1943) Forces Behind Food Habits and Methods of Change. *Bulletin of the National Research Council* 108: 35–65.

Lewin, K. (1948) *Resolving Social Conflicts.* Harper, New York.

Reason, P. & Bradbury, H. (Eds.) (2001) *Handbook of Action Research.* Sage, Thousand Oaks, CA.

Schein, E. H. (1987) *The Clinical Perspective in Fieldwork.* Sage, London.

Schein, E. H. & Bennis, W. (1965) *Personal and Organizational Change through Group Methods: The Experimental Approach.* Wiley, New York.

Senge, P. & Scharmer, O. (2001) Community Action Research: Learning as a Community of Practitioners, Consultants and Researchers. In: Reason, P. & Bradbury, H. (Eds.), *Handbook of Action Research.* Sage, Thousand Oaks, CA.

Shor, I. & Freire, P. (1987) *A Pedagogy for Liberation.* Bergen & Garvey, New York.

Torbert, W. R. (2001) The Practice of Action Inquiry. In: Reason, P. & Bradbury, H. (Eds.), *Handbook of Action Research.* Sage, Thousand Oaks, CA.

Trist, E. & Bamforth, K. W. (1951) Some Social and Psychological Consequences of the Longwall Method of Coal Getting. *Human Relations* 4: 3–38.

actor–network theory

Geoffrey Bowker

Actor–network theory originated in the 1980s as a movement within the sociology of science, centered at the Paris School of Mines. Key developers were Bruno Latour (Latour 1987), Michel Callon, Antoine Hennion, and John Law. It was sharply critical of earlier historical and sociological analyses of science, which had drawn a clear divide between the "inside" of a science (to be analyzed in terms of its adherence or not to a unitary scientific method) and its "outside" (the field of its application).

Actor–network theorists made three key moves. First, they argued for a semiotic, network reading of scientific practice. Human and non-human actors (actants) were assumed to be subject to the same analytic categories, just as a ring or a prince could hold the same structural position in a fairy tale. They could be enrolled in a network or not, could hold or not hold certain moral positions, and so forth. This profound ontological position has been the least understood but the most generative aspect of the theory. Second, they argued that in producing their theories, scientists weave together human and non-human actors into relatively stable network nodes, or "black boxes." Thus a given astronomer can tie together her telescope, some distant stars, and a funding agency into an impregnable fortress, and to challenge her results you would need to find your own telescope, stars, and funding sources. Practically, this entailed an agnostic position on the "truth" of science. Indeed, they argued for a principle of symmetry according to which the same set of explanatory factors should be used to account for failed and successful scientific theories. There is no ultimate arbiter of right and wrong. Third, they maintained that in the process of constructing these relatively stable network configurations, scientists produced contingent nature–society divides. Nature and society were not pre-given entities that could be used to explain anything else; they were the outcomes of the *work* of doing technoscience. Latour called this the "Janus face" of science. As it was being produced it was seen as contingent; once produced it was seen as always and already true.

Together, these three moves made the central analytical unit the work of the intermediary. There is no society out there to which scientists respond as they build their theories, nor is there a nature which constrains them to a single telling of their stories. Rather, the technoscientist stands between nature and society, politics and technology. She can act as a spokesperson for her array of actants (things in the world, people in her lab), and if successful can black-box these to create the effect of truth.

The theory has given rise to a number of concepts which have proven useful in a wide range of technoscientific analyses. It has remained highly influential as a methodological tool for analyzing truth-making in all its forms. The call to "follow the actors" – to see what they do rather than report on what they say they do – has been liberating for those engaged in studying scientists, who frequently hold their own truth and practice as if above the social and political fray. Their attention to the work of representation on paper led to the ideas of "immutable mobiles" and "centers of calculation," which trace the power of technoscience to its ability to function as a centralizing networked bureaucracy. Indeed,

the anthropological eye of actor-networked theorists – looking at work practices and not buying into actors' categories – has led to a rich meeting between the sociology of work, the Chicago School of sociology, and actor-network theory. Latour's later work on the distribution of political and social values between the technical world and the social institution has opened up a powerful discourse about the political and moral force of technology.

The actor-network theory itself has changed significantly in recent years, including Latour's (1999) tongue-in-cheek denial of each of its central terms and the hyphen connecting them. This has been in response to a number of critiques that the theory privileged the powerful, Machiavellian technoscientist as worldbuilder, without giving much opportunity for representing the invisible technicians within the networks and alternative voices from without (Star 1995).

SEE ALSO: Actor-Network Theory, Actants; Science and Culture; Science, Social Construction of; Technology, Science, and Culture

REFERENCES AND SUGGESTED READINGS

Latour, B. (1987) *Science in Action: How to Follow Scientists and Engineers Through Society*. Open University Press, Milton Keynes.
Latour, B. (1999) On Recalling ANT. In: Law, J. & Hassard, J. (Eds.), *Actor Network Theory and After*. Blackwell, Oxford, 15–25.
Star, S. L. (Ed.) (1995) *Ecologies of Knowledge: Work and Politics in Science and Technology*. SUNY Press, Albany, NY.

actor–network theory, actants

Steve Fuller

Actor-network theory has been the dominant school of science and technology studies since shortly after the English publication of Latour

(1987). It reflects the combined efforts of Michel Callon, an engineer turned economist, and Bruno Latour, a philosopher turned anthropologist, both of whom have worked since 1980 at the Center for the Sociology of Innovation at L'École Nationale Supérieure des Mines in Paris. Together, they have provided, respectively, the "hard" and "soft," or "policy oriented" and "academically oriented," versions of their joint intellectual standpoint. Actor–network theory has flourished in the context of the changing status of academic knowledge production in the European Union, where states influenced to varying degrees by neoliberalism have increasingly forced a traditionally protected higher education sector to justify itself by establishing ties with external "users and beneficiaries."

Its name notwithstanding, actor–network theory is less a theory than a method for mapping the patterns of "technoscience" that emerge from this neoliberal regime. However, the UK sociologist John Law, the main proponent of actor–network theory in the English-speaking world, has worked hard to convert the "theory" into a postmodern metaphysics presaging a complete makeover of the social sciences, in which networks become the stuff out of which both individual identity and social organization are constructed. While networks have long been recognized as an intermediate level of social organization between, say, a face-to-face group and an institution, actor–network theory at its most ambitious aims to redefine these multiple levels as networks of varying lengths, resiliency, and rates of growth. Unsurprisingly perhaps, this ambitious vision has found many followers in business schools, where "networking" is most naturally seen as constitutive of social reality.

The conceptual cornerstone of actor–network theory is the "actant," a term borrowed from semiotics. In the work of Greimas and Genette, it referred to anything that acts in a narrative setting. The term was coined to suspend issues about whether the actor is real or fictional, human or non-human, etc. What matters is simply the actant's role in an action context. Actor–network theory converts this methodological point into an ontological principle. Its import is that agency – and specifically responsibility – is distributed equally across

entities, including a host of non-human ones not normally seen as exercising agency at all. Consequently, actor–network accounts can appear animistic. In any case, they tend to undermine attempts to find a prime mover in a complex technoscientific "assemblage."

Sociologically speaking, actor–network theory is a classic beneficiary of others' miseries, in this case, a democratized and status-degraded French science and engineering profession. The godfather of structuralism in the human sciences, the philosopher Gaston Bachelard, turns out to be an inspirational figure because of his explicit portrayal of scientists and engineers as akin to a theoretically exploited proletariat, from whose labors philosophers try to extract surplus value in the form of such metaphysical positions as realism and idealism. This subaltern view suited French scientists and engineers after 1968, when Charles De Gaulle responded to the academic challenge to his presidency by multiplying universities, which succeeded in dividing the ranks of a previously elite profession along roughly class lines.

Actor–network theory was built on case studies of the success – and especially the failure – of technoscientific networks to translate their typically divergent interests into a workable product or course of action. Significant in the French science policy context were three failures: the electric car's failure to be marketable; the Minitel's failure to become integrated into global computer networks; and the failure of a computer-driven customized rail system to attract Parisian commuters (Latour 1993). In each case, the failure was traceable to an exaggerated confidence in what top-down management could accomplish without attending to the "interests" of those mediating entities – often but not always human – whose cooperation would have been necessary for the policy's implementation. Reflexively speaking, the actor–network theorist's own power here lies in her ability to temper actors' expectations, which in turn helps to maintain a rhythm to the circulation of elites that is tolerable by the society as a whole.

In terms of normative orientation, actor–network theory may be seen as turning Max Weber on his head. If, as Weber believed, the "modernity" of the state is marked by a reliance on scientifically authorized modes of legitimation, then instead of indulging their masters in the belief that policy regimes can be rendered efficient, duly authorized social scientists like Callon and Latour can both prove their usefulness and run interference on state policy by highlighting unforeseen obstacles on the way to policy implementation. They are thus able to manufacture a sense of integrity and even value-neutrality – along with a hint of radicalism – in a client-driven world: she can stare down her master while reinforcing the master's need for her services. A not inappropriate comparison is with the psychotherapist who strings along the patient for the material benefit of the former and the spiritual benefit of the latter. This opportunism, perhaps even cynicism, has been widely noted within science and technology studies without being decisively addressed.

SEE ALSO: Actor-Network Theory; Network Society; Semiotics; Technology, Science, and Culture

REFERENCES AND SUGGESTED READINGS

Bijker, W. & Law, J. (Eds.) (1992) *Shaping Technology/Building Society*. MIT Press, Cambridge, MA.

Callon, M., Law, J., & Rip, A. (1986) *Mapping the Dynamics of Science and Technology*. Macmillan, London.

Fuller, S. (2006) *The Philosophy of Science and Technology Studies*. Routledge, New York.

Latour, B. (1987) *Science in Action*. Open University Press, Milton Keynes.

Latour, B. (1993) *We Have Never Been Modern*. Harvard University Press, Cambridge, MA.

Addams, Jane (1860–1935)

Mary Jo Deegan

Feminist pragmatist, social settlement leader, and Nobel Laureate, Jane Addams was a charismatic world leader with an innovative intellectual legacy in sociology. She is one of the most important female sociologists who ever lived. From 1890 to 1935, she led dozens of women in sociology, although after 1920 most of these women were forced out of sociology and into other fields such as social work, home economics, applied psychology, pedagogy, and college administration.

Jane Addams was born on September 6, 1860, in the Midwestern small town of Cedarville, Illinois. She was profoundly influenced by her father, John Addams, a Hicksite Quaker, state senator, and mill owner, but she did not know her mother, Sarah Weber, who died when Addams was 2 years old. In 1877 Addams entered Rockford Female Seminary, in Rockford, Illinois, a pioneering college for women. After she graduated in 1881, her father died in August, and she became confused and despairing. She entered the Women's Medical College in Philadelphia in the fall, but she soon returned to Illinois. In poor health and surrounded by family problems, Addams drifted for a year. Finally taking some action, in 1883 she traveled to Europe, but she remained frustrated until she returned to Europe in 1887 and started new studies of society and culture. Accompanied by her college friend Ellen Gates Starr, Addams found a direction for her life after visiting the social settlement Toynbee Hall in London's East End. This group served the exploited working classes and supported artisans who harmonized their interests in art, labor, and the community. Toynbee Hall provided a model in 1889 for Addams and Starr to co-found their social settlement, Hull-House, in Chicago.

Hull-House became the institutional anchor for women's gender-segregated work in sociology and a liaison with the most important male sociological center during this era, the University of Chicago. Addams became a significant figure in an international social movement organized to bring together all classes, social groups, ages (especially the young and the elderly), and the oppressed to form a democratic community able to articulate and enact their ideals and needs. Addams led a worldwide network of activists, friends, and scholars. She powerfully described life there in *Twenty Years at Hull-House* (1910) and *The Second Twenty Years at Hull-House* (1930).

A groundbreaking sociological text, *Hull-House Maps and Papers* was published by Hull-House residents in 1895, predating and establishing the interests of the early Chicago male sociologists, including her friends and allies Albion W. Small, Charles R. Henderson, and George E. Vincent. She also helped establish the urban sociology and arts and crafts influence of the sociologist Charles Zueblin and his wife, Rho Fisk Zueblin. She profoundly influenced the work of George Herbert Mead, John Dewey, W. I. Thomas, and, to a lesser degree, Thorsten Veblen. She built a political and feminist epistemology parallel to their approach called symbolic interactionism or Chicago pragmatism. She was not acknowledged publicly as a colleague by Robert E. Park and Ernest W. Burgess, although her ideas and areas of specialization also influenced them.

Her combined thought and practice is called feminist pragmatism: an American theory uniting liberal values and a belief in a rational public with a cooperative, nurturing, and liberating model of the self, the other, and the community. Education and democracy are significant mechanisms to organize and improve society, to learn about one's community, participate in group decisions, and become a *citizen*. Feminist pragmatists study "social behavior" and believe each "individual" is born with rudimentary, flexible instincts or "impulses." Infants primarily learn by observing, imitating, and responding to the gestures of others, particularly their parents. They can abstract the meaning of "gestures," particularly "vocal gestures," and generalize about "the other, the group, the community, and institutions." This "process" allows the individual to develop a "mind, intelligence, a self, and the ability to take the role of the other." The self learns organized "attitudes" of "the community" towards "social situations." People sharing the same neighborhood and community develop "shared experience (which is the greatest of human goods)." The self emerges from others and is not in conflict with others unless it is taught to be in conflict.

Women who obey the rules governing the home and family follow "the family claim." When they work for others outside the home, they follow "the social claim." Conflicts between these claims create an instability in society, whereby "women become a resource for social change." Women in public life can utilize their cooperative worldview to implement the goals of democracy. The female world is based on the unity of the female self, the home, the family, and face-to-face interactions with neighbors in a community. Women can extend this pattern to nurturing others outside the home as "bread givers engaged in bread labor." Expanding their model for the home and family to the larger social situation is called "civic housekeeping." Women can be leaders in a new "social consciousness," indicated in "newer ideals of peace." A sign of this awakening consciousness is "the integration of the objective with the subjective." This is organized through "social movements in labor, social science, and women." The modern city is a new location for these social changes.

Women learn "folk wisdom" and share a culture based on female myths such as the Corn Mother. This unity crosses racial/ethnic lines while it supports and respects differences, including variation by class, age, race, religion, education, sexual preference, and disability. Democracy emerges from different groups, and represents these distinct perspectives, histories, communities, and characteristic structures of the self. Social change must articulate and respond to these various groups' commonalities and differences. "Old women" also learn and pass on legends, cherish the good in others, develop "woman's Memory," and engage in "perfecting the past." Because women are not full members of the male world, they are in an ideal situation to "challenge war, disturb conventions, integrate industry, react to life, and transform the past." "Women's obligation" is to help create and distribute the world's food supply. The modern woman's family claim is built on a "consumer role" that should critique and change industry. These concepts were discussed in several major books, including *Democracy and Social Ethics* (1902), *Newer Ideals of Peace* (1907), *The Spirit of Youth and the City Streets* (1909), *A New Conscience and an Ancient Evil* (1912), *The Long Road of*

Woman's Memory (1916), and *Peace and Bread in Time of War* (1922).

Addams's views on women were little understood then or now. Having a popular image as a "saintly" woman who worked for the poor, Addams believed that female values of nonviolence, cooperation, and nurturance were superior to male ones supporting violence, conflict, and self-centeredness and that a society built on feminine values would be more productive, peaceful, and just. Female culture was learned primarily and not biologically given. Thus, this is not an essentialist or biological argument, but one based on the assumptions of learned, symbolic behavior attained through socialization, especially public education. After the start of the Great War in Europe in 1914, Addams realized that she needed publicly to choose nonviolent values over any others, and this led to a different path than the one followed by her male sociological allies. This was an agonizing time for Addams. Committed to her values, based on female ideals, she maintained her pacifist position and was publicly shunned. The culmination of her politically untouchable status occurred in 1919, when she was targeted by the US government as the most dangerous person in America. Mead, Dewey, and Thomas separated from her from approximately 1916 until the war ended in 1918. Other male sociologists never healed the breach and her public role as a sociological leader was damaged severely. She was ostracized by succeeding generations of sociologists until recently.

In 1920, women were granted the franchise, and to Addams this was a major victory. Contrary to her expectation of a progressive and powerful women's vote, this decade led to an eclipse of the former power of women activists, including Addams. She gradually resumed her pubic leadership during the 1920s, but the devastating impact of the Great Depression called for new, radical social analysis and social change. Addams again became a distinguished world leader. Winner of the Nobel Peace Prize in 1931, she spoke for many of the values and policies adopted during the New Deal, especially in social security and other government programs which altered American capitalism. Dying in 1935, she was mourned worldwide as a great leader and interpreter of American thought.

There is a vast literature on Addams, most of it emphasizing her biography, social work, and public role in American society. This scholarship spans several fields, especially in women's studies, that criticizes white, middle-class women, early social workers, reformers, and philanthropists as conservative, exploitative, and oppressive. Addams is often the symbolic leader of these various groups and sometimes emerges as a contemporary symbol of the villainy of benevolent ignorance or intentional evil. Thus, some scholars stereotype her as a racist, assimilationist, essentialist, and atheoretical meddler. There is a serious lack of study of her intellectual apparatus: her theory of the arts, her lifelong commitment to political theory, and her vast influence in American race relations, especially between whites and people of color.

The general scholarship noted above contrasts with the early studies of Addams as a sociologist before 1920, when she was highly integrated into the sociological literature, frequently spoke before the American Sociological Society, and published in the *American Journal of Sociology*. Addams's stellar leadership in sociology was erased until the publication of Deegan (1988) and a series of related articles on the sociology of Addams and the cohort of women she inspired. The importance of rediscovering her role and influence in sociology is increasingly visible and understood within the profession. A comprehensive microfilm of the Jane Addams Papers, organized and collected by Mary Lynn McCree, provides expanded access to thousands of documents concerning Addams's life and contributions.

Addams's intellectual legacy as a feminist pragmatist has been obscured and sometimes distorted. She articulated radical changes in American life and politics, altering the possibilities for human growth and action for the poor, the working class, immigrants, people of color, youth, the aged, and women. Addams was a central figure in applied sociology between 1892 and 1920 and led a large and powerful cohort of women whom she profoundly influenced. Contemporary scholars often document and either praise or deplore

Addams's significant contributions to public life, but her intellectual stature is barely appreciated. Her profound influence on the course and development of sociology is only suggested in most sociological books and articles. A growing number of scholars are analyzing this great, alternative heritage and tradition in American sociology. They envision a new horizon for a more just and liberated society.

SEE ALSO: Chicago School; Dewey, John; Mead, George Herbert; Pragmatism

REFERENCES AND SUGGESTED READINGS

Brown, V. B. (2004) *The Education of Jane Addams.* University of Pennsylvania Press, Philadelphia.
Bryan, M. L. N., McCree, A., & Davis, F. (1990) *One Hundred Years at Hull-House.* Indiana University Press, Bloomington.
Bryan, M. L. N., Blair, B., & deAngury, M. (Eds.) (2002) *The Selected Papers of Jane Addams*, Vol. 1. University of Illinois Press, Chicago.
Deegan, M. J. (1988) *Jane Addams and the Men of the Chicago School, 1892–1920.* Transaction Books, New Brunswick, NJ.
Deegan, M. J. (2002) *Race, Hull-House, and the University of Chicago, 1892–1960.* Greenwood Press, Westport.
Deegan, M. J. & Hill, M. R. (Eds.) (1987) *Women and Symbolic Interaction.* Allen & Unwin, Boston.
Farrell, J. C. (1967) *Beloved Lady.* Johns Hopkins University Press, Baltimore.
Linn, J. W. (1935) *Jane Addams.* Appleton-Century Crofts, New York.

addiction and dependency

Emma Wincup

Terms such as addiction and dependency are frequently used to describe patterns of illicit drug use. However, there are no universal definitions of these terms and they are frequently used inconsistently and interchangeably. As a result, it is it difficult to estimate the number of drug users who can be described as addicted or dependent. Addiction tends to refer to dependence on a particular drug or drugs, which has developed to the extent that it has a severe and harmful impact on an individual drug user. The term implies that the drug user is unable to give up drug use without incurring adverse effects.

Dependency can refer to physical and/or emotional dependency and drug users may experience one or both forms. Drug users can become physically dependent on drugs, thus continuing with their drug use in order to avoid the physical discomfort of withdrawal. They can also become emotionally dependent on drugs; for example, relying upon drug use to seek pleasure or to avoid pain. Drugscope (a UK-based independent center for expertise on drugs) suggests the term addiction is inexplicably linked to society's reaction to drug users, and argues that there is an emerging consensus that the term dependency is preferable.

Sociologists have been influential in highlighting the importance of societal reaction to drug use. Drawing upon the insights of symbolic interactionism, Howard Becker's classic study *Outsiders: Studies in the Sociology of Deviance* (1963) drew attention to the processes by which individuals became drug users within a deviant subculture. Employing the notion of a career, he highlighted how the labeling of individuals as deviants by the public and agents of social control (including criminal justice agencies and medical professionals) helped to increase levels of drug use. He argued that by attaching a stigmatizing label to a drug user, the individual responds to this new identity. Other influential research, such as Jock Young's *The Drugtakers* he role of the media in amplifying drug use.

Sociological analysis of drug use has played a significant role in challenging the medicalization of so-called deviant behavior. Sociologists have challenged the practice of referring to drug use as a disease with the implication that it can be cured through medical treatment. In particular, feminist sociologists have been highly critical of this approach, which fails to recognize the links between women's subordinate position in society and their use of illicit drugs.

SEE ALSO: Deviance, Medicalization of; Deviant Careers; Drug Use; Drugs, Drug Abuse, and Drug Policy; Labeling; Labeling Theory

REFERENCES AND SUGGESTED READINGS

Barton, A. (2003) *Illicit Drugs: Use and Control.* Routledge, London.
Ettorre, E. (1992) *Women and Substance Use.* Macmillan, London.
Neale, J. (2001) *Drug Users in Society.* Palgrave Macmillan, London.
Taylor, A. (1993) *Women Drug Users: An Ethnography of a Female Injecting Community.* Clarendon Press, Oxford.
Wincup, E. (2005) Drugs, Alcohol and Crime. In: Hale, C., Hayward, K., Wahidin, A., & Wincup, E. (Eds.), *Criminology.* Oxford University Press, Oxford, pp. 203–22.

Adorno, Theodor W. (1903–69)

Markus S. Schulz

Theodor W. Adorno, a German-Jewish social theorist and cultural critic, is best known as a central protagonist in the development of the Frankfurt School's Critical Theory.

Born on September 11, 1903 as Theodor Ludwig Wiesengrund, the only son of a wealthy, Protestant German-Jewish wine merchant and an accomplished singer of Corsican-German descent, he pursued for much of his life a dual career as composer and academic thinker. He studied philosophy, sociology, and psychology at the University of Frankfurt and took lessons in composition with Alban Berg and piano with Eduard Scheuermann in Vienna, where he also met Arnold Schoenberg. Early friendships with Siegfried Kracauer, Max Horkheimer, and Walter Benjamin shaped profoundly his intellectual trajectory. Adorno wrote his dissertation at the University of Frankfurt under the supervision of Hans

Cornelius on Husserl's phenomenology (1924) and his *Habilitationsschrift* under Paul Tillich on Kierkegaard (1931). The publication of his Kierkegaard book coincided with the Nazi rise to power. He was dismissed from his junior faculty position at the University of Frankfurt and went to England, where he became an advanced student at Merton College, Oxford.

Adorno immigrated in 1938 to the US upon Horkheimer's offer to become a permanent member at the *Institut fuer Sozialforschung*, which had moved from Frankfurt to a building provided by Columbia University in New York, and a job in the Princeton Radio Research Project, led by Paul Lazarsfeld. The work in Lazarsfeld's music project proved conflictive. Adorno had no intention in helping to collect data that he thought would end up serving commercial-administrative purposes. His assessments of the cultural regression in the actual practices of listening to music on radio puzzled his colleagues in the project. The Rockefeller Foundation discontinued its funding for the music component of the project.

Adorno followed Horkheimer to Los Angeles, where they closely collaborated from 1941 to 1944 on a manuscript that was later published under the title *Dialectic of Enlightenment*. The authors traced the history of western rationality in a series of audacious chapters and excursions from ancient Greece to the present. The chapters on the *Odyssey* and the modern culture industry were mainly Adorno's contributions. It cast Homer's epos as enlightenment of the myth from which it was derived. Ulysses's ruse against the mythical sirens was interpreted as a first step of enlightenment's domination of nature and in the self-constitution of subjectivity. The modern culture industry was seen as tantamount to enlightenment becoming myth again in a totalitarian world of domination. The German edition of the book was available for many years only in the form of pirated copies. Its reprint in 1972 and its first translation into English made it an international academic bestseller. An improved new English translation appeared in 2002.

During his years in California Adorno also wrote most of the manuscripts for *Philosophy of Modern Music* (1949), *Minima Moralia* (1951), and *Composing for the Films* (with

Hanns Eisler, 1949), and provided musical consultation for Thomas Mann's *Doctor Faustus*. The *Minima Moralia* is seen by some as his most important work, as many of his key ideas are gathered in this collection of *Reflections from Damaged Life*. His dark time-diagnosis is captured in his verdict that there is "no beauty and no more consolation other than in the gaze that is directed at the horror, that withstands it, and that clings on to the possibility of the better in the unfettered consciousness of the negativity" (Adorno 1951: 26).

From 1944 on, Adorno worked also on the Berkeley Project on the Nature and Extent of Antisemitism. The resulting book, *The Authoritarian Personality* (with Frenkel-Brunswick, Levinson, and Sanford), was published in 1950 as part of the multi-volume *Studies in Prejudice* (edited by Horkheimer and Flowerman). This social psychological study was innovative in its integration of multiple empirical methods and theoretical approaches and pointed to a connection between internalized acceptance of authoritarianism and susceptibility to anti-Semitic prejudices.

Adorno returned to Germany in 1949 to become vice-director (in 1958, director) of the reestablished *Institut fuer Sozialforschung* and assumed a professorship for philosophy (from 1953 also for sociology) at the University of Frankfurt. He took on increasing responsibilities in the Institute's empirical research projects, which included studies of political culture, communities, and workplace relations. His collection of essays published under the title *Prisms* (1955) made him known to a larger audience as a cultural critic and social theorist. His *Jargon of Authenticity* (1964) was a sharp critique of Heidegger, whose work had been fashionable since the Nazi period. Adorno ridiculed the abstractness of Heidegger's existentialist philosophy as it subdued the concrete being.

In the course of the 1960s Adorno became an increasingly prominent public intellectual in West Germany, where he wrote frequently for the press and was heard on the radio and occasionally also seen on television. He served as the president of the *Deutsche Gesellschaft fuer Soziologie* (German Society for Sociology) from 1963 to 1968.

Although Adorno had helped to reestablish empirical social research in Germany after World War II, he found himself increasingly warning against what he regarded as objectifying uses of quantitative methods. Adorno's methodological critique culminated in a hefty dispute (later known as the *Positivismusstreit*) with Karl Popper and others about the proper ways of doing sociology (see Adorno et al. 1972). Adorno postulated that sociology should not restrict itself to a mere description of social conditions, but it should produce a critique of these conditions He warned that the fragmentation of sociology into separate fields would undermine the ability to grasp the social totality. He argued that quantitative methods were often mindlessly employed in studies that aspired to exact measurements of unimportant surface phenomena but forgot to consider what was relevant and failed to reflect on the context of research and on issues of power. Adorno's own social research methodology had been described as a "totality empiricism" (*Totalitaetsempirismus*) oriented at the "indices paradigm" (*Indizienparadigma*) (Bonss). In attempting to tackle the social totality, Adorno considered the complexity of social relations to be more graspable in multi-method case studies rather than mere quantitative opinion polls. The legitimation for this research would come ultimately from its transformative capacity.

Adorno provided a philosophically grounded justification of his theoretical approach in his *Negative Dialectics* (1966). Considered by many as his most elaborated work, in which his epistemological, methodological, ontological, and sociological positions, parts of which he had begun writing as far back as 1937, intersected, it does not offer a systematic theory but rather an "ensemble of model analyses." Adorno developed his arguments dialectically by engaging with Kant, Hegel, Marx, Nietzsche, and Heidegger through the method of interpretive "immanent critiques." Adorno reversed Hegel by maintaining that the whole social totality is what is false, yet he defended interpretive thought against the Marxist claim of its inconsequentiality by pointing to the lack of a viable revolutionary liberation project. Adorno maintained against positivism that the contradictions of the social totality make it impossible to present a non-contradictory theory about it. Adorno even refused to define his key terms. Their meaning was rather meant to be developed "mimetically" in the dialectical course of the argument. He argued that the identification of a concept with what it stands for represses the "non-identical" (*Nichtidentische*) and is essentially the same principle that reduces humanness to its exchange value, subdues the individual, and antagonizes society. The moments of hope for redemption that appear in the *Negative Dialectics* are in the negation of despair, in reference to the memory of fulfilled childhood days, and in high art.

Adorno's posthumously published *Aesthetic Theory* (1970) sums up his interest in visual art, literature, and music. The modern work of art has for him a double character. It is at once autonomous and yet in its autonomousness a reflection of its social conditioning. Adorno considered art as a sphere of experience that was not subservient to cultural criticism but equal to it. Adorno's work on music had earned him the title of a "father of the sociology of music," although he was ridiculed for his misunderstanding of jazz and much criticized for his inability to appreciate cultural excellence in musical genres that did not fit the compositional assumptions that he was trained in.

Adorno had a major impact on sociology and all of the humanities in Germany. He helped foment after World War II a critical sociology that is not content woith describing society as it is, but that sees the task of sociology above all as questioning the status quo and criticizing its shortcomings. Adorno's impact went far beyond academia. He had become in the 1960s increasingly a public intellectual who intervened in the debates on broadcasts and in the press. The West German student movement of the late 1960s and early 1970s saw in him a key source of inspiration, but later turned against him when he, unlike Herbert Marcuse at Berkeley, refused to participate in what he considered blind actionism. His perceived arrogance and arbitrary snobbishness came under heavy criticism. The conflict escalated in 1969 when he called in the police to evict students from the

Institute, whom he had feared to be in the process of occupying the building. Adorno died from a heart attack on August 6, 1969 while on vacation in Switzerland and was buried at Frankfurt's main cemetery.

Adorno's writings continue to attract the attention of sociologists, philosophers, musicologists, and cultural studies scholars. There is a huge and growing literature on Adorno. Contemporary sociology's growing interest in culture and postpositivist studies as well as in public sociology are likely to keep the interest in Adorno's work alive. His transcribed seminar lectures on the *Introduction to Sociology* (1993) were published a quarter century after his death and, like others of his works, were only recently translated or published as corrected translations into English.

SEE ALSO: Authoritarian Personality; Critical Theory/Frankfurt School; Culture; Culture Industries; Horkheimer, Max; Metatheory; Music and Media; Theory; Theory and Methods

REFERENCES AND SUGGESTED READINGS

Adorno, T. W. (1949) *Philosophie der neuen Musik.* J. C. B. Mohr, Tuebingen; trans. by A. G. Mitchell & W. V. Blomster as *Philosophy of Modern Music* (1973). Sheed & Ward, London.

Adorno, T. W. (1951) *Minima Moralia: Reflexionen aus dem beschaedigten Leben.* Suhrkamp, Frankfurt; trans. by E. F. N. Jephcott as *Minima Moralia: Reflections from Damaged Life* (1974). New Left Books, London.

Adorno, T. W. (1955) *Prismen: Kulturkritik und Gesellschaftstheorie.* Suhrkamp, Frankfurt; trans. by S. & S. Weber as *Prisms* (1967). Neville Spearman, London.

Adorno, T. W. (1964) *Jargon der Eigentlichkeit.* Suhrkamp, Frankfurt; trans. by K. Tarnowski & F. Will as *Jargon of Authenticity* (1973). Routledge & Kegan Paul, London.

Adorno, T. W. (1966) *Negative Dialektik.* Suhrkamp, Frankfurt; trans. by E. B. Ashton as *Negative Dialectics* (1973). Seabury Press, New York.

Adorno, T. W. (1970) *Aesthetische Theorie.* Ed. G. Adorno & R. Tiedemann. Suhrkamp, Frankfurt; trans. by R. Hullot-Kentor as *Aesthetic Theory* (1997). University of Minnesota Press, Minneapolis.

Adorno, T. W. (1970–) *Gesammelte Schriften* [Collected Writings], 23 vols. Ed. R. Tiedemann. Suhrkamp, Frankfurt.

Adorno, T. W. (1993) *Einleitung in die Soziologie*. Ed. C. Goedde (based on 1969 seminar lecture tapes and notes). Suhrkamp, Frankfurt; trans. by E. F. N. Jephcott as *Introduction to Sociology* (2000). Stanford University Press, Stanford.

Adorno, T. W. (1993–) *Nachgelassene Schriften* [Posthumous Writings], ca. 35 vols. Ed. T. W. Adorno Archiv, Frankfurt.

Adorno, T. W. & Eisler, H. (1949) *Composing for the Films*. Oxford University Press, New York; reprinted Athlone Press, London, 1994.

Adorno, T. W., Frenkel-Brunswick, E., Levinson, D. J., & Sanford, R. N. (1950) *The Authoritarian Personality*. Harper, New York.

Adorno, T. W., Dahrendorf, R., Pilot, H., Albert, H., Habermas, J., & Popper, K. R. (Eds.) (1972) *Der Positivismusstreit in der deutschen Soziologie*. Luchterhand, Darmstadt; trans. by G. Adey & D. Frisby as *The Positivist Dispute in German Sociology* (1976). Harper & Row, New York.

Buck-Morss, S. (1977) *The Origins of Negative Dialectics: Theodor W. Adorno, Walter Benjamin and the Frankfurt School*. Free Press, New York.

Gibson, N. & Rubin, A. (2002) *Adorno: A Critical Reader*. Blackwell, Oxford.

Horkheimer, M. & Adorno, T. W. (1947) *Dialektik der Aufklaerung: Philosophische Fragmente*. Querido, Amsterdam; trans. by J. Cumming as *Dialectic of Enlightenment* (1972). Herder & Herder, New York; new trans. (2002) by E. F. N. Jephcott. Stanford University Press, Stanford.

Jay, M. (1994) *Adorno*. MIT Press, Cambridge, MA.

Mueller-Doohm, S. (2003) *Adorno: Eine Biographie*. Suhrkamp, Frankfurt.

Schweppenhaeuser, G. (2000) *Theodor W. Adorno zur Einfuehrung*. Junius, Hamburg.

advertising

Lauren Langman

Advertising is the attempt to bring attention to a product or service using paid announcements in mass media that encourage people to purchase those goods or services.

The average person is exposed to innumerable advertisements. In addition to all the normal advertisements selling pharmaceuticals, cars, soft drinks, beer, and fast food, among many others, in an election year there will be many more ads "selling" candidates. Supporters argue that ads help consumers make informed decisions about all sorts of things, and indeed, advertising can provide people with a common basis for common goals, values, and a variety of gratifications. Opponents claim advertising leads to social fragmentation, alienation, hyperconsumption, and the resulting wanton destruction of the environment. All agree that ads are everywhere.

Since marketplaces first emerged, sellers have attempted to supply information to consumers to describe and promote their offerings. The in-house pictorial advertisements of Pompeii's brothels involve advertising particular services and their costs. For most of history, advertising consisted of the displays of wares closely tied to the place where sales or trades took place; what you saw was what you could get, whether fruits, vegetables, clothes, jewelry, pottery, prostitutes, or metal tools. By the Middle Ages, certain trades had distinct symbols of their products or services, the three balls in front of the pawn shop or striped barber's pole probably being the best-known examples.

As trade began to flourish, especially after the rise of printing-based literacy and newspapers, advertising and mass media soon became intertwined. In the eighteenth century, most such advertising consisted simply of announcements of product availability and descriptions. The first newspaper advertisement in the US appeared in 1702 offering an estate on Oyster Bay. About 40 years later, the *General Magazine*, founded by Benjamin Franklin, printed the first magazine advertisement. By the nineteenth century, advertising had become an important part of commerce. In 1841 the first ad agency opened in Philadelphia. By the Civil War, the sale of advertising space in newspapers and magazines had become a major business, pioneered in part by William Carlton, whose agency would eventually become known as J. Walter Thompson.

For the most part, early advertisements were often flowery product descriptions telling about quality, how well items were made and functioned, and/or the "trustworthiness" of the producer. With the spread of railroads and rural mail delivery came the home-delivered catalogues of Sears and Wards, who distributed their catalogues, and thus their goods, throughout the nation. The period toward the end of the century would see the growth of the department stores that soon became major advertisers in newspapers. The window displays themselves were advertisements of the "fantastic" life that could be purchased (Leach 1993). At this time there also occurred the growth of "branded" goods such as Campbell soup, Quaker Oats, Morton's salt, and Ivory soap. Soon outdoor signs and billboards heralding various goods, services, or events were found on buildings and along roads and highways. The turn of the twentieth century was marked by branded consumer products such as the Kodak Brownie or Gillette razor. Oldsmobile was the first mass-produced car and the Wright brothers flew the world's first airplane. So, too, was another innovation in the works. Electricity was becoming widely available and soon there were electrical home appliances from vacuum cleaners to refrigerators to sell and advertise.

From the 1920s or so on, there were four major innovations that would forever impact advertising and, in turn, society.

1 The rapid growth of cities, often tied to industrialization, created vast factories with better-paid workers and, in turn, markets for consumer goods and services workers could not produce for themselves. Advertising proliferated to "help" them make "informed" choices.

2 The rapid growth of radio, and the licensing of airwaves to private companies, led to the proliferation of radio programming that sold airtime to advertisers. Soon came an explosion of regular radio programs featuring various "stars" and, as a result, larger audiences for commercials encouraging consumption. The airwaves were soon flooded with jingles, songs and rhymes, testimonials, endorsements, and lofty promises.

3 Advertising began to change from textual descriptions to visual images and from selling the quality of the product to constructing and improving the nature of the consumer. Owning the product came to

have meanings for self-enhancement, status, recognition, and so on. Image slowly displaced substance. Advertised products promised to make one healthier, happier, more beautiful, and more "alluring." Otherwise said, advertising began to "colonize consciousness" and transform desire such that people believed purchasing certain things would provide self-gratifications that would make them happy (Ewen 1976; Ewen & Ewen 1982).

4 As a result of what has been said, the 1920s marked an important point of transition in which the technologies of mass production joined with mass-mediated entertainment. Consumerism spread from the elites to the masses. This new complex of production, mass-mediated advertising, and consumption would constitute modern consumer society with its elite-driven culture, extolled by advertising, in which the democratization of desire was realized.

While the proliferation of television was delayed by World War II, by the end of the 1950s most Americans owned a television set. By this time, advertising had largely completed the move from selling products per se to creating certain kinds of consumer-based identities that would lead to certain kinds of purchases. What one wore, drove, ate, or paid money to see/hear expressed one's group membership, who one was, and one's "distinction." Acquisition and consumption had become the means of achieving happiness (Leach 1993).

The post-World War II years in America saw a rapid expansion of the economy and, in turn, major corporate growth, rising disposable income, and an explosion of consumerism. Between pent-up demand and the new affluence, and a proliferation of government-backed mortgages that supported vast tracts of suburban housing construction, there were demands for all sorts of things including furnishings, appliances, cars, and, as a result of the boom in the ownership of automobiles, a national Interstate highway system. More than half of the economy was now based on advertising-inspired consumer demand for goods, services, and cultural consumption from records to foreign travel. By the 1950s, capitalism had achieved a major turning point: consumer society had arrived.

For many social observers, consumer society and its cornucopia of goods, championed by advertising, was a new stage of social development and a new form of domination. The new era of unending "spectacles" and manufactured events manipulated consciousness and fostered mass compliance to the world of better living through consumption (Boorstin 1962; Debord 1967). One of the key ways to understand this consumer society and the advertising that is so central to it has been the study of meanings and identities, namely what academics call semiotics. Thus, for example, certain meanings such as luxury, adventure, romance, sophistication, and even transgression come to be associated with certain brands or items. The advertisements suggest that if people buy this or that, eat this or that, or travel here or there, they will be considered classy, erudite, or sexy. The logic of advertising often borders on the "magical" in which a particular toothpaste makes one "popular" or an SUV renders one powerful. Similarly, many restaurants, theme parks, casinos, and hotels sell "themed environments" laden with meanings (Gottdiener 2001). In this realm of symbolic meanings, advertisements often challenge other advertisements and engage in what has been called "sign wars" (Goldman & Papson 1996).

How does advertising foster purchases? What mediates between advertised image, purchase, and emotions? Mass-mediated images impact not only consciousness, but unconsciousness as well. Advertising's images seem to go directly from the external source to the person's emotional realms, avoiding the cortical areas of reason and reflection. Thus if people hear the right words or songs, they feel that buying the suggested product will provide them with a positive feeling. Some critics of advertising suggest that many ads have subliminal messages and/or hidden sexual/aggressive imagery that encourage people to buy certain products, from popcorn during movie intermissions to clam dinners because of subliminal images of sex orgies. In any event, seeing or hearing ads, consciously or not, evokes certain feelings and desires. When shoppers see or seek out what is advertised,

they are disposed to reproduce that feeling – and quite often the purchase does indeed make them feel better, if only for a short period.

For many people, their narrative of self and identity is expressed in their styles of life, their clothes, home and its décor, cars (or other forms of transportation such as bicycles, motorcycles), food preferences, cultural tastes, and so on. Merchandisers today are less selling products than marketing "brands" that provide the consumer with certain lifestyle-based self-identities and memberships in the "imaginary communities" of, say, North Face adventurers, Ralph Lauren sophisticates, or Abercrombie and Fitch or Fubu's subcultures of transgression (Klein 2000).

Market researchers have devoted billions of dollars to targeting particular clusters of consumers. While social class (education, income) plays a major role in what one can afford and the aesthetic tastes one appreciates, for many Americans who consider themselves "middle class" selfhood is more complex, nuanced, and articulated in patterns of consumption that provide them with "distinction" (Bourdieu 1984). Thus, for example, "young bohemians" (urbanites in occupations like advertising) might well prefer to dine in the latest storefront restaurant serving Mexican Mongolian fusion food, while "the pool and patio" older, upper-middle-class suburbanites prefer Olive Garden or Chilies. Most tastes and preferences are not based simply on income but how people choose to dispose of it. Aesthetic tastes reflect lifestyles and identities. Products for the exploding youth market promise that consumers will be "cool"; the "marketing of cool" is a major strategy of advertising (Frank 1997).

The latest expression of branded selfhood is "celebrity ware," fashion lines "designed" and marketed by various media stars such as Jaclyn Smith, Jennifer Lopez, or Paris Hilton. Much like the magical thought called "imitative magic" among traditional peoples, the consumer imagines that if he or she dresses like a glamorous "star," then he or she too will be glamorous. Moreover, he or she might also need to enroll in that star's exercise program or diet plan and pick from recommended plastic surgeons.

There is little agreement on the consequences of advertising for individuals and society. Does consumption bring the personal happiness promised by the ads? Aristotle warned that since human wants are insatiable, wealth and possessions do not bring happiness. Tolstoy said much the same. Freud suggested that happiness came through love and work; indeed, the accumulation of goods was often a compensation for what was lacking within one's self or one's relationships. Yet advertising promises that consumption will provide idealized selfhood and the very happiness people seek, but when consumption does not gratify, people continue to buy things in the hope that the next purchase, the next "improved" version, will make them happy.

Whether or not advertising (and consumption) brings happiness, it has costs. One of the most enduring criticisms of advertising and the associated consumerism comes from various leftist critiques that see ad-dominated mass culture as an essential aspect of domination that sustains ruling-class interests, while the majority of people are not only exploited and alienated but also "dumbed down" and actively involved in reproducing their own subjugation. For Marx, religion served to keep people pacified and look forward to the next life. Today, consumerism serves many of the same functions. Consumerism not only provides most of the profits for the current economic system, it also secures political hegemony as it entraps people into the system.

As Marcuse (1964) argued, advertising produces "artificial needs" that are "gratified" in consumption that fosters an exaggerated concern with the self and personal pleasures. This self-centeredness leads to indifference to social costs and consequences on the larger community. Moreover, advertising fosters "one-dimensional" thought that erodes the power of critical reason and, in turn, encourages acceptance of domination rather than human freedom. Sut Jhally (1997) has argued that Americans, 6 percent of the world's people, consume 25 percent of its resources, leading to major environmental damage. We are approaching a point where our planet will see its ability to sustain humanity decline. Many experts have tied the intensity of recent hurricanes to global warming due to fossil fuel emissions and industrial pollutants.

Schudson (1984) argued that the function of advertising is not simply to sell goods, but further, advertising promotes "American realism," a notion that "the American way of life" provides more material abundance than that of any other society in the world. Not only is it "superior," but its future will be even better.

One of the most serious issues is political advertising, "selling" of candidates much like soap or toothpaste. Media consultants now play a major role in shaping political campaigns. Much like selling other products, they use focus groups, surveys, and audience responses to hone political images and messages to produce various soundbites and soundsights. Similar techniques are used to discredit the opponent. These political advertisements, like most other ads, appeal to feelings and emotions and, in turn, serious political questions are not subject to genuine debates.

At the same time, advertising has been used to promote such "worthy" causes from anti-slavery to suffrage to anti-sweatshop movements. But so too has advertising led to alienation and social fragmentation as well as social indifference to collective adversity. Yet whatever the opinions of critics, advertising has become a major component of the contemporary landscape.

SEE ALSO: Alienation; Department Store; Distinction; Hyperconsumption/Overconsumption; Identity: The Management of Meaning; Mass Culture and Mass Society; Mass Media and Socialization; Media and Consumer Culture; Semiotics

REFERENCES AND SUGGESTED READINGS

Boorstin, D. (1962) *The Image*. Random House, New York.

Bourdieu, P. (1984) *Distinction: A Social Critique of the Judgment of Taste*. Harvard University Press, Cambridge, MA.

Debord, G. (1967) *The Society of the Spectacle*. Black & Red Press, Detroit.

Ewen, S. (1976) *Captains of Consciousness: Advertising and the Social Roots of Consumer Culture.* McGraw-Hill, New York.

Ewen, S. & Ewen, E. (1982) *Channels of Desire: Mass Images and the Shaping of American Consciousness.* McGraw-Hill, New York.

Frank, T. (1997) *The Conquest of Cool.* University of Chicago Press, Chicago.

Goldman, R. & Papson, S. (1996) *Sign Wars: The Cluttered Landscape of Advertising.* Guilford, New York.

Gottdiener, M. (2001) *The Theming of America.* Westview, Boulder, CO.

Jhally, S. (1997) *Advertising and the End of the World.* Media Education Foundation, Northampton.

Klein, N. (2000) *No Logo: Taking Aim at the Brand Bullies.* Picador, New York.

Leach, W. (1993) *Land of Desire: Merchants, Power, and the Rise of a New American Culture.* Random House, New York.

Marcuse, H. (1964) *One-Dimensional Man.* Beacon Press, Boston.

Ritzer, G. (2005) *Enchanting a Disenchanted World: Revolutionizing the Means of Consumption,* 2nd edn. Pine Forge Press, Thousand Oaks, CA.

Schudson, M. (1984) *Advertising: The Uneasy Persuasion.* Basic Books, New York.

Twitchell, J. (1996) *Adcult: The Triumph of Advertising in American Culture.* Columbia University Press, New York.

aesthetics

Sam Binkley

Attempts to reconcile the concerns of sociologists with those of art historians and aestheticians have been among the most contentious of recent interdisciplinary efforts. The tendency of sociologists to reduce social "epiphenomena" to their independent variables in social structure impinges on the core belief of artists and aesthetes in the power of art to transcend the mundane. In its most reductionistic version the aesthetic is collapsed into a mechanism for the reproduction of class hierarchies and for the securing of legitimacy for social elites – a thesis most aggressively advanced in Marx's reduction of the cultural and ideological "superstructure" to a dependent relation to the economic "base." Such a deterministic view is taken up in the aesthetic theory of the Frankfurt School, most notably in the writings of Adorno. In a manner typical of mid-century cultural Marxism, Adorno differentiated between aesthetic productions before and after the arrival of capitalism and the expansion of commercial culture industries. Where aesthetics in the pre-capitalist period possessed moral and ethical value, the aesthetics of mass entertainment eroded the capacity for individual thought and action, reproducing conformity and docility in the population through the standardization of personal taste (Adorno 1991). Similar assaults on the autonomy of the aesthetic are recorded in Veblen's (1899) account of "conspicuous consumption," wherein objects of aesthetic value are read as expressions of "honorific waste," symbolic trophies of the dominance of one group over another.

Without a doubt, however, it is Pierre Bourdieu who has done the most to expand contemporary sociological understandings of the aesthetic realm. Bourdieu's sociology is suspicious of the reductionism of Veblen and Marx, but is also skeptical of the idealism implicit within aesthetic theory since Kant, and resonant within the Frankfurt approach. In *Distinction* (1984), his landmark inquiry into the social dynamics of taste, he discovers in the aesthetic realm logics of taste and aesthetic preference which correspond to and naturalize social hierarchies, without specifically being reducible to them. He arrives at this synthesis by viewing aesthetics as a contentious game of classification, in which taste is derived from acquired competencies (cultural capital) for the discerning of value in all objects of consumption, from art to food. Such competing modes of classification (tastes) are understood by Bourdieu to correspond to competing subordinate and dominant class fractions. For the middle classes, who enjoy a degree of distance from the brute demands of manual labor, taste follows a logic which celebrates a degree of removal from the obviousness or the directness of taste and aesthetic preference. Elite tastes prefer the thoughtful distance of high art to the sensory impact of popular entertainment. For the working classes, whose economic location places them in direct relation to immediate tasks and needs for survival, tastes in aesthetic preferences tend to emphasize the unmediated and the direct. Popular tastes refuse the logic of distance and reflection, preferring instead the excitement and directness of high sensory impact. Thus, the linkage Bourdieu establishes between social structure and aesthetics is not deterministic, but contentious: each aesthetic style valorizes and naturalizes the social location from which it derives. In short, lifestyles are rich symbolic metaphors meant both to legitimate but also to contest underlying social groupings, or, as Bourdieu handily put it: "Taste classifies the classifier."

While Bourdieu's work has inspired a groundswell of interest in the sociology of aesthetic production, other studies predate Bourdieu's influential work. Becker's *Art Worlds* (1982), for example, is credited with originating a sociological approach to the commercial and cultural system of museums and galleries through which contemporary art is legitimated and circulated. Similarly, Wolf's *Aesthetics and the Sociology of Art* (1993) traced many of the problematics surrounding a sociological approach to aethsthetics.

SEE ALSO: Adorno, Theodor W.; Art Worlds; Bourdieu, Pierre; Conspicuous Consumption; Cultural Capital; Distinction; Veblen, Thorstein

REFERENCES AND SUGGESTED READINGS

Adorno, T. W. (1991) On the Fetish Character in Music and the Regression of Listening. In: Bernstein, J. M. (Ed.), *The Culture Industry: Selected Essays on Mass Culture*. Routledge, London.
Becker, H. (1982) *Art Worlds*. University of California Press, Berkeley.
Bourdieu, P. (1984) *Distinction, A Social Critique of the Judgment of Taste*. Trans. R. Nice. Harvard University Press, Cambridge, MA.
Gronow, J. (1997) *The Sociology of Taste*. Routledge, New York.
Veblen, T. (1899) *The Theory of the Leisure Class*. A. M. Kelley, New York.
Wolff, J. (1993) *Aesthetics and the Sociology of Art*. University of Michigan Press, Ann Arbor.

affect control theory

Dawn T. Robinson

Affect control theory (ACT) is an empirically grounded, mathematical theory of social interaction. David R. Heise developed the theory in the early 1970s based on symbolic interactionist insights about the primary importance of language and of the symbolic labeling of situations. Inspired by the pragmatist philosophy of early symbolic interactionists, the theory begins with the premise that people reduce existential uncertainty by developing "working understandings" of their social worlds. The theory presumes that actors label elements of social situations using cultural symbols available to them. After creating this working definition, the theory further argues that actors are motivated to maintain it.

ACT assumes that our labeling of social situations evokes affective meanings. These are the meanings that we try to maintain during interaction. ACT makes use of three specific dimensions to measure the affective meanings associated with specific labels, a set of equations to describe how events change those meanings, and a mathematical function to show what actions will best maintain or restore original meanings. The theory is fundamentally contained in this three-part formalization: the measurement structure, the event reaction equations, and the mathematical statement of the control process. The theory is embodied in its mathematical expressions (i.e., the mathematical model predicts patterns that can then be tested empirically).

SCOPE

Scope statements specify the conditions under which a theory applies. ACT describes culturally situated social interactions. Therefore, the domain of the theory is quite broad. There are, however, some specific conditions that limit its applicability:

- *There is a directed social behavior.* This requires an Actor who generates the behavior, a target (or Object) of the behavior, and a Behavior that is directed toward the object-person. The behavior need not be observable to all: I could admire someone without anyone else knowing about this directed behavior. In such a case, the theory's predictions would apply only to my own responses to the event.

- *There is at least one observer who is a member of an identified language culture.* The observer can be the Actor, the Object, or a third party. It is from the perspective of this observer, or labeler, that ACT makes predictions. Participants may operate under vastly differing definitions of the situation, but always make predictions from a particular definition.
- *The theory applies only to labeled aspects of social experiences.* This scope condition excludes behaviors that are not witnessed or interpreted by observers or participants. Picture a child pointing and laughing at a man who is unaware that he has been sitting in wet paint. The paint on the man's pants will not enter into the man's predicted response unless it becomes part of his awareness. Picture another child shuffling across the floor to kiss her mother good night. Predictions about the feelings of the mother generated by the event *Daughter Kisses Mother* are within the scope of the theory. Predictions about the startle response that the mother might feel as a result of an electrostatic shock caused by the kiss are outside the scope of the theory.

SENTIMENTS

ACT assumes that people respond affectively to every social event – the *affective reaction principle*. The theory describes these affective responses along three dimensions of meaning: evaluation, potency, and activity. These are universal dimensions identified by Osgood and colleagues (1975) as describing substantial variation in the affective meaning of lexicons in more than 20 national cultures. These three fundamental dimensions of meaning serve as cultural abbreviations, describing important social information about all elements of an interaction – identities, behaviors, emotions, and settings.

- *Evaluation.* The evaluation dimension captures the amount of goodness or badness we associate with a concept. It is a bi-polar dimension of meaning that ranges from *nice, warm, good* to *nasty, cold, bad*.
- *Potency.* The potency dimension captures the amount of strength or weakness we associate with a concept. It is a bi-polar dimension of meaning that ranges from *big, strong, powerful* to *small, weak, powerless*.
- *Activity.* The activity dimension captures the amount of liveliness or quietness we associate with a concept. It is a bi-polar dimension of meaning that ranges from *fast, noisy, lively* to *slow, quiet, inactive*.

All social concepts evoke goodness, powerfulness, and liveliness. These affective meanings are referred to as *sentiments* in the theory. Sentiments are trans-situational, generalized affective responses to specific symbols that are widely shared in a culture or subculture. While the dimensions themselves are universal across cultures, symbol sentiments are products of a culture. Grandfathers come in a wide variety of shapes, sizes, colors, ages, and demeanors. Individuals within a culture may vary widely in attitudes toward and understandings about their *own* grandfathers. Nonetheless, members of mainstream US culture basically agree that the general meaning of the role-identity *grandfather* is good, powerful, and relatively quiet. In contrast, our culturally shared sentiments about accountants are more neutral on the first two dimensions, and our image of *rapist* is extremely negative on the evaluation dimension. It is our very agreement about the generalized meanings associated with specific symbols that allows us to communicate effectively with other members of our culture.

Sentiments vary cross-culturally, however. Within each culture, average evaluation, potency, and activity ratings are compiled into cultural "dictionaries" that contain generalized meanings. ACT researchers have developed these cultural dictionaries for the US, Canada, Japan, Germany, China, and Northern Ireland. There are profiles for hundreds of identities, behaviors, traits, emotions, and settings in each culture. These sentiment profiles locate these cultural symbols – potential elements of social events – in a three-dimensional affective space. The most important feature of these evaluation, potency, and activity profiles is that they represent *all* of the elements of a social interaction using the same metric. This unifying metric enables ACT's mathematical specification of social interaction.

IMPRESSIONS

After we define a social situation using culturally meaningful labels, the affective meanings change as social interaction unfolds. Picture a police officer interacting with a priest on a public sidewalk. The affect generated by the labels – *Police Officer* and *Priest* – help us know what actions we expect the two people to take. Now picture the *Priest Shoving the Police Officer*. In response to this event, our feelings about that priest, that police officer, and perhaps even what it means to shove someone, are temporarily altered because of our observation of that event. These situated meanings are called *transient impressions*: contextualized affective meanings that arise from labeling of specific social interactions.

ACT uses a full set of *impression formation* equations to predict changes in the impressions of Actors, Behaviors, and Objects on evaluation, potency, and activity as a result of their combination in social events. Taken as a set, these impression-change equations are empirical summaries of basic social and cultural processes. They capture important information about the ways in which social events temporarily transform the meanings of the symbolic labels that we use to define events. Along with the sentiment dictionaries, these equations provide the empirical basis for ACT's theoretical predictions. Currently, there are separate impression-formation equations for the US, Canada, and Japan.

CONTROL PRINCIPLE

Sentiments are the culturally shared, fundamental meanings that we associate with social labels. Impressions are the transient meanings that arise during social interaction. Discrepancies between sentiments and impressions inform us about how well current interactions are confirming cultural prescriptions.

Symbolic interactionism rests on the assumption that social actors try to maintain their working definitions of social situations. Inspired by Powers's (1973) work on perception control theory, Heise (1979) developed a control system theory to model this principle. ACT proposes that actors try to experience transient impressions consistent with their fundamental sentiments – the *affect control principle*. Fundamental sentiments act like a thermostat setting, a reference level for interpreting what happens in a situation. When impressions vary from that reference level (as the temperature might vary in a room), people act so as to bring the impressions back in line with cultural sentiments.

ACT defines *deflection* as the discrepancy between fundamental cultural sentiments and transient situated impressions in the three-dimensional evaluation, potency, and activity space. Deflection is operationalized as the squared distance between the sentiments and impressions. This mathematical expression allows manipulation of the impression-change equations to implement the affect control principle.

These transformed equations predict the behavior that optimally maintains initial cultural sentiments for the actors and objects. After an event disturbs meanings, solving for the behavior profile produces the creative response that an actor is expected to generate to repair the situation.

EMOTIONS AND TRAITS

The *impression-change equations* specify how events change impressions. The *behavioral-prediction equations* use the affect control principle to predict how actors are likely to behave for a given definition of the situation. *Labeling equations* tell us how actors or objects may be redefined as a result of observed interactions. In addition, there are *attribution equations* which solve for traits that, when added to an identity, can make sense of observed behaviors, and there are *emotion equations* that make predictions about the emotions that actors and objects are likely to feel during social interaction. Among other things, these equations imply that positivity of emotion is predicted by the positivity of the transient impression, as well as the positivity of the deflection produced by that transient impression. In other words, pleasant events make us feel happy. Events that are even better than our identities will make us feel even better. When events are identity-confirming, the pleasantness of an actor's emotion should reflect the goodness of his or her fundamental identity. Thus, the theory predicts that individuals operating in "nicer" identities will experience positive feelings more frequently than individuals operating in more stigmatized identities. The potency and activity equations reveal similar dynamics. When events push us higher in potency than our identities warrant, we experience more powerful emotions. Likewise, when events make us seem livelier than our identities warrant, we feel energized. In the case of perfectly confirming events, ACT predicts that the potency and activity of an actor's emotions will be roughly half of the potency and activity associated with that actor's fundamental identity.

THE INTERACT PROGRAM

Both the logic and the substance of ACT are contained in its mathematical specification. The empirically estimated equations contain crucial information about affective processing reflecting basic social and cultural processes of attribution, justice, balance, and response to deviance. The logic of the theory (for example, the affect control principle and the reconstruction principle) is implemented through mathematical manipulation of these equations. These mathematical manipulations produce predictions about behaviors, emotions, and labeling. A computer program, INTERACT, contains the equations and the dictionaries of culture-specific sentiments. This software allows researchers to work through implications of the theory. Simulation results using INTERACT can be taken as predictions of the theory and subjected to testing through empirical research.

RESEARCH

There is a large and growing body of empirical work in the ACT tradition. A number of recent studies focus on comparing affective dynamics cross-culturally. These studies find substantial similarity in the affective dynamics governing social interaction in various cultures. The differences, however, give us a way to characterize normative differences between cultures formally. Several empirical studies support predictions about the operation of the control process in social interaction. An extensive body of recent research supports the theory's predictions about the relationships between identity and emotions. Qualitative research in the ACT tradition reveals the way that bereavement and divorce support groups make use of the control process in the kinds of identity work they encourage and how gay and straight congregations invoke somewhat different rituals in order to optimally maintain meanings about key religious identities. For a recent review of this and other empirical research in the affect control tradition, see Robinson and Smith-Lovin (2006).

SEE ALSO: Emotion: Cultural Aspects; Emotion: Social Psychological Aspects; Impression Formation; Pragmatism; Scientific Models and Simulations; Symbolic Interaction

REFERENCES AND SUGGESTED READINGS

Heise, D. R. (1979) *Understanding Events: Affect and the Construction of Social Action.* Cambridge University Press, New York.

MacKinnon, N. J. (1994) *Symbolic Interactionism as Affect Control.* State University of New York Press, Albany.

Osgood, C. E., May, W. H., & Miron, M. S. (1975) *Cross-Cultural Universals of Affective Meaning.* University of Illinois Press, Urbana.

Powers, W. T. (1973) *Behavior: The Control of Perception.* Aldine, Chicago.

Robinson, D. T. & Smith-Lovin, L. (2006) Affect Control Theory. In: Burke, P. J. (Ed.), *Social Psychology.* Stanford University Press, Stanford.

Smith-Lovin, L. & Heise, D. R. (1988) *Analyzing Social Interaction: Advances in Affect Control Theory.* Gordon & Breach, New York.

affirmative action

David B. Bills and Erin Kaufman

The term affirmative action encompasses a broad range of voluntary and mandated policies and procedures intended to provide equal access to educational and employment opportunities for members of historically excluded groups. Foremost among the bases for historical exclusion have been race, ethnicity, and sex, although consideration is sometimes extended to other groups (e.g., Vietnam veterans, the disabled). Both the concept of affirmative action and its application have undergone a series of transformations and interpretations. These shifts have contributed to considerable ambivalence in levels of public support for and opposition to affirmative action policies.

There is no single model of affirmative action. Affirmative action efforts may be either public or private. Definitions of protected groups range from very restricted to very broad. Enforcement mechanisms may be quite rigorous or virtually non-existent. Oppenheimer (1989) identified a simple typology of affirmative action efforts that ranged from quite restrictive quota systems on one end to considerably less binding organizational commitments not to discriminate on the other. Situated between these ideal-typical extremes were a variety of preference systems, organizational self-examinations, and outreach plans.

Affirmative action is in many ways an outgrowth of the Civil Rights Movements. In particular, Title VII of the 1964 Civil Rights Act prohibited discrimination in any areas of employment that was based on race, color, creed, or sex. The year after the passage of the Civil Rights Act, President Lyndon Johnson signed Executive Order 11246, which prohibited discrimination against minorities by federal contractors. While American presidents had routinely been issuing similar Executive Orders for some time, EO 11246 was different in two important ways. First, it included sex rather than merely race as a protected category. Second, it established an enforcement mechanism, the Office of Federal Contract Compliance. While not a powerful entity, the OFCC was an important step in institutionalizing affirmative action.

Affirmative action received a further boost with the passage of the 1972 Equal Employment Opportunity Act. The EEOA required federal agencies to adopt affirmative action. By 2000, this legislation covered about 3.5 million federal employees (Harper & Reskin 2005).

Affirmative action has had substantial effects in both the educational and employment realms. Its impact has to a great degree been determined by several important Supreme Court decisions, although lower courts too have been instrumental in the direction that affirmative action has taken.

Perhaps the first broadly felt effects of affirmative action in education pertained to busing. Fourteen years after the landmark 1954 Supreme Court decision *Brown* v. *Board of Education* declared that government-mandated "separate but equal" schooling was unconstitutional, the Court decided in *Green* v. *County School Board* that schools needed to take affirmative steps to end racial discrimination. This led to the implementation of busing plans in many urban areas as a means to end racial discrimination in schools. Many of these were quite ambitious, but by the early 1990s these plans had been essentially discontinued.

Largely because of the steadily increasing centrality of higher education as a means to socioeconomic mobility (Sullivan 1999), affirmative action has been of critical importance in the allocation of educational opportunity. *University of California Regents* v. *Bakke* (1978) was a pivotal case regarding affirmative action in higher education. The University of California at Davis Medical School had two admissions programs, one general and one special. The general admissions program required that students have a 2.5 grade point average on a 4.0 scale for consideration. In contrast, the special admissions program, open to applicants who claimed economic or educational disadvantage and membership in a minority group, had no such grade point requirement. Allan Bakke, a white male, applied to the Davis Medical School in both 1973 and 1974. Bakke was rejected both times. In both years, special applicants with significantly lower qualifications than Bakke received admittance to the

Medical School. Although the Court failed to reach a consensus on the case, Justice Powell's opinion came to serve that function. While Powell's opinion overturned the special admissions program on the grounds that it violated the Equal Protection Clause of the 14th Amendment, the decision did allow the use of race as a factor in future admissions decisions so long as racial classifications were just one of many factors used to attain a diverse student body.

Standing in contrast to the *Bakke* case was *Hopwood* v. *State of Texas* (1996). In order to accommodate the large number of applicants to the University of Texas School of Law, the admissions program based its initial decisions largely on the applicant's Texas Index (TI) number, consisting of undergraduate grade point average and Law School Aptitude Test (LSAT) score. The TI score allowed the sorting of candidates into three categories: presumptive admit, presumptive deny, and discretionary zone. In order to consider and to admit more African American and Latino students, the Law School considerably lowered its TI score ranges for them. Hopwood, a white resident of Texas, was considered a discretionary zone candidate, but did not receive admission. Plaintiffs sued, claiming that the Law School's admissions program subjected them to unconstitutional racial discrimination. Rejecting Powell's *Bakke* opinion, the Court ruled that the consideration of race and ethnicity for the purpose of attaining a diverse student body was not a compelling interest under the 14th Amendment. The Court further stated that the use of racial classifications to attain a diverse student body hinders rather than helps the attainment of equal education.

The most recent Supreme Court affirmative action rulings in higher education were *Gratz et al.* v. *Bollinger et al.* (2003) and *Grutter* v. *Bollinger* (2003), both concerning admissions policies at the University of Michigan. In the first case, petitioners Gratz and Hamacher applied to the University of Michigan's College of Literature, Science, and the Arts. Although the college determined Gratz to be well qualified and Hamacher to be within the qualified range, both were denied admission.

In order to ensure consistency, Michigan's undergraduate admissions policy used a point system that awarded points to applicants for a variety of factors, including race. The admissions policy automatically awarded 20 of the 100 points needed for admission to African American, Latino, and Native American candidates; it was undisputed that the university admitted virtually every qualified applicant from these groups. Gratz and Hamacher sued on the grounds that the admissions policy violated the Equal Protection Clause of the 14th Amendment, Title VI of the Civil Rights Act of 1964, and 42 USC §1981. Citing Powell's opinion from *Bakke*, the Court agreed, finding the policy unconstitutional on the grounds that it was not narrowly tailored to achieve a diverse student body.

The second decision reviewed the admissions policy at the University of Michigan Law School. In order to achieve a diverse student body in accordance with the requirements that the *Bakke* decision outlined, the Law School admitted students through a flexible, individualized admissions policy. The policy took into account factors such as undergraduate grade point average, score on the LSAT, letters of recommendation, the applicant's personal statement, and an essay describing how the applicant would contribute to the school's life and diversity. While the admissions policy defined diversity in a broad manner, it did reaffirm the school's commitment to including African American, Latino, and Native American students. Grutter, a white Michigan resident, filed suit, claiming that the policy violated the Equal Protection Clause of the 14th Amendment, Title VI of the Civil Rights Act of 1964, and 42 USC § 1981. The Court disagreed, finding that the policy's narrowly tailored use of race to foster a diverse student body did not violate the Equal Protection Clause, Title VI, or §1981.

Affirmative action is also deeply embedded in the American workplace. The Equal Employment Opportunity Commission (EEOC) is the federal agency charged with ending employment discrimination. EEOC monitors compliance with and enforces civil rights legislation such as Title VII of the Civil Rights

Act of 1964; to do so, the agency can bring suit on behalf of alleged victims of employment discrimination. To prove employment discrimination, the EEOC must find one of the following: (1) disparate treatment, or an employer's intentional discrimination against an employee, or (2) disparate impact, which, while neutral in intent, shows that the policies of a particular employer have had a negative outcome for a particular employee or class of employees.

Griggs v. *Duke Power Company* (1971) was a major decision regarding racial discrimination in the workplace. Duke Power Company required most potential employees to have a high school diploma and to pass two aptitude tests. Current employees without a high school education could also qualify for transfer by passing two tests, neither of which measured the ability to learn to perform a particular category of jobs. Thirteen African American workers challenged Duke's practices on the grounds that they violated Title VII of the Civil Rights Act of 1964. The Court agreed, ruling that the Act prohibits employers from requiring a high school education or passing scores on an aptitude test as a condition of employment or transfer when (1) neither standard relates significantly to successful job performance, (2) both requirements serve to disqualify African Americans at a significantly higher rate than their white counterparts, and (3) the jobs in question had been filled solely by white employees due to longstanding practices of racial preference. Title VII prohibits artificial, arbitrary, and unnecessary barriers to employment when those barriers work to discriminate on the basis of racial or other impermissible classifications.

Another important case regarding affirmative action in the workplace was *United Steelworkers of America* v. *Weber* (1979). In 1974 United Steelworkers of America and Kaiser Aluminum & Chemical Corp. entered into a collective bargaining agreement. The agreement included an affirmative action, which reserved 50 percent of the in-house training program positions for African Americans. The plan was to remain in place until the percentage of African American craftworkers roughly equaled the percentage of African Americans in the local labor force. During the plan's initial year, seven African American and six white trainees entered the program, with the most senior African American having less seniority than several white production workers whom the program had rejected. Weber, one of the rejected production workers, alleged that the affirmative action program violated Title VII of the Civil Rights Act of 1964 through discriminating against qualified white applicants. The Court held that Title VII's prohibition of racial discrimination does not forbid all private and voluntary affirmative action plans that account for race.

Whether applied to employment or to education, affirmative action has been a politically sensitive issue. Much of the contention has been grounded in differing understandings and interpretations of affirmative action. In part these differences have emerged from the great diversity of affirmative action programs that have been in effect at any given time. Perhaps as important have been efforts by both proponents and opponents of affirmative action to frame it in ways most congenial to their own preferred remedies for redressing unequal access to social participation. While most participants in the affirmative action debate agree on the social benefits of racially and culturally diverse workforces and student bodies, they differ sharply on how to achieve this. Opponents of affirmative action often emphasize the apparent contradictions between group-based remedies and the American commitment to individualism and meritocracy. Many maintain that affirmative action unfairly stigmatizes members of protected categories, who can never be certain that their success was due to their individual merit (Steele 1991). Advocates discuss the benefits of more exclusive hiring and admissions criteria and the need in a fair society to provide reparations for indisputable histories of disadvantage.

SEE ALSO: Affirmative Action for Majority Groups; Affirmative Action (Race and Ethnic Quotas); *Brown* v. *Board of Education*; Discrimination; Labor Markets; Occupational Segregation; School Segregation, Desegregation

REFERENCES AND SUGGESTED READINGS

Harper, S. & Reskin, B. (2005) Affirmative Action at School and on the Job. *Annual Review of Sociology* 31: 357–79.

Oppenheimer, D. B. (1989) Distinguishing Five Models of Affirmative Action. *Berkeley Women's Law Journal* 4: 42–61.

Steele, S. (1991) *The Content of Our Character.* Harper, New York.

Sullivan, T. A. (1999) Beyond Affirmative Action: Algorithmic Versus Holistic Approaches to College Admissions. *Research in Social Stratification and Mobility* 17: 319–34.

affirmative action for majority groups

Mako Yoshimura

Affirmative action is generally a policy to give preferential treatment to minority groups (such as women, ethnic minorities, indigenous people, and handicapped persons) who are socially vulnerable and face structural discrimination in a society through the use of measures such as quota systems to provide for equality in employment, education, and so forth. In some countries, however, such as Malaysia, South Africa, and Fiji, there is affirmative action for majority groups that are perceived as being disadvantaged.

Malaysia has a population of around 25 million people, made up in 2000 of Malays (66 percent), Chinese (25 percent), Indians (8 percent), and "others" (1 percent). The Constitution defines certain special privileges for the Malays, and the New Economic Policy gives people defined as Bumiputera (literally, "sons of the soil," comprising Malays, indigenous people such as the *orang asli*, and ethnic minorities in Sabah and Sarawak) advantages with respect to capital ownership, employment, education, grants, licenses, and so on. These privileges are considered "sensitive issues" in Malaysia, and public discussion is prohibited.

During the British colonial period, Chinese came to Malaya to work in tin mines while Indians came to work as rubber tappers. Malays remained agricultural smallholders (planting rice, rubber, and coconuts) or fishermen in coastal areas, and argue that they were excluded from the country's economic development. When Malaya became independent in 1957, the major industries were dominated by western capital and there was a substantial economic imbalance between Malays and non-Malays.

Ethnic riots on May 13, 1969 showed the severity of the ethnic divide between Malays and Chinese. A government white paper, *Toward National Harmony*, blamed the "economic factor" for the ethnic clash, and also called for prohibition of public debate (even in Parliament) on "sensitive issues" such as Malay privileges, the position of Malay as the country's national language, the status of the Sultans, citizenship for non-Malays, and the use of non-Malay languages.

The government announced the New Economic Policy (NEP) in 1970, saying "the aims were to eradicate poverty and to restructure society so as to correct social and economic imbalances." The NEP aimed to increase Bumiputera employment in modern sectors of the economy (i.e., in manufacturing and services), and to build Bumiputera corporate equity. Employment was to be restructured to reflect more closely the country's ethnic composition. With regard to equity ownership, the targets were Bumiputera 30 percent, other Malaysians 40 percent, and foreigners 30 percent, compared with 1970 figures for corporate equity of Bumiputera 2.4 percent, other Malaysians 32.3 percent, and foreigners 63.3 percent. Bumiputera received preferential treatment in permits, grants, real estate ownership, education, and so on. The NEP remained in effect from 1971 until 1990. It was succeeded by the National Development Policy (NDP) from 1991 until 2000, and then the National Vision Policy (NVP), covering 2001 until 2010.

Special privileges for the Malay population originated during the colonial period with an enactment reserving certain lands for Malay ownership (Federated Malay States Enactment of 1913 and FMS Enactment of 1933 – Cap. 142 of the consolidated legislative code). Article 89 of the current Federal Constitution makes provision for Malay reservations.

In the early twentieth century, rubber planta-tions were developed by western capital and the Enactment on Malay Reservation was aimed at protecting Malays by reserving their land.

The quota system for Malays is based on Article 153 of the Constitution, which defines the responsibility of the king (the Yang di-Pertuan Agong) "to safeguard the special posi-tion of the Malays and natives of any of the States of Sabah and Sarawak" and "to ensure the reservation" for them of a reasonable pro-portion of "positions in the public service," as well as "scholarships, exhibitions, and other similar educational or training privileges" offered by the federal government, along with permits or licenses to operate "any trade or business" by federal law.

The All-Malaya Malay Youth Congress in 1955 and Bumiputera Economic Congresses in 1965 and 1968 demanded improvements in the economic status of Malays by providing spe-cial allotments and facilities for Malays. The recommendations of these three congresses seemed radical and unrealistic at the time, but the May 13 riot and the fear of ethnic instability created a political basis for acceptance. It was difficult for non-beneficiaries to accept this political economic policy, and the political party system, which consists of an alliance or National Front made up of the United Malays National Organization (UMNO), the Malayan Chinese Association (MCA), and the Malayan Indian Congress (MIC), was designed to absorb criti-cism and represent the interests of each ethnic group. At the same time, institutions of state power such as the Internal Security Act, Official Secrets Act, Printing Press Act, and Publications Act helped curtail public discus-sion. The prime minister between 1981 and 2002, Dr. Mahathir, wrote in his book *The Malay Dilemma* (1970) that Malays were geneti-cally inferior, and he later used this argument as a basis for rationalizing affirmative action for the Malays.

There have been objections to the imple-mentation of Malay privileges on grounds that they benefit only small groups of Malays. Other criticism suggests that Malays should try harder to improve their econo-mic performance rather than relying on legis-lated special privileges. Even Mahathir has complained that Malays take these privileges for granted.

The Republic of South Africa has a popula-tion of 44.83 million, comprising people defined as black (79 percent), white (9.6 per-cent), and colored (8.9 percent), along with a small Indian and Asian element (2.5 percent). The apartheid policy that discriminated against black Africans was abolished in 1991, and in 1994 an election in which all races partici-pated put a black government into power, end-ing 350 years of white rule.

The history of discrimination and unequal treatment in politics, economy, education, and human rights created not only segregation but also huge imbalances in income and political participation. Poor people who live on less than US$2.00 per day make up some 48 percent of the population, and most of them are black or colored. The acknowledged unemployment rate for this group is 38 percent, while the rate for whites is 4 percent, and the actual unemploy-ment rate in black and colored residential areas is thought to be as high as 50–60 percent.

When the African National Congress (ANC) came to power in South Africa in 1994, it iden-tified black economic empowerment as a major tool for addressing the economic injustices of apartheid. Besides the quota system of public servants, affirmative action policies for employ-ment became standard for all larger companies under an Employment Equity Act put into effect in 2000. Under the Broad-Based Black Economic Empowerment Act of 2003, "black people" is defined as a generic term that includes "Africans, Coloreds, and Indians." According to the Act, "broad-based black eco-nomic empowerment" – with an emphasis on "broad-based" – refers to the economic empow-erment of all black people including women, workers, youth, people with disabilities, and people living in rural areas.

Regarding ownership, the Black Economic Empowerment (BEE) Commission has recom-mended the following quotas for black people: 30 percent of productive land, 25 percent of the shares of companies listed on the Johannes-burg Stock Exchange (JSE), 40 percent of non-executive and executive directors of companies listed on the JSE, 50 percent of state-owned enterprises and government procurement, 30 percent of the private sector, and 40 percent of

senior and executive management in private sector companies (with more than 50 employees).

Yet, progress in extending black administra-
tion-level employment and black ownership,
according to a government document entitled
Towards a Ten-Year Review, remains slow.
While the government emphasizes the need
to empower the black population still further
by affirmative action, there has been criticism
that the policies are not helping the poorest
people, and the Congress of South African
Trade Unions (COSATU) and other groups
have highlighted problems arising from corruption and cronyism.

The third case is Fiji. Fiji has a population
of 830,000, made up of Fijians (51 percent),
Indians (44 percent), and others. The Constitution of Fiji and the country's Social Justice
Act sanction affirmative action for indigenous
Fijians in matters such as education, training,
land and housing, participation in business,
and employment in state services.

The original Fiji Constitution drafted in
London reserved privileges for indigenous
Fijians. The Alliance Party, widely supported
by Fijians, was in power from 1970, when the
country became independent, to 1987, when
the National Federation Party supported by
Indians and the Fiji Labour Party won power.
Two coups d'état followed in 1987, and a new
Constitution enacted in 1990 reserved certain
privileges and positions for Fijians, including
the post of prime minister. In 1997 this document was replaced by a new Constitution that
moderated the Fijian privileges, among other
things removing the restriction on who could
become prime minister. Following the putsch
of 2000, affirmative action policies were
encapsulated in a draft 20-Year Development
Plan that is to be introduced in Parliament.

Post-1987 affirmative action policies were
based on practices in Malaysia, where the ruler
had powers to safeguard the special position of
the indigenous people. The 1990 Fiji Constitution preserved quotas for the public service,
stipulating that not less than 50 percent of civil
service posts should be reserved for indigenous
Fijians. A *Nine Points Plan* introduced in 1988
and a *Ten-Year Plan for Fijian Participation in
Business* recommended ways for indigenous
Fijians to make financial investments and build
equity. The 1997 Constitution extended the

definition of the target group to "all groups or
categories of persons who are disadvantaged."

In 2000, the *Blueprint and Government's
Policy for the Enhancement of Indigenous
Fijians/Rotumans Participation in Commerce
and Business* (the *Blueprint*) aimed at economic
reform for creating a "multi-ethnic and multicultural society," fulfilling the "aspirations of
the Fijians and Rotumans," and respecting
"the paramountcy of their interests." A
Twenty-Year Development Plan (20-Y-Plan)
further developed the *Blueprint*'s proposals,
setting as a goal a 50:50 division within the
local economy between Fijians and other
groups by the year 2020.

As in South Africa, Fiji viewed the Malaysian policy of affirmative action in support of
a majority group as a sound model for economic development and political stability. Fiji
began emulating the Malaysian affirmative
action model as early as the 1980s, when the
Fijian Holdings Company was conceived by
the then prime minister, Ratu Sir Kamisesee
Mara, a close friend of the Malaysian prime
minister, Mahathir Mohamad. Following the
military coups in 1987, Fiji fervently
embraced the Malaysian model (Ratuva 2002:
131). South Africa also had a close relation
with Malaysia from 1994 and Mahathir was
positive in support of South Africa under the
South–South assistance.

When a country contemplates affirmative
action for a majority group, it generally assumes
that historical disadvantages the group has suffered have caused discrimination and an economic gap that cannot be overcome without
special measures. Yet it is difficult for non-
beneficiaries to consent to affirmative action
for a majority element since they bear no
responsibility for discrimination in the past,
and the measures are imposed by a dominant
group that holds political power. Moreover,
such policies can give rise to reverse racism or
reverse discrimination. Ratuva (2002) has
pointed out that affirmative action of this sort
can become a form of economic nationalism if it
is driven by political forces and justified by
political ideology aimed at consolidating the
interests of a particular ethnic group.

Affirmative action is generally understood to
be a program of contingent measures that will
be abolished when the pattern of opportunity

and treatment in a society improves. Yet it is difficult to decide when a program has met its objectives and should be ended. It is critical to set clear goals and a timetable based on a practical system of evaluation. Also, to lift the income standards of people disadvantaged by an affirmative action program, it is vital to set up social security programs and a social safety net that will sustain the poorest households and disadvantaged people in a society on the basis of income and needs, and not according to ethnic or racial standards.

SEE ALSO: Affirmative Action; Apartheid and Nelson Mandela; Ethnic and Racial Division of Labor; Indigenous Peoples; Race; Race and Ethnic Politics; Race (Racism)

REFERENCES AND SUGGESTED READINGS

Daniel, J., Habib, A., & Southall, R. (Eds.) (2003) *State of the Nation: South Africa, 2003–2004.* HSRC Press, Cape Town.

Hugo, P. (1990) Affirmative Action in the Civil Service. In: Schrire, R. (Ed.), *Critical Choices for South Africa: An Agenda for the 1990s.* Oxford University Press, Cape Town.

Jesudason, J. V. (1989) *Ethnicity and the Economy: The State, Chinese Business, and Multinationals in Malaysia.* Oxford University Press, Singapore.

Mahathir, M. (1970) *Malay Dilemma.* Donald Moore Press, Singapore.

Ratuva, S. (2002) Economic Nationalism and Communal Consolidation: Economic Affirmative Action in Fiji, 1987–2002. *Pacific Economic Bulletin* 17, 1 (May): 130–7.

Terreblanche, S. (2003) *A History of Inequality in South Africa, 1652–2002.* University of Natal Press, Pietermaritzburg.

affirmative action (race and ethnic quotas)

John Stone

Affirmative action is a term applied to policies designed to redress inequalities created by historical legacies of racial, ethnic, and other types of group discrimination and disadvantage. Such policies have also been called affirmative discrimination, usually by those opposed to such measures, or positive discrimination, by proponents of these strategies. Like most social action aimed at redistributing resources and opportunities between groups, affirmative action is generally a controversial set of procedures and can lead to violent protests and opposition. The scope of affirmative action can be applied to a variety of different social institutions, but access to (higher) education, employment opportunities, and political quotas are the major arenas where affirmative action has been used. Differential group access to educational or employment positions is nothing new as powerful groups in most societies have tended to monopolize life chances, even when the society claims to be based on egalitarian principles. What makes affirmative action so prone to conflict is that it represents an attempt to mitigate or reverse such inequalities for the sake of disadvantaged and generally less powerful groups.

In modern times, affirmative action policies were introduced in India, under British colonial rule, to compensate for the exclusion of lower-caste and dalit (outcaste) groups in employment and educational institutions in the 1890s. India has by far the longest experience of such measures in recent times and provides interesting illustrations of the strengths and weaknesses of these measures. Similar procedures were developed in the United States in the 1970s as a reaction to the perceived inadequacies of the Civil Rights legislation of the mid-1960s. Malaysia adopted affirmative action in the wake of the bloody ethnic riots between Malays and Chinese in 1969; Sri Lanka used the strategy during the Sinhalese–Tamil tensions following independence; and South Africa has employed the same approach to rectify some of the gross inequalities between whites and Africans after the end of apartheid in the early 1990s.

The main advocates of affirmative action argue that it is a necessary political initiative when group-blind policies fail to produce significant results in rectifying past inequalities. Even when formal measures have been passed to enshrine equality in the constitution, and in major areas of economic and social life, it is rare that theoretical equality can be rapidly transformed into a genuinely egalitarian society. This is because equality of opportunity is unlikely to lead to equality of outcomes – however approximately defined – after long periods of group domination, segregation, and discrimination. Large accumulations of human and social capital, wealth, knowledge, and influence may take generations to overcome. Situations of tense intergroup conflict, and delicate political and military balances of power, may lead to urgent calls for rapid and demonstrable changes in group resources, and affirmative action is often presented as a necessary, if not sufficient, strategy to bring about some tangible evidence of the success of such social engineering within a reasonable length of time.

The key debates are centered on a series of questions about whether affirmative action leads to effective results; helps to diminish, or actually enhances, group conflict; in practice merely substitutes one injustice for another; has unintended consequences that are more detrimental than the positive aspects of the policies; and raises complex questions of the morality of one generation paying the price for the sins of another. A number of comparative issues arise that appear to have relevance in most situations. Like other social policies, affirmative action has a mix of costs and benefits that are phased in a typical pattern: the former tend to be experienced immediately while the latter tend to be delivered at a much later date. This is particularly striking in cases, like the United States and India, where affirmative action is geared to redressing minority disadvantage rather than in societies where the beneficiaries are the disadvantaged majority, as in Malaysia or South Africa. In democratic political systems where the majority is prone to bear the "cost" of such policies, the electoral backlash against them, due to the timing problem, is a major obstacle.

Certain critics of affirmative action make the point that such policies tend to be cosmetic and do not address the fundamental problems generating inequality. Proposing targets or quotas in higher education or employment fails to rectify inequities in primary and secondary education, or in levels of technical skill and managerial expertise. Instead of fixing the basic problems, affirmative action policies divert attention away

from them and also may place underqualified individuals in a position where they can fail to meet minimum performance standards or complete academic courses. This sets in motion a self-fulfilling prophecy and feeds the stereotypes of those opposed to greater assistance to the disadvantaged.

Affirmative action policies also raise potentially difficult moral questions concerning intergenerational accountability, and individual as opposed to collective responsibility. While most accept the need to take some state action to compensate for past categorical discrimination, when specific individuals are confronted with situations where they lose out to those whom they perceive as "less qualified" members of other ethnic and racial groups there is a tendency to interpret this as "reverse racism." Pointing to the historical record, to the current legacy of unequal opportunities, or to the dubious nature of many "objective" indices of merit (SAT scores, IQ tests, etc.) provides little comfort to the individuals on the losing end of these decisions. In political systems where such individuals are part of the democratic majority, this invites a considerable political backlash.

Another issue that is frequently raised by both supporters and opponents of affirmative action is the skewed social class impact of many types of preferential policies. It can be argued that this is not a critical matter in the early stages of redistributional strategies as some inclusion of formerly disadvantaged elites is an essential first step in reducing ethnic violence and conflict. Apart from integrating these groups into the mainstream of society, they can also act as vital role models – Du Bois's "Talented Tenth" – to inspire hope and emulation. However, when an increasing economic chasm opens up between the newly affluent and a dangerously alienated underclass, the time has come to reassess the targeting of affirmative action policies to ensure a greater focus on economic, as much as ethnic and racial, justice. William J. Wilson's concern for the "truly disadvantaged" in America, and the Indian Supreme Court's rulings in the 1990s, reflected this realignment.

Opinions differ widely on whether affirmative action is the cause of or solution to ethnic and racial conflicts. The extent to which such conflicts are fostered by resource imbalances is also a matter of debate, but in many cases

economic and social inequities are closely associated with such conflicts. Attempts to rectify
these conditions are likely, as mentioned earlier, to stimulate immediate resistance, but in
the longer term can help to reduce some of
the causal factors underpinning racial and ethnic strife. Few would suggest that the degree
of inequality is the only variable involved, just
as few would maintain that affirmative action
is the sole cause of racial and ethnic strife.

There may be some indirect and often
unintended benefits, valuable side-effects,
from these policies. These include pressures
to expand opportunities; increasing the pool of
talent; improvements in efficiency; and the
encouragement of positive political mobilization. In the Malay case, it has been argued
that there has been an expansion of private
education and eventually public education, as
well as the beneficial exploitation of overseas
educational opportunities. Such benefits can be
seen as a result of the pressures created by the
Malay Rights policies. On the other hand,
critics maintain that attempts to radically alter
economic management and ownership inevitably produces incentives for bribery and corruption. In order to meet ethnic targets, existing
entrepreneurs appoint token directors and managers who simply add to costs and bring about
little structural change. The so-called "Ali-
Baba" corporations are a much cited example
in which bumiputera ("sons of the soil," i.e.,
Malay) directors are appointed as the official
owners of the business, but the actual organizations remain firmly in the hands of the Chinese
or Indian minorities. While it is true that this
often happens in the short run, it is necessary,
however, to evaluate the longer-term outcomes
of such regulations. In South Africa, Anglo-
American and other major conglomerates struck
deals with aspiring Nationalist (white Afrikaner) businessmen after 1948 which undoubtedly
enhanced Afrikaner entrepreneurial success
over the next few decades. After 1994, in the
newly democratic society, a similar process
developed with African entrepreneurs, like
the former ANC politician Cyril Ramaphosa,
moving into multiple business ventures as a
consequence of affirmative action for the African majority.

Another line of argument suggests that
public policy can be more effective in bringing
about greater ethnic equality by using non-
ethnic strategies. This is a parallel argument
to the advocates of class-based affirmative
action, and stresses the beneficial outcomes
of regional investment and location decisions
that attack ethnic inequalities in a more indirect manner. Such an approach has the added
advantage that it avoids the question of which
groups should be eligible for preferential treatment. In the United States, opinions differ on
whether affirmative action should be confined
to African Americans and Native Americans,
or whether Latinos, Asian Americans, and
women should also be included. Moskos and
Butler (1996), in their study of the American
military, argue that blacks should be the only
recipients of preferential policies; others disagree. The legitimate scope of affirmative
action is clearly an important and complex
question in post-apartheid South Africa, with
the claims of groups like the mixed-race Col-
oureds and the Indians, who were also discriminated against under apartheid, but not
perhaps as severely as the African majority,
subject to varying interpretations.

A particularly vital factor, as most of the
comparative evidence suggests, is the wider
economic context in which these policies are
pursued. Other things being equal, the faster
the rate of economic growth of the total economy, the less disruptive will be the process of
resource redistribution that lies at the heart of
the affirmative action strategy. Much of the
success of the Malaysian case, which at the
outset – in the wake of the 1969 race riots –
was hardly promising, can be attributed to the
sustained and rapid expansion of the economy.
By 2004 the policy, which is usually seen as a
temporary measure to bring about rapid social
change, was on the verge of being abolished.
A major criticism of affirmative action policies
is that they are introduced as temporary measures and then, once started, are politically
impossible to end. The Indian case offers examples where this is supported, the Malaysia
experiment suggests the reverse.

The politics of affirmative action in the
United States reflects the continuing American Dilemma. Developed as a response to the
lack of results flowing from the Civil Rights
struggles of the 1960s, preferential policies
were seen as a means to achieve greater equality

of outcomes among an increasingly diverse population. Like school busing, it has proved to be a controversial method toward the fulfillment of a generally approved social goal. Even if affirmative action goes the same way as busing, American society will still have to face the reality of the persistence of racial inequality.

SEE ALSO: Affirmative Action; Apartheid and Nelson Mandela; Assimilation; Conflict (Racial/Ethnic); Du Bois: "Talented Tenth"; Ethnic Groups

REFERENCES AND SUGGESTED READINGS

Adam, K. (2000) *The Colour of Business: Managing Diversity in South Africa*. P. Schlettwein, Switzerland.
Bowen, W. & Bok, D. (1998) *The Shape of the River: Long-Term Consequences of Considering Race in College and University Admissions*. Princeton University Press, Princeton.
Glazer, N. (1975) *Affirmative Discrimination: Ethnic Inequality and Public Policy*. Basic Books, New York.
Moskos, C. & Butler, J. (1996) *All That We Can Be: Black Leadership and Racial Integration the Army Way*. Basic Books, New York.
Sowell, T. (2004) *Affirmative Action Around the World: An Empirical Study*. Yale University Press, New Haven.
Stone, J. & Dennis, R. (Eds.) (2003) *Race and Ethnicity: Comparative and Theoretical Approaches*. Blackwell, Malden, MA.
Wilson, W. J. (1987) *The Truly Disadvantaged: The Inner City, the Underclass, and Public Policy*. Chicago University Press, Chicago.

age and crime

Peggy S. Plass

Of all the social characteristics associated with crime, age is perhaps the most powerful. Age has been found to be a strong predictor of involvement in crime for both victims and offenders. Crime is a phenomenon of the young – risk for involvement drops precipitously with age. While the patterns for both victimization and offending are the same, the explanation for age's effect on each is distinct.

In the United States, arrest rates generally peak for all crime in the early 20s. Generally, a bit more than half of offenders arrested in any given year are under the age of 30, and nearly 80 percent are under the age of 40. The elderly commit very few crimes (usually less than 1 percent of arrestees are age 65 or older). While juveniles (people under the age of 18) do *not* comprise a majority of those arrested for crimes in the United States, they do account for a disproportionately high level of arrests. Not surprisingly, then, juveniles have received a great deal of attention from social scientists and policymakers. In fact, a majority of theories which were developed in the twentieth century to explain criminal offending focused on the bad behaviors of youth (a focus probably fueled as much by concern for these young offenders as it was by the volume of offenses that occurred in this group). Among the best known of these explanations of criminal behavior in the young are Albert Cohen's strain theory (in which delinquency is seen as a reaction to failure, specifically in school), Walter Miller's subcultural theory (in which delinquents are seen as adhering to a different set of values), Sykes and Matza's techniques of neutralization (in which the techniques of youth for rationalizing or making sense of bad behaviors are examined), Sutherland and Cressey's differential association theory (in which children are seen as learning bad behaviors from those with whom they associate), and Travis Hirschi's social bond theory (in which the level and type of connection that youths have with legitimate institutions, values, and ways of doing things are portrayed as insulating them from involvement in crime) (Cohen 1955; Miller 1958; Sykes and Matza 1957; Sutherland & Cressey 1978; Hirschi 1969). A belief in the uniqueness of the needs of juvenile offenders fueled the development of a separate system of justice for these criminals, the juvenile justice system.

The first juvenile court was opened in 1899 in Cook County, Illinois. Not long after that, separate systems of justice for children were found in every state in the US. The degree to which young people should be held accountable for their criminal acts in the same way as are adults has, however, continued to be controversial in the United States. When rates of violent crime among juveniles began to rise in the 1980s, many states modified statutes, making it easier to try juveniles in the adult (criminal) courts. At the same time, there is also evidence that lawmakers continue to believe that children are different from adults. For example, in 2005 the US Supreme Court ruled that executions of those who were under the age of 18 when they committed their crimes are unconstitutional (*Roper* v. *Simmons*). Recent research regarding cognitive development in late adolescence has fueled debate as to whether or not teens are physically capable of the same criminal intent as are adults (ABA Juvenile Justice Center 2004). Undoubtedly, the issue of how these youngest offenders should be processed will continue to garner attention in the field.

Just as young people are more likely to commit crimes, they are also more likely to be victims. Since the early 1980s, the National Crime Victimization Surveys have found the highest rates of violent crime victimization to be among teenagers, with people in their early twenties having the next highest rates. Younger children are also at high risk for many types of criminal victimization (e.g., child abuse, family abduction, and the like), and recent evidence suggests that children of all ages comprise the majority of sexual assault victims in the US (Snyder 2000). Most explanations of the high rates of victimization among children focus on characteristics of the lifestyles of youngsters, who are generally more likely to engage in risky behaviors (e.g., Maxfield 1987). David Finkelhor, of the Crimes Against Children Research Center, also suggests that the high victimization rates of children can be explained by factors such as the level of dependence that children experience (e.g., children, unlike adults, are unable to choose where and with whom they live) and their smaller physical stature (Finkelhor & Hashima 2001).

SEE ALSO: Crime; Crime, Life Course Theory of; Criminal Justice System; Juvenile Delinquency; Race and Crime; Sex and Crime; Strain Theories

REFERENCES AND SUGGESTED READINGS

American Bar Association (ABA) Juvenile Justice Center (2004) *Adolescence, Brain Development, and Legal Culpability*. Chicago, American Bar Association.
Cohen, A. (1955) *Delinquent Boys: The Culture of the Gang*. Free Press, New York.
Finkelhor, D. & Hashima, P. (2001) The Victimization of Children and Youth: A Comprehensive Overview. In: White, S. O. (Ed.), *Law and Social Science Perspectives on Youth and Justice*. Plenum, New York.
Hirschi, T. (1969) *Causes of Delinquency*. University of California Press, Berkeley.
Maxfield, M. G. (1987) Lifestyle and Routine Activity Theories of Crime: Empirical Studies of Victimization, Delinquency, and Offender Decision Making. *Journal of Quantitative Criminology* 3: 275–82.
Miller, W. B. (1958) Lower-Class Culture as a Generating Milieu of Gang Delinquency. *Journal of Social Issues* 14: 5–19.
Snyder, H. (2000) *Sexual Assault of Young Children as Reported to Law Enforcement: Victim, Incident and Offender Characteristics*. BJS Report, NCJ 182990.
Sutherland, E. & Cressey, D. R. (1978) *Criminology*, 10th edn. Lippincott, Philadelphia.
Sykes, G. & Matza, D. (1957) Techniques of Neutralization: A Theory of Delinquency. *American Sociological Review* 43: 643–56.

age identity

Richard A. Settersten, Jr.

Age is important for societies, groups, and individuals (Settersten 2003a). For example, age underlies the organization of family, educational, work, and leisure institutions and organizations. Many laws and policies structure rights, responsibilities, and entitlements on the basis of age. Members of a society may share informal ideas about age and the changes that occur between birth and death, and individuals use these ideas to organize their lives. Age also shapes everyday social interactions.

Age is also linked to many aspects of self and personality, including "age identity" – that is, how individuals feel and think about themselves and others based on age. "Subjective age identification" was an especially lively tradition of research from the 1960s through the 1980s, but has only received scattered attention since (for an early review of this literature, see Barak & Stern 1986; for information on instruments and methods, see Cutler 1982; Settersten 1999). Several specific facets of age identity have been explored, including how old individuals feel, look, act (e.g., social roles and activities; interests and hobbies; functional capacities), and think (e.g., attitudes and values; intellectual functioning). Research in this tradition has also examined how individuals identify with or classify themselves into larger age groups, and how they compare themselves to age peers or stereotypes about people their age. It has also explored individuals' judgments about the "best," "optimal," and "desired" ages in life.

Research in this area has generally focused on late life, measured one or another of these types of age identity as single-item dependent variables, and then examined correlates or predictors in three categories – physical, psychological, and social – though rarely in a single study. Most studies have included gender, chronological age, and at least crude measures of physical health, psychological well-being, education, and income. A range of other factors has also been considered in isolated studies (such as marital status, employment status, transitions to widowhood or retirement, number and ages of children or grandchildren), though there is not enough evidence to reveal clear patterns.

Of the commonly included factors, the most consistent findings relate to self-rated physical health, which has a strong negative relationship with subjective age (that is, better physical health is associated with younger age identity, and poorer physical health is associated with older age identity). Indicators of self-rated psychological well-being (especially life satisfaction, which has been examined most often) also show consistent negative relationships with subjective age identity. Of course, physical health and psychological well-being are intimately connected (e.g., Freemont & Bird 2000), and these interrelationships have

often not been examined in research on subjective age identity.

Education and income also generally exhibit negative relationships with subjective age identity, though the evidence is not as strong or consistent as that for physical health and psychological well-being. It is important to note, however, that both physical health and psychological well-being are strongly connected to education, occupation, and income (e.g., Mirowsky et al. 2000), and these three dimensions of socioeconomic status may therefore have indirect rather than direct effects on subjective age identity via physical health and psychological well-being (Barrett 2003). Race has rarely been included in analyses of subjective age identity, but when it has, it has generally not been significant – though race, like dimensions of socioeconomic status, may exert its influence through physical and psychological health, for which there are many strong racial disparities (e.g., Smaje 2000).

The evidence for gender differences in subjective age identity is, surprisingly, even less consistent than socioeconomic status. Early studies speculated that women might have younger age identities and more often value youthful ages than men, particularly because of stronger cultural norms related to physical attractiveness for women. Studies in the 1980s and 1990s, however, have not found regular evidence of this gender difference and, in fact, one recent study found exactly the opposite (Kaufman & Elder 2003).

Early studies also suggested that chronological age and subjective age identity were positively related (that is, the older one is, the older one feels). Recent studies have instead suggested that there may be tendencies to identify with age groups other than one's own, particularly in early and late life (e.g., Goldsmith & Heiens 1992; Montepare & Lachman 1989). That is, teenagers and young adults may hold age identities that are older than their actual ages; adults through midlife may hold age identities that are relatively close to their actual ages; and adults in late life may hold age identities that are younger than their actual ages. In advanced old age, however, these discrepancies may vanish or reverse with the onset of significant health problems.

These assertions demonstrate the importance of expanding inquiry to younger periods and to dynamics across the life course (see also Kaufman & Elder 2002). To understand changes in subjective age identity within individuals adequately, prospective longitudinal data are needed. But such changes can also be assessed retrospectively, as individuals derive a sense of age identity at any given point by making internal comparisons between their current and former selves (Sherman 1994).

Inquiry in this area might also be expanded to address individuals' understandings of how other people view them (which may be incorporated into self-perceptions) and the views that individuals have of others. For example, studies of subjective age identity in late life suggest that respondents will classify others of the same chronological age as "old," but use younger terms to describe themselves (e.g., Connidis 1989). Younger adults tend to hold more negative views of aging than older adults, and many older adults who view the aging process as negative often do not apply this view to themselves. Generally, only those who are in poor health or isolated, or those who are very old, label themselves as old. This tendency may lead individuals to deny or insufficiently prepare for the hardships of aging.

Most research on subjective age identity has been conducted in the United States, and much remains to be learned about how these matters vary across cultures and nations. Not surprisingly, the few studies of subjective age identity in other countries have suggested that Americans have or strive for more youthful age identities (e.g., Uotinen 1998; Westerhof et al. 2003).

There is significant need to build multi-item measures of subjective age identity with sound psychometric properties, and to understand interconnections among the various types of subjective age outlined earlier. There is also great need to understand their differential correlates or predictors, as well as their differential outcomes. Measures of subjective age identity have rarely been viewed as independent variables, and are probably predictive of many physical, psychological, and social outcomes.

The last few decades have brought dramatic changes in the structure and content of the life course (for illustrations, see Settersten 2003a). These changes warrant renewed attention to subjective age identity and other age-related phenomena in contemporary societies – including age norms, age-related images and stereotypes, and the boundaries and markers of different life periods.

SEE ALSO: Age Prejudice and Discrimination; Aging and the Life Course, Theories of; Aging, Sociology of; Identity: Social Psychological Aspects; Life Course Perspective; Self; Social Identity Theory

REFERENCES AND SUGGESTED READINGS

Barak, B. & Stern, B. (1986) Subjective Age Correlates: A Research Note. *Gerontologist* 26(5): 57–8.
Barrett, A. E. (2003) Socioeconomic Status and Age Identity: The Role of Dimensions of Health in the Subjective Construction of Age. *Journals of Gerontology: Social Sciences* 58B(2): S101–S109.
Connidis, I. (1989) The Subjective Experience of Aging: Correlates of Divergent Views. *Canadian Journal on Aging* 8(1): 7–18.
Cutler, S. (1982) Subjective Age Identification. In: Mangen, D. & Peterson, W. (Eds.), *Research Instruments in Social Gerontology*. University of Minnesota Press, Minneapolis, pp. 437–62.
Freemont, A. M. & Bird, C. E. (2000) Social and Psychological Factors, Physiological Processes, and Physical Health. In: Bird, C. E., Conrad, P., & Freemont, A. M. (Eds.), *Handbook of Medical Sociology*, 5th edn. Prentice-Hall, Upper Saddle River, NJ, pp. 334–52.
Goldsmith, R. E. & Heiens, R. A. (1992) Subjective Age: A Test of Five Hypotheses. *Gerontologist* 32(3): 312–17.
Kaufman, G. & Elder, G. H., Jr. (2002) Revisiting Age Identity: A Research Note. *Journal of Aging Studies* 16(2): 169–76.
Kaufman, G. & Elder, G. H., Jr. (2003) Grandparenting and Age Identity. *Journal of Aging Studies* 17: 269–82.
Mirowsky, J., Ross, C. E., & Reynolds, J. (2000) Links Between Social Status and Health Status. In: Bird, C. E., Conrad, P., & Freemont, A. M. (Eds.), *Handbook of Medical Sociology*, 5th edn. Prentice-Hall, Upper Saddle River, NJ, pp. 47–67.
Montepare, J. M. & Lachman, M. E. (1989) "You're Only as Old as You Feel": Self-Perceptions of Age, Fears of Aging, and Life Satisfaction from Adolescence to Old Age. *Psychology and Aging* 4(1): 73–8.

Settersten, R. A., Jr. (1999) *Lives in Time and Place.* Baywood Publishing, Amityville, NY.

Settersten, R. A., Jr. (2003a) Age Structuring and the Rhythm of the Life Course. In: Mortimer, J. & Shanahan, M. (Eds.), *Handbook of the Life Course.* Kluwer Academic/Plenum, New York, pp. 81–98.

Settersten, R. A., Jr. (Ed.) (2003b) *Invitation to the Life Course.* Baywood Publishing, Amityville, NY.

Settersten, R. A., Jr., Furstenberg, F. F., Jr., & Rumbaut, R. (Eds.) (2005) *On the Frontier of Adulthood.* University of Chicago Press, Chicago.

Sherman, S. R. (1994) Changes in Age Identity: Self-Perceptions in Middle and Later Life. *Journal of Aging Studies* 8(4): 397–412.

Smaje, C. (2000) Race, Ethnicity, and Health. In: Bird, C. E., Conrad, P., & Freemont, A. M. (Eds.), *Handbook of Medical Sociology,* 5th edn. Prentice-Hall, Upper Saddle River, NJ, pp. 114–28.

Uotinen, V. (1998) Age Identification: A Comparison Between Finnish and North American Cultures. *International Journal of Aging and Human Development* 46(2): 109–24.

Westerhof, G. J., Barrett, A., Steverink, N. (2003) Forever Young: A Comparison of Age Identities in the United States and Germany. *Research on Aging* 25(4): 366–83.

age, period, and cohort effects

Norval D. Glenn

Age, period, and cohort effects must be considered as a package, because the three kinds of effects are so closely interrelated that it is impossible to deal empirically with one without also dealing with the others. Age effects are the consequences of growing older, either of human individuals or of other entities. Period effects are the consequences of influences that vary through time. And cohort effects are the consequences of being born (or coming into existence by some other means) at different times.

Assessing age effects is central to social gerontology, developmental psychology, and the sociological specialty of aging and the life course, in which fields hypotheses about the consequences of aging abound. For instance, it

is believed that participation in conventional crime diminishes due to declines in energy and risk-taking propensities associated with aging out of adolescence and young adulthood, and it is believed that voting and other forms of political participation typically increase as, and because, young adults take on greater work and family responsibilities. Estimating age effects is not easy, however, because these effects may be confounded with period or cohort effects in any kind of data used for the task. For instance, in a simple comparison of persons who are at different ages at one point in time (cross-sectional data), age effects may be confounded with cohort effects. For instance, older persons may be different from younger persons because they have always been different rather than because they have changed as they have grown older. In panel data, which result from the same persons being studied at different points in time, changes as the persons grow older may be age effects, or they may be period effects. For instance, changes in political attitudes from young adulthood to middle age may be the consequences of aging, or they may result from general changes in the political milieu throughout the society.

The confounding of age, period, and cohort effects is known as the age–period–cohort conundrum and is a special case of the "identification problem," which exists whenever three or more independent variables may affect a dependent variable and each of the independent variables is a perfect linear function of the others. This is the most extreme version of collinearity, because the multiple correlation of each independent variable with the others is unity. When all but one of the interrelated variables are controlled, the variance of the remaining one is zero. The identification problem is common in social research, being present, for instance, when the difference between two variables, as well as those two variables themselves, may affect a dependent variable. The classic case of the identification problem is when age, period, and cohort may all affect a fourth variable.

The age–period–cohort conundrum can be illustrated by the use of a standard cohort table, in which multiple sets of cross-sectional data relating age to a dependent variable are

Table 1 Percentage of women who were married, by age and year, United States

Age	Year			
	1968	*1978*	*1988*	*1998*
25–34	87.4	76.6	67.3	67.3
35–44	87.1	82.1	76.3	72.1
45–54	82.4	80.5	76.2	70.8
55–64	67.7	70.4	70.7	67.8
65–74	46.5	48.3	53.3	54.8

Source: Data are from the March Current Population Survey conducted by the US Census Bureau. The percentages are from, or are calculated from data in, US Census Bureau (1969, Table 37; 1979, Table 51; 1990, Table 49; and 1999, Table 63).

juxtaposed and in which the intervals between the periods for which there are data are equal in years to the range in each age category. For instance, in Table 1, in which the dependent variable is whether or not women were married, ten-year intervals and ten-year age categories are used. In such a table, the trend within a cohort can be traced by starting with any but the oldest age category in the left-hand column and reading diagonally down and to the right. For instance, according to the data in Table 1, in the cohort of women who were 25–34 years old in 1968, the percentage married went from 87.4 in 1968 to 82.1 in 1978 to 76.2 in 1988 to 67.8 in 1998. This decline of almost 20 percentage points could have been an age effect, because the cohort grew 30 years older; it could have been a period effect, reflecting general changes in the society during the three decades covered; or, more likely in this case, it may have been a combination of age and period effects. In other words, in this or any other cohort diagonal, age and period effects may be confounded. Likewise, age and cohort effects may be confounded in each column, and period and cohort effects may be confounded in each row, of a standard cohort table.

It is obvious that a simple inspection of Table 1 cannot reveal the extent and nature of any age, period, and cohort effects reflected in the data. What has not been evident to many researchers interested in the age–period–cohort conundrum is that no routinely applied statistical analysis of the data can, by itself, be relied on

to provide accurate estimates of the effects. Although one cannot put all three variables measured in the same way into a regression or similar analysis (the program will not run), various transformations of variables, manipulations of measurement, and simplifying assumptions can be used to get the analysis program to yield estimates of the effects of all three variables. For instance, two of the variables can be entered in continuous form while the third is converted into a set of dummy variables. Or one-year intervals between periods can be used while ten-year age categories are used. However, the resulting estimates are almost never meaningful; the linear dependence of the variables on one another is broken in the statistical model, but it remains in the real world.

The reason that statistical modeling cannot be relied on to distinguish the effects is illustrated by the different combinations of effects that could produce the data in Table 2, which is a standard cohort table reporting hypothetical data. The simplest interpretation of the data is that they reflect pure linear age effects, whereby each additional ten years of age produces a five-point increase in the dependent variable. For some dependent variables, this might be the only plausible interpretation, but as the alternative explanations at the bottom of the table indicate, it is not the only logically possible one. Rather, an infinite number of combinations of age, period, and cohort effects could produce the pattern of variation in the dependent variable shown in the table. When the pattern of variation in the dependent variable is not as simple as that in Table 2, which is usually the case, the combination of effects producing the data must be somewhat complex. It should be obvious that no mechanically applied statistical analysis can reveal which of the many possible complex combinations is the correct one.

Nevertheless, much time and effort has been devoted during the past 35 years to developing all-purpose techniques of statistical modeling to distinguish age, period, and cohort effects (APC). The method introduced by Mason et al. (1973) has been widely used, and unpublished papers describing at least two new APC modeling methods are being circulated.

Of the several statistical APC techniques, only the Mason et al. method has been demonstrated by simulation experiments to

Table 2 Pattern of data showing pure linear age effects, offsetting period and cohort effects, or a combination of age effects and offsetting period and cohort effects. (Numbers in the cells are hypothetical values of a dependent variable)

Age	Year					
	1950	1960	1970	1980	1990	2000
20–29	50	50	50	50	50	50
30–39	55	55	55	55	55	55
40–49	60	60	60	60	60	60
50–59	65	65	65	65	65	65
60–69	70	70	70	70	70	70
70–79	75	75	75	75	75	75

Alternative explanations:

1 Each 10 years of aging produces a 5-point increase in the dependent variable.

2 There is a 5-point per 10 years positive period effect on the dependent variable and a 5-point per 10 years negative cohort effect.

3 There is some combination of age and offsetting period and cohort effects on the dependent variable. An infinite number of combinations of such effects could produce the pattern of variation in the dependent variable shown in the table.

be able to produce accurate estimates, and it works only under very limited conditions. The method in its simplest form consists of (1) converting age, period, and cohort each into a set of dummy variables; (2) dropping one dummy variable from each set, as must always be done; and (3) dropping an additional variable from one of the sets. The simplifying assumption (identifying restriction) in this case is that the two dummy variables dropped from the same set have equal effects. If this assumption is precisely correct, if only one of the APC variables has effects, and if the effects are non-linear, then the method yields accurate estimates, but these conditions are very rarely met. If the simplifying assumption is even a moderate distortion of reality, the estimates will be grossly in error. And if there is any substantial linear component of the effects, the estimates are unlikely to be correct. How well the method works when there are non-linear effects of two or three of the APC variables has not been demonstrated.

A major limitation of all major methods of APC modeling is that they are based on the assumption that the effects are additive. In the real world, however, APC interactions are ubiquitous. There is a great deal of evidence, for instance, that young adults tend to respond more to stimuli for change than do older adults, so that period effects often vary by age and thus among cohorts of different ages. Furthermore, many kinds of age effects are likely to change through time and thus to vary among birth cohorts. Social expectations for behavior at various chronological ages have shifted considerably in recent decades, an example being an increased expectation for middle-aged and older people to be sexually active. Even biological aging has changed moderately with advancements in medical care and nutrition.

When cohort data are complex, and especially when there are interactions among the variables, their meaningful interpretation always requires knowledge of the phenomena being studied from sources other than the cohort data, or what Converse (1976) has called "side information." Some of this information may come from the same data set as the cohort data, but it usually comes from other sources. The data in Table 1 illustrate both the kinds of interactions that are common in cohort data and how side information is required for meaningful interpretation of complex cohort data. There are several interactions in the data, and statistically modeling the effects reflected in them would be difficult even if the identification problem did not plague the effort. However, the data are not mysterious to family demographers familiar with the relevant side information, namely, changes in marriage, divorce, and longevity in the United States in recent decades. The trends producing the data are (1) a substantial increase in the typical age at first marriage from the late 1970s through the 1980s; (2) a steep increase in divorce from the mid-1960s to around 1980 that involved long-term marriages only to a limited extent; (3) a decrease in the death rates of middle-aged and older men that began in the 1980s; and (4) the maturing into the older age brackets of cohorts with very high lifetime rates of marriage. To anyone not familiar with these trends, no statistical manipulation of the data in Table 1 could lead to much insight into the complex pattern of the data.

Figure 1 Happiness index[a] by age and sex, United States.
[a] Percentage of respondents who said they were "very happy" minus the percentage who said they were "not too happy."
Source: Pooled data from the 1972 through 2002 United States General Social Surveys.

The general meaning of simpler cohort data (but not the exact magnitude of effects reflected in them) may be evident once they are examined systematically. An example is data on reported personal happiness from the 1972 through 2002 American General Social Surveys. The relationship of reported happiness to age did not change systematically from 1972 to 2002, and thus pooled data from all of the surveys can be used to show that relationship, for males and females, respectively (see Fig. 1). For males, the relationship of happiness to age is positive and monotonic, but for females it is non-monotonic, being higher for middle-aged and early elderly persons than for either younger or older ones. The male–female difference relates to age in an almost perfectly linear fashion, with women reporting greater happiness than men in young adulthood and men reporting greater happiness than women beyond middle age. This cross-sectional variation in reported happiness by age could of course reflect either age or cohort effects, or both (and to some small extent might result from differential mortality).

At this point, one needs to ask what the over-all trend, and the trend among the youngest adults, would be if the observed age pattern of reported happiness were the result of cohort succession, that is, the result of each successive cohort that matured into adulthood being different from the ones before it. In the absence of offsetting period effects, the mean happiness of males would have declined, absolutely and relative to the happiness of females. In fact, however, the trends were in the opposite direction. The indicated happiness of males increased and that of females decreased from 1972 to 2002, both among adults as a whole and among those under age 35, resulting in a substantial and statistically significant increase in the relative happiness of males. The offsetting period effects explanation should not be summarily dismissed, because occasionally there are reasons to think that period and cohort effects may be in opposite directions. However, there is no reason to think that the happiness trends deviate from the usual pattern, whereby period and cohort effects result from common period influences and thus are same-signed components of change. (Here theory and side information are brought to bear in interpreting the data.) If the age pattern of happiness was the result of age effects, the happiness of males within cohorts as they grew older should have increased, absolutely and relative to the happiness of females. That is precisely what the data (not shown) indicate. The indicated intracohort trends are more than great enough to create the cross-sectional age pattern of reported happiness, probably because they reflect period effects as well as age effects and because intercohort trends reduced the cross-sectional age differences. Therefore, the cross-sectional data in Figure 1 apparently correctly indicate the direction of age effects on reported happiness, but they probably underestimate the magnitude of those effects.

Other cohort data require different analytic strategies, there being no formula or cookbook approach that works well in all cases. Rather, the analyst must use ingenuity and imagination to adapt the analysis to the problem at hand. Various statistics, ranging from simple to complex, may be useful, as long as the researcher is aware that the solution to the age–period–cohort conundrum cannot be solely a statistical one.

SEE ALSO: Aging, Demography of; Aging and the Life Course, Theories of; Aging, Longitudinal Studies; Aging, Mental Health, and Well-Being; Aging, Sociology of; Gerontology; Life Course Perspective; Secondary Data Analysis

REFERENCES AND SUGGESTED READINGS

Alwin, D. F., Cohen, R. L., & Newcomb, T. M. (1991) *Political Attitudes Over the Life Span: The Bennington Women After 50 Years.* University of Wisconsin Press, Madison.
Converse, P. E. (1976) *The Dynamics of Party Support: Cohort Analyzing Party Identification.* Sage, Beverly Hills, CA.
Glenn, N. D. (2004) *Cohort Analysis*, rev. edn. Sage, Thousand Oaks, CA.
Hirschi, T. & Gottfredson, M. (1983) Age and the Explanation of Crime. *American Journal of Sociology* 89: 552–84.
Mason, K. O., Mason, W. M., Winsborough, H. H., & Poole, W. P. (1973) Some Methodological Issues in the Cohort Analysis of Archival Data. *American Sociological Review* 38: 242–58.
Rosenstone, S. J. & Hansen, J. M. (1993) *Mobilization, Participation, and Democracy in America.* Macmillan, New York.

age prejudice and discrimination

Bill Bytheway

Agism is often defined as prejudice and discrimination against older people on the basis of age. Women are disadvantaged and oppressed as a result of sexism. Black and minority ethnic groups are disadvantaged and oppressed by racism. In similar ways age is held against older people due to agism.

The dominant social order of many contemporary societies has been radically changed by campaigns against sexism and racism. Many countries have legislation intended to end such discrimination and to ensure equal opportunities regardless of gender or ethnicity. In contrast there is comparatively little legal constraint relating to age.

Age discrimination is when people are denied resources or opportunities as a result of being judged to be old. Age prejudice is when older people are viewed in stereotypical and negative ways. At the individual level these actions are triggered either by chronological age or by the visual appearance of the person: face, body, and dress. Collectively, agism may be evident in the way in which services are organized, located, or described.

In his classic definition of agism as "a process of systematic stereotyping of and discrimination against people because they are old," Robert Butler (1975) did not see being old as problematic. However, as he goes on to observe: "Old people are categorized as senile, rigid in thought and manner, old-fashioned in morality and skills" and, in part, this is because the word itself enables "us" to characterize "them" in non-inclusive and homogenizing ways.

Increasingly, the word "older" is preferred to "old" or "elderly." Many have difficulty with this, however, using "older" as a euphemism for "old," or demanding a categorical definition based on chronological age. For those challenging agism this could be construed as evidence of success in that it is not so easy to stereotype and discriminate against such "ill-defined" categories. The turn to "older," however, also reflects a broader view of agism: as a set of deterministic beliefs about how people change biologically over the course of their whole lives. This conceptualization still parallels theories relating to racism and sexism in that biological differences are seen to underpin prejudicial assumptions, but it differs in that people of all ages are oppressed by agist assumptions about the aging process. Moreover, these beliefs legitimate the use of chronological age in determining expectations relating to personal growth and physical capacity.

Infants and very frail older people are unable to live independently in the modern world and most people would accept that they should be given proper care. Similarly, just as children need education so, in a well-ordered society, retired people are seen to need a pension. This and similar benefits and concessions are sometimes described as indications of positive agism. However, when chronological age is used to determine who is in need of care, education, or a pension, then legal status is transformed upon reaching certain birthdays and, regardless of whether such change is welcomed, these policies underpin demeaning attitudes and agist prejudice.

ORIGINS OF AGISM

Arguably, agism has existed in every society. Following anti-sexist and anti-racist action in the 1960s, however, it was perhaps inevitable that agism would be "discovered." At that time, social research was revealing the deplorable position of older people in so-called civilized societies. For example, in the US, there was Jules Henry's *Culture Against Man* (1965) and, in the UK, Peter Townsend's *The Last Refuge* (1962) and Barbara Robb's *Sans Everything* (1967). It was in 1969 that the word agism was coined, when Robert Butler commented on a controversy over the allocation of hi-rise blocks to old black people. In the angry debates that followed he heard echoes of the infamous intergenerational battles the previous year between students and police and, in a newspaper interview, he described the reaction to the housing proposals as a function of agism rather than racism (Butler 1989).

Such prejudice underpins the allocation of resources. Americans for Generational Equity (AGE) was formed in the 1980s to question governmental policies that seemingly prioritized the old at the expense of the young. It drew upon the work of Daniel Callahan, whose *Setting Limits* (1987) advocated using chronological age to weigh the provision of health care resources against older people.

Agism is about rights as well as inequalities. The ultimate human right is to life and, as Simone de Beauvour (1979) found in her review of ethnological evidence, many societies respect old people so long as they are competent, but abandon them when they become senile and infirm. At the beginning of the twentieth century, for example, the famous surgeon Sir William Osler backed Anthony Trollope's suggestion that men over 60 are useless and should be offered a peaceful departure through chloroform (Graebner 1980: 4–5). More recently, alarmed by forecasts of the impact of demographic change on the economy, various commentators have backed euthanasia for the aged. In 1984, for example, Governor Richard D. Lamm of Colorado argued that sick old people should "die and get out of the way."

The study of agism developed primarily in the US and, in the wider context, the policy agenda has focused on older workers and employment law. Many of those seeking to legislate against age discrimination have been patronizing towards "the old," and the historian Thomas Cole (1992) has argued that the attack on agism "originated in the same chorus of cultural values that gave rise to agism in the first place." In his view, agism is a conceptual tool that is "neither informed by broader social or psychological theory nor grounded in historical specificity" (pp. 228–9). The evidence of current sociology appears to support this claim: to date, sociological research into age has failed to match that which has focused on gender and ethnicity.

AGE PREJUDICE

Most of us have anxieties about the future and a fear of aging. Underpinning these are a number of beliefs: that the chances of illness and impairment will increase as we grow older; that old people are ugly; that they have failing memories, etc. With age, we lose not only those we are closest to, but people with whom we can share past experiences. There is a particularly strong fear of "losing one's faculties" and of becoming dependent on others for basic daily routines. These fears affect how we react to people of great age. Butler argued that agism allows younger people to see older people "as different from themselves" and as a result they "subtly cease to identify with their elders as human beings." The same is said of infants, but the difference is that in time infants are expected to become "full" human beings.

Since the publication in 1972 of a newspaper article by Susan Sontag, it has become widely accepted that appearance is constrained by agist values. Particularly for women, the youthful fashion model presents an image of the idealized body that is oppressive for women of all ages (Woodward 1999; Calasanti & Slevin 2001). Some older women have vividly described the experience of being made to feel "invisible" in an agist world (Macdonald & Rich 1983). Nevertheless, images of older people abound. Kathleen Woodward (1991: 1), for example, offers a telling anecdote about an exhibition that included the portrait of a thin naked old man. For some, the portrait confirmed and consolidated their prejudices and they indulged in agist humor. Others, however, Woodward noted, were forced to address their reaction to this image of their own possible future. Uncompromising images of the aging body can easily shock those who would normally look away. People often express their feelings of disgust and pity.

Prejudice is also evident in the ways in which chronological age is used in creating a summary identity. Just as a single photograph can categorize an individual as "male, old and white," for example, so the words "Applicant, 75, male" are sufficient to place the individual into an age and sex category and a stereotyped image comes to mind. In such ways chronological age and the image of the aging body combine to consolidate an age identity.

The above examples of prejudice feature an individual who is prejudged according to age. Agist prejudice can also apply to older people collectively. At a local level, housing can be reserved for "the elderly" and, as Butler observed, this might evoke in the local community the image of large numbers of "senile old people" invading the local community. In such instances, it is neither chronological age nor the sight of an older person that triggers the response, it is the stigma that goes with the crowd and words such as "elderly" and "senile."

AGE DISCRIMINATION

Whereas prejudice stigmatizes, discrimination divides and excludes. Exclusion implies a bar, something that is easier to demonstrate than stigma. Leaflets and advertisements often include age stipulations and clerks can point to these in explaining how we might be too old or too young to qualify. Typically, this kind of institutional discrimination depends upon chronological age. With each birthday, our status changes and regulatory doors open and close. Whether it is the cinema or the cardiology clinic, the temptation to lie about our age is always there.

There are many situations where chronological age is considered incidental. What really counts is appearance. In an agist society, older people are encouraged to pass as "youthful" and, in many settings, we only gain entry by conveying the right image. Gatekeepers in employment agencies, leisure centers, holiday camps, and night clubs have enormous discretion.

There are many sources of national statistics that can be used to illustrate the massive social and economic inequalities that result from such bureaucratic discrimination. For example, the UK Family Expenditure Survey demonstrates a strong association between age and household finance. There are striking differences between people aged 50 to 64 and people aged 75 or more. The older group has an average disposable income that is less than half that of the younger. The main sources of income of the . younger group are wages and salaries, whereas for the older they are predominantly pensions. Of the two groups, the older spends proportionately more on household essentials. People aged 75 or more are less able to cope with unexpected bills. These differences are caused by legal and regulatory restrictions on employment and income generation and it is in this way that institutional agism constrains the financial resources of older people. Many have less freedom to spend than they had previously and less than that enjoyed by younger generations.

METHODOLOGICAL ISSUES

As researchers, a key issue that we have to address is whether we see agism as a concept that helps explain inequality and discrimination, or as a political and cultural phenomenon. If the first, then we should consider carefully how we define and study it. We could conceptualize agism as something that includes "erroneous" beliefs about the "facts" of age and, following Palmore (1999), our aim would be to overcome agism through knowledge and education.

The second strategy, however, implies recognition that anyone and any organization can act against agism. As researchers we would not claim any authority in defining agism and how it should be challenged. We might encounter definitions that seem bizarre, based on an outdated vocabulary for example. Or, reflecting Cole's observation, we may encounter definitions of agism which, paradoxically, seem positively agist. Accepting that this is how discussion of agism is developing in the wider world, we would not seek to challenge this "mistaken" view of agism. Rather, we would attempt to account for its emergence and distinctive construction.

It is helpful to return to precedents relating to sexism and racism. In both, the lead has been taken by members of those groups that suffer the consequences. So campaigns against sexism have been led by women in a wide variety of contexts: ideological, academic, cultural, political, and economic. Men aligned to such campaigns have occasionally played a part, but it would be absurd to suggest that men have ever led, or should aspire to lead, such campaigns. Similarly, those who have led campaigns against racism have, with few exceptions, been members of oppressed racial groups. So the fight against agism defined as discrimination and prejudice against older people must be led by older people: people who have first-hand experience of the consequences.

Where does this leave us as sociologists concerned to challenge age prejudice and discrimination? We may have relevant first-hand experience of agism in the broader sense and we may encounter age prejudice within universities or similar institutions, but we are in a weak position to claim leadership in more broadly based campaigns against agism. It is only when we cease to be *employed* as sociologists and begin to share with others the experience of retirement and "being too old" that we can start to play an influential part in political action.

So the conclusion might be that sociologists have first-hand experience of aging and the oppressive use of chronological age, rather than of prejudice and discrimination against older people. It is in this context that sociologists employed as researchers can play a leading role in the continuing struggle against agism. To. this end, there are three directions that should be considered in planning future research (Bytheway 2002): moving away from a narrow focus on "the elderly" and "their needs," and towards aging in general and extreme age in particular; away from the planning and delivery of support services and towards the management of everyday life; and away from idealized models of the aging process and towards a focus on how people talk about and act upon their age.

SEE ALSO: Age Identity; Aging and the Life Course, Theories of; Aging and Social Policy; Aging, Mental Health, and Well-Being; Aging, Sociology of; Beauvoir, Simone de; Body and Society; Discrimination; Elder Abuse; Gerontology; Prejudice; Retirement; Stereotyping and Stereotypes; Stigma

REFERENCES AND SUGGESTED READINGS

Beauvoir, S. de (1979) *Old Age*. Penguin, Harmondsworth.

Binstock, R. H. (2003) The War on "Anti-Aging Medicine." *Gerontologist* 43(1): 4–14.

Butler, R. N. (1975) *Why Survive? Being Old in America*. Harper & Row, New York.

Butler, R. N. (1989) Dispelling Ageism: The Cross-Cutting Intervention. *Annals of the American Academy of Political and Social Science* 503: 138–47.

Bytheway, B. (1995) *Ageism*. Open University Press, Buckingham.

Bytheway, B. (2002) Positioning Gerontology in an Ageist World. In: Andersson, L. (Ed.), *Cultural Gerontology*. Greenwood Publishing, Westport, CT, pp. 59–76.

Calasanti, T. M. & Slevin, K. F. (2001) Gender, Social Inequalities and Aging. Alta Mira Press, Walnut Creek, CA.

Callahan, D. (1987) *Setting Limits: Medical Goals in an Aging Society*. Simon & Schuster, New York.

Cohen, E. S. (2001) The Complex Nature of Ageism: What is it? Who does it? Who perceives it? *Gerontologist* 41(5): 576–7.

Cole, T. R. (1992) *The Journey of Life: A Cultural History of Aging in America*. Cambridge University Press, Cambridge.

Graebner, W. (1980) *A History of Retirement*. Yale University Press, New Haven.

Macdonald, B. & Rich, C. (1983) *Look Me in the Eye: Old Women, Aging and Ageism*. Women's Press, London.

Nelson, T. (Ed.) (2002) *Ageism: Stereotyping and Prejudice against Older Persons*. MIT Press, Cambridge, MA.

Palmore, E. (1999) *Ageism: Negative and Positive*. Springer, New York.

Phillipson, C. (1998) *Reconstructing Old Age*. Sage, London.

Woodward, K. (1991) *Aging and Its Discontents: Freud and Other Fictions*. Indiana University Press, Indianapolis.

Woodward, K. (Ed.) (1999) *Figuring Age: Women, Bodies, Generations*. Indiana University Press, Indianapolis.

agency (and intention)

Stephan Fuchs

Agency is a fundamental and foundational category and puzzle in virtually all social sciences and humanities. Debates over agency have emerged together with these fields, and continue unabated into the present time, with no resolution or consensus in sight. While many agree that agency, action, and actor are basic in some sense, controversies persist over the definition, range, and explanatory status of these concepts. In addition, agency is contested because it connects to core questions in metaphysics, philosophy, and ethics, such as free will, moral responsibility, personhood, and subjective rights. Agency is tied to the legacy of liberal humanism that is part of the core of democratic citizenship.

In sociology, one result of these enduring conflicts has been a metatheoretical split into agency vs. structure, micro vs. macro, and individualism vs. holism. On the micro side of this divide are those who argue that, since only actors and their actions are real, all things social must ultimately be "reduced to," or "explained in terms of," agency. In contrast, those on the macro side defend the emergent and irreducible status of large-scale social entities, such as organizations, states, and social structures.

Underneath these disagreements are some common themes. Agency is the faculty for action. This faculty may be uniquely human. Action differs from the (mere) behavior of non-human organisms, which is driven by innate or conditioned reflexes and instincts. Non-human organisms have no or little control over how they behave. They do not have a sense of self or, if they do, it is not reflexive. Their behavior is caused by forces they cannot comprehend or influence. Human actors are different because they are conscious and aware of the world, themselves, and other actors. To some extent, what they do, and who they are, is up to them. They are open to the world, and not stuck in the immediately pressing here and now of a local niche. Human identity is not fixed from the start, and so human beings have to make themselves into who they will become. This makes predictions of actions difficult, if not impossible. Action is contingent; behavior is necessary. An actor can act, but also not, and can also act in different ways. While actors may have reasons for their actions, such reasons do not determine actions in the same rigid way that natural forces cause behavior.

The faculty for agency is located in the human mind. The mind is the seat of reflexivity, deliberation, and intentionality. Before we act, we rehearse possibilities and alternatives. The mind also houses the sense of who we are as individual persons. Humans have minds and selves, and these together are the sources for action. Action is motivated, but not caused, by intentions. These intentions give actions their meaning. To understand agency, action, and actors, sociology needs to understand and interpret the meanings and intentions that actions have for their actors. This is difficult, since intentions and meanings presumably are mental states inside the head, and so cannot be directly observed, unlike overt behavior. While each of us can introspect our own intentions, what happens in other minds may ultimately be inaccessible. In fact, for Freud, we do not even know, and chronically deceive ourselves, about what happens in our own minds.

RATIONAL CHOICE

Much depends on how this agentic core is developed. One possibility is rational choice and exchange theory. This holds person, intention, and action constant. In this tradition of scholarship, there is no genuine problem or difficulty with agency because it is settled by *fiat*. By axiom or definition, all actors are deemed rational. Rational actors always act out of a well-defined interest in their own personal welfare. Rational actors are very informed and knowledgeable. They know what they want, and what they want most. They also know how to get what they want in the most effective and efficient way. To do this, they must compete against other rational actors who want the same things. If two actors want something the other has, an exchange might occur. Such exchanges occur in markets. All social action is rational market exchange. To the extent that an actor needs something from another very badly, and cannot get that resource from someone else, the second actor has power over the first. Power results from dependence.

SYMBOLIC INTERACTIONISM

Very different from this rationalist and utilitarian theory of agency is symbolic interactionism, which owes much to American pragmatism. In this tradition, agency is more contingent and open-ended. It is not known or settled beforehand what action is and who the actors are. This is not for the external observer to decide, but emerges from the practice of social life itself. The self is not a homogeneous utility function, but a complex and multidimensional accomplishment. The most prominent theory of the self, that of Mead, reckons with three components of the self, each in an internal conversation with the others. The faculty for agency is not ready-made, but emerges through a process of social formation and re-formation. Social interaction is negotiation over definitions of the situation. Reality is socially constructed. Actors develop a sense of self, and present a certain side of themselves to others. They take each other's roles to manage the problem of double contingency. They see themselves through the perceptions of those others with whom they interact, particularly "significant" others.

To understand agency, one needs to take the "actor's point of view" and see the actors' worlds from their own perspectives. Since all action is symbolically structured, most importantly through language and culture, the key to agency and action is interpretation, not explanation. Understanding agency is akin to interpreting texts. The central method for interpreting social action and interaction is, therefore, participant observation. Sociologists are not free to impose their concepts on those they study, but must connect their understanding to the self-understanding of the actors they study.

ETHNOMETHODOLOGY

Symbolic interactionism works with a notion of agency that is similar to the idea of the subject in German idealism. The actor is a sovereign, in charge of who he or she is, and in control of the situation. The actor is a maker and author of the world. The world is the actor's will and representation. In contrast, the ethnomethodological notion of agency is indebted to continental phenomenology and existentialism (Husserl and Heidegger). Actors are not really in control of social life; rather, social life is in control of them. They are not subjects, but "members." Members of ordinary everyday society do not so much act as enact the social practices of common sense. There are very narrow limits on what actors can be consciously aware of and define or redefine. These practices continue and confirm themselves through members, much like the "habitus" in Bourdieu, which is a collective unconscious. Members are not the authors of these practices but one outcome of them. Members are the means by which society reproduces itself. Social practices cannot be defined and redefined at will. They establish a sense of facticity and normalcy over an abyss of uncertainty, contingency, and anxiety.

The way to study these practices is to disrupt them, and then observe how a sense of facticity repairs itself. Any social order is a local accomplishment. But it is not an accomplishment of actors and agency. Rather, social order emerges and maintains itself, and it does so through its members.

CONSTRUCTIVIST AGENCY

One difficulty with making agency, action, and actor the foundational concepts of the social sciences is that there are very many actors, doing very many different things, for many different reasons. There are about 6 billion actors alive today. It is impossible to know all of them, what all of them are doing, and why. Reasons and intentions are presumably inside the head, which makes them difficult to retrieve. One might ask them for their reasons, but the stated reasons may not be the real ones. Even if all this were knowable, it is still uncertain how one would get from an action to, say, the modern world-system. A society is not the result of anyone's doing. It cannot be "intended" as such or as a whole. Society does not really consist of persons or actors, in their full biographic totality. Even that which a single person does may have consequences that go far beyond any subjective meanings and plans.

One possible strategy to avoid such difficulties is a constructivist, rather than realist, notion of agency. Constructivism sees agency not as a faculty that is, in fact, had by actors but as a property that may, or may not, be ascribed to them. Agency then becomes an attribution, akin to the granting of a privilege that can also be withdrawn and withheld. Societies and cultures differ in how they distribute such privileges, and to what sorts of entities. Tribal societies with animistic cosmologies, for example, tend to grant agency to spiritual forces of nature that modern science sees as inanimate objects governed by physical laws. Historical sociology shows that different societies ascribe agency, and hence responsibility and accountability, to different persons in different ways, resulting in variable distinctions between adults and children, for example. Likewise, we tend to grant agency to our pets, but not to the microorganisms in our bodies. We tend to attribute agency to all other human persons, but on occasion withdraw this privilege, as happens to the insane or the comatose. Passionate conflicts rage over whether and when embryos have agency, and thus subjective rights that need to be protected. If all animals have agency and subjectivity, killing them for consumption might be murder.

This constructivist turn in the study of agency makes variation in attributions the key. Agency now becomes a second-order construct, not a first-order essence or natural kind. Allowing for variation might make it possible to render agency more amenable to empirical research, whereas up to now it has been bogged down in conceptual and semantic analysis.

SEE ALSO: Constructionism; Ethnomethodology; Micro–Macro Links; Rational Choice Theories; Structuration Theory; Structure and Agency; Symbolic Interaction

REFERENCES AND SUGGESTED READINGS

Bourdieu, P. (1990) *The Logic of Practice*. Polity Press, Cambridge.
Durkheim, É. (1984 [1893]) *The Division of Labour in Society*. Macmillan, London.
Emirbayer, M. & Mische, A. (1998) What is Agency? *American Journal of Sociology* 104: 962–1023.
Giddens, A. (1984) *The Constitution of Society*. Polity Press, Cambridge.
Mead, G. H. (1967) *Mind, Self, and Society*. Chicago, University of Chicago Press.
Stones, R. (2004) *Structuration Theory*. Palgrave Macmillan, London.
Weber, M. (1968) *Economy and Society*. Ed. G. Roth & C. Wittich. Bedminster Press, New York.

agenda setting

Darin Weinberg

The concept of agenda setting has become a term of art in the sociology of social problems largely through research concerning the effects of mass media on public opinion. However, it has also been applied beyond this particular area of research to consider how topics arise as matters of public concern more generally. Thus research on agenda setting focuses on the whole range of forces that influence public opinion on any given issue and the various ways in which issues become topical among policymakers themselves.

Research on agenda setting is predicated on the fact that there is not always a very strong relationship between scientific accounts of the prevalence and/or seriousness of a given social problem and the success with which that problem is publicized and/or made the focus of public policy. Often, putative problems that are not very widespread or significant get very high levels of public attention, while problems that are quite serious are comparatively ignored. If problems do not get placed on the public agenda simply by virtue of the fact that, objectively speaking, they warrant public attention, then there is a need to study the real reasons why some problems find their way onto the public agenda and others do not. Research based on this insight is often called social constructionist, to highlight its insistence that our beliefs about social problems do not derive as much from the objective characteristics of those problems as from the ways in which images of them are socially constructed in the mass media and elsewhere. Typically, the questions raised in the agenda-setting literature concern such issues as the social conditions under which a given problem arises as a matter of public concern, among whom it arises as a matter of concern, techniques used to get issues onto the public agenda, the resources with which this work is accomplished, the capacities of various audiences to attend to particular problems or problem sets, and the consequences (or the lack thereof) of various agenda-setting efforts.

The earliest research on agenda setting noted that because most of our information regarding what is happening in the community or the world at large derives not from first-hand experience but from the mass media, these media play an important gatekeeping role in determining which issues come to our attention. Some research has suggested that the mass media do not necessarily dictate exactly what we should think about the most important issues facing the community, but that they heavily influence whether an issue comes to be seen as important in the first place. This is accomplished through story selection and through decisions as to whether to continue coverage on a story or let it die. Research looking at the social structural conditions under which the news media work suggests these conditions strongly encourage a convergence of the various individual media outlets on similar sets of stories. Other research suggests that the power of the mass media goes considerably beyond merely establishing the salience of a problem to establishing the specific "frames" in light of which particular issues ought to be seen. For example, mass-media coverage of the problem of "drunk driving" not only places that issue on the public agenda but overwhelmingly tends to frame it as a problem concerning the personal habits of individual drivers. One might argue that this problem could just as easily be framed as a problem of inadequate road safety measures or public transportation provisions. Hence, researchers interested in agenda setting want to understand why one frame is promoted and/or adopted on a problem rather than another. Different media portrayals of a putative problem may suggest different causal explanations, levels of urgency, specifications of who is involved (as perpetrators, victims, or problem solvers), and possible remedies for the problem. Thus it is argued that the mass media can have an enormous influence not only on whether we regard a problem as important and worthy of public attention but also upon how we orient to that problem in all of its myriad dimensions.

In response to the argument that the mass media shape public opinion in this way, some have countered that the mass media merely reflect the interests and concerns of their consumers. Hence, one major debate in the agenda-setting literature has focused on the question of whether the mass media shape public opinion or public opinion shapes the content of the mass media. This formulation of the question has also been subject to the important criticism that neither the mass media nor public opinion are sufficiently uniform or consistent to speak of them in the singular. If we want to understand adequately whether public opinion has an influence on mass media content or vice versa, we must first specify which elements of "the public" we are speaking of and, likewise, which mass media. This point is equally true of research that would seek to explore the influence of the mass media on policymakers and vice versa. Contemporary research in this area acknowledges that these questions are seldom straightforward. Typically, various claims–makers are actively involved in vigorous struggles with one another as to whether a given issue belongs on the public agenda or not, and, if so, how that issue should be framed. These various claims-makers often have very different levels of access to the wide range of media outlets potentially available, different (and often very unequal) resources with which to promote their claims, and different levels of credibility among the various audiences they would hope to persuade. This more finely grained approach to research has also suggested that the very idea of a singular "public agenda" may need to be refined. If, in fact, the work of agenda setting is tailored to particular audiences that vary depending on the nature of the issues concerned, then it may be more appropriate to speak of many different public agendas, taking shape in many different practical arenas, rather than the singular and integrated public agenda of a given society.

SEE ALSO: Audiences; Awareness Contexts; Constructionism; Frame; Framing and Social Movements; Information Society; Media Literacy; Media Monopoly; Media and the Public Sphere; Mediation; Politics and Media; Propaganda; Public Opinion; Public Sphere; Reception Studies; Social Problems, Concept and Perspectives; Social Problems, Politics of

REFERENCES AND SUGGESTED READINGS

Dearing, J. W. & Rogers, E. M. (1996) *Agenda Setting*. Sage, Thousand Oaks, CA.

Goffman, E. (1974) *Frame Analysis*. Harvard University Press, Cambridge, MA.

Hilgartner, S. & Bosk, C. L. (1988) The Rise and Fall of Social Problems: A Public Arenas Model. *American Journal of Sociology* 94(1): 53–78.

Loseke, D. R. (1999) *Thinking About Social Problems: An Introduction to Constructionist Perspectives*. Aldine de Gruyter, New York.

McCombs, M. (2004) *Setting the Agenda: News Media and Public Opinion*. Polity Press, Cambridge.

Rochefort, D. A. & Cobb, R. W. (Eds.) (1994) *The Politics of Problem Definition: Shaping the Policy Agenda*. University of Kansas Press, Lawrence.

aggression

William J. Kinney

Aggression is any behavior that is directed toward injuring, harming, or inflicting pain on another living being or group of beings. Generally, the victim(s) of aggression must wish to avoid such behavior in order for it to be considered true aggression. Aggression is also categorized according to its ultimate intent. *Hostile aggression* is an aggressive act that results from anger, and is intended to inflict pain or injury because of that anger. *Instrumental aggression* is an aggressive act that is regarded as a means to an end other than pain or injury. For example, an enemy combatant may be subjected to torture in order to extract useful intelligence, though those inflicting the torture may have no real feelings of anger or animosity toward their subject.

The concept of aggression is very broad, and includes many categories of behavior (e.g., verbal aggression, street crime, child abuse, spouse abuse, group conflict, war, etc.). A number of theories and models of aggression have arisen to explain these diverse forms of behavior, and these theories/models tend to be categorized according to their specific focus. The most common system of categorization groups the various approaches to aggression into three separate areas, based upon the three key variables that are present whenever any aggressive act or set of acts is committed. The first variable is the *aggressor* him/herself. The second is the *social situation or circumstance* in which the aggressive act(s) occur. The third variable is the *target or victim* of aggression.

Regarding theories and research on the *aggressor*, the fundamental focus is on the factors that lead an individual (or group) to commit aggressive acts. At the most basic level, some argue that aggressive urges and actions are the result of inborn, biological factors. Sigmund Freud (1930) proposed that all individuals are born with a *death instinct* that predisposes us to a variety of aggressive behaviors, including suicide (self-directed aggression) and mental illness (possibly due to an unhealthy or unnatural suppression of aggressive urges). Other influential perspectives supporting a biological basis for aggression conclude that humans evolved with an abnormally low neural inhibition of aggressive impulses (in comparison to other species), and that humans possess a powerful instinct for property accumulation and territorialism. It is proposed that this instinct accounts for hostile behaviors ranging from minor street crime to world wars. Hormonal factors also appear to play a significant role in fostering aggressive tendencies. For example, the hormone testosterone has been shown to increase aggressive behaviors when injected into animals. Men and women convicted of violent crimes also possess significantly higher levels of testosterone than men and women convicted of nonviolent crimes. Numerous studies comparing different age groups, racial/ethnic groups, and cultures also indicate that men, overall, are more likely to engage in a variety of aggressive behaviors (e.g., sexual assault, aggravated assault, etc.) than women. One explanation for higher levels of aggression in men is based on the assumption that, on average, men have higher levels of testosterone than women. However, amounts vary across individuals depending on a variety of factors in addition to sex.

In contrast to the biological perspective on aggressors, the social learning perspective proposes that aggressive behaviors/tendencies are instilled in individuals when they observe aggression performed by others. One significant factor in this process is modeling, which is the tendency of individuals to imitate the behaviors displayed by others. Many experiments have shown that individuals are more likely to engage in aggression after witnessing acts of aggression (particularly portrayals of aggression that are shown in a positive light). It has also been shown that those who grow up in homes where domestic abuse has occurred are significantly more likely to engage in domestic abuse as adults. Researchers conclude that growing up in an abusive situation teaches some children that acts of physical aggression are appropriate. It may also serve to desensitize them at an early age to the outcomes of aggression.

Another component of social learning theory is that people may engage in aggressive acts because they can be rewarding. As individuals are socialized, behavioral patterns are established through a process known as "reinforcement." This means that we continue patterns of behavior that result in some type of reward, while we discontinue or decrease those behaviors that result in punishing or negative outcomes. Therefore, if one learns that aggression is more likely to result in a positive outcome (attention, approval, power, money, etc.) than a negative outcome, aggressive actions are more likely to be viewed as a viable means to a desired end.

A third explanation of aggressive behavior involves the phenomenon of psychopathology or sociopathology. These terms are frequently used interchangeably, since the conditions and symptoms are very similar in nature. The fundamental difference between the two is that psychopathology is thought to have a primarily biological basis, while sociopathology is thought to have a primarily social origin (such as childhood trauma). In either case, the individual experiencing this condition feels a kind of disconnection from the normative standards of the society around them. This disconnection is also generally accompanied by an inability to fully empathize with the experiences or feelings of others in their social environment. These combined factors may lead the individual to engage in patterns of behavior characterized by inappropriate and/or abnormal levels of verbal and physical aggression. Some propose that modern society is marked by such a high rate of significant life change, disruption, and social disconnection (e.g., frequent moves, divorce, the incidence of inadequate day care, etc.) that children today are more likely to experience factors conducive to this condition.

Apart from these key factors, research has shown that a wide variety of other influences, such as drugs, alcohol, verbal and/or physical provocation, arousal, etc., may have significant (though varying) impacts on the occurrence of aggressive behavior. The phenomenon of aggression is broad and complex, and many factors affect those who engage in it.

With these characteristics of aggressors in mind, we turn to the second key variable in determining aggression: the *situation*. A major consideration involving the situation is the presence of frustration or stress. Frustration is generally defined as the blocking of goal-directed behavior. In what came to be known as the *frustration–aggression hypothesis*, many early psychologists and social psychologists argued that frustration was a precursor to *all* acts of aggression. However, research on this issue proved that the presence of frustration does not necessarily result in aggressive acts. A complex interplay of factors determines whether the sensation of frustration ultimately translates into aggressive behavior. For example, if an individual perceives that an aggressive act will eliminate the cause of frustration, then the likelihood of that act being committed is increased. If aggression is not perceived as a possible remedy, the aggression is decreased.

Closely related to the phenomenon of frustration and aggression is the influence of environmental stressors. A prime example of the impact of stress on aggression is the relationship between high temperatures and various forms of violent crime. Research has shown that a variety of violent crimes (murder, assault, etc.) increase significantly during hot weather. Studies on the urban riots of the 1960s also show a clear correlation between high temperatures and the incidence of crowd violence. Laboratory experiments show that aggression is more likely to result from stressors such as heat and irritating noise, if the participant believes there is no escape from the stress. When participants perceive that they can modify or escape from the stressor, the occurrence of aggression decreases significantly. Other studies have shown a connection between a variety of environmental stressors (e.g., cigarette smoke, pollution, etc.) and the incidence of aggression.

The sociocultural perspective on aggression proposes that the fundamental situational determinant of aggression and violence is the nature and content of the popular culture in which one lives. It is hypothesized that factors such as the prevalence and availability of guns, governmental utilization of the death penalty, and the institutionalization of violence in sports (contact sports, in particular) foster a *culture of violence*. Another component of this culture is the frequency and portrayal of violence and aggression in the mass media. Numerous studies have documented the high frequency of such portrayals in various facets of the media. Most estimates show that the average American child has witnessed hundreds of thousands of violent acts, and tens of thousands of homicides, on television by the age of 18. Nearly every study on exposure to violence in the media shows a significant relationship with the tendency toward aggressive behavior (though direct causality remains difficult to prove). Thus, from a sociocultural perspective, the individual tendency toward aggression is largely a product of the norms people learn through social exposure.

The third key variable in aggression is the *target* or *victim* of the aggressive act. One aspect of this variable is the demographic characteristics of the target, namely, gender and race. These characteristics depend largely upon what type of aggression is being committed. For example, in examining the occurrence of crimes such as murder or assault, it is found that men are much more likely to be victims than women. However, if we focus more specifically on murder among spouses or cohabiting male/female couples, women are significantly more likely to be murdered than men. Regarding the issue of child abuse, it has been found that male and female children are abused in roughly equal rates. With regard to race and ethnicity, most aggression is intraracial, or directed within one's own racial/ethnic group. Most racial/ethnic minorities in the United States have higher rates of victimization than whites, though whites are more likely to be the victims of interracial aggression (such as murder, rape, and assault).

An important issue beyond the basic demographic dimension of aggression is the victim's capacity to retaliate against the aggressor.

Usually, if a victim has a significant ability to retaliate, the likelihood and severity of aggression is reduced. This dynamic is particularly relevant in cases of aggression that involve considerable thought and deliberation. In cases that involve strong emotion and/or the consumption of drugs or alcohol, rational considerations such as retaliatory capacity are less effective in reducing aggression. It is also thought that the low immediate retaliatory capacity of certain victims, such as abused children or rape victims, contributes to some degree in the occurrence of these crimes.

A final issue related to victims of aggression involves the psychological impact of aggression upon them, and the manner in which it may affect future behavioral patterns and coping strategies. One concept that exemplifies this concern is *learned helplessness*. Research on this phenomenon demonstrated that when animal subjects learned that aggression (such as electric shocks) was unavoidable, they quickly stopped trying to avoid it – even after escape became possible. The application of this concept to human behavior is mitigated by a variety of factors, but many believe that it holds relevance in explaining why some victims of aggression fail to free themselves from violent or abusive situations when the opportunity to do so is available. The primary problem encountered when examining the impact of aggression on victims in this manner is that it becomes easy to *blame the victim* for the aggression itself. However, by further understanding common responses to aggression, it also becomes possible to construct useful therapeutic programs and treatments for dealing with the phenomenon in a constructive way.

SEE ALSO: Learned Helplessness; Milgram, Stanley (Experiments); Rational Choice Theory: A Crime-Related Perspective; Social Learning Theory

REFERENCES AND SUGGESTED READINGS

Anderson, C. A. & Bushman, B. J. (2002) The Effects of Media Violence on Society. *Science* 295: 2377–80.

Ardrey, R. (1966) *The Territorial Imperative.* Atheneum, New York.

Bandura, A. (1973) *Aggression: A Social Learning Analysis.* Prentice-Hall, Englewood Cliffs, NJ.

Bandura, A., Ross, D., & Ross, S. (1961) Transmission of Aggression through Imitation of Aggressive Models. *Journal of Abnormal and Social Psychology* 63: 575–82.

Freud, S. (1930) *Civilization and Its Discontents.* Hogarth Press, London.

Lorenz, K. (1966) *On Aggression.* Harcourt Brace Jovanovich, New York.

Miller, N. E. (1941) The Frustration–Aggression Hypothesis. *Psychological Review* 48: 337–42.

Seligman, M. E. P. (1975) *Helplessness: On Depression, Development, and Death.* W. H. Freeman, San Francisco.

aging, demography of

Charles F. Longino, Jr. and Janet Wilmoth

Demography is the scientific study of human populations. Its origins are as old as those of science. The demography of aging, on the other hand, did not begin to emerge as a distinct subfield until the second half of the twentieth century, when low fertility and mortality rates were creating dramatic shifts in the age structure of developed countries. In 1980, Jacob Siegel devoted his presidential address to the Population Association of America to the topic of demography of aging, which he declared "brings demographers to focus holistically on a population group, the elderly, and a demographic process, aging" (1980: 345).

At that point, researchers in this area were in the early stages of defining old age and aging, documenting changes in the age structure, identifying mortality trends, describing the health status of older adults, explaining the geographical distribution and mobility of older adults, understanding the life course and cohort flow, and exploring living arrangements, family support, and retirement trends (Siegel 1980). Since that time demographers have become increasingly concerned with population aging as it relates to social transfer programs, social institutions such as the economy and the family, and the overall quality of life for different age groups (e.g., children, working-aged adults, older adults) (Preston & Martin 1994). Both formal demographers and social demographers have contributed to the sociology of aging. Their work on population aging worldwide and in the United States is reviewed below.

Formal demographers are primarily concerned with documenting the changing size, age/sex structure, and geographical distribution of the population, which are influenced by fertility, mortality, and migration rates. The first contribution demography makes to the sociology of aging, therefore, is documenting worldwide trends in population aging. Demographic transition theory explains the shifting fertility and mortality rates that accompany economic development. This transition involves three distinct phases. The first is characterized by high, fluctuating mortality rates and high, stable fertility rates. The age structure of the population is young and life expectancy at birth is low. In the second phase, childhood mortality declines. Typically, drops in fertility lag behind reductions in mortality, causing population growth and a reduction in the average age of the population. The final stage of the demographic transition is characterized by additional improvements in mortality, particularly mortality related to human-made and degenerative diseases that disproportionately affect older adults. Fertility fluctuates but remains low, often at below replacement levels. It is during this last stage that the population ages; specifically, the average age of the population increases as the proportion of the population that is older increases.

Historical evidence suggests this demographic transition occurred slowly in most developed countries. Consequently, developed countries, particularly in Western Europe and North America, experienced gradual population aging during the second half of the twentieth century. In contrast, developing countries are going through this demographic transition at a quicker pace, which means their populations are projected to age at a more rapid rate (United Nations 1999).

Another contribution demographers make to the sociology of aging is documenting national changes in mortality, morbidity, and disability. Mortality rates are related to life expectancy. Improvements in life expectancy *at birth* have been slowing, as the gains due to improved standards of living and health care have been realized and mortality rates due to infectious disease have decreased. However, in many countries improvements in life expectancy *at age 65* continue as mortality rates among the oldest-old decline. Life expectancy at age 65 tends to be highest in developed countries with more equitable wealth distributions, a higher percentage of gross domestic product that is allocated to old-age benefits and health care expenditures, and lower rates of tobacco consumption (Munnell et al. 2004).

Increasing life expectancy, particularly at age 65, raises questions about the quality of life during these additional years lived. Are older adults living longer, healthier lives or are they living longer in poor health? Healthy life expectancy, which is the number of years lived, on average, without disease and/or functional limitations, increases when improvements in morbidity and disability keep pace with, or exceed, improvements in mortality. In this scenario, morbidity is compressed into a shorter period of the life span such that older adults, on average, live longer and in better health.

In addition, the causes of disability often change as morbidity is compressed. Disability due to infectious and parasitic diseases tends to drop; however, disability due to noncommunicable diseases like cancer, heart disease, and neuropsychiatric disorders usually increases. This shift is expected to be particularly noteworthy in developing countries that are experiencing rapid population aging (Murray & Lopez 1997).

Social demographers focus on the social causes and consequences of demographic trends. They have attempted to address a range of issues related to population aging with international data. Three commonly addressed topics related to international population aging include the potential demand placed on health care systems, the impact of changing family structure on care provision, and the economic implications of an aging population.

The growth of the older adult population will not only place demands on health care in terms of the absolute number of people who need to be served, but it will also create shifts in the type of care that is required. The demand for treatment of non-communicable diseases and chronic conditions is likely to increase (Murray & Lopez 1997). This type of care is typically more technologically intensive and occurs over a longer period of time, which increases costs.

In terms of changing family structure and care provision, older adults in the future will have fewer adult children due to fertility declines. The education of women and their growing participation in the labor force worldwide, along with rising divorce rates in all developed countries, increase the complexity of family lives. The willingness and availability of adult children and extended family members to continue to provide the same level of support for their parents in the future is, therefore, called into question.

There is a common expectation that these population trends may come at a cost, particularly by slowing economic growth and raising demand for governmental support of older adults. For developing nations, rapid population aging in future decades may reverse hard-earned advances in economic development. In developed countries, continued population aging raises troubling questions about the viability of the pension and social security systems. Potential solutions would be to increase the retirement age, raise taxes to improve public pension fund solvency, lower benefits, and encourage private pension savings.

Another contribution of demography to the sociology of aging is that it documents in detail the trends in population aging that occurred in the United States. The most obvious is the growth of the older population. The percentage of the population age 65 or older increased from 4.1 percent in 1990 to 12.4 percent in 2000 and will be over 20 percent by 2060 (Himes 2001). Furthermore, the fastest-growing segment of the older adult population is among the oldest-old, who are age 85 and over. The percentage of older Americans who are age 85 and older has increased from only 5 percent in 1900 to 12 percent in 2000, and is expected to increase to 23 percent by 2050.

Over the past 50 years in the United States there have been substantial decreases in mortality, particularly in later life, and subsequent increases in life expectancy. Life expectancy at birth is now 74.3 years for men and 79.7 for women (National Vital Statistics 2004).

The leading causes of death in the United States continue to be due to degenerative diseases associated with aging, including heart disease, cancer, and stroke (Center for Disease Control 2003). The most common chronic conditions include arthritis, hypertension, hearing impairments, heart disease, and cataracts. Almost 45 percent of older adults are limited in activities because of a chronic condition (National Academy on an Aging Society 1999). Overall, however, demographic research on the health of older adults suggests Americans are living longer in better health.

A core concept in the sociology of aging is heterogeneity among the older adult population, which is substantiated by social demographic research on gender, racial, ethnic, and socioeconomic variation among older Americans.

In terms of gender, the ratio of men to women in later life is quite unbalanced and decreases dramatically with age. There are 70 males for every 100 females over the age of 65. Among those aged 85 and older, there are only 41 males for every 100 females (US Census Bureau 2000b). Consequently, many of the "problems of aging" are disproportionately experienced by women whose life course experiences shape their later life outcomes, including health conditions, economic status, and social relationships.

These outcomes also vary by race and ethnicity. The older US population is increasingly racially and ethnically diverse: 83 percent is currently non-Hispanic white but only 64 percent will be so by 2050. Rates of growth are fastest among older Hispanic and Asian populations (Federal Interagency Forum on Aging-Related Statistics 2000) due primarily to immigration trends, changing preferences for entry into the United States based on family status, and increases in the number of immigrants aged 60 or older.

Some of the differences in later life outcomes across racial and ethnic groups, of course, can be attributed to differences in socioeconomic status. Educational attainment is an indicator of socioeconomic status, and it has increased since 1950 more rapidly for non-Hispanic whites. Given the close connection between education attainment and income, it is not surprising that non-Hispanic white older adults are less likely to be in poverty and have more wealth in later life than other race and ethnic groups (US Census Bureau 2002). Furthermore, at all income and educational levels, non-Hispanic white older adults are more likely than minority older adults to own a variety of assets, including high-risk investments that can yield higher returns (Choudhury 2001). Perhaps more importantly, there is evidence that the economic disparities across racial and ethnic groups are increasing (Utendorf 2002).

Social demography also makes a contribution to the sociology of aging by systematically considering the consequences of population aging in the United States, particularly as it relates to labor force participation, retirement, and family ties.

Over the past 50 years, labor force participation among middle-aged and older men has dropped, while for middle-aged and older women labor force participation has increased (Federal Interagency Forum on Aging-Related Statistics 2000). For both men and women the age at retirement has declined. Among men the average age at retirement decreased from over 67 years in 1950–5 to 62 years in 1995–2000. Among women that average decreased from almost 68 years to approximately 62 years over the same time period (Gendell 2001).

This trend toward early retirement, in combination with increasing life expectancy, has substantially increased the average number of years retirees collect benefits: for men the average life expectancy at the median age of retirement in the early 1950s was 12 years, but this figure had increased to 18 years by the late 1990s, and among women the average life expectancy at the median age of retirement increased from nearly 14 years to 22 years during the same time period (Gendell 2001). Demographers speculate that even if age at retirement were to remain stable or increase somewhat, the average length of retirement is likely to increase due to projected improvements in life expectancy (US Census Bureau 2000a).

In terms of family ties, family members are a primary source of support to older adults. The majority of older Americans are embedded in a web of family relationships despite the increasing propensity to live independently. Over the twentieth century, the percentage of older adults living with family declined dramatically. This trend toward independent living is often attributed to preferences for living alone that have been realized through the improved economic and health status of the older population as well as changes in norms concerning non-family living arrangements (Pampel 1983). The likelihood of living alone tends to be lower among older adults who are minority group members or immigrants, are in poorer health, have fewer financial resources, and have more children.

Even though older adults are not likely to live with children, they tend to be in frequent contact with and live in close proximity to at least some family members. Current cohorts of older adults had relatively high marriage and fertility rates and therefore have relatively large family networks from which to draw support (Himes 1992). However, the trend toward lower fertility, in combination with longer life expectancy, is substantially restructuring American families. Although average family size is decreasing, multigenerational families are more prevalent (Bengston et al. 1995).

The complexity of family structure has been compounded by rising divorce rates, falling remarriage rates, and increases in the proportion of the population who have never married. This retreat from marriage has created a range of blended, alternative, and stepfamily arrangements. The long-term implications of the restructuring of the American family for family relationships and caregiving in later life have yet to be determined. However, some research suggests that divorce undermines affection and exchanges between parents and children, particularly between fathers and children (Amato & Booth 1996). Thus, future cohorts of older adults may not be able to rely as much on spouses and children for support.

In conclusion, the demography of aging primarily uses quantitative methods to document population aging worldwide and in the United States. In doing so, it provides a justification for studying older adults, identifies the social causes of aging, and considers the various consequences of shifting population age structure.

SEE ALSO: Aging and the Life Course, Theories of; Aging and Social Support; Aging, Sociology of; Demographic Data: Censuses, Registers, Surveys; Demographic Techniques: Population Pyramids and Age/Sex Structure; Demographic Transition Theory; Gender, Health, and Mortality; Gerontology: Key Thinkers; Healthy Life Expectancy; Race/Ethnicity, Health, and Mortality

REFERENCES AND SUGGESTED READINGS

Amato, P. & Booth, A. (1996) A Prospective Study of Divorce and Parent–Child Relationships. *Journal of Marriage and the Family* 58: 356–65.

Bengston, V., Rosenthal, C., & Burton, L. (1995) Paradoxes of Families and Aging. In: Binstock, R. & George, L. (Eds.), *Handbook of Aging and the Social Sciences*, 4th edn. Academic Press, San Diego, pp. 254–82.

Center for Disease Control (2003) *Chartbook on Trends in the Health of Americans*. Online. www.cdc.gov/nchs/data/hus/hus03cht.pdf. Accessed April 6, 2004.

Choudhury, S. (2001) Race and Ethnic Differences in Wealth and Asset Choices. *Social Security Bulletin* 64(4).

Federal Interagency Forum on Aging-Related Statistics (2000) *Older Americans: 2000. Key Indicators of Well-Being*. US Government Printing Office, Washington, DC.

Gendell, M. (2001). Retirement Age Declines Again in the 1990s. *Monthly Labor Review* 124(10): 12–21.

Himes, C. (1992) Future Caregivers: Projected Family Structures of Older Persons. *Journal of Gerontology* 47(1): S17–26.

Himes, C. (2001) Elderly Americans. *Population Bulletin* 54, 4 (April).

Munnell, A. H., Hatch, R. E., & Lee, J. G. (2004) Why Is Life Expectancy So Low in the United States? Issue Brief #21, Center for Retirement Research, Boston College.

Murray, C. J. L. & Lopez, A. D. (1997) Alternative Projections of Mortality and Disability by Cause 1990–2020: Global Burden of Disease Study. *Lancet* 349: 1498–1504.

National Academy on an Aging Society (1999) Chronic Conditions: A Challenge for the 21st Century. *Data Profile*, Series 1, No. 1.

National Vital Statistics Reports (2004) Table 12. Estimated Life Expectancy at Birth in Years, by Race and Sex. Online. www.cdc.gov/nchs/data/dvs/nvsr52_14t12.pdf. Accessed April 6, 2004.

Pampel, F. (1983) Changes in the Propensity to Live Alone: Evidence from Consecutive Cross-Sectional Surveys, 1960–1976. *Demography* 20: 433–47.

Preston, S. & Martin, L. (1994) Introduction. In: Preston, S. & Martin, L. (Eds.), *Demography of Aging*. National Academy Press, Washington, DC, pp. 1–7.

Siegel, J. (1980) On the Demography of Aging. *Demography* 17(4): 345–64.

United Nations (1999) *The Sex and Age Distribution of the World Populations, 1998 Revision*. United Nations, New York.

US Census Bureau (2000a) Projections of the Total Resident Population by 5-Year Age Groups, Race, and Hispanic Origin with Special Age Categories: Middle Series, 1999 to 2070. Online. www.census.gov/population/www/projections/natsum-T3.html. Accessed April 8, 2004.

US Census Bureau (2000b) QT-P1. Age Groups and Sex: 2000. Online. factfinder.census.gov/. Accessed April 8, 2004.

US Census Bureau (2002) Table 3. Poverty Status of People, by Age, Race, and Hispanic Origin: 1959–2002. Online. www.census.gov/hhes/poverty/histpov/.

Utendorf, K. (2002) The Upper Part of the Earnings Distribution in the United States: How Has It Changed? *Social Security Bulletin* 64(3): 1–11.

aging and health policy

Jill Quadagno and Brandy D. Harris

In many nations, people 65 and older are the fastest growing segment of the population, with the most rapid growth occurring among the oldest old: individuals aged 85 and older. Illness and disability are not an inevitable component of advancing age. Many people remain in good health into very old age, and early diagnoses and treatment of conditions associated with aging combined with healthy lifestyle choices can mitigate the effects of age-related diseases and conditions. Nonetheless, population aging raises critical health policy issues because the elderly have more hospitalizations and more chronic conditions than younger people and use more prescription drugs and medical services (Solomon 1999).

Demographic trends indicate that health care systems are likely to experience unprecedented demands in the near future because health policies have not kept up with these demographic changes (Victor 1991: 63). Until the twentieth century, the major causes of death for individuals of all ages was from an acute infectious disease, that is, an illness or condition with a sudden onset, sharp rise, and short courses, such as tuberculosis, diphtheria, gastrointestinal infections, and pneumonia. Death rates from these diseases dropped dramatically in developed countries between 1900 and 1970 due to antibiotics and immunizations and public health measures such as improved sanitation and purification of the water supply. As deaths from acute diseases declined, there occurred an increase in life expectancy along with a higher prevalence of chronic disease such as arthritis, heart disease, osteoporosis, Alzheimer's disease, emphysema, and diabetes. While some chronic diseases have an apparently sudden onset (e.g., heart attack), they may in fact have long latent periods before symptoms are manifested (Solomon 1999).

Many national health programs were enacted in the post-World War II period. Services focused on acute medical care, reflecting the most pressing health care needs at that time. Yet population aging and the increase in chronic health conditions have altered the nature of service demands. Even when coverage for acute care is adequate, in many countries, chronic care for elderly people is poorly coordinated and inadequately provided because health care systems were not originally oriented to these problems. Yet chronic care service needs differ considerably from those required for treating acute disease. How well the chronic care needs of older people are met depends on many factors. The generosity of routinely provided medical benefits, particularly long-term therapies and prescription drugs, as well as treatment patterns of health professionals, are part of the equation. Availability of a full range of health and social care services needed to support chronic care is another (Manton & Stallard 1996).

The US does not guarantee universal access to health care (Quadagno 2005). Most non-poor children and working-aged adults are covered by employment-based private health insurance, but anywhere from 14–18 percent lack medical insurance altogether (Hacker 2002). Government programs only cover people who are "uninsurable" in the private health insurance market. Medicare is a federal program that pays for hospital care and physician services for the elderly and disabled. It pays for approximately 54 percent of older Americans' health care expenses. Medicaid is a joint federal–state health insurance program for the very poor, but also pays for a substantial amount of nursing home care for the chronically ill. Because gaps in Medicare coverage (deductibles, co-payments, prescription drug costs, etc.) leave many acute health care needs unmet, two-thirds of elderly Medicare beneficiaries purchase supplemental "medigap" policies from private insurance companies. However, many beneficiaries of color are not able to purchase private supplemental insurance because of cost. They either rely on Medicaid for additional coverage or shoulder the burden themselves (Williams 2004).

How the prevalence of chronic disease and need for care among elderly people will be expressed in the future is unknown. If improved health behaviors and medical advances succeed in limiting or minimizing chronic conditions, there could be a compression of morbidity, with people experiencing fewer years of chronic illness and living longer, healthier lives (Manton & Stallard 1996). Alternatively, increased future longevity could be accompanied by longer periods of disabling chronic disease processes occurring, or more sick elderly people with a high need for long-term care services.

Research suggests that the compression of morbidity thesis is more accurate. People are living longer and experiencing fewer years of incapacitation. Results from the National Long Term Care Survey (NLTCS) reveal that from 1982 to 1999, disability rates among people over age 65 decreased about 2 percent per year (Fries 2003). The dilemma for health policy is that while a compression of morbidity may decrease the need for residential and institutional care, it may also increase dependence on technological interventions and prescription drugs to help sustain aging individuals' capacity for self-care. Between 1984 and 1999 the percentage of older Americans utilizing assistive devices for a disability increased from 13 percent to 26 percent (FIFARS 2004).

Further, overall trends mask significant differences in health care access and cost by race, income, and health status. Elderly people with more education and higher socioeconomic status are likely to experience a compression of morbidity, while low-income elderly and racial minorities may experience greater incapacity and thus rely more heavily upon the health care programs (Fries 2000). Past experience suggests that this is the case. Among Medicare enrollees age 65 and older (for 1992 to 2001), the average cost of health care for non–Hispanic blacks was higher than costs for either non–Hispanic whites and Hispanics. Moreover, Medicare enrollees who reportedly had no chronic health conditions paid approximately $11,900 less, on average, than those who reported five or more chronic conditions (CMS 2004).

Concerns about how governments will finance both the acute and chronic care costs of an aging population have been the central issue in most recent health policy debates. Many countries are struggling to integrate fragmented systems of treatment and community support to provide appropriate chronic care for their aging populations. Health care policymaking in the future is likely to involve some targeting of benefits to the older, poorer, more disabled population.

SEE ALSO: Aging and Social Policy; Aging and Social Support; Aging, Mental Health, and Well-Being; Aging, Sociology of; Health Care Delivery Systems; Health Maintenance Organization; Leisure, Aging and

REFERENCES AND SUGGESTED READINGS

Centers for Medicare and Medicaid Services (CMS) (2004) *2000 Medicare Current Beneficiary Survey (MCBS)*. CMS, Baltimore.

Federal Interagency Forum on Aging-Related Statistics (FIFARS) (2004) *Older Americans 2004: Key Indicators of Well Being*. US Government Printing Office, Washington, DC.

Fries, J. (1980) Aging, Natural Death, and the Compression of Morbidity. *New England Journal of Medicine* 303: 130–5.

Fries, J. (2000) Compression of Morbidity in the Elderly. *Vaccine* 18: 1584–9.

Fries, J. (2003) Measuring and Monitoring Success in Compressing Morbidity. *Annals of Internal Medicine* 139(5): 455–9.

Hacker, J. S. (2002) *The Divided Welfare State.* Cambridge University Press, Cambridge.

Manton, K. & Stallard, E. (1996) Changes in Health, Mortality, and Disability and Their Impact on Long-Term Care Needs. *Journal of Aging and Social Policy* 7(3): 25–51.

Quadagno, J. (2005) *One Nation, Uninsured: Why the US Has No National Health Insurance.* Oxford University Press, New York.

Solomon, D. H. (1999) The Role of Aging Processes in Aging-Dependent Diseases. In: Bengtson, V. & Schaie, K. W. (Eds.), *Handbook of Theories of Aging.* Springer, New York, pp. 133–50.

Victor, C. (1991) *Health and Health Care in Later Life.* Open University Press, Buckingham.

Williams, R. (2004) Medicare and Communities of Color. *National Academy of Social Insurance,* Medicare Brief No. 11.

aging and the life course, theories of

Angela M. O'Rand

The life course perspective provides an orienting framework for identifying the mechanisms that link lives and social structures in historical time. It focuses on the intersection between biography and history (Mills 1959). Accordingly, the conceptualization of time is a central concern. *Biographical time* is defined by the links between chronological age, psychophysical development and/or decline, and successive social statuses. *Biographies* are variable sequences of social statuses across the life span, with some statuses (but not all) highly correlated with chronological age. *Historical time* also has chronological and social components, with the latter tied to events or periods that exert differential influences on biographies.

Age, period, and *cohort* are core concepts in the life course perspective. Briefly defined, age refers to biographical time; period refers to historical time; and cohort refers to a group whose members experience a particular event at the same time in their lives. Persons born at the same time constitute a birth cohort. As they age they come to encounter historical events from a different social vantage point than other birth cohorts. So, for example, members of the US baby boom cohort, born between 1946 and 1964, face historical events such as the Vietnam War or the stock market bubble of the 1990s, and experience them differently from other birth cohorts because of their age and life course statuses during those events (Hughes & O'Rand 2004).

The life course framework is founded on three general principles. The first is the *age stratification principle* or the conceptualization that age is an independent social basis for differentiation and inequality across societies. First, age is a gauge of human development, marking some largely universal psychophysical transitions in the aging process from birth to death. Human development is a product of the coevolution of the brain and its cognitive capacity with a long life span, an extended period of juvenile dependence on parents/caretakers, and a complex familial organization for provisioning offspring until they reach adulthood (Kaplan et al. 2000). Hence, age has an underlying biological component that differentiates and stratifies developmental statuses. Second, age is also a social construction, defined by institutional arrangements that allocate individuals into social statuses, such as student, voter, and retiree, on the basis of age. Social allocation on the basis of age distributes resources and advantages unequally by defining rights and obligations.

The second principle may be termed the *heterogeneity principle*. This refers to processes of social differentiation as increasing functions of age. Birth cohorts may live through history together, but they do not experience that history similarly because of two sources of differentiation. First, birth cohorts are themselves heterogeneous in socially meaningful ways from the beginning. Gender, race, class, and geographical locations are among the initial differences within cohorts that anchor the

trajectories of lives and condition opportunities and actions over time. The baby boom cohort is not a homogeneous group, but one highly stratified by education, work history, race/ethnicity, and other meaningful social characteristics (Hughes & O'Rand 2004). Second, individual lives become increasingly differentiated within cohorts over time because later life statuses (such as wealth status or disability) are affected by social origins and by highly variable and interdependent transitions that intervene across several domains of life, including education, family, work and health, from birth to death. Levels of educational attainment, employment stability, marital stability, and health maintenance, along with personal responses to these life events across the life course, interact in complex ways to increase differentiation with age. These diverse life trajectories can also be deflected by historical events, which can have more severe consequences for some members of a cohort than for others. Glen Elder's extensive studies of the impacts of war, depression, and economic hardship repeatedly demonstrate the diversity of experiences with history within cohorts (e.g., Elder 1998; Conger & Elder 1995).

The *demographic principle* refers to changing aggregate patterns of lives that are responses to changing historical circumstances and stratified opportunities. These are the day-to-day behavioral responses of individuals to their life conditions that, in the aggregate, can exert forces for social change. For example, the baby boom was unexpected. Fertility behavior in the century before the baby boom and following it exhibited a long-term trend of declining fertility. However, the post-World War II economy and culture led to changes in fertility behavior including earlier and larger families. Since the post-World War II period, even more demographic changes have occurred, including increased labor force participation among young mothers, delayed fertility until middle age, and rising divorce and serial marriage, all of which are challenging traditional institutions associated with the family and the market.

This principle challenges the age stratification process that has differentiated the life course along strict age criteria. Matilda White

Riley and her colleagues (e.g., Riley et al. 1994) proposed a theory of structural lag in the 1990s, which argued that changing demographic patterns associated with increased active life expectancy and the delayed onset of disability (among other factors) have made age-based public policies associated with work and retirement obsolete and counterproductive for society. However, even more compelling was their argument that the life course is shifting in nearly every respect away from age differentiation to age integration. Figure 1 is an expanded version of the Riley age integration model of the new life course. It portrays the shift from an age-differentiated conception of the life course, in which social statuses in youth, middle age, and old age are strictly separated, to an age-integrated life course over which statuses and status transitions can recur and co-occur across ages and domains of life. Work and parenthood can occur early in life; education may continue later in life; parenthood may also extend to later life and be accompanied by family roles associated with assisting elderly parents; remarriage and new family formation can continue well into older

ages. In addition, changes occurring in one domain of life at any time (e.g., divorce in middle age) can trigger changes in other domains of life (e.g., returning to school, entering the labor force, a decline in mental health). The figure captures the dynamics among the three principles of the life course perspective noted earlier: age stratification, heterogeneity, and demographic pressure.

FROM PERSPECTIVE TO THEORY

These basic elements of the life course perspective are products of the convergence of several sociological traditions over the last three decades. Since Ryder's classic essay (1965), social demography has steadily contributed to the life course perspective through the development of dynamic models of life transitions such as marriage, fertility, and employment and their interdependence across historical contexts (e.g., Oppenheimer et al. 1997). Status attainment theory has moved in the same direction by steadily elaborating the relationship between social origins and later-life

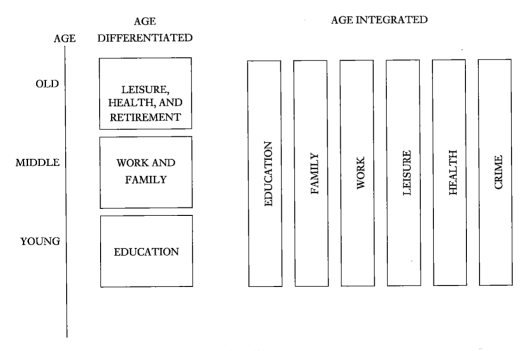

Figure 1 Expanded age integration model of the life course.

achievements across cohorts (Bernhardt et al. 2001). Criminology has developed trajectories of criminal careers and their turning points in varying contexts (Sampson & Laub 2003). And social gerontology has steadily turned to estimating the influences of earlier life patterns, including childhood origins, on later-life economic well-being and health (O'Rand 2001).

This convergence has not generated a unifying theory per se. Rather, efforts to develop middle-range theories within the life course perspective continue. Some of these are focused at the personological level. In this vein, Glen Elder and his colleagues have proposed several mechanisms of human development across the body of his work (e.g., Elder & Caspi 1990). The first two are borrowed from Ryder's (1965) classic paper on cohorts and social change, the remaining from life course research that has emerged over four decades.

- *The life stage hypothesis*: Social change and historical events have enduring (imprinting) impact on the lives of those in vulnerable and/or transitional statuses at the times of these events. The transition to adulthood is especially fateful in its long-term effects.
- *The situational imperative hypothesis*: The level of disruption and compelling severity of an event induces cohort variability. Exposures to wars, to large-scale depressions and similar big events, and to highly disruptive proximate events such as family dissolution, job loss, or incarceration, have greater effects on the life course than less severe events.
- *The interdependent lives hypothesis*: Social ties serve to diffuse experiences within a cohort such that long-term consequences are felt not only by individuals with direct experiences, but also by those associated with these individuals. Families share each other's experiences.
- *The accentuation principle*: New situations increase the salience of prominent individual attributes and lead to their reinforcement and accentuation over the life course. Ascribed attributes, and attributes developed early in life (such as temperament, aspiration, sociability), are reinforced

and amplified over the life course, and especially in the face of adversity.

Other efforts are generating theories at a structural level. One of the more provocative theoretical developments in this regard addresses life course stratification within cohorts based on the cumulative dis/advantage hypothesis (O'Rand 2002), which predicts that cohort differentiation over the life course is increasingly stratified in the direction of initial inequality (following Merton's "Matthew Effect"). Institutional processes preferentially reward early advantages and penalize early disadvantages over time in a cumulative fashion. These processes are embedded in normative schedules of achievement, organizational time-clocks of advancement, and socioeconomic compounding and discounting regimes that cumulatively appreciate or depreciate earlier achievements. They are observable in patterns of economic inequality and health disparities in mid- and late life in which socioeconomic origins and early educational achievements exert enduring independent effects on these later outcomes. These factors become embedded in historical contexts that can introduce obstacles to, or incentives for, cumulative effects.

In short, the life course perspective has been useful as an organizing framework for the study of lives over time with its focus on the intersection of biography with history. Its usefulness has spanned research on diverse domains of life, ranging from education to family, work, health, and even criminal careers. It has also spawned middle-range hypotheses to account for the changing temporal organization of lives over time.

SEE ALSO: Age, Period, and Cohort Effects; Aging, Demography of; Aging, Longitudinal Studies; Aging, Sociology of; Gerontology, Key Thinkers; Life Course and Family; Life Course Perspective

REFERENCES AND SUGGESTED READINGS

Bernhardt, A., Morris, M., Handcock, M. S., & Scott, M. A. (2001) *Divergent Paths: Economic Mobility in the New American Labor Market*. Russell Sage Foundation, New York.

Conger, R. D. & Elder, G. H., Jr. (1995) *Families in Troubled Times: Adapting to Change in Rural America*. Aldine de Gruyter, Hawthorne, NY.

Elder, G. H., Jr. (1998) The Life Course and Human Development. In: Lerner, R. M. (Ed.), *Handbook of Child Psychology*. Vol. 1: *Theoretical Models of Human Development*. Wiley, New York, pp. 939–91.

Elder, G. H., Jr. & Caspi, A. (1990) Studying Lives in a Changing Society: Sociological and Personological Explorations. In: Rabin, A. I., Zucker, R. A., & Frank, S. (Eds.), *Studying Persons and Lives*. Springer, New York, pp. 201–47.

Hughes, M. E. & O'Rand, A. M. (2004) *The Lives and Times of the Baby Boomers*. Russell Sage Foundation/Population Reference Bureau, New York and Washington, DC.

Kaplan, H., Hill, K., Lancaster, J., & Hurtado, A. M. (2000) A Theory of Human Life History Evolution: Diet, Intelligence and Longevity. *Evolutionary Anthropology* 9: 1–30.

Mills, C. W. (1959) *The Sociological Imagination*. Oxford University Press, New York.

Oppenheimer, V. K., Kalmijn, M., & Lim, N. (1997) Men's Career Development and Marriage Timing During a Period of Rising Inequality. *Demography* 34: 311–30.

O'Rand, A. M. (2001) The Cumulative Stratification of the Life Course: The Forms of Life Course Capital and their Interdependence. In: Binstock, R. H. & George, L. K. (Eds.), *Handbook of Aging and the Life Course*. Academic Press, New York, pp. 197–213.

O'Rand, A. M. (2002) Cumulative Advantage Theory in Life Course Research. In: Srystal, S. & Shea, D. (Eds.), *Annual Review of Gerontology and Geriatrics. Focus on Economic Outcomes in Later Life: Public Policy, Health and Cumulative Advantage* 22: 14–30.

Riley, M. W., Kahn, R. L., & Foner, A. (1994) *Age and Structural Lag: Society's Failure to Provide Meaningful Opportunities in Work, Family and Leisure*. Wiley, New York.

Ryder, N. B. (1965). The Cohort as a Concept in the Study of Social Change. *American Sociological Review* 30: 843–61.

Sampson, R. J. & Laub, J. H. (2003) Desistance from Crime over the Life Course. In: Mortimer, J. & Shanahan, M. (Eds.), *Handbook of the Life Course*. Kluwer Academic/Plenum, New York, pp. 295–310.

Sweeney, M. M. (2002) Two Decades of Family Change: The Shifting Economic Foundations of Marriage. *American Sociological Review* 67: 132–47.

aging, longitudinal studies

Duane F. Alwin

Historically, the concept of aging refers to changes to individuals that occur over time resulting from some combination of biological, psychological, and social mechanisms. The life span developmental perspective is a somewhat broader framework, as it considers aging to begin at birth and conceptualizes human development as multidimensional and multidirectional processes of growth involving both gains and losses. From this perspective, human development and aging are embedded in multiple contexts and are conceived of in terms of dynamic processes in which the ontogeny of development interacts with the social environment, a set of interconnected social settings, embedded in a multi-layered social and cultural context. In addition, the uniqueness of individual biographies and the diversity of life patterns have encouraged a life course approach to human development within the social sciences. The study of the life course is primarily concerned with the social pathways defined by events and transitions experienced by individuals and the sequences of roles and experiences followed by individuals over particular phases of their lives. Influences of development, maturation, and aging are usually identified with changes within individuals linked to their getting older, becoming more mature due to having lived more of life, having experienced a variety of different life course events, or due to physical, cognitive, or other kinds of developmental change. For simplicity, we often refer to all of these types of "within-person" change as the effects of (or consequences of) aging.

How do students of aging, life span development, and the life course study the causes and consequences of within-person change? Several different approaches have been used by researchers interested in the causes and consequences of within-person change with respect to outcomes of interest (outcomes typically related to health, disability, or cognitive functioning), but the emerging consensus among students of aging is that research designs that collect measurements on the same persons over time are a particularly valuable approach to studying the causes and consequences of aging. Any research design that locates and measures events and processes in time is referred to as *longitudinal*. There are a variety of types of longitudinal designs, including everything from complicated life-history calendars, which go to great lengths to date events, their timing and duration, on the one hand, to retrospective life histories presented in narrative form, on the other (see Scott & Alwin 1998).

Still, perhaps the most common approach in the study of aging is the one-shot cross-sectional study in which researchers simply compare age groups and from such comparisons draw inferences about aging. One of the critical problems with the one-shot cross-sectional studies is that they confuse the potential effects of aging with the influences of cohort factors (see Mason & Fienberg 1985). Persons of a particular age at a given point in time are also members of the same birth cohort (i.e., persons born during the same year). Members of a particular birth cohort share the experience of the life cycle; that is, they experience birth, infancy, and childhood, reach adolescence, grow into early adulthood, and mature into midlife and old age during the same historical time. In this sense, members of a birth cohort share a social history; that is, they experience the same historical events and the opportunities and constraints posed by society at a given time in history. A person's *cohort* membership may be thought to index the unique historical period in which a group's common experiences are embedded, and their behavior may have as much to do with their historical experiences as they do with their age.

It is important to realize that one-shot cross-sectional designs are *not* inherently limited, especially if they involve the replication of cross-sections over time. The existence of *diachronic* cross-sectional data for the same cohorts can be used as a legitimate basis for separating the effects of aging and cohort effects under certain circumstances (see Alwin et al. 2005). Another way to control for cohort differences is to study a single cohort over time. Eaton (2002) provides a strong rationale for studying a single

cohort from conception to death. In this type of single-cohort study, age variation occurs over time rather than cross-sectionally, and this permits an explicit focus on within-person change. However, development and aging do not occur in a historical vacuum, and while studying a single cohort over time does hold many variables constant, it is difficult to generalize about processes of aging because of the confounding influences of aging and history.

Having information on the same persons across a range of birth cohorts – a multiple cohort longitudinal study design – opens up several possibilities for analyzing the effects of aging across cohorts. The value of this type of longitudinal design is borne out by the vast number of research projects over the past few decades that locate and measure events and processes *in time* (see Young et al. 1991). Indeed, we have reached a point where there are several longitudinal data sets that permit the study of patterns and processes of aging in different historical and cultural contexts. For example, in the US, the series of panel surveys known as the Health and Retirement Study (HRS) provides a series of replicated longitudinal studies of a sequence of birth cohorts currently and in the future. The first of these began in 1992 as a panel survey of persons from cohorts born in 1931 through 1941 and re-interviewed biennially since then. The idea for the HRS derived from a growing awareness of the inadequacy of data available from the Retirement History Survey that began in 1969 and followed a set of cohorts of men and unmarried women born in 1906 through 1911 for ten years. Basing one's inferences about processes of aging, it was argued, on such a limited spectrum of historical cohorts had obvious limitations, given, for example, the growing participation of women in the labor force and related changes in the family. The collection of data on health and other antecedents of work and retirement decisions for more recent cohorts was viewed as essential to understanding experiences related to processes of aging in the more contemporary social context.

The assessment of change over time is fundamental to the quantitative study of aging, and longitudinal designs are vastly superior to cross-sectional studies in their ability to reveal causal influences in social processes because they can better pinpoint the temporal order of events, conditions, and experiences. Of course, even the best longitudinal data are unlikely to firmly resolve many substantive issues of this sort, in that there will still be relevant variables that are omitted from the design, limitations of sampling, measurement imperfections, and other impediments to drawing causal inferences. On the other hand, longitudinal data permit one to address far more interesting questions than is possible with cross-sectional data. Longitudinal data are also essential for examining issues linked to life course theory, which focuses primarily on the developmental or age-related patterns of change over the lifespan that are embedded in social institutions and subject to historical variation and change.

Generally, in research on aging and the life course virtually all the best designs for studying life course phenomena are *longitudinal* because they allow one to conceptualize more accurately the nature of the substantive phenomenon and locate lives in time. This requirement strongly implies the need for repeated longitudinal studies based on sequences of birth cohorts (see Alwin et al. 2005). Still, there are several major impediments to drawing inferences about change and its sources, even with longitudinal data. Perhaps the most fundamental of these is to be able to locate events and processes in time and specify their causal relation to consequences or outcome variables, while taking other causal factors into account.

Finally, longitudinal designs also fit well with the newer perspectives linking the demography of the life course to human development. If one takes a lifespan developmental perspective with respect to the study of processes of aging (including life cycle processes and life course events and transitions) and recognizes that human lives are embedded in social and historical contexts, it is clear that a range of ontogenic and sociogenic factors impinges on people's lives in ways that affect their well-being. Capturing the interlocking trajectories or pathways across the life span that are marked by sequences of events or social transitions which impact upon individual lives and relating them to measures of health and functioning (among other things), as well as linking them to underlying social

processes, is an important focus of a great deal of research on aging, and these are the major theoretical concerns that drive the present discussion of longitudinal methods for the study of aging and human development.

SEE ALSO: Aging, Demography of; Aging and the Life Course, Theories of; Aging, Sociology of; Life Course; Life Course Perspective

REFERENCES AND SUGGESTED READINGS

Alwin, D. F., Hofer, S. M., & McCammon, R. J. (2005) Modeling the Effects of Time: Integrating Demographic and Developmental Perspectives. In: Binstock, R. H. & George, L. K. (Eds.), *Handbook of Aging and the Social Sciences*, 6th edn. Academic Press, New York.

Alwin, D. F., McCammon, R. J., & Hofer, S. M. (2005) Studying Baby Boom Cohorts within a Demographic and Developmental Context: Conceptual and Methodological Issues. In: Whitbourne, S. K. & Willis, S. L. (Eds.), *The Baby Boomers at Midlife: Contemporary Perspectives on Middle Age*. Lawrence Erlbaum Associates, Mahwah, NJ.

Eaton, W. W. (2002) The Logic for a Conception-to-Death Cohort Study. *Annals of Epidemiology* 12: 445–51.

Mason, W. M. & Fienberg, S. E. (1985) *Cohort Analysis in Social Research: Beyond the Identification Problem*. Springer-Verlag, New York.

Scott, J. & Alwin, D. F. (1998) Retrospective Versus Prospective Measurement of Life Histories in Longitudinal Research. In: Giele, J. Z. & Elder, Jr., G. H. (Eds.), *Methods of Life Course Research: Qualitative and Quantitative Approaches*. Sage, Thousand Oaks, CA, pp. 98–127.

Young, C., Savola, K., & Phelps, E. (1991) *Inventory of Longitudinal Studies in the Social Sciences*. Sage, Newbury Park, CA.

aging, mental health, and well-being

Linda K. George

Social factors are strongly implicated in mental health and well-being throughout life, including old age. Sociologists argue that mental health and subjective well-being are powerful indicators of how well societies serve their members both individually and collectively. That is, effective societies not only meet the basic needs of their members, but also provide the conditions and opportunities that sustain emotional health and perceptions that life is good.

Three topics regarding aging, mental health, and well-being are reviewed here: descriptive information about the distribution and dynamics of mental health and subjective well-being in late life, evidence about the social antecedents of mental health and subjective well-being in late life, and the role of social factors in the course and outcome of late-life depression.

THE EPIDEMIOLOGY OF MENTAL HEALTH AND WELL-BEING IN LATE LIFE

The vast majority of Americans are relatively free of psychiatric or emotional symptoms and are generally satisfied with their lives. This pattern is at least as strong for older adults as for young and middle-aged adults. It is important to define the terms "mental health" and "subjective well-being" in both conceptual and empirical terms. Subjective well-being is the more straightforward of the two and is generally conceptualized as perceptions that life is satisfying and meaningful. Typical measurement strategies include a global self-assessment of life satisfaction (e.g., as unsatisfying, somewhat satisfying, and very satisfying), multi-item life satisfaction scales, and, more recently, multidimensional scales that tap several aspects of life quality (e.g., life satisfaction, purpose in life, self-acceptance). Each measurement strategy has characteristic strengths and weaknesses. The global rating is easily and quickly administered, but generates limited variability. Life satisfaction scales generate more variability than global self-ratings, but often include items that arguably measure the conditions that generate satisfaction with life in addition to subjective well-being. The conceptual and empirical clarity of multidimensional scales is even more problematic. For example, "high-quality social relationships" is one of the subscales of the most commonly used multidimensional scale. Most sociologists, however, view social bonds as a predictor of subjective well-being rather than an element of it.

Defining and measuring mental health is even more problematic. Although the label "mental health" is typically used, in fact investigators define and measure emotional distress and dysfunction rather than mental health. Two distinctions are sources of controversy among researchers. The first quandary is whether to measure overall psychological distress, regardless of the types of symptoms individuals experience, or whether to measure specific psychiatric syndromes such as depression and anxiety. At this point, both approaches are used, although the latter is more common. The second controversy is whether to use diagnostic measures of the presence or absence of mental illness or to use symptom scales that are used in continuous form. Again, there are countervailing advantages and disadvantages. Diagnostic measures have the advantage of identifying severe cases of mental illness, rendering findings of interest to clinicians and policymakers, as well as to sociologists. The disadvantage of diagnostic measures is that they have limited variability and ignore much of the significant distress caused by emotional symptoms that do not meet the criteria for a full-blown psychiatric diagnosis. In contrast, the advantage of symptom scales is that they capture the full range of psychiatric symptoms in the population, but focus on a distribution in which most "symptomatic" individuals suffer few if any functional consequences from their symptoms. Although discussion of these issues is often heated, empirical evidence suggests that the relationships between social factors and diagnostic vs. symptom scales of a specific syndrome vs. psychological distress are highly similar (Kessler 2002; Mirowsky & Ross 1989).

Sociologists initially hypothesized that older adults would be disadvantaged in life satisfaction relative to their younger counterparts as a result of the social and physical losses characteristic of late life. Contrary to this hypothesis, older adults report significantly higher satisfaction with life, on average, than young and middle-aged adults, although the differences are substantively modest (Campbell et al. 1976). These age differences have been consistent for more than 30 years and do not result from older adults being more advantaged than young and middle-aged adults in objective life conditions (Horley & Lavery 1995). Aspiration theory explains age differences in life satisfaction. According to this theory, individuals are satisfied with life when there is little discrepancy between their aspirations and their achievements and, conversely, are dissatisfied when there is a large discrepancy. Older adults' higher levels of subjective well-being result from their lower aspirations, on average, than those of young and middle-aged persons. It remains unclear whether these age differences result from cohort differences or the dynamics of aging.

One cannot understand age distributions of mental illness without taking into account the difference between organic and non-organic psychiatric disorders. Organic disorders involve structural changes in the anatomy of the brain and include dementia. These disorders are typically and appropriately not included in sociological investigations. Non-organic diagnoses include depressive disorders, anxiety disorders, psychotic disorders, and substance use disorders (alcohol, illegal drugs, abuse of prescribed medications). Most sociological studies focus on depression; thus, social epidemiology is primarily the study of the distribution of depression.

Depression in later life exhibits an epidemiologic paradox. Rates of depressive disorder (i.e., disorder meeting diagnostic standards) are lowest among older adults, highest among young adults, and intermediate among middle-aged adults. But a different pattern is observed for depressive symptoms, where the oldest old report higher levels of symptoms than adults of other ages (Blazer et al. 1991; Mirowsky & Ross 1989). Definitive evidence about the cause of this paradox of low diagnoses and high symptoms is lacking, but most observers believe that criteria other than the pure number of symptoms (e.g., persistence over time) exclude some older adults from qualifying for a diagnosis of depression.

SOCIAL ANTECEDENTS OF MENTAL HEALTH AND SUBJECTIVE WELL-BEING

A common, if not consensual, theory of the social precursors of depression in later life is emerging in the research literature (George 2004). Loosely speaking, it is a model of stratification or social disadvantage and stress. The general premise is that social disadvantage puts individuals on pathways that expose them to more proximate determinants of depression and distress. Although applications of the basic model utilize both cross-sectional and longitudinal data, it is a stage model of increasingly proximate predictors of psychiatric disorders in general and depression or distress in particular. There are five stages in the model.

The first, most distal stage includes basic demographic variables (e.g., age, sex, race, or ethnicity) that represent fundamental aspects of social location and are in fact bases of stratification in society. The second stage includes measures of early events and achievements, most commonly educational attainment and childhood traumas (e.g., child abuse, sexual abuse, parental divorce). The third stage includes indicators of later achievements, primarily SES (occupation, income) and family characteristics (marital status, fertility history). As a group, the first three stages provide fairly extensive information about social status. The general hypothesis is that disadvantaged status increases the risk of depression and distress.

The fourth stage of the model includes indicators of social integration. The most commonly used indicators measure personal attachments to social structure, such as organizational and religious participation. More recently, investigators have examined the effects of characteristics of the residential environment, such as measures of disorganization and transience, poverty levels, and rates of criminal victimization. Personal attachments to social structure are expected to decrease the risk of depression and distress; residence in disorganized, poor, and unsafe neighborhoods is expected to increase risk. The fifth stage of the model includes the most proximate antecedents of depression and distress and includes both vulnerability and protective factors. The major vulnerability or provoking factors investigated are chronic stressors and stressful life events. Two types of protective factors are typically examined. The first and most widely studied is social support: the tangible and intangible assistance that individuals receive from family and friends. Psychosocial resources such as self-esteem, mastery, and sense of control are also often included in models of the precursors of depression and distress.

This model is rarely tested in its entirety. Nonetheless, there is strong evidence supporting it. All of the social factors in the model are significant predictors of depression and distress, both in late life and in adulthood more broadly (e.g., George 1992; Holahan & Moos 1991). One of the advantages of the model is its stages of increasingly proximate predictors. Substantial evidence indicates that many of the variables in earlier stages of the model have limited direct effects of depression and distress, but have large indirect effects via more proximate predictors. The effects of demographic variables and SES are mostly indirect, exerting their effects on depression by increasing levels of stress exposure, including ambient, environmental stressors, decreasing the resources and assistance available from social support networks, and decreasing individuals' levels of psychosocial resources (e.g., Turner & Lloyd 1999).

Comparison of research based on older samples with those from age-heterogeneous samples reveals only a few rather subtle, but important differences. The most distinctive aspect of depression and distress in later life is the prominent role of physical illness and disability in increasing risk of depression. Many studies suggest that physical illness and/or disability is the strongest single predictor of depression and distress; in contrast, physical health is of negligible importance during young adulthood and middle age (George 1992). In contrast, demographic variables are weaker predictors of depression and distress in late life than earlier in adulthood. Racial or ethnic differences are minimally important during later life and even gender differences in depression, which are very large in young adulthood, narrow substantially by late life.

It is important to note that this model has proven useful in predicting both dichotomous diagnostic measures and continuous symptom scales. The strongest evidence of the power of social factors to predict depression comes from studies in which social factors are shown prospectively to predict the onset of depressive disorder among persons who are not depressed at baseline (i.e., in a true onset study). To date, there have been only a few studies of the onset of depressive disorder among older adults (George 1992; Green et al. 1992); their results strongly support this model of the social antecedents of depression.

The theoretical foundations of research on subjective well-being in late life are less sophisticated than those for depression and distress and were best articulated by Campbell, Converse, and Rodgers 30 years ago. Campbell and colleagues argued that perceptions of well-being are based on the objective conditions of life. Thus, they hypothesized that satisfaction with life would be a function of economic and social resources. They suggested that the major research questions of interest are whether the objective conditions relevant to self-appraisals of well-being differed across population subgroups and whether the levels of resources required for positive appraisals differed across population subgroups. Their research revealed that regardless of age, gender, education, and race or ethnicity, perceptions of well-being rested on the same basic set of life conditions. Economic security, high-quality social relationships, and health are, not surprisingly, the strongest predictors of subjective well-being. Other life domains, including leisure, the residential environment, and job satisfaction are significant, but substantially weaker predictors. Population subgroups differed, however, in the amount of resources needed to produce high levels of life satisfaction. For the purposes at hand, the most relevant finding is that older adults, on average, require substantially lower levels of resources than young and middle-aged adults to perceive their lives as satisfying (i.e., lower incomes, smaller social networks, less robust health). Note that these findings were based on cross-sectional data.

After three decades, findings from pioneering studies of subjective well-being have stood the test of time. Since then, research on

subjective well-being in late life has been aug-
mented in two primary ways. First, akin to
the "positive psychology" movement, some
sociologists suggest that if we want to study
mental health, rather than mental illness, subjective well-being is an appropriate outcome.
Consequently, recent investigations have
added many of the elements of the model of
the social antecedents of depression and distress to the study of subjective well-being,
especially stressors (e.g., Krause 1986). Results
of those studies indicate that high levels of
stress dampen levels of life satisfaction mod-
estly, but their effects are much weaker than
those for basic social resources such as economic security and health. Second, some
investigators have used longitudinal research
to determine the extent to which social losses
that frequently occur in later life (e.g., widowhood, retirement, illness onset) trigger corresponding declines in subjective well-being.
Results indicate that life satisfaction is relatively insensitive to these types of losses and
transitions (Kunzmann et al. 2000). As a
result, most investigators view subjective
well-being as a relatively stable assessment of
life as a whole (i.e., across domains of experience and across biographical time).

SOCIAL FACTORS AND THE COURSE AND OUTCOME OF DEPRESSIVE DISORDER

The vast majority of research on social factors
and depression in late life examines social
factors as predictors of depressive symptoms
disorder. The assumption in these studies is
that social location, social disadvantage, and
social stress increase the risk of depression.
It also is possible, however, that social factors
predict the course and outcome of depression
(e.g., recovery, time till recovery, chronicity)
among depressed older adults. Only a few
studies have examined the role of social factors in recovery from depression – and
although social scientists have conducted this
research, most of it has been published in
psychiatry journals. Evidence to date demonstrates that three social factors are strong predictors of recovery from depression. Social
stress impedes recovery from depression,
lowering the odds of recovery and increasing
time till recovery (McPherson et al. 1993).
The effects of social support are even stronger
and, of course, in the opposite direction. Perceptions of adequate social support increase
the odds of recovery and predict shorter time
until recovery (Bosworth et al. 2002; George
et al. 1989). Religious participation also increases
the odds of recovery and shortens the time
till recovery (Koenig et al. 1998). In general,
sociologists have paid insufficient attention to
the role of social factors in facilitating or imped-
ing recovery from both physical and mental
illness, despite the fact that the limited evidence
available suggests that this is a profitable area
of inquiry.

SEE ALSO: Aging and Health Policy; Aging
and Social Support; Aging, Sociology of;
Elder Care; Medical Sociology; Mental Disorder; Stress and Health; Stress, Stress Theories; Stressful Life Events

REFERENCES AND SUGGESTED READINGS

Blazer, D. G., Burchett, B., Service, C., & George,
L. K. (1991) The Association of Age and Depres-
sion Among the Elderly: An Epidemiologic
Exploration. *Journals of Gerontology* 46: M210–13.

Bosworth, H. B., Hays, J. C., George, L. K., &
Steffens, D. C. (2002) Psychosocial and Clinical
Predictors of Unipolar Depression Outcome in
Older Adults. *International Journal of Geriatric
Psychiatry* 17: 238–46.

Campbell, A., Converse, P. E., & Rodgers, W. L.
(1976) *The Quality of American Life*. Russell Sage
Foundation, New York.

George, L. K. (1992) Social Factors and the Onset
and Outcome of Depression. In: Schaie, K. W.,
House, J. S., & Blazer, D. G. (Eds.), *Aging,
Health Behaviors, and Health Outcomes*. Lawrence Erlbaum, Hillsdale, NJ, pp. 137–59.

George, L. K. (2004) Social and Economic Factors
Related to Psychiatric Disorders in Late Life. In
Blazer, D. G., Steffens, D. C., & Busse, E. W.
(Eds.), *Textbook of Geriatric Psychiatry*, 3rd edn.
American Psychiatric Publishing, Washington,
DC, pp. 139–61.

George, L. K., Blazer, D. G., Hughes, D. C., &
Fowler, N. (1989) Social Support and the Out-
come of Major Depression. *British Journal of
Psychiatry* 154: 478–85.

Green, B. H., Copeland, J. R. M., Dewey, M. E., Sharma, V., Saunders, P. A., Davidson, I. A., Sullivan, C., & McWilliams, C. (1992) Risk Factors for Depression in Elderly People: A Prospective Study. *Acta Psychiatrica Scandinavia* 86: 213–17.

Holahan, C. J. & Moos, R. H. (1991) Life Stressors, Personal and Social Resources, and Depression: A 4-Year Structural Model. *Journal of Abnormal Psychology* 100: 31–6.

Horley, J. & Lavery, J. J. (1995) Subjective Well-Being and Age. *Social Indicators Research* 34: 275–82.

Kessler, R. C. (2002) The Categorical versus Dimensional Assessment Controversy in the Sociology of Mental Illness. *Journal of Health and Social Behavior* 43: 171–88.

Koenig, H. G., George, L. K., & Peterson, B. L. (1998) Religiosity and Remission of Depression in Medically Ill Older Patients. *American Journal of Psychiatry* 155: 536–42.

Krause, N. (1986) Social Support, Stress, and Well-Being among Older Adults. *Journal of Gerontology* 41: 512–19.

Kunzmann, U., Little, T. D., & Smith, J. (2000) Is Age-Related Stability of Subjective Well-Being a Paradox? Cross-Sectional and Longitudinal Evidence from the Berlin Aging Study. *Psychology and Aging* 15: 311–26.

McPherson, H., Herbison, P., & Romans, S. (1993) Life Events and Relapse in Established Bipolar Affective Disorder. *British Journal of Psychiatry* 163: 381–5.

Mirowsky, J. & Ross, C. E. (1989) Psychiatric Diagnosis as Reified Measurement. *Journal of Health and Social Behavior* 30: 11–24.

Turner, R. J. & Lloyd, D. A. (1999) The Stress Process and the Social Distribution of Depression. *Journal of Health and Social Behavior* 40: 374–404.

aging and social policy

Debra Street

All developed countries have social policies designed to meet income, health, and social needs of older citizens. Most less-developed countries, too, have at least some public programs explicitly designed to serve elderly people. While the particulars of such policies differ from place to place, social policies for aging populations have in common collective national efforts to improve health and income security for older people. The scope and breadth of such social policies is an important influence on the overall well-being of each country's elderly citizens. From a sociological perspective, both country-specific and comparative social policy research have focused on understanding how different configurations of social policies create outcomes that minimize, reinforce, or exacerbate late-life inequalities arising from social class, race or ethnicity, and gender. Besides analyzing how these status categories influence inequality, sociologists also research and theorize how the interplay of institutionalized life courses and social policies contributes to age stratification.

HISTORICAL DEVELOPMENT OF AGE-BASED SOCIAL POLICIES

Before the development of the modern welfare state, older people depended on mainly informal mechanisms when age or frailty dictated withdrawal from employment or impeded the capacity to undertake daily activities. Wealthy elderly people had sufficient resources to obtain whatever help they needed to remain independent. The vast majority of elderly people, however, turned to family and kin networks to help them survive in old age, particularly in pre-industrial times. As industrialization progressed throughout Western Europe and North America, more elderly people were displaced from traditional family roles in farming communities as younger family members took advantage of opportunities to work in towns and cities. For lone elders or for elders whose families were unable or unwilling to offer assistance to them in old age, locally based institutions – including poorhouses, asylums, and almshouses – provided food and shelter to elders unable to maintain their independence, whether through poverty or frailty. Some communities provided subsidies to "deserving" elders to enable them to avoid institutionalization, although such local practices varied widely.

TWENTIETH-CENTURY DEVELOPMENTS

By the beginning of the twentieth century, complex socioeconomic factors combined with political windows of opportunity, fostering initiatives throughout the industrialized world to address problems of modern industrial economies. Modern welfare states emerged, characterized by benefit programs designed to address the problems that rapid social change and industrialization imposed on individuals and their families. Public education, social assistance, unemployment and disability insurance, and health insurance were social policies devised to meet the needs of working-aged families.

At the other end of the age spectrum, social policies designed to provide retirement income and health and long-term care for elderly people emerged as integral components of national welfare states. Pension policies developed because, at the same time as modern improved public health measures and living conditions contributed to increased longevity, most individuals were confronted by an industrial workplace having scant use for older workers. Although some early twentieth-century employers offered pensions for retiring workers, most did not. Business failures during the Great Depression created mass unemployment among people of all ages, but elderly workers who were displaced had even less chance than younger ones of finding any employment. Without secure pensions, elderly people who could no longer work due to frailty, ill health, or lack of employment opportunities risked destitution in old age. The practice of nearly universal *retirement* from paid work that became institutionalized in the latter half of the twentieth century required public pension systems that provided secure income in old age.

Thus, some modern social policies like pensions were designed to benefit elderly people directly. Public pension systems were developed to manage labor markets and to secure later-life income for individuals (and their dependents) when they retired from paid work. Age was one criterion used to establish eligibility for public pension benefits. Many contemporary long-term care programs require old age (sometimes in combination with disability or low income) to meet eligibility requirements. Some social assistance programs also use age as a criterion for eligibility in combination with low income, such as Guaranteed Income Support in Canada, or Supplemental Security Income in the US. And when sociologists in the 1970s drew attention to the social exclusion many elderly individuals experienced in modern societies, many countries enacted additional policies to foster participation of elderly people in community life. For example, policies implemented under the Older Americans Act in the US sought to promote participation by providing inexpensive transportation for elderly clients, subsidizing activities and information centers, and supporting other socially integrative activities. Other countries enacted similar policies to promote social inclusion.

For other social policies, age is irrelevant as a basis for establishing eligibility, yet elderly people often benefit indirectly. For example, national health insurance is available to residents of all ages in most countries, although elderly people arguably benefit disproportionately from such policies because they use more health services than other age groups. Elderly people in retirement may also benefit indirectly through national tax structures that skew taxation more heavily towards earned employment income, rather than investment or pension income as in the US. Whether program eligibility and level of benefit distribution should most appropriately be based on age versus need is a longstanding debate in social policy circles in modern welfare state regimes.

Welfare state regimes are country-specific combinations of social policies that shape the distribution and redistribution of income and wealth across and within age groups. Social policies composing national welfare states were developed during the first half of the twentieth century, in response to population-wide problems (like ill health, unemployment, disability, and inadequate old age income) arising in modern industrial economies. Social welfare policies are most generous in social democratic welfare states, typified by Scandinavian countries, where eligibility is usually based on citizenship and programs and benefits are universal, comprehensive, and generous. In corporatist welfare states, typified by countries like France or Germany, social policies support families and maintain workplace status hierarchies, but with relatively comprehensive universal entitlement to benefits. In contrast, liberal welfare states, such as Canada, Great Britain, and the US, are characterized by a predominance of targeted rather than universal social policies, designed to provide public subsistence benefits only to individual "labor market failures" with low incomes. Old age stands out most sharply as an influence on social policy when considering the quality and quantity of publicly provided income security, regardless of welfare state type. Even in liberal welfare states, where social benefits are usually low and means-tested, elderly individuals have been treated as a historically "deserving" group entitled to relatively generous universal public pensions.

Social policies beyond pensions are also vital for the well-being of elderly populations, particularly those addressing their health, long-term care, and social needs. Except for the US, all developed countries provide universal health insurance for citizens regardless of age. Canada and Western European countries often have additional age-based specialty programs, such as subsidies for obtaining prescription drugs or adaptive technologies like eyeglasses and hearing aids. In contrast to other countries, the US relies on a patchwork of employment-based health insurance for working-age families, Medicaid for the poor, and Medicare, the universal health insurance program for the elderly. The age-based entitlement to public health insurance under Medicare marks the US as unique among all developed countries in terms of the relationship between age and access to health care.

Social policies shaping social services and long-term care systems benefiting elderly people differ across nations. One truism is that, regardless of place, most elder care is provided privately, within families. Nonetheless, family provision alone cannot meet all the complex needs of aging populations. In places like Sweden, relatively comprehensive long-term care policies take the form of purposefully designed, age-integrated housing developments, where most services elders need are provided to them under one roof. Another approach provides public income subsidies and pension credits for care providers (even care providing family members) to support in-home supportive care when required, as in Germany. While all countries have some combination of public programs for frail elders, they are seldom well integrated. Most other countries' elder social services and long-term care provision is characterized by fragmentation of services and gaps in meeting service needs, as is the case in North America and Great Britain. Despite some social service programs that compensate for age-related frailty or poor health through self-care promotion, the extent of public provision is insufficient to meet need. Which types, how much, and where (whether in an individual's home, a congregate day site, or a nursing home or residential care setting) supportive social and long-term care services are publicly provided also varies substantially from country to country.

As important as such health and supportive long-term care policies have been for elders' well-being, the undeniable centerpiece of age-based social policies is the evolving system of national retirement income programs. National pension systems were initiated at different times, under different sociopolitical conditions, and with varying degrees of generosity and scope of coverage. Countries like New Zealand and the Scandinavian countries led the way in early development of comprehensive pension policies to address income adequacy for elderly citizens. In the aftermath of the Depression, the US implemented Social Security, a redistributive, earnings-related, universal public pension. Canada and Great Britain implemented flat-rate citizens' pensions prior to World War II, adding an earnings-related public pension tier only after the war. By the 1960s, most industrialized countries offered public pensions systems that offered an adequate floor of protection against destitution in old age; some offered generous public pensions. Other countries, like Great Britain and the US, relied heavily on private pensions to provide income adequacy in retirement. Parallel developments in private industrial pensions actually had a quasi-public character, in that they were state-regulated and subsidized in tax systems.

Throughout the twentieth century, public pension systems in industrialized countries were reformed, adapting to new conditions in workplaces and trends in national economies. In the relatively affluent and optimistic decades following the end of World War II, virtually all western countries expanded public pension systems and improved benefits. During the same period, industrial workplaces, particularly unionized ones, featured employers offering parallel systems of increasingly generous private employment-based pensions for long-serving employees. By the mid-1970s, enhancements to public pensions throughout the developed countries and the tandem expansion of public and private pensions created an apparent "golden age" of pensions, guaranteeing individuals the right to "cease work before wearing out" (Myles 1989).

Despite the 1970s optimism surrounding the institutionalization of retirement with secure pension income, feminist and critical sociologists' empirical studies demonstrated that the golden age of financially secure retirements was restricted, in most countries, to a pension elite having access to both public and private pensions. Race, ethnicity, gender, and characteristics of lifelong employment (employment sector, wage level, job tenure, etc.) meant that many elderly people, particularly women and racial or ethnic minorities, had incomes below the poverty line. By the 1980s the apparently limitless 1970s horizons of post-war pension expansion narrowed in the aftermath of worldwide economic downturn and dawning transformations from industrial to service economies. Serious gaps in pension provision, particularly for categories of disadvantaged workers, became increasingly obvious. As more women entered paid employment, and family forms changed (through single parenthood and increased rates of divorce), public pension systems that granted most women pension incomes as dependents of employed men – norms predicated on the employed male breadwinner/unpaid homemaker model – and which failed to take into account women's unpaid care work became increasingly irrelevant in terms of meeting women's future retirement income needs. Some public pension systems adapted policies to incorporate pension credits for periods of caregiving. Private pensions could not. Moreover, employers began replacing company administered, defined-benefit private pensions,

which featured risk-sharing and guaranteed benefits to individual retirement accounts known as defined contribution plans. Defined contribution plans promised portability and individual ownership, advantages for an increasingly mobile modern workforce, unlikely to experience lifetime employment at a single firm. But defined benefits also individualized risk, exposing individuals to the potential for low retirement income in the wake of poor investment choices, inadequate levels of participation and saving, or bad equities market luck. By the late twentieth century, policymakers and researchers had shifted their focus from explaining the development of age-based social policies in modern welfare states to other concerns. These included understanding how pension systems could continue to adapt to new socioeconomic conditions, fill gaps in coverage, and provide equitable and adequate incomes to retired individuals, regardless of gender. At the same time, sociologists increasingly focused research on understanding the potential implications of the increased risk implied by individualized retirement accounts.

TWENTY-FIRST CENTURY DEVELOPMENTS

The early twenty-first century finds the connections between age and social policies in a state of flux, with tensions between collective provision and individual responsibility playing out in most national debates about the appropriate relationships among age, need, and social policy. Universal social insurance programs have been retrenched in most (although not all) developed countries and the impetus in social policy appears to be opposite to the trend towards increased collective provision throughout the twentieth century. To the extent that social policies for elderly people are adapting to the post-industrial twenty-first century global economy, most trends seem to point towards retrenchment, increased privatization, and increased targeting of remaining spending programs. Among the socio-demographic realities influencing social policies are aging populations, burgeoning national budget deficits, slowed growth in national economies, and international uncertainty, all factors contributing to fiscal austerity shaping social policy innovations.

Welfare states are not particularly nimble in the face of rapid social change, but lessons from the twentieth century inform sociologists that social policies will surely adapt to new realities of aging in the twenty-first. Sociologists will make contributions to welfare state theory-building and comparative research as the outlines of transformed age-based social policies emerge. They will explore whether welfare state retrenchment reflects abandonment of collective provision or whether a more nuanced definition of retrenchment is warranted, one that acknowledges the need to marshal scarce resources until conditions improve. Innovations in targeting program resources efficiently to the neediest beneficiaries, a policy aspiration in most countries, implies that sociologists will need to develop better models to understand the complexities of the interplay between taxing and spending practices that create social policy outcomes. Such research may signal opportunities for policy-learning across innovating states whose national policy mixes best meet the needs of aging populations. Because all policy innovations create new sets of policy "winners" and "losers," sociologists will need to study how age and policy outcomes contribute to or undermine national political support for social policies. Finally, social policy innovations will provide research fodder for sociologists, who will continue pursuing their traditional core interest in inequalities, researching the implications of the relationships among age, social policy regimes, and social stratification, as current age-based policies are transformed and new ones enacted.

SEE ALSO: Aging, Demography of; Aging and Health Policy; Aging and Social Support; Aging, Sociology of; Elder Care; Gender, Work, and Family; Life Course and Family; Retirement; Social Policy, Welfare State; Welfare State, Retrenchment of

REFERENCES AND SUGGESTED READINGS

Calasanti, T. & Slevin, K. (2001) *Gender, Social Inequalities, and Aging.* AltaMira Press, Walnut Creek, CA.

Estes, C. L., Biggs, S., & Phillipson, C. (2003) *Social Theory, Social Policy and Ageing.* Open University Press, Buckingham.

Ginn, J., Street, D., & Arber, S. (Eds.) (2001) *Women, Work and Pensions: International Issues and Prospects.* Open University Press, Buckingham.

Harrington Meyer, M. (Ed.) (2000) *Care Work.* Routledge, New York.

Myles, J. (1989) *Old Age and the Welfare State.* University of Kansas Press, Lawrence.

Quadagno, J. (1988) *The Transformation of Old Age Security: Class and Politics in the American Welfare State.* University of Chicago Press, Chicago.

Shalev, M. (1996) *The Privatization of Occupational Welfare and the Welfare State in America, Scandinavia, and Japan.* Macmillan, London.

Walker, A. (1996) *The New Generational Contract: Intergenerational Relations, Old Age and Welfare.* Taylor & Francis, London.

aging and social support

Pearl Dykstra

Social support is a powerful predictor of living a healthy and long life. Large, well-controlled prospective studies show that social support has an impact on older adults' health independently of potentially confounded factors such as socioeconomic status, health-risk behaviors, use of health services, and personality (Uchino 2004). This entry discusses social support and then considers how it is related to aging.

Social support refers to positive exchanges with network members that help people stay healthy or cope with adverse events. Researchers typically distinguish the following types of supportive behavior: instrumental aid, the expression of emotional caring or concern, and the provision of advice and guidance.

Epidemiologists introduced the concept of social support in the 1970s to explain why people who are embedded in social networks enjoy better mental and physical health. More recent research has revealed that support is not the only pathway by which social relationships affect well-being (Berkman et al. 2000). Characteristic of social support is that it involves behavioral exchanges (giving and receiving) that are intended as helpful and are perceived as such. Social support needs to be distinguished conceptually from the other ways through which people benefit from having close relationships. The first is that networks provide opportunities for companionship and social engagement. Shared leisure activities serve as a source of pleasure and stimulation, whereas the participation in meaningful community activities brings social recognition. Social control is a second mechanism responsible for the healthful effects of social relationships. Social control operates directly when network members consciously attempt to modify a person's health behavior, or indirectly when people internalize norms for healthful behavior. Third, relationships provide access to resources that transcend an individual's means. To have relationships is to have access to other people's connections, information, money, and time. The different functions of relationships (social support, companionship, social control, and access to resources) are related to each other, and not easily separated in everyday life.

Social support is basically positive. Of course, not all our interactions with others are pleasant and enjoyable. Personal relationships can function as a source of stress, conflict, and disappointment. For that reason it is important to distinguish positive social exchanges (support) from negative social exchanges (Rook 1997). Examples of the latter are encounters characterized by rejection and criticism, violation of privacy, or actions that undermine a person's pursuit of personal goals. Ineffective assistance or excessive helping are other forms of negative interactions.

From the start, a major focus of social support research has been the question of how and why social support has salubrious effects. In this line of research social support is the independent variable. Two theoretical models have been dominant in the literature. The direct effects model maintains that social support operates at all times. The support people receive helps them maintain an overall sense of stability and self-worth and helps them in their efforts to improve their situation. According to the buffering effects model, social support operates when people are under stress. Social support helps people cope with setbacks and serves as a protective barrier against threats

to well-being. Underlying mechanisms are physiological, in the sense of moderating levels of cardiovascular reactivity, and psychological, in the sense of restoring self-esteem, mastery, and feelings of competence. The direct effects model and the buffering effects model are not competing theoretical frameworks. Each is couched in its own empirical tradition, and empirical support has been found for both (Cohen & Wills 1985). Tests of direct effects are generally based on data from the general population, whereas tests of buffering effects consider individuals undergoing stressful life events, such as a serious illness, marital problems, or the loss of a loved one.

Studies published in the 1980s showing that supportive behaviors at times have negative rather than positive consequences formed the impetus for new theoretical developments. One set of theoretical specifications pertains to the nature of support exchanges. For example, to better understand direct effects, researchers have suggested looking at the reciprocity of exchanges. Drawing upon equity theory, the idea is that receiving more support than one gives leads to distress and guilt. Over-benefiting is not only a violation of the norm of reciprocity but may also lead to a state of dependency. Whereas reciprocity focuses on the balance between support giving and support receiving, the optimal matching hypothesis, which is a specification of the buffering effects model, focuses on the kind of support received (Cutrona & Russell 1990). This hypothesis suggests that support is most effective when it matches specific needs. If people do not receive the right kind of support, then strains will not be reduced. A second set of theoretical specifications pertains to the meanings assigned to support exchanges. It has been suggested, for example, that the effects of receiving support are moderated by self-esteem. For some, receiving support has self-threatening qualities because it implies failure and an inability to cope on one's own. For others, receiving support has self-enhancing qualities such as evidence of love and caring. According to this perspective, people will react negatively to help if it causes damage to their self-esteem. A complementary perspective is that the perceived motivation for support exchanges determines their impact on well-being. Exchanges perceived to be motivated by affection rather than obligation or reciprocity are presumably most beneficial to the recipient.

A line of research that has been more prominent in the social gerontological literature has focused on explaining differences in the availability of social support. Here social support is the dependent variable. Questions about the access to support are particularly relevant to the elderly given that the loss or disruption of relationships is common in later life. Coinciding declines in older adults' health and mobility, leading to an increase in the support required from others, further underscore the relevance of the issue of how older adults negotiate transitions in their relationships. The convoy model of social support (Kahn & Antonucci 1980) emphasizes that pools of available contacts and needs for resources from others are patterned by older adults' life histories.

Network composition is a dependable indicator of the sources, the quantity, the quality, and the types of support to which older adults have access (Dykstra 1993). Relationships tend to be specialized in their support provisions. Knowledge about the different types of relationships composing networks provides insight into available support. According to the task-specificity model, different types of relationships best provide support that is consonant with their structures. Neighbors can best handle immediate emergencies because of their geographic proximity, kin can best perform tasks requiring long-term commitment, and friends can best be relied on for issues particular to a generation or life course phase that assume similarity in interests and values. The marital dyad can function in all the previously described task areas, since that unit shares proximity with neighbors, long-term commitment with kin and, frequently, similarity in interests and values with friends. In agreement with the task-specific model, available evidence indicates that partners are the primary providers of support in old age. Kin and non-kin generally differ in the support they provide. Family members are more likely than are friends to provide instrumental support such as help with transportation, shopping, and household chores. Family members are less likely than are friends to provide emotional support such as exchanging confidences, advice, or comfort.

There is also considerable overlap between kin and non-kin in the support they provide: family members can be major sources of emotional support and there are friends who provide long-term instrumental support. This happens when the usual primary providers are not available (spouseless and/or childless elderly). A compensatory hierarchy of support providers exists. Ties lower in the support hierarchy are invoked when higher-placed ties are not available. The position in the hierarchy follows socially shared views on who should provide help. The partner is generally the first to provide assistance when older adults are in need of help with the activities of daily living. In the absence of a partner or when the partner is impaired, adult children are likely to step in. In the absence of children or when they live too far away, support is likely to come from friends, siblings, or other family members, or neighbors. The hierarchical-compensatory model has been criticized for not keeping up with demographic reality. It is based on a conventional view of the family and fails to address the complexities in commitments that arise with divorce and new partnerships.

Though friends, members of the extended family, and neighbors often step in when needed, instrumental support provided by these relationships has a fragile basis. Given the absence of culturally prescribed obligations to provide such help to older network members, commitment and support expectations tend to be individualized within the relationships, and are subject to continuous negotiation. Relationships with peers are more susceptible to dissolution if exchanges are unbalanced than are parent–child relationships. The availability of friends, relatives, and neighbors for intense support-giving depends on the buildup of reciprocity over the course of their interactions with older network members (Wentowski 1981).

The hierarchical-compensatory and task-specificity models focus on types of relationships and the normative expectations to provide support associated with them. A drawback of the focus on relationship types is that the gendered nature of social life remains hidden.

Women are both expected to and do provide more support to aging family members. This is not to say that men do not undertake instrumental tasks. Though men and women do equal amounts of caregiving as spouses, men's participation in non-spousal caregiving is conditioned by their relationships with women (Calasanti 2003). Men often function as back-ups for their caregiving wives and sisters. Sons who act as primary caregivers are likely to be only children, to have no sister, or to have a sister living far away from the parent. Research shows a gender-typed specialization of the kind of support-giving tasks that are performed. Men are more likely to engage in activities such as odd jobs in and around the house, and paperwork, bills, and finances, whereas women are more likely to perform household tasks and personal care.

Family members provide the majority of the care that frail older adults receive. A long-standing debate is whether the emergence of formal services erodes the provision of informal support (Attias-Donfut & Wolff 2000). Empirical evidence favors the complementary hypothesis rather than the substitution hypothesis. Formal services increase the total level of support; they extend rather than replace informal support. With the introduction of formal care, informal support-providers appear to redirect their efforts to previously neglected or partially unfulfilled areas of support, rather than reduce their overall effort. Research shows furthermore that formal help is called in as a last resort. Though informal networks respond to increasing incapacity by expanding the scope of their assistance, there is a point beyond which the needs of the older adult exceed the resources of the network. At that point supplementary support is sought in formal services.

The imbalanced focus in the gerontological literature on help provided by children creates the impression that all older people need help and downplays their role as helpers in old age. Within families, more support goes down generational lines than goes up. Parents provide money, gifts, affection, and advice to their offspring until very late in life. A role reversal occurs only when the older generation encounters difficulties functioning independently. That is when the direction of exchange of assistance and services starts flowing predominantly from the bottom to the top.

Over the years there has been a methodological shift from relying on marital status, numbers of close friends and relatives, church membership, and other proxy variables to represent exposure to social support to more carefully examining the actual transactions in relationships. Nevertheless, a generally agreed upon measure of social support does not exist. This lack of consensus is not surprising given the wide range of disciplines in which social support is studied. Large epidemiological studies require brief measures. The crude nature of these measures leaves open what characteristics, structures, or processes of social interactions are most consequential for health. Psychologists tend to rely on measures of anticipated support: the belief that others will provide assistance in the future should a need arise. A criticism of these measures is that they might say more about the person than about the quality of his or her relationships. They are a way of measuring social support that makes it indistinguishable from a personality trait. In defense, one can argue that anticipated support is based on assistance that has actually been provided in the past. Sociologists (House et al. 1988) emphasize the necessity of distinguishing structural measures of support (existence or interconnections among social ties) and functional measures of support (actual exchanges of assistance and help). An issue that has yet to be resolved is whether to use global or relationship-specific measures. Global measures, whereby respondents are requested to rate supportive exchanges with their friends, neighbors, and relatives taken together, have the advantage that they are relatively easy to administer. The disadvantage is that they provide little insight into the relative importance of various social network ties. Relationship-specific measures, whereby an inventory is made of the supportive quality of selected relationships in the network, have the drawback that they are cumbersome to collect. Furthermore, their aggregation is not always straightforward (Van Tilburg 1990).

Social support researchers are faced with a constant tradeoff between breadth and depth of analysis. It is important to acknowledge that social support is amazingly complex. To advance our understanding of how social support works we need first to pay careful attention to our relationship measures, distinguishing tangible support exchanges from embeddedness. Secondly, we need to assess simultaneously the mechanisms that produce the positive outcomes hypothesized for social support. In doing so, we should more often make use of reports from multiple actors in the social network. Enriching information collected from one person with information from others helps uncover biases. A discrepancy between persons regarding the content and significance of their relationship might highlight conflicts or differences in dependencies.

Apart from a microsocial focus on the pathways by which social support influences well-being, there is a need for macrosocial analysis of the determinants of levels and types of social support. People's support networks are shaped in part by the locations they occupy in a larger social structure stratified by age, sex, and socioeconomic status and organized in terms of residential communities, work organizations, and religious and voluntary associations. Demographic developments such as the extension of life, the drop in birth rates, the increases in divorce and remarriage, and migration set limits for the potential availability of family support. Welfare arrangements influence the resources potentially available for redistribution through families and formal services. There is ample room for sociologists to make their mark in the social support literature, which so far has been dominated by psychologists and epidemiologists.

SEE ALSO: Aging, Mental Health, and Well-Being; Caregiving; Elder Care; Family Structure; Health Behavior; Life Course and Family; Social Integration and Inclusion; Social Network Analysis; Social Support

REFERENCES AND SUGGESTED READINGS

Attias-Donfut, C. & Wolff, F.-C. (2000) Complementarity between Private and Public Transfers. In: Arber, S. & Attias-Donfut, C. (Eds.), *The Myth of Generational Conflict: The Family and State in Ageing Societies.* Routledge, London, pp. 47–68.

Berkman, L., Glass, T., Brissette, I., & Seeman, T. E. (2000) From Social Integration to Health: Durkheim in the New Millennium. *Social Science and Medicine* 51: 843–57.

Calasanti, T. (2003) Masculinities and Care Work in Old Age. In: Arber, S., Davidson, K., & Ginn, J. (Eds.), *Gender and Ageing: Changing Roles and Relationships.* Open University Press, Maidenhead, pp. 15–30.

Cantor, M. (1979) Neighbors and Friends: An Overlooked Resource in the Informal Support System. *Research on Aging* 1: 434–63.

Cohen, S. & Wills, T. A. (1985) Stress, Social Support, and the Buffering Hypothesis. *Psychological Bulletin* 98: 310–57.

Cutrona, C. E. & Russell, D. W. (1990) Type of Social Support and Specific Stress: Towards a Theory of Optimal Matching. In: Sarason, B. R., Sarason, I. G., & Pierce, G. R. (Eds.), *Social Support: An Interactional View.* Wiley, New York, pp. 319–66.

Done, J. E., Farbe, C. M., Kail, B. L., Litwak, E., Sherman, R. E., & Siegel, D. (1979) Primary Groups in Old Age: Structure and Function. *Research on Aging* 1: 403–33.

Dykstra, P. A. (1993) The Differential Availability of Relationships and the Provision and Effectiveness of Support to Older Adults. *Journal of Personal and Social Relationships* 10: 355–70.

Finch, J. & Mason, J. (1990) Filial Obligations and Kin Support for Elderly People. *Ageing and Society* 10: 151–75.

House, J. S., Umberson, D., & Landis, K. R. (1988) Structures and Processes of Social Support. *Annual Review of Sociology* 14: 293–318.

Kahn, R. L. & Antonucci, T. C. (1980) Convoys Over the Life Course: Attachment, Roles and Social Support. In: Baltes, P. B. & Brim, O. (Eds.), *Lifespan Development and Behavior*, Vol. 3. Academic Press, New York, pp. 253–86.

Liang, J., Krause, N. M., & Bennett, J. M. (2001) Social Exchange and Well-Being: Is Giving Better than Receiving? *Psychology and Aging* 16: 511–23.

Litwak, E. (1985) *Helping the Elderly: The Complementary Roles of Informal Networks and Formal Systems.* Guilford Press, New York.

Rook, K. S. (1997) Positive and Negative Social Exchanges: Weighting their Effects in Later Life. *Journal of Gerontology: Social Sciences* 52B: S167–9.

Uchino, B. N. (2004) *Social Support and Physical Health: Understanding the Health Consequences of Relationships.* Yale University Press, New Haven.

Van Tilburg, T. G. (1990) The Size of the Supportive Network in Association with the Degree of Loneliness. In: Knipscheer, C. P. M. &

Antonucci, T. C. (Eds.), *Social Network Research: Substantive Issues and Methodological Questions*. Swets & Zeitlinger, Lisse, pp. 137–50.
Wentowski, G. J. (1981) Reciprocity and the Coping Strategies of Older People: Cultural Dimensions of Network Building. *Gerontologist* 21: 600–9.

aging, sociology of

Linda K. George

The sociology of aging is both broad and deep. The breadth of the field can be highlighted in several ways. First, the sociology of aging encompasses investigations of aging as a process, of older adults as a group, and of old age as a distinctive stage of the life course. Second, aging research is performed at multiple levels of analysis, from macro-level studies of age structure within and across societies, to meso-level studies of labor-force participation and family structure, to micro-level investigations of health and well-being. Third, aging research uses the full repertoire of methods that characterize the discipline, including life tables and other demographic methods, survey research, ethnographic methods, and observational studies. The depth of the field results from the accumulation of scientific studies that now span more than three-quarters of a century.

Any attempt to summarize concisely the state of the science in the sociology of aging will inevitably do justice neither to the breadth nor the depth of the field. Here, four major themes in theory and research on aging are reviewed. Selection of these themes is based on a review of appropriate reference works (e.g., handbooks, encyclopedias) and perusal of major journals and textbooks.

AGE STRUCTURE AND ITS IMPLICATIONS

Although primarily the province of demographers, both scientific and public interest in aging partially rests on the aging populations characteristic of the modern world. Age structure is based on the sizes of age groups in a given society. In turn, the sizes of age groups are a function of fertility and mortality rates. The *theory of the demographic transition* provides a portrait of the relationships between development (i.e., industrialization, urbanization, technological advances) and the age structures of societies (Bourgeois-Pichat 1979). According to this theory, the demographic transition occurs in three stages. In the first, prior to and during the early years of modernization, both fertility and mortality rates are high. The result is an age structure that takes the form of a pyramid, with the largest age group consisting of children, and older adults comprising the smallest group. During the process of modernization (the second stage), mortality rates decline, but fertility rates remain high. The result is larger populations in total size and a young population. The dependency ratio, which is the proportion of the population in the labor market relative to the number of children and older adults not in the labor market, is high, but consists primarily of children. As societies achieve modernization (third stage), mortality rates continue to decline, but fertility declines as well. The theory of the demographic transition hypothesized that the third stage would lead to a steady-state population size, in which fertility and mortality rates would be approximately equal and the age structure would take the form of a cylinder, with all age groups of approximately equal size, and the numerator of the dependency ratio including approximately equal numbers of children and older adults.

The first two stages of the theory of the demographic transition have been supported in empirical studies. Evidence for the hypothesized third stage is much weaker. Although both fertility and mortality rates have declined in modernized societies, fertility rates have declined faster than mortality rates, resulting in populations with disproportionately large numbers and percents of older adults. Two other demographic patterns have exacerbated the aging of the population in some societies. First, in the US and, to a lesser extent, in Western Europe and Australia, the end of World War II ushered in a decade or more of unusually high fertility, resulting in a baby boom, followed by the expected sizable declines in fertility. These unusually large cohorts delayed the expected declines in fertility, but because of the small cohorts that followed them, escalated the aging of the population. Second, countries in South America, Asia, and Africa have achieved substantial modernization with substantially smaller declines in fertility than expected.

The importance of the theory of the demographic transition is not its accuracy, but rather its attention to the age structures of societies and the effects of social change (in the form of fertility and mortality rates) on those age structures. Regardless of the indicator used (e.g., proportion of older adults, median age of the population), the population is aging rapidly in the US and other western societies.

Although initially slow to comprehend the significance of an aging population, both scientific and policy communities are now well aware of the challenges posed by an aging society. "Young" populations also pose problems for societies, but solutions to those problems (e.g., child welfare, schooling) evolved gradually in modern societies and became institutionally embedded in custom and law. The aging of modern populations occurred more rapidly, resulting in significant structural lag (Riley & Riley 1994) in institutional responses to the needs of older adults.

Demographic research has expanded substantially beyond questions of age structure per se. Most of what is now known about the prevalence, incidence, and course of disability is based on demographic research. Among the contributions of this research are findings that rates of disability among older adults have been gradually declining for approximately 20 years, that the higher rates of disability among women than men results from their greater longevity rather than higher incidence of disability onset, and that, although it is less common than the onset of disability, a sizable proportion of older adults recover or improve in functional status. The distinction between life expectancy (expected years of survival) and active life expectancy (expected years of disability-free survival) also is a high-priority issue. Interest in active life expectancy stems from concern that the increased longevity characteristic of modern

societies has been achieved by prolonging life after the onset of frailty and disability. Evidence suggests that the length of disability prior to death has not increased over the past several decades; however, there also has not been a decrease in the interval between the onset of disability and death. As these topics illustrate, demographers now devote a significant proportion of their efforts to understanding heterogeneity in the older population.

A large proportion of sociological research on aging rests on the challenges posed by an aging society, although that impetus is not always explicit. Studies of public and private transfers of money, time, and in-kind services rest in large part on their salience for sustaining an aging population. Studies of health, disability, and quality of life are important not only because they address threats to well-being, but also because they shed light on the factors that keep older adults from excessive reliance on public programs. Even studies of the caregivers of impaired older adults rest not only on concern about the health risks of chronic stress, but also on the desire to enable families to bear as much of the cost of care as possible, thus relieving public programs. Thus, age structure and its social implications is a significant and far-reaching arm of aging research.

AGING AS CONTEXT: THE SIGNIFICANCE OF COHORTS

Multiple forces, both social and non-social, determine the process and experience of aging. Historically, there was a tendency to attribute the aging process and the experience of late life to inherent biological and developmental processes. Most of us are relatively ignorant of the extent to which the process and experience of aging vary across historical time, finding it difficult, for example, to imagine a time when there was no retirement or when the odds of dying were essentially the same during childhood, adulthood, and old age. And yet, retirement as a predictable life course transition and odds favoring survival to old age both emerged in the twentieth century. The concept of cohort allows us to distinguish conceptually and empirically between inherent components of the aging process and patterns that result from social factors, especially social change and unique historical events or circumstances.

Although cohort membership can be based on any event, the term is typically used for birth cohorts (i.e., for persons born at the same or approximately the same time). Cohorts share more than the timing of their births; they also experience the same historical events and social structures throughout their lives. Cohorts share collective experiences that often differ from those shared by earlier and later cohorts. Thus, there often are sizable cohort differences in the process and experience of old age.

Cohort differences, often observed across cohorts born in relative proximity, can be generated by multiple conditions. First, cohorts can differ substantially in size and composition. Substantial evidence documents that unusually large and unusually small cohorts differ substantially, especially in economic opportunities, with the latter more plentiful in smaller cohorts. Cohort composition can be affected by many factors, including excess male mortality during wars, different birth rates across racial/ethnic groups, and changes in immigration policies.

Second, historical events can substantially alter the experiences of cohorts. When many cohorts experience the same historical event, effects differ depending on age at the time of the event (e.g., wars most strongly affect young men). Even in the absence of dramatic events or dislocations, historical developments imprint cohorts differently, creating persisting differences (e.g., racial identity among African Americans before and after the Civil Rights Movement). Substantial evidence suggests that historical events and social change generally affect adolescent and young adult cohorts more than they affect younger and older cohorts.

Third, social change creates cohort differences and the more rapidly social change occurs, the greater the differentiation across cohorts. Social change, of course, takes many forms, ranging from changes in public policies (e.g., Social Security and Medicare created large cohort differences in economic status during later life), changes in the norms governing social behavior (e.g., norms concerning the acceptability of fertility outside of marriage and cohabiting), and major structural changes such as the shift from an industrial to a service economy. Technological change also generates cohort differences, with varying implications for the older population. For example, devices that save household labor or provide assistance in compensating for disabilities enhance the likelihood that older adults can live independently. Conversely, diffusion of general technological changes often takes longer to reach older adults, distancing them from younger cohorts (e.g., personal computers and related use of the Internet).

Fourth, older cohorts are inevitably affected by the composition of and changes occurring in younger cohorts. Responses to those changes can create related changes in older cohorts. For example, the prevalence of custodial grandparents, although still uncommon, increased dramatically over the past two or three decades. This change in older cohorts is a direct result of changes in fertility and childcare practices of younger cohorts.

Cohort comparisons comprise a substantial proportion of sociological research on aging. An issue that receives considerable attention is comparisons of the assets and liabilities that different cohorts bring to late life. To date, research findings paint a rosy picture of this form of cohort change. For at least half a century, successive cohorts have entered old age with higher levels of resources and fewer liabilities than the cohorts that preceded them. This pattern has been especially consistent for health, education, wealth, and the availability of social support, all of which are valuable assets in late life. As Uhlenberg and Minor (1996) note, there is no reason to believe that this pattern will continue indefinitely. Indeed, some scholars predict that baby boomers will enter old age more disadvantaged than their parents; other scholars predict that the pattern will not reverse until the children of the baby boomers reach old age – but most scholars expect the pattern of increasingly resource-rich older cohorts to peak at some point during the next 50 years.

The large volume of cohort comparison studies is too large to detail here, but includes issues as diverse as political affiliation and voting behavior, family structure (primarily cohort differences in divorce, remarriage, and single-parent mothers), cognitive abilities, alcohol consumption, and rates of depression. Cohort comparisons also are important for policy planning and analysis. Comparison of cohorts before and after a major policy change, such as the enactment of Medicare, is one of the primary strategies used to evaluate the impact of broad-scale public policies. Cohort comparison studies also remind us that public policies targeted at older adults are not the only policies that create differential advantage or disadvantage across cohorts. Policies that enhance educational attainment during adolescence and young adulthood have long-term benefits, creating cohorts that are more advantaged as they enter old age than were older cohorts. The GI Bill, first made available to World War II veterans, for example, created dramatic increases in the educational attainment and economic resources with which those cohorts entered late life.

At the same time that cohort comparison studies have enjoyed success, a related body of research examines *intracohort variability*. Although there are often large differences across cohorts, cohorts are not homogeneous. Paralleling sociology more broadly, increased attention to heterogeneity has characterized aging research for the past quarter century. Intracohort variability has received both conceptual and empirical attention. Two bodies of research have contributed most to this research base.

First, the attention paid to social location, as indexed by basic ascribed and achieved statuses, has increased dramatically. Thirty years ago or so, gender differences, racial/ethnic differences, marital status differences, and socioeconomic (SES) differences typically were examined perfunctorily, if at all. It was not until the mid to late 1970s, for example, that women's retirement received empirical attention. There is now general consensus that age, race/ethnicity, gender, and SES represent basic social structural categories and are forms of social stratification. Investigation of these multiple forms of stratification has been incorporated into aging research and into the discipline more broadly.

Second, a compelling body of research demonstrates that historical events or conditions do not have uniform effects on cohort members. Some cohort subgroups are strongly affected by historical events; others are largely untouched by them. Several important studies demonstrated that the Great Depression had the strongest contemporaneous and long-term effects on late adolescents whose families experienced the greatest economic deprivation (Elder 1999); that relatively few young adults participated in the political activism of the 1960s, but that there were persisting differences in the life patterns of those who did and did not (McAdam 1989); and that veterans' emotional problems in middle and late life were largely a function of amount of combat exposure during World War II (Elder et al. 1997). Broad-based cohort effects also have been observed for these and other historical events or conditions (e.g., the "children of the Great Depression" had greater concerns about financial security than earlier and later cohorts, regardless of the amount of deprivation experienced), but there is also great heterogeneity in the effects of historical events on cohort members.

Intercohort comparisons and studies of intracohort variability are arguably the core of sociological aging research. These studies demonstrate that aging is not solely – or even primarily – a biological process, but rather that the aging process and the experience of late life are shaped by social and historical context.

AGING AND WELL-BEING

The vast majority of aging research falls under the general topic of aging and well-being, with well-being broadly defined to include any social asset (e.g., economic resources, life satisfaction). Social scientific interest in aging was spurred by concerns about the well-being of older adults in both absolute and relative (to other age groups) terms. This is probably not surprising. The history of sociology in general has been driven by concerns about social disadvantage – its prevalence, antecedents, and consequences.

The types of well-being examined in relation to aging are numerous. A partial list of the forms of well-being frequently studied in late life include longevity, physical health, disability, mental health, subjective well-being, economic status, and identity or sense of self.

Self-perception during late life is an important and understudied topic relative to studies of physical and mental health and subjective well-being. Two primary dimensions of self-perception are especially important: a sense of self-worth (typically measured as self-esteem or self-acceptance) and a sense of competence (usually measured as self-efficacy, mastery, or sense of control). These self-perceptions are important in their own right – most of us consider adequate self-esteem and sufficient self-efficacy essential components of well-being. In addition, these self-perceptions mediate many of the relationships between social factors and other forms of well-being, including physical and mental health and subjective well-being. For example, self-esteem has been shown to mediate the effects of education on health (Murrell et al. 2003), of social support on subjective well-being and self-rated health (Bisconti & Bergeman 1999), and of social stress on functional status (Forthofer et al. 2001). Traditionally, sociologists tended to view self-perceptions as the province of psychology. There is now plentiful evidence, however, that the antecedents of these self-perceptions are primarily social and that their distributions are concordant with multiple stratification systems. Adequate sociological explanations of variability in well-being will need to take these psychosocial processes into account.

Three major research strategies underlie most research on aging and well-being. First, some studies examine the well-being of older adults relative to that of younger age groups. Examples of this kind of research include age comparisons of rates of poverty, chronic physical illness, disability, and mental illness and levels of subjective well-being, self-esteem, and self-efficacy across age groups at a single point in time. These studies are of limited use in understanding the aging process because it is unclear whether differences across age groups are due to age per se or to cohort differences. But comparisons across age groups can be useful for both providing basic descriptive information about the relative status of older adults and for identifying issues important to public policy (e.g., whether it makes sense to target income-maintenance programs at specific age groups). That is, policymakers typically are more concerned about the unmet needs of older adults than they are about disentangling age and cohort effects.

A second strategy for understanding the effects of aging on well-being is to study adults longitudinally as they move from middle age to late life and from being young-old to being old-old. The advantage of this strategy, of course, is that age-related changes in well-being are directly observed. These studies focus on the status of the elderly relative to earlier points in their lives, rather than relative to younger age groups. The limitation of these studies is that findings may be cohort-specific, rather than reflecting a consistent developmental pattern. In theory, if one samples a large number of cohorts and studies them over long periods of time, investigators can determine whether patterns of change and stability are similar across cohorts. Unfortunately, few, if any, data sets are of sufficient breadth in both the number of cohorts studied and number of measurements over time to permit conclusions about whether patterns of change and stability are generalizeable or cohort-specific.

Patterns of change and stability in the multiple forms of well-being that have been studied to date cannot be detailed here. Importantly, however, there is no consistent pattern of age-related decline across all forms of well-being. Declines are the modal pattern for some forms of well-being, such as income and the prevalence and onset of chronic illnesses. Stability or increases are the modal pattern for other types of well-being, including self-esteem and life satisfaction – at least until very late life (i.e., age 80 and older).

A third strategy is to focus on variability within the older population – to assess variability in well-being among older adults and to identify the antecedents of that variability. Either cross-sectional or longitudinal data can be used to study heterogeneity among older adults, but only longitudinal data permit investigators to establish temporal order between well-being and its presumed antecedents. Note that age is not the independent variable in studies of this type; instead, the independent variables are the presumed causes of variability in well-being.

Compared to studies of age structure and cohort comparisons, the theoretical underpinnings of studies of aging and well-being are typically richer and more complex. A broad range of theories is used in studies of well-being in late life. Most of these theories are imported in whole or in part from other domains of sociology. For example, stratification theories are used to examine both income dynamics and health inequalities in later life, stress theory is used in studies of physical and mental illness, network theory is used to understand older adults' patterns of social support, and aspiration and equity theories are used in studies of subjective well-being. In addition to importing theories from other domains of sociology, a substantial proportion of research on aging and well-being rests on theories developed to highlight the distinctive conditions of later life. Examples include activity theory, which posits that multiple forms of well-being are enhanced in late life by sustaining high levels of activity and engagement – and adding new forms of activity to compensate for losses that often accompany aging; the double-jeopardy hypothesis, which predicts that the combined statuses of being old and a member of a racial/ethnic minority have more damaging effects on health and well-being than their purely additive effects; and socioemotional selectivity theory (Carstensen 1995), which suggests that declines in social contacts in late life are a purposeful and effective strategy for sustaining high-quality relationships. Clearly, the theories used to explain variations in well-being among older adults are rich and varied.

The independent variables used in studies of well-being during late life are typically measures of social status, social context, and social resources. Social context, as indexed by age, race, and gender, is related to economic well-being, physical and mental health, and longevity. Only the more social psychological forms of well-being, such as self-esteem and life satisfaction, are either not significantly related or are weakly related to these basic demographic characteristics. As expected, traditional indicators of socioeconomic status are significant predictors of longevity, physical and mental health, self-esteem and self-efficacy, and subjective well-being. Social resources, especially social integration (e.g., organizational and religious participation) and social support

also have positive effects on longevity, health, sense of self, and subjective well-being. As this brief description illustrates, we know a lot about the factors that explain heterogeneity in well-being in later life. These same social factors also explain much of the variability in well-being among young and middle-aged adults. As the body of research that compares predictors of well-being across age groups documents, the distinctive feature of well-being in late life is not the specific antecedents of well-being, but rather the distribution of those antecedents across historical and biographical time.

AGING AS THE CULMINATION OF THE LIFE COURSE

During the past 20 years, the life course perspective has assumed increasing influence in sociological research, especially research on aging. The core of the life course perspective is the proposition that lives unfold over time and that events and conditions at earlier phases of the life course have persisting effects at later phases – either continuing direct effects or indirect effects via more temporally proximate events and conditions. Taking temporality seriously changes research questions and research methods in multiple ways (George 2003). Most importantly, perhaps, long-term patterns of change and stability, often conceptualized as trajectories, are the primary focus of analysis. Investigators can study trajectories of independent variables (e.g., marital history), trajectories of dependent variables (e.g., patterns of recovery, remission, and chronicity in depressive symptoms), or both. In addition to the "shape" of trajectories, duration in states of interest also may be important (e.g., length of time till recovery from disability).

Methodologically, life course studies require either multiple measurements over long periods of time or retrospective data about earlier phases of the life course. Longitudinal data are more accurate than retrospective data, but most life course investigators are willing to use retrospective data if they are all that is available. The statistical techniques most frequently used in life course studies (e.g., latent growth curve analysis) are newer and more complex than those used in cross-sectional or short-term longitudinal studies. Other methodological problems, ranging from substantial attrition in sample size to difficulties in selecting measurement tools that are applicable across adulthood, emerge when using longitudinal data covering long periods of time. Nonetheless, it is the way that research questions are conceptualized that is the hallmark of life course studies.

Life course studies provide important information about trajectories of vulnerability and resilience. At their best, they also incorporate the processes by which early events and conditions have persisting effects on outcomes of interest measured decades later. Work by Elder and colleagues on the long-term effects of combat exposure provides a compelling illustration of the knowledge generated by life course studies (Elder et al. 1997). This research is based on the Terman men, a sample of unusually intelligent males tested on multiple occasions from childhood to early old age. Most of these men participated in World War II, although not all of them were exposed to combat – and among those who were in combat, the amount of exposure varied widely. Elder and colleagues demonstrate that combat exposure is a significant predictor of physical and (especially) mental health problems 40 years later, controlling on other known predictors of physical and mental health in later life. They also identified the life course achievements that allowed some of these combat veterans to avoid or minimize subsequent health problems. Men who achieved greater socioeconomic success, those who sustained contacts with other combat veterans, and especially those who had lasting, high-quality marriages were able to avoid or minimize the health risks posed by combat exposure. This research demonstrates the benefits of life course research, documenting both the persisting effects of early trauma and the mechanisms that allowed some men to avoid those risks.

In aging research, the life course perspective has been used most frequently to understand the effects of life course patterns of socioeconomic status on multiple forms of well-being in later life. The conceptual framework underpinning most of this research is the *theory of cumulative advantage/disadvantage*. This theory was developed nearly a half-century ago by Robert Merton (1957), as a framework for understanding occupational success among college and university professors. Merton observed that, at job entry, assistant professors looked very similar on standard measures of productivity and occupational success, regardless of the status of the institutions in which they were employed. Over time, however, variability increased dramatically in levels of productivity and occupational success among professors, with those employed at resource-rich schools exhibiting patterns of increasing success and those at resource-poorer schools exhibiting steady declines in productivity. Merton referred to the pattern of increasing success as cumulative advantage and the trajectory of declining productivity as cumulative disadvantage. In colloquial terms, the theory of cumulative advantage/disadvantage posits that "the rich get richer and the poor get poorer."

In general, what Merton observed among professors is true for socioeconomic status (SES) over the adult life course. That is, SES differences are smallest during young adulthood and largest during late life (Crystal & Shea 1990). This is true for income and SES differences are even more dramatic for wealth. Thus, cumulative advantage/disadvantage generates increasing economic heterogeneity over the adult life course.

The life course perspective also has been valuable in accounting for health inequalities across the life course. As is true for income and wealth, SES differences in health are minimal during young adulthood. By middle age, however, there are large differences in health between the lowest and highest SES quartiles in the US. Evidence is less clear during old age, with some investigators reporting that SES differences in health continue to widen during late life (Ross & Wu 1996). Other researchers, however, report that SES differences in health are largest during middle age and narrow somewhat during old age, although they remain significant (House et al. 1994). At some point in late life, SES differences in health are likely to narrow as the result of selective mortality (i.e., the earlier deaths of many lower SES individuals).

Some of the mechanisms that account for SES differences in health also have been identified. The benefits of education, occupational status, income, and wealth are, of course, much of the basis of SES differences in health. Other mechanisms that mediate the effects of SES on health include health behaviors; stress, including life-long accumulation of stressors; and psychological resources such as self-esteem and mastery.

In addition to long-term trajectories of assets and liabilities, the life course perspective also focuses attention on the persisting effects of early life events and conditions. For example, evidence demonstrates that parental SES predicts health during middle and late life, over and above the effects of individuals' own SES trajectories (Hayward & Gorman 2004). Indeed, limited evidence suggests that fetal growth *in utero* plays a substantial role in health during late life (Barker et al. 2000). In addition to economic resources, lack of emotional support from parents during early childhood increases the risk of both depression and chronic physical illnesses in late life (Shaw et al. 2004). Similarly, a variety of childhood traumas – including child abuse, sexual abuse, and parental divorce – are known to increase the risk of depression many decades later, even with other known risk factors taken into account (Kessler et al. 1997).

Although the volume of life course research that extends to late life has increased dramatically during the past two decades, many other topics could be profitably addressed in a life course framework. For example, although there is compelling evidence that social relationships are powerful predictors of health and well-being in late life, little is known about the relative importance of life-long patterns of social bonds as compared to the contemporaneous effects of social networks during late life. Similarly, religious participation has been demonstrated to be a strong predictor of mortality and morbidity in late life (Koenig et al. 1999). But this research is based on studies in which *current* religious involvement is measured. Virtually nothing is known about how length of exposure to religious participation affects health. In other words, we do not know how long individuals must participate in religious activities before health benefits are observed.

The life course perspective also renders the usual distinction between social selection and social causation moot. Studying the life course is the equivalent of studying patterns of selection and causation as they unfold across personal biography. And, of course, the effects of social causation observed earlier in the life course become selection effects for outcomes observed later in life.

The life course perspective focuses on the complex links between social/historical change and personal biography. In addition, the life course perspective is ideally suited to linking macro- and meso-level social conditions to individual behaviors and well-being, to tracing the effects of both structural opportunities and constraints of human agency (i.e., personal choices) over the long haul, and documenting the many ways that the past is indeed prologue to the future. Thus, life course research is an important and exciting part of the sociology of aging.

SEE ALSO: Age, Period, and Cohort Effects; Aging, Demography of; Aging and the Life Course, Theories of; Aging, Mental Health, and Well-Being; Aging and Social Policy; Aging and Social Support; Chronic Illness and Disability; Cultural Diversity and Aging: Ethnicity, Minorities, and Subcultures; Demographic Transition Theory; Life Course; Life Course Perspective

REFERENCES AND SUGGESTED READINGS

Barker, D. J., Shiell, A. W., Barker, M. E., & Law, C. M. (2000) Growth *in utero* and Blood Pressure Levels in the Next Generation. *Journal of Hypertension* 18: 843–6.

Bisconti, T. L. & Bergeman, C. S. (1999) Perceived Social Control as a Mediator of the Relationships among Social Support, Psychological Well-Being, and Perceived Health. *Gerontologist* 39: 94–103.

Bourgeois-Pichat, J. (1979) The Demographic Transition: Aging of Population. In: *Population Science in the Service of Mankind*. International Union for the Scientific Study of Population, Liege, pp. 211–39.

Carstensen, L. L. (1995) Evidence for a Life-Span Theory of Socioemotional Selectivity. *Current Directions in Psychological Science* 4: 151–6.

Crystal, S. & Shea, D. (1990) Cumulative Advantage, Cumulative Disadvantage, and Inequality among Elderly People. *Gerontologist* 30: 437–43.

Elder, G. H., Jr. (1999) *Children of the Great Depression*, 25th anniversary edn. Westview Press, Boulder.

Elder, G. H., Jr., Shanahan, M. J., & Clipp, E. C. (1997) Linking Combat and Physical Health: The Legacy of World War II in Men's Lives. *American Journal of Psychiatry* 154: 330–6.

Forthofer, M. S., Janz, N. K., Dodge, J. A. et al. (2001) Gender Differences in the Associations of Self-Esteem, Stress, and Social Support with Functional Health Status among Older Adults with Heart Disease. *Journal of Women and Aging* 13: 19–36.

George, L. K. (2003) What Life Course Perspectives Offer the Study of Aging and Health. In: Settersten, R. A. (Ed.), *Invitation to the Life Course*. Baywood Publishing, Amityville, NY, pp. 161–90.

Hayward, M. D. & Gorman, B. K. (2004) The Long Arm of Childhood: The Influence of Early-Life Social Conditions on Men's Mortality. *Demography* 41: 87–107.

House, J. S., Lepkowski, J. M., Kinney, A. M. et al. (1994) The Social Stratification of Aging and Health. *Journal of Health and Social Behavior* 35: 213–34.

Kessler, R. C., Davis, C. G., & Kendler, K. S. (1997) Childhood Adversity and Adult Psychiatric Disorder in the US National Comorbidity Survey. *Psychological Medicine* 27: 1101–19.

Koenig, H. G., Hays, J. C., Larson, D. B., George, L. K., Cohen, H. J., McCullough, M. E., Meador, K. G., & Blazer, D. G. (1999) Does Religious Attendance Prolong Survival? A Six-Year Follow-Up Study of 3,968 Older Adults. *Journal of Gerontology: Medical Sciences* 54A: M370–6.

McAdam, D. (1989) The Biographical Consequences of Activism. *American Sociological Review* 54: 744–60.

Merton, R. K. (1957) Priorities in Scientific Discovery: A Chapter in the Sociology of Science. *American Sociological Review* 22: 635–59.

Murrell, S. A., Salsman, N. L., & Meeks, S. (2003) Educational Attainment, Positive Psychological Mediators, and Resources for Health and Vitality in Older Adults. *Journal of Aging and Health* 15: 591–615.

Riley, M. W. & Riley, J. W. (1994) Structural Lag: Past and Future. In: Riley, M. W., Kahn, R. L., & Foner, A. (Eds.), *Age and Structural Lag*. New York, Wiley, pp. 15–36.

Ross, C. E. & Wu, C. E. (1996) Education, Age, and the Cumulative Advantage in Health. *Journal of Health and Social Behavior* 37: 104–20.

Shaw, B. A., Krause, N., Chatters, L. M. et al. (2004) Emotional Support from Parents Early in Life, Aging, and Health. *Psychology and Aging* 19: 4–12.

Uhlenberg, P. & Minor, S. (1996) Life Course and Aging: A Cohort Perspective. In: Binstock, R. H. & George, L. K. (Eds.), *Handbook of Aging and the Social Sciences*, 3rd edn. Academic Press, San Diego, pp. 208–28.

aging and technology

Stephen J. Cutler

Aging and technology stand in a reciprocal relationship to each other. On the one hand, technological change has numerous implications for older persons and for how they experience the process of aging. On the other hand, individual aging and population aging may be viewed as catalysts shaping the nature of technological development and change.

To illustrate, technological developments in the areas of health and medicine (including advances in birth control technology) have been among the factors contributing to increases in life expectancy and to population aging. Initially concentrated in western societies, population aging has now become a worldwide phenomenon as birth rates decline and life expectancy increases in nations across the globe. As environments (e.g., one's home or neighborhood) become more taxing, demanding, and challenging because of frailties and mobility limitations associated with aging, technology can redress such imbalances, reduce what Lawton and Nahemow (1973) refer to as environmental press, and enhance person–environment fit. Various types of assistive devices can compensate for sensory and mobility problems that are more prevalent at the older ages, lengthen the period of independence, and reduce reliance on informal and formal caregivers. The advent of personal computing and the emergence of the Internet can facilitate social interaction and social integration, place a wealth of information at the fingertips of older persons, and allow for new modes of social, political, and economic participation. Online networks of social support are flexible, overcome barriers to participation in support groups created by time and distance, and have been shown to reduce strains and burdens associated with caregiving.

Technology is not without negative consequences. According to some modernization theorists (e.g., Cowgill 1974), population aging – a product of technological developments – led to increased competition between generations for jobs, provided a rationale for the institutionalization of retirement as a life stage, and contributed to a decline in the status of older persons. Rapid changes in health care technology have been accompanied by periods of normative indeterminacy in the appropriateness of using technology with older patients. Costs associated with the use of advanced medical technology in end-of-life care have led some to propose using age as a basis for rationing scarce, expensive health care.

Other dimensions of technological development are proving to be problematic for older persons. Suburbanization, for instance, was a process predicated in large measure on the availability of the automobile as a means of transportation. With the aging of suburbs and the "aging in place" of its residents, mobility can be a challenge to older persons in the absence of alternative means of transportation. This is an example of what Riley et al. (1994) refer to as structural lag: a situation where societal opportunity structures have not kept pace with changes in the circumstances and conditions of the older population. A variation of structural lag is what Lawton (1998) refers to as individual lag, which is when social structures and environments change more rapidly than people's abilities (e.g., the challenges of keeping abreast of rapid changes in communications and information technology).

These several examples point to ways that technology acts as a causal agent in affecting the lives of elders and in influencing the nature of the aging process. Yet aging can also be viewed as a force influencing technological development. Most observers agree that technology generally tends to be developed by young persons and is aimed at a young market, but there are signs of growing interest in the development and application of technologies specifically for the elderly. Some of this interest stems from a recognition of commercial and market implications of social and demographic trends such as the aging of baby boomers and a likely "graying" of the labor force. That the prevalence of functional limitations and related health problems increases with age points to continued growth in the market for assistive and other enabling technologies.

Numerous studies have documented that older persons have been slower to acquire and adopt some forms of technology than younger persons have. Notable examples are communications and information technologies. Might processes of cohort succession and cohort change diminish if not eradicate such age differences in the future, or will processes accompanying intra-cohort aging lead to the persistence of age differences?

It is safe to conclude that some portion of observed age differences in technology use is due to the operation of cohort effects. In school and workplace settings, as well as at home, both the young and the middle aged have had much greater exposure to information technology than current cohorts of older persons. Familiarity with cell phones and automated systems such as ATMs among the young and middle aged likely means that these and related skills will be brought with them to their later years. Furthermore, adopting and using new technology is related to socioeconomic factors, especially education and income. That future cohorts of older persons will certainly have higher levels of educational attainment and perhaps greater levels of economic security also suggests that age differences may diminish in coming years.

On the other hand, if the types of cognitive, sensory, and motor changes that typically accompany aging persist, these may lead to the continuation of age gradients. For example, the additional features that are usually part of revised or new versions of technology often add to their complexity, and trends toward miniaturization may present visual and motor control challenges. Until the objectives embodied in transgenerational and universal design are realized, changes that accompany normal aging may work against adoption and use of tomorrow's new and enhanced, but more complicated technologies.

Finally, fascination with technology must not cause us to overlook inequalities in access. The potential benefits of the technology embodied in "smart" houses are impressive, but more fundamental for many elders are basic housing issues of availability, affordability, and adequacy. Navigational systems, already available in high-end automobiles, may make it easier to reach destinations safely and benefit some segments of the older population. For many others, however, the availability, accessibility, and cost of *any* form of transportation are more immediate issues. Thus, for persons living on limited, fixed incomes, the fruits of technological change may prove to be inaccessible, thereby creating and/or perpetuating a "technological divide" as a further form of social inequality within and between age groups.

SEE ALSO: Aging and Health Policy; Aging, Mental Health, and Well-Being; Aging and Social Support; Aging, Sociology of; Information Technology; Technology, Science, and Culture

REFERENCES AND SUGGESTED READINGS

Charness, N. & Schaie, K. (Eds.) (2003) *Impact of Technology on Successful Aging.* Springer, New York.
Cowgill, D. (1974) Aging and Modernization: A Revision of the Theory. In: Gubrium, J. (Ed.), *Late Life: Communities and Environmental Policy.* Charles C. Thomas, Springfield, IL, pp. 123–46.
Cutler, S. (forthcoming) Technological Change and Aging. In: Binstock, R. & George, L. (Eds.), *Handbook of Aging and the Social Sciences,* 6th edn. Elsevier, San Diego.
Lawton, M. (1998) Future Society and Technology. In: Graafmans, J., Taipale, V., & Charness, N. (Eds.), *Gerontechnology: A Sustainable Investment in the Future.* IOS Press, Amsterdam, pp. 12–22.
Lawton, M. & Nehemow, L. (1973) Ecology and the Aging Process. In: Eisdorfer, C. & Lawton, M. (Eds.), *Psychology of Adult Development and Aging.* American Psychological Association, Washington, DC, pp. 464–88.
Morrell, R., Mayhorn, C., & Echt, K. (2004) Why Older Adults Use or Do Not Use the Internet. In: Burdick, D. & Kwon, S. (Eds.), *Gerotechnology: Research and Practice in Technology and Aging.* Springer, New York, pp. 71–85.
Pew, R. & Van Hemel, S. (Eds.) (2004) *Technology for Adaptive Aging.* National Academies Press, Washington, DC.
Riley, M., Kahn, R., & Foner, A. (Eds.) (1994) *Age and Structural Lag: Society's Failure to Provide Meaningful Opportunities in Work, Family, and Leisure.* Wiley-Interscience, New York.

aging and work performance

Melissa Hardy

In the US, work performance, narrowly defined, is measured by productivity; more broadly conceived, it denotes how well individual workers master requisite skills, complete tasks, execute instructions, interact with colleagues, and contribute to the success of the enterprise. Perhaps as a holdover from the earlier part of the twentieth century, older workers often are assumed to be less productive than their younger counterparts. When worker productivity was a function of the speed of repetitive tasks in physically demanding jobs, and the "innovations" of the shorter work week led to a faster pace on the production line, the age-related declines in strength and endurance likely would have created age-related reductions in productivity. In part, these changes involved a growing role of innovative technology in the workplace; however, it was not the technological change, per se, that made work more difficult for older workers. It was the speed at which the machines were operated.

The current research literature that deals with changes in productivity as workers age is inconclusive, and many of the studies refer to dated production technologies. Productivity can best be assessed in specific work contexts, not only because it is job-specific productivity that is at issue, but also because expertise and experience – two factors that tend to increase with age – can be job or even task specific. Unfortunately, neither employers nor workers are particularly willing research subjects. Because reliable data that include contextual factors are not available, the relationship between age and job performance is not well understood (Aviolo 1992; Czaja 1995, 2001). Even so, current assessments suggest that age accounts for a small fraction of the between-individual variability in performance; productivity levels are highly variable among older workers; and experience appears to be a better predictor of job performance than age (Aviolo et al. 1990).

A growing literature documents age-related decline in acuity in all five senses (vision, hearing, touch, taste, and smell), age-related decline in motor abilities, and changes in cognition that can affect work performance. For example, rates of visual impairment increase with age, including a loss of static and dynamic visual acuity. Loss of contrast sensitivity, reduction in color sensitivity, greater sensitivity to problems of glare, and declines in dark adaptation are also age-related. Many older adults experience age-related hearing losses, including difficulty understanding speech and increased sensitivity to loudness. And, aging has been linked to slower response times, disruptions in coordination, loss of flexibility, and other declines in motor skills, such as reductions in strength, endurance, and dexterity (Rogers & Fisk 2000).

Decrements in intellectual functions such as working memory, attention, and perception may also decline with age. Memory, learning, thinking, and language use are cognitive functions that have received considerable attention from researchers. With aging, the sensoriperceptive system linked to the intake of information, the cognitive system that processes information, and the motor systems that translate thoughts into actions all appear to slow with aging, although not uniformly. Working memory, problem solving and reasoning, inference formation, encoding and retrieval in memory, and information processing have all been shown to decline with age (Park 1992). These changes in cognitive processing make it more difficult for older workers to shift their attention between displays, more difficult to multitask, and more difficult to maintain a rapid pace of information processing, but the evidence supporting these findings is largely experimental, performed in laboratory settings.

Changes in physical work capacity associated with aging include changes in the cardiovascular and musculoskeletal systems, body structure, and sensory systems. Although there are large individual differences here as well, certain patterns of aggregate decline are apparent. For example, maximum oxygen consumption shows a clear, linear decline with age, although it is also responsive to regular exercise and can therefore be better maintained through adherence to a schedule of routine cardiorespiratory exercise.

Many of these declines can be attenuated, reversed, or compensated for by individual behavior, workplace modification, and job redesign. For example, even workers performing physically demanding work require positive physical exercise to maintain an average fitness level for their age. Regular physical exercise can keep physical capacity nearly unchanged between ages 45 and 65; however, failure to engage in regular exercise can make a 45-year-old worker less fit than an active 65-year-old (Ilmarinen 1992). Improved workplace lighting, larger characters, acoustical adjustments, and ergonomically designed work tools can make important differences to aging workers. In addition, workers develop strategies as they age, and their accumulated experience and knowledge can compensate for slower speeds; practice can also compensate for declines in working memory and declines in perception and attention (Salthouse 1997; Czaja 2001). In addition, cognitive functions such as processing complex problems in uncertain circumstances can actually improve with age. And the process of learning is not dependent on age, although the specific features of this process relative to brain structure may change with age, and the speed of learning may slow (Baltes & Smith 1990; Salthouse 1997).

To the extent that work performance is linked to speed, skill, and expertise, training that updates workers' skills is particularly important for an aging workforce. Negative stereotypes of older workers as inflexible, unable to use new technologies, incapable of learning new skills, and unable to provide sufficient returns for the training cost provide employers with an argument against investing in retraining older workers, who are underrepresented in employer-provided training programs. Because workers learn differently as they age (Hardy & Baird 2003), training programs should take these differences into account. By presenting material at a somewhat slower pace, using active learning strategies that apply concepts within specific work contexts, building on existing skills, and allowing workers some say in structuring their own training, the effectiveness of the training can be increased.

Unfortunately, the United States Age Discrimination in Employment Act of 1967 (ADEA) has not been able to prevent the frequent exclusion of older workers from these retraining programs. The US Department of Labor attempted to consolidate the nation's fragmented employment and training system into an integrated employment and job-training service. These "one-stop" centers allow workers and job-seekers to locate an extensive range of information at a single site, including descriptions of employment opportunities, skill requirements for jobs, and education and training programs. The Workforce Investment Act of 1998 institutionalized and expanded the One-Stop Career Center System.

As aging workers experience changes in physical and mental functioning, they also encounter changes in work techniques and the tools of the trade, work expectations and workloads, the introduction of new technologies and different methods of organizing the labor process (e.g., team approaches versus sequential, individually performed operations). Although the complex connections among work experience, work performance, and aging have not been fully developed, some research reports that older workers are as productive as younger workers, and that older workers and younger workers can be equally productive in both skill-demanding and speed-demanding jobs (Spirduso 1995). Ilmarinen (1999) argues that many workers become physically weaker but mentally stronger as they age, and these changes should be reflected in work responsibilities that are less physically demanding but draw on the cognitive functions that improve with age. The concepts of *work ability* and *employability*, introduced by those at the Finnish Institute of Occupational Health (Ilmarinen 1992), address the connection between the capabilities of workers, the structure of job tasks, and the design of the work environment. The work ability index

can be a tool for human resource managers and serve as a guide for how employers can build in adjustment periods that permit the identification of sources of friction in the new regime. Then they can develop appropriate training and design ergonomically superior work settings that allow work to flow smoothly. Japan, for example, is providing federal support to companies that retool the workplace (*kaizen*) to accommodate aging workers, allowing innovative ergonomic design to minimize the effects of changes in functional ability.

As our workforce ages, we will need to better understand how features of work environment, physiology, and cognition account for variability in work performance and how the tools, workplaces, and tasks can be redesigned to enable rather than limit workers. Because of the range of systems involved, an interdisciplinary approach will be required, and employers and workers will have to become much more accepting of and accessible to research. Unlike Taylorism, which transformed production lines in the early part of the twentieth century by micro-managing the labor process and severely restricting workers' discretion in determining how to perform their tasks, innovative approaches to employment practices in the beginning of the twenty-first century can develop dynamic approaches to workplace design that will enhance workers' abilities and create flexibility in both the process and the structure of the work day.

SEE ALSO: Age Prejudice and Discrimination; Aging, Mental Health, and Well-Being; Aging and Social Policy; Aging and Technology; Employment Status Changes; Labor–Management Relations; Labor Markets; Leisure, Aging and

REFERENCES AND SUGGESTED READINGS

Aviolo, B. J. (1992) A Levels of Analysis Perspective of Aging and Work Research. In: Schaie, K. W. & Lawton, M. P. (Eds.), *Annual Review of Gerontology and Geriatrics*. Springer, New York, pp. 239–60.

Aviolo, B. J., Waldman, D. A., & McDaniel, M. A. (1990) Age and Work Performance in Nonmanagerial Jobs: The Effects of Experience and

Occupational Type. *Academy of Management Journal* 33: 407–22.

Baltes, P. & Smith, J. (1990) Toward a Psychology of Wisdom. In: Stenberg, R. J. (Ed.), *Wisdom: Its Nature, Origin, and Development*. Cambridge University Press, New York, pp. 87–120.

Czaja, S. (1995) Aging and Work Performance. *Review of Public Personnel Administration* 15(2): 46–61.

Czaja, S. (2001) Technological Change and the Older Worker. In: Birren, J. E. & Schaie, K. W. (Eds.), *Handbook of the Psychology of Aging*, 5th edn. Academic Press, New York, pp. 547–56.

Hardy, M. (2005) Older Workers. In: Binstock, R. H. & George, L. K. (Eds.), *Handbook of Aging in the Social Sciences*. Academic Press, San Diego.

Hardy, M. & Baird, C. L. (2003) Is It All About Aging? Technology and Aging in Social Context. In: Charness, N. & Schaie, K. W. (Eds.), *Impact of Technology on Successful Aging*. Springer, New York, pp. 28–41.

Ilmarinen, J. E. (1992) Job Design for the Aged with Regard to Decline in their Maximal Aerobic Capacity. *International Journal of Industrial Ergonomics* 10: 53–77.

Ilmarinen, J. E. (1999) *Ageing Workers in the European Union: Status and Promotion of Work Ability, Employability, and Employment*. Finnish Institute of Occupational Health, Ministry of Social Affairs and Health, Ministry of Labor, Helsinki, Finland.

Ilmarinen, J. E., Louhevaara, V., Korhonen, O., et al. (1991) Changes in Maximal Cardiorespiratory Capacity Among Aging Municipal Employees. *Scandinavian Journal of Work, Environment, and Health* 17: 99–109.

Park, D. C. (1992) Applied Cognitive Aging Research. In: Craik, F. I. M. & Salthouse, T. A. (Eds.), *The Handbook of Aging and Cognition*. Lawrence Erlbaum, Mahwah, NJ, pp. 449–94.

Rogers, W. A. & Fisk, A. D. (2000) Human Factors, Applied Cognition, and Aging. In: Craik, F. I. M. & Salthouse, T. A. (Eds.), *The Handbook of Aging and Cognition*, 2nd edn. Lawrence Erlbaum, Mahwah, NJ, pp. 559–91.

Salthouse, T. A. (1997) Implications of Adult Age Differences in Cognition for Work Performance. In: Kilborn, A., Westerholm, P., & Hallsten, L. (Eds.), *Work After 45?* Vol. 1. Arbete och Halsa. Arbetslivsinstitutet, Solna, pp. 15–28.

Schieber, F. (2003) Human Factors and Aging: Identifying and Compensating for Age-Related Defects in Sensory and Cognitive Function. In: Charness, N. & Schaie, K. W. (Eds.), *Impact of Technology on Successful Aging*. Springer, New York, pp. 42–84.

Spirduso, W. W. (1995) Job Performance of the Older Worker. In: Spirduso, W. W. (Ed.), *Physical Dimensions of Aging*. Human Kinetics, Champaign, IL, pp. 367–87.

AIDS, sociology of

Susan Kippax and Heather Worth

AIDS or acquired immune deficiency syndrome is caused by a retrovirus identified in 1984, the human immunodeficiency virus (HIV). Twenty years later, it is estimated that over 20 million people have died of AIDS and 40 million people are living with HIV, with 95 percent living in developing countries. The world is facing a global pandemic: a pandemic marked by inequalities of class, gender, race, and sexual preference. The spread of HIV and AIDS is not evenly distributed and prevalence rates range from less than 1 percent of the adult population in much of the developed world to more than 30 percent in some southern African countries. Some countries in northwestern Europe and Australia have "local" epidemics mainly confined to gay men; some such as Botswana, Namibia, South Africa, and Zimbabwe are experiencing "generalized" epidemics where the entire sexually active population is affected; others such as Russia are experiencing an accelerating epidemic initially confined to transmission among injecting drug users but now becoming generalized; while still others such as the United States and some countries in South America are experiencing multiple epidemics – among people who inject drugs, among gay men, and increasingly among the poor. In Asia and the Pacific regions the patterning of the epidemic continues to emerge, but there are fears that some countries, such as India, will experience a generalized epidemic.

Globalization has played a central and unique role in both the spread of and the response to the AIDS pandemic, and presents both risks and opportunities for future action. As AIDS has become an intensely globalized problem, a number of pressing issues have come to the fore, not only economic but also political, social, cultural, and security issues. By the mid-1990s serious concerns were being raised about the massive global debt being incurred by developing countries in their fight against HIV and AIDS. While widespread financial and donor support for HIV programs is now available, particularly through the Global Fund for TB, Malaria, and HIV and international donors, the World Bank and the International Monetary Fund were slow to recognize the severity of the economic toll AIDS would exact and thus slow to fund.

Structural adjustment policies, set up as a condition for receiving loans, required that countries adopt austerity programs – including major cuts in health spending. Critics have argued that this helped create the very social and economic conditions and forces that contributed to the spread of HIV infection in developing countries. There is no doubt that many nations will experience severe economic downturn because of AIDS. In Africa, there has already been a decline in agricultural output and a threat to food security. Ill health means: less time spent on growing crops and more time spent caring for the sick; a concomitant decline in household expenditure on education; a return to rural areas to die, thus adding to the problem of scarce village resources; a dramatic increase in health expenditure; and, as a consequence of parental deaths, a rapid increase in the number of children orphaned.

While pressure is being exerted by developing countries over their right to parallel import and produce their own anti-retroviral AIDS drugs under the emergency conditions of the AIDS crisis, the World Trade Organization (WTO) TRIPS agreement concerning patent protection to pharmaceutical companies may substantially widen the gap in global access to such therapies. In November 2001 in Doha, the Ministerial Conference of the WTO declared that the TRIPS should be interpreted to support public health and allow for patents to be overridden if required to respond to emergencies such as the AIDS epidemic.

Massive global flows of population (forced and by choice) are an integral part of globalization and the spread of HIV is implicated in these transient flows of populations. The war in the region of the Horn of Africa in the early 1980s as well as the 1994 war in Rwanda brought into sharp relief the connection between refugees and HIV. The worldwide number of refugees and internally displaced people has been estimated at over 22 million, with an HIV prevalence rate of up to 5 percent in some countries. Migration for work also renders men and women vulnerable to HIV because of their living and working conditions – poverty, powerlessness, precarious family situations and separations, and inadequate access to health services.

AIDS is an issue of global governance involving various UN agencies, medical establishments, pharmaceutical companies, researchers, governments, non-government and community-based organizations. The global politics, policies, and practices of AIDS prevention and support radically affect nationally based health care systems and education programs, as well as local grassroots efforts.

HIV PREVENTION

As a blood-borne virus, HIV is most commonly transmitted by sexual practice, particularly penetrative intercourse (vaginal and anal) with an HIV-infected person. It is also transmitted by the sharing of HIV-contaminated needles and syringes, from an HIV-positive mother to her child during birth and breast-feeding, and via the transfusion of infected blood and blood products. The population most affected by HIV is young men and women of reproductive age.

Although in 1996 treatments – in the form of anti-retroviral therapy (ART) and fusion inhibitors that block HIV from entering the body's immune cells to effectively slow the progression from HIV to AIDS to death – were developed, there is at present no cure for AIDS or an effective prophylactic vaccine for HIV. Perinatal transmission (sometimes referred to as "mother-to-child" transmission) can be dramatically reduced by using anti-retroviral therapy, while changes in sexual practice and injection drug use can almost completely prevent HIV transmission. These changes in practice include abstinence (from sex and from injecting drug use), the use of condoms for sex, and the use of clean needles and syringes for drug injection.

There is now indisputable evidence that countries which have established needle and syringe programs supplying clean needles and syringes to people who inject drugs have curbed injecting drug-related HIV transmission. Embracing this "harm reduction" approach has proved far more effective than abstinence-based and related drug supply reduction programs, such as the "war on drugs," and there is little evidence to support the claim that needle and syringe programs promote illegal behaviors.

In countries and regions, for example, in much of Western Europe and in the United States, Australasia, Thailand, Cambodia, Senegal, and Uganda, where condom promotion has been successful, there has been a dramatic decline in HIV prevalence. In these countries, the adoption of condoms has proved more effective than abstinence or reliance on monogamy. In other words, "safe sex" (sometimes "safer sex") rather than no sex has been effective. It is also clear that where there are or were barriers to condom uptake, HIV prevalence rates are high, with some countries exhibiting prevalence levels of 30 to 35 percent among their sexually active populations.

HIV prevalence rates fall in countries where governments: acknowledge HIV is a virus that affects everyone; are committed to and fund prevention and health promotion including education programs; promote condom use and needle and syringe programs; support social movements by funding at-risk communities to combat HIV transmission; and provide treatment, care, and support to all those living with HIV and AIDS. In the absence of these factors, prevention efforts falter.

Nonetheless, debate continues about the provision of needle and syringe programs and the content of sex and relationship education for the young, some arguing that young people have the right to sex education that recognizes the central role of condoms in halting HIV transmission, with others claiming that sex education should focus on promoting abstinence. Moral agendas in many countries thwart prevention efforts: some governments claim that sex education promotes sexual activity among the young; others, particularly those with religious affiliations, promote monogamy, which is now acknowledged to be a risk factor – at least for married women.

The conservative policies of some countries, including the United States, and the related advocacy of abstinence and monogamy, have had a profound and, many would claim, negative impact on HIV prevention and education programs.

AIDS AND HUMAN RIGHTS

The promotion and protection of human rights constitute an essential component in preventing transmission of HIV and reducing vulnerability to infection and to the impact of HIV/AIDS. Because HIV most affects stigmatized and marginalized populations, human rights issues have been central to the response to HIV. Denying the rights of people living with HIV and those most at risk imperils not only their well-being, but also life itself. Human rights violations include sexual violence and coercion faced by women and girls, stigmatization of men who have sex with men, abuses against sex workers and injecting drug users, refugees, and migrants, lack of access to condoms and harm reduction measures in prisons, and violations of the right of young persons to information on HIV transmission. Human rights violations constitute a major barrier to both prevention efforts and access to treatments and care.

HIV exacerbates the differential power between men and women and the gendered patterns of social and economic dependency. Social structures and the beliefs, customs, and practices that define "masculine" and "feminine" attributes play a central role in who is vulnerable to infection, and who will receive care, support, or treatment. In the early years of the pandemic men accounted for the majority of those living with HIV. However, this is changing: to the end of 2004 in Sub-Saharan Africa, 57 percent of all adults living with HIV were women.

For men and boys, institutions and structures that form societal expectations about gender create social pressure for men to take sexual risks, putting them at risk of HIV. In many countries, men's labor takes them far from families, increasing their (and their partners') vulnerability to HIV. The problems facing men are often overlooked because of their apparent physical and emotional invulnerability. A disregard for their own health and that of their sexual partners puts men in danger. Young men have the greatest number of unprotected sexual acts, are most likely to inject drugs, are most likely to engage in male sex work, and to be the victims of male-to-male sexual violence. On the other hand, older men may seek very young women as partners and wives because they believe they are less likely to be HIV-positive, thus placing young women at increased risk of becoming infected.

Women have less access than men to education and economic resources, which significantly reduces their capacity to fight HIV, but at the same time women are often positioned as vectors of HIV. In some societies, there is a belief that women and girls should be both ignorant about sex and passive during sex. Lack of knowledge of sexual matters is often viewed as a sign of purity and innocence, and prevents young women from seeking information about sex. On the other hand, girls are often pressured by boys to have sex as a proof of love. Data on HIV transmission indicate that in much of Africa and in countries such as India, most married women are infected as a consequence of normal marital sexual relations with their husbands. It is estimated that some 60 to 80 percent of African women in steady relationships who become infected with HIV have one sexual partner – their husband or regular partner.

Women's subordinate place and the emphasis on women's innocence make it difficult for them to discuss sex and safe sex openly with their partners. Women may also have little control over how, when, and where sex takes place, which considerably constrains their ability to insist on safe sex. Further, violence against girls and women, including rape, exacerbates their susceptibility to HIV, and this increases in times of conflict and war.

People living with HIV and AIDS are particularly subject to stigmatization and discrimination in society, including in the workplace and in access to government services. Fundamental human rights, such as the right to non-discrimination, equal protection and equality before the law, privacy, liberty of movement, work, equal access to education, housing, health care, social security, assistance, and welfare, are often violated based on known or presumed HIV/AIDS status. The Commission on Human Rights in 2001 and again in 2002 confirmed that access to AIDS medication is a key component of the right to the highest attainable standard of health, enshrined in the Universal Declaration of Human Rights, the International Covenant on Economic, Social, and Cultural Rights, and the Convention on the Rights of the Child.

On a political level, the response to the AIDS pandemic is hindered by countries which do not recognize freedoms of speech and association, nor the right to information and education by infected and affected groups and by civil society as a whole. Respect, protection, and fulfillment of human rights are central to the AIDS agenda, and equally, HIV/AIDS needs to be at the center of the global human rights agenda.

While some uncertainties remain as to why some countries have a higher prevalence than others, and why some countries have managed to reduce prevalence levels radically, it is evident that a successful response to HIV is dependent on a human rights approach that empowers civil society and ensures the communities have a secure place within the national dialogue. In general, in the developed world and also, in some instances, in the developing world, where a modern public health approach has been adopted, an approach in which communities encourage and support individuals, understood as rational agents, to reduce harm to themselves and others, and where people have access to prevention education and treatment, HIV transmission has been slowed. On the other hand, economic and social disadvantage and civil disruption, and associated marginalization and stigma, increase vulnerability to HIV.

HIV TREATMENTS

The issue of human rights is central to treatment access: all who are infected with HIV have the right to treatment. In the developed world where most people living with HIV have access to these therapies, there has been an 80 percent fall in deaths related to AIDS. In the developing world, however, only approximately 5 percent of those who are infected are currently receiving the most effective therapy. Prospects for access to treatments continue to be thwarted by poverty and global inequalities despite the recent moves for treatment "access for all": the Global Fund's commitment to buy and distribute cheap generic drugs to poor countries; and the "3 by 5" initiative of the World Health Organization (WHO) to provide ART therapy to 3 million people by 2005. To the middle of 2004, only 400,000 of the 3 million had been treated with ART.

The "3 by 5" initiative, although welcomed by many, has placed an additional burden on much of the developing world – the burden to test their populations. There are estimates that between 180 million and 300 million people will need to be HIV tested at least once in order to reach the target of 3 million people on ART. People have been slow to come forward for testing, however, because of the stigma and discrimination often associated with an HIV-positive diagnosis. As a result of the poor response, routine "opt-out" testing is being adopted in countries with high prevalence rates. While some interpret this response as necessary, others are concerned that the pressure to test will undermine human rights and increase stigma and discrimination rather than reduce it.

An added incentive to treatment rollout is the possibility that if treatment uptake is extensive, then ART may also act in a preventive fashion. It is yet to be proven whether widespread testing and subsequent uptake of treatment among those who are HIV-infected will reduce the population viral load and hence make HIV transmission less likely. In the developed world, high uptake of treatment has not led – at least not initially – to a reduction in HIV transmission. In some countries such as the United States and Australia, treatment uptake is related to a relaxation in "safe sex" and an apparent concomitant increase in HIV incidence.

The current push for routine testing and treatment carries with it the risk of downplaying prevention. In recognition of this problem, some are advocating prevention in the clinic – voluntary counseling and testing have become a site for prevention. While prevention in the clinic may be a useful addendum to health promotion, it is unlikely to succeed alone. What is needed to sustain changes in sexual and drug injection practice is cultural and normative authority, and such authority is best achieved in the social realm. The clinic is by its very nature private, confidential, and individualistic and thus unlikely to provide the appropriate environment for sustained prevention. More importantly – perhaps most importantly – extending testing so as to make it a major prevention tool will give governments the excuse to draw back from HIV, the excuse not to have to deal with and face the complexities of talking about sex and drugs, the excuse not to train teachers and those in contact with the young, to raise issues in connection with HIV transmission. It will excise the public and collective voice.

The current conservative global climate appears to be producing a flight from "behavioral" prevention. While it is imperative that the quest continue for a cure to HIV and AIDS and for an effective prophylactic vaccine and other prevention technologies, it is equally vital that such endeavors do not undermine the gains already made. The challenge for modern public health is to address the social, cultural, and economic dimensions of health, to address issues of power between and within countries, and to attack discrimination and prejudice.

SEE ALSO: Drug Use; Gender, Development and; Globalization, Sexuality and; Health Risk Behavior; HIV/AIDS and Population; Human Rights; Prevention, Intervention; Safer Sex

REFERENCES AND SUGGESTED READINGS

Barnett, T. & Whiteside, A. (2003) *AIDS in the Twenty-First Century: Disease and Globalization.* Palgrave, New York.

Bayer, R. (1989) *Private Acts, Social Consequences: AIDS and the Politics of Public Health.* Rutgers University Press, New Brunswick, NJ.

Bloor, M. (1995) *The Sociology of HIV Transmission.* Sage, London.

Crimp, D. (Ed.) (1988) *AIDS: Cultural Analysis, Cultural Activism.* MIT Press, Cambridge, MA.

Epstein, S. (1996) *Impure Science: AIDS, Activism, and the Politics of Knowledge.* University College Press, Berkeley.

Global HIV Prevention Working Group (2004) *HIV Prevention in the Era of Expanded Treatment Access.* Gates Foundation/Kaiser Family Foundation.

Kippax, S. & Race, K. (2003) Sustaining Safe Practice: Twenty Years On. *Social Science and Medicine* 57: 1–12.

Moatti, J.-P., Souteyrand, Y., Prieur, A., Sandfort, T., & Aggleton, P. (Eds.) (2000) *AIDS in Europe: New Challenges for the Social Sciences.* Routledge, London.

Patton, C. (2002) *Global AIDS/Local Context.* University of Minnesota Press, Minneapolis.

Rofes, E. (1998) *Dry Bones Breathe: Gay Men Creating Post-AIDS Identities and Cultures.* Harrington Park Press, New York.

Rosenbrock, R., Dubois-Arber, F., Moers, M., Pinell, P., Schaeffer, D., & Setbon, M. (2000) The Normalization of AIDS in Western European Countries. *Social Science and Medicine* 50: 1607–29.

Treichler, P. (1999) *How to Have Theory in an Epidemic: Cultural Chronicles of AIDS.* Duke University Press, Durham, NC.

UNAIDS (2004) *Global Summary of the HIV/AIDS Epidemic: Joint United Nations Programme on HIV/AIDS.* UNAIDS, Geneva.

UNHCR (2002) *HIV/AIDS and Refugees: UNHCR's Strategic Plan 2002–2004.* United Nations High Commissioner for Refugees, Geneva.

WHO (2005) *"3 by 5" Progress Report, December 2004.* World Health Organization, Geneva.

al-Biruni (973–1048)

Syed Farid Alatas

Abu Rayhan Muhammad ibn Ahmad al-Biruni was born in the city of Khwārazm (modern Khiva) in what is today known as Uzbekistan, but during his youth was part of the Iranian Samanid Empire. He spent his early years under the patronage of various rulers until finally becoming part of the court of Mahmud Ghaznavi (979–1030), the ruler of an empire that included parts of what is now known as Afghanistan, Iran, and northern India. Al-Biruni went to India with the troops of Mahmud and remained there for many years. During this time, he studied Sanskrit, translated a number of Indian religious texts, and conducted research on Indian religions and their doctrines. Al-Biruni was the first Muslim and probably the first scholar to provide a systematic account of the religions of India from a sociological point of view. Furthermore, his work is considered to be a vital source of knowledge of Indian history and society in the eleventh century, providing details of the religion, philosophy, literature, geography, chronology, astronomy, customs, laws, and astrology of India.

Typical of the great scholars of his period, al-Biruni was multitalented, being well versed in physics, metaphysics, mathematics, geography, and history. He wrote a number of books and treatises. Apart from his *Kitab ma li al-hind (The Book of What Constitutes India)*, he also wrote *Al-Qanun al-Masudi* (on astronomy and trigonometry), *Al-Athar al-Baqia* (on ancient history and geography), *Kitab al-Saidana (Materia Medica)*, and *Kitab al-Jawahir (Book of Precious Stones)*. His *Al-Tafhim-li-Awail Sina'at al-Tanjim* gives a summary of mathematics and astronomy. His important work sociologically speaking is his *Kitab ma li al-hind*, in which he presents a study of Indian religions. Al-Biruni died in 1048 CE at the age of 75.

The history of Central Asia during the tenth and eleventh centuries provides an important backdrop for the understanding of al-Biruni's intellectual development. He was born in the environs (Persian, bīrūn) of Kāth, one of the two main cities of Khwārazm, the other being Jurjāniyya. The title of Khwārazmshāh had been held for a long time by the ruler of Kāth. But in 995 the ruler of Jurjāniyya killed his suzerain and appropriated the title for himself. During the civil war, al-Biruni fled the area for a few years. Various dynasties that once flourished around Khwārazm, such as the Sāmānids to the southeast, the Buwayhids to the west, and the Ziyārid state in between, were gradually absorbed by the Ghaznavids under the leadership of Sultan Mahmūd in central Afghanistan by 1020. During his flight and after, it is likely that al-Biruni lived in places such as Rayy (near modern Tehran), Bukhara, and Gurgān. In Bukhara he met the famed physician and philosopher ibn Sina (Avicenna). By 1022, Sultan Mahmūd had conquered large parts of India including Waihand, Multan, Bhatinda, and the Ganges valley up to near Benares. It was during this time that al-Biruni developed an interest in Indian society, living in an empire that conquered large areas of the Indian subcontinent and having the opportunity to travel and take up residence there (Kennedy 1970).

The work of al-Biruni that can be considered as sociological is his study of India. His *Kitab ma li al-hind* (*The Book of What Constitutes India*) aimed to provide a comprehensive account of what he called "the religions of India and their doctrines." This included the religion, philosophy, literature, geography, science, customs, and laws of the Indians. Of special interest to sociology is al-Biruni's construction of the religions of India.

Al-Biruni considered what we call "Hinduism" as a religion centuries before Europeans recognized Hinduism as not mere heathenism. In attempting a reconstruction of al-Biruni's construction of "Hinduism," it is necessary to point out that it is inadequate to rely on Sachau's English translation of the Arabic original. The translation, which was undertaken in the late nineteenth century, reads into Arabic terms nineteenth-century European ideas about what Hinduism was. For example, in his preface in the Arabic original, al-Biruni refers to "the religions of India and their doctrines" (*adyān al-hind wa madhāhibuhum*) (Al-Biruni 1377/1958 [ca. 1030]: 4), while this is translated by Sachau as "the religions and doctrines of the Hindus" (Sachau 1910: 6). Throughout the translation Sachau uses the term "Hindu," leading one to assume that al-Biruni conceived of a single religion called Hinduism. For example, the second chapter of the *Tahqīq ma li al-hind* was translated by Sachau as "On the Belief of the Hindus in God," whereas the Arabic original has it as "On their Beliefs in God, Praise be to Him." Moreover, the term Hindu does not appear in the Arabic text and the term "*hind*" did not have religious connotations.

The account of the creed of the Indians begins in chapter 2 with an exposition of their belief in God, by which al-Biruni means the same God that is worshipped by Jews, Christians, and Muslims. The exposition begins with an account of the nature of God, with reference to his speech, knowledge, and action (Sachau 1910: 27–30; al-Biruni 1377/1958 [ca. 1030]: 20–2).

We are then told that this is an account of the belief in God among the elite. Here al-Biruni is making a distinction between ideas associated with a high tradition and ideas held by the common people, as far as the conception of God is concerned (Sachau 1910: 31–2; al-Biruni 1377/1958 [ca. 1030]: 23–4).

What we get so far is a picture of a monotheistic religion based on a determinate number of books, the *Patañjali*, *Veda*, and *Gita* (Sachau 1910: 27, 29; al-Biruni 1377/1958 [ca. 1030]: 20–1). The *Veda* was "sent down" to Brahma (*anzalahu 'alā brāhma*) (Sachau 1910: 29; al-Biruni 1377/1958 [ca. 1030]: 21). Sociologically speaking, a distinction has to be made between the abstract, metaphysical ideas of the high tradition and the literalist, anthropomorphic ideas of the common people.

From the chapter headings of the *Kitab ma li al-hind*, it is obvious that by "the religions of India and their doctrines" al-Biruni means something much broader than "religion" as understood in sociology today. He is clearly referring to the entire corpus of Indian beliefs and practices, including the various branches of knowledge that are not seen by modern sociology to be part of religion. These include theology, philosophy, literature, metrology, geography, astronomy, chronology, and the study of manners and customs.

RELEVANCE TO THE HISTORY OF CONTEMPORARY SOCIOLOGY

Al-Biruni's studies on Indian religions are important for three principal reasons. One is that he pioneered the comparative study of religion. Al-Biruni was extremely versatile as a scholar. In his work in the exact sciences such as in his *Kitab al-Jawahir* (*Book of Precious Stones*), he was an experimental scientist. But he was well aware that such methods were not suitable for the study of religion and, therefore, employed a comparative approach in his study of India. For example, when he makes the distinction between the abstract, metaphysical ideas of the elite and the anthropomorphic ideas of the masses, he clarifies that this dichotomy is to be found among the ancient Greeks, Jews, Christians, and Muslims (Sachau 1910: 24, 111). In other words, the dichotomy is a universal tendency found in all religions.

Second, his work on India is an example of an early sociological study conscious of the necessity for objectivity. Al-Biruni was an impartial observer of Indian society. This can be seen from the full title of his study: *Kitab al-Biruni fi tahqiq ma li al-hind min maqbulat fi al-'aql aw mardhulat*, that is, *The Book of What Constitutes India as derived from Discourse which is Logically Acceptable or Unacceptable.* Al-Biruni's approach was to make assessments based on what was logically acceptable. He was fully aware of the need to refrain from making value judgments about Indian religions from an Islamic perspective. He attempted to present Indian civilization as understood by Indians themselves (Sachau 1910: 25; al-Biruni 1377/1958 [ca. 1030]: 19). Al-Biruni quotes extensively from Sanskrit texts which he had either read himself or which were communicated to him.

Third, al-Biruni's work on India is important from a methods point of view because it contains ideas pertinent to social statistics, applied social research, and the issue of numerical evidence (Boruch 1984). These come under the categories of errors in information, data sharing, the limits of knowledge, and statistics. On errors in information, he was concerned with fixing limits to guesswork and the problems of translation as he relied greatly on Sanskrit sources (Boruch 1984: 826). He also raised the problem of response bias that arises from ethnocentrism, lying, corroboration, the question of the validity of information (Boruch 1984: 828–30), and the types of misrepresentations.

On data sharing, al-Biruni was critical of those who resisted doing so, saying that the Indians "are by nature niggardly in communicating that which they know, and they take the greatest possible care to withhold it from men of another caste among their own people, still much more, of course from any foreigner" (Sachau 1910: 22, cited in Boruch 1984: 836). On the limits of knowledge, he listed various impediments such as knowledge

of languages, carelessness of scribes, a metrical system of writing, and religious insularity (Boruch 1984: 837). On statistical technique, Boruch notes that although al-Biruni was obviously not familiar with concepts of relative frequency distribution, there is an attempt to articulate an embryonic notion of that when he discusses rare events (Boruch 1984: 838).

In cautioning us against the various types of lies and misrepresentations, al-Biruni refers to the example of the critics of the Mu'tazila school of theology in Islam. He once called upon a scholar by the name of Abu Sahl 'Abd al-Mun'im Ibn 'Ali Ibn Nuh al-Tiflisi, who spoke of the misrepresentation of the Mu'tazila school. According to the Mu'tazila, God is omniscient and, therefore, has no knowledge (in the way that man has knowledge). The misrepresentation is that God is ignorant (Sachau 1910: 5)! It is the same scholar who urged al-Biruni to write a work on the religions of India because of the misrepresentations of India that were found in contemporary works among Muslims (Sachau 1910: 6–7).

Also on methods, al-Biruni makes an interesting case for hearsay as opposed to eyewitness. We are used to thinking of eyewitness accounts as more reliable than hearsay. Al-Biruni concurs when he says that "the eye of the observer apprehends the substance of that which is observed, both in the time when and the place where it exists, whilst hearsay has its peculiar drawbacks" (Sachau 1910: 3). However, he notes that had it not been for the drawbacks, hearsay would be preferable to eyewitness. The reason for this is that "the object of eye-witness can only be *actual* momentary existence, whilst hearsay comprehends alike the present, the past, and the future, so as to apply in a certain sense both to that which *is* and to that which is *not*" (Sachau 1910: 3). In this sense, al-Biruni notes, written tradition is a type of hearsay and the most preferable, observing that if a report regarding an event were not contradicted by logic or physical laws, then its truth or falsity depends on the "character of the reporters, who are influenced by the divergency of interests and all kinds of animosities and antipathies between the various nations" (Sachau 1910: 3).

While it is true that his study was narrow in that his sources were mainly textual, what is interesting from the sociological standpoint is the definition of *dīn* (plural, *adyān*), the complexity of which is lost when translated into the modern "religion." This then raises the question as to whether al-Biruni imposed an Islamic conception of religion onto his Indian data or derived this broad conception from his Indian textual sources or informants. This issue has so far not been dealt with by scholars of al-Biruni or of Hinduism.

It has been noted that al-Biruni utilized Muslim categories in his study of Indian thought. As Lawrence suggests, the introductory chapters on theology and philosophy of the *Kitab ma li al-hind* suggest an organizational principle and selection criteria based on the Islamic understanding of God (Lawrence 1978: 6). However, this cannot be seen as an imposition of Muslim categories as al-Biruni did not read Islamic meanings into the religions of the Indians. It is interesting that al-Biruni's translator, Edward C. Sachau, observed that al-Biruni's method was not to speak himself "but to let the Hindus speak, giving extensive quotations from their classical authors" (Sachau 1910: xxiv), while Sachau himself does not always allow al-Biruni to speak when he reads modern European meanings into al-Biruni's Arabic text.

Al-Biruni had a universal conception of *dīn*, which he applies to religions other than Islam, at a time when the Latin *religio* was only applied to Christianity. At the same time, al-Biruni does not intellectually or culturally Islamize the religions of the Indians by reading into the Indian material an Islamic model or Islamic meanings.

SEE ALSO: Hinduism; Islam; Khaldun, Ibn; Religion; Religion, Sociology of

REFERENCES AND SUGGESTED READINGS

al-Biruni, Abu al-Rayhan Muhammad bin Ahmad (1377/1958 [ca. 1030]) *Kitab al-Biruni fī tahqīq ma li al-hind min maqbūlat fī al-'aql aw mardhūlat.* Majlis Da'rāt al-Ma'ārif al-Uthmāniyyah, Hyderabad.

Boruch, R. F. (1984) Ideas about Social Research, Evaluation, and Statistics in Medieval Arabic Literature: Ibn Khaldun and al-Biruni. *Evaluation Review* 8(6): 823–42.

Jeffery, A. (1951) Al-Biruni's Contribution to Comparative Religion. In: *Al-Biruni Commemoration Volume AH 362–AH 1362.* Iran Society, Calcutta, pp. 125–60.

Kennedy, E. S. (1970) Al-Biruni. In: C. C. Gillispie (Ed.), *Dictionary of Scientific Biography*, Vol. 1. Scribner, New York, pp. 147–58.

Lawrence, B. B. (1978) Al-Biruni's Approach to the Comparative Study of Indian Culture. *Studies in Islam* 11(1): 1–13.

Sachau, E. C. (Trans.) (1910) *Alberinu's India: An Account of the Religion, Philosophy, Literature, Geography, Chronology, Astronomy, Customs, Laws and Astrology of India about AD 1030.* Low Price Publications, Delhi.

alcohol and crime

Hung-En Sung

Alcohol is the most widely abused psychoactive substance in the United States. It is the only legally available non-prescription addictive drug that dangerously alters the mind and behavior. The term "alcohol-related crime" refers to violations of laws regulating the sale or use of alcohol and also covers other criminal activities that involve alcohol.

Underage drinking and drunk driving are the most prevalent alcohol-specific offenses in the US. In 2003, more than three-fourths of students had consumed alcohol by the end of high school, and more than half of 12th graders had been drunk at least once in their lifetime (Johnston et al. 2004). Apart from being illegal, underage drinking – binge drinking in particular – has led to very high rates of drunk driving among adolescents. Youths between ages 16 and 20 are more than twice as likely to be involved in alcohol-related car accidents. Young male drivers, people with drinking problems, those who begin drinking at younger ages, and drivers who do not wear safety belts are disproportionately likely to be involved in alcohol-related fatal accidents.

There are more than 82 million incidents, but only 1.5 million arrests for drinking and driving each year (Hingson & Winter 2003). Law enforcement has not been effective in deterring drunk driving: at least two-thirds of the fatal alcohol-involved accidents are caused by repeat drink drivers. Effective measures for controlling drunk driving and alcohol-related accidents include lowering legal blood alcohol concentrations, controlling liquor outlets, nighttime driving curfews for minors, educational treatment programs combined with license suspension for offenders, and court monitoring of high-risk offenders.

Data demonstrate the close association between alcohol and violent crimes. Nationally, about 30 percent of violent crimes involved an offender who had been drinking according to victimization data (Bureau of Justice Statistics 2004). At the macro-level, alcohol availability rates and alcohol consumption rates are associated with violent crime. Yet at the micro-level, alcohol increases the risk of violent behavior only for certain individuals and under some social situations or cultural influences. For example, drinking is conducive to aggression when alcohol intoxication is celebrated as a display of masculinity and male togetherness or when certain situational cues, such as weapons or hostile peers, are present.

Although perpetrators are far more likely than victims to be intoxicated, the role of alcohol in violent victimization is largest among groups that, if not intoxicated, are normally less vulnerable to violence: whites, males, and persons of higher socioeconomic status. Difficult temperament, hyperactivity, hostile beliefs, history of family violence, poor school performance, delinquent peers, criminogenic beliefs about alcohol's effects, impulsivity, and antisocial personality disorder are risk factors that increase the likelihood of alcohol-related violence and could appear in childhood and adolescence as its precursors.

Alcohol use typically co-occurs with domestic violence. Two-thirds of victims reported alcohol being a factor. Recent findings have also corroborated the role of alcohol in female-to-male and same-sex partner violence. Although moderate drinkers are more frequently engaged in intimate violence than are light drinkers and abstainers, only heavy and/or binge drinkers are involved in the most chronic and serious forms of aggression. The odds, frequency, and severity of physical attacks are highest on days of alcohol use. Relationship stress, deficient

conflict/anger management skills, and a history of physical abuse heighten risks of violence due to alcohol abuse or dependence in an intimate relationship. Clinical data attest that violence decreases after behavioral marital alcoholism treatment.

The role of parental alcohol abuse in the perpetration of physical or sexual child abuse has not been conclusively established. However, some research indicates that parental alcohol abuse may increase a child's risk of experiencing physical or sexual abuse. Potential contributors to alcohol-induced child abuse include low socioeconomic status, relationship stress between parents, and parental history of violence.

Alcohol is also a contributor to nuisance, loitering, panhandling, and disorderly conduct in open spaces. The prevalence of alcohol use is high among the homeless and street youths. The mere sight and smell of alcohol-related incivilities instill a sense of insecurity in the citizenry. Policing alcohol-related street disorder and enforcing compliance checks of alcohol-dispensing businesses have proved promising in reducing citizens' fear of crime and preventing further deterioration of community safety.

A particular alcohol-organized crime connection was seen after 1919 when the ratification of the 18th Amendment outlawed the production, sale, and transportation of alcoholic beverages across the US. The emergence of a national market for bootlegged liquor increased the visibility, influence, lethality, and wealth of criminal organizations and severely corrupted the enforcement apparatus (Miron 2004). Homicide rates grew dramatically in major urban areas during the 1920s. Public health gains of Prohibition were achieved at a public safety cost that the society was unwilling to tolerate. The 21st Amendment repealed the 18th in 1933.

The mere co-occurrence of alcohol use and violence does not prove that alcohol use causes violence. In some cases, the desire or plan to use violence may actually trigger alcohol consumption (i.e., drinking to embolden oneself before attacking someone). Moreover, certain common factors may lead to both alcohol consumption and violence (i.e., some youth gangs encourage both heavy drinking and fighting). The *causal* pathways between alcohol and human violence in diverse contexts remain to be determined.

SEE ALSO: Alcoholism and Alcohol Abuse; Crime; Drug Use; Drugs, Drug Abuse, and Drug Policy; Drugs and the Law; Drugs/ Substance Use in Sport; Juvenile Delinquency

REFERENCES AND SUGGESTED READINGS

Acierno, R., Coffey, S., & Resnick, H. S. (Eds.) (2003) Interpersonal Violence and Substance Abuse Problems. Special issue. *Addictive Behaviors* 28(9).

Bureau of Justice Statistics (2004) *The Role of Alcohol in Crime Victimization*. Online. www.ojp. usdoj.gov/bjs/cvict_c.htm#alcohol.

Gordis, E. (Ed.) (2001) Alcohol and Violence. Special issue. *Alcohol Research and Health* 25(1).

Greenfeld, L. A. (1998) *Alcohol and Crime: An Analysis of National Data on the Prevalence of Alcohol Involvement in Crime*. Bureau of Justice Statistics, Washington, DC.

Hingson, R. & Winter, M. (2003) Epidemiology and Consequences of Drinking and Driving. *Alcohol Research and Health* 27: 63–78.

Johnston, L. D., O'Malley, P. M., Bachman, J. G., & Schulenberg, J. E. (2004) *National Survey Results on Drug Use from the Monitoring the Future Study, 1975–2003*. Vol. 1: *Secondary School Students*. Vol. 2: *College Students and Adults Ages 19–45*. NIH Publications 04-5507 and 04-5508. National Institute on Drug Abuse, Bethesda, MD.

Miron, J. A. (2004). *Drug War Crimes*. The Independent Institute, Oakland, CA.

Zhang, Z. (2003). *Drug and Alcohol Use and Related Matters Among Arrestees, 2003*. National Institute of Justice, Rockville, MD.

alcoholism and alcohol abuse

Paul Roman

Evidence of the presence of alcohol in human societies extends to the beginning of recorded history. Nearly all human societies have discovered and used some form of beverage alcohol (Heath 2000). Ethanol, the genre of alcohol consumed by humans, occurs as a natural product of the fermentation of common foods. In decaying fruit, sugar converts to ethanol, and likewise with grain and potatoes, where decay and fermentation move from starch to sugar to ethanol. Thus ethanol's production and discovery of its psychoactive effects likely occurred accidentally when humans attempted to store food for later consumption. The discovery of the psychoactive effects of this substance likely led quite quickly to the deliberate production of alcoholic beverages.

The normative structures surrounding the use of alcohol have varied greatly over time and geography. Many settings have been observed by social scientists where drinking almost solely accompanies rituals of celebration and social solidarity (Bacon 1943). In many settings alcohol is consumed regularly as a part of normal diet. Some preparations, especially beers, have significant nutritional value, while consumption of diluted wine, via the purifying effects of alcohol, allows for safe use of otherwise marginal water supplies.

Together with evidence of positive social effects of alcohol use, there is a long historical record of events of drunkenness with varying consequences. The potential adverse effects of alcohol consumption are recognized in its prohibited use throughout Islamic and other religious groups. In an early biblical account, Noah is recorded as having shamed himself before his sons after a drinking bout that celebrated completing the construction of the Ark. Many historical records describe damage and destruction associated with excessive drinking, and there are occasional references to persons whose chronic excessive drinking prevented them from fulfilling expected social roles. In general, however, the historical record suggests many centuries' socially integrated use and relatively few problems in those cultures where alcohol was manufactured and used.

The emergence of concepts of alcohol-related problems in the form of alcoholism and repeated patterns of alcohol abuse are social developments of the past 500 years. This transformation has raised complex questions for sociological analysis, for within most societies patterns of socially integrated alcohol use have been sustained in parallel to emerging social concerns and problems. From a broad perspective, the emergence of alcohol problems and the definition of alcohol dependence accompany combinations of industrialization, urbanization, immigration, and population growth (Heath 2000).

Deviant uses of alcohol involve failures to perform expected roles and/or destructive or anti-social behaviors. Sociologically, alcohol abuse is any use of alcohol that is contrary to social norms governing the circumstances where the drinking occurs (i.e., alcohol abuse is not an objective phenomenon, but is largely socially constructed) (Gusfield 1996). These behaviors can range from breaking the rules of small groups to committing murder in an intoxicated rage. The significance of alcohol abuse lies in the combination of (1) its relative prevalence within a certain population or subgroup of that population, (2) repeated and/or escalating patterns of abuse by individuals, (3) the extent to which the social and physical consequences of abuse touch upon moral codes or key values of communities or subcultures within them, and (4) the manner in which the local culture interprets the causal relationship between the presence of alcohol and adverse outcomes.

Alcoholism (or alcohol dependence) can be viewed as a subcategory of severe alcohol abuse, while others define alcoholism as a distinctive disease condition that is triggered by the interaction of alcohol with physiological characteristics that biological researchers are yet to agree upon (Jellinek 1960). The key feature of alcoholism is repeated events of alcohol consumption (typically alcohol abuse) despite notable physical, psychological, and social costs that accompany such consumption (Bacon 1973). That this behavior is seemingly irrational and beyond the individual's control is one of the bases used to define it as a disease condition.

Alcohol abuse and alcoholism are behavioral patterns that can be found today in nearly all societies that have moved into some phase of industrialization. This seeming universality is an artifact of the globalization of patterns of western social and economic organization. There is great variability across cultures and nations in drinking and problematic drinking patterns, and such variations are important topics for sociological analysis (Heath 2000). For example, it has been observed that

unanticipated drinking problems may emerge in industrializing nations where regular alcohol consumption has been normative for centuries. Problems emerge not from alcohol consumption per se, but from the adoption of new patterns of drinking, such as the consumption of distilled spirits when drinking customs had been centered for centuries on beer or wine, or through patterns of daily drinking in commercial bars following completion of work in settings when drinking had been traditionally restricted to festivals or other similar occasions of social celebration.

Sociological interest in ethnic differences in drinking patterns and problems has led to studies to understand why some ethnic groups have very low rates of abstinence from alcohol consumption accompanied by low rates of alcohol problems. Orthodox Jews are a particularly striking example of this phenomenon, and analyses have revealed unique patterns of social control that encourage alcohol use but respond sharply to incidents of intoxication or abuse (Glassner & Berg 1980). Research of this genre has also revealed that cultural groups with significant rates of abstinence are usually marked by significant alcohol problems, with abstinence norms being a signal for the relatively weak mechanisms of social control over deviant drinking behavior.

Since alcohol is a potent drug, it is not surprising that age is a social variable that generates substantial social control efforts in industrialized societies such as the US, with concerns about drinking among American college students and its consequences approximating a level of social panic in the late twentieth and early twenty-first centuries (Wechsler & Wuethrich 2002). Drinking patterns are linked to gender. While in most societies alcohol use and abuse is concentrated among males, industrialization, women's employment, and movement toward social equality for women appear to lead to increasingly similar drinking patterns between men and women, although parity of drinking between men and women is essentially non-existent in any society (Wilsnack & Wilsnack 1997).

Sociologists have had a longstanding interest in the dynamics of family relationships associated with alcohol dependence. Research produced a model describing how family structures adapted to the behavior of the alcoholic husband and father, focusing upon the changes in role expectations and role relationships that often kept families intact despite dramatically deviant behavior on the part of this adult male (Steinglass et al. 1987). Stemming from these studies has been the concept of "enabling" behaviors that has widely diffused into both technical and popular literatures.

Research by sociologists has also focused upon employed persons with drinking problems, approaching this issue from two distinct perspectives. One framework looks at the stressors built into jobs and organizations, and the manner in which heavy drinking is a response to these conditions, used in a manner that can be aptly called self-medication (Martin et al. 1992). A second approach parallels the research literature on the family, looking at the group dynamics and power relationships in work settings that tend to "normalize" deviant drinking behaviors and reduce the likelihood of identification (Roman & Blum 2003). Several recent studies have examined the roles of labor unions in these dynamics. This research has helped formulate strategies for peer intervention that build upon workers' relationships that might otherwise impede the process of providing assistance to the problem drinker.

It is clear that control is a major theme in discussing the use of alcohol in human society. Thus, in multiple nations on multiple occasions, the prohibition of the manufacture and use of alcohol has been seen as the sweeping solution for the problems that drinking brings to different social institutions. The American experience of the emergence of a major temperance movement that ultimately led to national Prohibition has been well documented (Clark 1976). Reasons for the repeal of Prohibition are more complex than is implied by assertions that the social experiment was a failure. One of the dynamics that emerged along with Prohibition's repeal was the diffusion of the idea that certain drinkers were unable to control their drinking because they suffered from the "disease" of alcoholism (Jellinek 1960). Such a concept effectively undermined the need for Prohibition for the entire population and instead called for identification of treatment of the small minority which was unable to drink "normally."

Sociology has a long tradition of critical perspectives on the dominant definitions of alcohol-related problems and accompanying social policies (Roman 1988). There is considerable skepticism about the disease model of alcohol dependence, largely because the successful treatments of such dependence are primarily centered on the personal "will" in the achievement of abstinence rather than through external medical interventions. Related studies have examined the dynamics of the processes surrounding alcohol dependence and recovery through intense conceptual and empirical examination of Alcoholics Anonymous (Denzin 1986).

Given its potentially harmful effects, its widespread use, and the legality of its use for most adults, it is clear that there is considerable ambivalence around the notions of appropriate and inappropriate uses of alcohol in most of the world today. The possibility of prohibition has been largely abandoned in most locations and thus appropriate controls become the central issue. Most current sociological research is oriented toward these practical considerations, focused on the design and evaluation of prevention and treatment strategies, with extensive recent attention to curbing the "binge drinking" of college students, drinking and driving, and methods to reduce or eliminate youthful alcohol consumption often associated with crime and delinquency.

SEE ALSO: Addiction and Dependency; Alcohol and Crime; Chronic Illness and Disability; Deviance, Medicalization of; Deviance, Theories of; Deviant Careers; Drugs, Drug Abuse, and Drug Policy; Health Risk Behavior; Labeling Theory; Marginalization, Outsiders; Moral Entrepreneur; Sick Role; Social Epidemiology; Stigma

REFERENCES AND SUGGESTED READINGS

Bacon, S. D. (1943) Sociology and the Problems of Alcohol: Foundations for a Sociologic Study of Drinking Behavior. *Quarterly Journal of Studies on Alcohol* 4: 402–45.

Bacon, S. D. (1973) The Process of Addiction to Alcohol: Social Aspects. *Quarterly Journal of Studies on Alcohol* 34: 1–27.

Clark, N. H. (1976) *Deliver Us From Evil: An Interpretation of American Prohibition.* Norton, New York.

Denzin, N. K. (1986) *The Alcoholic Self.* Sage, Beverly Hills, CA.

Glassner, B. & Berg, B. (1980) How Jews Avoid Alcohol Problems. *American Sociological Review* 45: 647–64.

Gusfield, J. R. (1996) *Contested Meanings: The Construction of Alcohol Problems.* University of Wisconsin Press, Madison.

Heath, D. (2000) *Drinking Occasions: Comparative Perspectives on Alcohol and Culture.* Brunner-Mazel, Philadelphia.

Jellinek, E. M. (1960) *The Disease Concept of Alcoholism.* College and University Press, New Haven.

Martin, J. K., Blum, T. C., & Roman, P. M. (1992) Drinking to Cope and Self-Medication: Characteristics of Jobs in Relation to Workers' Drinking Behavior. *Journal of Organizational Behavior* 13: 55–72.

Roman, P. M. (1988) The Disease Concept of Alcoholism: Sociocultural and Organizational Bases of Support. *Drugs and Society* 2: 5–32.

Roman, P. M. & Blum, T. C. (2003) Employee Assistance Programs and Other Workplace Preventive Strategies. In: Galanter, M. & Kleber, H. D. (Eds.), *Textbook of Substance Abuse Treatment,* 3rd edn. American Psychiatric Press, Washington, DC.

Steinglass, P., Bennett, L. A., Wolin, S. J., and Reiss, D. (1987) *The Alcoholic Family.* Basic Books, New York.

Wechsler, H. & Wuethrich, B. (2002) *Dying to Drink: Confronting Binge Drinking on College Campuses.* Rodale Press, Emmaus, PA.

Wilsnack, R. W. & Wilsnack, S. C. (Eds.) (1997) *Gender and Alcohol: Individual and Social Perspectives.* Publications Division of the Rutgers Center of Alcohol Studies, New Brunswick, NJ.

alienation

Randy Hodson

Alienation is the social and psychological separation between oneself and one's life experiences. Alienation is a concept originally applied to work and work settings but today is also used to characterize separation from the political sphere of society. To be alienated is to live in a society but not to feel that one is a part of its ongoing activities.

Theories of alienation start with the writings of Marx, who identified the capacity for self-directed *creative activity* as the core distinction between humans and animals. If people cannot express their *species being* (their creativity), they are reduced to the status of animals or machines. Marx argued that, under capitalism, workers lose control over their work and, as a consequence, are alienated in at least four ways. First, they are alienated from the *products* of their labor. They no longer determine what is to be made nor what use will be made of it. Work is reduced to being a means to an end – a means to acquire money to buy the material necessities of life. Second, workers are alienated from the *process* of work. Someone else controls the pace, pattern, tools, and techniques of their work. Third, because workers are separated from their activity, they become alienated from *themselves*. Non-alienated work, in contrast, entails the same enthusiastic absorption and self-realization as hobbies and leisure pursuits. Fourth, alienated labor is an isolated endeavor, not part of a collectively planned effort to meet a group need. Consequently, workers are alienated from *others* as well as from themselves. Marx argued that these four aspects of alienation reach their peak under industrial capitalism and that alienated work, which is inherently dissatisfying, would naturally produce in workers a desire to change the existing system. Alienation, in Marx's view, thus plays a crucial role in leading to social revolution to change society toward a non-alienated future.

The study of alienation has probably inspired more writing and research in the social sciences than any other single topic. Today, the core of that research has moved away from the social philosophical approach of Marx, based on projecting a future that *could be*, and toward a more empirical study of the causes and consequences of alienation within the world of work as it *actually exists*. Although less sweeping than Marx's original vision, this approach has produced insights that are largely consistent with his views. The contemporary approach substitutes measures of job satisfaction for Marx's more expansive conception of alienation. Related concepts include job commitment, effort bargaining, and, conversely, resistance. In the political sphere voting behavior and a sense of political efficacy have emerged as central empirical indicators of underlying alienation from society's power structures.

The intellectual movement from a social philosophy of alienation to a social science of alienation has produced a wealth of research on the causes of job satisfaction and related empirical measures of political and social disengagement. Autonomy to decide on the details of one's own work tasks and freedom from oppressive supervision have been identified as among the most important determinants of experiencing satisfaction and meaning in one's work. Other determinants of job satisfaction include both positive foundations for self-realization, such as perceptions of justice at work and supportive co-workers, and corrosive factors, such as large organizational size, bureaucracy, and control of local operations by remote corporate entities. The absence of work can also generate a sense of alienation because one has no useful role in society. High levels of unemployment have been empirically linked with increased depression, higher rates of illness, and even suicide. Globalization has contributed to job loss for many workers who are displaced by workers elsewhere in the world who either have access to better technology or are willing to accept lower pay.

In the political sphere alienation arises from a sense of estrangement from political power. Such estrangement arises because political institutions have become increasingly distant in large complex societies, but also, importantly, because effective channels of participation have been blocked for many people or simply do not exist. The role of individual and corporate wealth as determinants of political influence has led many people to a lack of confidence and trust that the political institutions of society either represent their interests or are open to their participation. Political alienation appears to be on the increase. In western nations, particularly in the United States, the proportion of people who bother to vote has fallen to a historic low. In the 1960s in the United States about three quarters of the population felt that the government

was run for the benefit of all. Today, this number has fallen to roughly one quarter.

Even for those who have good jobs and some opportunity to exercise political power, overwork and the experience of feeling chronically rushed and pulled in multiple directions have become increasingly common sources of disaffection. Such stresses can lead to feelings of alienation and separation from one's life. In spite of widespread overwork, however, surveys indicate that many people prefer work activities over family and leisure activities, further contributing to overwork even in the face of work that may be less than fulfilling. It appears that at least some work in modern society may compete well with alternative activities in the private spheres of life. If people prefer work to family and leisure, does this imply that alienation from work has ended? Or does it simply suggest that the roles of community and family are fading as these assume a smaller and smaller place in people's lives? These changes, if true, present a challenge to traditional alienation theory as it struggles to understand the increasingly diverse experience of life in modern society.

Theories of alienation, as scientific explorations of the causes of job satisfaction and political behavior, serve a pivotal function in moving us beyond workplace and societal practices that destroy human motivation and toward practices that liberate human involvement and creativity. Theories of alienation, as exercises in social philosophy, help to keep alive questions about the future of society by envisioning possible alternatives that do not yet exist. Such exercises are necessary if the social sciences are to retain a transformative potential beyond the tyranny of *what is* and toward *what could be*.

SEE ALSO: Anomie; Capitalism; Class Consciousness; Dialectic; Gramsci, Antonio; Industrial Relations; Labor Process; Marcuse, Herbert; Marx, Karl; Mass Culture and Mass Society; Political Sociology

REFERENCES AND SUGGESTED READINGS

Bottomore, T. B. (1963) *Karl Marx: Early Writings*. McGraw-Hill, New York.

Fromm, E. (1966) *Marx's Concept of Man*. F. Ungar, New York.

Hodson, R. (2001) *Dignity at Work.* Cambridge University Press, New York.

Marx, K. (1971 [1844]) The Economic and Philosophic Manuscripts of 1844. In: Jordon, Z. A. (Ed.), *Karl Marx.* Michael Joseph, London.

Seeman, M. (1959) On the Meaning of Alienation. *American Sociological Review* 24, 6 (December): 783–91.

Shepard, J. M. (1971) *Automation and Alienation: A Study of Office and Factory Workers.* MIT Press, Cambridge, MA.

alliances

Siegfried P. Gudergan

The concept of alliance has been used widely in a variety of contexts with definitions generally being discipline-bound. Theoretical and empirical research into alliances has had extensive interdisciplinary appeal. Research into alliances has been conducted in a multitude of disciplines, including sociology, psychology, economics, political science, law, strategic management, and organizational behavior. The word alliance has a set of meanings, including a confederation described as the act of forming an alliance; a formal agreement establishing an association or alliance between nations or other groups to achieve a particular aim; a coalition, being an organization of people, nations, or businesses involved in a pact or treaty; a bond, being a connection based on kinship or common interest; and a confederation as a state of being allied or confederated. We define alliances as a unified effort involving two or more organizations, groups, or individuals to achieve common goals with respect to a particular issue. This view of alliances is closely related to its sociological roots and suggests that an alliance has a number of defining features. First, an alliance brings together two or more individual parties – whether people or organizations. Second, an alliance requires these parties to be interconnected in some way with resource dependencies. Interconnectedness is a state of being connected reciprocally. Third, the alliance must share common goals, interests, or

values. Fourth, there is an assumption that the individual parties maintain at least some level of autonomy.

The functioning of alliances involving autonomous parties is based on shared norms and behavioral expectations (Macneil 1980). Drawing on sociological foundations, researchers such as Macaulay (1963) and Macneil (1978, 1980, 1981) have examined behavior in alliances being shaped by norms, obligations, and reciprocity. The work of Clegg and his co-authors (2002) on alliance cultures and associated value systems supports this notion; so do Dyer and Singh (1998), Gudergan et al. (2002), and Ring and Van de Ven (1992, 1994). Common to a lot of work is that alliances can be characterized by social dilemmas where one party's interest can be in possible conflict with the common interest of the alliance.

Social relations that underlie alliances explain the nature of the connection between the parties to an alliance and possible tensions. These relations are characterized by different levels of chemistry, politics, and associated political and professional relations, dealings and communications. They are associated with human action and activity within groups and can be viewed as a union of political organization comprising social and political units. This suggests that an alliance is the state of being allied or confederated, reflecting unification and coalition. Associated bonds reflect the attachment representing a connection that fastens alliance activities. Group actions, or activities by the parties in alliances, are those taken by a group of individuals and/or organizations. While such actions are associated with transactions and communalism, they are also characterized by embedded conflict.

Social control plays a vital role in alliances and is defined as the control exerted actively or passively by group action. Such control in alliances is reflected in the power, management, and leadership occurring in alliances affecting duties, responsibilities, obligations, and accountabilities. Social and other institutional enforcement mechanisms applying to the alliance influence the extent of compliance with agreements.

Agreements entailing explicit and implicit understandings result from oral and written alliance statements of an exchange of promises. Oral alliance contracts are agreements that are not in writing and are not signed by the parties, but are real, existing contracts that lack only the formal requirement of a memorandum to render them enforceable in litigation. Written agreements are legal documents summarizing the agreement between parties. Associated alliance communications, messages, and contents are subject to the parties' social interpretations. The resultant social contract is an implicit agreement among people within the alliance that results in the organization of alliance activities.

Mental processes of the alliance parties include interaction and internalization processes. Interpersonal chemistry – the way individuals relate to each other in the alliance – affects the nature of social relations and the extent to which mental processes result in implied alliance contracts. Implied contracts in alliances assume a meeting of minds and community of interests. Political relations – social relations involving authority and power – in turn influence compliance with implied alliance contracts. Legal relations – professional relations that are regulated by law and are based on the fiduciary system – influence how one alliance party justifiably places reliance on the other, whose contribution is sought in some manner. Reliance on alliance agreements is based on an understanding characterized by comprehension, discernment, and empathy. These social settings explain the process by which explicit and implicit agreements are formed and social or implied contracts evolve that affect compliance with alliance agreements.

The potential existence of ethnocentricity and individualistic and selfish action can be counterbalanced by procedures that secure a dialectical process toward increased tolerance and mutual understanding (Etzioni 1988). The interaction patterns developed through procedures of communicative activities are used as the basis on which alliance norms can be created. These norms give predictability in the specific setting of future alliance action, and managers responsible for the exchange serve as guarantors of norm fulfillment.

Although established alliance-specific norms may result in well-functioning alliances, the creation of such norms may demand substantial effort at the personal level, particularly when it involves parties from different macro-cultures. Hence, personal relationships and reputations between boundary-spanning alliance parties play an important role in facilitating and enhancing the functioning of the alliance. There is also risk involved in increased manager–organization dependency where the alliance is too closely connected to the specific individuals involved in the process.

The development of alliance norms is consistent with interactional psychology (Endler & Magnusson 1976) and social psychology (Kelman 1961). The interaction of parties and associated oral alliance contracts leads to a sense of obligation and *de facto* accountability that is based on social norms. In addition, the specification and acceptance of written alliance contracts result in parties forming an informal understanding of alliance prerogatives. Important to note here is that each party to the alliance might interpret a written contract differently because of ambiguity and differences in their macro-culture. As such, the informal understanding about carrying out obligations may be viewed differently by the other party to the alliance. This understanding is mirrored in a sense of obligations and *de jure* accountability that is based on a fiduciary system. A party's sense of obligation and accountability – embedded in the implied alliance contract – increases with the bi-directional communications in the alliance. While parties form a sense of obligation and accountability, they also form expectations about the other party's sense of obligation and accountability. This in turn influences the confidence in that party devoting appropriate inputs to the alliance.

In summary, alliances are socially embedded where this embeddedness determines processes that characterize the alliance. The specific understandings underlying the alliance functioning are socially constructed, resulting in the parties' sense of obligation and accountability that comprise the implied alliance contract.

REFERENCES AND SUGGESTED READINGS

Clegg, S. R., Pitsis, T., Rura-Polley, T., & Marosszeky, M. (2002) Governmentality Matters: Designing an Alliance Culture of Inter-Organizational Collaboration for Managing Projects. *Organization Studies* 23(3): 317–37.

Dyer, J. & Singh, H. (1998) The Relational View: Cooperative Strategy and Sources of Interorganizational Competitive Advantage. *Academy of Management Review* 23(4): 660–79.

Endler, N. & Magnusson, D. (1976) Toward an Interactional Psychology of Personality. *Psychological Bulletin* 83: 956–74.

Etzioni, A. (1988) Normative-Affective Factors: Toward a New Decision-Making Model. *Journal of Economic Psychology* 9(2): 125–50.

Gudergan, S., Devinney, T., & Ellis, S. R. (2002) An Integrated Theory of Alliance Governance and Performance. In: Trick, M. A. (Ed.), *Mergers, Acquisitions, Alliances and Networks*. Carnegie Mellon University Press, Pittsburgh.

Kelman, H. C. (1961) Process of Opinion Change. *Public Opinion Quarterly* 25: 57–78.

Macaulay, S. (1963) Non-Contractual Relations in Business: A Preliminary Study. *American Economic Review* 28(1): 55–69.

Macneil, I. R. (1978) Contracts: Adjustment of Long-Term Economic Relations Under Classical, Neoclassical and Relational Contract Law. *Northwestern University Law Review* 72: 854–905.

Macneil, I. R. (1980) *The New Social Contract: An Inquiry into Modern Contractual Relations*. Yale University Press, New Haven.

Macneil, I. R. (1981) Economic Analysis of Contractual Relations: Its Shortfalls and the Need for a "Rich Classificatory Apparatus." *Northwestern University Law Review* 75(6): 1018–63.

Ring, P. S. & Van de Ven, A. (1992) Structuring Cooperative Relationships Between Organizations. *Strategic Management Journal* 13: 483–98.

Ring, P. S. & Van de Ven, A. (1994) Developmental Processes of Cooperative Interorganizational Relationships. *Academy of Management Review* 19(1): 90–118.

Tetlock, P. (1985) Accountability: The Neglected Social Context of Judgment and Choice. *Research in Organizational Behavior* 7: 297–332.

alliances (racial/ethnic)

Benjamin P. Bowser

An alliance is "a close association for a common objective" or "for mutual benefit," synonymous with the idea of a league, a confederacy, or a union (Friend & Guralnik 1960). One will find research on alliances between business organizations and between clients and therapists in psychotherapy. Here the focus is on alliances in social movements. Despite the importance of alliances in the success of any social movement, there is no tradition of focused research on the topic. For example, in social science research in the US, it is touched on in now classic social movement studies such as Ted Gurr's *Why Men Rebel* (1970), Anthony Oberschall's *Social Conflict and Social Movements* (1973), and Francis Piven and R. Cloward's *Poor People's Movements: Why They Succeed, How They Fail* (1977). Ralf Dahrendorf in *Class and Class Conflict in Industrial Society* (1954) explored the idea of alliances only briefly while explaining why conflict has not happened as Karl Marx predicted in the post-World War II period. One central objective of this work is to present the underlying processes and principles by which social movements mobilize, are sustained, and then demobilize.

A variety of theoretical perspectives emerged out of efforts to follow up on these studies and present even clearer ideas of social movements which could also assist in our understanding of alliances. For example, social movement theorists have explored a number of issues and problems related to alliances: studies of levels of relative deprivation (Stouffer et al. 1949; Pettigrew 1964), of ethnic solidarity (Bonacich & Modell 1980), and of resources to mobilize (Tilly 1978). The shortcomings of these post-war theories have led to a more theoretically diffuse approach which uses primarily ethnographies and case studies in order to derive new insights into social movements and alliances. This can be seen in chapters of Michael Jones-Correa's edited volume, *Governing American Cities: Interethnic Coalitions, Competitions, and Conflict* (2001). In this collection of case studies, what is clear is that appeals to color and minority status are no longer sufficient in the post-civil rights era. Rather, authentic appeals to important issues and interests across groups are necessary for successful coalitions and to avoid the intense conflict that occurs whenever one or the other group is excluded. For this reason, biracial coalitions may not be enough; such coalitions must now be all inclusive. Memphis is another example to illustrate this point. Until 1991 Memphis was the only major US city with a majority-black population that had not elected a black mayor. Infighting and competition among black city leaders and citizen aversion to candidates who attempted cross-racial appeals were all explanations. A black finally was elected mayor and worked to overcome these obstacles, and was able to hold an interracial coalition together for two terms. Several popular theories of voting and election strategy in urban elections were examined – black threat theory, urban regime theory, and deracialization. The urban setting was found to be the most important factor, suggesting that each site is unique enough and that no one theory can describe the prospects for or against multiracial political alliances (Venderleeuw et al. 2004).

Others have pointed out that it is rare for racial commonalities to overcome interminority tensions, highlighting the limits of race-based coalitions; institutional barriers such as competition for jobs and different media images are more than sufficient to push intergroup dynamics against alliances (Rogers 2004). Women seem better able to mobilize around institutional barriers. There is something about black women's multiple social identities that links multiracial blackness (African, Pakistani, and Caribbean) in Britain as a unified oppositional identity which can be invoked by black women activists in order to mobilize collective action (Sudbury 2001).

In looking at movements focused on economic inequality and for social justice between 1930 and 1990, data were analyzed on 2,644 "left" protest events that occurred on US college campuses. The availability of resources was important to the successful formation of within-movement coalitions but not to the formation of cross-movement coalitions. Local

threats inspire within-movement coalition events, but it took larger threats such as the war in Vietnam and the draft to affect multiple constituencies and inspire cross-movement coalition formation. This research demonstrated that political threats sometimes inspire protest and that organizational goals do influence strategic action (van Dyke 2003). There are also examples where alliances resulted in bringing the power of the state to protect minorities. The alliance of Canadian Jews and political liberals, following World War II, was very strategic. This alliance prompted politicians to adopt the view that racial prejudice was a social problem resulting from an individual's pathology, and led to laws being passed against it. In doing so, they managed to get discriminatory practices prohibited and set a standard of non-discrimination for the law-abiding population. This universalist philosophy has led to other minority groups which are now experiencing racial/ethnic discrimination to join the original coalition to continue legal reform (Walker 2002).

The potential for theoretically fruitful work on alliances will require investigators to go beyond the familiar black–white racial antagonism model. There are many more variations of ethnic antagonism, segregation, social identities, and even attitudes toward intermarriage that play into the potential for inter- and intraracial alliances (Hirschman 1986). In addition, it is now a necessity for social movements to expand beyond national boundaries and move toward an international stance (Bowser 1995). For those who worry about the scope of western economic, political, and cultural structures and their worldwide domination, it can be assumed that these structures and domination can only be effectively influenced and challenged by counterinternational structures and alliances (Waterman 2005). Given the little that we know about alliances, there is an extraordinary challenge ahead for both social movements and those who study them.

SEE ALSO: Alliances; Biracialism; Black Urban Regime; Ethnic Groups; Ethnic, Racial, and Nationalist Movements; Majorities; Polyethnicity; Race and Ethnic Politics; Separatism; Social Movements

REFERENCES AND SUGGESTED READINGS

Bonacich, E. & Modell, J. (1980) *The Economic Basis of Ethnic Solidarity: Small Business in the Japanese American Community*. University of California Press, Berkeley.

Bowser, B. (Ed.) (1995) *Racism and Anti-Racism in World Perspective*. Sage, Thousand Oaks, CA.

Friend, J. & Guralnik, D. (Eds.) (1960) *Webster's New World Dictionary of the American Language*. World Publishing, New York.

Hirschman, C. (1986) The Making of Race in Colonial Malaya: Political Economy and Racial Ideology. *Sociological Forum* 1(2): 330–61.

Pettigrew, T. (1964) *A Profile of the American Negro*. Van Nostrand, Princeton.

Rogers, R. R. (2004) Race-Based Coalitions Among Minority Groups. *Urban Affairs Review* 39(3): 283–313.

Stouffer, S. et al. (1949) *The American Soldier*. Princeton University Press, Princeton.

Sudbury, J. (2001) (Re)constructing Multiracial Blackness: Women's Activism, Difference, and Collective Identity in Britain. *Ethnic and Racial Studies* 24(1): 29–49.

Tilly, C. (1978) *From Mobilization to Revolution*. Addison-Wesley, Reading, MA.

van Dyke, N. (2003) Crossing Movement Boundaries: Factors that Facilitate Coalition Protest by American College Students, 1930–1990. *Social Problems* 50(2): 226–61.

Venderleeuw, J., Liu, B., & March, G. (2004) Applying Black Threat Theory, Urban Regime Theory, and Deracialization: The Memphis Mayoral Elections of 1991, 1995, and 1999. *Journal of Urban Affairs* 26(4): 505–19.

Walker, J. W. (2002) The "Jewish Phase" in the Movement for Racial Equality in Canada. *Canadian Ethnic Studies* 34(1): 1–29.

Waterman, P. (2005) The Old and the New: Dialectics Around the Social Forum Process. *Development* 48(2): 42–7.

Althusser, Louis (1918–90)

Kenneth H. Tucker, Jr.

Louis Althusser was a French Marxist philosopher, best known for his structuralist reinterpretation of Marxism in the 1960s. He was also important as a strong intellectual influence on many of the poststructuralist authors such as Michel Foucault, Jacques Lacan, and Jacques Derrida, who became central figures in social scientific and literary studies in Europe and the US in the 1970s.

In two of his major books, *Lire le Capital* (1965), translated as *Reading Capital*, and *Pour Marx* (1965), translated as *For Marx*, Althusser criticized the overly romantic versions of Marxism that became prominent in the 1960s. He was particularly disparaging of the "humanist" Marxism of thinkers such as Antonio Gramsci and the Frankfurt School, who viewed Marx as a theorist of alienation concerned with the quality of life under capitalism. For Althusser, this romantic Marxism undermined Marx as a scientist. In Althusser's view, Marx attempted to scientifically analyze the capitalist mode of production, as well as other forms of social organization. While Marx was concerned with issues such as alienation in his writings as a young man, including the *Paris Manuscripts of 1844*, this was a youthful folly which Marx abandoned after 1845. Althusser labels this intellectual change in Marx's writings an *epistemological break*, as Marx moved from romanticism to science, culminating in his masterwork *Capital*. Althusser argues that in *Capital* Marx examined the economic structure of the capitalist mode of production, developing a new type of science that not only analyzed capitalism but also explained its own conditions of development. Even Marx was limited in what he accomplished and what he could understand, however. Althusser believes that he supplies the missing dimensions of a Marxist science.

Althusser was dismissive of many Marxists' fascination with the ideas of the philosopher Hegel, such as the theory of the dialectical progression of history and the notion that the whole determines its parts. These abstract ideas Althusser thought to be scientifically useless. He also found Marxism's dichotomous pairing of economic base and cultural and ideological superstructure to be problematic. He replaced these terms with his ideas of *contradiction* and *overdetermination*. Althusser argues that capitalism is an inherently contradictory system, as workers struggle with capitalists, private interests conflict with public goods, and the like. But Marxist analysis must move beyond concerns with economic analysis. In Althusser's language, every contradiction is overdetermined, as there are a number of different contradictions in politics, ideology, and economics which influence one another. Each of these realms is relatively autonomous, with its own internal dynamics. Yet they influence one another, so that what happens in the political realm can affect economic activities and decisions. For Althusser, there is no center to the mode of production. The ideological, economic, and political elements of the social structure cannot be explained solely by economic factors. While the economic level is indeed the determining factor in any mode of production, this is only in the last instance, which rarely occurs.

One of Althusser's major contributions to Marxism is his theory of ideology. For Althusser, ideology is not simply a misguided interpretation of social life; rather, ideology produces conscious awareness for individuals. It is no accident that Althusser seems much like Freud here, for he also argues that ideologies are unconscious, tied to the emotional dimensions of people's existence, such as their hopes and fears. Althusser also draws on the psychoanalyst Lacan's notion of the imaginary, which is a world of mirrors and illusions, organized around the images and fantasies that we have of ourselves and of others. We take this imaginary to be real, and relations between individuals are converted into imaginary relationships. Ideology operates in the realm of the imaginary. Much of ideology's content and power is based on unconscious assumptions, beliefs, and desires.

What Althusser calls "ideological state apparatuses," major institutions ranging from the family to governments, generate ideologies which individuals internalize. Ideologies convince us that we are individuals freely making choices. In Althusser's vocabulary, we are *interpellated* as individuals with free choice, as subjects. Ideology is dependent on the idea of a subject, indeed ideologies create us as subjects. We are addressed as subjects, named as subjects, so we think of ourselves as free individuals. We live ideology, as we engage in ideological practices such as rituals and

traditions which tie us to universal ideas such as God and the Nation, and the institutions which these ideas represent. But these beliefs, like the idea of the subject, are myths. Individuals are "bearers of structure," as structures influence individuals rather than vice versa. We are determined by material constraints beyond our consciousness, such as the division of labor and the movement of private property, but also by non-material structures that we are not aware of, such as language and sexuality.

Althusser's analysis of ideology and his embrace of Freud helped guarantee that his influence extended beyond the confines of Marxism. He has been especially influential in the poststructuralist school of his student Foucault, and other figures such as Derrida, though these thinkers are not Marxists. They have adopted variants of his ideas that individuals are the creation rather than the creators of structures, and that language determines our existence. Like Althusser, they see society in terms of a "decentered totality," where economic, political, and ideological elements interpenetrate in every social formation with no one dimension having priority over the other. Foucault et al. also reject any teleological or progressive version of history, for no social formation gives birth to its successor.

While Althusser remained popular in the US throughout the 1970s and the early 1980s, his influence in France waned after the student revolts of 1968. Althusser sided with the French Communist Party against the students, for he did not see the demonstrations as indicators of a truly revolutionary movement. Students and intellectuals abandoned his thought as they turned against the Communist Party. His life took a very tragic turn when he murdered his wife in 1980. He was institutionalized until 1983, as he was believed unfit to stand trial. He lived a lonely life upon his release until his death in 1990.

SEE ALSO: Base and Superstructure; Critical Theory/Frankfurt School; Derrida, Jacques; Foucault, Michel; Freud, Sigmund; Gramsci, Antonio; Hegel, G. W. F.; Ideology; Lacan, Jacques; Marx, Karl; Poststructuralism; Structuralism

REFERENCES AND SUGGESTED READINGS

Althusser, L. (1969 [1965]) *For Marx*. Trans. B. Brewster. Pantheon Books, New York.

Althusser, L. (1972 [1969]) *Lenin and Philosophy, and Other Essays*. Trans. B. Brewster. Monthly Review Press, New York.

Althusser, L. (1984 [1976]) *Essays on Ideology*. Trans. B. Brewster. Verso, London.

Althusser, L. & Balibar, É. (1977 [1965]) *Reading Capital*. Trans. B. Brewster. New Left Books, London.

Kaplan, E. A. & Sprinker, M. (Ed.) (1993) *The Althusserian Legacy*. Verso, New York.

Montag, W. (2003) *Louis Althusser*. Palgrave Macmillan, New York.

Poulantzas, N. (1975) *Political Power and Social Classes*. Humanities Press, Atlantic Highlands, NJ.

Resch, R. P. (1992) *Althusser and the Renewal of Marxist Social Theory*. University of California Press, Berkeley.

Thompson, E. P. (1978) *The Poverty of Theory and Other Essays*. Monthly Review Press, New York.

ambivalence

Gad Yair

Ambivalence denotes contrasting commitments and orientations; it refers to simultaneous conflicting feelings toward a person or an object; and it is commonly used to describe and explain the hesitance and uncertainty caused by the juxtaposition between contradictory values, preferences, and expectations. Layperson use follows intuitive psychological explanations which refer to ambivalence interchangeably with personal hesitation, confusion, indeterminacy, and agitation. In contrast, sociological use suggests that although ambivalence is a bi-polar, subjective experience, its causes are social and hence understandable and predictable. True, most sociological uses of the term maintain its conflictual denotations, but this volatile experience is treated as the result of contrasting social pressures exerted on actors.

The concept of sociological ambivalence has been strategically used to show that structural functional theory is not blind to conflicts and contradictions in social structure. Specifically, Merton (1957) proposed the concept as part of his role-set and role-relations theory. He suggested that while societies have a functional need to enable most people most of the time to go about their business of social life, without encountering extreme conflict in their role-sets, normative contradictions and contrasting expectations are nonetheless inherent in social structure. Ambivalence is therefore a normal part of social life, expected and even routinized. As Merton suggested, sociological ambivalence refers to incompatible normative expectations, attitudes, beliefs, and behavior assigned to a status or to a set of statuses. According to this role-set approach, sociological ambivalence results from such incompatible normative expectations incorporated in a *single* role of a *single* social status. Hence, ambivalence is not a pathological situation because it normally results from the social definition of roles and statuses. Therefore, Merton advocated that in explaining inconsistent behaviors and feelings sociologists need to expose the latent and the manifest contradictions in social structure.

Merton's structural functional approach is general and ahistorical. It aims to explain contradictions, tensions, and inconsistency in all manners of social life, in all periods and societies. In contrast, Bauman (1991) historicizes the phenomenon, suggesting that the experience of ambivalence is a child of late modernity, of fluid modernity. While modernity aspired to order, control, and predictability, its most recent phases have harbored disorder, confusion, and even randomness. Bauman's take on ambivalence suggests that in late modernity ambivalence-as-incoherence became a *Zeitgeist* – "the spirit of the time" – a general cultural orientation that is loosely identified with postmodernity. Instead of Merton's social psychological approach, Bauman's approach is phenomenological. Where Merton pointed to normative micro-level contradictions in social structure, Bauman focuses his attention on the blurring of cognitive categories and the mixing up of genres. He suggested that ambivalence – a structural condition – confounds calculation of events and confuses the accuracy and even the relevance of past action patterns (Beilharz 2001). He further argues that historically ambivalent times result from the inadequacy of linguistic tools and from the blurring of social categories. Under these conditions, perceptions become hazy, inconsistent, and confused. Consequently, action turns mute, while thinking becomes numb.

Applications of the concept of ambivalence in empirical studies follow these traditions. Most studies measure the concept as a phenomenological experience denoting confusion, conflict, hesitancy, contradictory feelings, and behaviors. They frame it as a dependent variable of prior structural conditions: changing family configurations, restructuring of labor markets and organizations, and contrasting political commitments (Yair 2005). Their unique contribution – as Merton envisioned – is in tying together different units of conceptualization and analysis – actors and social structures. In doing so, they provide a meaningful explanation for seemingly paradoxical behaviors, attitudes, and feelings.

SEE ALSO: Merton, Robert K.; Modernity; Role; Structural Functional Theory

REFERENCES AND SUGGESTED READINGS

Bauman, Z. (1991) *Modernity and Ambivalence.* Polity Press, Cambridge.

Beilharz, P. (Ed.) (2001) *The Bauman Reader.* Blackwell, Oxford.

Merton, R. K. (1957) The Role-Set: Problems in Sociological Theory. *British Journal of Sociology* 8: 106–20.

Yair, G. (2005) In a Double Bind: Conflicts Over Education and Mayoral Election Outcomes. *Local Government Studies* 31(2): 167–84.

American Dilemma, An (Gunnar Myrdal)

Peter Kivisto

In 1944 the Swedish economist Gunnar Myrdal published a monumental study on the social conditions of African Americans. Encyclopedic in its effort to cover all aspects of black life, *An American Dilemma* was a volume of over 1,000 pages that included analyses of major demographic, political, economic, and cultural forces that shaped the black experience in the United States. Furthermore, it provided extended discussions of social inequality and social stratification and the persistent role of prejudice and discrimination. It examined the institutional structure of the black community, including an analysis of patterns of leadership and prospects for collective action aimed at redressing a long legacy of racial hostility and oppression. After presenting a vast body of data regarding the past and present circumstances of blacks, Myrdal provided tempered, but nonetheless generally optimistic, conclusions about the future.

The study was commissioned by the Carnegie Corporation, a philanthropic organization established by the estate of the industrialist Andrew Carnegie, which wanted to derive from the study its implications for the formulation of social policy. Although it was not entirely clear why the corporation hired a foreigner who had conducted no prior research on race relations in the United States or elsewhere, a primary reason appears to have been the desire to obtain a novel, outsider's perspective on the topic. Myrdal had substantial monetary support, ample office space in New York City's Chrysler Building, and the participation of many prominent American scholars, including several black activists and intellectuals.

The overarching thesis advanced in the study was noteworthy in several ways. Despite the range and complexity of the topics treated, Myrdal's conclusions about the future of race relations derived from a remarkably simple claim: the dilemma produced by the conflict between the American ideals of freedom and equality and the reality of black oppression would be resolved in favor of the realization of American values. Myrdal was an assimilationist who based his assessment of the future of race relations on the assumption that the nation had a unified culture with commonly shared core values. He referred to this as the American Creed, which involved generalized values rooted in the Christian tradition and the national ethos. A dilemma existed in the United States insofar as the American Creed was not realized in the everyday lived experience of white Americans, which involved complex patterns of behavior and thought that led to the perpetuation of prejudice, discrimination, and racial subordination. The race problem was located in the white mind, which, as long as it harbored prejudicial attitudes that were translated into discriminatory actions, would ensure that the dilemma persisted. Thus, the solution to the race problem would occur when whites rooted out their own racism and treated blacks in a manner congruent with the core cultural values.

But Myrdal did not think that consciousness-raising was all that was needed to cure the nation of white racism. On the contrary, he understood that the historical legacy of racial oppression had to be remedied. He called for the federal government to play a critical role in promoting policies intended to improve the social conditions of African Americans. A dedicated democratic socialist, he had played a pivotal role in the creation of Sweden's welfare state. He was an unapologetic proponent of social engineering. This position had not been a particularly prominent feature of American social science, but it was congruent with the expanded role of the state being advanced by advocates of the New Deal. It contrasted with the *laissez-faire* views that Myrdal associated not only with William Graham Sumner, but also with virtually all important scholars of race relations, including Robert E. Park, W. I. Thomas, and W. Lloyd Warner. He thought that these scholars shared Sumner's contention that the mores cannot be legislated – or in other words, that laws do not change the way people think and feel. Such a position led to governmental acquiescence regarding the existing state of race relations. Myrdal's position starkly refuted this claim. In his opinion, government could and should involve itself in improving the living conditions and life chances of blacks, through expanded educational opportunities, job training, and the like. In the process, it could play a salutary role in changing white attitudes and behaviors such that they ended up being congruent with the American Creed.

Myrdal called for racial integration. He abandoned Booker T. Washington's approach, which had opted for promoting black socioeconomic development within the confines of a racial caste society. Prior to Myrdal commencing his research, Roy Wilkins of the NAACP expressed concern that Myrdal might promote a renewed commitment to the Washingtonian position of development within the framework of a segregated world. Instead, Myrdal endorsed the quest most closely associated with the views of W. E. B. Du Bois for the dual objectives of advancement and integration.

Myrdal placed relatively little emphasis on black activism as a means for challenging their subordinate place in American society. For critics such as Ralph Ellison, this was part of a larger problem with the work, which was that it significantly downplayed the role of blacks as sociohistorical agents shaping their own lives and that of the society they inhabited. When Myrdal discussed the presence of protest organizations within the black community, especially the NAACP and the Urban League, he stressed the importance of their interracial character. He was sympathetic to such organizations and suggested that more organizations with somewhat different political orientations would be welcomed. Nonetheless, his general view was that due to their lack of power and experience, such organizations would necessarily play an essentially secondary role in the move to redefine the roles that blacks would play in the future. He did not appear to anticipate the profound significance of the Civil Rights Movement, which began to have a major impact on the existing racial formation within a decade of the publication of *An American Dilemma*. Despite this shortcoming, the book stands as a landmark of sociological analysis and a clarion call for government intervention on behalf of racial equality and harmony.

SEE ALSO: Assimilation; Civil Rights Movement; Consumption, African Americans; Discrimination; Du Bois, W. E. B.; Park, Robert E. and Burgess, Ernest W.; Prejudice; Race; Race (Racism)

REFERENCES AND SUGGESTED READINGS

Ellison, R. (1964) *Shadow and Act*. Random House, New York.

Lyman, S. M. (1972) *The Black American in Sociological Thought*. Capricorn, New York.

Lyman, S. M. (1998) Gunnar Myrdal's *An American Dilemma* After a Half Century: Critics and Anticritics. *International Journal of Politics, Culture, and Society* 12(2): 327–89.

Myrdal, G. (1944) *An American Dilemma: The Negro Problem and Modern Democracy*. Harper & Brothers, New York.

Smith, C. V. & Killian, L. M. (1990) Sociological Foundations of the Civil Rights Movement. In: Gans, H. (Ed.), *Sociology in America*. Sage, Newbury Park, CA, pp. 105–16.

Southern, D. W. (1987) *Gunnar Myrdal and Black–White Relations: The Use and Abuse of An American Dilemma, 1944–1969*. Louisiana State University Press, Baton Rouge.

Wacker, R. F. (1983) *Ethnicity, Pluralism, and Race: Race Relations Theory in America Before Myrdal*. Greenwood Press, Westport, CT.

American Sociological Association

Michael R. Hill

The American Sociological Association (ASA) is currently the largest and most influential membership organization of professional sociologists in the US. The ASA began its organizational life in 1905 when a small group of self-selected scholars representing several existing scholarly organizations (including the American Economic Association, the American Historical Association, and the American Political Science Association) proposed a separate and independent American Sociological Society (ASS) ("Organization of the American Sociological Society" 1906). The first ASS annual meeting convened December 27–29, 1906, in Providence, Rhode Island, with 115 members and a full program of scholarly papers. In 1959 the organization's name was formally changed from the American Sociological Society to the American Sociological Association. As of 2004, the ASA reported 13,715 paid members and an investment portfolio valued at $7.1 million.

Corporately, the first ASS presidents comprised the major white, male, intellectual architects of what became the American sociological tradition and included (with institutional affiliations and dates of ASS presidency): Lester Frank Ward (Brown University, 1906–7), William Graham Sumner (Yale University, 1908–9), Franklin Henry Giddings (Columbia University, 1910–11), Albion Woodbury Small (University of Chicago, 1912–13), Edward Alsworth Ross (University of Wisconsin, 1914–15), George Edgar Vincent (University of Minnesota, 1916), George Elliott Howard (University of Nebraska, 1917), and Charles Horton Cooley (University of Michigan, 1918). The pioneering work of the ASS and its ever-growing membership is chronicled in the 23 volumes of the *Papers and Proceedings of the American Sociological Association* (1906–28) and in the pages of the *American Journal of Sociology* (*AJS*). The *AJS*, founded in 1895 by Albion W. Small and published by the University of Chicago Press, predated the ASS. The *AJS*, under Small's editorship, became the voice of the ASS and reprinted many of the articles and official reports appearing in the *Papers and Proceedings* (Meroney 1930a).

From the beginning, ASS membership grew steadily from 115 in 1906 to 1,812 in 1930, with the largest proportion of members (41.7 percent and 41.5 percent, respectively) coming from the Middle West and the East. In the early years, to 1922, annual meetings focused single-mindedly on a topic chosen and organized by the Society's president for that year, with an average of only 43 members participating on the program of any given meeting. These relatively small gatherings provided maximum opportunities for detailed discussions and face-to-face interaction between presenters, discussants, and the attendees as a whole. When Columbia's Franklin H. Giddings presided at the 1911 meeting in Washington, DC, for example, the program roster included 14 participants, an all-time low. The introduction of separate sectional meetings (organized around special topics) within the ASS began in 1922, resulting in larger total numbers of program participants during annual meetings and, simultaneously, a trend away from extended discussions of the presentations toward the reading of large numbers of formal papers per se (Meroney 1930b), a pattern that continues today. By 2004 there were 43 separately organized sections, representing such diverse fields as teaching and learning; medical sociology; Marxist sociology; sociology of emotions; mathematical sociology; history of sociology; animals and society, etc.

Despite the existence of numerous female sociologists during the first years of the twentieth century, the ASS was overwhelmingly a male club. When women were invited to participate on the annual programs it was typically as discussants rather than as major presenters (albeit the programs organized by Edward A. Ross (1914 and 1915) and William I. Thomas (1927) were more inclusive of women). Men dominated governance of the ASS during its first 25 years. Women rarely reached the inner sanctum of the ASS Executive Committee. The few who did were Emily Green Balch (1913–14), Julia Lathrop (1917–18), Grace Abbott (1920–23), Susan M. Kingsbury (1922–25), Lucile Eaves (1924–26), and Ethel Stugess Dummer (1927–30). Foreshadowing the end of what Deegan (1991) called the "dark era of patriarchal ascendancy" in American sociology, extending from 1920 to 1965, Dorothy Swaine Thomas became in 1952 the first woman elected to the ASS presidency. Since 1969, members of Sociologists for Women in Society (SWS) have lobbied for wider participation by women in governing the ASA. Subsequent female ASA presidents include Mirra Komarovsky (1973), Alice S. Rossi (1983), Matilda White Riley (1986), Joan Huber (1989), Maureen T. Hallinan (1996), Jill Quadagno (1998), and Barbara F. Reskin (2002). As of 2001, women comprised approximately 52 percent of the ASA membership.

African American sociologists also experienced variable inclusion within the ASA membership and governance structures. For example, W. E. B. Du Bois, America's most noted and prolific African American sociologist, neither attended ASA meetings nor held any ASA office. Indeed, Du Bois was professionally ostracized due to the ideological opposition of Robert E. Park, an ASA president (1925) and an influential faculty member of the sociology department in the University of Chicago. Park favored perspectives advocated by Booker T. Washington and this made room for limited African American participation within organized sociology. Partly in consequence, E. Franklin Frazier, with a doctorate from the University of Chicago, became – in 1948 – the first African American ASA president. Nonetheless, Frazier later recounted instances of racial discrimination at ASS meetings. Little changed during subsequent years. In 1968 the Black Caucus, led by Tillman Cothran, was organized to confront the continuing marginalization of African Americans within the ASA. As of 2001, African Americans comprised approximately 6 percent of the ASA membership. Two additional African Americans have been elected to the ASA presidency: William Julius Wilson (1990) and Troy Duster (2005). Compounding sexism with racism, no African American woman has ever been elected to the ASA presidency (Deegan 2005).

When the ASS was first proposed in 1905, Edward A. Ross, then a professor at the University of Nebraska, endorsed the idea but also wrote: "As the *American Journal of Sociology* will no doubt publish the best part of the proceedings, I see no reason for our group doing any publishing." By 1935, however, a disgruntled faction within the ASS chafed at the editorial control exercised over the *AJS* by the University of Chicago, as well as the Chicago department's unbroken administrative lock on the ASS office of secretary-treasurer. By a two-to-one vote at the annual business meeting in December 1935, the ASS membership established a new journal, the *American Sociological Review* (*ASR*) – and it remains an official ASA journal today. Of those supporting this change, Frank H. Hankins (of Smith College) was made the first editor of *ASR*, Henry P. Fairchild (of New York University) was elected ASS president, and Harold Phelps (a non-Chicagoan from Pittsburgh) was elected secretary of the Society. It was a clean sweep for the rebels (Lengermann 1979). Nonetheless, the strong Chicago influence within the ASA continued. For example, of the 25 ASA presidents elected from 1946 to 1969, fully 12 (48 percent) had earned their doctorates at Chicago. Harvard University, the only significant challenger to Chicago's enduring dominance, trained six (24 percent) ASA presidents during this period and seven other schools trained but one ASA president each (Kubat 1971: 582).

The 1935 "rebellion" against Chicago exemplifies numerous quarrels characterizing sociology generally and the ASA specifically, among them internal departmental conflicts between powerful professors (e.g., Talcott Parsons vs. Pitirim Sorokin at Harvard; Philip Hauser vs. Donald Bogue at Chicago); elite departments competing with each other (e.g., Chicago vs. Harvard vs. Columbia, ad infinitum); academics from large schools vs. small schools; so-called "pure" scientists vs. "applied" researchers; large vs. small ASA sections; radicals vs. liberals vs. conservatives, etc. The fight over Pitirim Sorokin's nomination and election to the ASA presidency (1965) is an illuminating case study of organizational turmoil (Johnston 1987). More recently, the 1976 ASA president, Alfred McClung Lee, fought heatedly with the ASA Council and subsequently decamped to form the Society for the Study of Social Problems (SSSP), a more openly liberal, action-oriented sociological organization (and when Lee discerned that the SSSP had in his view become too much like the ASA, he again bolted to co-found the Association for Humanist Sociology). It is a curious fact that the status, prestige, and power struggles among sociologists are so little studied by a discipline in which such matters are otherwise standard inquiries.

Over the long century since the founding of the ASA, countless former sociologists have been lured away by cognate disciplinary organizations. This silent disciplinary migration includes many who are now identified as social workers, criminologists, urban planners, geographers, anthropologists, demographers, rural sociologists, prison administrators, gerontologists, statisticians, economists, political scientists, high school and community college social science teachers, and the like, who have clubbed together in their own independent groups. As a result, the ASA is neither as intellectually robust nor as professionally diverse as it might otherwise be. For the most part, the ASA today is largely an organization by and for tenured academic sociologists at large universities and elite colleges, not to mention a modicum of researchers and administrators employed by well-endowed private foundations and large government agencies. The ASA's professional services, programs, awards, annual meetings, special conferences, and publications directly reflect the needs and interests of this bureaucratically sophisticated, well-educated, upper-middle-class constituency.

The ASA publishes several academic serials and currently requires subscription to at least one major ASA journal as a condition of ASA membership. These serials include *American Sociological Review*, *Contemporary Sociology* (a journal of book reviews), *American Sociologist*, *Journal of Health and Social Behavior*, *Social Psychology Quarterly*, *Sociology of Education*, *Teaching Sociology*, *Sociological Theory*, *Contexts*, *City and Community*, and *Sociological Methodology*. The association's professional newsletter, *Footnotes* (begun in 1973), is distributed to all members. Additional publishing projects include the *Rose Series in Sociology* (formerly the *Rose Monograph Series*), an annual *Guide to Graduate Departments*, a bi-annual *Directory of Departments*, a monthly *Employment Bulletin*, a bi-annual *Directory of Members*, the *Final Program* for each yearly ASA meeting, and a variety of miscellaneous publications on special topics.

Day-to-day operations of the association are administered by the ASA Executive Officer, who is selected and hired by the ASA Council (the Council is itself elected by the ASA membership from a slate of candidates selected by an elected Committee on Nominations; write-in candidacies are possible, but rare; and ASA membership is essentially open to anyone willing to pay the annual dues). The first full-time ASA Executive Officer, Gresham Sykes, was hired in 1963 with offices in Washington, DC. From that point forward, the ASA executive office, as a formal bureaucratic organization in its own right – with the vested interests inherent in all such organizations – grew in size, complexity, and influence. Sally T. Hillsman, who became the ASA Executive Officer in 2002, is the ninth full-time appointee to hold the position. As of 2005, the ASA executive office included some 25 paid staff members. With the rise of the executive office, the ASA President has become much less responsible for ordinary bureaucratic tasks and typically concentrates his or her energies on chairing the Program Committee and presiding at Council meetings. As an ongoing bureaucratic entity, the ASA executive office frequently represents the collective face of American sociology to legislators, government agencies, courts of law, private industry, media, research foundations, other non-profit associations, and to practicing sociologists and would-be sociologists. For good or ill, the ASA executive office has itself become a consequential force in shaping and promoting the public image of disciplinary sociology in the US.

It must be noted that the structure and constraints of the ASA, as an organization, are not congruent with the particular needs and goals of all sociologists as sociologists. A variety of independent organizations serve special interests and agendas not met by the ASA and include, for example, the Society for the Study of Social Problems, Society for the Study of Symbolic Interaction, Association for Humanist Sociology, Rural Sociological Association, Association of Black Sociologists, Sociologists for Women in Society, Association for the Sociology of Religion (formerly the American Catholic Sociological Society), the Harriet Martineau Sociological Society, and the Clinical Sociology Association, among many others. These organizations, some larger than others but all smaller relative to the size of the ASA, collectively represent a significant number of dedicated sociologists. Further, whereas the ASA is national in scope, several regional and state sociology organizations provide meetings and professional outlets on a more local level. Many sociologists participate in both the ASA and one (sometimes more) of the smaller sociological organizations or regional societies. Some of these organizations work in tandem, alongside the ASA, some in splendid isolation, and yet others largely within the ASA.

The history, politics, and activities of the American Sociological Association are the subject of numerous short studies and scholarly articles (see Centennial Bibliography Project Committee 2005). Two in-house histories have been sponsored by the ASA itself (Rhoades 1981; Rosich 2005), but no independent

comprehensive studies have yet appeared. A new archival depository for ASA records has been arranged at Pennsylvania State University, but few official records prior to 1950 are extant (save reports published in the *Papers and Proceedings of the American Sociological Society* and materials surviving in the personal papers of various ASS members and officers).

SEE ALSO: British Sociological Association; Chicago School; Cooley, Charles Horton; Du Bois, W. E. B.; Komarovsky, Mirra; Park, Robert E. and Burgess, Ernest W.; Parsons, Talcott; Patriarchy; Small, Albion W.; Sorokin, Pitirim A.; Sumner, William Graham; Ward, Lester Frank

REFERENCES AND SUGGESTED READINGS

Centennial Bibliography Project Committee, American Sociological Association Section on the History of Sociology (2005) A Brief Centennial Bibliography of Resources on the History of the American Sociological Society/Association. Online. www.mtholyoke.edu/courses/etownsle/HOS/Bib.pdf.

Deegan, M. J. (1991) Early Women Sociologists and the American Sociological Society: The Patterns of Exclusion and Participation. *American Sociologist* 16 (February): 14–24.

Deegan, M. J. (2005) Women, African Americans, and the ASA, 1905–2005. In: Blasi, A. J. (Ed.), *Diverse Histories of American Sociology*. Brill, Leiden, pp. 178–206.

Johnston, B. V. (1987) Pitirim Sorokin and the American Sociological Association: The Politics of a Professional Society. *Journal of the History of the Behavioral Sciences* 23 (April): 103–22.

Kubat, D. (Ed.) (1971) *Paths of Sociological Imagination: The Presidential Address before the American Sociological Association from 1946–1969*. Gordon & Breach, New York.

Lengermann, P. M. (1979) The Founding of the *American Sociological Review*: The Anatomy of a Rebellion. *American Sociological Review* 44 (April): 185–98.

Meroney, W. P. (1930a) Index to the Sociological Papers and Reports of the American Sociological Society 1906–30. *Publications of the American Sociological Society* 25: 226–58.

Meroney, W. P. (1930b) The Membership and Program of Twenty-Five Years of the American Sociological Society. *Publications of the American Sociological Society* 25: 55–67.

Organization of the American Sociological Society (1906) *American Journal of Sociology* 11 (January): 555-69.

Rhoades, L. J. (1981) *A History of the American Sociological Association, 1905–1980.* American Sociological Association, Washington, DC.

Rosich, K. J. (2005) *A History of the American Sociological Association, 1981–2004.* American Sociological Association, Washington, DC.

analytic induction

Norman K. Denzin

Originally associated with the work of Florian Znaniecki (1934), analytic induction is an interpretive strategy that seeks universal explanations of the phenomenon in question. Analytic induction involves a process of generating and then testing hypotheses against each successive case or instance of the phenomenon. Its decisive feature "is the analysis of the exceptional or negative case, the case which is deviant to the working hypothesis" (Buhler-Niederberger 1985). Negative case analysis may be regarded as a "process of revising hypotheses with hindsight" (Lincoln & Guba 1985). Analytic induction directs the investigator to formulate processual generalizations that apply to all instances of the problem. This differentiates analytic induction from other forms of causal analysis, including the multivariate method where concern is directed to generalizations that apply, not to all instances of the phenomenon at hand, but rather to most or some of them.

DESCRIPTION OF ANALYTIC INDUCTION

Strategically, analytic induction represents an approximation of the experimental model to the extent that explicit comparisons are made with groups not exposed to the causal factors under analysis. Conceptually, this represents the classic "before-after" experimental design, and when employed in the field method it calls for the investigator to search for empirical instances that negate the causal hypothesis. This general strategy, which combines the method of agreement and the method of difference, involves the following steps (see Robinson 1951; Buhler-Niederberger 1985; Schwandt 2001; Silverman 1993; Flick 2002):

1 A rough definition of the phenomenon to be explained is formulated.
2 A hypothetical explanation of that phenomenon is formulated.
3 One case is studied in light of the hypothesis, with the object of determining whether or not the hypothesis fits the facts in that case.
4 If the hypothesis does not fit the facts, either the hypothesis is reformulated or the phenomenon to be explained is redefined so that the case is excluded.
5 Practical certainty can be attained after a small number of cases have been examined, but the discovery of negative cases disproves the explanation and requires a reformulation.
6 This procedure of examining cases, redefining the phenomenon, and reformulating the hypotheses is continued until a universal relationship is established, each negative case calling for a redefinition or a reformulation.

Alfred Lindesmith's (1947, 1968) research on opiate addiction provides an illustration of this method. The focus of his investigation was the development of a sociological theory of opiate addiction. He began with the tentatively formulated hypothesis that individuals who did not know what drug they were receiving would not become addicted. Conversely, it was predicted that individuals would become addicted when they knew what they were taking, and had taken it long enough to experience distress (withdrawal symptoms) when they stopped. This hypothesis was destroyed when one of the first addicts interviewed, a doctor, stated that he had once received morphine for several weeks, was fully aware of the fact, but had not become addicted at that time. This negative case forced Lindesmith (1947: 8) to reformulate his initial hypothesis: "Persons become addicts when they recognize or perceive the significance of withdrawal distress which they are experiencing, and that if they do not recognize withdrawal distress they do not become addicts regardless of any other consideration."

This formulation proved to be much more powerful, but again negating evidence forced its revision. In this case persons were observed who had withdrawal experiences and understood withdrawal distress, but not in the most severe form; these persons did not use the drug to alleviate the distress and never became addicts. Lindesmith's (1947: 8) final causal hypothesis involved a shift on his part from "the recognition of withdrawal distress, to the use of the drug after the insight had occurred for the purpose of alleviating the distress." The final hypothesis had the advantage of attributing the cause of addiction to no single event, but rather to a complex chain of events. All the evidence unequivocally supported this theory, and Lindesmith (1947: 165) concluded: "This theory furnished a simple but effective explanation, not only of the manner in which addiction becomes established, but also of the essential features of addiction behavior, those features which are found in addiction in all parts of the world, and which are common to all cases."

ADVANTAGES OF ANALYTIC INDUCTION

Before reaching the conclusion that his theory explained all cases of opiate addiction. Lindesmith explicitly searched for negative cases that would force revision or rejection of the theory or the definitions of central concepts. Analytic induction provides a method by which old theories can be revised and incorporated into new theories as negative evidence is taken into account. The method, with its emphasis on the importance of the negative case, forces a close articulation between fact, observation, concept, proposition, and theory. It leads to developmental or processual theories, and these are superior to static formulations which assume that variables operate in either an intervening or an antecedent fashion on the processes under study.

Still, as Turner (1953) has suggested, analytic induction is too frequently employed in a definitional rather than a causal fashion. For example, predictions concerning who would take a drug and who would not, or under what conditions withdrawal symptoms would be severe or not severe, are not contained in Lindesmith's theory. Instead, it is a predictive system that explains the behavior of persons who have taken opiates.

The goal of seeking interpretations that apply to all instances of a phenomenon is admirable, as is the use of negative cases to reach that goal. As a strategy for interpreting qualitative materials, analytic induction has a great deal in common with grounded theory analysis and the constant comparison method (Glaser & Strauss 1967; Lincoln & Guba 1985; Silverman 1993; Schwandt 2001).

SEE ALSO: Emic/Etic; Experimental Design; Experimental Methods; Hypotheses; Methods; Negative Case Analysis; Znaniecki, Florian

REFERENCES AND SUGGESTED READINGS

Buhler-Niederberger, D. (1985) Analytische Induktion als Verfahren qualitativer Methodologie. *Zietschrift fur Soziologie* 14(4): 475–85.

Flick, U. (2002) *An Introduction to Qualitative Research*, 2nd edn. Sage, London.

Glaser, B. & Strauss, Anselm L. (1967) *The Discovery of Grounded Theory*. Aldine, Chicago.

Lincoln, Y. S. & Guba, E. G. (1985) *Naturalistic Inquiry*. Sage, Beverly Hills.

Lindesmith, A. (1947) *Opiate Addiction*. Principia Press, Bloomington.

Lindesmith, A. (1968) *Addiction and Opiates*. Aldine, Chicago.

Robinson, W. S. (1951) The Logical Structure of Analytic Induction. *American Sociological Review* 16: 812–18.

Schwandt, T. (2001) *Dictionary of Qualitative Inquiry*, 2nd edn. Sage, Thousand Oaks, CA.

Silverman, D. (1993) *Interpreting Qualitative Data*. Sage, London.

Turner, R. H. (1953) The Quest for Universals in Sociological Research. *American Sociological Review* 18: 604–11.

Znaniecki, F. (1934) *The Method of Sociology*. Farrar & Rinehart, New York.

anarchism

Chamsy El-Ojeili

Anarchism signifies the condition of being without rule. Anarchism, then, has often been equated with chaos. This interpretation was lent weight by the period of anarchist "propaganda by deed" towards the end of the nineteenth century. For most anarchists, though, their political allegiances involve opposition to the intrusiveness, destructiveness, and artificiality of state authority, the rejection of all forms of domination and hierarchy, and the desire to construct a social order based on free association. Anarchism is, however, a heterogeneous political field, containing a host of variations – for instance, organization versus spontaneity, peaceful transition versus violence, individualist versus collectivist means and ends, romanticism versus science, and existential versus structural critique of domination.

Although anarchism has been traced back, say, to millenarian sects of the Middle Ages, anarchism is properly a nineteenth-century ideology and movement, and anarchists are perhaps best remembered through Marx's encounters with Max Stirner, Pierre-Joseph Proudhon, and Mikhail Bakunin. Nevertheless, anarchism and communism were not clearly distinguished as varieties of socialism until the period after the Second International. From this time onwards, Marxists equated anarchism with extreme individualism, with opposition to any form of organization or authority, and with mistakenly taking the state (instead of capital) as primary in understanding exploitation and domination.

The equation of anarchism with individual rebellion has some justification in the case of thinkers like Max Stirner and Emma Goldman, and certainly in the case of the "anarcho-capitalism" of Murray Rothbard and Robert Nozick. However, prominent anarchist thinkers such as Mikhail Bakunin, Peter Kropotkin, Rudolph Rocker, and Alexander Berkman were collectivist and socialist in orientation, did not reject political organization, and were deeply critical of capitalism. If this draws anarchists nearer to Marxists, anarchists after Bakunin were wary of the possibility of a new dictatorship by Marxist intellectuals, seeing Marxian politics as statist, centralist, and "top-down," against their own "bottom-up" and decentralist conception of transitional struggle and post-revolutionary social organization (say, a federation of communes).

In the twentieth century, anarchism provided the underpinnings of larger movements and rebellions – for instance, revolutionary syndicalism (the trade unions as revolutionary weapons and models of a future social order) in strongholds such as France, Spain, and Italy; and the collectivization of land and factories during the Spanish Civil War. MIT linguist and political activist Noam Chomsky is probably the best-known contemporary representative of this strand of anarchist thought.

Between 1914 and 1938, anarchism as an ideology and a movement went into serious decline. However, it was widely viewed as at least implicit in the counter-cultural opposition of the 1960s and 1970s. From this period, Murray Bookchin developed a sophisticated anarchist theory containing a social ecology perspective that emphasized diversity and locality; and, more recently, "primitivist" anarchists connected modernity's obsessions with science and progress with the domination of human beings and nature and with the loss of authenticity and spontaneity. For some, poststructuralism has strong anarchist resonances – underscoring difference against totalizing and scientistic Marxian theory and politics, decentralist, and attentive to the micro-operations of power. Finally, the anti-globalization movement is sometimes said to represent a "new anarchism," opposing neoliberal capitalism and statism, decentralist and localist in its aims, and characterized by openness and by "horizontal" organizational tendencies.

SEE ALSO: Capitalism; Communism; Direct Action; Goldman, Emma; Nozick, Robert; Socialism; Utopia

REFERENCES AND SUGGESTED READINGS

Bookchin, M. (1998) *The Third Revolution: Popular Movements in the Revolutionary Era*, 2 vols. Cassell, London.

Carter, A. (1971) *The Political Theory of Anarchism.* Routledge & Kegan Paul, London.

Guerin, D. (1970) *Anarchism.* Monthly Review Press, New York.

Marshall, P. (1992) *Demanding the Impossible: A History of Anarchism.* HarperCollins, London.

Sonn, R. D. (1992) *Anarchism.* Twayne, New York.

Woodcock, G. (1962) *Anarchism.* Penguin, London.

Woodcock, G. (Ed.) (1977) *The Anarchist Reader.* Harvester Press, Brighton.

Anglo-conformity

Toni-Michelle C. Travis

As a nation founded by European immigrants, the United States had to grapple with the concept of what it means to be an American. In seeking to become American, many immigrants adopted one model of assimilation, Anglo-conformity. This model promoted subordination of immigrant cultural values and customs to American holidays, civic rituals, and the English language which was stressed by the public school system. Even in colonial times multiple cultures were evident, although the dominant culture was British with the values of speaking English, governing based on common law, and practicing Protestant Christian beliefs. The goal was to emulate the cultural traits of white Anglo-Saxon Protestants (WASPS).

Theories held that the process of assimilation would follow one of two routes, Anglo-conformity or blending into American society as part of the "melting pot." Both routes led to fast-track assimilation and Americanization.

Anglo-conformity was an underlying premise of the Immigration Act of 1924, which reinforced the primacy of European immigration. It established national quotas, which favored immigrants from Northwestern Europe. Asian immigrants, however, were excluded from the US beginning with the Chinese Exclusion Act of 1882, followed by the Act of 1924 that barred Japanese entry by denying them a quota. Two groups already present in American society were not part of this assimilation process. Both Native Americans and

African Americans were excluded. Native Americans were confined to reservations, while African Americans faced segregation.

Since the Immigration Act of 1965 the Anglo-conformity model of assimilation has been challenged by the rise of ethnic consciousness. Immigrants in the post-1965 wave came primarily from Africa, Asia, and Latin America. These immigrants caused a reexamination of what it means to be American. Was the criterion for becoming American merely to speak English or to conform to an antiquated image of American equaling white, a synonym for European-looking? The new immigrants, often referred to as people of color, confounded the notion that all Americans looked like the earlier European immigrants.

Anglo-conformity is now just one of many ways of being American. In a multicultural society a growing number of Americans may not speak English as their primary language and prefer to retain the cultural traditions of their ancestors. The formation of American identity continues to be an evolving process.

SEE ALSO: Acculturation; Assimilation; Eurocentrism; Melting Pot; Multiculturalism; Pluralism, American; Race and Ethnic Consciousness

REFERENCES AND SUGGESTED READINGS

Alba, R. D. (1990) *Ethnic Identity: The Transformation of White America.* Yale University Press, New Haven.

Glazer, N. & Moynihan, D. P. (1963) *Beyond the Melting Pot.* MIT and Harvard University Press, Cambridge, MA.

Gleason, P. (1990) *Speaking of Diversity: Language and Ethnicity in Twentieth-Century America.* Johns Hopkins University Press, Baltimore.

Gordon, M. (1964) *Assimilation in American Life.* Oxford University Press, Oxford.

Haney Lopez, I. F. (1994) *White By Law.* New York University Press, New York.

Hollinger, D. A. (1995) *Postethnic America: Beyond Multiculturalism.* HarperCollins, New York.

Lieberson, S. & Waters, M. C. (1988) *From Many Strands: Ethnic and Racial Groups in Contemporary America.* Russell Sage Foundation, New York.

Novak, M. (1972) *The Rise of the Unmeltable Ethnics: Politics and Culture in the Seventies.* Macmillan, New York.

Zack, N. (1993) *Race and Mixed Race.* Temple University Press, Philadelphia.

Zelinsky, W. (2001) *The Enigma of Ethnicity.* University of Iowa Press, Iowa City.

animal rights movements

Robert Garner

Concern for the rights of animals dates back to at least the nineteenth century, but the modern animal rights movement emerged in the 1970s, initially in Britain. It can be distinguished from a more moderate concern for animal welfare, both in terms of objectives and strategy. Reasons for the rise of the animal rights movement include factors such as affluence, changes in the occupational structure, and the influence of gender that are only indirectly related to the public's concern for animals and what is done to them. More specific explanatory variables include the intellectual ballast provided by academic philosophers, and the greater awareness of what is done to animals and the ways in which they can suffer.

The first national law designed to protect animals was carried in Britain in 1822. The legislation itself was very moderate but established the principle that animals can be directly harmed and that the law could be used in certain circumstances to reduce their suffering. Since then, animal welfare in Britain and elsewhere has become an important political issue and most areas of animal use are subject to a complex legislative and bureaucratic framework (Garner 1998).

For the animal rights movement, however, the law does no go far enough. This was particularly evident in the abolitionist demands of the anti-vivisectionist organizations that emerged in the nineteenth century. However, concern for animals in general declined at the beginning of the twentieth century and did not reemerge until the 1960s and 1970s in Britain, and a decade later in the US. The revitalization of the animal protection movement can be measured in terms of a marked increase in the number of groups existing and the membership of new and existing groups, growing income, and the existence of an increasingly attentive public prepared to donate to groups and support their objectives.

This revitalization of the animal protection movement was characterized by a greater radicalism as traditional animal welfarism was challenged by an emphasis on animal rights. In Britain, the anti-vivisectionist organizations were reinvigorated and new national animal rights groups were created (e.g., Animal Aid and Compassion in World Farming). In the US there were two streams to the development of the animal rights movement. One centered on New York and Henry Spira's well-documented campaigns against laboratory animal exploitation, while the other centered on the creation of People for the Ethical Treatment of Animals (PETA), now by far the largest animal rights organization in the US.

The animal rights movement can be distinguished from animal welfarism by its objectives and strategy. It is characterized by its abolitionist objectives. In practice, this means the end of raising and killing animals for food, their use as experimental subjects, and as sources of clothing and entertainment. Animal welfare proponents, by contrast, can be characterized by a belief in eliminating the unnecessary suffering of animals. By implication, of course, this assumes that some suffering – that which provides significant human benefits – is necessary.

This ideological difference has resulted in conflict, sometimes severe, between the welfare and rights wings of the animal protection movement, the arena for this conflict in Britain often being the Royal Society for the Prevention of Cruelty to Animals (RSPCA). The animal rights movement is also characterized by its willingness to engage in grassroots campaigning. While the older welfare groups (such as the RSPCA and the Fund for the Replacement of Animals in Medical Research) tend to be more elitist, relying on the expertise of their full-time staff, animal rights groups encourage and facilitate grassroots activism. What has emerged is a network of activists only loosely connected to the national groups who try to provide leadership and direction. For example, recent British animal rights campaigns against the export of live agricultural animals and the Huntingdon Life Sciences contract research laboratory have involved locally formed groups with little formal structure and hierarchy. In America, similarly, the new radical groups have encouraged individual activists to participate in mass campaigns and civil disobedience. This was the fundamental characteristic of the Spira-inspired campaigns which launched the modern animal rights movement in the US.

Because of the characteristics noted above, the animal rights movement may be an example of a new social movement, distinguished from an old social movement by its decentralization, disorganization, rejection of the old political divisions based on capital and labor, and stress on wider cultural changes as opposed to merely seeking piecemeal legislative change. This is a pretty accurate description of the animal rights movement, if not the animal protection movement in general. It should be noted though that some of the above characteristics imputed to new social movements are not particularly new − witness some of the animal protection campaigns in the nineteenth century. Some scholars (e.g., Jordan & Maloney 1997) doubt its explanatory utility.

Animal rights grassroots activism is a reflection both of the urgency to right what are perceived to be appalling wrongs and the animal rights movement's lack of "insider" status with government. A moral imperative is also behind the pursuit of direct action by a small number of animal rights activists. Direct action was particularly associated with the Animal Liberation Front, formed in a number of countries from the 1970s onwards. More recently, animal rights militants have been organized in specific campaigns against animal research establishments, most notably Huntingdon Life Sciences in the UK. Assessing the validity of direct action depends principally, of course, upon the type of action undertaken. Most argue that civil disobedience, such as sit-ins, is a valuable part of

democratic culture. At the other end of the spectrum, violence or threats of violence directed at those who use animals is deemed by most within the animal rights movement as unacceptable, whatever the moral imperative that causes it. Very few activists, it should be said, have undertaken this kind of terrorist activity.

There is a role for social scientists in seeking to explain the emergence of the modern animal rights movement over the past few decades, although there has been a general paucity of scholarly works by political scientists and sociologists on the animal rights movement. Two US-based studies are Nelkin and Jasper's *The Animal Rights Crusade* (1992) and Finsen and Finsen's *The Animal Rights Movement in America* (1994).

Jasper and Poulsen (1995) have sought to utilize the animal rights movement as a case study of social movement recruitment, mobilization, and maintenance. One of their principal arguments is that people are recruited into the animal rights movement through moral shocks, often provided by the movement's own literature. Images of animal exploitation have influenced people to participate in animal rights activism. This, they argue, contrasts markedly with other new social movements (e.g., the anti-nuclear movement) where activists tend to be recruited through preexisting networks.

Arguments employed to explain the emergence of the animal rights movement are general or specific. In the former category is the explanation associated with Inglehart (1977), which sees the possession of post-material values as the reason behind a growth in concern for non-material quality of life issues such as the well-being of animals. Inglehart explains the growth of post-material values in terms of post-war affluence. Certainly, this approach would seem to have considerable explanatory power as far as the animal protection movement is concerned, not least seeming to account for its historically uneven development − buoyant in times of prosperity, less so in times of economic depression.

Inglehart's explanation is not entirely convincing or, at least, comprehensive enough to account for the rise of the animal rights movement. In the first place, surveys suggest that animal rights activists do not tend to be the most affluent members of society. Rather, given the preponderance in the animal rights movement of those in the non-productive service sector – teachers, doctors, and so on – it may be, as Cotgrove and Duff (1980) have suggested, that the most important explanatory variable is occupation rather than affluence. Alternatively, a key explanatory variable could be gender, given that a preponderance of animal rights activists are women. Here, it might be argued that the culturally defined role of women, with its emphasis on nurturing and caring, and the greater consciousness women have of their political status, has led many to lend their weight to a cause with which they can identify (Donovan & Adams 1996).

Other explanations provide room for the independent explanatory validity of people's genuine concern for animals and what is done to them, as opposed to being byproducts of affluence, occupation, or gender. Surely of some importance, for instance, is the development of a radical philosophy for animals, which has given the movement academic respectability and has aided the recruitment of articulate people from academe and other professions.

The emergence and development of the animal rights movement have been accompanied and encouraged, then, by the work of academic philosophers and, more recently, by legal scholars. Especially important influences on the animal rights movement have been *Animal Liberation* (1975), written by the Australian philosopher Peter Singer, and *The Case for Animal Rights* (1984), by the American philosopher Tom Regan. Somewhat ironically, since he has been feted for providing the Bible of the animal rights movement, Singer is in fact a utilitarian thinker, eschewing the notion of rights, and has been criticized by Regan and others for failing to provide a cast-iron basis for the abolition of animal exploitation. More recently, a second generation of animal ethicists – including Pluhar (1995), DeGrazia (1996), and Rowlands (1998) – has emerged, providing important contributions to the academic debate, although less influential in the development of the animal rights movement. Equally important has been the contribution

of legal scholars, principally Francione (1995) and Wise (2000), who have suggested that the objectives of the animal rights movement cannot be achieved while animals remain, in law, as the property of humans.

Of course, ideas by themselves do not have an impact without a receptive social climate. This is where cultural, occupational, and gender explanations come in. Another factor is that far more now is known about the capabilities of animals. This has the effect of making the radical philosophical arguments more convincing. This greater knowledge goes beyond a simple recognition that animals can feel pain. The fact that at least some species have been shown to have considerable cognitive ability makes it much harder to justify many of the ways in which humans exploit animals.

Knowledge of animal capabilities leads in turn to a greater recognition that they are more like us than we had previously thought. The decline of theological separatism and the influence of Darwin's theory of evolution are crucial here (Rachels 1990). Moreover, that the public are now much more aware of both the capabilities of animals and what is actually done to them is primarily a product of the greater coverage of animal issues in the media. This is also partly a product of the movement's efforts to get the issues onto the political agenda.

SEE ALSO: Anthrozoology; Direct Action; Environmental Movements; Gender Oppression; Human–Non-Human Interaction; Moral Shocks and Self-Recruitment; New Social Movement Theory; Popular Culture Forms (Zoos); Social Movements

REFERENCES AND SUGGESTED READINGS

Cotgrove, S. & Duff, A. (1980) Environmentalism, Middle-Class Radicalism and Politics. *Sociological Review* 28: 333–51.

DeGrazia, D. (1996) *Taking Animals Seriously: Mental Life and Moral Status.* Cambridge University Press, Cambridge.

Donovan, J. & Adams, C. (Eds.) (1996) *Beyond Animal Rights: A Feminist Caring Ethic for the Treatment of Animals.* Continuum, New York.

Francione, G. (1995) *Animals, Property and the Law*. Temple University Press, Philadelphia.

Garner, R. (1998) *Political Animals: Animal Protection Politics in Britain and the United States*. Macmillan, Basingstoke.

Inglehart, R. (1977) *The Silent Revolution: Changing Values and Political Styles Among Western Publics*. Princeton University Press, Princeton.

Jasper, J. & Poulsen, J. (1995) Recruiting Strangers and Friends. *Journal of Social Problems* 42(4): 493–512.

Jordan, G. & Maloney, W. (1997) *The Protest Business*. Manchester University Press, Manchester.

Pluhar, E. (1995) *Beyond Prejudice: The Moral Significance of Human and Nonhuman Animals*. Duke University Press, Durham, NC.

Rachels, J. (1990) *Created From Animals*. Oxford University Press, Oxford.

Regan, T. (1984) *The Case for Animal Rights*. Routledge, London.

Rowlands, M. (1998) *Animal Rights: A Philosophical Defence*. Macmillan, Basingstoke.

Singer, P. (1975) *Animal Liberation*. Jonathan Cape, London.

Wise, S. (2000) *Rattling the Cage: Toward Legal Rights to Animals*. Perseus Books, Cambridge, MA.

animism

Gaetano Riccardo

Already used by Stahl in 1707 in his work *Theoria medica vera* (*True Medical Theory*) to denote, in the medical field, the theory that identifies the soul with the life principle, in anthropology animism refers to Tylor's concept of religion, which he expounded in *Primitive Culture* (1871). In anthropology the term animism has also been used not to indicate a theory of religion but, more usually, the beliefs concerning the existence of many spiritual beings. Finally, in psychology, animism is conceived by Piaget as a typical concept of the world corresponding to a precise step in children's cognitive development.

To remain in the anthropological realm, Tylor's opinion was that the idea of soul would have been the starting point for more complex religious beliefs. Animism would have arisen from reflection upon universal experiences such as dreams and death. In particular, the fact that people remain motionless while dreams provide the sensation of acting, moving, and interacting with others, including the dead, would have suggested to primitive people the existence of something surviving death, a kind of "double" able to abandon the human body. This is exactly what happens when people sleep. There is a feeling of temporarily leaving the body, only to return to it later. This element is precisely the soul or vital force, which in time came to be regarded as belonging not only to human beings but also to inanimate objects and animals. Thus primitive humans in their dreams would have imagined that life does not stop with physical death but continues. This would have suggested the idea of the existence of a parallel world beyond the material one.

If these souls are at first conceived as being attached to material things, the idea that some of them, the spirits, are totally immaterial leads them into what will become for humans the religious sphere. At this stage it is possible to verify a progressive hierarchization and differentiation of such spiritual beings, on the basis of ways that, starting from animism, reach polytheism and finally monotheism. This is to give a purely intellectual explanation for religious beliefs. Religion would be a kind of primitive philosophy. From this point of view, Tylor's animism is not very different from other theories aiming to find the kind of belief underlying more sophisticated religious forms. Other authors identified it with fetishism (Comte), magic (Frazer), or totemism (Durkheim).

The fact that Tylor's view, in contrast with other theories, was built on reflections on universal and immediate experiences, like dreams and death, could explain its great success during an age in which evolutionistic images of cultural facts were fashionable. Most of these theories aimed to discover the most archaic form of religion. The opposing arguments put forward by others referred not only to this approach, but also to the choice of one or another belief as representative of the most archaic form of religion. The various theories were more similar than different and the arguments against them always followed the same course. So, in the case of animism too, one of the first arguments against it consisted in stressing that it was not universal. It was noted that many cultures had no word equivalent to the western idea of the soul. Studies of other peoples showed that the notion of the soul presupposed other even simpler notions. So what Tylor considered original was derived.

One of the first authors to stress this kind of argument against animism was Marett (1909), who spoke of pre-animism. His reflections were based on studies of the Melanesians conducted by Codrington (1891) regarding the notion of *mana*, an impersonal power contained in all things. Among the other arguments against animistic theory, a very special place is occupied by that formulated by Durkheim in *Les Formes élémentaires de la vie religieuse* (1912). He showed that many of Tylor's statements were based on presuppositions whose attribution to the primitive peoples was scarcely probable. But Durkheim also stresses the merits of Tylorian theory, such as that of submitting the soul notion to a historical analysis. With Tylor the notion of the soul ceased to be an immediate datum of the conscience, as it was in most philosophical arguments, becoming rather a subject investigated as a product of mythology and history.

In spite of this progress in the debate, Durkheim stressed how it was anti-historical to assign to primitive peoples the idea of soul as something completely separate from the body, as is the case with the idea of the double. It was also scarcely probable for Durkheim that the notion of soul as double was originated by the experience of dreams, which would have suggested to primitive people the idea of the existence of a self parallel to the self dwelling in the body. Stressing the relation that often exists between dreams and actual experiences, Durkheim emphasizes that certain oneiric images are only possible on the condition of presupposing the existence of religious thought, and they cannot be conceived as a cause. Above all, echoing a remark made by Jevons (1896), Durkheim stresses how the belief in the double does not automatically imply the belief in its being sacral, destined to worship. Finally, to explain religion as starting from the experience of dreams would be, notes Durkheim, to trace it to a hallucinatory and not a real element. But it

is not evident why this hallucinatory element, and not a real one, connected with life in society, would be at the basis of the various religious systems.

Although Durkheim shares with Tylor the concern to find the most archaic form of religion, his consistent critique of animism yet implies the kind of reflections that, developed afterwards by functionalism, will eventually diminish the interest in every debate aiming to trace the presumed original form taken by religion, leading scholars' reflections to more properly sociological and pragmatic problems.

SEE ALSO: Anthropology, Cultural and Social; Comte, Auguste; Durkheim, Émile; Early History; Fetishism; Magic; Popular Religiosity; Religion; Sacred; Totemism

REFERENCES AND SUGGESTED READINGS

Codrington, J. H. (1891) *The Melanesians: Studies in their Anthropology and Folk-Lore*. Clarendon Press, Oxford.
Durkheim, É. (1912) *Les Formes élémentaires de la vie religieuse*. Alcan, Paris.
Evans-Pritchard, E. E. (1965) *Theories of Primitive Religion*. Clarendon Press, Oxford.
Jevons, F. B. (1896) *An Introduction to the History of Religion*. Methuen, London.
Marett, R. R. (1909) *The Threshold of Religion*. Methuen, London.
Tylor, E. E. (1871) *Primitive Culture: Researches into the Development of Mythology, Philosophy, Religion, Art, and Custom*. Murray, London.

Annales School

John R. Hall

The group of interdisciplinary historians that emerged in France in the first quarter of the twentieth century became known as a school named for the journal that Marc Bloch and Lucien Febvre started in 1929 – *Annales de l'histoire économique et sociale*, now called *Annales: Histoire, Sciences Sociales*. Annales historians have been eclectic in their methods and topics. Their shared perspective (1) subordinates traditional narrative history centered on political, military, and religious elites (e.g., the "scientific history" of the nineteenth-century German Leopold von Ranke) and (2) embraces wide-ranging sources of data and social science methodologies and theories. The diverse results of their scholarship are a testament to the power of colleagues, mentors, and students encouraging one another in manifold interdisciplinary inquiries, even on topics sometimes alien to their own.

Scholars like Tocqueville, Marx, and Weber already had eclipsed Ranke with broader sociological visions of history. But the Annales School consolidated that tendency for history proper with their journal and their informal collegial network centered in the École Pratique des Hautes Études, which gained stronger institutionalization in the Boulevard Raspail's Maison des sciences de l'homme – the Paris building finished in 1970 that houses a complex of research centers and institutes. Peter Burke describes three generations of the Annales: the founding one initiated by Bloch and Febvre; the generation led by Fernand Braudel; and a third generation, many of them appointed by Braudel when he took up leadership of the *VIème section* upon Febvre's death in 1956, and later served as the first director of the Maison des sciences de l'homme.

The founding scholars wrote imposing studies that challenged core assumptions about the subject matter of history. Marc Bloch ranged widely, writing about a persisting superstition – the king's supposed ability to heal by touch – and exploring feudalism, a social institution that endured for centuries. Similarly, Lucien Febvre studied topics from biography to geography. The classic Annales exemplar remains Fernand Braudel's *The Mediterranean and the Mediterranean World in the Age of Philip II*, written in notebooks while he was a prisoner of war in Germany, and published in French in 1949. The book maps the Mediterranean region by its environmental and human ecology and enduring social formations, offering a conventional narrative history of Philip only at the end. In the 1960s, Braudel theorized three temporal "levels": ecological history (*la longue durée*), institutional history, and the history of events.

To address the connection between levels, he invoked an orchestral metaphor: Multiple historical temporalities, he argued, compose a grand symphony of History to be charted on the grid of objective time (Hall 1989).

The Annales is better understood as a school than as a paradigm because it connects radically different approaches, e.g., geography, economics, sociology, and social and cultural anthropology. Despite the systemic features of Braudel's model, Annales scholars avoid the term "system." As Georg Iggers (1997: 53–5) observes, they have borrowed from French structuralism, specifically from Émile Durkheim and more broadly from anthropological and linguistic structuralisms. To be sure, theirs is a *historicist* structuralism that views structures as enduring arrangements *in* history. Ironically, though, an affinity with Ranke is thereby retained. Like Ranke, Annales scholars largely embrace the historicist view that shuns any formal theoretical "laws" of development or social process. They differ from Ranke more in scope than methodological assumptions. Thus, Fernand Braudel's model incorporates a diverse range of social, institutional, and ecological events within a multi-scale yet realist framework of linear time. Like Braudel's, much other work within the Annales tradition has been averse to any strong use of theory.

Nevertheless, the sociological character of Annales studies would be hard to miss in structural histories like Georges Duby's investigation of medieval European rural economy. With achievements such as this, the Annales School became unrivaled in the detailed, almost archeological, delineation of social forms and practices. Yet the Annales program for correcting preoccupations with the history of events succeeded perhaps too well (Iggers 1997: 56). What Jack Hexter once suggested for Braudel's *The Mediterranean* is more widely salient: Annales structural analyses tend to remain disconnected from interplay with the concrete lives of human beings. Cultural structures are dissociated from life.

From the 1960s onward, Annales scholars participated in an international (and increasingly poststructuralist) dialogue that shifted the agenda of cultural history in relation to social history, history "from below," Foucault's archeology, and what Italian historians called *microhistoria*. They produced a rich vein of studies such as Le Roy Ladurie's fascinating cultural inventory of local Pyrenees village life in the late thirteenth and early fourteenth centuries – *Montaillou: The Promised Land of Error* (1979), and Roger Chartier's history of reading. However, cultural history was hardly new to the Annales. Marc Bloch published his study of the "royal touch" in the early 1930s, and Febvre's 1942 study of religious thought artfully turned the question of whether Rabelais was an atheist into a study of *mentalités* – about what collective meaning unbelief would hold in sixteenth-century Europe.

The Annales School gained prominence in historical sociology in the 1970s when Immanuel Wallerstein invoked Braudel's *The Mediterranean* in formulating his world-system theory. More widely, along with other exemplars, the Annales School inspired the emerging post-1960s generation of historical sociologists to embrace diverse new practices and topics. The Annales School is best known for the studies of its participants. However, the challenge it poses for historical sociology and for sociology more generally concerns how to conduct social *science* under (historicist) conditions in a world where enduring traditions and practices, and durable social institutions and structures of life, frame both everyday and "historic" events.

SEE ALSO: Braudel, Fernand; Historical and Comparative Methods; Marx, Karl; Weber, Max

REFERENCES AND SUGGESTED READINGS

Burke, P. (1990) *The French Historical Revolution: The Annales School, 1929–89*. Cambridge, Polity Press.

Burke, P. (2003) The Annales, Braudel and Historical Sociology. In: Delanty, G. & Isin, E. (Eds.), *Handbook for Historical Sociology*. Sage, London, pp. 58–64.

Carrard, P. (1992) *Poetics of the New History: French Historical Discourse from Braudel to Chartier*. Johns Hopkins University Press, Baltimore.

Hall, J. R. (1989) *Cultures of Inquiry*. Cambridge University Press, Cambridge.

Iggers, G. (1997) *Historiography in the Twentieth Century*. Wesleyan University Press, Hanover, NH.

Stoianovich, T. (1976) *French Historical Method: The Annales Paradigm*. Cornell University Press, Ithaca, NY.

anomie

Mathieu Deflem

Anomie refers to the lack or ineffectiveness of normative regulation in society. The concept was first introduced in sociology by Émile Durkheim (1893) in his study on the social dimensions of the division of labor. Contrary to Marx, Durkheim argued that the division of labor is not problematic as long as it is sufficiently regulated. However, under exceptional circumstances, Durkheim maintained, the division of labor will take on an anomic form, either because there is a lack of regulation or because the level of regulation does not match the degree of development of the division of labor. Durkheim saw such anomic forms present during periods of industrial crises, in the conflict between labor and capital, and in the lack of unity and excessive degree of specialization in the sciences.

In his famous study on suicide, Durkheim (1897) extended the anomie perspective when, next to altruistic and egoistic suicide, he identified the anomic type of suicide. Durkheim argued that anomic suicide takes place when normative regulations are absent, such as in the world of trade and industry (chronic anomie), or when abrupt transitions in society lead to a loss in the effectiveness of norms to regulate behavior (acute anomie). The latter type explains the high suicide rate during fiscal crises and among divorced men.

Durkheim's anomie concept was not widely influential in sociology until it was adopted and expanded in Robert K. Merton's (1938, 1968) theory of deviant behavior and opportunity structures. Differentiating between society's culturally accepted goals and its institutionalized means to reach those goals, Merton argues that a state of anomie occurs as a result of the unusually strong emphasis in US society on the cultural goals (individual success) without a corresponding emphasis on the legitimate norms (education, work). Anomie refers to the resulting demoralization or deinstitutionalization of a society's legitimate means, leading people in some social categories, depending on their socioeconomic conditions, to be more likely to adopt illegitimate and often illegal means to reach culturally approved goals.

Based on Merton's work, anomie became among the most discussed and applied concepts in American sociology during the 1950s and 1960s. Working broadly within the structural functionalist framework, various theoretical extensions and reformulations were introduced and applied in empirical research. Theoretically, anomie was perceived among non-Marxists as a useful alternative to alienation. In matters of empirical research, an important development was the introduction of the concept of anomia. First introduced by Leo Srole (1956), anomia refers to the social psychological mental states of individuals who are confronted with social conditions of anomie. Throughout the 1960s, the concept of anomia was widely adopted in empirical research, in part because it was easily measurable on the basis of the anomia scale Srole had introduced. At the same time, applications of Merton's anomie theory were also popular, especially in the area of crime and deviance. Caught between the polarization of micro and macro perspectives, the relation between anomia and anomie at a theoretical level has never been adequately addressed.

During the 1970s and early 1980s there was a general decrease in the popularity of structural functionalism, and the concept of anomie was much less applied and discussed. Since the late 1980s, however, there has been a revival of the sociological use of the anomie concept in at least two areas of inquiry. First, Merton's perspective of anomie and social structure is now widely recognized as one of the most influential contributions in criminological sociology (Adler & Laufer 1995; Passas & Agnew 1997). Along with Merton's various theoretical reformulations since 1938 and its extensions by others, the theoretical approach has now been broadened as comprising an anomie theory as well as a strain theory (Featherstone & Deflem 2003). Whereas Merton initially presented the two theoretical components as inextricably linked, that perspective is generally no longer accepted. Anomie refers to a state of social organization, whereas strain is a mechanism that induces deviant behavior. Strain can only occur under conditions of anomie, but the social condition of anomie can be accompanied by a variety of mechanisms that lead to deviance. In contemporary criminological sociology, strain theory is much more influential than anomie theory.

Second, less widespread but no less significant is the recent adoption of the anomie concept in research on societies undergoing rapid social and economic change. This perspective particularly grew out of sociological efforts to account for the drastic changes that have been taking place in many Eastern European countries since the collapse of communism. This notion of anomie largely relies on the work of Durkheim, who introduced the concept a century before to denote similar events of transition and upheaval. It remains to be seen if and how this renewed concept of anomie will integrate with the related literature on globalization and inequality that is traditionally rather hostile toward Durkheimian and functional structuralist theories. Perhaps a new integrated perspective can emerge that will transcend the prior dichotomies between anomie and rival concepts such as alienation.

SEE ALSO: Alienation; Durkheim, Émile; Merton, Robert K.; Norms; Strain Theories; Structural Functional Theory

REFERENCES AND SUGGESTED READINGS

Adler, F. & Laufer, W. S. (Eds.) (1995) *The Legacy of Anomie Theory: Advances in Criminological Theory, Volume 10*. Transaction, New Brunswick, NJ.

Durkheim, É. (1933 [1893]) *The Division of Labor in Society*. Trans. G. Simpson. Free Press, Glencoe, IL.

Durkheim, É. (1952 [1897]) *Suicide: A Study in Sociology*. Trans. J. A. Spaulding & G. Simpson. Routledge & Kegan Paul, London.

Featherstone, R. & Deflem, M. (2003) Anomie and Strain: Context and Consequences of Merton's Two Theories. *Sociological Inquiry* 73: 471–89.

Merton, R. K. (1938) Social Structure and Anomie. *American Sociological Review* 3: 672–82.

Merton, R. K. (1968) *Social Theory and Social Structure*, enlarged edn. Free Press, New York.

Passas, N. & Agnew, R. (Eds.) (1997) *The Future of Anomie Theory*. Northeastern University Press, Boston.

Srole, L. (1956) Social Integration and Certain Corollaries: An Exploratory Study. *American Sociological Review* 21: 709–16.

ANOVA (analysis of variance)

Paul T. Munroe and Neil J. Salkind

Analysis of variance (or ANOVA) is a statistical technique that tests the difference between more than two sample means. It is one of the simpler of the techniques that fall within the larger category "general linear model."

In the basic case, a sample is divided into groups based on their values on one independent variable, usually a discrete variable with a relatively small number of categories. Within each group, the means for a second variable, the dependent variable, are calculated. The difference in the means for the different groups is calculated and is then compared to the variation of the individual cases within each group around that group's mean. The larger the difference in the means (relative to the variation around each mean), the more likely it is that the means are significantly different – that is, the less likely that one would make a Type I (alpha) error by saying that the groups have different means in the population from which the sample is drawn.

To calculate ANOVA, an F test is performed. The F statistic comprises the ratio of the variance between groups and the variance within groups as follows:

$$F = \frac{Variance\ Between\ Groups}{Variance\ Within\ Groups}$$

When the source of variance between groups (reflecting the strength of the treatment) is larger than the source of the variance within groups (reflecting individual variability), then the F value increases and approaches statistical significance. If both sources of variance are equal, the resulting F value is equal to 1, which one would expect by chance.

The manual computation of F is too detailed for this presentation, but below is the output from a simple one way analysis of variance computed using the Data Toolpak from Excel.

SUMMARY

Groups	Average
Column 1	4.67
Column 2	3.24
Column 3	6.43

ANOVA

Source of variation	SS	df	MS	F	F crit
Between groups	107.27	2	53.63	43.71	3.15
Within groups	73.62	60	1.23		
Total	180.89	62			

The above output shows: the average for each of the three groups or levels of the one independent variable source of variance (between and within groups); Sums of Squares (SS) and Mean Squares (MS), both variance estimates and the degrees of freedom (df); F value, which is a ratio, as stated earlier; and critical F value or that needed for significance.

In this example, the F value is greater than the critical value (that would be expected by chance alone) and the difference between the three groups is statistically significant. Since the F test is a robust test (an overall test of the significance between three means), follow-up tests (often called post-hoc comparison) need to be conducted to learn where this difference lies. These tests compare all combinations of means.

As with all general linear model techniques, there are some assumptions that must be met before one can make reliable inferences about the population based on the sample. The most important of these assumptions is random sampling. It is assumed that the sample was drawn randomly from the population. It is also assumed that the distribution of the dependent variable is not skewed in either direction around the mean(s), but is normally distributed.

More complicated techniques have been developed based on the reasoning of analysis of variance, including multivariate ANOVA (MANOVA), which allows one to test simultaneously for the effects of two or more discrete variables, and possible interaction effects among these variables, on the dependent variable; ANCOVA (analysis of covariance), which allows for simultaneously testing the effects of one or more categorical and one or more continuous variables on a continuous dependent variable; and repeated measures ANOVA, which allows one to look for differences in means when individuals can be in two groups at the same time, for example the changes in means for the same people over time.

SEE ALSO: General Linear Model; Quantitative Methods; Statistics

REFERENCES AND SUGGESTED READINGS

Agresti, A. & Finlay, B. (1997) *Statistical Methods for the Social Sciences*, 3rd edn. Prentice-Hall, Upper Saddle River, NJ.

Harris, M. B. (1994) *Basic Statistics for Behavioral Science Research*. Allyn & Bacon, Boston.

Knoke, D. & Bohrnstedt, G. (1994) *Statistics for Social Data Analysis*, 3rd edn. F. E. Peacock, Itaska, IL.

Salkind, N. (2003) *Statistics for People Who (Think They) Hate Statistics*. Sage, Thousand Oaks, CA.

anthropology, cultural and social: early history

Bernd Weiler

The traditional subject matter of anthropology (from the Greek *anthropos*, human being, and *log-*, study of) has been the study of non-western, "exotic," and "nonliterate" peoples. As in other social sciences and humanities, the beginnings of western anthropology go back to Greco-Roman antiquity. It was in the wake of the Greek colonization of the Mediterranean world, commencing around 750 BCE, that questions arose regarding the history, the inhabitants, and the fauna and flora of the newly discovered lands. This intellectual interest reached its first peak in the works of Hecataeus of Miletus (ca. 550–490 BCE) and Herodotus of Halicarnassus (ca. 480–425 BCE), often considered the "fathers" of western ethnography, and eventually led to a well-developed body of doctrines that constitutes the classical heritage of anthropology (Müller 1980; Lovejoy & Boas 1997).

As in antiquity, the rise of anthropological thinking in early modern times was intimately linked to the expansion of European powers, beginning with the Portuguese expeditions to West Africa in the mid-fifteenth century, followed by the epochal "discovery" of the "New World" in 1492, and continuing with the voyages of the sixteenth century. The exploration and conquest of the Americas instigated numerous debates regarding the historical origin, the legal and theological status, the cultural achievements, and the psychobiological and "racial" makeup of its indigenous population. Because of its biblical implications the rivalry between monogenesis and polygenesis, a rivalry that may be viewed as a special variant of the "grand" controversy between universalism and relativism, assumed particular importance. Early modern comparative ethnological analyses are thus said to have emerged in the course of the sixteenth century, represented by thinkers such as de Vitoria, Las Casas, and de Acosta (Pagden 1999). Antedating, but apparently only loosely connected with, these developments were the famous accounts of inland travelers to Asia (e.g., Rubruck, Polo), as well as the insightful ethnological works of medieval Islamic scholars of the thirteenth and fourteenth centuries (e.g., Ibn Batuta, Ibn Khaldun).

In the sixteenth and early seventeenth centuries knowledge about the "other" – it might suffice to point to Montaigne and Campanella – was also increasingly employed in a strategic manner to support moral skepticism, to criticize the values of one's own culture, and to foster utopian visions: a normative use of anthropological "facts" that has continued to the very present. Apart from utopian thought and cultural criticism, anthropological considerations were also central to the development of political philosophy and international law (e.g., Grotius, Hobbes), especially for theories concerning the state of nature and natural rights.

As in other intellectual fields, anthropological thinking flourished in the Age of Enlightenment. The worldwide expansion of trade, the activity of scientific-minded missionaries (e.g., de Lafitau), and the famous naval explorations (e.g., de Bougainville, Cook) contributed to a wealth of new ethnographic material that stimulated comprehensive comparative social analyses (e.g., Montesquieu). Though degenerationist and "primitivist" ideas figured prominently in various social theories and fictional accounts, by and large the anthropological discourse of the Enlightenment was embedded in a progressivist framework. By combining the belief in the universality of reason and in the "psychic unity of mankind" with the idea of perfectibility and of the orderliness of the world, the contemporary "savage" was conceptualized as a distant ancestor and representative of prehistoric times. "In the beginning," so John Locke claimed in his *Two Treatises of Government* (1690), "all the world was America." As cultural differences were interpreted as temporal differences, many eminent Enlightenment thinkers, such as Turgot, Millar, and Smith, tried to reconstruct the successive stages of humanity (e.g., hunting and gathering, pastoralism, agriculture, industry) and to rank the various peoples on this universal ladder of development (Meek 1976). A thorough critique of this progressivist orientation can be found in the so-called Counter-Enlightenment, for example in Herder's early historicist pamphlet *Another Philosophy of History* (1774), and in the Romantic movement. Partly in opposition to the claim that the rest of the world was lagging behind the *grand nation*, Herder argued that every nation had its "center of happiness within itself." Though still adhering to the doctrine of "human brotherhood," Herder rejected the temporal interpretation of differences by emphasizing the plurality, relativity, and incommensurability of cultures, thus paving the way for the famous opposition of *Kultur* and *Zivilisation*.

The second half of the nineteenth century saw the founding of a number of important anthropological journals, professional organizations, international conferences, and ethnographic museums and may thus be regarded as the period when anthropology emerged as an autonomous academic discipline. Preceded by the widening of the temporal horizon through the science of geology, modern anthropology built upon and united four lines of research which had developed in the late eighteenth and early nineteenth centuries: namely, the field of comparative philology and linguistics (e.g., Jones, von Humboldt, Schlegel, Bopp), the anatomical study of human "races" (e.g., Linnaeus, Blumenbach), prehistoric archeology (e.g., Thomsen), and the ethnographic accounts of missionaries, travelers, and explorers. The prime concern of the anthropologists of this period, often referred to as "armchair anthropologists" because they drew upon material collected by others, was to describe and explain the social evolution of humanity and its various institutions such as marriage, law, and warfare from the "origins" to the present or at least to the times covered by ancient historians. These endeavors rested upon the assumption that social phenomena, like natural ones, were governed by uniform laws, and that within the natural and the social world one could witness a steady growth from, as Spencer famously put it, "incoherent homogeneity" to "coherent heterogeneity." That the social evolution from the "savage" to the "civilized" also implied a "moral uplift" was a truth held to be self-evident by the majority of thinkers. Important works written at the beginnning of this period and generally discussed under the heading of "social evolutionism" include Maine's *Ancient Law* (1861), Bachofen's *Das Mutterrecht Primitive Marriage* (1865), Lubbock's *The Origin of Civilisation and the Primitive Condition of Man* (1870), Tylor's *Primitive Culture* (1871), and Morgan's *Ancient Society* (1877). One of the last and maybe the best-known work of "classical" social evolutionism was the voluminous *The Golden Bough* (1890–1936) by Frazer.

From an ideological viewpoint social evolutionist ideas often emphasized the need to elevate the "savage" from his or her miserable condition and were hence employed to justify imperialist endeavors, colonial policies, and a variety of allegedly "civilizational missions."

At the end of the nineteenth and the beginning of the twentieth centuries anthropology experienced an "anti-evolutionist" turn. Arguing that cultures could not be viewed as self-contained entities in which a more or less invariant series of "independent inventions" took place and which developed according to *one* grand scheme, Boas and his school of cultural anthropology in North America (e.g., Kroeber, Lowie, Spier, Goldenweiser) emphasized the actual historical relationships and the diffusion between "primitive" cultures. These relationships that constantly crisscrossed the allegedly conjectural history of social evolutionism should be studied by tracing the distribution of traits in well-circumscribed geographical territories, the so-called culture-areas, an idea that owes much to Ratzel's anthropogeographical work. By rejecting social evolutionism as well as ideas of innate "racial" differences and by asserting that different histories accounted for cultural differences, Boas and his school, often subsumed under the heading "historical particularism," contributed decisively to the contemporary relativistic and pluralistic concept of culture (Stocking 1982). At the same time, Boas stressed the need for prolonged fieldwork to gather sufficient and reliable data as well as to understand the "native's point of view." Diffusionist ideas were also at the heart of the German *Kulturkreislehre* or "Culture Circle Theory" (e.g., Graebner, Ankermann, Frobenius), the Viennese School of Ethnology (e.g., Schmidt, Koppers), and, though with a rather speculative bent, of the works of Rivers, Smith, and Perry in Britain.

Around 1900 the French sociologist Émile Durkheim had become increasingly interested in the study of "primitive" societies in order to better understand the fundamental nature of social cohesiveness or solidarity. Though they were innovative theorists, Durkheim himself and his early students (e.g., Mauss, Hertz) contributed little to ethnographic fieldwork. By shifting the focus, however, from the historical reconstruction to the study of the functional interrelations that existed between society's institutions and belief systems at a given time, the Durkheimian school anticipated the "synchronic and nomothetic revolution" in anthropology. In Britain this new orientation is intimately linked to the work of Malinowski and Radcliffe-Brown, the "fathers" of British social anthropology and the most influential theorists of functionalism from the 1920s to the early 1950s. Among their most famous students, some of whom later diverted from their ideas, are Firth, Evans-Pritchard, Fortes, Nadel, Gluckman, Schapera, Mair, and Richards. Whereas Malinowski, whose ethnography on the Trobriand Islanders is often regarded as the archetypal fieldwork, argued that culture essentially functioned as a response to individual basic needs, Radcliffe-Brown was interested in the contribution of a recurrent activity or institution to the structural continuity of the society as a whole. In Germany, Thurnwald is commonly considered the main functionalist theorist of the interwar period. A trend toward a synchronic anthropological orientation, frequently fused with ideas from *Gestalt* psychology and Freudian ideas, is also noticeable among some of Boas's students in the 1920s and 1930s, most famously in Benedict's *Patterns of Culture* (1934). In contrast to the British functionalists, however, the North American so-called "culture and personality" researchers, which, apart from Benedict, include Sapir, Kardiner, Linton, and Mead, adhered to an idiographic orientation by arguing that each culture was characterized by a unique configuration or pattern.

SEE ALSO: Biosociological Theories; Boas, Franz; Colonialism (Neocolonialism); Cultural Relativism; Culture; Durkheim, Émile; Ethnocentrism; Feminist Anthropology; Indigenous Peoples; Malinowski, Bronislaw K.; Mead, Margaret; Progress, Idea of; Radcliffe-Brown, Alfred R.

REFERENCES AND SUGGESTED READINGS

Adams, W. Y. (1998) *The Philosophical Roots of Anthropology*. CSLI Publications, Stanford.

Asad, T. (Ed.) (1973) *Anthropology and the Colonial Encounter*. Ithaca Press, London.

Barnard, A. (2001) *History and Theory in Anthropology*. Cambridge University Press, Cambridge.

Barnard, A. & Spencer, J. (Ed.) (1996) *Encyclopedia of Social and Cultural Anthropology*. Routledge, London.

Barth, F. et al. (2005) *One Discipline, Four Ways: British, German, French, and American Anthropology*. University of Chicago Press, Chicago.

Bitterli, U. (2004 [1976]) *Die "Wilden" und die "Zivilisierten": Grundzüge einer Geistes- und Kulturgeschichte der europäisch-überseeischen Begegnung*, 3rd edn. Beck, Munich.

Clifford, J. & Marcus, G. E. (Eds.) (1986) *Writing Culture: The Poetics and Politics of Ethnography*. University of California Press, Berkeley.

Hodgen, M. T. (1964) *Early Anthropology in the Sixteenth and Seventeenth Centuries*. University of Pennsylvania Press, Philadelphia.

Hollis, M. & Lukes, S. (Eds.) (1982) *Rationality and Relativism*. Blackwell, Oxford.

Kuper, A. (1989) *Anthropology and Anthropologists: The Modern British School*. Routledge, New York.

Lovejoy, A. O. & Boas, G. (1997 [1935]) *Primitivism and Related Ideas in Antiquity*. Johns Hopkins University Press, Baltimore.

Meek, R. L. (1976) *Social Science and the Ignoble Savage*. Cambridge University Press, Cambridge.

Müller, K. E. (1980 [1972]) *Geschichte der antiken Ethnographie und ethnologischen Theoriebildung*, 2 vols. Steiner, Wiesbaden.

Padgen, A. (1999 [1982]) *The Fall of Natural Man: The American Indian and the Origins of Comparative Ethnology*. Cambridge University Press, Cambridge.

Stocking, G. W. (1982 [1968]) *Race, Culture, and Evolution: Essays in the History of Anthropology*. University of Chicago Press, Chicago.

Stocking, G. W. (1991) *Victorian Anthropology*. Free Press, New York.

Stocking, G. W. (1996) *After Tylor: British Social Anthropology, 1888–1951*. Athlone Press, London.

Stocking, G. W. & Handler, R. (Eds.) (1983–2003) *History of Anthropology*, 10 vols. University of Wisconsin Press, Madison.

anthrozoology

Adrian Franklin

Anthrozoology is the study of human–animal relations. The field of human–animal relations is fast becoming one of the hot areas of debate in the social sciences and is beginning to forge the sort of attention once held only by "the environment." A mere glance at the recent literature shows that this new area is advancing on several fronts. These include, for example, the philosophy and sociology of animal rights; genetically modified animals and "laboratory life"; histories of human–animal relations; animal foods, diets, and risk; animals, nature, and gender; consumptive relations in hunting and fishing sports; pets (or companion species) and health; companion animals, domestication, and human co-evolution and animals and human representation.

It is a relatively young interdisciplinary field dating back to the 1980s, and particularly to the founding of two dedicated anthrozoological journals, *Anthrozoos* (est. 1987) and *Society and Animals* (est. 1993). It draws on a very wide range of disciplines (including anthropology, sociology, geography, veterinary medicine, history, ethology, art and literature, cultural studies, human medicine, psychology, and human medicine) and anthrozoological writing is itself characterized by multidisciplinarity or drawing on more than one discipline.

It originated in two separate but now overlapping sources. Its first wave derived from the groundswell of interest in animal rights and welfare which itself belongs to the broader series of social movements based on the politics of postmaterialism and the extension of *rights*. The possibility of animals rights focused attention on how little we knew about our relations with animals. These important relationships were never studied before because they fell between the scientific study of the animal and the social scientific study of human relationships. The new debates were driven by extremely powerful, influential, and wealthy international organizations such as People for the Ethical Treatment of Animals, the World Wildlife Fund, the International Fund for Animal Welfare, and Greenpeace. While much of the ferment was new, it was long in the making and includes contributions from such diverse origins as Henry Salt and the formation of the Vegetarian Society in the 1890s, Walt Disney's persistent pro-animal works in film and television in the twentieth century, and Peter Singer's hugely influential book, *Animal Liberation*, of 1975. Although the changing nature of human–animal relations resulting from the animal rights movement is one of the leading dimensions to anthrozoology, the possibility of perfect consistency in the realm of human–animal relations is less likely than differentiations. Social anthropology teaches that humans have always used animals to shape human differentiation and that is no different today. That is, for any one culture, the "animal world" is never seen as one indivisible category but as a historically constituted, contingent, and morally loaded field of meanings that derive from the human habit of extending/imposing social logics, complexities, and conflicts onto the natural world and particularly onto animals other than ourselves. In modern nation-states the possibilities for differentiations in meaning and practice in human–animal relations are multiplied by the social differentiations that stem from class, ethnicity, region, gender, and religion (amongst others). A sociology of human–animal relations also includes how animals are/have been appropriated socially into a range of modern human projects: the use of animals in establishing and manipulating national identity, politics, and citizenship; the use of animal categories as signifiers of taste, belonging, and distinction and the use made of animals and categories of animals in framing moral and ethical debates (e.g., in popular television documentaries and children's books).

A second strand to anthrozoology, and certainly a key theoretical inspiration, stems from one of sociology's leading subdisciplines, science and technology studies (STS). In the past 25 years the writers who cluster under this heading have consistently refused to continue *humanist* sociological investigations that assume humans and human society can be isolated and studied independently from non-humans. While this *posthumanism* asserts the importance of the agency of all non-humans, and this includes machines, texts, technologies, and objects of all kinds, it has of course considerably changed the ontological status of animals and encouraged studies that investigate the potency of their interaction with humans (see Haraway 1989, 1991). There are landmark studies of humans and microbes (Latour 1988), humans and scallops (Callon

1986), and humans and laboratory mice and dogs (Haraway 1991, 2003). This has raised the field of anthrozoology to new levels of ontological debate, and in addition to theorizations of change in human–animal relations (Franklin 1999) there is now investigation into the very nature of the relation between them: Baker (2000) and Lippit (2000), for example, discuss the implications of Deleuze and Guattari's concept *becoming animal* for contemporary art, literature, and relations with the animal other.

In a related way, geographers and sociologists of the city have begun to describe urban spaces as neither human nor animal but both. From the writings of Mike Davis on Los Angeles (especially *Ecology of Fear*) to new animal geographies of the city (Sabloff's work on Toronto; see Sabloff 2001), we are beginning to appreciate the extent to which we are entangled with animals on an everyday basis and the fact that this entanglement matters.

The scope for anthrozoology is thus established by the increasingly contentious and conflictual nature of human–animal relations across a number of sites in the twenty-first century and ontological debates within sociology itself.

SEE ALSO: Actor-Network Theory; Actor-Network Theory, Actants; Animal Rights Movements; Human–Non-Human Interaction; Nature; Science and Culture; Society and Biology

REFERENCES AND SUGGESTED READINGS

Baker, S. (2000) *Postmodern Animal*. Reaktion, London.
Callon, M. (1986) Some Elements of a Sociology of Translation: Domestication of the Scallops and the Fishermen of St. Brieuc Bay. In: Law, J. (Ed.), *Power, Action, and Belief: A New Sociology of Knowledge?* Routledge & Kegan Paul, London.
Davis, M. (1998) *Ecology of Fear*. Picador, London.
Franklin, A. S. (1999) *Animals and Modern Cultures*. Sage, London.
Haraway, D. (1989) *Primate Visions: Gender, Race, and Nature in the World of Modern Science*. Routledge, New York.
Haraway, D. (1991) *Simians, Cyborgs, and Women: The Reinvention of Nature*. Routledge, New York.

Haraway, D. (1997) *Modest_Witness@Second_Millennium.FemaleMan© Meets OncoMouse*™. Routledge, London.

Haraway, D. (2003) *The Companion Species Manifesto: Dogs, People, and Significant Otherness.* Prickly Paradigm Press, Chicago.

Latour, B. (1988) *The Pasteurization of France.* Trans. J. Law & A. Sheridan. Harvard University Press, Cambridge, MA.

Latour, B. (1993) *We Have Never Been Modern.* Harvester, New York.

Lippit, A. M. (2000) *Electric Animal.* University of Minnesota Press, Minneapolis.

Ritvo, H. (1987) *The Animal Estate: The English and Other Creatures in the Victorian Age.* Harvard University Press, Cambridge, MA and London.

Sabloff, A. (2001) *Reordering the Natural World.* University of Toronto Press, Toronto.

Singer, P. (1995) *Animal Liberation.* Pimlico, London.

anti-Semitism (religion)

John P. Bartkowski

Anti-Semitism (also antisemitism) consists of hostility or hatred directed at Jews. Anti-Semitism may be manifested as prejudicial attitudes or discriminatory actions toward Jews because of their racial, ethnic, and/or religious heritage, as well as perceptions about their economic standing or political power. History records many incidences of anti-Semitism, culminating in the attempted genocide perpetrated against Jews during the Holocaust prior to and throughout World War II.

From a sociological perspective, anti-Semitism is not reducible to individual prejudicial attitudes or discriminatory acts against a Jewish person. Although anti-Semitism may be perpetrated by a particular individual or may target a specific victim, the question of interest to sociologists is how anti-Semitic attitudes and actions are collectively facilitated, culturally supported, and institutionally legitimated. Thus, even if a particular person or small group of "extremists" within a society exhibits anti-Semitic beliefs or behaviors, a sociological approach to this phenomenon seeks to account for the broader group influences (e.g., definitions of race, norms of authoritarianism,

sources of religious conflict) that legitimate such ideas and actions.

The Holocaust is the most horrific outgrowth of anti-Semitism, given the aim of its architects to commit "judeocide" (that is, the genocide of all Jewish people living in Europe). However, the precise role and scope of anti-Semitism in the Holocaust has provoked a debate of sorts among historians and social scientists (e.g., Smith 1998; Brustein 2003). One theory, dubbed "intentionalism," attributes the Holocaust to a clique of mad extremists not representative of German culture or society. Another theory, more functionalist in nature, traces the Holocaust and the rise of Nazi fascism after World War I to obstacles that inhibited Germany's modernization and undermined the nation's economic development. A third perspective charges that "eliminationist anti-Semitism," a virulent hatred of Jews that aimed to achieve nothing short of genocide, was widespread among the German population. According to this perspective, then, only Germany and its unique political culture could have spawned the Holocaust. There is some evidence to support each of these theories.

William Brustein's (2003) work on anti-Semitism, particularly as it relates to the Holocaust, is especially instructive. Brustein suggests that there are four different forms (or sources) of anti-Semitism: religious, racial, economic, and political anti-Semitism. Religious anti-Semitism is rooted in the unique elements of Judaism (the Jewish faith), while racial anti-Semitism is linked to socially defined perceptions about Jews' distinctive physical appearance. Economic anti-Semitism is most common in moments of economic crisis and during periods when Jewish commerce was perceived to threaten the welfare of other groups. Finally, political anti-Semitism often results from perceptions about Jewish influence on or threats toward the realms of governance and law (e.g., charges of Jewish involvement in the Communist Party during the twentieth century). Each form of anti-Semitism has been manifested in Europe at periods prior to the Holocaust, though it is the combination of these four types of anti-Semitism – such as that in pre-Holocaust Germany – that provokes the most virulent hatred of Jews. Thus, current cross-national studies of anti-Semitism suggest that it is important to identify the type of anti-Semitism found in particular locales, and the precise determinants that foster anti-Jewish sentiments and practices in specific contexts (Brustein & King 2004).

Research demonstrates that anti-Semitism also has a long history in the United States, although support for the tenets of this ideology has declined markedly during the past several decades (Dinnerstein 1994, 2004; Blakeslee 2000; Weiner & King 2005). For example, in 1964, 48 percent of Americans believed that Jews have irritating faults and are more willing than others to engage in "shady" practices, while only about half this number support such views in the contemporary United States (Smith 1993). Moreover, whereas 29 percent of Americans were regarded as "hardcore anti-Semites" by the Anti-Defamation League in 1964, only 17 percent were considered to fit this profile in 2002, which is a slight increase from the low of 12 percent in 1998 (Dinnerstein 2004). Thus, while anti-Semitism is at historically low levels, some observers argue that survey evidence suggesting that nearly 20 percent of the American population is anti-Semitic points to alarmingly high levels of anti-Jewish sentiment (Simon 2003). It is worth noting that the Anti-Defamation League's operationalization of an anti-Semite is based on an 11-point scale measuring agreement with various stereotypes of Jews (e.g., Jews "always like to be at the head of things," "are more loyal to Israel than America," "have too much power in the business world," "don't care what happens to anyone but [their] own kind," "are just [not] as honest as other business people"). Based on the Anti-Defamation League definition, hardcore anti-Semites are those who answer in the affirmative to six or more of the items on this 11-point scale. Other scales of anti-Semitism commonly include a selection of these items.

Despite the decline in Americans' hostility toward Jews during the past several decades, some groups within the United States are still more inclined to hold anti-Semitic views than others (Dinnerstein 2004; Weiner & King 2005). Gender differences in anti-Semitism have been observed, such that men exhibit more hostility toward Jews than do women. Americans who are older, rural dwellers, and Southerners are generally more anti-Semitic than those who are young, urbanites, and those residing outside the South. Blue-collar workers are more inclined toward anti-Semitism than are white-collar professionals. Education is widely viewed as the key to diminished anti-Semitism among those in the professional class, because higher levels of education tend to erode support for anti-Semitism while bolstering a commitment to liberal viewpoints and tolerance for others. Anti-Semitic views generally increase in locales with a higher proportion of Jews and declining economic conditions (Weiner & King 2005), a pattern that is commonly observed for other minority groups as well. As minority groups grow in number, concerns typically increase about the "threats" they may pose to local politics, economic opportunities, and social life in general.

There are also racial and religious variations in anti-Semitic attitudes. Research reveals greater support for anti-Semitic views among black Americans than among their white counterparts. Sociologists generally interpret blacks' stronger negative attitudes toward Jews as a function of African Americans' blocked opportunities in American society, which contrast markedly with the high economic status that Jews in the US tend to enjoy. Where religion is concerned, some research traces American anti-Semitism to the pervasiveness of Christianity in the US, particularly the conservative (fundamentalist) brand of Protestantism that is so prominent in the South. Interestingly, conservative Christians, who are generally distinguished by their view of the Bible as the inerrant word of God, seem to be of two minds concerning Jews (Smith 1999). While conservative Christians tend to embrace the biblical depiction of Jews as a "chosen people" and strongly support the existence of a Jewish state, they also believe that Jews should be converted to Christianity and tend to believe that Jews are overly focused on monetary gain.

Within the United States, efforts to promote Holocaust education to reduce anti-Semitism seem to have met with mixed success (Simon 2003). Between 80 and 90 percent of Americans believe that valuable lessons can be learned by studying the Nazis' efforts to eradicate the Jewish population in Europe during the Holocaust. However, these courses may be of limited value in reducing anti-Semitism because students who take such courses enter them already having low levels of anti-Semitism and high levels of political tolerance. Thus, while such courses can provide beneficial knowledge about the Holocaust, students who take them are not very anti-Semitic in the first place. Those who could most benefit from such courses are likely to avoid enrolling in them because of their prejudice against Jews.

Finally, given the heterogeneity of cultural practices and viewpoints among different types of Jews (Conservative, Orthodox, Reconstructionist, Reform, and secular), it is worth noting that religious variations have been observed in perceptions of and reactions to anti-Semitism among American Jews (Djupe & Sokhey 2003). In one study of Jewish rabbis, Orthodox rabbis and those linked to Jewish advocacy organizations perceived anti-Semitism to be a greater problem and more frequently express concerns about this problem in public speech than those affiliated with other branches of Judaism.

SEE ALSO: Anti-Semitism (Social Change); Discrimination; Ethnicity; Genocide; Hate Crimes; Holocaust; Judaism; Pogroms; Prejudice; Race; Race (Racism)

REFERENCES AND SUGGESTED READINGS

Blakeslee, S. (2000) *The Death of American Anti-semitism*. Praeger, Westport, CT.
Brustein, W. I. (2003) *Roots of Hate: Anti-Semitism in Europe Before the Holocaust*. Cambridge University Press, Cambridge.
Brustein, W. I. & King, R. D. (2004) Anti-Semitism as a Response to Perceived Jewish Power: The Cases of Bulgaria and Romania Before the Holocaust. *Social Forces* 83: 691–708.
Dinnerstein, L. (1994) *Anti-Semitism in America*. Oxford University Press, New York.
Dinnerstein, L. (2004) Is There a New Anti-Semitism in the United States? *Society* 41: 53–8.
Djupe, P. A. & Sokhey, A. E. (2003) The Mobilization of Elite Opinion: Rabbi Perceptions of and Responses to Anti-Semitism. *Journal for the Scientific Study of Religion* 43: 443–53.

Simon, C. A. (2003) The Effects of Holocaust Education on Students' Level of Anti-Semitism. *Educational Research Quarterly* 27: 3–17.
Smith, R. B. (1998) Anti-Semitism and Nazism. *American Behavioral Scientist* 9: 1324–63.
Smith, T. W. (1993) Actual Trends or Measurement Artifacts? A Review of Three Studies of Anti-Semitism. *Public Opinion Quarterly* 57: 380–93.
Smith, T. W. (1999) The Religious Right and Anti-Semitism. *Review of Religious Research* 40: 244–58.
Weiner, M. & King, R. (2005) Group Position, Collective Threat, and Anti-Semitism in the US. Paper presented at the annual meetings of the American Sociological Association, Philadelphia.

anti-Semitism (social change)

William I. Brustein

To account for the rise of anti-Semitism in the West in the modern period we can turn to the evolution and popularization of its four principal roots. The four roots, religious, racial, economic, and political, contain within themselves four distinct anti-Semitic narratives, each of which entailed its own set of themes depicting Jewish malfeasance. Anti-Semitism in the years prior to 1870 was largely characterized by a dislike based primarily on religious differences and perceived Jewish economic practices. After 1870, both religious and economic anti-Semitism continued – albeit with new themes – to be joined by the rising racial and political strains.

Of the four roots of anti-Semitism, religious anti-Semitism has the longest history in western Christian societies. Religious anti-Semitism encompasses hostility derived from the Jewish people's refusal to abandon their religious beliefs and practices, and, specifically within Christian societies, from the accusation of Jewish collective responsibility for the death of Jesus Christ. By the eighteenth century, the religious root would expand to include the French Enlightenment's critique that Judaism was responsible for the anti-progressive and exclusionist characters of its followers.

Official Christian antipathy toward Judaism began to gather steam within one hundred years of the death of Christ. Christian bitterness may have stemmed largely from the new religion's competition with Judaism for a following. The competition between the two religions was unlike that between quite *dissimilar* religions, such as Buddhism and Christianity or Hinduism and Christianity, for Jesus Christ had been a Jew and Christianity saw itself replacing Judaism as the inheritor of God's covenant with Abraham.

Since the birth of the Christian faith, numerous deeds of malfeasance have been leveled against the Jews. For centuries, Jews were held responsible for the crucifixion of Christ; chastised for not accepting Christ as the messiah; accused of a series of acts and practices, including practicing a ritual of killing Christian children in order to use their blood to make matzoth during the Jewish holiday of Passover; causing the "Black Plague" of the Middle Ages by poisoning the wells of Europe; desecrating the host (stealing and destroying communion wafers after the eucharist ceremony); serving as agent of the Antichrist; and, at various times, being usurers, sorcerers, and vampires.

With the advent of the Enlightenment, religious anti-Semitism took on a new leitmotif emanating interestingly from the attacks leveled on the Jewish religion by such eminent secularists as Voltaire, Diderot, Montesquieu, von Dohm, and d'Holbach. In their critique of the roots of Christianity, they condemned Judaism for remaining a fossilized religion, persisting in a self-image of its special "election," and upholding anti-progressive beliefs. In this way, the Enlightenment may have contributed to modernizing and secularizing anti-Semitism. During the nineteenth century, many secularists felt betrayed by Jews, who, in their eyes, failed to abandon their distinctive beliefs and practices after having been emancipated and granted civil rights. Whereas traditional religious anti-Semitism appealed largely to a less-educated public, the secularist critique attracted a more highly educated following.

Whether one drew upon the traditional religious prejudice against Jews or the secular argument, the common assumption held that once Jews converted to Christianity or abandoned the Jewish faith, the "Jewish problem" would disappear. However, as the nineteenth century unfolded, a new form of anti-Semitism emerged that would not see conversion or rejection of the faith as a sufficient solution to the "Jewish problem." For among the followers of this new form of anti-Semitism, Jews constituted a separate and pernicious race, and only through enforced social isolation or physical removal could the problem of the place of Jews in society find a resolution.

During the latter half of the nineteenth century, Jews were increasingly depicted as members of a unique race rather than as members of a separate religious group. Spurred on by European colonialism, nationalistic fervor, and fear of immigration, the new science of race dug deep roots into European mass culture. Scientific racism, or race science, referred to the ideology that differences in human behavior derive from inherent group characteristics, and human differences can be demonstrated through anthropological, biological, and statistical proofs. In the nineteenth century, race science rose and gained respectability. Proponents of racial theory held a firm belief that there were inexorable natural laws beyond the control of humans governing individuals and cultures. Arguments that territorial national sovereignty should be based on a culturally identifiable nation and that the superior cultures of Europe had the right and duty to colonize non-European areas of the world found justification in scientific racism. The impact of scientific racism on European Jewry would be profound, for racial science permitted anti-Semites to attire their hatred of Jews in the disguise of science.

How is it then that anti-Semitism became increasingly interwoven with racial thinking? By themselves, the advent of European colonialism and the project of national unification could hardly constitute a fertile context in which racial anti-Semitism would flourish. Moreover, before 1881, the relatively small Jewish population of Western Europe seemed, in the minds of many Gentiles and Jews, to be on the road to assimilation. This was, however, about to change with the westward march of Russian and East European Jewish immigrants. The wave of East European and

Russian Jewish immigration fueled a firestorm of racial anti-Semitism.

In the contexts of a spreading European colonialism, rising nationalism, and Eastern European Jewish immigration combined with the emergence and popularization of the new science of race, racial anti-Semitism gained adherents throughout the nations of Europe. For many of those embracing racial anti-Semitism, Jews should no longer be considered simply as a minority with their own religious beliefs, rituals, and customs within the national territory of established nations. In the new thinking, Jews constituted a separate race and, as a race, the Jews were inferior to Aryans but also the most dangerous of the inferior races.

Over the centuries, Jews have been variously characterized as miserly, manipulators of money, ultra-materialist, and possessors of extraordinary wealth. The pervasiveness of the link between Jews and unsavory economic practices can be seen in the not too distant past in the usage of such unflattering verbs as "to Jew" (to cheat or to overreach) and "to Jew down" (to drive down the price unfairly by bickering) in one of the definitions of the word "Jew" (i.e., "applied to a grasping or extortionate usurer") found in the authoritative *Oxford Universal Dictionary*, at least until 1955.

The history of the economic root of anti-Semitism, while not quite as old as that of the religious root, dates back to the Christian medieval period in Europe. Warnings against middleman practices are found in the writings of early Christian fathers like John Chrysostom and Augustine. It wasn't until the Lateran Council of 1139 that the Catholic Church assigned a negative significance to usury. In the decisions reached at the Lateran Council, usury took the meaning of charging excessive or illegal interest on a loan. The Lateran Council asserted that those who practiced usury, or those who practiced it but failed to repent, would be refused a Christian burial.

European Jews increasingly found themselves the object of charges of usury as well as a host of other economic sins, including dishonest practices in petty commerce and secondhand trade, and the pursuit of parasitic and non-productive commercial activities. Why did this occur? There is no question that Jews were overrepresented as moneylenders, peddlers, and merchants in Christian Europe. Though it officially condemned usury, the Roman Catholic Church throughout the Middle Ages derived benefits from the existence of usury and from Jews as usurers. In the eyes of the Church, Jews, having cut themselves off from the saving grace of Jesus Christ, were a likely group to perform the necessary but sinful practice of moneylending. Moreover, the Crown, cognizant of the Christian Church's prohibition against usury for good Christians, encouraged Jewish moneylending in its pursuit of its own prosperity and revenues. In that the Crown considered Jews its own private property, it saw fit to compel Jews to serve the role of moneylenders.

Moneylending was only one of the professions open to Jews in Christian Europe. More and more Jews were restricted to those economic activities considered the least desirable, like moneylending, and to those which did not engender competition for Christian guilds. For instance, medieval merchant guilds successfully blocked Jews from selling their goods in shops or at the marketplace, while craft guilds prevented Jews from manufacturing goods. Consequently, Jews were left to peddle goods in the street or countryside and to buy and sell secondhand wares, particularly clothing. Prior to the Holocaust, much had been made of the fact that Jews rarely pursued the farming profession. The dearth of Jews in farming in Europe has a foundation in medieval European prohibitions against Jewish property ownership. Land constituted a principal source of power and status in the Middle Ages in Christian Europe, and he who owned land had power over the serfs and a say in the selection of local priests. The Christian Church also depended on the payment of a tithe and feared that Jewish landholders might refuse to pay the Church tithe. To that end, the Church strongly discouraged its faithful from selling land to Jews or offering land to Jews in exchange for their debts. While Jews confronted obstacles in owning land, they were permitted and frequently encouraged by the Crown or nobility to manage large estates. Especially in East Central Europe, Jews became prominent as administrators of large noble estates. By standing as intermediaries between the nobility and the serfs, Jews served as convenient buffers and scapegoats in times of growing economic tension.

By virtue of their experience as moneylenders or estate agents, numbers of Jews found employment as royal usurers of the princes or "court Jews," largely responsible for managing the personal finances of the aristocracy throughout much of Europe. Illustrative of the famous "court Jews" was Joseph Süss-Oppenheimer, who, in mid-eighteenth-century Germany, arose from court agent of Duke Karl Alexander of Württemberg to the high post of privy councilor. Oppenheimer would become the *Jud Süss* of later anti-Semitic legends. Even more famous than Oppenheimer, Meyer Amschel Rothschild, the patriarch of the famous Rothschild banking family, began as a court agent in 1769 to William, Prince of Hessen-Kassel.

Before the nineteenth century, popular economic anti-Semitism in Europe typically embodied accusations about alleged unethical business practices in secondhand trade, petty commerce, and moneylending conducted by Jews. As the nineteenth century unfolded, economic anti-Semites would add the charge that Jews inordinately controlled the major means of production and, by virtue of this power, successfully manipulated both the domestic and foreign policies of states. Though a number of Jewish families in Europe had acquired sizable fortunes before the advent of the nineteenth century, principally as court agents of aristocratic families, the myth of Jewish economic dominance truly gained widespread currency as a result of several key factors, including Jewish emancipation and European industrialization. The emancipation of European Jewry opened to Jews previously blocked access to higher education and the professions. More equal access to education and the professions bred increased competition between Jews and Christians, leading often to resentment. Europe's industrialization opened new domestic and global investment opportunities for entrepreneurs. The removal of barriers to trade allowed capital to flow across borders, financing railways and mines in a fashion never before experienced.

The new investment opportunities led to the accumulation of phenomenal wealth for the fledgling banking industry. Jews were well represented in the banking industry, given their prior background as moneylenders and court agents, and many Jewish families benefited greatly from the new investment opportunities. This is certainly not to say that wealthy Gentile fortunes did not exist. But rather, it was the number of wealthy Jewish families in proportion to the overall Jewish population, and the concentration of Jewish wealth in a small number of arenas like banking, that likely cast Jewish economic dominance in a particular light. Take, for instance, the case of the state of Prussia in 1908, where it was reported that 55 of the 200 millionaires were of Jewish origin, of which 33 had made their money in finance and banking. The accumulation of extraordinary wealth, particularly through profits from investment, elicited vitriolic resentment within many quarters. That several prominent Jewish families became prime beneficiaries of this new wealth gave new legs to the myth of Jewish economic dominance. Yet the banking industry wasn't the only economic enterprise in which wealthy Jewish families appeared to dominate. Notable European Jewish families held substantial control over the department store industry, grains, real estate, and the cattle, fur, pearl, jewelry, diamond, and ready-made clothing trade, and perhaps most importantly, the news medium.

Not only did trade become global after 1840, but local or national economic crises became, for the first time, worldwide. In the pre-industrial economy, abrupt price fluctuations were typically caused by natural disasters like droughts or floods and tended to be local in nature, whereas in the new industrial economy, financial crises more often were linked to trade and became cyclical, more spatially diffused, and increasingly severe in their impact. It was during and after these periodic recessions or depressions that attention focused on the alleged negative role that the wealthy Jewish banking houses played in the creation of the economic crisis. In contrast to earlier epochs of economic crises, during the Industrial Age, with the existence of multinational financial houses managing the international flows of capital and buying and selling stocks, the physical presence of Jews was no longer a necessary requisite for economic chaos in the minds of many anti-Semites. The 1873 Depression unlocked a wave of resentment against the free-market policies of the 1850s and 1860s – policies that had become associated with Jewish banking interests. The 1873 Depression also unleashed public displeasure by virtue of the series of accompanying stock market collapses and bank failures – in which several prominent Jews had played a role. The Great Depression of the 1930s evoked heightened economic antipathy toward Jews for a number of reasons. In a time of high unemployment, the immigration of thousands of Eastern European Jews constituted an economic threat to financially hard-pressed Gentiles. For others open to the possibility of Jewish perfidy, the Jews were seen as both manipulators and beneficiaries of the worldwide economic collapse as foretold in the notorious but popular *Protocols of the Learned Elders of Zion*.

At various times throughout the modern period, the myth of a "Jewish world conspiracy" has attracted adherents. Jews have been accused of plotting to take over the world by undermining the existing social and political order. The myth of the "Jewish world conspiracy" springs from diverse sources. Before the emergence of revolutionary socialist parties in the last decades of the nineteenth century, subscribers to the myth that the Jews covertly planned to take control of the world believed they had proof in what they perceived was the inordinate Jewish presence as "court Jews" advising and financing rulers, and the role Jews allegedly played as leaders and members of the supposedly anti-Church and liberal Freemasons. In more recent times, Jews were assumed to be the backers or originators of radical and subversive movements whose chief aim was allegedly to bring down the reigning national political order.

Political anti-Semitism, defined as hostility toward Jews based on the belief that Jews seek to control national and/or world power, experienced a momentous upsurge after 1879 in Europe. The dramatic rise in political anti-Semitism between 1879 and the Holocaust can largely be attributed to the emergence and

rapid development of an international socialist movement and, concomitantly, to the popularization of the notorious *Protocols of the Elders of Zion* in the aftermath of the Bolshevik Revolution. During the last half of the nineteenth century, a host of newly established political movements and parties marked the European political landscape. Many of these new political groups advocated radical programs aimed at redressing social and political inequalities. Among these new movements or parties were the socialist or Marxist groups, which steadily gained prominence in Europe after 1879. These parties were perceived to represent major threats to the interests of elite and middle-class groups as well as to the Christian religious faithful.

Socialism was disliked by many people across the social spectrum because of its apparent antipathy toward religion, patriotism, and nationalism. Jews and socialism were inextricably tied in the eyes of anti-Semites for numerous reasons. The link between socialism and Jews requires exploration. To begin with, it is worth repeating that the "red menace," namely, the fear that a worldwide subversive communist movement sought to gain world power, had dominated western thinking until 1989. Belief in the "red menace" reached epidemic levels in the wake of socialism's first major success, the Bolshevik Revolution of 1917, and again in the aftermath of communism's success in Eastern Europe and China after World War II. That prominent Jews played key roles from the beginning in the socialist and communist movements provided the European anti-Semitic crusade considerable nourishment and momentum.

After 1917, acknowledgment of the existence of a link between Jews and revolutionary socialism reached pandemic proportions. The seizure of power by the Russian Bolsheviks in 1917, followed by a series of left-wing uprisings elsewhere in Europe in the aftermath of World War I, ushered in a wave of anti-Marxist and anti-Semitic hysteria. During the chaotic period following the termination of World War I, many political leaders and major newspapers portrayed the Bolshevik Revolution and the wave of left-wing revolutionary attempts to seize power elsewhere as part of the overall Jewish plan to take control of the world. Jews were shown to have dominated the leadership of the Russian Bolshevik Party and leftist revolutionary parties in other European states. The purported link between Jews and revolutionary socialism grew ironically to include rich Jewish financiers, such as the American shipping magnate Jacob Schiff and the German banker Max Warburg. In the opinion of many in the anti-Semitic camp, wealthy Jews were alleged to have engineered and funded the revolutionary movements in Russia in order to bring down the despised and intensely anti-Semitic Czarist regime. Much has been made of the position Jews held in the leadership of the Russian Bolshevik Party and the fact that these Jews employed pseudonyms. In time, Trotsky, Zinoviev, Kamenev, and Radek became household names throughout the West, and Jew and Bolshevik became synonymous. The fact that these Jewish revolutionaries employed aliases convinced many in the West that they were deceitfully trying to hide the Jewish nature of the Russian Revolution. The popular association between Jews and Bolshevism made inroads far beyond the masses of ardent anti-Semites and the uneducated.

During the peak of the revolutionary socialist upheaval in the years following the conclusion of World War I, political anti-Semitism received a substantial boost from the worldwide publication and translation of the infamous forgery, the *Protocols of the Elders of Zion.* (In 1919, the earliest German and Polish editions appeared, and in 1920, the first English edition was released in London and Boston.) The *Protocols* described an elaborate Jewish plan of world conquest through the creation of worldwide unrest, culminating in the ascent to world power of the Jewish House of David. In particular, the Russian Revolution, by ushering in a period of European-wide revolutionary upheaval, civil war, and the birth of an international communist movement, transformed a relatively obscure pamphlet into a powerful vehicle, giving credibility to the myth of "Judeo-Bolshevism" and linking anti-Semitism and anti-Bolshevism for decades. No other factor did more to galvanize political anti-Semitism after World War I

than the fear of revolutionary socialism. By advocating social and economic leveling, dismissing religion, and opting for internationalism over nationalism, revolutionary socialists spawned substantial resentment among many groups in society who failed to share their vision.

The western world's anti-Semitism contributed to the Holocaust. As we embark upon a new millennium, we may wonder if anti-Semitic prejudice could once again raise its ugly head to the extent that world Jewry would again be threatened with mass annihilation. Do recent European events including negative portrayals of Israeli policy in the Middle East and attacks on Jewish persons and property conjure up a revival of European anti-Semitism on the scale of the 1930s? The likelihood of history repeating itself vis-à-vis the Jews within the West is highly unlikely. Indeed, the recent upsurge in anti-Semitic acts in Europe has more to do with the Israeli–Palestinian dispute than with what some commentators refer to as the reawakening of Europe's ancient anti-Semitic demon. These attacks on Jews and Jewish property emanate almost exclusively from particular segments of Europe's Muslim population.

A more optimistic assessment of the future of Jewish–Gentile relations within Europe is not based solely upon beliefs in the value of learning, but largely because of the attenuation of the underlying foundations of the four roots of anti-Semitism within the West. Much has occurred in the Christian–Jewish relationship since 1945 to dampen Christian religious anti-Semitism. In particular, the *Nostra Aetate* declaration embraced by the Second Vatican Council in October 1965, withdrawing the blanket accusation of Jewish guilt for the murder of Christ, and the public pronouncements of Pope John Paul II, documenting the historical mistreatment of Jews by Christians, have eliminated official Christian support for anti-Semitism. The science of race, which had successfully dug deep roots into western society before World War II, has been convincingly debunked. Few serious scholars would today pay heed to such notions as a hierarchy of races and inferior and superior races. Clearly, the racial basis of anti-Semitism has largely disappeared. With the collapse of the Soviet Union and the state socialist system in Eastern and Central Europe, the foundation for political anti-Semitism has been dealt a mortal blow. Revolutionary socialism provided anti-Semites a key weapon in their assault on Jews given the magnitude of the perceived threat from revolutionary socialism and the alleged association of Jews and the political left. Perhaps no other fact has done more to alleviate anti-Semitism than the collapse of communism.

The fate of economic anti-Semitism diverges from the other forms. Economic anti-Semitism, while somewhat abated, still appears to draw adherence. Economic anti-Semitism in the West today is more implied and subtle than before World War II. Murmurings about Jewish inordinate influence in banking, the media, and the arts are less common now, but still present. Recent events in Russia and the Ukraine point to the resiliency of resentment of large segments of the population toward the alleged economic power of Jews. Equally disturbing has been the tendency of some in the anti-globalization camp to blame Jews for the purported evils of globalization. However, these anti-Semitic voices have failed to resonate widely – a big difference from the pre-World War II period, when anti-Semitic attitudes were widely held by respected elites and the lower and middle classes.

If, on the one hand, popular anti-Semitism in Europe has lost considerable steam by virtue of the attenuation of the religious, racial, and political roots, it has, on the other hand, gained strength from popular resentment toward Israeli policies in the Middle East. Increasingly, the distinction between a dislike of Israeli policies and a dislike of Jews has become blurred in the minds of many people. Even more alarming is the explosive rise of anti-Semitism within the Islamic world. While Christian–Jewish relations have vastly improved since the Holocaust, Muslim–Jewish relations have fallen upon hard times. Fueled largely by the Israeli–Palestinian dispute, anti-Jewish antipathies wrapped in religious, racial, economic, and political narratives have entered the public discourse throughout the Muslim

world. The curtain of history has yet to drop on society's longest hatred.

SEE ALSO: Anti-Semitism (Religion); Conflict (Racial/Ethnic); Fascism; Holocaust; Judaism; Prejudice; Race (Racism); Racist Movements; Religion

REFERENCES AND SUGGESTED READINGS

Almog, S. (1990) *Nationalism and Anti-Semitism in Modern Europe, 1815–1945.* Pergamon, Oxford.

Brustein, W. (2003) *Roots of Hate: Anti-Semitism in Europe Before the Holocaust.* Cambridge University Press, Cambridge and New York.

Fein, H. (1979) *Accounting for Genocide: National Responses and Jewish Victimization During the Holocaust.* Free Press, New York.

Katz, J. (1980) *From Prejudice to Destruction: Anti-Semitism, 1700–1933.* Harvard University Press, Cambridge, MA.

Lindemann, A. S. (1997) *Esau's Tears: Modern Anti-Semitism and the Rise of the Jews.* Cambridge University Press, Cambridge and New York.

Marrus, M. R. & Paxton, R. O. (1981) *Vichy France and the Jews.* Stanford University Press, Stanford, CA.

Massing, P. W. (1949) *Rehearsal for Destruction: A Study of Political Anti-Semitism in Imperial Germany.* Harper & Brothers, New York.

Mosse, G. L. (1985) *Toward the Final Solution: A History of European Racism.* University of Wisconsin Press, Madison.

Oldson, W. O. (1991) *A Providential Anti-Semitism: Nationalism and Polity in Nineteenth-Century Romania.* American Philosophical Society, Philadelphia, PA.

Poliakov, L. (1971) *The Aryan Myth: A History of Racist and Nationalist Ideas in Europe.* Trans. E. Howard. Basic Books, New York.

Pulzer, P. (1992) *Jews and the German State: The Political History of a Minority, 1848–1933.* Blackwell, Oxford.

Volovici, L. (1991) *Nationalist Ideology and Antisemitism: The Case of Romanian Intellectuals in the 1930s.* Pergamon, Oxford.

Wilson, S. (1982) *Ideology and Experience: Anti-Semitism in France at the Time of the Dreyfus Affair.* Farleigh Dickinson University Press, Rutherford, NJ.

Wistrich, R. S. (1991) *Anti-Semitism: The Longest Hatred.* Pantheon, New York.

Zucotti, S. (1987) *The Italians and the Holocaust: Persecution, Rescue, and Survival.* Basic Books, New York.

anti-war and peace movements

Kristina Wolff

Anti-war and peace movements are social movements that concentrate on many issues related to war, armed conflict, and violence. Often, they focus on calling for an end to a specific conflict, the abolition of war, and the elimination of weaponry, as well as the creation of nonviolent mechanisms to solve conflicts. Historically, strategies for change have included violent acts such as assassination, self-immolation, and/or the destruction of property. However, the vast majority of people participating in these movements utilize nonviolent tactics. These approaches include wide-scale boycotts, protests and marches, sit-ins, speeches, letter-writing campaigns, education and outreach, and voting.

Motivations for resisting war and promoting peace vary and include concerns over the ideological reasons behind the war, the immorality of killing people, violations of human rights, and the destruction of lives, property, and/or the environment, as well as the financial costs. Individuals and groups organize in a variety of ways, including through local churches, schools, and organizations. Recently, many protesters have joined together for specific events such as the meeting of government officials who are conducting a war. With the emergence of the Internet and other advances in technology, coalition building has been expanded, as it is easier to reach people around the globe. There has been a significant increase in simultaneous protests happening around the world, as demonstrated by protests against trade practices and the World Trade Organization, and continual opposition and protests against the war in Iraq.

Researchers have noted that anti-war and peace movements succeed in affecting public debate and the opinions and actions of government officials, but they rarely stop wars (Marullo & Meyer 2004). One example of this is the amount of opposition against the Vietnam War. While each war that the US has waged has had some level of public resistance, the anti-war and peace movement of the 1960s and 1970s galvanized the nation and created enough pressure on government officials to change their actions concerning the war. Part of this success was the number of people within government and politics who were openly against the war and worked to end it as soon as possible. The progression of the scale of opposition increased with the length of time spent in Vietnam, the growing number of casualties, and the expense of the war. This is a common trend, which can also be seen in the growth of visible opposition to the war with Iraq.

SEE ALSO: Civil Rights Movement; Gay and Lesbian Movement; Peace and Reconciliation Processes; Social Movements; War; Women's Movements

REFERENCES AND SUGGESTED READINGS

Addams, J. (2002) *The Jane Addams Reader.* Ed. J. Elshtain. Basic Books, New York.
Cooney, R. & Michalowski, H. (1987) *The Power of the People: Active Nonviolence in the United States.* New Society Publishers, Philadelphia.
Epstein, B. (2003) Notes on the Antiwar Movement. *Monthly Review* 55(3): 109.
Evans, S. (1980) *Personal Politics.* Vintage Books, New York.
Fendrich, J. (2003) The Forgotten Movement: The Vietnam Antiwar Movement. *Sociological Inquiry* 73(3): 338.
Marullo, S. & Meyer, D. (2004) Antiwar and Peace Movements. In: Snow, D., Soule, S., & Kriesi, H. (Eds.), *The Blackwell Companion to Social Movements.* Blackwell, Oxford, pp. 641–65.
Wittner, L. (1984) *Rebels against War: The American Peace Movement, 1933–1983.* Temple University Press, Philadelphia.
Zinn, H. (1994) *You Can't Be Neutral on a Moving Train: A Personal History of Our Times.* Beacon Press, Boston.

apartheid and Nelson Mandela

Kogila Moodley and Kanya Adam

Apartheid is a uniquely South African policy of racial engineering with which European colonizers tried to ensure their supremacy between 1948 and 1994. Invented by the Afrikaner section of the minority white population, it also aimed at advancing exclusive Afrikaner nationalism. Prior to the institutionalized racialism, Anglo-type informal segregation had achieved similar effects, although racial mixing and miscegenation was widespread in a rapidly industrializing society. The apartheid ideology, strongly influenced by evolutionist, hierarchical, and racial supremacist ideas, justified the formal separation between racialized groups in South Africa. The Afrikaner Nationalist Party, particularly under its leader Hendrik Verwoerd, systematized these practices into a coherent doctrine. Afrikaner newspapers, such as *Die Burger*, preachers, and intellectuals used the suppression of the Afrikaans language by the assimilationist United Party as a mobilizing tool, subsequently supplemented with a program of capital accumulation ("buy Afrikaans only") for fledgling Afrikaner building societies and banks.

When the Nationalists unexpectedly came to power through a restricted franchise in 1948, Afrikaners formed 57 percent of the white population controlling 29 percent of total personal income, as against the English-speaking whites who held 43 percent. Africans, although comprising 68 percent of the population, commanded only 20 percent of total personal income (Giliomee 2003: 489). The Nationalist "poor whites," distinctly underprivileged vis-à-vis English speakers, also had to compete with African jobseekers, who were considered cheaper and more pliant by English-dominated corporations. Faced with the threat of nationalization, a compromise was struck to guarantee poor whites job reservation and higher wages in mining enterprises ("civilized labor policy") as well as preferential employment on the railways and in the post offices.

Racial legislation took the form of categorizing the population into four racial groups: whites, coloreds, Asians (Indians), and Africans. In 1949, the Prohibition of Mixed Marriages Act made it illegal to marry across the color line. Later this was followed by the Immorality Act, which declared it an offense to have any intimate contact across racial groups. The Population Registration Act required the carrying of identification documents; the Group Areas Act of the 1960s designated separate residential and commercial areas for each group; the Suppression of Communism Act, which gave extraordinary power to the state to ban organizations considered to be "communist," and the Bantu Education Act controlled access to segregated education for each racial group.

Longstanding communities comprising people of all groups who had come to live together were destroyed by these measures. The residential segregation particularly affected the Indian and colored property owners more than it did Africans, who had already been excluded earlier under the Urban Areas Act preventing them from acquiring any land in the urban areas and "white" South Africa, comprising 83 percent of the total territory. The rationale offered for this was twofold; firstly, that whites had submitted petitions complaining about Indian and colored penetration into their areas with the consequent drop in their property values. Secondly, it was argued that groups would be more inclined to live harmoniously with one another when they reside among members of their own group. The same logic was to pervade the case for separate educational facilities, at first at the primary and secondary levels.

Unlike any other country, South Africa imposed group membership, regardless of individual association. Without self-identification such labeling stigmatizes people, especially where differential privileges and forcible separation are concerned. This is all the more so where groups have lived in close proximity to one another and shared culture, language, and religion, as was the case with the 10 percent so-called coloreds in the Cape. Often there were few discernible differences and degrading practices such as pencil tests – namely, to see if a pencil when inserted into hair would fall out or be held by more curly African-type hair – were used to decide if one was colored or white.

Through a process of ethnicization, black ethnic groups were separated from one another and disaggregated, while non-blacks with diverse ethnic origins were homogenized through racialization into one group, as whites, for political advantage. Apartheid utilized different histories and cultures to divide the population through the program of separate development. Whites held the monopoly of political control over a disenfranchised "non-white" majority. Economic power was initially concentrated in the hands of the people of English origin but later increasingly included Afrikaner capitalists through state patronage.

The franchise was the privilege of white South Africans only, as others were excluded from the political process. Instead Africans were to have circumscribed citizenship rights within the segregated enclaves designated for each group, known as Bantustans. Freedom of movement from these impoverished rural areas into urban centers was curtailed through influx control and pass laws.

European penetration of the African hinterland had destroyed most of the traditional African subsistence economy. Squeezed into ever more overcrowded reserves, its inhabitants increasingly relied on remittances of migrant workers in the cities. At the beginning of industrialization, Africans had to be forced into poorly paid work on the mines through head and hut taxes which British administrators first introduced in the Eastern Cape. Later it was sheer rural poverty that drove blacks into the city slums, dormitories, and compounds. Migrant labor not only destroyed the African peasantry but also undermined the traditional family. The competition among ethnically housed migrants in the insecure urban settings encouraged tribalism as a form of kinship solidarity and own group protection in a tough struggle for survival.

In 1910 the African National Congress (ANC) was founded. Among the first goals of the ANC was the battle for African unity against tribalism. Under the influence of supportive white and Indian liberals and communists, this priority was later extended to colorblind non-racialism. A moderate black elite,

educated at Christian missionary schools, repeatedly pleaded with the government for recognition. A much-celebrated Freedom Charter of 1955 claimed the right of all South Africans to the land of their birth. A Gandhian-type civil disobedience campaign against new pass laws was tried in Natal, but failed when the government simply imprisoned the peaceful protesters. The National Party government responded with ever more repressive legislation. The 1960 Sharpeville massacre of some 60 protesters marked a turning point. The ANC and its rival, the more radical Pan African Congress (PAC), decided to go underground, revert to sabotage without hurting civilians, and establish an exile presence for the anti-apartheid struggle after they were outlawed inside the country. After a few years in hiding, Nelson Mandela and his comrades were caught and sentenced to life imprisonment, to be freed only after 27 years on Robben Island in 1990.

In 1983 the National Party had split and shed its conservative wing. In 1989, the hardline president P. W. Botha was replaced with a new National Party leader, F. W. de Klerk, who had finally realized that apartheid was not sustainable. The costs outweighed the benefits. Influx control of blacks into the cities had failed; business needed ever more skilled employees who also had to be politically satisfied; a powerful union movement had taken over from the banned political organizations since the late 1970s; restless townships could not be stabilized, despite permanent states of emergencies; demographic ratios changed in favor of blacks, with more whites emigrating and draining the country of skills and investments; the costs of global sanctions, particularly loan refusals, and moral ostracism of the pariah state were felt. The collapse of communism and the end of the Cold War in 1989 provided the final straw for the normalization of South Africa. The National Party decided to negotiate a historic compromise from a position of relative strength while the whites were still ahead. With the loss of Eastern European support, the ANC also had to turn away from the armed struggle and seek a political solution. A perception of stalemate on both sides prepared the ground for a constitutionally mandated agreement to share power for five years. The first free democratic elections in 1994, 1999, and 2004 provided the ANC with a two-thirds majority.

NELSON ROLIHLAHLA MANDELA (B. 1918)

Nelson Mandela, perhaps the most generally admired political figure of our time, was born on July 18, 1918 into the Thembu royal family in Transkei. Groomed to become a chief, he attended Healdtown, a mission school of the Methodist Church, which provided a Christian and liberal arts education, and later the University College of Fort Hare, which was a beacon for African scholars from all over Southern, Central, and Eastern Africa. For young black South African leaders including Oliver Tambo and Robert Mugabe, Fort Hare became the center of early anti-colonial sentiments and liberation strategies. At the end of his first year, Mandela became involved in a boycott of the Students Representative Council against the university's policies and was expelled. After moving to Johannesburg as an impoverished student, Mandela studied law at the University of the Witwatersrand, where he was the only African student in the law faculty, and, in partnership with Oliver Tambo, set up the first black law practice in Johannesburg in 1952.

As a young student, Mandela became increasingly involved in political opposition to the white minority government's denial of political, social, and economic rights to South Africa's black majority. Together with Walter Sisulu, Oliver Tambo, and others, Mandela was active in the ANC Youth League, of which he became national president in 1950. He helped organize the passive resistance campaign against the laws that forced blacks to carry passes and kept them in a position of permanent servility, calling for non-violent protest for as long as it was effective. This led to his first arrest and suspended sentence under the Suppression of Communism Act. Despite his ban from political activity, Mandela succeeded in reorganizing the ANC branches into small cells for their expected underground functioning.

In 1956 Mandela was charged with high treason along with 156 political leaders following the anti-pass campaign and demonstrations against the Declaration of the Republic. Following the banning of the ANC and PAC in 1961, Mandela went underground and traveled to Addis Ababa, Algeria, and London where he attended conferences and held discussions with various political leaders.

A few weeks following his return to South Africa in July 1962, Mandela was arrested and charged with incitement and for leaving the country illegally. At the notorious Rivonia trial of 1964, he was sentenced to life imprisonment together with his fellow conspirators on June 12. His statement from the dock stirred the conscience of many:

> During my lifetime I have dedicated myself to the struggle of the African people. I have fought against white domination, and I have fought against black domination. I have cherished the ideal of a democratic and free society in which all persons live together in harmony and equal opportunities. It is an ideal which I hope to live for and to achieve, but, if needs be, it is an ideal for which I am prepared to die.

The rallying cry "Free Nelson Mandela" became the slogan associated with opposition to apartheid for anti-apartheid campaigners around the world in subsequent years.

On February 11, 1990, after nearly 27 years in prison, Mandela was finally released unconditionally following delicate negotiations, sustained ANC campaigning, and international pressure that led to both his freedom and the beginning of the end of apartheid. He had refused earlier offers of conditional release in return for renouncing the armed struggle. After more than two decades of imprisonment, Mandela quickly filled a vacuum in the heterogeneous ANC camp. His leadership unified the oldest and most popular liberation movement as he straddled the divide between a militant youth and older traditionalists, revolutionaries and pragmatists, African nationalists and liberal universalists, orthodox socialists and social democratic capitalists. He succeeded in rallying the ANC's skeptical constituency behind the new politics of negotiation, suspending the armed struggle, and allaying fears of nationalization and redistribution. Mandela's remarkable lack of bitterness and steady moderation were also critical in convincing the white minority to share political power with a disenfranchised majority.

As the first ever democratically elected president of South Africa, he presided over the transition from minority rule and apartheid, from May 1994 to June 1999, winning international respect for his advocacy of national and international reconciliation. At the same time, Mandela was criticized for his support of Arafat's PLO, Libya's Gadhaffi, and Cuba's Castro, whom he referred to as his "comrades in arms." Some critics alleged that the world's most famous prisoner was in danger of becoming a symbol more powerful behind bars than in the world of *realpolitik*. Many were also disappointed with his government's ineffectiveness in dealing with a looming AIDS crisis. However, he subsequently engaged in a massive campaign to address the AIDS pandemic and in so doing admonished his successors for their silence on this question.

After his retirement as president in 1999 and handing over to his successor, Thabo Mbeki, Mandela went on to become an advocate for a variety of social and human rights organizations. On his 80th birthday he married Graca Machel, widow of the former Mozambican president, and travels the world to raise funds for major causes. He has been honored in countless countries with a host of prestigious awards. As a universally revered hero and global conscience, he speaks out against injustice on the world scene, from criticizing US unilateralism to peacemaking in Burundi. He spoke out against the Zimbabwean government for its human rights abuses while other African leaders maintained silence. Mandela almost assumed the role of informal opposition leader along with fellow Nobel laureate Desmond Tutu while simultaneously remaining a loyal member of the ANC.

For countless people around the world Nelson Mandela stands as an international hero whose lifelong struggle to end racial oppression in South Africa represents the triumph of dignity and hope over despair and hatred. His unprecedented moral authority and iconic status resemble the influence of Mahatma Gandhi nearly half a century earlier. Like Gandhi, an honorable Mandela remains faithful to his party's ideals of non-racialism, inclusiveness, and reconciliation for his beloved South Africa.

SEE ALSO: Burundi and Rwanda (Hutu, Tutsi); Color Line; Conflict (Racial/Ethnic); Racial Hierarchy; Race; Race (Racism); Truth and Reconciliation Commissions

REFERENCES AND SUGGESTED READINGS

Adam, H. & Moodley, K. (1993) *The Opening of the Apartheid Mind*. University of California Press, Berkeley.

Giliomee, H. (2003) *The Afrikaners*. University of Virginia Press, Charlottesville.

Mandela, N. (1994) *Long Walk to Freedom: The Autobiography of Nelson Mandela*. Little, Brown, New York.

Sampson, A. (2000) *Mandela: The Authorized Biography*. HarperCollins, London.

arcades

Keith Hayward

Originating in Paris in the 1820s, arcades were decorative passages or walkways through blocks of buildings. Typically glass-roofed and supported by ornate ironwork columns, arcades served as a form of interior street; a site of conspicuous consumption for the wealthy, and a place of marvel and spectacle for the poor. Hemmed in by antique shops, concession stands, and an eclectic array of emporia, arcade shop fronts offered the observer a chaotic visual experience of illuminated shop-signs, *objets d'art*, and a cornucopia of commodities and artifacts from around the world. In sociological terms, the importance of the Parisian arcades lies in their purported role as progenitor of modern consumerism and more tangentially as a prototype of the contemporary shopping mall.

The unearthing of the arcade as a site of sociological and philosophical importance is closely associated with the work of the German literary theorist Walter Benjamin. Benjamin was fascinated by the "mythical" qualities of the arcades, viewing them as both "threatening" and "alluring" – places in which the emotions were stimulated and where the social constraints of public and private life were simultaneously blurred and challenged. In his fragmentary work *The Arcades Project* (*Das Passagen-Werk*) he viewed the arcades as a metaphor that could help us understand the composition and dynamic form of high modern industrial capitalism. Benjamin described arcade shop fronts as "dream houses," where everything desirable becomes a commodity (frequently on the first floor of the arcades, sexual pleasures could be bought and drinking and gambling were common). For Benjamin, the continual flow of goods, the "sensual immediacy" of the displays, the utopian forms of new technology, and the novelty and visual appeal of transitory fashions were all fragments of the "commodity fetish." Yet, while newness itself becomes a fetish, the modern commodity has a built-in obsolescence: the novel inevitably becomes the outmoded. This tension is apparent when one considers the fate of the arcades themselves. Following Baron George Haussman's "creative destruction" of Second Empire Paris in the 1860s, most of the arcades were destroyed to make way for the wide boulevards and imposing facades that characterize Paris today. Likewise, by the time of Benjamin's research, the arcades had already been superseded by the more organized modern department store, which in turn served to further "democratize demand" and usher in the rationalized forms of mass urban consumption that we know today (Ritzer 2004, 2005). However, surviving examples of original arcades can still be found in Paris today.

SEE ALSO: Benjamin, Walter; Conspicuous Consumption; Consumption; Critical Theory/ Frankfurt School; *Flânerie*; Marxism and Sociology; Shopping Malls

REFERENCES AND SUGGESTED READINGS

Benjamin, W. (1999) *The Arcades Project*. Ed. R. Tiedemann. Harvard University Press, Cambridge, MA.

Buck-Morss, S. (1989) *The Dialectics of Seeing: Walter Benjamin and the Arcades Project*. MIT Press, Cambridge, MA.

Geist, J. F. (1983) *Arcades: The History of a Building Type*. MIT Press, Cambridge, MA.

Ritzer, G. (2004) *The McDonaldization of Society*. Pine Forge Press, Thousand Oaks, CA.

Ritzer, G. (2005) *Enchanting a Disenchanted World: Revolutionizing the Means of Consumption*, 2nd edn. Pine Forge Press, Thousand Oaks, CA.

Arendt, Hannah (1906–75)

Peter Murphy

PERSONAL HISTORY

Hannah Arendt was born in Hanover and grew up in an assimilated German-Jewish social democratic household in Königsberg, then East Prussia, today Kaliningrad in Russia. She attended university (1924–8), completing a year at Marburg where her teacher, and briefly her lover, was Martin Heidegger; a semester at Freiburg with Edmund Husserl; and then on to Heidelberg to complete a doctoral dissertation under Karl Jaspers. Arendt had a gift for friendship. She remained close to Jaspers all her life. She even maintained a tense contact with Heidegger after the war, despite his embrace of Nazism. After university, Arendt lived in Berlin and married the leftist philosopher Günter Stern (pen-name Anders) in 1929, fleeing Nazi Germany for France in 1933, divorcing Stern in 1937. She worked in Paris for Jewish relief organizations and became acquainted with the rising French intellectuals of the day (Aron, Sartre), as well as Jewish intellectual émigrés such as Walter Benjamin, whose manuscripts she carried from France and edited (in 1968) after Benjamin's suicide. She met her second husband, the Berliner and communist Heinrich Blücher, in 1936. In 1940, Blücher and Arendt fled Nazi-occupied France for the US, finally arriving in 1941 in New York, the city that would be her home for the rest of her life. She became a US citizen in 1951.

In the US Arendt did political journalism (1941–5), directed research for Jewish cultural reconstruction organizations (1944–6, 1949–52), and was a chief editor at Schocken Books (1946–8) where, among other projects, she published a German edition of Franz Kafka's *Diaries*. After the success of *The Origins of Totalitarianism* in 1951, Arendt began a career of visiting professorships and lecture engagements at American universities. Skeptical of academic conformism, she resisted any permanent appointment until 1967. She taught peripatetically at Berkeley (1955), Princeton (1959), Columbia (1960), Northwestern (1961), Wesleyan University's Center of Advanced Studies (1961–2), the University of Chicago's Committee on Social Theory (1963–7), and at the New School for Social Research (1967–75). She presented Princeton University's Christian Gauss Seminar Lectures (1953), the Walgreen Lectures at the University of Chicago (1956), and the Scottish Universities' Gifford Lectures (1973).

INTELLECTUAL AND SOCIAL CONTEXT

Arendt progressed through some of the most important intellectual milieus in the twentieth century – from inter-war German universities, to wartime Paris, to post-war New York and Chicago. Possibly the most decisive of all of Arendt's intellectual environments was her childhood town of Königsberg – a place that was the seedbed of an astonishing intellectual progeny. On the far eastern side of the Baltic, this old port and university town not only produced Immanuel Kant but also Hermann Minkowski (the geometer who provided the mathematical basis for Einstein's theory of space-time) and Theodor Kaluza (whose geometry laid the foundation for string theory in physics). Copernicus came from the nearby port town of Frombork.

Arendt rebelled against German high schooling. She organized teenaged study circles with her friends to read and translate Greek texts. Expelled from high school, she took refuge in University of Berlin classes, most notably those of Romano Guardini.

Later, in Berlin and Paris, she had extensive contact with Jewish intellectuals, including influential Zionist (Jewish homeland nationalist) advocates such as Kurt Blumenfeld and Salmon Schocken. Arendt, who likened herself to a self-conscious pariah, admired the Zionist critique of Jewish assimilation in Protestant and Catholic Europe, but remained to the end of her life an anti-nationalist and a federalist. Her ideal of Israel was a settler federation encompassing Jews, Arabs, and other nationalities. In the 1940s she criticized the appeasement of the Nazis by some Jewish leaders and repeated this charge, to great controversy, in her report *Eichmann in Jerusalem* (1963).

Though she followed events in Europe closely, her intellectual life after 1951 was an American one. She became a paradigmatic example of a New York intellectual of the 1950s and 1960s. Her many New Yorker friends included the poets Randall Jarrell and W. H. Auden. Her closest friend from that world was the Catholic-American novelist Mary McCarthy, with whom she shared many judgments on modern "mass society."

SUBSTANTIVE CONTRIBUTIONS

Arendt's masterpieces are *The Human Condition* (1958) and *On Revolution* (1963). They are classics – elegant, timeless, and profound. Her other major works circulate like orbs around these twin suns. The essay collections *Between Past and Future* (1961) and *Crises of the Republic* (1972) underscore and amplify the themes of *On Revolution*. *The Life of the Mind* (1981) develops ideas originally sketched in *The Human Condition* into a multivolume work. Arendt's life's work has a marvelous unity throughout. Observations about twentieth-century fascist and communist revolutions in *The Origins of Totalitarianism* (1951) were the starting point for her study of the eighteenth-century French Revolution in *On Revolution*. The triptych structure of *The Human Condition* echoes the anti-Semitism–imperialism–racism structure (the "three pillars of hell") of the totalitarianism book, and is replayed in the tripartite meditation on thinking, willing, and judging in *The Life of the Mind*.

In *The Human Condition* Arendt divides human doing into three dimensions: labor, work, and action. Each dimension of this typology represents a confluence of social psychology, behavior, and institutions. Labor conjoins need psychology, survival behavior, and bureaucratic institutions. Human beings labor in order to consume – and consume in order to survive. Bureaucracies developed to coordinate labor on a large scale. History has seen many kinds of bureaucratic society, from early patrimonial to late imperial societies. Arendt observed how twentieth-century totalitarian states like the Soviet Union and China also gravitated around the organization and ideology of labor. These were "body" politics in which a bureaucratic class that owed its existence to a political party orchestrated industrial and rural and prison-slave labor on a vast and often irrational scale.

In Arendt's eyes, labor had a number of defining characteristics, each of which were negated in work or action:

- Laboring is done with the human *body*. Its telltale sign is exhaustion.
- Labor's products are *transient*. Whatever it produces is consumed more or less immediately. Labor is constantly needed to maintain and reproduce life. Some societies are dominated by laboring; in others, it shrinks to modest proportions. But no matter its social weight, the consumption goods it produces barely survive the act of being produced. Bread lasts a day. It is ephemeral – subject to swift decay. It leaves nothing behind.
- A labor-centric society produces *nothing lasting*. It creates no durable artifices. Its building or its manufacture is notoriously shoddy. Its time horizons are short-term. The fixation of the totalitarian party-state on "five year plans" was typical of this.
- Labor is *repetitive*. Human beings labor to rest, and rest to labor. They consume in order to labor, and labor in order to consume. Labor has no beginning or end. It is unending toil. Its tasks are repeated day in and day out. The utopia of labor is abundance; a state where life's necessities are easily come by, without backbreaking toil.

- Labor is *private*. The products of labor are immediately incorporated and annihilated by the body's life processes. Human beings hide from public attention the toil and sleep, pain and elation, consumption and defecation that dominate the life process. Labor fulfills needs that all human beings have, and yet these needs cannot be shared (my hunger can never be your hunger) and cannot even be fully communicated (how can I really describe my pain?).
- Labor is *urgent*. Human beings must eat and sleep. Labor serves the need to survive, but the desperation to survive also readily turns into its opposite: a lust for cruelty and death.

Class societies emerged when some individuals found ways of making peasants and slaves labor while others worked, traded, and ruled. Interestingly, though, Arendt did not regard labor-centric societies as limited to patrimonial or totalitarian types. Even when labor in the field and factory shrank dramatically in modern automated societies, the ghostly imprint of labor remained when, as Arendt insisted, modern bureaucracies produced nothing of lasting significance, modern buyers were hooked on instant gratification, and modern industries produced goods that instantly wore out.

Permanence mattered to Arendt. Only through work are lasting things created. Work creates things or objects – artifices – that are durable. This is important because the human species makes its world out of these artifices. There is a crucial difference, Arendt insisted, between producing bread that lasts a day and building a temple that lasts centuries. The former appears and then disappears almost in the same instant; the latter endures through time. Just as the loaf of bread is ephemeral, so are human services and bureaucratic functions – even modern automated ones. Often, their only material effect is records. Information technologies and systems are one of the few ways human beings objectify intangible services and functions. Bureaucracy is only immortalized through its files. Arendt observed that even thinking (the activity of the philosopher) left nothing behind it. It took others (Plato, etc.) to make something of the thoughts of Socrates – to create a work from the labor of thought.

On the whole, Arendt preferred work to labor, and action to work. Labor satisfied hungers. Work produced durable objects. Action created new beginnings. Action was the highest form of human behavior. This was because human beings, Arendt thought, have an impulse to be "unique." They believe their identities (the symbolic representation of their selves) to be distinctive. It is action that allows a person to disclose to others "who I am" by beginning something new – something that is not a retread of what has come before. This happens on small and large scales. Yet action risks futility. Initiatives frequently fail either because they have no support or else because no one records them. A person can begin something new but fail to make it last. Unlike artifacts, actions have a will-o'-the-wisp quality if they cannot be objectivated in institutions and stories.

Action is like Socrates' thoughts without Plato to record them. The human challenge is: how can my "I" last? In other words, how can "I" be remembered? How can "my" self be immortalized? One answer is that human beings perform acts that are sufficiently memorable that someone will tell a story about those acts. Storytelling turns acts into worldly artifices. To become worldly, human deeds and events and patterns of thought must be reified. They must be turned into things or objects – books, paintings, sculptures, monuments, or documents. Human beings witness deeds. They remember them. They reify the memory of those deeds. The fleeting moment is thus materialized. This materialization is a kind of workmanship. The worldliness of a material record ("what's in the file") provides reliability of recall that human memory cannot match. Everyone knows how unreliable human recollection is – notwithstanding the memory feats of oral societies. What makes the human world, including materialized memories, reliable is that things in the world that surround human beings are relatively permanent. These worldly things are more permanent than the actions they record, and more permanent than actors' lives and deeds.

Human beings constantly tell stories about each other's doings. The storytelling – and ultimately the books – of the novelist or the playwright fix this for generations in the case of great heroes. But, mostly, human beings are not great heroes. Most stories told about them are not art but institutional narratives – from the Domesday book to corporate storytelling. Some narratives are stories of failure – the doomed initiative, the project that went awry. Some are stories of achievement. The latter tell us how individual actions are turned into worldly structures. Some of these stories are gripping. They show us how many of the greatest achievements in history were almost failures.

Arendt sought to explain that initiatives or "actions" succeed only when others pledge themselves to carry forward the initiative. That's how power is created. A leader initiates and others commit themselves to abide by and expand the initiative. When initiative and commitment persist, a worldly structure like a city or state, institution or association comes into being. Few human beings are present in the heroic moment "right at the very beginning" of this process. There are few Solons or Henry Fords. But those who come later replicate the initiatives and commitments of the founder-titans. Most people are remembered not for their heroism but for participating in an ongoing collective artifice or world-making. Those who "participate in power" are remembered for their collective achievement. Stories are told about the making of great republics, commonwealths, towns, cities, and institutions. We do remember the Athenians and the Venetians. Their characters are distinctive. They do escape oblivion.

One of the most important things Arendt realized is that the story of great collective achievement applied with equal force to the New York and Chicago of her day as it had done to Paris in the nineteenth century or to Berlin in the early twentieth century. She understood without illusion that power had crossed the Atlantic from Europe to America. Mid-twentieth-century Europe had produced violence instead of power – on a daunting scale. The totalitarianism of the Nazis and Stalinists had substituted destruction for self-sustaining action. With this in mind, Arendt set out in *On Revolution* to explain the different political trajectories of Europe and the US in the modern age.

In Europe, the idea of revolution arose out of the mental ideals of laboring. Jacobin and communist outpourings from the French Revolution seized on "bread" rather than freedom as the major objective of revolution. This explained the difference between the American and European conception of politics. The American beginning was prosperous, Arendt noted. Colonists had access to plenty of land and good wages. Poverty – "the social question" – did not affect America in its early days. Europe, in contrast, was bedeviled by poverty. Thinking they would end this scourge, Europeans encouraged the poor to enter the public realm. European modernity recognized "the rights of man." Political entitlements were due to all human beings, including the dispossessed by reason of birth or nature. Arendt was skeptical of this. She wondered aloud whether "by birth or by nature" was not loaded dice. Arendt equated nature with life – with pre-political bodily processes. When the modern continental revolutions opened the public realm to the poor, they unwittingly opened the door to desperation. For "the rights of man" became the rights of the hungry. Churches, noblesse oblige, and civic charities outside the political realm had previously cared for the downtrodden. When the rights of man prevailed, the idea of revolution acquired the force of nature. It suddenly appeared in history as an implacable torrent-like force – making the same insistent demands on a mass scale that the hungry and the desperate made on an individual or group scale. The French idea of revolution took up where the bodily processes of life and labor left off. Social movements that were raging frenzies drove it. When the poor entered the public realm en masse for the first time in human history, politics became the politics of neediness. It acquired an urgent, insistent, violent, crushing character. History became surrounded by an aura of inevitability. Freedom became a kind of necessity. Terror and mass murder were legitimated by this necessity. In this atmosphere, the political philosophies of Hegel and Marx were born.

Arendt contrasted three alternative models to the French Revolution. The first was the great historic city oligarchies ruled by citizen peers – from Aristotle's Athens to Machiavelli's Florence. The second was Edmund Burke's England, where the rights of man were resisted in favor of the historical rights of an "English person" embodied in an unwritten constitution. Arendt drew a certain tacit flavor from Burke: she was enduringly skeptical about the declarations and proclamations of human rights. She had been a stateless person, and understood the fragility of that condition. Rights not embodied in the law of the state were worthless. Humanity was an inherently stateless condition. She cautioned against wooly schemes to create a world state. Who wants to live under a world police, she reasoned?

The third model that Arendt contrasted to the French Revolution was the American Revolution. This was the model that Arendt most cherished. It represented a public order that (in Burke's sense) was not universal but that nonetheless was capable of enlargement. Arendt loved America and the American Revolution because they promised new worlds and new beginnings, yet also ways of stabilizing what was new and making it permanent.

New beginnings were a kind of disclosure. In political action, actors disclose who they are by beginning something. The impetus of the American Revolution was to extend the "right to act" to all Americans – no matter whether they were old or young, rich or poor, high or low, wise or foolish, ignorant or learned. The Europeans, including the famous observer of America Alexis de Tocqueville, thought of this as "democracy." The Americans in contrast thought of it as "republicanism." The difference in terminology mattered. The American republic retained something of the spirit of the ancient and Renaissance city republics. This was echoed in the American passion for distinction. Distinction requires public life. The public realm is the place where actors can excel, and thereby distinguish themselves. At times Arendt hinted that the public realm and the republic were virtually identical. She never identified the American republic with its written constitution.

Arendt agreed that law was a restraint on despotism, and that classical republics always thought of themselves as the enemies of despotism. But she did not think of a republic just as a negation of tyranny. She thought of it as a positive force that induced public happiness, not merely freedom from dictatorship. Public happiness was created by the widespread participation of citizens – and resident aliens – in the public realm. The public sphere was the space where individuals could appear. It was the worldly artifact where citizens and others could reveal and display their initiative – their freedom to begin. The law of the constitution helped create the boundaries of the public space. But public happiness depended not on law but on participation in the public realm. Public happiness depended on human selves being lifted out of the obscurity of private life into the visibility of the public. Such a lift could be nerve-wracking. Public speaking rates as most people's greatest fear. What Arendt reasoned, though, was that only in the public realm could individuals gain recognition for their distinctive abilities and characters. Human beings gained recognition when their initiatives drew the attention or support of their fellows. It was these initiatives that allowed individuals to distinguish themselves and to be remembered by their peers.

Only those who "act" will be remembered, because they will have stories told about them. Others will be forgotten. Notorious criminals and dictatorial mass murderers are cited by history. But they are remembered only for their failure to leave anything constructive behind them. They create mayhem but no power. They leave a trail of violence but no achievement. Creating worldly structures requires finding others to cooperate in initiatives. For this, a public realm is crucial. Why the American Revolution succeeded and the French Revolution failed was that the Americans found a way of replacing violence with power – through public action and promise making.

Privacy, Arendt believed, was for subjects, not citizens. In private, persons could be happy. She herself was a private person who enjoyed the company of her family and friends. She also knew that duty weighed heavily on great public figures. But she rejected the idea that private matters of welfare and property were the proper ends of government. Thus, she wondered aloud, whether the outcome of the American Revolution – two centuries on – had not been ambivalent. It could hardly

be denied that contemporary Americans judged government according to whether it delivered prosperity and welfare ("jobs and insurance"). This propensity, though, was not born of a history of poverty. Need did not become a factor in American life till the great immigrant waves of the nineteenth century. By that time, American political ideals were already in place. Arendt instead thought that a fatal passion for sudden riches haunted American public life. She couldn't quite make up her mind where this passion came from.

She acknowledged that a good republic needed to be liberated from poverty, otherwise necessity would rule politics. But she knew that liberation did not by itself produce a successful system of power. Liberation did not cause people to act in concert. Americans were good at acting in concert, but also – seemingly – were distracted from this by their passion for consumer wealth. Arendt's explanation of this was that the poor had their own vision of wealth, and that vision had inveigled its way into American life. The poor idealized material abundance and endless consumption. Arendt found herself in agreement with the "mass society" critics of the 1950s: America had developed a passion for consumption, the wealth of a laboring society. Its counter was a Doric interpretation of republicanism that said that freedom and luxury were incompatible, and that frugality was the mainstay of freedom. In short, prosperity, through the medium of luxury, threatened the public realm.

This argument could easily be stood on its head, though. It is equally plausible that wealth is a byproduct of "acting in concert," and that American capitalism was bounteous because of – and not despite – its civic foundations. Arendt would not have agreed. For her, prosperity and necessity destroyed republics. Both turned human beings into private creatures. Prosperity encouraged the private life of consumption, while necessity justified the isolated life of violence. Both were inimical to the public realm.

Revolutions of the French type demonstrated the fateful relation between necessity and violence and privacy. Such revolutions substituted violence for power. Violence was the medium of those who stood alone. Power, in contrast, was a product of public life.

Power arose out of cooperation and interaction between persons. The thing that most distinguished the French-type revolutions, as they spread around the world, was not the power of those who participated in them but their powerlessness. Notwithstanding their awesome effects, terror and destruction were impotent. They always ended in social demoralization and depression.

Arendt had a high opinion of power. She did not share the view of most twentieth-century intellectuals that power corrupts. Equally, she rejected the idealization of impotence. Impotence always leads to rage and infatuation with violence. She was skeptical of the *enragés* who reveled in self-pity, powerlessness, and humiliation, and who created movements and states that were violent but impotent. Impotence could be seen in the inability of such movements and states to leave anything worldly and lasting behind them. Constructive acts in the human domain require cooperation. Cooperation is a public medium. It emerges through interaction in public space. Public actors start things. Others perpetuate these beginnings through stories and commitments. Stories and commitments are public media. When the capacity to begin is combined with the capacity to tell stories and to make commitments to things that are ongoing, power is created. Successful societies endow their institutions with power. Societies that are impotent substitute violence and terror for power.

The ultimate failure of impotent revolutions is their inability to create and grow power. This, Arendt judged, was one of the reasons why the American Revolution had been so successful. It was a mistake then to equate America with "limited government." Yes, its legislators and administrators are subject to the rule of law. Yes, it has a written constitution that regulates relations between the various branches and levels of government. But the point of all of this is not to limit government but to augment power.

The American system of power began in a simple public covenant, the Mayflower Compact, drawn up by the pilgrims as they crossed the Atlantic on their way to settle in America. In response to proposals, and through mutual promises, the pilgrims created a "civil body politic" and the instruments of government.

Power is precisely the union of initiative and commitment. It is different from strength, which is the capacity of individuals in isolation to resist pressure and violence. Power is also different from violence. Violence is born of isolation. The suspicious nature and paranoia of dictators tell us much about the isolative character of violence. Power comes into being when persons join together for purposes of action. By combination and mutual promise human beings create stable worldly structures to house their combined power of action. Americans created a lot of these worldly structures. They created towns, cities, counties, and states. But they didn't just create worldly structures – they combined them. Out of multiple states, for example, they created a federal union of states – the United States.

Arendt thought Americans were sometimes neglectful. They missed opportunities to incorporate cities into the federal union and they often forgot about their revolutionary past. Yet they also had a genius for increasing or augmenting power. Part of that genius rested on respect for grassroots action. The origin of American power was "the people." "The people" are a collective character – persons who come together in order to act. This image of popular action was immortalized by Tocqueville's depiction of the American talent for voluntary association. But Americans created vast numbers of compulsory and collective bodies as well: states and cities. Just as crucially, they discovered an ingenious way of combining these powers through mechanisms of balance or equilibrium. They were inspired to do this by ancient political theories. Such arrangements enabled power to be stopped when it went astray, but to be preserved and increased at the same time. The Americans found a way of enlarging their republic without simply relying on expansion or conquest. The idea of a union of states laid the basis for a republic that had features akin to the classic city-republics but which was of unprecedented size. Beyond its borders, the US achieved further enlargement of its power through alliances and treaties. Like the original promises that created America's first institutions, treaties and alliances created durable worldly structures across the face of the earth. This allowed America to reach out on a global scale without encountering the disadvantages that attend a world state.

Power does many things. It builds, it organizes, and it legislates. But how does it legitimate itself? Power invariably attracts critics. How do those with power justify their acts? They can appeal to the origin of power in "the people." This justification often faces practical impediments, though. A "people" may pledge to create and maintain a legislature, but lawmakers can still make bad laws. Thus, holders of power have to justify their acts independent of "the people." They do this in a number of ways: appealing to transcendental justifications for their acts, to self-evidence, and to beginnings. Arendt rejected transcendental justifications of action, such as the appeal to the higher law of God or the higher law of the Revolution that the Jacobins, Nazis, and Bolsheviks relied on. Transcendence equaled necessity, and thus confounded freedom. Arendt also rejected self-evidence as a satisfactory justification of power. She admired Jefferson, but took issue with his formula "We hold these truths to be self-evident." Self-evidence is a kind of mathematical necessity, and Arendt was suspicious of any necessity in politics – even in the American Declaration of Independence. While geometric axioms might be self-evident, the principles of politics, Arendt thought, were not. If "we" freely agree, then "our" agreement should not be coerced by truth. Politics is properly a function of opinion not of truth.

This was one of the weaker aspects of Arendt's theorizing. It is not clear that opinion is always an effective medium for lending initiatives support. Jefferson was right. Self-evidence plays a powerful role in mobilizing allegiance. Why Arendt missed this is pretty obvious. From storytelling to promising, all her media of politics are linguistic in nature. But self-evidence works through showing, not saying. Arguments and opinions can pressure and threaten. So can images that "send a message." Self-evidence, though, relies not on delivering messages but on showing patterns that everyone already intuitively knows. Like much of ancient Greek thought, Plato's republic rested on the tacit geometry of proportionality. Arendt was skeptical of Plato's "public worker," the demiurge, who she

thought created a political artifact like a carpenter builds a table – keeping a pattern in mind. This smacked of violent behavior (hammering) carried on in isolation (by the lonely artisan). But, in fact, the most complex types of voluntary cooperation (e.g., creating and maintaining a city) work because actions can be framed in terms of self-evident patterns that do not require articulation or verbal agreement. Unsurprisingly, then, many of the American founders were deists, including Jefferson. Arendt interpreted this as a residual attempt by them to justify actions by appeals to the rewards and punishments of heaven. But, given Jefferson's Epicureanism, Arendt's interpretation makes no sense.

American deism simply asserted that there were absolutes in nature: not commandments, but self-organizing pattern or order. Arendt, however, was skeptical of all appeals to nature. Nature equated with urgency. Urgency equated with violence. Thus, the authority of American power could not rest on self-evidence. Nonetheless, it was erected on an absolute. This absolute, Arendt argued, was not coercive. It was the absolute of beginnings. Not nature, but the natal condition legitimated power. Power existed to provide the worldly house of action. Action provided the justification of power. The initiative of the lawmaker or the policymaker was justified by the idea of inauguration or beginning (again). Here Arendt entered into difficult but productive terrain. At first glance her argument looks contradictory. When people act, they begin something new. Action is fragile. Its products can evaporate; its deeds can be forgotten. Power allows persons to perpetuate their acts. Power derives from agreements among people whose desire to act is such that they will bind themselves to their own creations. This suggests that durability trumps change and that permanence overwrites initiative. In fact, if they do not, the effort to initiate and create has been pointless: time will erode our deeds and turn our life from something meaningful into something meaningless. Arendt sought to escape the paradox of "the new and the lasting" in this way: the thing that is most lasting in a state is the act of foundation. The foundation is an act that lasts. All the best deeds in a state imitate this act that lasts.

The ultimate justification of law and policy is to initiate something that lasts.

Arendt thought that the Americans took the idea of the act that lasts from the Romans. Central to Roman religion was the notion of being bound back to the beginning of Rome. This piety provided authority for the city-state. This authority was invested, most visibly, in the Roman Senate. The Roman "people" had power, and the Roman Senate exercised authority. The authority of the Senators stemmed from their origins in the citizen ruling class of early republican Rome that had overthrown kingship. The Americans relied on something analogous – and not simply because they ousted the English Crown. Take the case of the American Supreme Court. It is a power that checks the behavior of other powers in the Republic by interpreting and applying constitutional law. Its power, however, rests on authority. Its authority – what legitimates its power – derives from it being tied back to the original act of constitution making. The American Constitution was an act of the American people – an initiative agreed to in a popular vote. The authority of the Supreme Court derives from the unbroken line that ties the present-day Constitution back to the original act of making the Constitution. Importantly, though, this continuity is also a procession of change. The US Constitution is a worldly legal artifice that is periodically revised, amended, and added to. It is an act that has lasted; it has lasted because it is subjected to periodic initiatives that alter it. The voting public accepts some initiatives and rejects others. Amendments augment the Constitution. Augmentation is the key to the authority or legitimacy of power, Arendt thought. Augmentation permits the old and the durable to be changed without being disposed of. This makes change an expression of stability, and innovation a manifestation of permanence. Thus, Arendt could conclude that the "absolute" lies in the beginning, because the beginning is conservative while conservation is achieved through alteration.

This dialectic of initiative and stability is neither prosaic nor procedural. Rather, it is a great drama and the stuff of brilliant stories. What *On Revolution* did was to tell America's foundation story in philosophical terms.

Arendt's model for this was Virgil's story of the wanderings of Aeneas after the burning of Troy. As the story goes, Aeneas' joining of Latins and Trojans prefigures Rome's creation out of the merger of Latins and Sabines. But this act of foundation, though a new beginning, is replete with the myth-history of earlier Greek heroes and gods. This myth-history placates the arbitrariness implicit in any beginning. What is new can be intensely willful. It can start processes that have unintended and even dreadful consequences. To the extent that initiative relies on will, it is arbitrary. Its philosophical conundrum is: why this and not something else? The answer, Arendt thought, was to reinsert the act of foundation back into a temporal continuity that the will otherwise destroys. The idea of foundation as a refoundation – America as a new Rome – achieves exactly this.

Arendt stressed that refoundation was different from the Christian idea of the beginning of things as an act of creation that is entirely new. In Arendt's Virgilian model, the act of foundation is a creation out of something, not a creation out of nothing. In this manner, Arendt attempts to answer the question of how we can civilize the arbitrariness inherent in all beginnings. If this civilizing does not happen, then new beginnings may simply license the human potential for crime. Every despot proclaims a new order. This new order always ends up being a horrible, chaotic, violent mess. It is a beginning that plunges society into violence and bestiality. It is a beginning that is devoured by its own effects. It is a beginning that ends in murder. One way of logically avoiding this is to say that the legitimate absolute is the new beginning that is not an absolute new beginning. Thus, Virgil's mythical Rome was a creation that was in part a recreation of the fraternal compact of Aeneas' Trojan expatriates. America was the creation that was in part a recreation of Rome. All birth, which naturally equips human beings to begin, is also a matter of lineage.

Arendt observed that America after the colonial and revolutionary eras broke with the classical past. It began down its own path of "absolute novelty." Given its several beginnings (compacts, independence, revolution, constitution) it no longer needed to cast itself as a recreation of the past. It now entered history as a *sui generis* actor. It had its own past filled with foundation acts. What saved these acts of beginning from their own arbitrariness is that each act of beginning carried its own principle within itself. Each act of beginning was an absolute. Each was an absolute because it inspired subsequent deeds that replicated the "first" beginning. Arendt imagines a circle of legitimation: what happens afterwards validates the inaugural act, while later acts are validated by first beginnings. This circle of American history was a pragmatic absolute. The absolute was absolute because it worked.

RELEVANCE TO SOCIOLOGY

Arendt casts light on many of the great problems of classical sociology, ranging from the nature of labor in Marx to the nature of the state in Weber. But, more crucially still, she adapts these themes, which had begun as European questions, to the horizon of the "new world." By doing this, she creates an indispensable model for any future "sociology of the new world." In this sociology, America rivals Europe for the production of themes. As the phrase indicates, the master theme of any "new world" sociology is the question of the creation of "new worlds" and all of the paradoxes such an idea invariably generates.

Arendt was a philosopher of social creation. Her principal European peer in this was Cornelius Castoriadis. His work has similar resonances for sociology. The most powerful thing that distinguishes Arendt's work from Castoriadis's is that Castoriadis's rumination on creation was a reflection on the West and its fading energies – what he called its rising tide of insignificance. Arendt likewise knew in her bones that Europe had become impotent after the plague of totalitarianism. With her spiritual home in America, though, she was also in a position to see that the new world had what Europe had lost – escalating energies and power.

Thus, among her many contributions, perhaps her greatest achievement was to begin to chart ways of thinking about new world societies. Arendt was schooled in European social

thought, so there never could have been a question of her postulating an absolute hiatus between Europe and America. Not that there was one in any case. But nobody thought harder, more deeply, or more seriously about what it means to create a "new world" in the new world. For any future Weber of North American or Australasian sociology, the paradoxes that Arendt posed – the paradoxes of time and creation, change and permanence, arbitrariness and principle – will be forever the inescapable beginning of understanding the social constitution of the strange new worlds of the migrants who settled on distant shores and the Europeans who left Europe and its discontents behind them.

SEE ALSO: Communism; Fascism; Political Sociology; Revolutions; Totalitarianism

REFERENCES AND SUGGESTED READINGS

Arendt, H. (1951) *The Origins of Totalitarianism*, 1st edn. Harcourt, Brace, New York.
Arendt, H. (1958) *The Human Condition*. University of Chicago Press, Chicago.
Arendt, H. (1961) *Between Past and Future*. Viking Press, New York.
Arendt, H. (1963) *Eichmann in Jerusalem*. Viking Press, New York.
Arendt, H. (1963) *On Revolution*. Viking Press, New York.
Arendt, H. (1972) *Crises of the Republic*, 1st edn. Harcourt Brace Jovanovich, New York.
Arendt, H. (1981) *The Life of the Mind*. Harcourt Brace Jovanovich, San Diego.
Young-Bruehl, E. (1982) *Hannah Arendt: For Love of the World*. Yale University Press, New Haven.

Aron, Raymond (1905–83)

Dusko Sekulic

Raymond Aron was a French sociologist, philosopher, political actor, and commentator. Before World War II, he lectured at several

French universities, including Le Havre and Bordeaux. In 1930 he defended his doctoral thesis, *Introduction to the Philosophy of History*, which was published as a book and widely reviewed in Europe and the United States. After graduating, he spent the period 1930–3 in Germany and observed the rise to power of National Socialism. In 1935 he published *German Sociology*, in which he made the distinction between "systematic" and "historical" sociology. Systematic sociology was concerned with "fundamental social relations, types of social groups [and] the static structure of society," while historical sociology focused on the "laws, or at least the theory, of the development of the bourgeois society" (Aron 1957 [1935]: 2).

Within systematic sociology he distinguished between formal sociology (Simmel and von Wiese), the sociology of society and community (Tönnies), phenomenological sociology (Vierkandt), and universalistic sociology (Spann). Within historical sociology he classified Oppenheimer, the cultural sociology of Alfred Weber, and Mannheim's sociology of knowledge. The greatest attention and praise, however, was paid to Max Weber, "without any doubt, the greatest of German sociologists" (Aron 1957 [1935]: 67). Weber's influence is present in all of Aron's work and Aron's stature in modern sociology has been compared with that of Max Weber. When Aron was presented with the Goethe Prize in 1979, Dahrendorf declared: "Raymond Aron is the only social scientist of recent decades who ... may be compared in terms of significance with Max Weber" (Dahrendorf 1989: 30).

The analogy with Max Weber can be extended to intellectual preoccupations. Like Weber, Aron "became a sociologist in a long and intense debate with the ghost of Karl Marx" (Albert Salomon in Gurvitch & Moore 1945: 596). Aron's sociology is a constant debate with the heirs of Marx in their communist totalitarian form. This consistent theoretical criticism of Marxism earned Aron a certain isolation within French sociology, which was heavily influenced by Marxism. However, that did not diminish his influence on the general intellectual and political scene in France.

In 1940, Aron joined *Free French* in England and from 1940 to 1944 was editor of *La France Libre*. After the war he continued to write as a journalist (with *Figaro* from 1947), was a member of editorial boards of influential journals like *Combat* and *Les Temps modernes*, and held political positions such as *directeur de cabinet* in Malraux's Ministry of Education. In 1955 he was appointed professor of sociology at the Sorbonne, and in 1970 he became professor of sociology at the Modern Civilization Collège de France. He was also co-editor of the *European Journal of Sociology*.

As subtitles of Colquhoun's (1986) biography indicate, before the war Aron was more preoccupied with the philosophical problems where (especially after his appointment to the Sorbonne) his writing went more in a "sociological direction." Aron (1978) himself divided his contribution to sociology into four major areas: (1) the analysis of contemporary ideologies with *The Opium of the Intellectuals* (1955), the most comprehensive example of that problem; (2) the analysis of the concept of industrial society in *Eighteen Lectures on Industrial Society* (1963) and *The Industrial Society* (1966); (3) the analysis of international relations and warfare in *The Century of Total War* (1951), *Peace and War* (1961), *The Great Debate* (1963), *De Gaulle, Israel, and the Jews* (1968), *The Imperial Republic* (1973), and *Clausewitz* (1976); and (4) the analyses of modern political systems and movements in *Democracy and Totalitarianism* (1965), *An Essay on Freedom* (1965), *The Elusive Revolution* (1968), and *Progress and Disillusion* (1969).

At the beginning of the 1960s Aron wrote an influential introduction to sociological theory, *Main Currents in Sociological Thought* (first volume in 1960, the second in 1962). Beside treatments of Comte, Marx, Pareto, Weber, and Durkheim, there is an extensive discussion on Montesquieu with special emphasis on Alexis de Tocqueville. The idea for this book came to him as a consequence of attending the World Congress of Sociology at Stresa, in Northern Italy, in September 1959. Aron wondered whether there were commonalities between Marxist sociology, advocated by the sociologists from Eastern Europe, and empirical sociology, especially in its American tradition. The purpose of that book was a "return to origin," to show that sociology, Marxist or otherwise, has a common origin, and that Weber could not be understood without Marx, or Durkheim without Comte.

The inclusion of Tocqueville was unusual because he was not usually considered one of the "fathers" of sociology. But one sentence explains Aron's affinity for Tocqueville: "Instead of giving priority either to industrial reality, as Comte did, or to the capitalist reality, as Marx did, he gave priority to the democratic reality" (Aron 1969: 183). For him, the political was always an autonomous dimension of social life. The mode of concentration or dispersion of political power and the relation of such concentration or dispersion to freedom and liberty were the key elements of his analysis. For him, political institutions and processes were not mere reflections of the industrial base or capitalist relations. They are independent spheres of human action and also a dimension for evaluation of different societal types.

Aron can be rightly called a great liberal of modern sociology. For him, liberty and reason were not abstract concepts, dogmas, or ideologies but the epitome of old republican virtues embedded in social institutions. Ideologies, the "opium of the intellectuals," were the perversion of the spirit of reason and liberty, and they constituted the greatest threat to the institutions on which these great virtues are based. In that sense, Aron is one of the last great sociologists of the Enlightenment, although without the naïve belief in endless progress, as demonstrated in *Progress and Disillusion* (1968).

SEE ALSO: Communism; Ideology; Marxism and Sociology; Tocqueville, Alexis de; Totalitarianism; Weber, Max

REFERENCES AND SUGGESTED READINGS

Anderson, C. B. (1999) *Raymond Aron: The Recovery of the Political*. Rowman & Littlefield, Lanham, MD.
Aron, R. (1957 [1935]) *German Sociology*. Trans. M. & T. Bottomore. Heinemann, London.
Aron, R. (1969) *Main Currents in Sociological Thought*, Vol. 1. Penguin, New York.
Aron, R. (1978) Introduction. In Conant, M. B. (Ed.), *Politics and History: Selected Essays by Raymond Aron*. Free Press, New York.
Colquhoun, R. (1986) *Raymond Aron*. Vol. 1: *The Philosopher in History*. Vol. 2: *The Sociologist in Society*. Sage, Newbury Park, CA.
Dahrendorf, R. (1989) The Achievement of Raymond Aron. *Encounter* (May): 29–35.
Gurvitch, G. & Moore, W. E. (1945) *Twentieth-Century Sociology*. Philosophical Library, New York.

art worlds

Diana Crane

One of the most influential ideas in the sociology of art, the concept of an art world provides the basis for a sociological orientation for understanding the arts, in contrast to artist-centered approaches favored in other disciplines. Art worlds have both social and cultural components. The concept of an art world implies that art is a collective activity, rather than the product of solitary genius. The cultural bases for cooperation among actors in art worlds are shared commitments to artistic conventions that define what is considered to be art in a specific period and how it should be produced.

The production and distribution of art in art worlds is characterized by an extensive division of labor. Many people who do not define themselves as artists provide some essential material or service that is required for the creation or dissemination of artworks. A partial list of occupations on which painters depend include manufacturers of painting equipment, art dealers, art collectors, museum curators, critics, aestheticians, state bureaucrats, members of the public, and other painters. Placing the artist in the context of an art world demystifies art and artistic genius because it reveals that the creative process is similar for major and minor artists. The process of creating an artwork is not confined to activities that take place in an artist's studio but involves a variety of opportunities and constraints that are shaped by the nature of the social organization of the art world to which the artist belongs.

This approach rejects the conventional analysis of meaning in artworks, based on an evaluation of their social or aesthetic significance. Artworks are not interpreted as reflecting or commenting on social life. Instead, the meanings of artworks are embodied in the conventions that are used to create them. The formulation of aesthetic judgments by sociologists of art is not acceptable. Aesthetic assessments are part of the collective activity of art worlds. Through their interactions with one another, artists develop shared agreements about the worth of the works they are creating.

The concept of an art world was defined and extensively analyzed by Howard Becker, using a wide range of materials drawn from many different types of art, both popular and elite. The publication of his book *Art Worlds* in 1982 marked the beginning of a renewed interest among American sociologists in the sociology of art. The concept is powerful because it can be applied to many different types of creative activities, ranging from the plastic arts, literature, music, photography, and fashion, to culture industries such as film, television, and popular music. Issues related to different aspects of art worlds that sociologists have explored and debated in the past two decades include the following.

Culture creators and support personnel. Becker identified four categories of artists, each of whom had a different relationship with contemporary art worlds: integrated professionals, mavericks, folk artists, and naïve artists. Artists who belong to art worlds are "integrated professionals." They are confronted with similar types of constraints and opportunities, which affect their access to resources for making art. Artists who are not "integrated professionals" are relegated to the margins of the art world. Mavericks generally begin their careers in conventional art worlds but, because of their commitment to types of innovations that are too radical for members of those art worlds to accept, they withdraw from those social networks and lose the types of support they provide. By contrast, folk artists are not members of conventional art worlds and do not think of themselves as artists producing artworks. Instead they generally belong to local communities of people engaged in the same type of activity. Becker uses the example of quilting as performed by housewives in farm communities. Finally, naïve artists have also had no contact with conventional art worlds and no artistic training but tend to work by themselves. Some of their works resemble certain types of conventional painting while others are virtually unique.

A number of studies have attempted to show how "outsider" artists working in non-elite art worlds are similar to or different from "integrated professionals." Finney (1997) suggests that, given the multiplicity of art worlds today, the terms "insider" and "outsider" are relative. For the individual, the definition of insider and outsider depends on her location in a particular art world. For those who take a larger perspective, the terms are inherently unstable, shifting over time in response to sociological, cultural, and aesthetic trends.

Conventions or shared understandings of what cultural works should be like. Becker approaches the meaning of artworks through an analysis of the conventions on which they are based. For example, he contrasts the artist's conventions with those of the craftsperson. The conventions embodied in art objects are lack of utility, absence of virtuosity, indifference to beauty, and uniqueness in the sense that the artist is constantly challenging and replacing conventions for specific forms of art and cherishes her autonomy in relation to collectors and dealers. The conventions of the craftsperson are exactly the opposite: uniformity in the production of series of objects, demonstration of skill in the creation of useful or beautiful objects, and fidelity to the client's demands. Failing to observe conventional procedures is a way for an artist to express her autonomy and freedom but it is likely to impede recognition. Breaking artistic conventions often disturbs an artist's relationships with other actors in the art world and with the public. Familiarity with conventions is an important indicator of differences among art publics as well.

Organizations in which artworks are displayed, performed, or produced. Three types of organizations that perform important roles in the production of artworks have been identified (Gilmore 1987). Small organizations embedded in social networks of artists provide settings for continuous feedback among creators and between creators, critics, and audiences. This seems to be especially conducive for the creation of works that are either aesthetically original or ideologically provocative or both. Small profit-oriented businesses encourage artists to produce works that are pleasing and profitable. Non-profit organizations tend to emphasize the preservation of existing artistic traditions rather than the creation of new ones. Funds from federal, state, and local governments that contributed to the support and expansion of the organizational infrastructure of avant-garde art worlds have greatly diminished, with negative consequences for the continued production of this type of art (Pagani 2001).

Gatekeepers, who evaluate cultural works. To sell their work and extend their influence beyond the confines of their immediate social networks, creators must obtain a nucleus of supporters or a "constituency" in the art world or on its periphery. In the case of the artist, this is usually drawn from art galleries, museums, art journals, collectors, and corporations. Three models of the gatekeeping process have been proposed: objective appraisal in terms of existing aesthetic criteria, cultural persuasion based on the development of new aesthetic criteria, and social influence in which success is engineered through personal influence and the availability of material resources (Mulkay & Chaplin 1982). Studies of artistic careers indicate that the first model, which Becker calls "the conventional theory of reputation," is least likely to explain artistic success (Finney 1997).

Audiences. Becker differentiates between serious and occasional audiences on the basis of how much they know about the nature of artistic conventions, about how they are being used, and about how they are changing at a particular time. People's experience of art is strongly influenced by their awareness and understanding of the conventions on which it is based. The values they express in their judgments about art reflect their level of understanding of artistic conventions.

Characteristics of potential audiences are a major factor in determining what types of cultural works are displayed, performed, or sold in a particular urban setting. Artworks produced in different types of organizational contexts vary depending on the social class of the audiences that typically consume them (Crane 1992). Cultural products directed at audiences drawn primarily from the middle or upper class tend to be defined as "high culture," while those aimed at minority or lower-class groups tend to be defined as ethnic or popular culture.

Comparisons of art worlds. Many studies have examined how art worlds vary within cities, in large as compared to small cities, in different countries, and in elite and non-elite art forms. Implicitly or explicitly, the avant-garde art world in New York is generally used as the exemplar against which other types of creative activities are compared. For example, studies of non-elite art worlds generally show that they include some but not all aspects of the components of elite art worlds.

Critiques and new directions. Becker's analysis of how an art world operates is central to our understanding of the production of culture but it has been criticized for overemphasizing the social and organizational aspects of artistic creation, for reducing elite arts to the status of non-elite arts, and for neglecting the impact of social and political institutions. Others claim that its treatment of aesthetic issues and meaning is superficial. In its original form, this approach emphasized consensus, cooperation, and coordination in art worlds rather than conflicts among artists and other actors who control material and symbolic resources. This orientation discouraged attention to artistic controversies, as well as ideological and political aspects of the arts.

For some observers, the weaknesses in Becker's concept of an art world are the strengths of Bourdieu's (1993) concept of a cultural field. While both concepts are designed to characterize the relationship between creators and their social environments, Bourdieu's approach emphasizes the opposition between elite and non-elite arts, their connections with social class, and their ideological and aesthetic foundations. Recent work is moving toward a synthesis of the two approaches, including a conceptualization of the aesthetic and ideological foundations of the arts that overcomes the limitations of an approach based mainly on artistic conventions.

Methods. Studies of art worlds have generally been based on interviews and ethnographic research. Following Becker, researchers have tended to interpret their data by constructing typologies of different types of artists or of activities related to the production and dissemination of art. The focus of most studies has been on the activities of small groups of creators, small organizations involved in display, performance, or dissemination of artworks in urban settings, and the publics for these works. The concept has been less useful for understanding cultural production in large organizations located in cultural industries, where creators are faced with different types of pressures and rewards.

SEE ALSO: Culture; Culture, Production of

REFERENCES AND SUGGESTED READINGS

Alexander, V. (2003) *Sociology of the Arts: Exploring Fine and Popular Forms.* Blackwell, Malden, MA.

Becker, H. (1982) *Art Worlds.* University of California Press, Berkeley.

Bourdieu, P. (1993) *The Field of Cultural Production.* Columbia University Press, New York.

Crane, D. (1992) *The Production of Culture: Media and Urban Arts.* Sage, Newbury Park, ch. 6.

Finney, H. C. (1997) Art Production and Artists' Careers: The Transition from "Outside" to "Inside." In: Zolberg, V. L. & Cherbo, J. M. (Eds.), *Outsider Art: Contesting Boundaries in Contemporary Culture.* Cambridge University Press, Cambridge.

Gilmore, S. (1987) Coordination and Convention: The Organization of the Concert World. *Symbolic Interaction* 10: 209–27.

Mulkay, M. & Chaplin, E. (1982) Aesthetics and the Artistic Career: A Study of Anomie in Fine-Art Painting. *Sociological Quarterly* 23: 117–38.

Pagani, J. (2001) Mixing Art and Life: The Conundrum of the Avant-Garde's Autonomous Status in the Performance Art World of Los Angeles. *Sociological Quarterly* 42: 175–203.

'asabiyya

Georg Stauth

'Asabiyya (of Beduin, pre-Islamic, secular origin: from *'asaba,* to bind, to fold, to wind, and *'asâba,* the group of male relatives) is one of the most important concepts of the social history of the Arabs and of Islam. Meaning a basic form of social and material human relations, it is a concept which integrates biological, geographical, social, and cultural terms. It is central to Ibn Khaldun's (1332–1406) theory of civilization ('umran), as discussed in his famous *Muqaddima* (Ibn Khaldun 1967, I: 269–8, 313–27). *'Asabiyya* became one of the most daring sociological concepts. Today, it is of importance with respect to global issues and intracultural discourse between Islam and the West and about the "heritage" of political structures in Muslim societies.

Rosenthal's (1932) translation of the *Muqadimma* reads *'asabiyya* in mere terms of "group feeling." Diverse French and German translations use "esprit de corps," "idea of nationhood," "cohesiveness," or "solidarity" among segmentary tribal or nomadic groups. Schimmel (1951) would refrain from translating it at all. A complex reading associates *'asabiyya* not only with group solidarity but also with the striving for sovereignty within and among tribal or family groups. In this sense, *'asabiyya* also means strong societal effects of solidarity determining the vitality of dynastic or state institutions. In fact, *'asabiyya* could be referred to merely in terms of sociopolitical vitality, not only with respect to the condition of states (nomadism, urbanism), but also to the foundation and expansion of religious doctrine, and of knowledge, rationality, and science. In its most abstract and absolute sense *'asabiyya* seems to be identical with "power," including the reflection of the social sources of power formation (Simon 1959: 48 ff.).

Durkheim, with his concept of mechanical solidarity, seems to have considered the *'asabiyya* problematic. He departed from the classical view on societal formation and in contrast to Hobbes's self-interest and the respective approaches on individualism, he focused on "solidarity." He seems to have been influenced by Ibn Khaldun in this. A well-debated French translation of Ibn Khaldun's *Muqaddima* by W. M.-G. de Slane (Paris 1862–8) existed in Durkheim's lifetime. Taha Hussayn, the influential Egyptian nationalist philosopher, was a student of Durkheim's in Paris. He submitted his dissertation, however, as late as in 1917, the year when Durkheim died (Hussein 1917). *'Asabiyya* is a theorem about the irreducibility of the social which resembles Durkheim's thesis of the community as the prior element of the social. Without any doubt, it is through Durkheim that the concept of *'asabiyya* gained new importance both in Middle Eastern as well as in western sociology.

In Ibn Khaldun's "sociological studies" – "antedating modern European sociology by more than four centuries" (Grunebaum 1953: 339) – *'asabiyya* is central to his cyclical model of civilizational construction. Modern sociologists depended on the metaphorical and structural translations of his formula, specifically with respect to the "Community–Society" (*Gemeinschaft–Gesellschaft*) divide in twentieth-century social theory. "*'Asabiyya* is a sociopolitical structure which marks the transition from classless to a class society. The tribal aristocracy holds power only in so far as it is still integrated into egalitarian structures" (Lacoste 1984: 116).

'Asabiyya stands at the center of an empirical foundation of a general cyclical law inherent in processes of civilization. It includes a specific concept of social dynamism: tribal solidarity is the motor of renewing bloodless urban structures and institutions. Since nomads in general are people of desert lands and countryside, marginals in the real sense, sociology often understood *'asabiyya* wrongly as a pure concept of social cohesion of tribal or local communities and similarly Islam as the religion of communal holism and static societies. Starting from this angle and neglecting the urban sources of Islam and the urban inclinations of *'asabiyya* would mean giving little justice to Ibn Khaldun's civilizational theory and the fundamental position of *'asabiyya* in it. Ibn Khaldun was the first to explain history and to take social development as the subject of theoretical consideration.

From there, *'asabiyya* is involved in a type of rationality which in its reference to the broadest real institutional and visionary expansions remains tied to concerns of family and local group relations and their inherent genealogical sense; not preventing any type of functional-technical rationality, however, but subsuming it to solidarity of (male) groups and the genealogy of blood-ties and vitality.

'Asabiyya, in its conceptual generality, incorporates a variety of fields of social construction which renders it an ambiguous and paradoxical concept in the global field of sociology today. First, *'asabiyya* appears as the very secular foundation of social dynamics between (tribal) egalitarianism and (dynastic) power construction. This denotes an ambiguous field of tension between solidarity and power. The concept is grounded in egalitarian kinship and brotherhood relationships, in which the extent of social cohesion becomes largely dependent on solidarity sentiments, "group feeling," and socio-ecological conditions. The existence of the social group and its organization, *'asaba*, is the material social condition of *'asabiyya*. In this sense, *'asabiyya* also appears as an abstracted idea of solidarity groupings within fragmented strata of urban civilization, as well as of military, political, and religious "chieftaincies whose composition varies greatly" (Lapidus 1990). On the other hand, Ibn Khaldun understands *'asabiyya* in general as the moving force in social development; in a way, as an absolute turning point for gaining superiority of men, tribes, and nations over others, it moves towards kingship. Lack of *'asabiyya* leads to loss of power. For Ibn Khaldun, the dialectics of "solidarity and kingship continue to be essential for the formation and sustenance of all political regimes" (Mahdi 1957: 198). More specifically, Ibn Khaldun distinguishes components of order and continuity and the effects of growing social differentiation. Kinship and group solidarity – whether real or imagined – support the sustenance of life. State power in its various forms depends largely on securing and reflecting immediate social ties of life sustenance. It is important to trace with *'asabiyya* a kernel of a theory of "bio-politics," state power moving from abstracted ideas of territorial control to genealogy, nutrition, and

strength of the population. In this sense, 'asabiyya puts into the forefront of power construction a category which is at the center of the modern discourse of power: the sustenance, flourishing, and encapsulating of "naked life" (Agamben, Foucault) – here, of course, in the sense of a collective body.

In fact, 'asabiyya relates to a sociopolitical concept of vitality of populations and their inherent institutional bondage. In this context, to describe 'asabiyya and nomadism in terms of vitality of marginal "collective bodies" and their potential to create equivalents to organized "war-machines" (Deleuze & Guattari 1992) is interesting and reminds us of Foucault's similar description of the mass movements of the Iranian Revolution.

Second, 'asabiyya, although secular in its base, remains a concept which is strongly involved in religious constructions of the social: group solidarity needs to be underscored by religion. The dialectic of 'asabiyya and religion unfolds its regime in that religion extends and intensifies the power of 'asabiyya-groups on the one hand while, on the other, there is no flourishing of religion without 'asabiyya. Prophecy and Mahdism would not be possible without 'asabiyya support. However, 'asabiyya-based tribal groups can only gain and maintain dynastic power with the support of religious propaganda (Ibn Khaldun 1967, I: 320).

When Ibn Khaldun speaks of religion and 'asabiyya, what counts is the holistic sense of the theocracy of the state; individual or group piety or enhancement for the transcendental world are not the essential elements here. That is what makes his perspective so strange among medieval thinkers: he delivers an objective evaluation of the social significance of religion and religious law; in fact, a functionalist concept of both: religion and solidarity.

Third, there is the dimension of charisma in Ibn Khaldun's concept of 'asabiyya. Social, political, and economic energy derive from blood-relation and the genealogical foundation of the individual's status within the line of such relationships. This is the paradox: 'asabiyya – despite its bondage to the social as such – also relates to individualist power constructions in the specific terms of kingship and prophetism. Here, obviously, we may

trace a very special characteristic of charisma, in that it roots in the (tribal) genealogy of blood-ties as a "natural gift," but even more as a means of securing social support, while individual charisma appears to be only a function to this general social condition of charisma. Creative power and vitality depend on the group and its genealogy and the maintenance of its energy over generations with respect to social, political, and economic achievements. The blood-relation and the genealogical formation of blood-ties and thus the individual's status within such a line of relationships form a decisive foundational basis for any concept of charisma. In contrast to Weber's individualist explanation of charisma (depending on the "gifts" of the individual and personal extraordinariness), it is the "social fact" of the genealogy of the kin-group that founds the formative aspect of all social movement.

'Asabiyya as a concept of dynamism differs from Weber's idea of charisma, for Weber's idea depends on an individualistic transcendental absolutism. He sees the inner strength of the individual, its drives, its extraordinary abilities and their routinization as a source and an essential condition for modern bureaucratism and professionalism. In contrast, 'asabiyya represents a sort of communal totalism based on genealogy and descent. What is of a broader interest with respect to social theory is that 'asabiyya as a source of charisma relates in a very ambiguous sense to immediacy, bondage to face-to-face relations, human solidarity instincts and their effects on power and state formation. This seems to contrast concepts like restraint and rationality, modulation of affects, civilization or general regulation and bureaucracy. In this anthropological perspective, the actively thriving human group tends to absorb the social sphere of regulating institutions, and everything melts within 'asabiyya – not the other way around, as Gehlen and Luhmann would have it (if one takes their system–lifeworld dichotomy in this context).

Thus, 'asabiyya can be discussed beyond the spirit of social cohesion, beyond the prevailing local family or group networks, in terms of a specific type of rationality; namely, causal rationality, which operates in a controlled social field in which cause and effect, success and defeat remain visible. However, at the same time, the system of visible causal rationality seems to be not only coexistent within functionally differentiated systems, but also it tends to make use of it and to profit from it. In this condition, *'asabiyya* signifies that any input-raising into the rational func-tional system would also lead to a test of its effectiveness in keeping up with local perso-nalized networks. This would not lead to any strategic gain on both sides. The strategic gain of *'asabiyya* in this figure of thought would lie in immediate controlling of causes and effects. *'Asabiyya* is quite in agreement with ontologi-cal theories about the clash of systems of functional-technical causality with prevailing family and mafia structures in Southern Italy that Luhmann (1995) described. Indeed, to view *'asabiyya* in terms of Luhmann's South–North dimension is helpful, as it would come close to imagining modern culture as a deterritorialized arena combining latent east-ern and western structures based on discrete patterns of vitality without engaging in an open clash about fundamentals and value.

Fourth, and beyond the three paradoxes of *'asabiyya* in relation to egalitarianism/power, solidarity/religion, and individual charisma/group, genealogy, and causal rationality, there seems to be a further dimension of sociological concern with *'asabiyya* in the way in which it relates to knowledge and professional groups. In a strange turn of the sociological proble-matic of *Gemeinschaft* – similar to Machiavelli's *virtù* – there is a momentum which crystal-lizes in its intensity and situational expression as an "emotional component" in intersubjec-tive relations and collective experience with respect to the construction of knowledge. *'Asabiyya* appears here as a multi-layered con-cept, including faithfulness to the community, will for defense, readiness for self-sacrifice, internal unity, common will for power, and national passion, but also religious fanaticism: "feeling of solidarity" as a source of knowl-edge and vice versa. In this sense, *'asabiyya* turns into an abstracted concept, which seems also ethically overcharged.

'Asabiyya here also turns into an idea of the solidarity of the "finer natures," "two friends," the "warm feeling of friendship," solidarity among immediate social groups,

which also operate in modern social and pro-fessional life up to national and religious soli-darity circles (Ritter 1948). Following this elitist transposition of the concept, *'asabiyya* could also relate to modern types of socially constituted solidarity, designating "a true irra-tional solidarity circle" within a modern uni-versalist perspective. Athough it is considered that *'asabiyya* could generate the negative effects of delimiting a general, universal value to the strict borderlines of a social group, the readiness of group members to help and sacri-fice themselves without expecting any return, generating true altruism, should be stressed. However, restricted to group solidarity, help and sacrifice can ignore injustice and create double moral codes leading to separate inter-nal and external application of rules (ibid.).

The positive emotional values and intensi-ties of feeling within the solidarity circles could potentially lead to fanaticism and the loss of the objective value of things. Again, positive inner-group feelings could lead to coolness, indifference, enmity, hatred, and moments of pitiless behavior toward outsiders. There is no external validity of morals and the solidarity circle has moral boundaries (ibid.).

'Asabiyya describes the friend–enemy, insi-der–outsider valuation that irrational solidarity groups apply to moral values, which on the other hand leads to dividing good from evil, just from unjust, in a way that may turn out to be a great obstacle for objective knowledge.

Solidarity presents itself in varying degrees of strength, which could turn into aggression, feud, and war. When Ritter (1948) points to the Arabs and Islam, to the leadership of Muhammad and Umar in organizing the Islamic conquests, he speaks of pure solidarity, not of irrational solidarity groups. However, he shows that solidarity, despite its legitimate function, often appears to be intermingled with less noble motives. "Interests" enter, where pure emotions are rare in real life.

In this sense, the feeling of solidarity comes about in practical life, through blood relation-ship, face-to-face social interaction and reci-procal testing and trying, through common occupations and neighborhoods. A higher *'asabiyya* points to the common education solidarities, or breakthrough solidarities tying the founder-generations together versus the superficial solidarities of later strands (maintaining good relations for selfish purposes) (ibid.). This "orientalist" transposition of *'asabiyya* into a universalist outlook, as the momentum of western "irrational solidarity groups" – mirrored within a framework of Islamic history as worked out by Ayad (1930) and Rosenthal (1932) and showing similarities with Machiavelli's concept of *virtù* – is based on reflections on European history and disasters, specifically World War II.

In a very specific interpretation of *'asabiyya* and religion, the "Ibn Khaldunian mode" has recently received new attention with respect to interpreting Saudi Wahabism and Islamic movements. Lapidus's (1990) warning, that conquest movements which "represented a fusion of clan, religious, and political identities rather than lineage *'asabiyya*" were the driving force in the Islamization of the Greater Middle East, seems to support such a perspective. This would lead to a reinterpretation of contemporary Muslim society in terms of varying expressions and combinations of *'asabiyya*, sectarian movements, and tribal utopianism. Gellner's reading of *'asabiyya* as interacting with a learned urban elite, pedantic scripturalist and urban classes to be muted by desert utopianism and *'asabiyya*-based tribal segments (Zubaida 1995) could be viewed as a first stage in this perspective. For Gellner (1981), it is the coincidence of tribal movements and urban Islamic spirituality that strengthens the position of civil society in Muslim countries. For Gellner, this relative strength of civil society founded on the merging of Islam and tribal solidarity patterns, together with the gradual transformation of oriental despotism and the growth of modern institutions, was to lay the ground for a strong and real pattern of modernity in Middle Eastern societies. This is Islamic utopia, which in this context puts Ibn Khaldun's treatment of religion in a position of increasing importance. However, much of the debate on Islamic civil society, with its often essentialist concepts of civil or public religion, stands in contrast to Ibn Khaldun, for whom religion is instrumental to broadening the social effects of tribal (secular) solidarity and *'asabiyya*. For Ibn Khaldun, religion is secondary to power, it is functional to power; however, it is dependent on power.

Recent theory exploits this Khaldunian split between *'asabiyya* and religion. Gellner defined the dynamism of Islamic society in terms of the decline of tribalism and therefore insisted that *'asabiyya* comes to be substituted by the religious ethos of urban educated classes challenging secular power. For Gellner, this forms the historical background to the current surge of Islamism in politics. Eisenstadt (2002) departs from a fundamental concept of "separation between the religious community and the ruler" in Islamic societies. He perceives *'asabiyya* as the case of tribal religious protofundamentalism in traditional Islam. In insisting on an inherent entwinement between *'asabiyya* and religion, Eisenstadt believes that it is this tribal-religious element which cyclically transforms society and creates new political regimes (Voll 1991).

This inner connection between tribal elements and Islamic religious political visions – presenting the "symbol of pristine Islam" – is seen here as the inherent model of Islamic societies where primordial Islamic utopia gives rise to patrimonial or imperial regimes, establishing anew the "'old' Ibn Khaldun cycle" (Eisenstadt 2005). Thus, the antinomies of Ibn Khaldun's theory of *'asabiyya* have been explained as an essential, undeniable, and authentic trait of the social dynamic in Islamic societies; where one sees some modernist elements implanted, however, all explanations of recent social unrest on a world scale related to Islam seem to have caught sight of an involuted "tradition" of cultural specificity in the "Khaldunian sense" of cyclical revolt (Ruthven 2002) and tribal utopianism (Eisenstadt 2002).

Indeed, Ibn Khaldun's stand is ambiguous. On the one hand, he considers the solidarity of kin (*'asabiyya*) to be the basis for the spread of religion, and on the other hand, he sees the prophetic tradition of Islam as the real monotheistic religion, functioning to broaden solidarity among kin-groups. In this, however, Ibn Khaldun provides for the clear distinction between *'asabiyya* and religion as two different fields of social contention.

A comparative analysis of modern societies would obviously have to deal with the more general and enlightening global issues of *'asabiyya*, East and West, with respect to rationality, knowledge, and science as much as with its impact on relations between state and society, with respect to individualism, sovereignty, and "naked life" and their varying social and jurido-political expressions.

SEE ALSO: Agency (and Intention); Body and Cultural Sociology; Civil Religion; Islam; Khaldun, Ibn; Religion

REFERENCES AND SUGGESTED READINGS

Ayad, M. K. (1930) *Die Geschichts- und Gesellschaftslehre Ibn Halduns*. Forschungen zur Geschichts- und Gesellschaftslehre, Stuttgart.

Deleuze, G. & Guattari, F. (1992) *Tausend Plateaus. Kapitalismus und Schizophrenie. Aus dem Französischen übersetzt von Gabriele Ricke und Ronald Voullié*. Merve Verlag, Berlin.

Durkheim, É. (1992 [1933]) *Über soziale Arbeitsteilung. Studie über die Organisation höherer Gesellschaften*. Suhrkamp-Verlag, Frankfurt am Main.

Eisenstadt, S. N. (2002) Concluding Remarks: Public Sphere, Civil Society, and Political Dynamics in Islamic Societies. In: Hoexter, M., Eisenstadt, S. N., & Levtzion, N. (Eds.), *The Public Sphere in Muslim Societies*. State University of New York, Albany, pp. 139–61.

Eisenstadt, S. N. (2005) Culture and Power – A Comparative Civilizational Analysis. *EWE* 1–14.

Gellner, E. (1981) *Muslim Society*. Cambridge University Press, Cambridge.

Grunebaum, G. E. von (1953) *Medieval Islam: A Vital Study of Islam at Its Zenith*, 2nd edn. University of Chicago Press, Chicago.

Hussein, T. (1917) *Étude analytique et critique de la philosophie sociale d'Ibn Khaldoun*. Dissertation, Paris.

Ibn Khaldun (1967) *The Muqaddimah: An Introduction to History*, 3 vols. Trans. F. Rosenthal. Routledge & Kegan Paul, London.

Lacoste, I. (1984) *Ibn Khaldun: The Birth of History and the Past of the Third World*. Verso, London.

Lapidus, I. (1990) Tribes and State Formation in Islamic History. In: Khoury, P. S. & Kostiner, J. (Eds.), *Tribes and State Formation in the Middle East*. University of California Press, Berkeley, pp. 25–47.

Luhmann, N. (1995) Kausalität im Süden. *Soziale Systeme* 1: S7–28.

Mahdi, M. (1957) *Ibn Khaldun's Philosophy of History*. George Allen & Unwin, London.

Ritter, H. (1948) Irrational Solidarity Groups: A Socio-Psychological Study in Connection with Ibn Khaldun. *Oriens* 1: 1–44.

Rosenthal, E. (1932) *Ibn Khalduns Gedanken über den Staat. Ein Beitrag zur Geschichte der mittelalterlichen Staatslehre*. Beiheft 25 der Historischen Zeitschrift, Berlin.

Ruthven, M. (2002) The Eleventh of September and the Sudanese Mahdiya in the Context of Ibn Khaldun's Theory of Islamic History. *International Affairs* 78(2): 339–51.

Schimmel, A. (1951) *Ibn Chaldun. Ausgewählte Abschnitte aus der Muqaddima. Aus dem Arabischen von Annemarie Schimmel*. J. C. Mohr (Paul Siebeck), Tübingen.

Simon, H. (1959) *Ibn Khalduns Wissenschaft von der menschlichen Kultur*. VEB Otto Harrassowitz, Leipzig.

Tönnies, F. (1970 [1935]) *Gemeinschaft und Gesellschaft. Grundbegriffe der reinen Soziologie*. Wissenschaftliche Buchgesellschaft, Darmstadt.

Voll, J. (1991) Fundamentalism in the Sunni Arab World: Egypt and the Sudan. In: Murray, M. and Appleby, R. S. (Eds.), *Fundamentalism Observed*. University of Chicago Press, Chicago, pp. 345–403.

Zubaida, S. (1995) Is There a Muslim Society? Ernest Gellner's Sociology of Islam. *Economy and Society* 24(2): 151–88.

asceticism

Giuseppe Giordan

The concept of asceticism shows the unity of efforts through which an individual desires to progress in his moral, religious, and spiritual life. The original meaning of the term refers to any exercise, physical, intellectual, or moral, practiced with method and rigor, in hopes of self-improvement and progress. Notwithstanding the great flexibility that characterizes the application of asceticism, the concept always alludes to a search for perfection based on the submission of the body to the spirit, recalling the symbolic distinction between exterior and interior life.

Following the evolution of the concept of asceticism within different historical and social contexts, it is possible to see its strategic importance within the social sciences, especially in regard to understanding the western world. Aside from the combination of physical and intellectual exercises, which have always had their own social relevance, asceticism refers to the complex relationship between nature and culture, as well as to the classic religious relationship between faith and reason; such aspects are the fruit of a continual and dynamic negotiation that develops within concrete social and cultural contexts.

THE HISTORICAL ASPECTS

A comprehensive look at the historical evolution of the concept of asceticism allows for a description of what one refers to when using the term. Etymologically, the term comes from Greek and it was Homer who used it only to describe artistic technique and production. Herodotus and Thucydides used the term in reference to physical exercises and effort undertaken by athletes and soldiers in order to keep their bodies fit. Coupled with this physical aspect of asceticism is the moral dimension, where a constant and prolonged effort is what leads intellect to wisdom and virtue. The methodical training of the spirit, which was celebrated by nearly all classical philosophers, involves the progressive liberation of the soul from the body, which was considered bad and deviant.

It is with the Pythagoreans that the concept of asceticism is used in a specifically religious sphere, referring to the perfecting exercises the soul undertakes in order to deserve the contemplation of God. Already in the classical world the concept had pieced together the physical with moral and religious dimensions: exercising the body, controlling the passions, mortification through abstinence and renunciation, and good works were considered subsequent stages that educated the virtuous man.

In early Christianity, all the above elements were interpreted and organized in a coherent manner. Especially within monastic life, almost as if to substitute the bloody sacrifices of the early martyrs, penance and asceticism become necessary to win the struggle against sin and to gain particular graces from God.

Perceived in this manner, Christian life becomes an austere struggle that combines suffering and renunciation in a continual effort to overcome temptations of the flesh. Just such control of the instincts, and sometimes even of the legitimate inclinations of desires, marks the particular relationship that the ascetic has with his own body. Besides poverty and obedience, in the first centuries of Christian life chastity was advised, which sometimes manifested itself in extreme forms of radical hostility toward sexuality. Aside from corporal mortification, especially within the Benedictine and Cistercian traditions, work, silence, and prayer together with fasting and vigils were characteristic elements of asceticism.

In the Middle Ages, ascetic practices left the monasteries to involve groups of laypeople, who, imitating the great religious orders such as the Dominicans or Franciscans, came together to give birth to the Third Orders. Asceticism in this period became further refined, developing new methods designed to perfect the exercises of the spiritual life. Among these a special place was devoted to mental prayers, which included the continual repetition of simple prayer formulas such as the rosary or brief invocations to the saints. Together with the repetition of oral formulas were repeated exterior acts of veneration, such as genuflection, often practiced with a deep penitential spirit, and the use of the hair shirt and other means of mortification.

ASCETICISM AND MYSTICISM

With the advent of the modern era, especially with the Reformation, a radical critique of asceticism as it was conceived in the Middle Ages can be found. However, Luther's doctrine of justification, which denied the worthiness of human efforts to obtain salvation, did not lead to ethical and moral indifference. The Reformation promoted a new understanding of asceticism, which changed from physical discipline and was manifested in the workplace, married life, respect for parents, and the undertaking of political responsibilities, obviously alongside prayer and meditation on the Bible. Max Weber (1958) discusses

Protestant ethics in terms of this worldly asceticism and considers modern capitalism as an expression of the Puritan Calvinist mentality.

Even Catholics realized the excessiveness and the risks of an indiscriminate application of asceticism. The Church warned against excesses, distancing itself from the most gruesome and inhumane practices. Even in the theological field a new sensitivity developed, which, notwithstanding the necessity of human effort, stressed the preeminence of God's actions. What was important was not human actions but passive human acceptance of the works of the Spirit. The excessive willingness of asceticism was replaced by a mystical attitude that valued physicality, affections, and the emotions of the person, thus overriding an openly dualistic and often Manichean vision. However, asceticism and mysticism were not to be considered as being opposed to one another, but as two aspects of the same spiritual journey. Especially from modern times on, this journey did not privilege mortification of the body and the passions but underlined the importance of the individual's harmonious development, in both physical and spiritual dimensions. Starting from renunciation for its own sake, there is a movement from a choice that is functional toward the fulfillment of a more harmonious and balanced personality.

THE SOCIOLOGICAL APPROACH

The founding fathers of sociology showed great interest in both asceticism and mysticism, above all particular forms of religious cohesion that developed from these two experiences throughout the centuries. Interest in these issues remains alive even in the contemporary world, and sociologists find it not only within new religious experiences but also in connection with different fields such as caring for the body or political activism.

Max Weber contrasts asceticism and mysticism, specifying that the former considers salvation as the result of human actions in the world, while the latter refers to a particular state of enlightenment, which is reached only by a few select people through contemplation. While asceticism calls people to actively dedicate themselves in the world to incarnate the religious values in it, in the mystical perspective the world loses importance in order to give way to a union with God. The logic of mysticism is to run away from the world, while the logic of asceticism has a belligerent attitude toward the world full of sin. Weber points out how asceticism is a broad and, in certain aspects, ambiguous sociological category. On the one hand, it means the systematic and methodological effort to subordinate natural and worldly instincts to religious principles. On the other hand, it refers to the religious criticism of the often utilitarian and conventional relationships of social life. Therefore, it is possible to distinguish two different forms of asceticism. One is founded on a highly negative perception of the world. The second considers the world as God's creation. Even though the world is the place where humans can sin, it is also the concrete situation where the virtuous person fulfills his vocation with a rational method. According to the second definition of asceticism, the individual, in order to find confirmation of his own state of grace and privilege, lives his existence in the world as if he were an instrument chosen by God.

Asceticism, when it is put into concrete practice in the life of a religious group, as is the case with Calvinism or in the various Protestant sects, can become a forcefully dynamic element of social and cultural transformation, instigating reform or revolutionary movements. Starting from the distinction between asceticism and mysticism, Weber points out the difference between western and eastern religions. Even though it is not a strict contrast, eastern religions rely on mysticism, while western religions are centered on ascetic ideals and ethics. This does not mean that in western Christianity there are no mystical experiences, especially within the Catholic sphere, which determine ascetic practices that reinforce the authority of the hierarchical Church. Jean Séguy (1968) hypothesizes that in Catholicism, the sociological category of mysticism is often functional in order to affirm obedience as a virtue, and, therefore, intended as asceticism.

Reworking Weber's distinction between the Church and the various sects, Ernst Troeltsch

(1992) uses the concept of asceticism to verify the plausibility of each part. With such a goal in mind, he proposes a detailed analysis of all the forms of Christian asceticism according to different historical periods, economic and social contexts, and types of religious groups. First, there is the heroic asceticism of the early Christians. Based on Christ's ethics more than on hostility toward the world, it consists of a feeling of indifference toward what is bound to disappear. It then follows that the definition of asceticism, based on Augustine's pessimistic view of the world, devalues the material world in comparison to the interior world, making it necessary to stop and or discipline the impulses of the flesh. Medieval Christianity sought to establish a compromise with mundane reality; while monks practiced fleeing from the world, laypeople had to accept its dynamics. Lutheranism successively proposed a secular asceticism that considered the effort of transforming the world as an instrument of continuous conversion, while Calvinism considered work and professional achievement as signs of divine election. Finally, within the sects, asceticism mainly became a renunciation of the world, expressed in various ways from indifference to hostility and resignation. Asceticism in this particular light is not the repression of the senses but, rather, a denial of established power.

ASCETICISM IN THE CONTEMPORARY WORLD

Far from disappearing, asceticism is present in the contemporary world, and not only in the context of oriental religious experiences such as some practices of Hinduism and Buddhism. While in a strictly religious sphere new forms of asceticism could be tantric practices or yoga, Deborah Lupton (1996) relates asceticism to the issue of food and awareness of the body, and Enzo Pace (1983) puts it in the context of political activism.

According to Lupton, in western cultures food and diet are interpreted in a dialectic that puts asceticism and hedonistic consumption as the two extremes. Eating, together with the corporeal experience, demands the continual exercise of self-discipline: such

ascetic practices of diet, besides having over the centuries a typically religious value, represent a means to build one's own subjectivity. Furthermore, as in religion ascetic renunciations are rewarded by God's grace, so self-control and self-denial with regard to food are rewarded by a healthy, slim, and fit body. Fitness, body building, and dieting would then be the ascetic practices of the contemporary era, where it is considered morally good to eliminate the need for bad or unhealthy food. Even today temptation of the flesh, considered as food and no longer as an entity opposed to the soul, must be energetically resisted through a rigorous dietetic asceticism.

Enzo Pace reflects on the relationship between religion and politics within the Italian context, with reference to the Democrazia Cristiana Party. He hypothesizes that the predominance of an ascetic attitude in the political arena, which characterized dissent in a few Catholic groups, was succeeded by a mysticism typical of charismatic movements, which separate their faith from any presence in society and politics to give space to the acts of the Spirit. Lay neo-asceticism promoted subjective adhesion to one's faith rather than objective membership of a specific institution: such subjective tension rediscovered the ethical religious basis of one's own choice founded on personal contact with the Bible, and therefore not controlled by an ecclesiastical institution. This form of political asceticism underlines the importance of social and political dedication, experienced in terms of Christian vocation, starting with workers and those in marginalized situations and poverty openly criticizing the progressive secularization of the Church, which made political compromises with the state party, Democrazia Cristiana. The interesting point of this hypothesis, which goes beyond the concrete Italian context, is that it shows that the worldly asceticism of political dedication permits interpretation of one's own political actions as being connected to the evangelical message of equality, justice, and solidarity, even if such religious identity is no longer perceived as directly dependent upon a religious institution that guarantees it.

Analyzing the role of asceticism in the Protestant sphere, Jean Séguy (1972) highlights that it is not necessarily connected to work ethics but can assume other modes of expression, such as giving up tobacco or alcohol, a particular way of dressing, the adornment of a place of worship, or decoration of one's home. Séguy's observations, integrating Weber's interpretive scheme, still leave open the inquiry on the role of asceticism in the modern world.

SEE ALSO: Body and Cultural Sociology; Buddhism; Christianity; Durkheim, Émile; Hinduism; Martyrdom; Popular Religiosity; Religion; Sexuality, Religion and; Weber, Max

REFERENCES AND SUGGESTED READINGS

Lupton, D. (1996) *Food, the Body and the Self.* Sage, London.
Pace, E. (1983) *Asceti e mistici in una società secolarizzata.* Marsilio, Venice.
Séguy, J. (1968) Ernst Troeltsch ou de l'essence de la religion à la typologie des christianismes. *Archives de Sociologie des Religions* 25: 3–11.
Séguy, J. (1972) Max Weber et la sociologie historique des religions. *Archives de Sociologie des Religions* 33: 71–104.
Troeltsch, E. (1992) *The Social Teachings of the Christian Churches,* 2 vols. John Knox Press, Louisville.
Weber, M. (1958) *The Protestant Ethic and the Spirit of Capitalism.* Charles Scribner's Sons, New York.
Weber, M. (1963) *The Sociology of Religion.* Beacon Press, Boston.

Asch experiments

William J. Kinney

Solomon Asch (1907–96) conducted pioneering social psychological experiments on conformity in group settings, and the processes by which we form impressions of other people. His conformity experiments are of particular importance, in that they displayed how the desire to conform to social pressures may be so great that it overrides our own perceptions. Asch emigrated from Poland to the United States in 1920, completed a PhD at Columbia University in 1932, and worked for 19 years as a faculty member at Swarthmore College. In addition to his seminal research on conformity and person perception, he wrote the classic text *Social Psychology* (1952). This text had a profound impact on the early development of the field.

Asch is primarily known for his experiments on conformity in group settings. In these experiments, college students were told that they were participating in a study on visual perception. The students (in groups of varying sizes, but usually ranging from seven to nine) were seated around a table, and shown a succession of "stimulus cards" with a series of lines on them. They were informed that their task was to match the length of a single line on a card displayed on an easel with one of three lines (labeled A, B, and C) displayed on a separate card. The experiment was structured so that the lengths of the three comparison lines varied to the extent that there was an extremely low probability of error. Students gave their answers aloud and responded in the order they were seated around the table.

In truth, this experiment was not designed to measure the students' visual perception. It was intended to measure the extent to which they would conform to group norms and perceptions, even when those norms/perceptions conflicted with their own interpretation of reality. In the primary version of this experiment, all of the students except one in each test group were in fact confederates in the study. The individual participant in each group was seated last, so that all other members of the group would give their verbal responses before the participant. At specific intervals, the confederates in the experiment were instructed to intentionally give identical answers that were clearly wrong. The participants were thus faced with the dilemma of providing a response that was correct based on their own perception, or a response that they personally believed was incorrect but that matched with the apparent perception of the entire group, excluding themselves.

Asch expected that the participants involved in the study would display a high level of independence from the influence of the group. The results of the study therefore came as somewhat of a surprise. About one third of the participants conformed to the group's incorrect answers in a majority of the trials, while about one fourth refused to conform in any of the trials. The rest of the participants conformed in some instances, though less than a majority. Of all the judgments made by all of the participants, approximately one third reflected conformity to the group (i.e., the answers were incorrect), while two thirds reflected independence from the group (i.e., the answers were correct). Though these findings do indeed indicate a higher incidence of independence than conformity, it must be kept in mind that the incidence of conformity constitutes a significant minority of the responses. This significance is enhanced when keeping in mind that the specific act of conformity resulting from this experiment involves denying one's own perception of reality. It is also noteworthy that, while the majority of the *individual responses* given in the experiment reflected independence from the group, three fourths of the *participants* conformed *at least once* during the course of the experiment. A clear majority of the participants therefore displayed a capacity to engage in this extreme form of conformity at least once during the course of the experiment.

Given these results, Asch sought to determine what factors and motivations may have played a role in the conforming behaviors of his experiment participants. Follow-up interviews with the participants revealed three different responses to the group pressures they encountered. First, some of the participants appear to have experienced an altered or distorted *perception* as a result of the group influence. As the majority opinion became clear, they viewed this as the genuinely correct interpretation and failed to attribute their incorrect perception to group influence. Second, a large number of the participants experienced a distortion in *judgment*. For these people, the majority opinion indicated that their own perception of the situation must simply be incorrect. Their actions were therefore based on faith in the majority, and uncertainty regarding their own individual perspective. A majority of the participants fell into this category. And, third, some of the participants distorted their *actions* to comply with the group pressure. These individuals continued to believe in their own perception, regardless of the group influence. However, they acted contrary to what they perceived in order to avoid negative consequences from the group (ridicule, embarrassment, etc.).

Another important facet of Asch's conformity experiment involved his exploration of the group dynamics and processes that may *decrease* the likelihood of conformity. More specifically, he sought to examine the impact of dissent and minority influences on group unanimity and conformity. In one variation of his experimental procedure, he instructed all but one of the confederates to give the wrong answer. One lone confederate was instructed to give the correct answer. In this circumstance, when the naïve participant in the experiment had just one corroborator from the rest of the group, the rate of conformity dropped dramatically (by approximately three fourths). In another variation, Asch examined the influence of a minority on the majority by instructing nine confederates in a group of 20 students to vote incorrectly (thus, 11 of the participants were naïve non-confederates). In this case, none of the naïve participants complied with the minority (i.e., all of the participants gave the correct answer). However, their reaction to the confederate minority was respectful and considerate (in contrast to the ridicule and laughter encountered by lone confederate dissenters).

The impact of these experiments on the early development of the field of social psychology was enormous. They inspired a wide-ranging body of studies and experiments on the phenomenon of conformity that continue to this day. A variety of studies have explored how personal or individual qualities (e.g., personality type, gender, nationality, status, etc.) may influence the likelihood of conformity. Other studies have examined the impact that various situational factors (e.g., group size, fear, ambiguity, etc.) may have on the phenomenon. In addition, the Asch conformity experiments served as an inspiration for other, future research (e.g., Stanley Milgram's experiments on obedience to authority, Phillip Zimbardo's mock prison study at Stanford University, etc.) that was to have equally profound consequences in the social sciences.

Though not as widely recognized as the conformity experiments, Asch also conducted a series of experiments on our perceptions of other people that had an equally profound impact on the early theoretical development of social psychology. In these experiments, a list of personality descriptors was read to participants. The participants in turn were asked to write a brief essay on their perception of the hypothetical person possessing these traits, as well as pick a variety of additional traits (from a predetermined list) that they felt would also describe this person based on the preliminary perception they had formed.

Asch found that, when certain key traits were changed between different experimental groups, it created radically different impressions in the participants' minds. For example, one test group was read a list that contained the traits: *cautious, determined, industrious, intelligent, practical, skillful,* and *warm.* Another group was read the same list, except *warm* was replaced with *cold.* In the test group that was read the trait *warm,* 91 percent of the participants responded that the person being described would also be *generous.* Only 9 percent of the group that was told the person was *cold* also felt he/she would be *generous.* The alteration of this one trait was so important that it ultimately changed the participants' perception of the hypothetical person on 12 out of 18 key personality traits.

Based on these findings, Asch concluded that certain perceived characteristics (such as *warm/cold*) are weighted more heavily in the minds of most people, and play a much greater role than other traits in determining our overall evaluations of others. He deemed such characteristics to be *central traits.* Characteristics that are less likely to alter our overall perception of others are *peripheral traits.* In addition, it was concluded that our perceptions of others are generally composed of structures of perceived traits, many of which are inferred. Complex expectations and impressions of others are thus formed based on the assumption that certain traits or sets of traits are associated with one another. This pioneering set of experiments formed the foundation of what came to be known as implicit personality theory, a crucial component of

modern social psychological theory on person perception.

Solomon Asch's body of work served as inspiration for the creation of the Solomon Asch Center at the University of Pennsylvania in 1998. The Center's mission is to advance the work of social scientists in understanding and resolving violent intergroup conflicts.

SEE ALSO: Authority and Conformity; Decision-Making; Group Processes; Milgram, Stanley (Experiments); Social Psychology; Zimbardo Prison Experiment

REFERENCES AND SUGGESTED READINGS

Anderson, C. A. & Sedikides, C. (1991) Thinking about People: Contribution of a Typological Alternative to Associationistic and Dimensional Models of Person Perception. *Journal of Personality and Social Psychology* 60: 203–17.

Asch, S. E. (1946) Forming Impressions of Personality. *Journal of Abnormal and Social Psychology* 41: 258–90.

Asch, S. E. (1951) Effects of Group Pressure upon the Modification and Distortion of Judgments. In: Guetzkow, H. (Ed.), *Groups, Leadership, and Men.* Carnegie Press, Pittsburgh, PA, pp. 8, 12.

Asch, S. E. (1952) *Social Psychology.* Prentice-Hall, New York.

Asch, S. E. (1955) Opinions and Social Pressure. *Scientific American* (November): 31–55.

Asch, S. E. (1956) Studies of Independence and Conformity: A Minority of One Against a Unanimous Majority. *Psychological Monographs* 70 (Whole No. 416).

Grant, P. R. & Holmes, J. G. (1981) The Integration of Implicit Personality Schemas and Stereotype Images. *Social Psychology Quarterly* 44: 107–15.

Wegner, D. M. & Vallacher, R. R. (1977) *Implicit Psychology: An Introduction to Social Cognition.* Oxford University Press, New York.

assimilation

Richard Alba and Victor Nee

Assimilation is reemerging as a core concept for comprehending the long-run consequences of immigration, both for the immigrants and their descendants and for the society that receives them.

This new phase could be described as a second life for a troubled concept. In its first life, assimilation was enthroned as the reigning idea in the study of ethnicity and race. In the United States, where the theoretical development of assimilation mainly took place, this period began with the studies of the Chicago School in the early twentieth century and ended not long after the canonical statement of assimilation theory, Milton Gordon's *Assimilation in American Life*, appeared in the mid-1960s. In this first phase, assimilation did double duty – on the one hand, as popular ideology for interpreting the American experience and, correlatively, an ideal expressing the direction in which ethnic and racial divisions were evolving in the US; and, on the other, as the foundational concept for the social scientific understanding of processes of change undergone by immigrants and, even more, the ensuing generations.

This dual role inevitably produced irreconcilable tensions that undermined the social scientific validity of assimilation. As a critical sociology arose in response to the Vietnam War and to the deeply embedded racism in the US revealed by the race riots of the late 1960s, assimilation came to be seen as the ideologically laden residue of an intellectually exhausted functionalism. The very word seemed to conjure up a bygone era, when the multiracial and multi-ethnic nature of American and other western societies was not comprehended. By the early 1990s, Nathan Glazer (1993) could write an essay tellingly entitled, "Is Assimilation Dead?"

Yet, as social scientists and others attempt to understand the full ramifications of the new era of mass immigration, which began for the societies of North America and Western Europe in the two decades following the end of World War II, they are resurrecting the assimilation idea, but now in forms that take into account the critiques of the preceding decades. To be useful as social science, as a means of understanding contemporary social realities and their relationship to the past and future, this rehabilitation requires that the concept of assimilation be stripped of the normative encumbrances that it had acquired

in its prior existence. At the same time, it requires the recognition that the pattern of assimilation is not the only modality of incorporation evident in immigration societies, that pluralism and racial exclusion exist also as patterns by which individuals and groups come to be recognized as parts of these societies.

THE POST-WORLD WAR II SYNTHESIS

As the paradigmatic concept for research on the incorporation of immigrants and their descendants, assimilation can be credited to the Chicago School of Sociology of the early twentieth century and especially to the work of Robert E. Park, W. I. Thomas, and their collaborators and students. Yet, by the middle of the twentieth century, when assimilation attained its zenith as an expression of American self-understanding (a.k.a. the "Melting Pot"), its formulation in social science had not yet crystallized into a set of clear and consistent operational concepts that could be deployed in measurement. Part of the problem, as Milton Gordon demonstrated, was that assimilation is multidimensional; and the solution required disentangling distinct, if interrelated, phenomena, a task he set for himself in *Assimilation in American Life* (1964). It is with this book that a canonical account emerges, and it has proven so compelling that, despite several problematic aspects that have provided handholds for subsequent critics, it remains very influential.

Acculturation, Gordon argued, was the dimension that typically came first and was inevitable to a large degree. He defined acculturation in a very broad manner, as the minority group's adoption of the "cultural patterns" of the host society – patterns extending beyond the acquisition of the host language and such other obvious externals as dress to include aspects normally regarded as part of the inner, or private, self, such as characteristic emotional expression or key life goals. In the US, the specific cultural standard that represented the direction and eventual outcome of the acculturation process was the "middle-class cultural patterns of, largely, white Protestant, Anglo-Saxon origins," which Gordon also described as the "core culture."

In his view, acculturation was a largely one-way process: the minority group adopted the core culture, which remained basically unchanged by acculturation. Only the area of institutional religion was exempt: he had no expectation that the fundamental religious identities – e.g., Catholic, Jewish – of different immigrant groups to the US would be given up as a result of acculturation.

Acculturation could occur in the absence of other types of assimilation, and the stage of "acculturation only" could last indefinitely, according to Gordon. His major hypothesis was that structural assimilation – i.e., integration into primary groups – is associated with, or stimulates, all other types of assimilation. In particular, this meant that prejudice and discrimination would decline, if not disappear, that intermarriage would be common, and that the minority's separate identity would wane. All told, Gordon identified seven dimensions of assimilation – cultural, structural, marital, identity, prejudice, discrimination, and civic.

Yet seven proved not enough. As subsequent analysts attempted to apply an assimilation framework in empirical research, they spotted gaps in Gordon's design and added other dimensions to fill them in, while still remaining faithful to the fundamental premises of the schema. One obvious omission was socioeconomic assimilation, and researchers quickly identified it as a distinct and critical dimension. Indeed, the view that cultural and socioeconomic assimilation are inevitably linked was a key premise in the classic literature on assimilation that predated Gordon's synthesis – for example, W. Lloyd Warner and Leo Srole's *The Social Systems of American Ethnic Groups* (1945). One drawback, however, was that socioeconomic assimilation was generally equated with attainment of average or above-average socioeconomic standing, as measured by indicators such as education, occupation, and income. Since many immigrant groups, especially those coming from agricultural backgrounds such as the Irish, Italians, and Mexicans in the US, entered the social structure on its lowest rungs, this meaning of socioeconomic assimilation conflated it with social mobility. This conception has become problematic in the contemporary era of mass immigration because immigrant groups no longer start inevitably at the bottom of the labor market: present-day immigration includes numerous groups that bring financial capital, as well as substantial educational credentials, professional training, and other forms of human capital.

Another addition to the repertoire of assimilation dimensions involved residential mobility. Douglas Massey's "spatial assimilation" model formalized the significance of residence for the assimilation paradigm (Massey 1985). Its basic tenet holds that as members of minority groups acculturate and establish themselves in labor markets, they attempt to leave behind less successful members of their groups and to convert socioeconomic and assimilation progress into residential gain, by "purchasing" residence in places with greater advantages and amenities. However, because good schools, clean streets, and other amenities are more common in the communities where the majority is concentrated, the search by ethnic minority families for better surroundings leads them toward greater contact with the majority. In the US, this has also meant their suburbanization, since the suburbs are where middle-class majority families are found.

In the end, though, the post-World War II synthesis suffered from other blind spots that were not easily remedied without changes to its foundations, and these became the basis for a series of withering criticisms of the entire assimilation corpus. One concerned the seeming inevitability of assimilation. Warner and Srole exemplify this premise – according to them, American ethnic groups are destined to be no more than temporary phenomena, doomed by the assimilatory power of the American context.

Interestingly, Gordon himself did not believe this: while he saw acculturation as mostly inevitable, he argued that ethnic groups still had a social structural role in providing for many non-economic needs of individuals. Nevertheless, the inevitability of assimilation seemed to many scholars the default assumption, and it made assimilation into the natural endpoint of the process of incorporation into the receiving society. Even black Americans, blocked by the racism of US society from full pursuit of the assimilation goal, were presumed to be assimilating, albeit at a glacial pace. Further, by equating assimilation with full or successful incorporation, assimilation scholars viewed racial minorities as, in effect, incompletely assimilated, rather than as incorporated into the society on some other basis. After the racial turmoil in the US of the 1960s, this view seemed untenable.

Another blind spot could be described as a profoundly ethnocentric bias. The post-war synthesis in effect assumed that minority groups would change to become more like the ethnic majority, which, aside from absorbing the new groups, would remain unaffected. In cultural terms, it elevated the cultural model of the "core" ethnic group, in the US, middle-class Protestant whites of British ancestry, to the normative standard by which other groups are to be assessed and toward which they should aspire. Assimilation then was a decidedly one-directional process, as Gordon in fact proclaimed. What was lacking was a more differentiated and syncretic concept of mainstream culture, a recognition that it could be a mixture, an amalgam of diverse influences, that continues to evolve with the arrival of new groups.

A further implication of this ethnocentric bias was that the chances and rate of assimilation for any group varied in accordance with its phenotypic similarity to the core group. In the US, this was not just a problem for African Americans. Warner and Srole laid out in systematic fashion a hierarchy of racial and cultural acceptability, with English-speaking Protestants in the top rank. For groups deviating from this ethnic prototype in any significant respect, assimilation would be prolonged, if not doubtful. Thus, the assimilation of "dark-skinned" Mediterranean Catholics, such as the Italians, was expected to demand a "moderate" period, which Warner and Srole equated with six generations or more! Given such arguments, it was not difficult to criticize the assimilation perspective for uncritically reflecting the racism of the larger society.

NEW CONCEPTUALIZATIONS

The writings of the Chicago School offer another different starting point for the formulation of a new concept of assimilation, one better suited than the post-war synthesis for societies as diverse and fluid as the United States, especially under the impress of contemporary immigration. The founders of the Chicago School were responding to the transformative changes and social problems associated with the mass immigration of their time, which have some similarities with those of today. Their definition of assimilation envisioned a diverse mainstream in which people of different ethnic/racial origins and cultural heritages evolve a common culture that enables them to sustain a common national existence. This more flexible and open-ended specification of assimilation largely receded into the background in Gordon's synthesis.

Contemporary scholars are taking up the challenge of refashioning the concept. Rogers Brubaker (2001), for example, defines assimilation as one group "becoming similar (in some respect)" to another group. For their definition, Richard Alba and Victor Nee (2003) start from the recognition of assimilation as a form of ethnic change. As the anthropologist Frederick Barth emphasized, ethnicity is a social boundary, a distinction that individuals make in their everyday lives and that shapes their actions and mental orientations toward others. This distinction is typically embedded in a variety of social and cultural differences between groups that give an ethnic boundary concrete significance. According to Alba and Nee, assimilation, as a form of ethnic change, can be defined as the decline of an ethnic distinction and its corollary cultural and social differences. "Decline" means in this context that a distinction attenuates in salience, that the occurrences for which it is relevant diminish in number and contract to fewer and fewer domains of social life. As ethnic boundaries become blurred or weakened, individuals' ethnic origins become less and less relevant in relation to the members of another ethnic group (typically, but not necessarily, the ethnic majority group); and individuals from both sides of the boundary mutually perceive themselves with less and less frequency in terms of ethnic categories and increasingly only under specific circumstances. Assimilation, moreover, is not a dichotomous outcome and does not require the disappearance of ethnicity; consequently, the individuals and groups undergoing assimilation may still bear a number of ethnic markers. It can occur on a large scale to members of a group even as the group itself remains as a highly visible point of reference on the social landscape, embodied in an ethnic culture, neighborhoods, and institutional infrastructures.

Boundaries are obviously important for assimilation processes; this observation raises the possibility that features of social boundaries may make assimilation more or less likely and influence the specific forms that it takes. Aristide Zolberg and Long Litt Woon (1999) have introduced an extremely useful typology of boundary-related changes that sheds light on different ways that assimilation can occur. Boundary crossing corresponds to the classic version of individual-level assimilation: someone moves from one group to another, without any real change to the boundary itself (although if such boundary crossings happen on a large scale and in a consistent direction, then the social structure is being altered). Boundary blurring implies that the social profile of a boundary has become less distinct: the clarity of the social distinction involved has become clouded, and individuals' location with respect to the boundary may appear indeterminate. The final process, boundary shifting, involves the relocation of a boundary so that populations once situated on one side are now included on the other: former outsiders are thereby transformed into insiders.

Boundary blurring and shifting represent possibilities not adequately recognized in the older literature. Boundary shifting is the subject of the recent whiteness literature, which discusses how various disparaged immigrant groups, such as the Irish and Eastern European Jews, made themselves acceptable as "whites" in the US racial order: indicated is a radical shift in a group's position (Jacobson 1998). Boundary blurring may represent the most intriguing and underexplored possibility among the three: blurring entails the ambiguity of a boundary with respect to some set of individuals. This could mean that they are seen simultaneously as members of the groups on both sides of the boundary or that sometimes they appear to be members of one and at other times members of the other. Under these

circumstances, assimilation may be eased insofar as the individuals undergoing it do not sense a rupture between participation in mainstream institutions and familiar social and cultural practices and identities. Blurring could occur when the mainstream culture and identity are relatively porous and allow for the incorporation of cultural elements brought by immigrant groups, i.e., two-sided cultural change.

Another innovation is the concept of "segmented" assimilation, formulated by Alejandro Portes and Min Zhou (1993). They argue that a critical question concerns the segment of a society into which individuals assimilate, and they envision that multiple trajectories are required for the answer. One trajectory leads to entry to the middle-class mainstream. But, in the US, another leads to incorporation into the racialized population at the bottom of the society. This trajectory is followed by many in the second and third generations from the new immigrant groups, who are handicapped by their very humble initial locations in American society and barred from entry to the mainstream by their race. On this route of assimilation, they are guided by the cultural models of poor, native-born African Americans and Latinos. Perceiving that they are likely to remain in their parents' status at the bottom of the occupational hierarchy and evaluating this prospect negatively because, unlike their parents, they have absorbed the standards of the American mainstream, they succumb to the temptation to drop out of school and join the inner-city underclass.

CONCLUSION

One profound alteration to the social scientific apparatus for studying immigrant-group incorporation is that it is no longer exclusively based on assimilation. Very abstractly, three patterns describe today how immigrants and · their descendants become "incorporated into," that is, a recognized part of, an immigration society: the pattern of assimilation involves a progressive, typically multigenerational, process of socioeconomic, cultural, and social integration into the "mainstream," that part of the society where racial and ethnic origins have at most minor effects on the life chances of individuals; a second pattern entails racial exclusion, absorption into a racial minority status, which implies persistent and substantial disadvantages vis-à-vis the members of the mainstream; a third pattern is that of a pluralism in which individuals and groups are able to draw social and economic advantages by keeping some aspects of their lives within the confines of an ethnic matrix (e.g., ethnic economic niches, ethnic communities). A huge literature has developed these ideas and applied them to the ethnic and generational groups arising from contemporary immigration.

In the US, all three patterns can be found in the record of the past, and all are likely to figure in the present and future, though not in ways identical to those of the past. The pattern of assimilation has been the master trend among Americans of European origin. The pattern of racial exclusion characterized the experiences of non-European immigrant groups, such as the Chinese, who were confined to ghettos and deprived of basic civil rights because American law, up until the 1950s, defined them as "aliens ineligible for citizenship." The pattern of pluralism is evident in the minority of European Americans whose lives play out primarily in ethnic social worlds, which remain visible in the form of ethnic neighborhoods in such cities as New York and Chicago.

In contemplating contemporary immigration to the US, most observers readily concede the continued relevance of the patterns of racialization and pluralism. The first reappears in the new concept of segmented assimilation; and the second has been elaborated in old and new forms, in the guise of such concepts as "ethnic economic enclaves" and "ethnic niches." It is the pattern of assimilation whose continued significance has been doubted or rejected. But it is increasingly apparent that all three remain relevant. It may be unlikely that the assimilation pattern will achieve the hegemonic status that it did for the descendants of the prior era of mass immigration: in the long term, it applied even to many descendants of Asian immigrants, despite the racial exclusion from which the immigrants themselves initially suffered. But it is not outmoded, as a great deal of evidence about such matters as linguistic assimilation and

intermarriage demonstrates. Any reflection on the American future must take assimilation into account, and the same will undoubtedly prove true in other immigration societies.

SEE ALSO: Acculturation; Anglo-Conformity; Boundaries (Racial/Ethnic); Immigration; Melting Pot; Whiteness

REFERENCES AND SUGGESTED READINGS

Alba, R. & Nee, V. (2003) *Remaking the American Mainstream: Assimilation and Contemporary Immigration*. Harvard University Press, Cambridge, MA.

Brubaker, R. (2001) The Return of Assimilation? Changing Perspectives on Immigration and Its Sequels in France, Germany, and the United States. *Ethnic and Racial Studies* 24: 531–48.

Glazer, N. (1993) Is Assimilation Dead? *The Annals* 530: 122–36.

Gordon, M. (1964) *Assimilation in American Life*. Oxford University Press, New York.

Jacobson, M. F. (1998) *Whiteness of a Different Color: European Immigrants and the Alchemy of Race*. Harvard University Press, Cambridge, MA.

Massey, D. (1985) Ethnic Residential Segregation: A Theoretical Synthesis and Empirical Review. *Sociology and Social Research* 69: 315–50.

Portes, A. & Zhou, M. (1993) The New Second Generation: Segmented Assimilation and Its Variants. *The Annals* 530: 74–96.

Warner, W. L. & Srole, L. (1945) *The Social Systems of American Ethnic Groups*. Yale University Press, New Haven.

Zolberg, A. & Woon, L. L. (1999) Why Islam is Like Spanish: Cultural Incorporation in Europe and the United States. *Politics and Society* 27: 5–38.

atheism

Patrick Michel

An atheist is one who does not believe in the existence of God or who denies God's existence. The difficulty of defining atheism results from the whole range of nuances that the concept appears to subsume. Whether it results from active denial or whether it derives from a real or supposed vacuum, whether it is therefore "positive" or "negative," atheism is fundamentally conceived as unbelief. But this only renders the problem more complex: how can one devise a history or a sociology of the "negative"? If atheism, placed as it is under the sign of privacy, is nothing more than the other side of belief, only the latter can be a positive concept. Atheism is thus an integral part of a system organized around a central reference to a religion which exhausts the concept of belief. Ultimately, any sociology of atheism is a sociology of religion.

The difficulty of accounting for unbelief (or non-belief) independently of what is supposed to provide its foundations explains why the concept of atheism has been studied by theologians and philosophers, psychologists and psychoanalysts, far more than by sociologists and historians. (This does not take into account the abundant literature – pertaining more to propaganda than to science – dedicated to this subject in the Soviet Union and its satellite countries.) There is no doubt that the phenomenon has a very long history: 2,500 years before our era, there were thinkers in India who claimed that the skies were empty. Lucretius and Epicure, Epictetus and Parmenides, Heraclitus and Xenophanon of Colophon held similar assumptions. More than 2,000 years before Nietzsche, Theodorus the Atheist proclaimed the death of God. Moreover, from the atheism of antiquity to that of the Enlightenment and the "Masters of Suspicion" (Ricoeur's expression for Marx, Nietzsche, and Freud), the history of non-belief is also that of the deepening of the distinction between the sacred and profane, lay and religious.

However difficult it may be to reduce it to a unique definition, atheism as an indicator and an instrument of the secularization of societies occupies a pivotal position in this process of disenchantment which, mostly in Europe, constructed the individual as an autonomous category and as the central subject of history. In that sense, atheism, as invented by modernity, is a pure product of the Christian West, even if its occurrence is

well attested in other contexts. Strongly condemned and attacked by the churches, which saw it as the epitome and the culmination of all the errors of modern times, as this "absurd enterprise which is the construction of a world without God" denounced by Louis Veuillot, this atheism derives simultaneously from materialism, rationalism, and more modern trends going from immanentism to phenomenology and from Marxism to existentialism. Some identify within it the expression of four tendencies: a scientistic atheism (science does not need the hypothesis of God to explain the laws of nature); a moral atheism (there is a contradiction between God and evil: "The only excuse God has, therefore, is that He does not exist," a formula Sartre borrows from Stendhal); a humanist atheism (from Bakunin to Nietzsche and from Proudhon to Lukács or to Merleau-Ponty); and an ontological atheism (Nietzsche, once again, but also Hölderlin or Heidegger). And there is even a "methodological atheism," which should be scrupulously respected in any scientific description of phenomena related to belief.

Atheism cannot possibly be grasped today in the same terms as those used by the seventeenth-century Encyclopedists or, nearer to us, by Marxism or existentialism. Nor can it be grasped in the terms we use to approach these thinkers. If atheism remains· in certain societies legally impossible or socially difficult, and thus an object of scandal, what everywhere else was once a marginal attitude has now become an established social fact, provided one interprets atheism not as the militant denial of God, who is relevant to only a small number of our contemporaries, but as aprofound indifference which can take on many different forms. As pointed out by the Japanese Buddhist monk, theologian, and philosopher Hôseki Shinichi Hisamatsu (1996), "the fundamental characteristic of the modern era is atheism."

This is not because a solution has been found to the question of the existence or non-existence of God. It is that this question appears to have lost its organizing capacity. The radical individualization which characterizes our contemporary relation to meaning deprives religion of the centrality it claimed to embody. Such an evolution, seen against the backdrop of a massive distancing from the institutionalization of belief, entails two major consequences: the ever-increasing difficulty of sustaining the distinction between believer and non-believer when there is no longer, except in theory, a "content" to belief which can be taken as an ultimate frame of reference; and therefore the loss of sociological relevance of a concept of atheism, the meaning of which demands that very frame of reference.

Theology itself has made use of these trends. Apart from the currents which, in the perspective opened up by Dietrich Bonhoeffer, try to define an a-religious Christianity (especially in the English-speaking world and under diverse forms), some have suggested that the term "unbeliever" should be replaced by "believer in a different way." Others even go so far as to consider unbelief as a new paradigm for theological research, and even as a new model for the comprehension of faith.

In the field of sociology itself, the substantial developments observable within our societies suggest an end to the bias which consists in identifying belief with religion and the latter with institutionalized religion. Maintaining this approach implies that the only way of outlining the contours of contemporary belief is to use the analytical tools devised for the study of institutionalized religion. An approach through membership, based on the proximity or the distance from a specified content of belief, seems unable to account for the trends just mentioned. To take only one example, a very large majority of French people claim to be Catholic, but 40 percent of them simultaneously state that they "have no religious affiliation." Along these same lines, approximately one third of the teenagers who identify themselves as Catholics assert that they "do not believe in God."

The contemporary landscape, in which belief is governed by subjectivism, is made up entirely of fluid currents which remain highly resistant to any structuring reference to a form of stability, unless stability is perceived as strictly operational. The goal is not to reach a "religious identity," seen as stable (and

indispensable to understand an "a-religious" identity). What is now at stake is the relation to experience (and the priority of the latter over the content of belief); to authenticity (and the priority of the latter over truth); to a refusal of violence and to belief constituted as a "comfortable" space, kept at a distance from constraints and norms.

Of course, individualization is not a new process, nor is individuality a modern invention, nor individualism a contemporary discovery. This is not the question. The rather enigmatic status of religion today (should the term be used in the singular or the plural? Is religion on its way out or making a comeback? Is it ultimately reducible to politics or is it the converse?) does not proceed from an overriding individualization of the relation to meaning, but from the social legitimatization of the latter. Even the great names of sociology, from Durkheim to Weber and from Tocqueville to Marx, are of little help in understanding this phenomenon because it is – if not a radical or unexpected novelty – at least a brutal acceleration of the movements which stir our contemporary societies, and via globalization, even those beyond our western societies, which have been the cradle of the individualization of belief.

If the concept of atheism does not appear to make sense today as a sociological tool, it continues however to make sense as a political category. We are not thinking here specifically of the effort to eradicate religion pursued in the communist system, where the official policy of forced atheization was a necessary part of the construction and consolidation of the legitimacy of the regime. "Opium of the masses," religion was construed as the prime indicator of social suffering. If its disappearance would have demonstrated the advent of the harmonious society sought for by the regime, its resilience proved how difficult it was to achieve such a program. Only one country, Albania, followed this logic inherent to the communist project to the bitter end, by declaring religion unconstitutional.

With the collapse of the Soviet Union and its empire, the reference to atheism has taken on a different political significance. If yesterday it was linked to communism, it now testifies to the perversion and decadence of western society. This type of discourse, often associated with a radical interpretation of Islamism, presents the secularization of societies as an outgrowth of Christian civilization. In the last instance, it aims at stigmatizing "democracy" as the official institutionalization of pluralism and therefore of a presumed relativism. From the same perspective, it also denounces a domineering West imposing its own order on the rest of the world.

SEE ALSO: Civil Religion; Civilizations; Communism; Cultural Relativism; Deinstitutionalization; Globalization, Religion and; Humanism; Individualism; Modernity; Postmodernism; Religion, Sociology of; Sacred, Eclipse of the; Sacred/Profane; Secularization; Values

REFERENCES AND SUGGESTED READINGS

Certeau, M. de (1987) *La Faiblesse de croire* (The Weakness of Believing). Seuil, Paris.
Desroche, H. (1968) *Sociologies religieuses* (Sociologies of Religion). PUF, Paris.
Gauchet, M. (1985) *Le Désenchantement du monde – Une histoire politique de la religion* (The Disenchantment of the World: A Political History of Religion). Gallimard, Paris.
Hisamatsu, H. S. (1996) *Una religione senza dio – Satori e Ateismo* (A Religion without God: Satori and Atheism). Il melangolo, Genova.
Michel, P. (1999) Religion, nation et pluralisme – Une réflexion fin de siècle (Religion, Nation and Pluralism: A "Turn of the Century" Reflection). *Critique internationale* 3: 79–97.
Michel, P. (2003) La Religion, objet sociologique pertinent? (Is Religion a Sociologically Pertinent Object?). *Revue du Mauss* 22: 159–70.
Minois, G. (1998) *Histoire de l'athéisme – Les incroyants dans le monde occidental des origines à nos jours* (History of Atheism: Unbelievers in the Western World from their Origins to the Present). Fayard, Paris.
Pace, E. (1994) *La Sociologie des religions* (Sociology of Religion[s]). Cerf, Paris.
Ramet, S. P. (1993) *Religious Policy in the Soviet Union.* Cambridge University Press, Cambridge.
Van Den Bercken, W. (1989) *Ideology and Atheism in the Soviet Union.* Walter de Gruyter, Berlin.

attitudes and behavior

Frances G. Pestello

Since the early days of the twentieth century, scholars have pondered the role of mental conceptions and evaluations in guiding social action. This has been an enduring question in social psychology and one that has implications for all of sociology. Most social scientists have conceptualized this as the relationship between attitudes and behavior. Two competing paradigms have emerged to explain this relationship. They diverge theoretically and methodologically. One approach to the study of attitudes and behavior is grounded in positivism and deductive theorizing. The competing paradigm is inductive and phenomenological, emphasizing process and construction. The central disputes, in these competing approaches, involve the importance placed upon social context and how attitudes are conceptualized.

These competing approaches to the study of attitudes emerged almost immediately in psychology and social psychology. Attitudes are identified by early writers as a foundational concept in social psychology. Herbert Spencer used the concept. Thomas and Znaniecki wrote about the scientific study of subjective dispositions, which they called "attitudes." They defined attitudes as the subjective component of situations and as a critical component of the social landscape. Situations undergird all behavior. Behavior is never separate and distinct from the situations in which it occurs. In *The Polish Peasant* (1918) they provide the foundation for a situational, processual approach to the understanding of behavior, in which there are three kinds of data a social actor considers in forming actions: the objective conditions, preexisting attitudes, and the definition of the situation. Faris (1928) too articulates the processual nature of attitudes, as a residue of past action as well as a precursor to future actions. Faris emphasizes the importance of imagination in the construction of action.

However, it was Gordon Allport in the mid-1930s who posited what proved to be the seminal definition of attitudes as mental states which direct one's response to objects and situations. This definition put attitudes in a causal, directive relationship with behavior, and lay the groundwork for a deductive, scientific approach to the relationship between attitudes and behavior. From this perspective attitudes are intrapersonal, psychological tendencies expressed through the favorable or unfavorable evaluation of objects. Initially the core component of an attitude was affective. As the concept developed, some researchers articulated a tripartite model, including a cognitive or mental piece, a conative or directive or guiding component, and an affective or emotional aspect to attitudes.

The dominant contemporary model in the attitude–behavior literature was developed by Martin Fishbein and Icek Ajzen, who called it the theory of reasoned action. The theory of reasoned action is a four-stage, recursive model, in which the immediate determinant of volitional behavior is intention. Intentions are dependent upon attitudes and subjective norms, which are one's perception of how relevant others would view the performance of the behavior in question. Attitudes and subjective norms, in turn, are determined by "beliefs." In short, if behavior is not coerced and one intends to do something, then behavior should follow, if nothing else intervenes. The line of research promulgated by the theory of reasoned action is probably the most visible and cited exemplar of this approach to work on attitudes. The core assumption of this approach to attitudes is consistency. Attitudes are conceptualized as generic, trans-situational, psychological expressions that guide behavior across circumstances. Attitudes, if measured correctly, predict behavior. The social context in which the behavior is expressed is largely irrelevant.

Early on the invisibility of attitudes as an individual, mental construct created a measurement problem for researchers. The dilemma was how to get people to reveal their inner attitudes in a reliable and valid way. This led to the development of attitude scaling techniques, which generated reproducible results. These techniques have become the backbone of sociological data collection strategies. Likert, Thurstone, Guttman, and Osgood pioneered the operationalization and measurement of attitudes. The common core of all these techniques is asking questions about how respondents evaluate target objects through survey or interview questions.

Considerably less attention has been paid to the conceptualization and measurement of behavior in attitude–behavior research. Given its visibility, behavior appears to be a more straightforward and obvious concept that is easily measured. Some, such as Fishbein, discourage the measurement of actual behavior and opt for the measurement of behavioral intention instead. Intentions, like attitudes, can be revealed through the answers to carefully worded questions. Researchers have therefore come to rely primarily upon survey instruments to measure behavior. Through a question format, respondents are asked to reveal what they intend or expect to do, or, through self-reports, what they remember doing at some earlier time. Although a causal relationship is hypothesized, most researchers accept the simultaneous measurement of attitudes and behavior in their designs.

Sometimes attitudes were found to predict behavior. Other times, no relationship was found. Surprisingly, based on theoretical predictions, sometimes there was an inverse relationship between attitudes and the related behavior. In the mid-1960s, some researchers, like Albrecht, began to focus on intervening variables that might interfere with or enhance the relationship between one's attitudes and subsequent behavior. It was believed that such a focus might help explain the inconsistent findings in the attitude–behavior literature. The thrust of this research is that some conditions, largely attributable to the social context, may impact the relationship between attitudes and behavior. The relationship would be more clearly understood if researchers looked not simply at whether attitudes and behaviors are related, but under what conditions they were related. Social constraint, opportunity, reference group, and the public or private nature of the situation are some of the variables considered in these analyses.

The primary critique of the scientific approach to the study of attitudes rejects the notion of consistency. Both attitudes and behaviors are believed to be interpersonal.

In this approach to the problem the role of social context is prominent. Richard LaPiere challenged the core assumption of the positivist approach in an early article entitled "Attitudes vs. Action." He discovered in a field study that the way in which respondents' thought and talked about a despised minority did not always match their actions. He demonstrated this anomaly by traveling around the Western United States with a Chinese couple, members of a group that was experiencing high levels of prejudice and discrimination at the time. As they traveled, he observed how his Chinese companions were treated in actual service situations. The Chinese couple was refused service only once. In addition, the service they received was reasonably good throughout their travels.

He followed up these observations by sending a questionnaire to all the establishments the Chinese couple had visited with him throughout their travels. The surveys indicated that the Chinese couple would not receive service at almost every establishment they had visited, a sharp contradiction with actual experience. His conclusion was that prejudicial attitudes toward the Chinese did not predict their treatment in actual situations. By using a qualitative and inductive approach to the attitude–behavior relationship, LaPiere established the basis for an entirely different approach to the study of attitudes and behavior. Merton produced similar findings in a study on African Americans. This approach assumes that attitudes are complex and situational.

LaPiere anticipated the work of Herbert Blumer, who challenges the very idea of a bivariate, objective, intrapersonal conceptualization of either attitude or behavior. Blumer was unwilling to see attitudes as input and behavior as output. For him the key to understanding the relationship between mental conceptualizations and actions is embedded in the actor's definition of the situation. Actors are continually interpreting and reinterpreting the situations in which they find themselves, in order to create and coordinate their line of action with others. This approach, perhaps because of the more laborious methodology and the non-deterministic assumptions upon which it is based, has failed to generate anywhere near the volume of research the theory of reasoned action has.

Irwin Deutscher begins with the conundrum posed by the work of LaPiere and draws on Blumer in his 1973 review and critique of the current state of theoretical and methodological thinking on the relationship between attitudes and behavior. Deutscher struggles with the generic problem of how words and deeds are connected. He concludes with an advocacy of a situational approach to the study of attitudes and behavior, in which social actors construct their behavior and give it meaning in specific social situations. Deutscher emphasizes that "it's what's in between attitude and behavior" that counts in understanding the relationship. In a 1993 sequel to *What We Say/What We Do*, Deutscher and his colleagues find a great deal of evidence that merits the continued use of the phenomenological approach in the study of attitudes and behavior. From their perspective, situations are open, indefinite, and subject to continuous interpretation, reinterpretation, and modification by the social actors embedded in them. People imbue situations with meaning, then act on the basis of that meaning. Behavior is constructed in concert with others, not solely by individuals. Social action is almost always in collaboration with others.

The concept of attitude has been used to explain behavior in a variety of contexts. Attitude change has also been used as a means of hypothesizing and explaining behavioral change. Relevant studies appear in almost every field of sociology, including law, criminology, family, and substance use. Given the affective and motivational nature of attitude conceptualization, work in the sociology of emotions, motive, and language has relevance for understanding the complexity of this relationship and resolving some of these intellectual disputes in understanding the relationship between thoughts and actions.

SEE ALSO: Accounts; Blumer, Herbert George; Definition of the Situation; Emotion: Social Psychological Aspects; Interaction; Language; Psychological Social Psychology; Social Cognition; Symbolic Interaction; Thomas, William I; Znaniecki, Florian

REFERENCES AND SUGGESTED READINGS

Albrecht, S. L. (1973) Verbal Attitudes and Significant Others' Expectations as Predictors of Marijuana Use. *Sociology and Social Research* 57: 426–35.

Allport, G. W. (1935) Attitudes. In: Murchison, C. (Ed.), *Handbook of Social Psychology*. Clark University Press, Worcester, MA, pp. 798–844.

Blumer, H. (1955) Attitudes and the Social Act. *Social Problems* 3: 59–65.

Blumer, H. (1969) *Symbolic Interactionism: Perspective and Method*. Prentice-Hall, Englewood Cliffs, NJ.

Dawes, R. M. & Smith, T. L. (1985) Attitude and Opinion Measurement. In: Lindzey, G. & Aronson, E. (Eds.), *The Handbook of Social Psychology*, Vol. 1, 3rd edn. Random House, New York, ch. 10.

Deutscher, I. (1973) *What We Say/What We Do: Sentiments and Acts*. Scott, Foresman, Glenview, IL.

Deutscher, I., Pestello, F. P., & Pestello, H. F. G. (1993) *Sentiments and Acts*. Aldine de Gruyter, New York.

Faris, E. (1928) Attitudes and Behavior. *American Journal of Sociology* 34: 271–81.

Fishbein, M. & Ajzen, I. (1975) *Belief, Attitude, Intention, and Behavior: An Introduction to Theory and Research*. Addison-Wesley, Reading, MA.

Guttman, L. (1947) The Cornell Technique for Scale and Intensity Analysis. *Educational and Psychological Measurement* 7: 247–79.

La Piere, R. T. (1934) Attitudes vs. *Action. Social Forces* 13: 230–7.

Likert, R. (1932) The Method of Constructing an Attitude Scale. *Archives of Psychology* 140: 44–53.

Merton, R. K. (1940) Fact and Factiousness in Ethnic Opinionnaires. *American Sociological Review* 5: 13–27.

Osgood, C. E. (1952) The Nature and Measurement of Meaning. In: Snyder, J. G. & Osgood, C. E. (Eds.), *Semantic Differential Technique: A Sourcebook*. Aldine, Chicago, pp. 1–3.

Pestello, F. G. & Pestello, F. P. (1991a) Ignored, Neglected, and Abused: The Behavior Variable in Attitude–Behavior Research. *Symbolic Interaction* 14: 341–51.

Pestello, F. P. & Pestello, F. G. (1991b) Precision and Elusion: The Saga of the Attitude Variable in Attitude–Behavior Research. *Studies in Symbolic Interaction* 12: 255–80.

Spencer, H. (1862) *First Principles*. Burt, New York.

Thomas, W. I. & Znaniecki, F. (1918) *The Polish Peasant in Europe and America*. Badger, Boston.

Thurstone, L. L. (1928) Attitudes Can Be Measured. *American Journal of Sociology* 33: 529–44.

attraction

Christabel L. Rogalin and Bridget Conlon

Attraction is a positive attitude one holds for another person. Attraction also refers to the positive behaviors an individual displays in response to another person over a prolonged period of time. Positive behaviors can include the experience of positive emotions or feelings in conjunction with the other, enhancing the welfare of the other, and trying to maintain close proximity to the other. Little work has been done to expand on the theoretical construct of attraction. Rather, the literature has tended to address the question of why people are attracted to each other and why people find some people more attractive than others.

From this body of literature, several principles of attraction have emerged: familiarity, proximity, reciprocity, similarity, and physical attractiveness. Empirical support for all of these conditions has been found by experimental studies and naturalistic studies. In other words, empirical support for these conditions has been established in studies among relative strangers and among actual relationships (either friendship or intimate).

Familiarity is the principle that individuals tend to like people who are familiar to them. The more exposure effect is the consistent research finding that people, under most conditions, tend to like familiar people and objects more than people and objects they have not seen before. The more individuals are exposed to a given person, the more attracted they are to that person.

Proximity is the second principle of attraction. Proximity refers to the location of individuals – either physical or functional distance. The closer individuals are physically, the more likely attraction will occur. Proximity is influential in the development of attraction because it allows opportunity for individuals to interact. Attraction cannot occur without interaction. In other words, interaction is a necessary condition in order for attraction between individuals to occur. Proximity is related to familiarity in that individuals who are geographically close are more likely to be familiar than those individuals who are geographically distant. The closer individuals are, the more likely they are to interact with one another. As the number of interactions between individuals increases, they become more familiar to one another. While being physically close to another person increases the likelihood of interaction, being functionally close to another person has a greater impact on whether or not a relationship develops. In the classic study by Festinger et al. (1950), the authors investigated the impact of the physical layout of an apartment complex on the development of friendships among married couples. They found that couples were more likely to form friendships with their next-door neighbors compared to neighbors who lived two doors away. The further any two couples lived, the less likely they were to develop a friendship. But, they found that functional distance was a stronger predictor than physical distance as to whether or not relationships developed. Couples who lived by the mailboxes or stairways tended to develop more friendships than couples who did not live near the mailboxes or stairways. Proximity is influenced by institutional structures (i.e., school tracking) and preferences (i.e., similar interests cause individuals to end up at the same place at the same time).

Reciprocity is another principle of attraction. People tend to like people who like them. Balance theory (Heider 1953) asserts individuals are motivated to maintain a cognitive balance among a set of sentiments. Sentiment refers to the way an individual feels (or evaluates) another individual or object. Balance theory argues that relationships tend toward a balanced state, in which there is no stress. If a person, A, believes that another person, B, likes A, A will start to like B. Relationships are supposed to be reciprocated. When a relationship is not reciprocated, the relationship ceases to exist.

Similarity is the fourth principle of attraction. People tend to like others who hold similar attitudes. Balance theory offers an explanation as to why people like others who hold similar attitudes. Balance theory's principle of consistency argues that individuals strive to maintain relationships that are consistent (congruent) with one another, rather than relationships that are inconsistent (incongruent). If inconsistency does arise between cognitive elements, individuals are motivated to restore harmony between elements. Inconsistency is presumed to be unpleasant and stressful; this is why individuals are motivated to minimize stress. Another explanation for similarity is social comparison. People compare their beliefs to the beliefs of others. When attitudes and beliefs are similar, people's beliefs and attitudes are validated.

Not only do people tend to like others with similar attitudes, they also tend to like others who are similar to them in terms of demographic characteristics. This tendency is captured in the principle of homophily. *Homophily* refers to the principle that individuals are more likely to interact with those who are similar to them, rather than with those who are dissimilar to them (McPherson et al. 2001). It is a well-documented research finding that individuals tend to both initiate and maintain relationships with similar others. This does not necessarily mean that individuals choose to interact with those who are similar to them rather than those who are dissimilar to them. Furthermore, the more individuals interact, the more similar they become over time. Common characteristics in which individuals tend toward similar others are sex, race, ethnicity, age, class background, and educational attainment. Studies looking at naturally occurring relationships have consistently found that individuals are more likely to be friends with those who are similar to them than those who are dissimilar.

Homogamy is the research finding that in addition to being attracted to similar others, individuals tend to marry similar others. Marriage partners tend to share similar characteristics, including education and race.

Physical attractiveness is the final principle of attraction. People tend to like individuals who are physically attractive more than those who are less physically attractive. The primary explanation for this principle can be summarized with the stereotype, "what is beautiful is good." What one considers to be physically attractive is culturally dependent and changes over time, both within and across cultures. The matching hypothesis asserts that individuals tend to be attracted to individuals of similar levels of attractiveness.

Some researchers argue that there is an evolutionary component as to what traits are considered to be physically attractive. Buss (1989) argues there are sex differences in biology that give rise to psychological differences in attraction between men and women. In a study of 37 cultures, he found that women tend to value economic stability, ambition/drive, social status, and older age. He found that men tend to value youth and physical attractiveness. Physical attractiveness signals fertility (reproductive value). The two traits that are key in physical attractiveness are clear skin and symmetric features. Work by Eagly and Wood (1999) contradicts the work by Buss. They find that individuals choose their mates within the constraints of the role structure – that people choose good exemplars for their culture's definition of a good mate (either wife or husband). They reanalyzed Buss's 37 culture study. Specifically, they looked at the variability in the amount of sex differences in cultures. They asserted that if it is truly biology that causes the gender differences in mate selection preference, there should not be variation across cultures. However, they found that gender differences in mate selection are not found in societies in which there is gender equality. Specifically, the more similar the gender roles are for women and men in a given society, the greater the tendency to choose a mate like oneself. Rather than biology impacting mate selection, according to their social structural theory, gender roles impact mate selection.

The majority of research within the area of interpersonal attraction has focused on the conditions under which attraction occurs. The exception to this has been the development of theories of love, for example Sternberg's (1986) triangular theory of love. The triangular theory of love asserts that there are three basic components of love: intimacy, passion, and decision/commitment. Intimacy is the feeling of a close emotional bond with a person. Passion refers to the physical and sexual component of love. Decision/commitment is the conscious choice to love a person in the short term and the declaration of a longer-term promise. Each of these three components is combined in different ways to yield eight types of love.

A growing area in current research focuses on the intersections of class, race, and ethnicity on attraction. Specifically, research has started to focus on whether or not there are differences across class and racial and ethnic groups in the factors that influence attraction. Also, research has started to focus more on relationships (friendship or intimate) in which people differ. Specifically, there has been an increase within the literature on interracial friendships and intimate relationships (see, e.g., Hallinan & Williams 1989).

SEE ALSO: Cognitive Balance Theory (Heider); Friendship: Interpersonal Aspects; Friendship: Structure and Context; Networks; Social Exchange Theory; Social Network Analysis; Social Network Theory; Sociometry

REFERENCES AND SUGGESTED READINGS

Buss, D. (1989) Evolutionary Hypotheses Test in 37 Cultures. *Behavioral and Brain Sciences* 12: 1–49.

Eagly, A. H. & Wood, W. (1999) The Origins of Sex Differences in Human Behavior: Evolved Dispositions versus Social Roles. *American Psychologist* 54: 408–23.

Festinger, L., Schachter, S., & Back, K. (1950) *Social Pressures in Informal Groups: A Study of Human Factors in Housing.* Stanford University Press, Stanford.

Hallinan, M. T. & Williams, R. A. (1989) Interracial Friendship Choices in Secondary Schools. *American Sociological Review* 54: 653–64.

Heider, F. (1953) *The Psychology of Interpersonal Relations.* Wiley, New York.

McPherson, M., Smith-Lovin, L., & Cook, J. M. (2001) Birds of a Feather: Homophily in Social Networks. *Annual Review of Sociology* 27: 415–44.

Quillian, L. & Campbell, M. E. (2003) Beyond Black and White: The Present and Future of Multiracial Friendship Segregation. *American Sociological Review* 68: 540–66.

Sternberg, R. J. (1986) A Triangular Theory of Love. *Psychological Review* 93: 119–35.

attribution theory

Abdallah M. Badahdah

As interest in consistency theories waned in the 1960s, new approaches to cognitive research emerged. In the 1970s, and to a lesser extent in the 1980s, attribution research became a dominant force in the field of social psychology. There is no one theory of attribution; rather, several perspectives are collectively referred to as attribution theory. Attribution theory explains how perceivers explain human behaviors by inferring the causes of those behaviors.

Frtiz Heider (1958) provided social psychologists with the building blocks for developing attribution research. Heider argued that people strive to understand, predict, and control events in their everyday lives. Laypeople have their own theories about the reasons why certain events occur. Heider encouraged social psychologists to learn from the commonsense, causal reasoning that was presumed to guide their behaviors. Among his important contributions to attribution research was his proposal that in their search for causal structures of events, people attribute causality either to elements within the environment (external attribution) or to elements within the person (internal attribution). Moreover, Heider noted that people have a tendency to overestimate the power of internal causes, such as needs and attitudes, when explaining others' behavior. Another insight was his distinction between intentional and unintentional behaviors and his assumption that people tend to make an internal attribution of causes if they view an action as intentionally caused. However, Heider did not articulate and develop a systematic theory of his attribution principles.

Jones and Davis (1965) were the first to decipher some of Heider's principles and translate them into testable hypotheses. Correspondence inference theory identifies the conditions under which an observed behavior can be said to correspond to a particular disposition or quality within the actor. In other words, "correspondence inference" refers to the perceiver's decision about whether the actor's behavior matches or corresponds to particular personal traits. The process of correspondence inference works backward and is divided into two stages: the attribution of intention and the attribution of dispositions. First, to determine whether the actor had intended to produce the observed effects, the observer's responsibility is to find out whether the actor knew about the act's observed effects and had the ability and freedom to produce those effects. Second, the observer seeks to conclude that the act was caused by internal or dispositional factors by comparing the effects of chosen and non-chosen actions. Cultural desirability plays a role at this stage. If an act's given effect is expected and considered culturally desirable (in-role), then it is less informative and plays a lesser role in correspondence inference. However, if the effects contradict generally held expectations, then more information can be gained and an attribution to personal dispositions is made. Sometimes chosen and non-chosen acts produce similar results, which complicates the attribution process. The principle of non-common (unique) effects of the intended act is helpful in this case. When a given act has fewer non-common or unique consequences, the observer's confidence in his or her attribution increases.

Correspondence inference is also influenced by two factors related to the observers: hedonical relevance and personalism. The consequences of an act are said to be hedonically relevant to the observers if they benefited from or were harmed by the act. The more hedonically relevant the consequences of an act are to the observers, the more likely that inferences will be correspondent. Personalism influences correspondence inference if observers perceive that they are the act's intended target. The more strongly the observers believe that they are the act's intended target, the more likely they will attribute the act to personal dispositions.

Kelley's (1967) theory of covariation analysis is concerned with the accuracy of attributing causes to effects. His theory hinges on the principle of covariation between possible causes and effects. The causes can be persons, entities, or times. Three types of information are used to make causal attribution: consensus, distinctiveness, and consistency. Consensus refers to whether all people act the same way toward the same stimulus or only the observed person. Distinctiveness concerns whether the observed person behaves in the same way to different stimuli. Consistency refers to whether the observed person behaves in the same way toward the same stimulus over time and in different situations. One can score high or low on these three qualities. The attribution to personal or environmental factors depends on the combination of these qualities. For example, an attribution is most likely to be made to a personal quality within the actor if consensus and distinctiveness are low and consistency is high. However, if consensus, consistency, and distinctiveness are high, then the attribution is more likely made to external factors.

Kelley acknowledged, however, that observers might have limited information, or lack the motivation or time needed to sort through multiple observations. In such cases, observers use their past experiences and theories about the relationships between causes and effects, which he called "causal schemata," to make attributions. Two principles are associated with these causal schemata. The discounting principle states that the role of a particular cause in producing a given outcome is minimized if other plausible causes are present. The augmentation principle argues that observers are more likely to attribute a given effect to the actors if the effect is produced under inhibitory conditions, such as risk or cost. Thus, if a given effect is produced despite the risk and cost involved, then perceivers are more likely to attribute the cause to the actors.

Kelley and Michela (1980) called the above theories, which focus on the antecedents–attribution link, "attribution theories." Bernard Weiner's (1986) theory of achievement and emotion, which focuses on the emotional and behavioral consequences of the attribution process, is labeled attributional theory. Weiner's theory suggests three dimensions of perceived causality: the locus of the cause (within the person versus outside the person), the stability of the cause (stable versus unstable), and the controllability over the cause (controllable versus uncontrollable). Individuals will pay attention to and search for a causal attribution if the outcome is negative, unexpected, and/or important. The resultant

emotions depend on the type of attribution that observers make. Weiner distinguished between two groups of affective consequences of causal attribution. First, "outcome-dependent" affects, such as feeling happy for succeeding in a task or sad for failing a task, are experienced because of the attainment or non-attainment of the outcome, and not by the cause of that outcome. The second group, "attribution-linked" affects, are the product of appraisal and the assignment of a cause. For example, successful outcomes that are attributed to one's internal quality, such as effort, are more likely to engender high self-esteem than success that is attributed to external factors, such as good luck. Similarly, attributing one's failure to an internal quality may cause lower self-esteem than failure that one attributes to external factors.

In the process of making attributions, people make errors by either overestimating or underestimating the impact of situational or personal factors when explaining their behaviors or the behaviors of others. These errors are termed biases in attribution. One prominent bias is the correspondence bias, which refers to observers' tendency to exaggerate or overestimate the influence of dispositional factors when explaining people's behavior. This bias is so ubiquitous that in the social psychology literature, it is known as the fundamental attribution error. Even though there is no one preferred or accepted explanation for this bias, several have been suggested. One explanation of correspondence bias is that in explaining an individual's behavior, observers are more likely to focus on the actor rather than situational cues. Another explanation suggests that when people attempt to explain others' behaviors, they proceed through two steps. In the first step, the observers make dispositional inferences, which is relatively easy and effortless. In the second step, the observers revisit their inferences to correct or adjust them after scrutinizing the situation. Revisiting the first step for the purpose of correction might be difficult or impossible if the observers are busy or distracted. Another type of error is the actor–observer difference, in which actors tend to attribute the cause of their behaviors to external factors, while observers of the same behaviors tend to attribute causality to stable, dispositional factors within the actors. One explanation for this bias is the amount of information available to actors and observers. Actors have more intimate information about themselves and their present and past behaviors than observers. Self-serving bias is the third type of bias, and it refers to a situation in which people attribute their own successes to dispositional factors, but attribute their failures to external factors. One reason for engaging in self-serving bias is to increase or maintain self-esteem; another is to enhance one's self-presentation.

Attribution research has been criticized for being individualistic and for paying little attention to social context. Studies at the interpersonal level have focused on issues related to marriage, such as the relationship between attribution and marital satisfaction (Bradbury & Fincham 1990). For example, it was found that spouses in happy relationships tend to use more relationship-enhancing attributions (e.g., attributing negative behaviors to external factors), whereas spouses in unhappy relationships tend to use more distress-marinating attributions (e.g., the negative behaviors are attributed to internal, stable traits). At the intergroup level, attribution theories provide insights into the field of intergroup relations. For example, attribution theories explain the tendency for in-group members to attribute positive outcomes to causes that are internal to the group, while negative outcomes are attributed to environmental factors. This tendency is known as the ultimate attribution error. At the societal level, attribution is seen as an ingredient of social representations. That is, members of a given society share beliefs about the causes of societal problems, such as homelessness and unemployment (Hewstone 1989).

Attribution research also has examined several of its basic assumptions in cross-cultural studies. While many social psychologists view attribution biases as a cultural universal, cross-cultural research has indicated that this is not the case. Research has indicated that attribution biases are prominent in western cultures, which stress individuality and view the self as independent and autonomous. In these cultures, individuals are encouraged to ascribe behavior to dispositional factors and underestimate external ones. In Asian cultures, however,

socialization stresses the importance of group membership and conformity. Individuals in these collectivistic cultures are aware that their behaviors are largely governed and intended to please their in-group. Hence, when they make attributions, they are more attentive to the role of situational factors. Undoubtedly, individuals in collectivistic cultures do make personal attributions, but they tend to be more sensitive to external forces.

Attribution theories have much to contribute to the study of many sociological phenomena, such as labeling, accounts, impression management, and stratification (Grittenden 1983; Howard & Levinson 1985). Recently, Weiner's attributional theory has focused on the dimension of controllability in the study of stigma, providing an interesting insight that might complement sociologists' work on this topic.

SEE ALSO: Accounts; Labeling Theory; Marriage; Self-Esteem, Theories of; Stigma

REFERENCES AND SUGGESTED READINGS

Bradbury, T. N. & Fincham, F. D. (1990) Attributions in Marriage: Review and Critique. *Psychological Bulletin* 107: 3–33.

Grittenden, K. S. (1983) Sociological Aspects of Attribution. *Annual Review of Sociology* 9: 425–46.

Heider, F. (1958) *The Psychology of Interpersonal Relations*. Wiley, New York.

Hewstone, M. (1989) *Causal Attribution: From Cognitive Processes to Collective Beliefs*. Blackwell, Cambridge, MA.

Howard, J. A. & Levinson, R. (1985) The Overdue Courtship of Attribution and Labeling. *Social Psychology Quarterly* 48: 191–202.

Jones, E. E. & Davis, K. E. (1965) From Acts to Dispositions: The Attribution Process in Person Perception. In: Berkowitz, L. (Ed.), *Advances in Experiential Social Psychology*. Academic Press, New York, pp. 219–66.

Kelley, H. H. (1967) Attribution Theory in Social Psychology. In: Levine, D. (Ed.), *Nebraska Symposium on Motivation*. Lincoln, University of Nebraska Press, pp. 192–238.

Kelley, H. H. & Michela, J. L. (1980) Attribution Theory and Research. *Annual Review of Psychology* 31: 457–501.

Weiner, B. (1986) *An Attributional Theory of Motivation and Emotion*. Springer Verlag, New York.

Weiner, B. (1993) On Sin versus Sickness: A Theory of Perceived Responsibility and Social Motivation. *American Psychologist* 48: 957–65.

audiences

Pertti Alasuutari

The audience is a central concept in media research. Typically, the audience refers to a large, loosely connected mass on the receiving end of the media, and in most cases it is used in association with electronic media, such as radio or television. The concept's centrality in media research stems from the fact that as a notion it provides a link between academic theory, industry practice, and media policy. In public service broadcasting politics, the audience is the public whose freedom of speech and whose access to the public sphere are at stake, for whom high-quality and educational programs are made, and in whose name laws controlling and regulating the media are passed. For commercial broadcasting, the audience ratings and the demographic features of a program's audience are of crucial economic importance. For academic research, the concept of audience is important in addressing these questions: the audience is the arena in which the effects of mass communications are played out, or the place where the meanings and pleasures of media use are ultimately realized. More recently, media research and theory have questioned the self-evident character of the notion of the audience. The audiences are not natural things; they are constructed by audience-rating techniques and by various notions of the audience. Different notions of audiences are part of the working of the media in contemporary societies. Developments in information and communication technology have also made the notion of audience in its traditional sense problematic and made media researchers question when it is sensible to speak of communication technology users as audiences.

The English word *audience*, denoting the assembled spectators or listeners at an event, first appeared in the fourteenth century, but it was not until the mid-nineteenth century that the word took on a more modern meaning by denoting the readers of a particular author or publication. With the advent of electronic media in the early twentieth century the word was adapted to include the far-flung listeners of radio and television. As a theoretical concept, the idea of a mass audience crystallized in the 1930s.

Paul Lazarsfeld started a brand of communication research in the 1930s commonly known as the Lazarsfeld tradition or the mass communication research (MCR) tradition, which significantly influenced the way academics and media practitioners came to see audiences and audience research. In this approach, the audience was conceived as a rather heterogeneous collection of people who were mostly unknown to each other, to be captured with the help of statistical research and revealed by quantifying selected attributes of individual audience members and aggregating the results. The idea in Lazarsfeld's studies was to try and explain how people make choices between available alternatives. In addition, the mass communication tradition was concerned with studying the effects of mass communication. It addressed public concerns about the effects of the media; for instance, how moving pictures affect the young or how the media is used for propagandistic purposes. The theme of the effects of mass communication was also behind marketing research dealing with radio and later television audiences: commercial broadcasting companies wanted to study how effective these media are for advertising.

The MCR tradition conceives of mass communication in terms of a transmission model. Developed by Shannon and Weaver (1949), the elements of the model are succinctly expressed in Lasswell's (1948) well-known verbal version: "Who says what in which channel to whom with what effect?" The model is simple, generalizable, and quantifiable and it fits within a commonsensical conception of communication as transportation of information.

However, there are shortcomings in this mechanistic model of communication, which the MCR tradition tried to overcome by modifying and developing it. Human communication is poorly described as sending packages of information to a receiver, because interpretation of the contents by the receivers is an essential element, which is a condition for the effects that communication may have. Because there was no theory of language in the original model, the effects of mass communication were a mystic black box. Accordingly, from the viewpoint of the effects, the transmission model was commonly labelled as the "magic bullet" or "hypodermic needle" theory, and later became known as the stimulus-response theory. Empirical research showed that there are several intervening factors that modify the response to messages. Recipients of mass communication are not isolated individuals, but are influenced by family members, friends, and work colleagues. Drawing on these findings, Katz and Lazarsfeld developed the two-step flow theory of mass communication, which asserts that information from the media flows in two stages. First, certain people who are heavy or regular users of the mass media receive the information. Second, these people, called opinion leaders, pass the information along to others who are less exposed to the media, through informal, interpersonal communication. Later, it has been noted that there are different sets of opinion leaders for different issues. Also, research that is more recent has shown that the spreading of ideas is not a simple two-step process. A multiple-step model is now more generally accepted (Rogers 1962).

Despite modifications, in the transmission model of communication the audiences have a passive role as recipients of information. Either directly or indirectly, through opinion leaders, audience members are pictured as individuals influenced by mass communication.

Unlike the mass communication research tradition's main strand, the uses and gratifications (U&G) tradition conceives of audiences as active agents and approaches the mass media from the other end of the chain of communication. Instead of asking "what media do to people" it is concerned with "what people do with media." U&G researchers are interested in the various functions that mass communication has for individuals.

U&G arose originally in the 1940s as part of the MCR tradition. The first studies were based on qualitative interviews, from which the researchers inferred and named the different functions that the media served for respondents. Later, from the late 1950s onward, U&G became part of the dominant survey research paradigm. Instead of using open-ended questions, researchers used ready-made lists of functions such as social information, entertainment, and passing time. Respondents were asked to assess how well these functions characterize their media use, and researchers analyzed how different functions correlated with different programs and segments of the population. After an interval the tradition underwent a revival in the 1970s and 1980s. It presents the use of media in terms of the gratification of social or psychological needs of the individual. For instance, in 1974 Bulmer and Katz suggested that individuals might choose and use a program for diversion, personal relationships, personal identity, surveillance, and information. According to U&G researchers, the mass media compete with other sources of gratification, but gratifications can be obtained from a medium's content, from familiarity with a genre, from general exposure to the medium, and from the social context in which it is used. U&G theorists argue that people's needs and personality types influence how they use and respond to a medium. Within the U&G tradition, the lists of different uses and gratifications have been extended, particularly as new media forms have come along.

James Lull's (1980a,b) ethnographic study about the social uses of television can be seen as a return to the origins of the U&G tradition. Based on participant observation in households, Lull's study suggests that television has several uses. It can be a companion for accomplishing household chores and routines and used for background noise as an environmental resource. Second, television can be used as a "behavioral regulator," by which Lull means that activities such as mealtimes and chore times are punctuated by television. These are both "structural" uses, in addition to which Lull identifies "relational" uses.

They relate to the ways in which audience members use television to create practical social arrangements. "Communication facilitation" means that family members can use television in order to help them to talk about difficult or sensitive issues. By "affiliation/avoidance" Lull refers to television as a facilitator of physical or verbal contact or neglect. An example of this would be a moment of intimacy with a couple while watching television, or at least with the television switched on. "Social learning" refers to uses of television making decisions, modeling behavior, solving problems, disseminating information, and transmitting values. Finally, "competence/dominance" includes role enactment, which is reinforced by the parent regulating the watching of television programs as a gatekeeper.

The emergence of reception theory can be dated to an article by Stuart Hall (1973). It was important in inspiring reception research in media studies, in accordance with the cultural studies approach of the Birmingham Centre for Contemporary Cultural Studies. Like the older communication models, the reception model approaches (mass) communication as a process where certain messages are sent and then received with certain effects. However, the reception paradigm meant a shift from a technical to a semiotic approach to messages. A message was no longer understood as some kind of a package or a ball that the sender throws to the receiver. Instead, the idea that a message is encoded by a program producer and then decoded (and made sense of) by the receivers means that the sent and received messages are not necessarily identical, and different audiences may also decode a program differently. The model does not dismiss the assumption that a message may have an effect, but the semiotic framework introduced means that one moves away from a behavioristic stimulus-response model to an interpretive framework, where all effects depend on an interpretation of media messages. With this linguistic or semiotic turn the arguments about effects are sort of swallowed up or at least made dependent upon people's interpretations or thought processes.

The reception theory has inspired empirical studies about the reception of television programs by different audiences, the first one of which was David Morley's *The "Nationwide" Audience* (1980). By selecting different groups of people and showing them the *Nationwide* public affairs television program, Morley could more or less confirm and develop Hall's ideas about different codes audiences use for decoding media messages. Morley's seminal study was soon followed by studies about the reception of (especially) romantic serials and literature (e.g., Radway 1984; Ang 1985). What became known as qualitative audience reception studies typically meant that one analyzes a program, film, or book and studies its reception among a particular audience group by conducting "in-depth" interviews of its viewers or readers.

The turn from a causal to a semiotic framework of communication meant that the active role of the receiver became emphasized. John Fiske's optimism in the face of television viewers' possibilities to actively produce their readings and interpretations is often considered as an extreme example. Fiske (1987) even talks about television's "semiotic democracy," by which he refers to the delegation of production of meaning to viewers. On the other hand, Fiske does recognize the imbalance of cultural power. Although the semiotic or cultural power of the dominant is sharply limited by the semiotic guerrilla tactics of the powerless, there is an inequality in people's ability to circulate their meanings simply because there is inequality of access to the media.

In reception research there has been a gradual shift from studying the reception of a particular program within an audience group to studying the role of different media in the everyday life of people (e.g., Morley 1986). These studies concentrate on the politics of gender, on the discourses within which gender is dealt with in the programs and how women viewers interpret and make use of the offered readings against the background of their everyday lives and experiences. Feminist scholarship has had an important role in this change. At the expense of a diminishing interest in program contents, in what became known as audience ethnography, more emphasis is laid on the functions of the medium, for instance how television use reflects and reproduces (gendered) relations of power in family life. Within audience ethnography researchers also started to look at reception from the audience's end of the chain. One does not try to explain a reception of a program by probing into an "interpretive." Instead, one studies the everyday life of a group, and relates the use of (a reception of) a program or a medium to it. One studies the role of the media in everyday life, not the impact of the everyday life on the reception of a program.

From the late 1980s onward there was a new turn in the field of audience research when a number of writers began to question and discuss the premises of audience ethnography. For instance, Allor (1988), Grossberg (1988), and Radway (1988) emphasized that there really is no such thing as the "audience" out there. Instead, *audience* is, most of all, a discursive construct produced by a particular analytic gaze. This constructionist turn broadened the frame within which one conceives of the media and media use. One does not necessarily abandon ethnographic case studies of audiences or analyses of individual programs, but the main focus is not restricted to finding out about the reception or "reading" of a program by a particular audience. Rather, the objective is to grasp our contemporary "media culture," particularly as it can be seen in the role of the media in everyday life, both as a topic and as an activity structured by and structuring the discourses within which it is discussed. One is interested in the discourses within which people conceive of their roles as the public and the audience, and how notions of programs with an audience or messages with an audience are inscribed in both media messages and in assessments about news events and about what is going on in the world. This means resumed interest in the programs and programming, but not as texts studied in isolation from their usage as an element of everyday life. Furthermore, the constructionist turn adds a layer of reflexivity to the research on the reception of media messages by addressing the audiences' notions of themselves as the audience.

Related to the constructionist turn, there has been an increased interest in analyzing how notions of the audience are related to media policy and politics (Ang 1991, 1996). It has been pointed out that different notions of audiences also provide the discourses by which to legitimate different program policies

(Hellman 1999). For instance, the problematization of the distinction between "high" and "low" brow in media research reflects, perhaps also contributes to, the international and especially European deregulation of media policy. Similarly, the celebration of the active audience and the emancipatory potential of different programs and genres can be seen as a discourse useful in justifying or opposing media policies and politics.

A further challenge to the notion of the audience and audience research has emerged from the development of information and communication technology, which has meant that electronic mass media such as radio, television, film, and video are amalgamated with interactive media such as telephones and the Internet. Since many researchers who used to do media audience research have now moved to researching people's use of information and communication technology (e.g., Silverstone et al. 1991), it is inadequate to call it audience research. For instance, using the Internet may at times entail "audiencing," when an individual reads, views, or hears texts, programs, films, or music, but at other times or simultaneously it may mean that he or she is engaged in two-way communication or in gaming. Additionally, the local context in which this takes place may include other people who play an active part in using the Internet resources. In this way audience research is intertwined with what is called user research of information and communication technology.

SEE ALSO: Birmingham School; Encoding/ Decoding; Lazarsfeld, Paul; Media; Media Literacy; Public Opinion; Radio; Ratings; Semiotics; Television

REFERENCES AND SUGGESTED READINGS

Alasuutari, P. (Ed.) (1999) *Rethinking the Media Audience: The New Agenda*. Sage, London.

Allor, M. (1988) Relocating the Site of the Audience. *Critical Studies in Mass Communication* 5: 217–33.

Ang, I. (1985) *Watching Dallas: Soap Opera and the Melodramatic Imagination*. Methuen, London.

Ang, I. (1991) *Desperately Seeking the Audience.* Routledge, London.

Ang, I. (1996) *Living-Room Wars: Rethinking Media Audiences for a Postmodern World.* Routledge, London.

Fiske, J. (1987) *Television Culture.* Methuen, London.

Grossberg, L. (1988) Wandering Audiences, Nomadic Critics. *Cultural Studies* 2(3): 377–92.

Hall, S. (1973) Encoding and Decoding in the Television Discourse. Centre for Contemporary Cultural Studies, Stencilled Occasional Paper No. 7. University of Birmingham, Birmingham.

Hellman, H. (1999) Legitimations of Television Programme Policies: Patterns of Argumentation and Discursive Convergencies in a Multichannel Age. In: Alasuutari, P. (Ed.), *Rethinking the Media Audience: The New Agenda.* Sage, London, pp. 105–29.

Hermes, J. (1995) *Reading Women's Magazines: An Analysis of Everyday Media Use.* Polity Press, Cambridge.

Lasswell, H. D. (1948) The Structure and Function of Communication in Society. In: Bryson, L. (Ed.), *The Communication of Ideas.* Institute for Religious and Social Studies, New York.

Lull, J. (1980a) The Social Uses of Television. *Human Communication Research* 6: 197–209.

Lull, J. (1980b) Family Communication Patterns and the Social Uses of Television. *Communication Research* 7(3): 319–34.

Morley, D. (1980) *The "Nationwide" Audience.* British Film Institute, London.

Morley, D. (1986) *Family Television.* Comedia, London.

Radway, J. A. (1984) *Reading the Romance: Women, Patriarchy, and Popular Literature.* University of North Carolina Press, Chapell Hill.

Radway, J. A. (1988) Reception Study: Ethnography and the Problems of Dispersed Audiences and Nomadic Subjects. *Cultural Studies* 2(3): 359–76.

Rogers, E. M. (1962) *Diffusion of Innovations.* Free Press, New York.

Shannon, C. E. & Weaver, W. (1949) *A Mathematical Model of Communication.* University of Illinois Press, Urbana.

Silverstone, R. (1991) From Audiences to Consumers: The Household and the Consumption of Communication and Information Technologies. *European Journal of Communication* 6: 135–54.

Silverstone, R., Hirsch, E., & Morley, D. (1991) Listening to a Long Conversation: An Ethnographic Approach to the Study on Information and Communication Technologies in the Home. *Cultural Studies* 5(2): 204–27.

auditing

Thomas A. Schwandt

The notion of auditing is associated with social science methodology and with social theory. Generally defined, auditing is a procedure whereby an independent third party systematically examines the evidence of adherence of some practice to a set of norms or standards for that practice and issues a professional opinion. Thus, for example, financial auditors examine a corporation's financial statements against a set of standards for generally accepted accounting practices and issue a professional opinion (called an attestation) as to the dependability, integrity, and veracity of those statements. This general idea has been borrowed from the discipline of accounting and adopted in discussions of social science method. An auditing procedure has been suggested as a means to verify the dependability (cf. reliability) and confirmability (cf. warrantability) of claims made in a qualitative study (Lincoln & Guba 1985; Schwandt & Halpern 1989). The researcher is advised to maintain an audit trail (a systematically organized documentation system) of evidence including the data, processes, and product (claims, findings) of the inquiry. A third-party inquirer then examines that audit trail to attest to the appropriateness, integrity, and dependability of the inquiry process and the extent to which claims made are reasonably grounded in the data.

In the field of social program evaluation, the general idea of auditing has influenced practice in two ways. First, program and performance auditing that is routinely performed at state and national levels. As defined by the Comptroller General of the United States (US GAO 1994), a performance audit is "an objective and systematic examination of evidence . . . of the performance of a government organization, program, activity, or function in order to provide information to improve public accountability and facilitate decision-making." A program audit is a subcategory of performance auditing in which a key objective is to determine whether program results or benefits established by the legislature or other authorizing bodies are being achieved. Second, metaevaluation – a third-party evaluator examines the quality of a completed evaluation against some set of standards for evaluation. These standards are, more or less, guidelines for the conduct of evaluation and are promoted by various national and international evaluation agencies and organizations (e.g., the American Evaluation Association, the Canadian Evaluation Association, the African Evaluation Association, the European Commission, OECD).

The significance of auditing to social theory arises as program and performance auditing practices have proliferated (e.g., in hospitals, schools, universities, etc.) in contemporary society. An auditing mentality is closely associated with neoliberal theories of governance and the ideology of New Public Management (NPM). NPM emphasizes a programmatic restructuring of organizational life and a rationality based on performance standards, accountability, and monitoring. By being submitted to formal audit procedures the work of organizations is held to be more transparent and accountable. A variety of criticisms based in empirical and conceptual investigations are directed at the audit society, audit culture, or the culture of accountability as the latest manifestation of the infiltration of technological, means-end, and instrumental rationality into the forms of everyday life. Auditing is viewed as an example of what Lyotard called the performativity that is characteristic of modernity – that is, the drive for efficiency, perfection, completion, and measurement that strongly shapes conceptions of knowledge, politics, and ethics. Some scholars argue that auditing (and associated practices such as total quality management, performance indicators, league tables, results-oriented management, and monitoring systems) is not simply a set of techniques but a system of values and goals that becomes inscribed in social practices, thereby influencing the self-understanding of a practice and its role in society. To be audited, an organization (or practice like teaching or providing mental health care) must transform itself into an auditable commodity. Auditing thus reshapes in its own image those organizations and practices which are monitored for performance (Power 1997). Others argue that audit culture or society promotes the normative ideal that monitoring systems and accountability ought to replace the complex social-political processes entailed in the design and delivery of social and educational services and the inevitably messy give-and-take of human interactions. Still others contend that the growing influence of an audit culture contributes to the disappearance of the idea of *publicness* as traditional public service norms of citizenship, representation, equality, accountability, impartiality, openness, responsiveness, and justice are being marginalized or replaced by business norms like competitiveness, efficiency, productivity, profitability, and consumer satisfaction.

SEE ALSO: Authenticity Criteria; Norms; Reliability

REFERENCES AND SUGGESTED READINGS

Lincoln, Y. S. & Guba, E. G. (1985) *Naturalistic Inquiry*. Sage, Newbury Park, CA.
Power, M. (1997) *The Audit Society: Rituals of Verification*. Oxford University Press, Oxford.
Schwandt, T. A. & Halpern, E. S. (1989) *Linking Auditing and Metaevaluation*. Sage, Newbury Park, CA.
Strathern, M. (2000) *Audit Cultures: Anthropological Studies in Accountability, Ethics, and the Academy*. Routledge, London.
US General Accounting Office (GAO) (1994) *Government Auditing Standards*, revd. US General Accounting Office, Washington, DC.

authenticity criteria

Yvonna S. Lincoln

Authenticity criteria are criteria for determining the goodness, reliability, validity, and rigor of qualitative research. They may be contrasted with trustworthiness criteria on foundational grounds. Trustworthiness criteria were developed in response to conventional quantitative and statistical concerns for rigor, including internal validity, external validity (or generalizability), reliability (or replicability), and objectivity. Each of the four dimensions of trustworthiness parallels each of the four rigor dimensions of quantitative methods. Trustworthiness criteria, therefore, may be said to be foundational because they respond to the foundations of conventional scientific research.

Authenticity criteria emerged in response to the call for criteria which were responsive not to conventional quantitative research, but rather to the reformulated philosophical premises of phenomenological, constructivist, or interpretivist inquiry. Such criteria were neither proposed nor self-evident. Attempts to tease out such criteria resulted in five proposals for judging the fidelity of phenomenological or interpretivist qualitative research to its underlying philosophical principles or axioms. Those five proposals included fairness and balance, ontological authenticity, educative authenticity, catalytic authenticity, and tactical authenticity.

FAIRNESS AND BALANCE

The mandate that interpretivist (or constructivist) research collect the constructions of all stakeholders or research participants implies that these participants will be actively sought out and solicited for their views on the research problem at hand. This does not imply that "anything goes," or that standards will not be brought to bear when weighing the information and sophistication level of the accounts; merely that all accounts will be sought, and judged later. Community derived standards, with the input of the researcher, can be developed for testing the various accounts or constructions against some tests for information accuracy, misinformation, biases, stereotypes, or lack of information. But such testing of accounts is conducted after accounts from all participant or respondent groups have been invited and elicited.

Balance is the characteristic of case studies or ethnographies (the usual product of qualitative research methods) which demonstrates, within the text, that accounts have been sought, and that all viewpoints, whether consensual or competing, are being fairly represented. Balance requires, first, that those viewpoints be expressed, although the researcher may not

agree with them, and second, that discussions of methodology explain the efforts of researchers to seek out and obtain those constructions. Occasionally, some stakeholding or participant groups will elect not to provide their constructions of the phenomenon being researched. Efforts to persuade them otherwise may fail, but researchers must explain and describe their efforts fully in the case study or ethnography.

ONTOLOGICAL AUTHENTICITY

In qualitative research, it is frequently the case that interviewees and research respondents will be asked questions which they have never formulated for themselves. Occasionally, when that happens, respondents will find themselves expressing ideas or thoughts which never consciously occurred to them previously. The experience of coming to know how an individual feels about some issue – when she or he never thought about the issue before – is an encounter with one's own personal consciousness, which is termed ontological authenticity. This self-understanding or self-knowledge is one of the intended outcomes of the process of phenomenologically oriented inquiry, and is therefore a criterion for judging the fidelity of the process of such inquiry. It is not necessary for each and every respondent to discover something new about her own thinking on some matter, but if no respondents make such discoveries, then the inquiry could fairly be called superficial.

EDUCATIVE AUTHENTICITY

A second criterion for judging interpretive and qualitative research is the extent to which all members of stakeholding groups come to understand the constructions of all the others, and indeed, members of different stakeholding groups (e.g., parents and teachers and school administrators) understand the value positions and/or constructions of other groups. This suggests that researchers need to plan for anonymous reporting venues which make all stakeholding groups aware of the sensemaking of other groups, whether through formal reporting venues, or more informal periodic portrayals of group data.

This widespread sharing of constructions (although never individual respondents' names or other identifiers) runs counter to conventional inquiry, where in certain kinds of inquiries, particularly evaluations, data are shared only between researcher and managers and/or funders. The purpose, however, of interpretive inquiry is to ensure that all participants come away from the inquiry with richer, more textured, more informed, and more highly sophisticated understandings. In this manner, when decisions must be made by a community, each participant is operating with high levels of accurate information, and sound understanding of the viewpoints, constructions, and value positions of other community members.

CATALYTIC AUTHENTICITY

Catalytic authenticity refers to the possibility that research or evaluation study participants may wish to take action of some sort on their own behalf. For instance, as a result of some piece of research, parents may decide that their children need more formal instruction on ways to prevent sexually transmitted diseases. The research has acted as a catalyst to prompt greater concern on the part of parents for sexually active teenagers, and they may decide to address the school board on requested changes in the high school health and safety curriculum. Or research participants who are recipients of various community services may come to understand that social workers want to be responsive to their clients' needs, but struggle under enormous caseloads, and therefore attend to what appear to be the most desperate or dire circumstances. Research participants who are the targets of some social policy may desire to petition a state for more case workers in an agency to meet the needs of a growing community. In this instance, the understanding of overworked and overloaded case workers prompts the request for additional lines to serve the agency's and targets' need in this community.

Catalytic authenticity indexes a study's intent to address genuine or compelling social problems, likely those identified by some community of stakeholders, and to find meaningful possibilities for addressing the problems which can be understood and acted upon by those for whom it is a problem. Catalytic research frames research problems in ways which enhance the likelihood that problems will be understood by all stakeholders, creates a language and a discourse which can be shared by all involved in studying the problem, but especially participants, and poses meaningful strategies (in cooperation with stakeholders) for addressing the issues. Catalytic authenticity ensures that community questions are a part of the activities of researchers, and that real-world solutions can be acted upon.

TACTICAL AUTHENTICITY

Sometimes, stakeholders understand the issues all too well, but do not fully understand how to address the issues, or to whom potential solutions might be posed. When this occurs, researchers and evaluators – most of whom understand quite well how to "speak truth to power" or to get themselves on public agency agendas – may be called upon to train research or evaluation participants appropriate means and modes for getting their concerns addressed. Far from being "activist," as such researchers who work with participants are often labeled, they are doing little more than simply leveling the playing field so that participants and stakeholders with less power and voice may actively participate in the kinds of dialogue and processes to which any middle-class family has access. This is a form not only of authenticity to the democratic and participatory aspects of naturalistic and phenomenological inquiry, it is a kind of *balance*, in that it rebalances power relations within a community via community and adult education in democratic process (Guba & Lincoln 1989).

Authenticity criteria are not the only metric for assessing the reliability, trustworthiness, validity, or fidelity to some real-life context for a study. Authenticity criteria address the quality of process in a phenomenological study, and additional quality criteria have been extrapolated from a variety of writers and theoreticians reflecting on their own work (Lincoln 1995). Those quality criteria include the communitarian nature of the inquiry, that is, whether the inquiry process supports community building or whether it is anti-communal; whether a text has achieved poly-vocality, or whether it remains "the voice from nowhere, and the voice from every-where"; whether a text demonstrates critical subjectivity, reciprocity, and sacredness; and whether there is any sharing of the benefits of research from those who provided the answers to the inquirer's questions.

Clearly, many criteria remain to be ex-plored. Equally clearly, the rather spartan set of criteria which characterizes positivist, or experimental, inquiry is insufficient for a para-digm of inquiry which seeks community and participatory forms of knowing.

SEE ALSO: Auditing; Naturalistic Inquiry; Paradigms; Trustworthiness

REFERENCES AND SUGGESTED READINGS

Guba, E. G. & Lincoln, Y. S. (1989) *Fourth Generation Evaluation*. Sage, Thousand Oaks, CA.
Lincoln, Y. S. (1995) Emerging Criteria for Quality in Qualitative and Interpretive Research. *Qualitative Inquiry* 1(3): 275–89.

author/auteur

Laurence Simmons

The concept of authorship seemed uncompli-cated, or was at least unexplored, until the second half of the twentieth century, since when it has become the site of much theore-tical discussion. Modern literary criticism has not simply underwritten the authority of authors. The American New Critics of the 1930s and 1940s, Cleanth Brooks and Robert Penn Warren in their *Understanding Poetry* (1938), ruled out the study of biographical materials as a substitute for study of the lit-erary text itself. They raised the issue of

whether the reconstruction of an author's intention from the text was at all possible, and, if possible, whether it is even relevant. Soon after, in a famous essay entitled "The Intentional Fallacy" (1954), the American critics William Wimsatt and Monroe Beardsley forbade critics to refer to authorial intentions in the analysis of literature, arguing that the literary work itself contained all the informa-tion necessary for its understanding, and that appeals to authorial intention or biography (disparaged as "Shakespeare's laundry list") were at best irrelevant, at worst downright misleading.

In 1968, the year of student and worker unrest in Paris, French literary critic Roland Barthes published a short article, "The Death of the Author," in which he argued that the traditional notion of an author is a product of rationalist thought that ascribes central impor-tance to the individual human being. This idea of the author, Barthes went on to suggest, is tyrannical in that it encloses the text within a single meaning tied to the author as expres-sive origin. Barthes's view of the author is intimately tied up with his notion of *écriture*, which translates, rather unsatisfactorily, into "writing" in English. For Barthes (1977: 42), writing "is that neutral, composite, oblique space where our subject slips away, the nega-tive where all identity is lost, starting with the very identity of the body writing." Texts are not produced by authors but by other texts, and here Barthes presages the ideas of later poststructuralists such as Julia Kristeva's "intertextuality." The text is irreducibly plural, a weave of voices or codes which can-not be tied to a single point of expressive origin in the author. It is language which "speaks," not the author. For Barthes, the classic texts of modernism, such as the poetry of Stephane Mallarmé or the prose of Marcel Proust, reach such a point where language can be said to be "speaking itself."

Shortly after Barthes's intervention, in 1969 before members and guests of the *Société fran-çaise de philosophie*, Michel Foucault delivered a paper entitled "What is an Author?" Begin-ning with a quotation from Samuel Beckett ("What does it matter who is speaking"), Foucault explored his indifference to the con-cept of the author as the motivation and fundamental ethical principle in contemporary writing. What is in question in writing, he suggested, is not so much the expression of a subject as the opening up of a space in which the subject who writes can only but disappear: "the mark of the writer is reduced to nothing more than the singularity of his absence" (Foucault 2000: 207). The quotation from Beckett, as Foucault realized, contained a contradiction, and it was contradiction that remained the hidden theme and motor of his seminar. "'What does it matter who is speaking,' someone said, 'what does it matter who is speaking.'" Even though he or she might be anonymous and without face, there is someone who has offered up this enunciation, someone without whom this thesis, which negates the importance of who speaks, could not have been formulated. That is, the same gesture that refutes any relevance of the identity of the author nevertheless affirms its irreducible necessity. The author who Barthes had wanted to kill off comes back as a ghost.

At this point Foucault was able to clarify the direction of his understanding of the problem. This was founded upon the distinction between two notions that are often confused: the author as "real" person (who must remain outside the field) and the "author-function" who will be the subject of Foucault's essay. The name of the author was not simply a proper name like others, neither on the descriptive level nor on the level of designation. According to Foucault: "As a result, we could say in a civilization like our own there are a certain number of discourses endowed with the 'author-function' while others are deprived of it...The author-function is therefore characteristic of the mode of existence, circulation and functioning of certain discourses" (Foucault 2000: 211). The various features of the author-function derive from this: a regime that attributes rights to an author and at the same time allows for the possibility that he or she might be persecuted and punished for what is written; the possibility of distinguishing between literary texts and scientific texts; the possibility of authenticating texts by placing them in a canon; the possibility of constructing a transdiscursive function which constitutes the author beyond the limits of his or her own text as the

instigator of a discourse (thus now the name Marx represents much more than the author of *Das Kapital*).

Two years later Foucault was to deliver this paper again at the University of Buffalo in a modified form in which he opposed even more rigorously the author as real individual with the "author-function." "The author is not," he declared on that occasion, "an indefinite source of significations that fill a work; the author does not precede the works; he [*sic*] is a certain functional principle by which, in our culture, one limits, excludes, and chooses; in short, by which one impedes the free circulation, the free manipulation, the free composition, decomposition, and recomposition of fiction" (Foucault 2000: 221). This radical separation of the author-subject from the apparatus that governs its function within society was read by many hostile critics as a profound indifference on Foucault's part to the flesh-and-blood subject in general and it led to a charge that he was simply "aestheticizing" the living subject. But Foucault was perfectly conscious of this dilemma and this aporia. For him, the subject as living individual is always present if only through the objective processes of subjectification which construct it, and the apparatus which writes it and captures it within mechanisms of power. As Foucault never tired of repeating, "the trace of the writer lies only in the singularity of his absence." The author is not dead, but to present oneself as an author is to occupy the place of the dead. An author-subject exists, but he or she exists through the traces of absence.

In 1976 Jacques Derrida was to publish a small book on the French experimental poet Francis Ponge entitled *Signéponge/Signsponge* (1984). The title of this book punned on the *sponge*-like nature of *Ponge*'s poetry, which sucked up watery *signs* and was, it could be said, "signed by the sponge." In this challenging text, among other things Derrida looked at the different ways an author signs a text and how an author's signature is a textual element as well as being a mark of the author – he calls these "signature effects." Derrida specified three distinct senses of the word signature. First of all, the literal sense of the signature: the name of the author that is articulated and readable (a director's name on the credits at the beginning of a film, a painter's signature on a painting, an author's name on the cover of a book). At first sight this may seem simple and straightforward and its use is rather like the way in which we sign our own names on checks or documents countless times each day. But, as Derrida points out, there are plenty of dud checks in circulation. That is, the signature may be a forgery, or it may not directly indicate ownership, as in the case of the Orson Welles's film *A Touch of Evil* (which Welles himself was to disown due to his exclusion by the studio from the final editing), or it may divert one's attention from the real author, as in the use of pseudonyms (where, for example, George Eliot gives the "wrong" indication about the author's gender). In Derrida's second sense, the signature is the set of marks or motifs left in the work, the style peculiar to one author or painter or film director. (Jackson Pollock's particular use of splattered paint is his signature in this context; the narratively inexplicable shots of driving rain that appear in most of Andrei Tarkovsky's films function in a similar way.) Third, there is what Derrida calls "the signature of the signature": those moments in a text when it points to the processes of representation and its own construction. These are metatextual moments of a sort of self-reflexive pointing in a text to the text itself, a pointing to the act of production of that text. Derrida's meditations on the "signature effect," where the author is an active element at work within the text, provided a useful corrective to the extreme negation of Barthes's "death of the author."

In film studies there has been an equally complex debate around the concept of the author (generally taken to be the film director). In fact we can go as far back as to Germany in 1913 to find the term "author's film" (*Autorenfilm*), meaning then, however, that a film was to be judged the work of its literary author or screenwriter rather than the person responsible for directing it. In the 1950s a group of French film critics and future film directors associated with the magazine *Cahiers du cinéma* initiated a debate on the *politique des auteurs* arguing the opposite, that despite its

collective or industrial production the director was the sole author of the finished product of the film, and that to fully understand any film we must focus on the figure of the director, in contrast to, say, its scriptwriter. So while they still recognized that filmmaking was an industrial process, the film criticism of the *Cahiers* critics stressed the *mise-en-scène* (the elements a director might manipulate in front of and with the camera), and the director's mastery of the codes of cinema that gave his or her films an individual touch (Derrida's "signature as style"). *Politique* here might be translated as "policy" (as much as "politics"), since it involved a conscious decision to look at films in a certain way and to value them in a certain way. During the German occupation of France in World War II, American films had been banned, but in the immediate aftermath of the war hundreds of heretofore unseen films flooded in. As they avidly consumed these films, the *Cahiers* critics bestowed auteur status and artistic respectability on directors such as Alfred Hitchcock, Howard Hawks, John Ford, and Samuel Fuller, most of whose films had only been awarded scant recognition in their countries of origin up until this point.

In the early 1960s Andrew Sarris, a film critic writing for the *Village Voice*, but also the English editor of *Cahiers du cinéma*, began to use the French "auteur theory" to reexamine Hollywood films, thus replacing the star or the producer or studio as the criterion of critical value with that of the director. Not only did Sarris assert that a creative artist could work within the constraints of Hollywood, but also that what had been considered commercial products up until this point could be thought of as works of art. Like his French counterparts, Sarris was the first to argue that these Hollywood films were worthy of serious critical attention and that popular directors like Alfred Hitchcock, Howard Hawks, Vincente Minnelli, and Nicholas Ray merited critical attention. In Sarris's hands auteurism also became an argument for the superiority of American cinema over that of the rest of the world and, indeed, the individualizing and formalist emphasis of auteur theory persists in popular journalism and general film culture in the US today. Back in Europe the debate around auteurism was picked up in the light of the impact of structuralism, which had shifted attention to the codes employed and the structures of a text rather than a hidden or intentional (authorial) meaning. So in British film theory of the 1970s (associated with the magazine *Screen*) there was a shift from the notion of the author or director as a creative source of a work to the idea of a film as a set of structural relationships which *interact* to produce the author's worldview, rather than merely reflect or implement it. With this structuralist approach two notions are brought together that seem contradictory: on the one hand, the individual as director, a singular voice; on the other, the individual as director enmeshed in a number of social, aesthetic, linguistic structures that affect the organization of meaning in a text. For example, the films of John Ford were read through sets of binary oppositions that played out across them: European/Indian, settler/nomad, civilized/savage, book/gun, East/West. The master antinomy was taken to be that between nature and culture borrowed from the structural anthropologist Claude Lévi-Strauss. Auteur structuralism shifted the emphasis from *mise-en-scène* to narrative structures and also displaced the auteur from the center of the work to become but one structure among several others making up the filmtext.

At first sight, the auteur frame would not appear to translate easily to the study of television and other media or popular culture texts. The names of television directors, with the exception of quality drama programs like *Twin Peaks* (which involved the film director David Lynch), are not well known to the general public, whereas those of actors often are. In the study of television the critical frame most employed is that of genre, which is often referred to as the other side of the auteurist coin. Nevertheless, the notion of the author/auteur, if only as a site of reaction, has an important place in media sociology and sociological theory, which may be credited with the latest theoretical twist and turn of the author/auteur. This is actor-network theory, most prominently associated with the French sociologists of science Bruno Latour and Michel Callon. The theory's aim is to describe a society of humans and nonhumans as equal actors tied together into networks built and maintained in order to achieve a particular goal, for example the development of a product. Latour recognized that semiotically both human actors and nonhuman participants (whether artifacts or naturalized constructs like bacteria) were equally "actants" (the term is borrowed from narrative semiotics): they were defined by how they acted and were acted on in the networks of practices. The important fact here is not that humans and nonhumans are treated symmetrically but that they are defined relationally as functions in the network, and not otherwise. An actor network, then, is the act linked together with all of its influencing factors (which again are linked), producing a network. The similarities and resonances with Barthes's demise of the subject, Foucault's "author-function," and Derrida's "signature effect" will be obvious. Actor-network theory opens up a new approach to cultural production, which is no longer to be understood in any individualistic way (the author as subject), but is rather shaped by the social and material organization of work, the means of communication, and the spatial arrangements of institutions. It is also important that, for Latour, actor-network theory attempts to overcome the major shortfalls of modernism. The epistemology of modernism divided nature and society into two incommensurable poles. Nature was only observed, never man-made; whereas society was only made by humans. The two poles were indirectly connected by language which allowed us to make stable references to either one of them. It is Latour's goal to show that the separation introduced by modernism is artificial. Because (technological) reality is simultaneously real, like nature, narrated, like discourse, and collective, like society, it does not follow the clean divisions envisioned by modernism, and Latour has claimed that *We Have Never Been Modern* (1993).

A number of people have contributed to this encyclopedia, but, it might be argued, all under the direction of George Ritzer. This could imply that this is *his* encyclopedia and that he is therefore the *author*, but as most of the words are not his own, it is fairly clear that he could not be regarded as the author. If this was a film, and George Ritzer was the director, we might argue as to whether his direction of the process was so complete as to overpower any input from his collaborators, or whether it is in fact difficult, perhaps impossible, to assert his authorship because of the overwhelming nature of the collaborative process: the roles of advisers, consulting editors, famous experts in their fields, etc. A second issue to consider is one of organizational control: if this encyclopedia is a product of Blackwell Publishing, any claim George Ritzer might have to be its creator, or director of operations, might be nullified, in the same way that a studio system might influence the input of any director to their finished film. So perhaps the best theory might be that George Ritzer is simply some actor in a network of practices. Whatever the solution, even here at the opening of the twenty-first century, it is clear that the claims and complexities of the arguments around the notion of author/auteur will not go away.

SEE ALSO: Actor-Network Theory; Actor-Network Theory, Actants; Barthes, Roland; Cultural Reproduction; Derrida, Jacques; Foucault, Michel; Poststructuralism; Structuralism

REFERENCES AND SUGGESTED READINGS

Barthes, R. (1977) The Death of the Author. In: *Image Music Text*. Fontana, London.
Brooks, C. and Penn Warren, R. (1938) *Understanding Poetry*. Henry Holt, New York.
Derrida, J. (1984) *Signéponge/Signsponge*. Trans. R. Rand. Columbia University Press, New York.
Foucault, M. (2000) What Is an Author? In: Faubion, J. (Ed.), *Aesthetics, Method and Epistemology: Essential Works of Foucault 1954–1984*, Vol. 2. Penguin, London (this translation includes both the Paris and Buffalo versions of the text).
Latour, B. (1993) *We Have Never Been Modern*. Prentice-Hall, London.
Law, J. & Hassard, J. (1999) *Actor Network Theory and After*. Blackwell, Oxford.
Wimsatt, W. K. & Beardsley, M. C. (1954) The Intentional Fallacy. In: *The Verbal Icon*. University of Kentucky Press, Lexington.

authoritarian personality

Thomas F. Pettigrew

The authoritarian personality is a psychological syndrome of traits that correlates highly with outgroup prejudice. Three personality traits in particular characterize the syndrome: deference to authorities, aggression toward outgroups, and rigid adherence to cultural conventions. Thus, authoritarians hold a rigidly hierarchical view of the world.

Nazi Germany inspired the first conceptualizations. The Frankfurt School, combining Marxism, psychoanalysis, and sociology, introduced the syndrome to explain Hitler's popularity among working-class Germans. An early formulation appeared in Erich Fromm's (1941) *Escape from Freedom*. American social psychologists soon demonstrated the syndrome in the United States. In 1950, the major publication, *The Authoritarian Personality*, appeared. The product of two German refugees (Theodor Adorno and Else Frankel-Brunswik) and two American social psychologists (Daniel Levinson and Nevitt Sanford) at the Berkeley campus of the University of California, this publication firmly established the concept in social science. The volume offered both clinical and questionnaire evidence. But it was the easily administered F (for fascism) Scale that led to an explosion of more than 2,000 published research papers.

Critics immediately disparaged the work on political, methodological, and theoretical grounds. Right-wing detractors questioned the finding that political conservatives averaged higher scores on the F Scale. They argued that there was widespread authoritarianism on the left as well. To be sure, the Berkeley investigators were politically liberal, and the syndrome exists on the left. But research repeatedly shows that the syndrome is preponderantly found among those on the political right. Indeed, a modern measure is simply called the Right-Wing Authoritarianism Scale.

Methodological critics unearthed a host of problems. For example, the clinical evaluators were not blind to the F-Scale scores of their interviewees. Consequently, their assessments were not independently derived. No probability samples of respondents were tested – only samples of convenience (usually college students). The F Scale itself has problems. All the items are worded positively, so that agreement indicates authoritarian tendencies. This allows response sets to invalidate some scores, because some respondents agree or disagree regardless of the item content.

The Authoritarian Personality also provoked theoretical criticism. Its Freudian foundation is difficult to test directly. Many objected to its nominalist approach – the use of extreme categories based on the highest fourth of F-Scale scores labeled "authoritarians" and the lowest fourth labeled "equalitarians." The Berkeley co-authors virtually ignored the middle half of their subject distribution. The most important theoretical objection concerned the 1950 study's neglect of the social context. Authoritarianism rises in times of societal threat, and recedes in times of calm. Crises invoke authoritarian leadership and encourage equalitarians to accept such leadership. Moreover, the syndrome's link to behavior is strongly related to the situational context in which authoritarians find themselves.

Many of these criticisms have merit. Nonetheless, research throughout the world with various F Scales shows that authoritarians reveal similar susceptibilities. In particular, high scorers are more likely than others to favor extreme right-wing politics and exhibit prejudice against outgroups. Three key questions arise: Just what is authoritarianism? What are its origins? And why does it universally predict prejudice against a variety of outgroups?

This remarkable global consistency of results, despite the problems involved, suggests that the authoritarian personality is a general personality syndrome with early origins in childhood that center on universal issues of authority. A plethora of theories attempt to define the personality type and its origins. The original Berkeley study viewed it as a personality type with particular characteristics. Relying on psychoanalytic theory, it stressed the effects of a stern father in early life. Later formulations emphasize the syndrome's focus on strength and weakness, its intense orientation to the ingroup, and the

importance of modeling of authoritarian behavior by parents. The most recent work on the syndrome's origins connects authoritarianism with attachment theory. Rejection by an early caregiver, often the mother, leads to an avoidance attachment style that closely resembles the authoritarian personality. Recent survey data with a probability sample of German adults reveal a strong relationship between the syndrome and a strong desire to avoid interpersonal closeness.

These German surveys also suggest why authoritarianism is universally related to outgroup prejudice. Developed early in life, authoritarianism later leads to conditions and behaviors that in turn generate intergroup prejudice. For example, authoritarians more often feel politically powerless ("political inefficacy") and that modern life is too complex and bewildering ("anomia") – both predictors of prejudice. Situational factors are also involved. Authoritarians tend to associate with others who are prejudiced. And they tend to avoid contact with outgroup members – a major means for reducing prejudice.

Thus, the authoritarian personality concept is an important tool for social science to understand a range of important social phenomena. For all its problems, it has stood the test of time and an abundance of research. But it operates at the individual level of analysis. Writers often erroneously employ it to explain societal phenomena – a compositional fallacy that assumes societal processes are mere composites of individual behavior. However, when authoritarianism is combined with situational and societal perspectives, it gains explanatory power in accounting for such phenomena as extreme right-wing politics and intergroup prejudice.

SEE ALSO: Adorno, Theodor W.; Critical Theory/Frankfurt School; Fromm, Erich; Holocaust; Race; Race (Racism); Scapegoating; Slurs (Racial/Ethnic)

REFERENCES AND SUGGESTED READINGS

Adorno, T. W., Frankel-Brunswik, E., Levinson, D. J., & Sanford, R. N. (1950) *The Authoritarian Personality*. Harper & Row, New York.

Altemeyer, B. (1988) *Enemies of Freedom: Understanding Right-Wing Authoritarianism*. Jossey-Bass, San Francisco.

Christie, R. & Jahoda, M. (Eds.) (1954) *Studies in the Scope and Method of "The Authoritarian Personality."* Free Press, Glencoe, IL.

Fromm, E. (1941) *Escape from Freedom*. Rinehart, New York.

Pettigrew, T. F. (1999) Placing Authoritarianism in Social Context. *Politics, Group, and the Individual* 8: 5–20.

Sales, S. (1973) Threat as a Factor in Authoritarianism: An Analysis of Archival Data. *Journal of Personality and Social Psychology* 28: 44–57.

Sanford, R. N. (1973) Authoritarian Personality in Contemporary Perspective. In: Knutson, J. N. (Ed.), *Handbook of Political Psychology*. Jossey-Bass, San Francisco, pp. 139–70.

Strong, W. F., Lederer, G., & Christie, R. (Eds.) (1992) *Strength and Weakness: The Authoritarian Personality Today*. Springer-Verlag, New York.

authoritarianism

Esperanza Palma

The concept of authoritarianism has been used mainly to refer to a type of authority whose power is exercised within diffuse legal, institutional, or de facto boundaries that easily leads to arbitrary acts against groups and individuals. Those who are in power are not accountable to constituencies and public policy does not derive from social consent.

Within sociology and political science, particularly within comparative politics, authoritarianism has been understood as a modern type of political regime. Therefore, the concept focuses on the way of accessing, exercising, and organizing power, on the nature of the belief system, and the role of citizens in the political process. This notion has had an important conceptual development since the 1970s, which clarified some ambiguities within political analyses that tended to mix up this type of regime with fascism and other forms of totalitarianism. The concept of authoritarianism has included a range of regimes, from personal dictatorships such as Franco's in Spain in the 1930s, hegemonic party regimes like the Mexican regime founded after the

1910 Revolution, and the military governments of South America established during the 1960s and 1970s. The context in which this type of regime was founded was generally a protracted situation of instability such as a revolution (Mexico), a civil war (Spain), a democratic crisis (Chile), and deterioration of the economy and political polarization (Argentina). Most countries where an authoritarian regime was founded had neither a liberal democratic rule nor an opportunity to develop a state of law, and the construction of the nation was mediated not primarily by the concept of the citizen but rather by the notion of "the people."

As part of non-democratic politics, authoritarianism does not fulfill the two theoretical dimensions of polyarchy defined by Robert Dahl (1971), public contestation and inclusiveness, which translate into eight requirements: freedom to form and join organizations, freedom of expression, right to vote, eligibility for public office, right of political leaders to compete for support, alternative sources of information, free and fair elections, and institutions for making government policies depend on votes and other expressions of preference.

Authoritarianism does not allow either public contestation (organization of opposition) or participation of all citizens (extension of the suffrage). Even though these dimensions can develop to some extent, they are always restricted because the political monopoly of the group in power cannot be placed at risk. Elections might be held under some authoritarian regimes, as was the case in Mexico where universal suffrage was guaranteed, and yet their function is not to allow citizens to decide who will govern but rather to corroborate the permanence of a group in power, and to allow recycling of the members of the same political elite. In some other cases like South Africa under apartheid, contestation was effective but a racial group was excluded from participation.

Although it has been clear that all forms of non-democratic regimes do not fulfill the requirements of polyarchy, it has been less clear what the differences are between authoritarianism and totalitarianism. In academic debate, there have been key authors and works that, based on comparative analyses, have developed a theory of authoritarianism and that have specified its method of functioning. These authors are, among others, Juan Linz, who first studied the case of Spain under Franco, and Guillermo O'Donnell, who made a crucial contribution to the understanding of some Latin American cases by analyzing the regimes that followed military coups of the 1960s and 1970s in Argentina, Brazil, Uruguay, and Chile. From these analyses he developed the concept of "bureaucratic authoritarianism."

In a seminal article, Linz (1964) proposed a typology of political regimes which clearly distinguished among totalitarianism, authoritarianism, and democracy. The main contribution of this work is that it poses the view that authoritarianism is not a form of transitional regime but, rather, a stable institutional arrangement which resolves in a particular manner the obtaining of obedience, legitimacy, social control, relation to social groups, and recruitment of the political elite, among others. As Linz (1975) points out in an essay in which he treats thoroughly the differences between authoritarianism and totalitarianism, the borderline between non-democratic and democratic regimes is a rigid one that cannot be crossed by slow and imperceptible evolution but almost always requires a violent break. The definition of authoritarianism excludes totalitarian regimes, traditional legitimate regimes or oligarchies, and nineteenth-century semi-constitutional monarchies. It also excludes earlier stages of modern democracies where suffrage was restricted to some layers of the male population.

Authoritarianisms are political systems with limited, not responsible, political pluralism; without elaborate ideology, but with distinctive mentalities; without extensive or intensive political mobilization, except at some points in their development; and in which a leader or occasionally a small group exercises power within formally ill-defined, but actually quite predictable, limits (Linz 1975: 255). Totalitarian regimes, by contrast, have an ideology, a single mass party, and other mobilizational organizations, and concentrate power in an individual and his collaborators.

In contrast to the unlimited pluralism of democracies, the *limited pluralism* under authoritarian regimes does establish legal or de facto limits to political and/or interest groups. Yet, there might be some institutionalization of political participation of a limited number of independent groups that might lead to complex patterns of semi-opposition. Limited pluralism could have its expression in a number of organizations or in the composition of a political elite that can have diverse origins and viewpoints; however, in some cases it is neither illegitimate nor legitimate – in the sense that citizens can organize and freely express their preferences – but rather tolerated by the authoritarian rulers.

Authoritarian elites hold a *mentality* rather than an ideology, which is a system of thought more or less intellectually elaborated and organized, often in written form, by intellectuals. Mentalities are ways of thinking and feeling, more emotional than rational, that provide non-codified ways of reacting to different situations. Ideologies have a strong utopian element and capacity for mass mobilization whereas mentalities are more difficult to diffuse among the masses. The founding group or leader of the regime has few ideological commitments except some vague ideas about defending order, uniting the country, modernizing the nation, overthrowing a corrupt regime, or rejecting foreign influences. Vis-à-vis limited pluralism and the absence of an ideology, the distinction between state and society is not fully obliterated.

Generally speaking, the absence of an ideological commitment translates into *low political mobilization*. Yet, some types of authoritarian regimes needed mobilization at the time of their founding. The historical and social context of the establishment of the regime favors or demands such a mobilization through a single party and its mass organizations. Struggle for national independence from a colonial power or the defeat of a highly mobilized opponent led to the emergence of mobilizational authoritarian regimes of a nationalist, populist variety, like the case of Mexico, whose regime was preceded by a revolution. However, once established, the political elite promotes demobilization and apathy.

Power is concentrated in a group and there cannot be rotation in power, although it does not have to be concentrated in a party. Given limited pluralism and absence of an ideology, the political elite is not so exclusive. There might be some semi-opposition that is willing to participate in power without challenging the regime.

From this general framework of analysis some subtypes of authoritarian regimes are derived. Linz takes two main variables for distinguishing among cases: (1) limited pluralism, taking into account which groups and institutions are allowed to participate and which ones are excluded, and (2) the nature of the limited mobilization. These two dimensions give several subtypes (Linz 1975: 278): bureaucratic-authoritarian regimes, organic statism, mobilizational authoritarian regimes, post-independence mobilizational authoritarian regimes, racial and ethnic "democracies," pre-totalitarian political situations, and post-totalitarian authoritarian regimes.

If we take the dimension of limited pluralism, political power is controlled by certain social forces and channeled through different organizational structures. On that account authoritarian regimes range from those dominated by a military-technocratic elite to those in which there is a single dominant party. If we turn to the other dimension, we find that in a bureaucratic-military regime there are few, if any, channels for participation. There are also regimes that attempt to mobilize the citizens to participate through a single or dominant party. The circumstances under which mobilizational authoritarian regimes have appeared, such as an independent movement from foreign domination, must be taken into account.

Bureaucratic-military authoritarian regimes, which have developed neither a more complex institutionalization of limited pluralism in the form of organic statism nor a single party contributing to the recruitment of the top-level elite serving as an instrument of control and as a channel for participation of citizens, are the paradigmatic authoritarian regimes. The most important analyses of bureaucratic-military authoritarian regimes have been developed by O'Donnell and one of the most important debates has been aired in the book compiled by David Collier, *The New Authoritarianism in Latin America* (1979), which presents crucial works and a collective debate held by Guillermo O'Donnell, Fernando Enrique

Cardoso, Albert Hirschman, and Robert Kaufman, among others.

The military coups of the 1960s and 1970s put into question the central assumption of modernization theory that democracy was associated with industrialization. Contrary to this theory, Brazil (1964) and Argentina (1966 and 1976) showed high levels of industrialization at the time of their coups. Uruguay and Chile (1973) used to have institutionalized, strong democracies. These cases posed the need to rethink and analyze the new authoritarianism that was becoming institutionalized. Thus, after the resurgence of authoritarianism in the 1960s and 1970s, some Latin American countries were facing a paradox: they were becoming more modern and at the same time more authoritarian (Cardoso 1979: 39).

Also a central characteristic of the debate on Latin American authoritarianism during the 1970s was the need for a new concept for understanding this regime in order to distinguish it from previous experiences of authoritarian forms of exercising power in the region. *Caudillismo* as a form of authoritarian leadership has always been present in Latin America, and yet what was new in the 1960s and 1970s was that the military as an institution took power in order to restructure the society and the state under a national security doctrine. Hence, the concept of bureaucratic authoritarianism. The concept was useful to characterize cases where a military intervention took place. To the extent that situations preceding military coups were economic crisis, hyperinflation, and political polarization, military governments envisioned their task and justified their actions as the need to restore order and normalize the economy (O'Donnell 1997a: 98).

Some of the distinctive characteristics of bureaucratic authoritarianism are that, unlike European fascism, it aimed to promote political apathy among the population, annihilated political parties, and the state did not take a corporativist form (Cardoso 1979: 290). Political domination was supported by the high bourgeoisie, and it was a system based upon exclusion of a previously active popular sector and the suppression of the citizenry. Expertise of coercion played a decisive role within government, which implemented a supposedly neutral technical rationale for saving capitalism and eliminating groups that were responsible for "social diseases" by taking highly repressive measures (O'Donnell 1997b).

Most authoritarian regimes in Southern Europe and Latin America, as well as Eastern European regimes, were swept away by the third wave of democratization (Huntington 1991) during the 1970s and 1980s as the result of complex processes of legitimacy crisis, the spread of democratic values, international pressure, growth of opposition movements, and divisions within authoritarian elites. Democratizing processes inaugurated new lines of political and sociological research. One of them was the debate on the characteristics of authoritarianism and to what extent these characteristics and differences among cases determined a diversity of paths of transitions to democracy. For instance, it was an issue whether a more institutionalized authoritarian regime like that in Mexico made a more lengthy transition than a regime that depended to a great extent on a dictator, as in Spain. Another important trend that transitions to democracy brought into academic debate was the process of democratization itself and what could be learned about political and regime change in general from the third wave (O'Donnell & Schmitter 1989). A current research area is the concern for the conditions under which democracies would be stable and become consolidated (Mainwaring et al. 1992). Some cases in Latin America from the beginning of the twenty-first century, where democracy seems to be at stake, bring attention to further empirical research within political science on the conditions that prevent democratic breakdowns which in the past facilitated the emergence of authoritarian solutions. Some of this empirical research focuses on institutional design and arrangements, such as form of government, presidential or parliamentary democracy, electoral and party systems, and types of opposition (Mainwaring & Schugart 1997).

SEE ALSO: Apartheid and Nelson Mandela; Authority and Legitimacy; *Caudillismo*; Democracy; Fascism; Modernization; Political Sociology; Totalitarianism

REFERENCES AND SUGGESTED READINGS

Cardoso, F. (1979) Sobre la caracterización de los regimenes autoritarios en América Latina. In: Collier, D. (Comp.), *The New Authoritarianism in Latin America*. Princeton University Press, Princeton, pp. 39–62.

Collier, D. (Comp.) (1979) *The New Authoritarianism in Latin America*. Princeton University Press, Princeton.

Dahl, R. (1971) *Polyarchy: Participation and Opposition*. Yale University Press, New Haven.

Huntington, S. (1991) *The Third Wave*. University of Oklahoma Press, Oklahoma.

Linz, J. (1964) A Theory of Authoritarian Regime: The Case of Spain. In: Allardt, E. & Littunen,Y. (Eds.), *Cleavages, Ideologies, and Party Systems*. Transactions of the Westermarck Society, Vol. X, Helsinki, pp. 291–341.

Linz, J. (1975) Totalitarian and Authoritarian Regimes. In: Greenstein, F. & Polsby, N. (Eds.), *Macropolitical Theory: Handbook of Political Science*, Vol. 3. Wesley, Reading, MA, pp. 175–411.

Mainwaring, S. & Schugart, M. S. (Comp.) (1997) *Presidentialism and Democracy in Latin America*. Cambridge University Press, Cambridge.

Mainwaring, S. et al. (1992) *Issues in Democratic Consolidation: The New South American Democracies in Comparative Perspective*. University of Notre Dame Press, Notre Dame, IN.

O'Donnell, G. (1997a) Las fuerzas armadas y el estado autoritario del Cono Sur de América Latina. In: *Contrapuntos*. Paidós, Argentina, pp. 97–127.

O'Donnell, G. (1997b) Notas para el estudio de procesos de democratización política a partir del estado burocrático-autoritario. In: *Contrapuntos*. Paidós, Argentina, pp. 199–217.

O'Donnell, G. & Schmitter, P. (1989) *Transitions from Authoritarian Rule*. Johns Hopkins University Press, Baltimore.

authority and conformity

Mark Konty

A common phenomenon in social groups (some would say a requirement) is the existence of authority: the right or power to give orders and enforce standards. Authority is only meaningful if people comply with those rules and orders. Conformity, compliance with orders and standards, is the corollary to authority.

Early sociological views of authority and conformity examined their role in meeting the rational or functional requirements of a society (e.g., the maintenance of social order). Weber's (1968) discussion of legitimate authority is a good example of this line of thinking. Among other things, Weber wanted to explain how authority induces conformity in a society. On the one hand, coercion can ensure compliance with authority. People in a group will conform to the dictates of authority if they are threatened with physical or economic harm. On the other hand, Weber believed that societies could not rely totally on coercion. Instead, he argued, the people in a society had to view the authority as legitimate so that conformity to the orders and standards is voluntary and not coerced.

Weber outlined three types of legitimate authority. *Rational–legal* authority ensures conformity by creating a system of rules and procedures by which everyone is bound. Conformity is given voluntarily because the greatest benefit is obtained within the system. *Traditional* authority produces conformity because people view the position and succession of authority as a product of the past and thus as an arrangement that should continue to exist. There is no rational calculation of benefits, simply the recognition that all is as it should be. *Charismatic* authority encourages conformity by convincing group members that the person in the position of authority possesses some unique qualities and the authority should thus be obeyed. Authority of this type exists only as long as the charismatic person exists and with that person's demise the authority simply disappears or may transform into traditional authority passed through a line of successors. By any of these three mechanisms a society's members conform to the authority of the leader without the threat of coercion because they believe the authority is legitimate and thus the demands are legitimate.

MICRO-LEVEL PERSPECTIVES

After World War II many German citizens and soldiers charged with war crimes responded with the claim that they were not responsible for their actions because they were simply "following orders." Responsibility for war crimes was mitigated by the position that conformity to authority is natural and thus the individual could not be held responsible for the consequences of obedience. This claim led to a new line of inquiry examining the micro-level relationship between authority and conformity. American social scientists questioned the argument that people conform to authority as a matter of course. They argued that any rational individual would recognize the heinous consequences of his actions and resist the call of authority to commit atrocities.

Asch (1955) began this line of inquiry with a series of conformity studies. Asch believed that people would not conform to group consensus if their senses told them that the group was wrong. Asch's subjects came into a room with a number of other subjects who were actually confederates of the experimenter. The group was presented with three lines of different lengths and asked which line is similar in length to a comparison line. At first all of the participants seated at the table selected the correct line. After a few trials, however, the confederates begin to choose the obviously wrong line. When the confederates chose the correct line the subjects had less than a 1 percent error rate. When the confederates chose the incorrect line the subjects' error rate increased to almost 40 percent.

All of the subjects reported that they knew the correct line to choose, but they began to question their own judgment in the face of group consensus and decided to conform to the group rather than break consensus. Interestingly, if only one other person in the room confirmed the subjects' choice, the error rate fell below 10 percent. Confirmation by one other person was enough to break conformity to an obviously wrong choice. Asch discovered that people will defy their own senses to conform to the group, but can dissent with the support of others.

Milgram (1974) designed an experiment intended to show that people could resist authority if the demands of that authority are repugnant to the individual. The experiments required naïve subjects to administer increasingly more severe punishments to another person engaged in a learning experiment.

The person receiving the shocks was a confederate of the experimenter and no real punishment was administered, but the subject believed the punishment was real. Most subjects followed instructions and administered a level of shock listed as "extreme intensity" and a large majority willingly administered a level of shock above "danger," listed as "XXX" on the voltage dial. All of the subjects expressed some level of unease with administering such obviously painful punishment, but verbal prodding by the experimenter is all that was required to raise the level of punishment.

Milgram thus demonstrated the opposite of what he predicted: people are willing to conform to authority even if that conformity requires the commission of a harmful act. Milgram concluded that the university setting, the researcher in a lab coat, and the seriousness of the actions undertaken by the subject all combined to give the subject the impression that the experimenter had the authority to demand conformity, which is precisely what the subjects did. Both Asch and Milgram found that people will set aside their own senses and beliefs to conform to the group or individual authority.

Zimbardo (1972) took the authority and conformity paradigm a step further to see if authority and conformity emerged from individual traits or characteristics of the situation. Zimbardo believed that the situation signals to the individual the types of behavior that are expected. Individuals then act on those expectations; they conform to the expectations of the situation. To test this hypothesis Zimbardo and his colleagues created a mock prison and randomly assigned experimental subjects to play a role as either a guard or a prisoner within this setting. Even though the situation was contrived, the subjects conformed to the expectations of their roles as if they were in a real prison setting. Guards began to abuse prisoners and prisoners began to rebel against the oppression. Zimbardo had to stop the experiment after only a few days because the guards had become too abusive and the prisoners began to show signs of mental strain.

The prison experiment demonstrated that authority is a property of a social position, not individuals, and that conformity is not an individual trait but rather a common motivation that manifests in even the most contrived situations. These findings shed some light on Asch and Milgram's observations. Asch's study demonstrated the power of conformity to overcome even an obvious definition of reality. Milgram's study demonstrated that authority comes from social positions and that this authority can induce conformity even when it violates the individual's own values and beliefs. As Milgram (1974: 139) himself states: "The power of an authority stems not from personal characteristics but from his perceived position in a social structure." The force of the situation can overcome whatever individual traits are brought to the setting.

These results on conformity raise an interesting question: when do people resist authority and not conform? As Asch discovered, the presence of allies increases resistance to authority. This was also confirmed in some of Milgram's studies. Another way to approach this question is to look at the mechanisms influencing conformity. Within a situation people are influenced by the extant social structure. Milgram argued that if people believe that the higher-status person has "legitimate" authority then conformity is more likely. Milgram (1974: 133) viewed responses to legitimate authority as an "agentic state ... the condition a person is in when he sees himself as an agent for carrying out another person's wishes." The basic mechanism is that the lower-status individual believes that responsibility for any subsequent act rests with the legitimate authority. The lower-status person is absolved of any responsibility for committing heinous acts in the name of the legitimate authority.

Another set of studies using Milgram's obedience paradigm, the Utrecht studies, specifically tested for this mechanism (Meeus & Raaijmakers 1995). When the low-status person is under "legal liability" for his actions the rate of obedience is significantly lowered. That is, when the low-status person becomes solely responsible for her actions, she is less likely to obey. The converse is also demonstrated in these studies: when the low-status person is given "legal cover" the rate of obedience returns to baseline levels. These results are consistent with some other studies showing that low-status persons will not obey if the act directly harms them (for reviews of this and other variations on the Milgram obedience paradigm, see Miller et al. 1995; Blass 2000).

These lines of research all point to the power of the situation to influence people. Researchers posit many kinds of "authority" (Blass 2000), but all influence to conformity has a common characteristic: it is social in nature. A broader theoretical paradigm examining authority and conformity is "social influence." While there are many theoretical veins in this paradigm, the basic premise is that the authority of the social group influences the behavior of group members (Zanna et al. 1987). Ceteris paribus, group members are inclined to conform to the expectations of their social group. Social identity theory (Abrams & Hogg 1999) is one theory of social influence that is integrated into sociological social psychology (Stets & Burke 2000). Theories of social influence will likely direct future micro-level explanations for the construction of authority and its influence on conformity.

CURRENT MACRO PERSPECTIVES

With the emergence of globalization and related social problems like global terrorism, sociologists have new reason to examine the macro-level implications of authority and conformity. The massive international corporate structures that both create and sustain globalization represent a type of authority with tremendous influence. The authority of these organizations is not vested in a single individual, but rather within the structure of the organization itself. Conformity takes the form of workers complying with corporate dictates, as well as the effect the corporations have in homogenizing culture.

The McDonald's corporation, to take one example, not only introduces a structure for doing business to which all its subsidiaries and franchises around the world conform, but in each locale where a McDonald's is located a little bit of the local culture is homogenized with the "global" culture that McDonald's

brings (Ritzer 2000). This attempt to produce conformity on a global scale is often met with stiff resistance from other macro-level sources of authority such as religion and clan ties. These two forces, corporate authority and religious authority, induce conformity in seemingly opposite directions and often produce a high level of conflict between the competing worldviews (Barber 1995).

The US's "war on terror" produced its own startling example of macro-level authority and conformity. In late 2003 the world became aware that US military forces were engaged in interrogation techniques that many defined as torture. Some of the soldiers' actions were visually recorded and the images created a political scandal over who was responsible for the acts; that is, on whose authority the acts were carried out. In a hierarchical structure like the US military it is assumed that all authority is top-down. The political administration, however, denied giving orders to carry out these actions. No evidence of authority ordering these acts was ever found. However, there is substantial evidence that the political leaders at the time created an organizational mandate to effectively press the war on terror by almost any means necessary, including "outrages against personal dignity." Many of the soldiers charged with abusing prisoners claimed that they were simply conforming to the expectations of the military and political command and that it was the organization itself that fostered the belief that this kind of activity was promoted from the highest levels of authority (Hooks & Mosher 2005).

Globalization continues to expand the reach of all kinds of authority, from corporate and media influences to religious evangelism. The demands of group membership and hierarchical structures continue to produce heinous acts around the world. As new and old sources of authority influence conformity, theory and research into these phenomena maintain an important role in understanding local and global transformation.

SEE ALSO: Asch Experiments; Deviance; Group Processes; Milgram, Stanley (Experiments); Social Control; Social Influence; Weber, Max; Zimbardo Prison Experiment

REFERENCES AND SUGGESTED
READINGS

Abrams, D. & Hogg, M. A. (Eds.) (1999) *Social Identity and Social Cognition*. Blackwell, Oxford.
Asch, S. H. (1955) Opinions and Social Pressure. *Scientific American* 193: 5.
Barber, B. R. (1995) *Jihad vs. McWorld*. Ballantine Books, New York.
Blass, T. (Ed.) (2000) *Obedience to Authority: Current Perspectives on the Milgram Pardigm*. Lawrence Erlbaum Associates, Mahwah, NJ.
Hooks, G. & Mosher, C. (2005) Outrages Against Personal Dignity: Rationalizing Abuse and Torture in the War on Terror. *Social Forces* 83(4): 1627–46.
Meeus, Wim H. J. & Raaijmakers, Q. A. W. (1995) Obedience in Modern Society: The Utrecht Studies. *Journal of Social Issues* 51: 155–75.
Milgram, S. (1974) *Obedience to Authority: An Experimental View*. Harper & Row, New York.
Miller, A. G., Colins, B. E., & Brier, D. E. (Eds.) (1995) Perspectives on Obedience to Authority: The Legacy of the Milgram Experiments. *Journal of Social Issues* 51: 3.
Ritzer, G. (2000) *The McDonaldization of Society*. Pine Forge Press, Thousand Oaks, CA.
Stets, J. E. & Burke, P. J. (2000) Identity Theory and Social Identity Theory. *Social Psychological Quarterly* 63: 224–37.
Weber, M. (1968) *Economy and Society*. Ed. G. Roth & C. Wittich. Bedminster, New York.
Zanna, M. P., Olson, J. M., & Herman, C. P. (Eds.) (1987) *Social Influence*. Lawrence Erlbaum Associates, Hillsdale, NJ.
Zimbado, P. G. (1972) *The Stanford Prison Experiment: A Simulation Study of the Psychology of Imprisonment*. Phillip G. Zimbardo, Stanford.

authority and legitimacy

Stephen Turner

Authority is often defined as legitimate power, and contrasted to pure power. In the case of legitimate authority, compliance is voluntary and based on a belief in the right of the authority to demand compliance. In the case of pure power, compliance to the demands of the powerful is based on fear of consequences or self-interest. But beyond this, there is considerable disagreement and variation of usage.

Because legitimacy is a concept from monarchic rule, deriving from the right of the legitimately born heir to rule as monarch, authors as diverse as Hannah Arendt and Carl Schmitt have argued that it is not applicable to modern politics. But it is nevertheless commonly applied, even in ordinary political discussion, to many situations, such as voluntary compliance to taxation, that go far beyond the original meaning.

Both "legitimate" and "authority" are terms which appear in sociology as a neutralized or value-free form of a concept that is normative or valuative in ordinary usage and in political theory. In its normative form, it distinguishes mere power from authority that is genuinely justified. One approach to sociologizing the term builds on these theories. Normally these are theories of representation, in which a person holding authority merely does so as a representative or delegate of the originating power.

The relations of representation that figure in governing ideologies have, historically, been very diverse. In the western political tradition, for example, kings were held to have "two bodies," one being their body as representative of the nation, which legitimately exercised authority, the other their personal body, which did not (Kantorowicz 1957). In modern western political thought, parliaments and presidents are supposed to represent the will of the people. In Islamic political thought, God is the final basis of political authority, and the people are his caliphs or representatives, themselves subservient to Divine Law. Some sociological approaches to legitimacy, such as Habermas's (1975), are attempts to consider the social conditions of genuine deliberative democracy, and treat these as representing genuine legitimacy and their absence as explanations for "crises" of legitimacy.

The most influential approach to the transformation of legitimacy into a sociological, descriptive concept was performed by Max Weber, who provided a famous classification of forms of legitimate authority in terms of the defining type of legitimating belief. Weber (1978: 36–8) identifies four distinct "bases" of legitimacy, three of which are directly associated with forms of authority. The fourth – value-rational faith – legitimates authority indirectly by providing a standard of justice to which particular earthly authorities might claim to correspond. The forms of authority are charismatic, traditional, and rational-legal. Each of these forms can serve on its own as the core of a system of domination. Traditional authority is based on unwritten rules; rational-legal authority on written rules. Unwritten rules may be justified by the belief that they have held true since time immemorial, while written rules are more typically justified by the belief that they have been properly enacted in accordance with other laws. Charismatic authority is command which is not based on rules. The charismatic leader says "it is written, but I say unto you," as Jesus said. What the charismatic leader says overrides and replaces any written rule. Charismatic authority originates in the extraordinary qualities of the person holding this authority, not in another source, such as the will of the people (pp. 212–54).

Weber also points to a variety of practical motives for adherence to a legal order that are not "legitimating" but which may make a powerful causal contribution to the acceptance of the order. These may include the pragmatic value of adherence and the fear of punishment. The element of legitimating belief necessary to sustain a legal order, consequently, may in many circumstances not need to be particularly large, as long as the regime assures compliance or acceptance in other ways. Weber largely ignored, and has been criticized for ignoring (Beetham 1974: 264–9), the idea of democratic legitimacy, because he considered democracy in its pure form to be possible only in small communities, and suggested that modern democracies typically involved a complex mixture of beliefs in which procedural rationality or "rational-legal" authority was central, but which also involved charismatic authority, for example in the context of elections and leadership.

The concept of legitimate authority has many extended uses. Legitimacy is often viewed in modern political sociology as similar to trust, as a resource that regimes have and can employ to gain acceptance of policies. One can distinguish "input" or procedural sources of legitimacy from output sources, such as effectiveness, for example, and see both as

alternative sources of trust (Scharpf 1999). In the case of expertise, for example, cognitive authority might be said to derive from the procedural fact of peer review or from the successful application of expertise.

SEE ALSO: Authority and Conformity; Belief; Democracy; Expertise, "Scientification," and the Authority of Science; Legitimacy; Norms; Power Elite; Representation; Ruling Relations; Weber, Max

REFERENCES AND SUGGESTED READINGS

Beetham, D. (1974) *Max Weber and the Theory of Modern Politics.* George Allen & Unwin, London.

Beetham, D. (1991) *The Legitimation of Power.* Humanities Press International, Atlantic Highlands, NJ.

Easton, D. (1975) A Reassessment of the Concept of Political Support. *British Journal of Political Science* 5: 435–57.

Habermas, J. (1975) *Legitimation Crisis.* Beacon Press, Boston.

Kantorowicz, E. (1957) *The King's Two Bodies: A Study in Mediaeval Political Theology.* Princeton University Press, Princeton.

Lukes, S. (1991) Perspectives on Authority. In: *Moral Conflict and Politics.* Clarendon Press, Oxford, pp. 141–54.

Peters, R. S. (1958) Authority. *Proceedings of the Aristotelian Society* 32: 207–24.

Scharpf, F. W. (1999) *Governing in Europe: Effective and Democratic?* Oxford University Press, Oxford.

Weber, M. (1978 [1968]) *Economy and Society: An Outline of Interpretive Sociology,* 3 vols. Ed. G. Roth & C. Wittich. University of California Press, Berkeley.

Zelditch, M. & Walker, H. (1998) Legitimacy and the Stability of Authority. In: Berger, J. & Zelditch, M., Jr. (Eds.), *Status, Power and Legitimacy: Strategies and Theories.* Transaction Publishers, New Brunswick, NJ, pp. 315–38.

autoethnography

Stacy Holman Jones

Autoethnography is a theoretical, methodological, and (primarily) textual approach that seeks to experience, reflect on, and represent through evocation the relationship among self and culture, individual and collective experience, and identity politics and appeals for social justice. In investigating these relationships, autoethnography fuses personal narrative and sociocultural exploration. Autoethnographic inquiry and writing has long been practiced by journalists and novelists, historians and biographers, travelers and journal writers. However, development of the theoretical, methodological, and textual concerns and conventions of autoethnography among researchers and scholars in the human disciplines is more recent.

Autoethnography, as the term suggests, is closely aligned with ethnography, which in turn is most notably associated with anthropological explorations of cultural practices beginning in the twentieth century (though ethnographic writing dates to the sixteenth century and perhaps earlier). Such explorations focused on cultures as whole systems, subsuming individual and personal experience within larger, often monolithic structures of kinship and interaction. As practitioners of ethnography began to question the possibility and politics of western writers and scholars' claims to objectively and authoritatively investigate and represent exotic "others," ethnographic research and writing moved toward more partial, partisan, local, and personal accounts of culture. Beginning in the 1970s and intensifying in the 1980s, concerns about what any research team or single author can know, verify, and responsibly present as cultural "truth" came to be known as the crises of legitimation, representation, and praxis. These crises prompted a rethinking of the form and purpose of sociocultural investigation and description. Researchers called for accounts that foregrounded dialogue, incompleteness, the impossibility of separating or collapsing life from/into texts, and an ethical responsibility to the "subjects" of ethnography. Such accounts reflect the experience of a postmodern world in which the authority, autonomy, and independence of social, cultural, and personal institutions and practices is shifting and decentered. These accounts also evidence the development of poststructural theory interested in explaining, critiquing, and refiguring relationships among

identity, language, and systems of discourse and power. With these shifts, then, ethnographers recognized the need to explore, understand, evoke, and critique the relationship among not only individuals and cultures but also the subjects, authors, and readers of ethnographic representations.

Renewed interest in individual experience as it is situated in larger cultural systems led ethnographers to reconsider the power and import of personal narrative. In particular, autoethnographic texts feature concrete action, are reflexive and self-critical, and strive to create an emotionally and intellectually charged *engagement* of selves, bodies, texts, and contexts. To create such texts, autoethnographers adopt the conventions of literary writing, calling upon the power of personal narrative and storytelling to conjure how selves are constructed, disclosed, silenced, implicated, and changed in the acts of telling and reading. Autoethnographic texts also self-consciously stage an encounter of subjects, authors, and readers who are often classified as *other* by virtue of their race, class, gender, sexual preferences, religious affiliations, physical abilities, and other mutually implicated identity categories. Such encounters are opportunities to testify to and witness how selves are differently situated, understood, experienced, and changed within and outside such categories. These encounters are also occasions for debating and exchanging ideas about how to create more satisfying, creative, and just ways of being in the world. In this way, autoethnographic texts strive to be *performative* – to demonstrate how selves-in-cultures and cultures-in-selves are not constituted outside of or beyond discourse, language, and history, but are instead created and recreated in the moments of their telling. The performative autoethnographic text evokes how life stories are implicated in the social, cultural, and political contexts in which they are told, as well as how texts – as sites of dialogue and debate – are *themselves* spaces that are questioned and struggled over. In addition, autoethnographic texts are increasingly created *as performances* and thus literally stage encounters among authors, readers, performers, and subjects toward such contested and potentially productive ends.

Given the intellectual, social, and cultural contexts in which autoethnography emerged and the resulting concerns of autoethnographic practices and writing, establishing stable, all-encompassing, and mutually agreed-upon criteria for what constitutes an effective autoethnographic text is a difficult (and perhaps unwelcome) task. However, there are some intersections among the criteria offered for effective autoethnography. Such work should strive to create a visceral lifeworld and a charged emotional and intellectual atmosphere; a relationship of mutual responsibility among subjects, authors, and readers; aesthetic and analytical strategies that generate opportunities for dialogue (rather than an exhibition of mastery); a felt obligation to explain and critique existing systems and discourses of power; and an embodied commitment to act through and on the knowledges of the text. These criteria constitute current challenges facing autoethnographers and act as points of departure for staging more evocative, ambitious, and charged texts.

SEE ALSO: Critical Qualitative Research; Ethnography; Performance Ethnography; Representation; Writing as Method

REFERENCES AND SUGGESTED READINGS

Bochner, A. P. (2000) Criteria Against Ourselves. *Qualitative Inquiry* 6: 266–72.
Bochner, A. P. (2001) Narrative's Virtues. *Qualitative Inquiry* 7: 131–57.
Conquergood, D. (1991) Rethinking Ethnography: Towards a Critical Cultural Politics. *Communication Monographs* 58: 179–94.
Denzin, N. (1997) *Interpretive Ethnography: Ethnographic Practices for the 21st Century.* Sage, Thousand Oaks, CA.
Diamond, E. (1996) Introduction. In: Diamond, E (Ed.), *Performance and Cultural Politics.* Routledge, London, pp. 1–12.
Ellis, C. (2004) *The Ethnographic I: A Methodological Novel about Teaching and Doing Autoethnography.* Alta Mira Press, Walnut Creek, CA.
Holman Jones, S. (2005) Autoethnography: Making the Personal Political. In: Denzin, N. K. & Lincoln, Y. S. (Eds.), *Handbook of Qualitative Research*, 3rd edn. Sage, Thousand Oaks, CA, pp. 763–91.
hooks, b. (1995) Performance Practice as a Site of Opposition. In: Ugwu, C. (Ed.), *Let's Get It On: The Politics of Black Performance.* Bay Press, Seattle, pp. 210–21.
Pollock, D. (1998) Performing Writing. In: Phelan, P. & Lane, J. (Eds.), *The Ends of Performance.* New York University Press, New York, pp. 73–103.
Richardson, L. (2000) Writing: A Method of Inquiry. In: Denzin, N. K. & Lincoln, Y. S. (Eds.), *Handbook of Qualitative Research*, 3rd edn. Sage, Thousand Oaks, CA, pp. 923–48.

autopoiesis

Jens Zinn

The neurobiologists Humberto R. Maturana and Francisco J. Varela introduced the term *autopoiesis* in the 1970s in order to describe how living systems (e.g., human, plant, cell, or microbe) produce and reproduce themselves. Combining the idea of autonomy and production, autopoiesis means in short the continual self-production of living systems. The components of an autopoietic system reproduce themselves and the relations between them by these components and relations (Maturana et al. 1974; Maturana & Varela 1987). It is therefore operationally closed: the system determines the rules of reproduction relatively independently of its specific environment.

Since an autopoietic system is determined by its internal organization of reproduction, it cannot be changed directly from the outside – that would destroy it. It can only be "perturbed." The outside can affect it, but the state of a system itself determines what and how such perturbations will affect it. As a result of ongoing non-destructive perturbations, autopoietic systems become structurally coupled to their environment or to other systems. That does not mean that they blend with a specific environment, but they are loosely coupled. They have only to fit insofar as it allows them to maintain their autopoietic reproduction. (Human beings can live in a wide range of environments from the North Pole to the equator as long as they can nourish themselves on the environment.) From this perspective, social phenomena appear as a result of structurally coupled systems which mutually perturb one another over a period of time.

The concept of autopoiesis supports constructivist ideas of reality. Behaviour is not what a system is doing, but it is ascribed by an *observer*. The observer's observations are at the same time determined by his or her own autopoiesis.

The concept was very influential in several disciplines. In sociology, Luhmann (1989, 1995) took up the concept of autopoietic organization and transferred it into systems theory. Functional systems conceptualized as autopoietic systems cannot influence each other directly. They only notice information that can be transformed into something that is relevant for the respective reproduction of a system. For example, truth as the core element of science is only recognized by the economic system insofar as it can be transformed into money. Such systems are autonomous, but they might become structurally coupled when they mutually constitute relevant environments. Many scientific innovations are obviously very relevant for economic success, while the money provided by the economic system supports scientific research.

Maturana and Varela (1987) were very reluctant to see their concept transformed into the framework of social systems theory. Instead, they prefer to see the concept as strictly bound to biological systems.

SEE ALSO: Constructionism; Luhmann, Niklas; System Theories

REFERENCES AND SUGGESTED READINGS

Luhmann, N. (1989) *Ecological Communication.* Polity Press, Cambridge.
Luhmann, N. (1995) *Social Systems.* Stanford University Press, Stanford.
Maturana, H. R. & Varela, F. J. (1987) *The Tree of Knowledge: The Biological Roots of Human Understanding.* Shambhala, Boston.
Maturana, H. R., Varela, F. J., & Uribe, R. (1974) Autopoiesis: The Organization of Living Systems, Its Characterization and a Model. *Biosystems* 5: 187–96.

awareness contexts

Stefan Timmermans

In their 1965 landmark study *Awareness of Dying*, Barney Glaser and Anselm Strauss introduced awareness context as "what *each* interacting person knows of the patient's defined status, along with his recognition of the others' awareness of his own definition... *awareness context*...is the context within which these people interact while taking cognizance of it." Studying the process of dying in six San Francisco Bay area hospitals, Glaser and Strauss were struck by how little information patients possessed about their impending death, even though the staff were often aware that the patient might be dying. They analyzed the organizational-structural conditions for secrecy, its resulting interactions, changes in awareness, and consequences of the interactions for the participants and the setting. Drawing from the symbolic interactionist tradition, Glaser and Strauss intended to capture the work of managing and negotiating social change within the structural context of the hospital.

Glaser and Strauss distinguished four awareness contexts: *closed awareness, suspicion awareness, mutual-pretense awareness,* and *open awareness*. In a closed awareness context the patient is unaware of pending death while the staff know. Glaser and Strauss found that most patients in the early 1960s died in closed awareness (Glaser & Strauss 1968). Closed awareness reflects a patronizing approach in medicine in which authorities determine what is good for others to know. Ultimately, because it depends on staff and relatives keeping the secret from an unsuspecting patient, closed awareness is an unstable condition that can change into other awareness when the united front breaks down. In a context of suspicion awareness the patients suspect with varying degrees of certainty that the staff consider them dying. Staff and relatives might unwittingly flash clues or even drop hints and patients might search out diagnostic information. Closed and suspicion awareness contexts put much strain on the interactions between nursing staff, relatives, and patients. The most isolating context, however, is the mutual-pretense awareness context when patients and staff know that the patients are dying but pretend otherwise. Both parties might send tentative signs about death which are met with non-response in the daily bustling of the hospital. Finally, when both parties know that the patient is dying, the context changes to open awareness. This context is the prerequisite for Elizabeth Kubler-Ross's psychodynamic stage theory of coping with death (Kubler-Ross 1969). While in open awareness patients know they are dying, uncertainty about the time and manner of dying might still persist with staff and patient managing prognostic knowledge and expectations about appropriate dying styles. Still, in an open awareness context a patient has the opportunity to say farewell to loved ones and take care of estate planning.

Glaser and Strauss's awareness contexts theory was significant as the first comprehensive sociological exploration of the process of dying and helped foster a US social movement of death and dying activism in the early 1970s. Reflecting on Glaser and Strauss's observation that dying patients were often ignored in North American hospitals and the work of Elizabeth Kubler-Ross and Cicely Saunders (Saunders 1978), death activists challenged the patronizing approach to terminal illness and death in institutions. Glaser and Strauss's study in particular gave rise to a subdiscipline of communicating bad news in clinical encounters. Physicians in training increasingly received pointers on how to break bad news. As a consequence, the incidence of the closed, suspicion, and mutual-pretense awareness contexts gradually declined in American and some other western hospitals (Cassileth, Zupkis, et al. 1980). These changes have been explained by an ethos of individualism and a climate of doubt about the beneficence of medical experts. Other countries, notably Japan and Italy, have maintained dying in closed awareness (Gordon 1990; Kai, Ohi, et al. 1993).

Glaser and Strauss framed the interaction around the deathbed in terms of knowledge about pending death. Yet, researchers noted that even when patients and their relatives were increasingly informed, they absorbed the information differently. One person's open awareness was the other's closed awareness:

some people seemed to persist in denial even when they were informed. Based on introspective ethnographies of their own encounters with dying relatives, Stefan Timmermans and Laura Mamo suggested modifications to the open awareness context (Timmermans 1994; Mamo 1999). Timmermans argued that open awareness could be suspended when patients and relatives block out the information provided about the terminal condition. In addition, the information, often provided with qualifiers, might be questioned for accuracy in an attempt to maintain hope. Glaser and Strauss's open awareness context could be subdivided into *suspended open awareness*, *uncertain open awareness*, and *active open awareness*. Mamo argued for a stronger link between the emotional and cognitive aspects of managing, negotiating, and acting upon information about a terminal condition.

In addition to setting a sociological agenda for the study of the dying process, the theory of awareness context has been relevant as an illustration of *grounded theory*, a qualitative data analysis method based on coding schemes and memo-writing aimed at generating theory (Glaser and Strauss 1967). *Awareness of Dying* demonstrated grounded theory's emphasis on inductive conceptualization in a systematic manner to understand a range of interactions. The authors' data gathering in different hospitals was guided by the developing conceptual framework, a strategy they would refer to as *theoretical sampling*, and ongoing comparisons with alternative settings.

Glaser and Strauss intended their theory not only as a substantive theory of death and dying but also as a flexible theory of managing secrets and interpreting suspicious signs in larger and more intimate settings. Their theory has been applied in a study of the early stages of Alzheimer's disease when patients, their relatives, and caregivers learn to distinguish signs of disease from the normal forgetfulness and confusion that comes with old age. In this situation, no party has firm knowledge about Alzheimer's but everyone has to try to reconcile possible with probable Alzheimer's disease and then incorporate this information in personal and group identities (Hutchinson, Leger-Krall, et al. 1997). The theory has also been used to shed light on the disclosure of adoption to adoptive children and people out-side the nuclear family (Hoffman-Riem 1989), and the disclosure of single women's preg-nancy in Ireland (Hyde 1998).

SEE ALSO: Death and Dying; Grounded Theory

REFERENCES AND SUGGESTED READINGS

Cassileth, B. R., Zupkis, R. V., et al. (1980) Infor-mation and Participation Preferences among Can-cer Patients. *Annals of Internal Medicine* 92(6): 832–6.

Glaser, B. G. & Strauss, A. L. (1967) *The Discovery of Grounded Theory*. Aldine, New York.

Glaser, B. G. & Strauss, A. L. (1968) *Time for Dying*. Aldine, Chicago.

Gordon, D. R. (1990) Embodying Illness, Embody-ing Cancer. *Culture, Medicine, and Psychiatry* 14: 275–97.

Hoffman-Riem, C. (1989) Disclosing Adoption. *Society* 26(4): 26–31.

Hutchinson, S. A., Leger-Krall, S., et al. (1997) Early Probable Alzheimer's Disease and Aware-ness Context Theory. *Social Science and Medicine* 45(9): 1399–409.

Hyde, A. (1998). From Mutual Pretense Awareness to Open Awareness: Single Pregnant Women's Public Encounters in an Irish Context. *Qualita-tive Health Research* 8(5): 634–43.

Kai, I., Ohi, G., et al. (1993) Communication between Patients and Physicians about Terminal Care: A Survey in Japan. *Social Science and Medicine* 36: 1151–9.

Kubler-Ross, E. (1969) *On Death and Dying*. Macmillan, New York.

Mamo, L. (1999) Death and Dying: Confluences of Emotion and Awareness. *Sociology of Health and Illness* 21(1): 13–36.

Saunders, C. (Ed.) (1978) *The Management of Term-inal Disease*. Arnold, London.

Timmermans, S. (1994) Dying of Awareness: The Theory of Awareness Contexts Revisited. *Sociol-ogy of Health and Illness* 16(4): 322–39.

B

ba

Takami Kuwayama

In Japanese, *ba* means "place" or "field." It has, however, so many other meanings that it is difficult to find a single English word for it. Furthermore, it is associated with the Japanese belief that a person's behavior is induced or actually caused by the place in which that person is situated. Thus, *ba* not only indicates a physical space, but also illuminates the Japanese notion of accountability. When applied in the analysis of social relationships, *ba* explains how Japanese groups are organized.

Nihon Kokugo Daijiten (*Comprehensive Dictionary of Japanese*, 2nd edn, 2001) defines *ba* under ten categories. Among the most relevant are: (1) site; whereabouts; place; garden; seat; (2) place where an event takes place; place where a meeting is held; venue; seat in a meeting or its atmosphere; (3) situation or circumstances at each moment; plight; occasion; time; (4) scene in a play or a movie; portion of a theatrical performance that is complete in itself with no change occurring in the background scene; (5) mental state or emotional condition; stage or level of a skill; (6) term used in psychology to refer to the environment or condition that affects a person's behavior or response; and (7) area where a given physical quantity has a value according to each point set in a space (e.g., electric field; magnetic field; gravitational field; stress field; nuclear field); power field. These definitions show that the term *ba* is used primarily to designate "place" in the widest sense of the word, but, by extension or by implication, it also means the power of a place to induce a particular state of the mind or actual behavior among the people who, purposely or by accident, have gathered in that place. Furthermore, in some situations, *ba* has a temporal dimension.

Clinical psychologist Hiroshi Yamane regards *ba* as comparable to the Greek idea of *topos*. He explains that the term *basho*, written in two characters, one meaning "*ba*" and the other meaning "site," mainly indicates a physical space, whereas *ba* is more inclusive because it also signifies the atmosphere prevailing in a particular place. According to Yamane, *basho* is transformed into *ba* by some recognizable factors. Among them are the ways a given place is used in everyday life, the social meanings attached to that place, and the personalities of the people who gather in that place. *Ba* is, therefore, not simply a physical concept, but a social one as well, whose meaning is dependent on the relationship of the people present at a particular place. Yamane further contends that *ba* is spontaneously created, instead of being manipulated for specific purposes, which makes it difficult to control. In other words, *ba* has a structure of its own, which is often invisible even to the people involved, and exerts its influence independently. In clinical settings, *ba* helps mentally suffering people recover by allowing them to interact spontaneously with other patients and therapists. On the other hand, *ba* may suppress the patients' autonomy by creating a hostile atmosphere, experienced as a collective pressure for conformity, from which they find it difficult to escape.

We may say that *ba* has a logical structure that makes a given place, rather than the individual who is there, accountable for his or her thought and action. As such, it exemplifies the widely shared Japanese belief that the self is acted upon by an external entity, whether animate or inanimate, rather than acting upon that entity. This belief contrasts with the modern western conception of the self, which places the individual at the center of the universe, regarding him or her as the ultimate source of action. Clifford Geertz (1983) best explained this perspective when he described the western self as "a bounded, unique, more or less integrated motivational and cognitive universe, a dynamic center of awareness, emotion, judgment, and action organized into a distinctive whole and set contrastively both against other such wholes and against its social and natural background."

The Japanese concept of *ba* is related to the so-called "situationalism" or "particularism" of the Japanese people. A classic study of this subject is found in Ruth Benedict's *The Chrysanthemum and the Sword* (1946). During World War II, Benedict was astonished to find that Japanese soldiers, known for their loyalty to the emperor, had suddenly changed their attitudes after being captured and became very cooperative with their enemies, disclosing many of Japan's military secrets. Interviews with these soldiers revealed that they had considered themselves socially dead and behaved according to the new circumstances in which they were placed. Put another way, the dramatic change in the prisoners of war's attitudes had been demanded by the complete change in their situation. Similar changes were repeatedly observed after Japan's surrender, when, for example, the wartime slogan of "fighting to death with bamboo spears" was replaced overnight with a warm welcoming of the occupation forces. Benedict thus called Japanese ethics "situational" and "circumstantial." This ethics is parallel to the idea of *ba*, which requires behavior appropriate to a particular place. Instead of consistency across situations, it encourages "malleability," holding the place accountable for a person's emotion, thought, and action.

In sociology and anthropology, Chie Nakane presented a most powerful theory of *ba*. Nakane, author of *Japanese Society* (1970), one of the most influential books in the study of Japan, translated *ba* as "frame" and explained that it could be "a locality, an institution or a particular relationship which binds a set of individuals into one group." Thus, she extended the meaning of *ba* to indicate human relationships that develop in a particular social setting. In Nakane's work, *ba* or frame is contrasted with *"shikaku"* or "attribute," which includes both ascribed and achieved characteristics. Being a member of X Company, for example, refers to frame, while working there as an office clerk refers to an attribute. The former concerns the individual's group membership, whether president or a clerk, while the latter points to that individual's specific capacity. According to Nakane, these two criteria overlap in actual contexts, but frame is far more important than attribute in the organization of Japanese groups.

Nakane maintained that the frame blurs the distinction between people with different attributes. In her mind, Japan's traditional family called *"ie"* is the best example of this blurring. In the *ie*, often translated as "household," the most important factor in deciding membership is common residence for the purpose of satisfying needs and maintaining the household line, rather than the blood relationship. Thus, the household head's brother, for example, who has married and established his own household, is an outsider (i.e., non-member), whereas his adopted son is an insider (i.e., member), even if they are genealogically unrelated. In this example, the household refers to frame, and kinship to attribute. To support her thesis, Nakane cited the Japanese saying, "The sibling is the beginning of a stranger."

Regarding the *ie* as the basic unit of Japanese society, Nakane contended that larger groups, including the corporation and even the entire nation, are structural extensions of the *ie*. Because the Japanese group is, in Nakane's analysis, organized by the principle of frame, which emphasizes common membership, individuals tend to be totally involved in group activities. From this emerges the so-called "group consciousness" of the Japanese, namely, the feeling of being one unit within the frame. This feeling, in turn, generates a strong attachment to the group. Nakane explained the success of post-war Japanese corporations in terms of this strong group identity of the Japanese people.

Cross-culturally speaking, the idea that one is acted upon by an external entity, rather than acting upon that entity, is not peculiar to Japan. Nor is the conception of self as part of a larger whole, whether of the human group or the place surrounding it, exclusively found among the Japanese. Indeed, in the anthropological literature, the non–western self has frequently been described as "situational," "relational," "undifferentiated," "sociocentric," and so forth. Particularly interesting is Edward Hall's report that, among Spanish Americans, mental illness is a foreign idea because they tend to think that the individual will act peculiarly when he or she is put in a certain set of circumstances. Thus, according to Hall, they try to keep the individual away from situations that are not good for him or her, while denying that he or she is mentally ill (Hall 1976). Although not identical, this notion is similar to that of *ba*. Comparative research utilizing *ba* as a frame of reference may reveal unexpected cross-cultural similarities in the relationship between human beings and the place, or, more generally, the environment.

SEE ALSO: *En*; *Ie*; *Nihonjinron*; *Seken*; Self; *Tatemae/Honne*

REFERENCES AND SUGGESTED READINGS

Bachnik, J. M. & Quinn, C. J. (Eds.) (1994) *Situated Meaning*. Princeton University Press, Princeton.
Geertz, C. (1983) Native's Point of View. In: *Local Knowledge*. Basic Books, New York.
Hall, E. (1976) *Beyond Culture*. Anchor Press, New York.
Rosenberger, N. (Ed.) (1992) *Japanese Sense of Self*. Cambridge University Press, Cambridge.
Yamane, H. (2000) *Ba (Toposu) o Ikasu (Using Ba or Topos)*. In: Yamane, H. et al., *Hito to Shüdan/Ba (Person and Group/Ba)*. Miwa Shoten, Tokyo.

balkanization

Polly S. Rizova

The term "balkanization" has come to mean a process of dividing an area, a country, or a region into several small hostile units. It was first coined by the *New York Times* in the aftermath of World War I to denote the disbanding of the Habsburg Empire into small, antagonistic states. The name is derived from the region that comprises the southeastern part of Europe, the Balkan Peninsula. Because of its geographical location and historical situation on the boundary between the Ottoman and Habsburg empires, the various states in this area have been subjected to constant conquest and political manipulation by outside powers. The Balkans comprise the states of Albania, Bosnia and Herzegovina, Bulgaria, Croatia, Greece, Republic of Macedonia, Romania, Serbia and Montenegro. Sometimes Slovenia and the European part of Turkey are also included.

The diversity of the region's population, the ever changing political boundaries, and a history of severe ethnic, national, and religious conflicts make up the characteristics that give the term its special meaning. In the twentieth century, the region was at the center of the two major European conflicts: Archduke Franz Ferdinand of Austria was assassinated in Sarajevo in 1914, an event that triggered the start of World War I. The region was also heavily involved in the conflict between the Western Allies and the Soviet Union against Nazi Germany during World War II. At the end of the first conflict, the Ottoman and Habsburg empires were destroyed and Yugoslavia, together with a series of other independent states, was created. With the exception of Greece and Turkey, all of these fell under the sphere of influence of the Soviet Union between 1945 and 1989. After the collapse of the Soviet Union, more ethnic violence erupted as the component parts of the former Yugoslavia struggled to realign themselves in the new political vacuum. The massacre in Srebrenica, the siege of Sarajevo, the conflicts in Kosovo, and the appearance of Slobodan Milosevič at the War Crimes Tribunal in the Hague, all helped to reestablish the image of the region as one of deep-seated ethnic and religious divisions and long-standing historical animosities.

In reality, the types of processes often subsumed under the term balkanization are as old as human conflicts. They are often found in imperial settings where the colonial powers have used the tactic of "divide and rule" to divert the attention of the colonized from the primary source of their exploitation. The system of indirect rule, employed by the British in many of their colonies, illustrates a carefully calculated policy to prevent the emergence of a united opposition to foreign rule. This took many forms, such as: playing one ethnic or religious group off against another; favoring one region at the expense of another; importing laborers from other colonies of different religious or linguistic backgrounds to work in specific economic niches; or making sure that the local military or police forces were only recruited from a single minority or tribal background. Such tactics were commonplace throughout the British Empire and, while they clearly served a useful function for the colonizers, they created a dangerous legacy of ethnic strife and conflict in the postcolonial era. In fact, it could be argued that much of independent Africa's instability in the post-war period is a direct result of, or at least strongly nurtured by, colonial policies to fragment and balkanize the continent. It has also been argued that similar tactics have been used in the postcolonial period and particularly as a result of the Cold War competition between the West and the Soviet Union that encouraged rivalries to undermine their opponent's allies and support their friends on the continent.

Subdividing states on ethnic, national, or religious grounds does not necessarily produce violence and conflict, and in some cases may be used as a means of conflict resolution in an effort to protect minority rights or safeguard regional, linguistic, or religious autonomy. Federal constitutions have often successfully managed to preserve the integrity of multinational states, as the classic example of Switzerland's canton structure illustrates. In this case, German-, Italian-, and French-speaking units have held together for centuries and even Hitler and Mussolini, at the height of their expansionist powers, did not choose to annex the German- or Italian-speaking parts of the Swiss Federation. While the Swiss case is clearly unusual, there are other examples where subdividing an already divided state has been used to diffuse conflict in the aftermath of a civil war. At the end of the unsuccessful secessionist war by the southeastern region (Biafra) of the newly

independent Nigeria in the 1960s, a series of constitutional measures was enacted to increase the number of political units from the three basic regions, each dominated by a single ethnic group, to 12 states in 1967 and to 19 in 1976. In this way, it was intended that the rivalries between the three major ethnic groups – Ibo, Yoruba, and Hausa-Fulani – would be diffused in the many subunits of the new federal state. As Horowitz has argued, creating multiple states can result in several outcomes that may help to reduce the destructive power of ethnic conflicts. The new arrangements help to transfer some of the conflict from the center to the local levels; the new more numerous states foster arenas where intra-ethnic conflicts may develop; more opportunities are created for interethnic cooperation and alliances; as the new states strive to promote their own interests non-ethnic issues start to emerge; and, finally, separate state bureaucracies open up employment opportunities for groups previously excluded from the federal civil services. While hardly definitive, the Nigerian experiments in different types of federalism suggest that a form of benign balkanization can be employed to counterbalance and diffuse the tensions created by the legacy of a colonial history of divide and rule.

SEE ALSO: Conflict (Racial/Ethnic); Ethnic Cleansing; Ethnonationalism; Self-Determination; Tribalism

REFERENCES AND SUGGESTED READINGS

Denitch, B. (1994) *Ethnic Nationalism: The Tragic Death of Yugoslavia*. University of Minnesota Press, Minneapolis.

Glenny, M. (2001) *The Balkans: Nationalism, War and the Great Powers, 1804–1999*. Penguin, Harmondsworth.

Horowitz, D. (1985) *Ethnic Groups in Conflict*. University of California Press, Berkeley and Los Angeles.

Sekulic, D. (1997) The Creation and Dissolution of the Multinational State: The Case of Yugoslavia. *Nations and Nationalism* 3(2): 165–79.

Todorova, M. (1997) *Imagining the Balkans*. Oxford University Press, New York.

bankruptcy

Claudia W. Scholz and Juanita M. Firestone

Bankruptcy or insolvency is a legal status in which a debtor is deemed unable to meet obligations to creditors. Bankruptcy usually involves some combination of debtor asset liquidation, payment rescheduling, and the discharge of remaining debts. Legal frameworks governing bankruptcy around the world vary in the degree to which they seek to serve the interests of creditors, debtors, or society at large.

Legal systems that favor the creditor tend to regard excessive debt in moral terms or as a form of deviant behavior. In many Latin American countries bankruptcy law is not clearly separated from criminal law, which strongly discourages many from pursuing bankruptcy status. Canadian bankruptcy law emphasizes credit counseling as a means of "reforming" the debtor. In contrast, some legal systems view bankruptcy as a fresh start for debtors, emphasizing debt discharge over the rescheduling of payment. For example, in the US over a million individuals filed for debt liquidation (Chapter 7) in 2004, while less than half that number filed for debt reorganization (Chapter 13). Under US debt liquidation provisions a considerable proportion of a debtor's assets, usually including his or her home, is exempt. Under Chapter 7 debtors are protected from further action by creditors even if monies generated from the sale of the debtor's assets do not fulfill all existing obligations. Some have argued that US bankruptcy protection takes the place of a social safety net, serving as a last resort for families faced with economic hardship.

While considerable variation remains, bankruptcy laws around the world seem to be converging. With the passage of the Bankruptcy Abuse Prevention and Consumer Protection Act of 2005, the US began to shift away from a debtor-centric bankruptcy framework. In contrast, many European countries with little history of consumer bankruptcy law are adopting US-style debtor-friendly laws as higher proportions of their populations fall into

credit-card debt. In addition, the United Nations Commission on International Trade Law (UNCITRAL) has been coordinating efforts to provide an international legal framework to deal with bankruptcies involving transnational corporations.

Sociological studies of consumer bankruptcy filings in the US indicate that debtors span all socioeconomic and demographic categories. Nevertheless, many bankruptcy filers may be classified as middle class based on educational attainment and other characteristics. Most bankruptcy filings are precipitated by transformative life events such as job loss, illness, or family disruption (divorce or death of spouse). In the US certain debt burdens, including federal educational loans and child support payments, cannot be discharged through standard bankruptcy proceedings. Personal bankruptcy remains on a debtor's credit report for 10 years, resulting in significant negative consequences for access to credit, services and, in some cases, employment.

Chapter 11 is the most common US bankruptcy protection status for businesses. Bankruptcy allows a firm to reorganize and restructure its debt obligations, including certain leases and contracts. Typically, a business may continue to operate while in Chapter 11, although it does so under the supervision of the Bankruptcy Court. In recent years several high-profile bankruptcy decisions have resulted in widespread layoffs and the transfer of a number of large pension programs to the federal government's overburdened Pension Benefit Guarantee Corporation.

SEE ALSO: Consumption; Credit Cards; Inequality, Wealth; Money; Wealth

REFERENCES AND SUGGESTED READINGS

Manning, R. D. (2000) *Credit Card Nation: The Consequences of America's Addiction to Credit.* Basic Books, New York.
Niemi-Kiesiläinen, J. & Ramsay, I. (1997) Changing Directions in Consumer Bankruptcy Law and Practice in Europe and North America. *Journal of Consumer Policy* special issue 20(2).

Sullivan, T. A., Warren, E., & Westbrook, J. L. (2000) *The Fragile Middle Class: Americans in Debt.* Yale University Press, New Haven.

Warren, E. and Tyagi, A. W. (2003) *The Two-Income Trap: Why Middle-Class Mothers and Fathers Are Going Broke.* Basic Books, New York.

Barthes, Roland (1915–80)

Nick Perry

Roland Barthes is best known as a literary critic and essayist and as a member of that generation of internationally distinguished French intellectuals (*maîtres à penser*) that includes the philosopher/historian Michel Foucault, the psychoanalyst Jacques Lacan, and the anthropologist Claude Lévi-Strauss. His relevance for sociology derives above all from the way his writings (1) served to construct linkages between semiology (the study of sign systems), ideological processes, and social structures; (2) made plain just how the possible objects of inquiry of such a "social semiology" might be massively extended; and (3) contributed to the interpretation of readership as social practice.

In his consciously quirky and playful exercise in autobiography, Barthes's own laconic summary of his life was "studies, diseases, appointments" (Barthes 1977a: 184). As a student at the Sorbonne his initial academic interest was in classics and French literature. An ongoing struggle with pulmonary tuberculosis, however, a struggle that would last until his early thirties, prevented him from sitting the examination that was the path to, and prerequisite for, an orthodox academic career. In 1947, unable to find work in Paris, he accepted a post as librarian and subsequently as a teacher in L'Institut français in Bucharest, Romania. When the institute's staff were expelled by the Romanian government in 1949, Barthes succeeded in being appointed to a position at the University of Alexandria in Egypt. It was here that he was first introduced to contemporary linguistics by the semiologist A. J. Greimas. Both men would eventually go on to join the faculty of the École des Hautes Études in Paris. In Barthes's case, his initial appointment – to a postgraduate-only institution that was also his first French academic post – was not until 1960. By then he was in his mid-forties and had published three books and numerous articles, worked briefly in publishing, and held scholarships in lexicology, and subsequently sociology, at the CNRS (Centre national de la recherche scientifique). He was granted tenure at the École in 1962, and appointed as *directeur d'études* in "the sociology of signs, symbols, and representations." By the time of his election in 1976 to France's most prestigious academic institution, the Collège de France, Barthes had become the country's most famous literary critic. The title he chose for his chair was Professor of Literary Semiology. It was a post that he would hold until his death following injury in a traffic accident in 1980.

Although Barthes is most renowned for his contributions to literary theory and criticism, the influence of his more than 20 books and collections of essays reaches across a number of disciplines in the humanities and the social sciences. His writings also traverse and interrogate a variety of theoretical approaches, ranging from an early enthusiasm for existentialism, through structuralism and poststructuralism, to the phenomenological singularities of his last works. *Mythologies*, his third book and the work which above all served to secure him a place within Anglo-American media sociology and the analysis of popular culture, was seen as an exemplar of structuralism. Published in France in 1957, it consisted of short essays that had first appeared as a series of magazine articles (literally, "Mythologies of the Month") that were retrospectively integrated by a lengthier, concluding theoretical essay. The short essays were eclectic, ranging widely across, and engaging with, an emergent consumer culture and featuring such topics as all-in wrestling, soap powder advertising, *Elle* magazine, Einstein's brain, electoral photographs, wine, and French toys.

The publication of *Mythologies* in English in 1972 broadly coincided with the emergence of British cultural studies. The combination of belated translation and the peculiarities of (especially) English culture both served to skew the terms of its reception and allowed it to exert a liberating impact upon those working in, or drawn to, this field (cf., e.g., Hebdige 1979; Masterman 1984). Practitioners of cultural studies were predisposed to read Barthes's book *against* the prevailing literary-derived and narrowly academic definitions of Englishness. Hence what they read it *for* was its matter-of-fact selection of everyday objects of inquiry; its perceived even-handedness as between high and popular culture; its recognition of the political and ideological import of signifying practices; its methodological promise – as well as for the sheer exuberance and wit of the writing. The overall effect was to facilitate the assimilation of the themes of Barthes's collection to a more explicitly empirical idiom and to a more nearly sociological methodology.

Mythologies was thus interpreted as having provided a methodological model that could be generalized so as to reveal how all manner of everyday objects and images are invested with ideological meanings. There is an irony about this consolidation of novelty into orthodoxy. For what most of the subsequent commentators on Barthes have sought to show is that what he particularly valued and was especially alert to was the repudiation of conventional models and methods of writing.

The approach that he developed in *Mythologies* was derived from, but decisively extended, Saussure's notion of the sign. In Saussure's account, a sign was understood to be the relation between two elements. These two elements were not, however, a thing and a name, but rather a concept or idea (the signified) that is materialized by a vocal or graphic mark, such as a photograph or print on a page (the signifier). The distinction between signifier and signified is an analytic one; they are united by the sign and hence they always arrive together. The relation between them is, however, in no way natural, but rather an arbitrary or conventional one that is given by the culture in which they circulate.

What Barthes added to Saussure's model was the notion that the signs (i.e., signifier + signified) of this first-order system acted as the signifiers for a second-order system of signs (again, signifier + signified) that operate on the level of myth. As such, the signs in this second-order system are perforce associated with *new* concepts (or signifieds). These second-order signs function ideologically to "establish blissful clarity," capitalizing upon the apparent naturalness of the first order so as present themselves as if they were facts of nature. Barthes famously illustrates the operation of this process with an example drawn from a photograph on the cover of *Paris Match* nial boy soldier in French military uniform giving a disciplined salute, "his eyes uplifted, probably fixed on a fold of the tricolour." At the first level it is simply a colonial boy soldier in uniform. But at the second level of myth, what it signifies, says Barthes (1972: 116), is "that France is a great empire, that all her sons, without any colour discrimination, serve faithfully under her flag." Yet myth and its attendant ideology always has access to the alibi which the first order provides – in this case, that "it's just a picture."

In this early work, Barthes's structuralist-informed objective was to demythologize mythmaking process; to tell just how showing can become a form of telling; to say just what "it-goes-without-saying" is being made to say; to expose how the purportedly natural is thoroughly conventional and how it thereby acts to sustain a particular social formation and the interests that it serves. What he subsequently argued, however, from a more clearly post-structuralist perspective (in an essay whose initial publication in French had actually pre-dated *Mythologies*' appearance in English) was that, insofar as such unmaskings had become routine, then they were effectively complicit with mythology (Barthes 1977b: 165–9). Rather than the more or less transparent ideology of myth, the proper object of critique was the sign itself, with its investigation sustained by a full recognition of the density, ambiguities, and fissures of language. As he would phrase it some years later:

> Whether in science, in economics, in linguistics, in sociology, the present task is less to be sure of the main principles than to be able to describe imbrications, relays, returns, additions, exceptions, paradoxes, ruses: a task which very quickly becomes a combative one, since it comes to grips with a henceforth reactionary force: *reduction*. (Barthes 1985: 102, italics in original)

For Barthes, those forms of critical inquiry which aspired to recover what a given author *really* meant were instances of just such a reduction. Inasmuch as they were predicated upon the revelation of clear and stable meaning, purportedly anchored and sustained by the notion of authorial intent, then they were supportive of a social order that seeks to regulate or suppress the very notion of difference which language and writing serve to make available. Thus what Barthes proposed was a shift of attention away from the closed singularity of "the work" and toward the contested plurality of "the text" (Barthes 1977b: 155–64); away from "the author" and toward "the reader" (Barthes 1977b: 142–8).

There are affinities between such themes and the contributions of other writers associated with poststructuralism such as Derrida, Foucault, and Kristeva. The influence upon sociology of this aspect of Barthes's writing is linked to this larger movement and the "linguistic turn" with which it is associated. Its impact thus appears as altogether more diffuse and indirect than that of *Mythologies*. Certainly with respect to the sociology of pre-Internet media, it is *Mythologies* that has proved to be his most consequential contribution. It is noteworthy, for example, that it is routinely incorporated into analyses of television (cf., e.g., Fiske & Hartley 1978; Perry 1994) – notwithstanding that the essays effectively predate the medium's general availability and hence do not engage with its characteristic flow of images. But then it may be that, as Barthes – always the writer – once observed, the image always has the last word.

SEE ALSO: Author/Auteur; Ideology; Photography; Poststructuralism; Semiotics; Structuralism

REFERENCES AND SUGGESTED READINGS

Barthes, R. (1972) *Mythologies*. Selected and Trans. A. Lavers. Jonathan Cape, London.
Barthes, R. (1977a) *Roland Barthes by Roland Barthes*. Trans. R. Howard. Hill & Wang, New York.
Barthes, R. (1977b) *Image, Music, Text*. Selected and Trans. S. Heath. Fontana, London.
Barthes, R. (1985) Day by Day with Roland Barthes. In: Blonsky, M. (Ed.), *On Signs*. Blackwell, Oxford, pp. 98–117.
Fiske, J. & Hartley, J. (1978) *Reading Television*. Methuen, London.
Hebdige, D. (1979) *Subculture: The Meaning of Style*. Methuen, London.
Masterman, L. (Ed.) (1984) *Television Mythologies: Stars, Shows and Signs*. Comedia, London.
Perry, N. (1994) *The Dominion of Signs*. Auckland University Press, Auckland.
Sontag, S. (Ed.) (1982) *A Barthes Reader*. Hill & Wang, New York.

base and superstructure

Rob Beamish

The base and superstructure metaphor did not originate with Karl Marx – Scottish Enlightenment thinkers Adam Ferguson, Adam Smith, and others conceptualized different modes of subsistence, with particular structural characteristics, as foundational to societies – but Marx (1904, 1980) wrote the classic statement. Humankind distinguishes itself from nature and animals when it produces its means of subsistence – indirectly producing its actual material life. Production is substantial and eternal to human life; its form is historical. In the same year Darwin's *Origin of the Species* appeared, Marx (1980: 99) sketched the "guiding thread" to his work: humankind enters determinate, necessary social relations of production appropriate to a determinate developmental stage of the material forces of production. These two relations – comprised of real individuals, their activity, and the material conditions in which they live – constitute the "economic structure," the real basis of the legal and political superstructure and determinate forms of social consciousness. Consciousness does not determine social being, being determines consciousness.

Rejecting claims that new ideas or changes in the superstructure were fundamental to social transformation, Marx argued the material infrastructure was the real locus of, and for, change. The social relations of production – or property relations – initially facilitate but later fetter development in the material forces of production, leading to social transformation. With the ensuing changes "in the economic foundation, the whole immense superstructure sooner or later revolutionizes itself" (Marx 1980: 100). This formulation suggested to some the infrastructure's direct determination of the superstructure.

After Marx's death, Engels rejected simple, deterministic interpretations of Marx's Preface, arguing the base was determinate "only in the last instance." But Engels's scientific socialism and the Marx/Darwin parallels he had drawn supported those espousing a narrow, mono-causal, deterministic Marxism. Bernstein (1961) was among the first to reject claims that socialism would emerge from a purely objective, evolutionary process – capitalism's economic breakdown through the falling rate of profit, over-production/under-consumption. Karl Kautsky, Heinrich Cunow, Michael Tugan-Baranowsky, Louis Boudin, Rosa Luxemburg, Henryk Grossmann, and others defended the inevitability of the "breakdown theory" or mildly qualified its determinism. In contrast, Karl Korsch emphasized the subject/object dialectic and praxis.

Interpreting Marx's statement that "der materiellen naturwissenschaftlich treu zu konstatirenden Umwälzung" as "the material transformation, determined with the precision of science" (e.g., see Stone's interpretation, Marx 1904: 12) rather than "the material, scientifically diagnosable, transformation in the economic conditions of production" (Marx 1980: 101) and separating that from the ideological forms – implicitly not scientifically diagnosable – in which humankind becomes conscious of the conflict, the determinists argued the economic base is the focus of historical materialism. Changes in the superstructure would follow axiomatically.

Careful attention to Marx's Preface, let alone his other works, demonstrates that the Second International's economic determinism was misguided. The dynamic relation Marx sketched was changes within the material forces of production (consisting of the means of production – raw materials, machinery, technology, production facilities, and geographic spaces – and human labor power). Contrary to dialectically

materialist, technological, or economic determinist claims, the subject, as labor power, the social relations of production, including workers' aggregation in increasingly larger factories, and class consciousness were all within the internal dynamic fueling pressure for change. Praxis was always within Marx's guiding thread.

One must also read the scientific diagnosis of the "material transformation in the economic conditions of production" in context. The Preface introduced Marx's first, long awaited (almost 15 years), published critique of political economy. He almost had to justify why a socialist revolutionary must wade through the ensuing dry economic analysis. The compressed sketch proclaimed that political economy's diagnostic precision could reveal capitalist production's fundamental contradictions. Properly grasped, practical action focused on those fissure points could create a revolutionary transformation of capitalism's basic infrastructure.

Marx (1980: 101) recognized it was in "the legal, political, religious, artistic or philosophical, in short, ideological forms" that humankind became "conscious of this conflict," but emphasized that it was the social relations of production that required fundamental transformation:

> A social formation does not collapse before all the forces of production, of which it is capable, are developed and new, superior relations of production do not take their place before the material conditions of existence have matured in the womb of the old society itself. Therefore humankind always sets for itself only the tasks that it can solve, since closer examination shows that the task itself only arises where the material conditions for its solution are already at hand or at least in the process of being grasped. (Marx 1980: 101)

In 1969, Louis Althusser argued that capitalist reproduction is key to the base/superstructure metaphor. He maintained that ideology (contrasted to ideologies), endowed with a structure and function, is an omni-historical reality, operating through ideological state apparatuses (ISAs). Ideology provides an "imaginary relation" to the relations of production that functionally reproduces those relations rather than exposing the relations of production themselves. Interpellating subjects into an (ideological) subject, the ISAs repress real understanding and reproduce the relations of production, leaving the base determinate in the last instance. By replacing conscious, historical subjects with a system of structures, Althusser misinterprets Marx's guiding thread in a different way than those in the Second International.

SEE ALSO: Althusser, Louis; Capitalism; Capitalism, Social Institutions of; Labor/Labor Power; Marx, Karl; Materialism

REFERENCES AND SUGGESTED READINGS

Bernstein, E. (1961 [1899]) *Evolutionary Socialism: A Criticism and Affirmation*. Trnas. E. Harvey. Schocken Books, New York.

Cohen, G. (1978) *Karl Marx's Theory of History*. Princeton University Press, Princeton.

Korsch, K. (1922) *Kernpunkte der materialistische Geschichtsaufassung* [Key Points of the Materialist Conception of History]. VIVA, Leipzig.

Korsch, K. (1938) *Karl Marx*. Chapman & Hall, London.

Marx, K. (1904 [1859]) *A Contribution to the Critique of Political Economy*. Trnas. N. Stone. Charles H. Kerr, Chicago.

Marx, K. (1980 [1859]) Vorwort, Zur Kritik der politischen Ökonomie (Preface, Towards the Critique of Political Economy). In: Institute for Marxism-Leninism (Ed.), *Karl Marx Friedrich Engels Gesamtausgabe [Karl Marx–Friedrich Engels Complete Works]*, Pt. II, Vol. 2. Dietz Verlag, Berlin, pp. 99–105.

Sweezy, P. (1970) *The Theory of Capitalist Development*. Monthly Reader Paperbacks, New York.

Bataille, Georges (1897–1962)

Michael Presdee

Georges Bataille was born in Billon, Puy-de-Dôme, in central France and converted to Catholicism on the eve of World War I, serving in the army from 1916 to 1917. Later he joined the seminary at Saint-Fleur and spent a period with the Benedictine congregation at Quarr on the Isle of Wight in Britain. In 1922, Bataille became the deputy keeper at the Bibliothèque Nationale in Paris, a position he held until 1944, later becoming a librarian in Carpentras in Provence in 1949 and then in Orléans in 1951. Through his editorship of *Critique*, he gave space to new intellectuals such as Foucault, Barthes, Derrida, and Deleuze.

Intellectually, Bataille was an uneasy member of the Surrealist movement during the 1920s, calling himself "the enemy within," and through the work of Nietzsche became preoccupied with the notion of eroticism, horror, and obscenity, writing on topics such as transgression, excess, evil, sacrifice, de Sade, and desire. Bataille always involved himself in intellectual edge-work, having a "thirst for excess and violence" and the "unacceptable." From Nietzsche he learned that "the secret for harvesting from existence the greatest fruitfulness and the greatest enjoyment is ... to live dangerously" (Nietzsche 1974: 228).

Bataille's work on transgression was his most important intellectual legacy to modern sociology and criminology. It showed that he had an intimate understanding of the effects of the march of rationalization on a controlled and constrained society, where carnival, the fête, and collective celebration have become necessary for the formation of individual identity. Transgression, crime, antisocial behavior all became for him essential characteristics of advanced capitalism, and he concluded that "there is no prohibition that cannot be transgressed ... the nature of the taboo ... makes a world of calm reason possible but is itself basically a shudder appealing not to reason but to feeling, just as violence is" (Bataille 2001: 63–4). Here is the beginning of the modern debate about the fascination yet fear of doing social edge-work, of the sublime feeling that comes from doing crime and transgressing. "Men are swayed by two simultaneous emotions: they are driven away by terror and drawn by an awed fascination. Taboo and transgression reflect these two contradictory urges. The taboo would forbid the transgression but the fascination compels it" (Bataille 2001: 68). This "delightful terror" achieved through transgression Bataille saw as emanating from violence and eroticism, with the realization that the darkness of social life is a place where we live out our lives, that there is nothing else. "Cruelty and eroticism are conscious intentions in a mind which has resolved to trespass into a forbidden field of behaviour ... Cruelty may veer towards eroticism" (Bataille 2001: 80). It is here in violence and eroticism where we acquire the energy for social life and creativity.

SEE ALSO: Criminology; Cultural Criminology; Deviance; Deviance, Criminalization of; Foucault, Michel; Nietzsche, Friedrich; Pornography and Erotica; Sadomasochism; Transgression; Violence

REFERENCES AND SUGGESTED READINGS

Bataille, G. (1949) *The Accursed Share*, Vol. 1. Trans. R. Hurley. Zone Books, New York.
Bataille, G. (1982) *Story of the Eye*. Penguin, Harmondsworth.
Bataille, G. (1985) *Visions of Excess: Selected Writings, 1927–1939*. Trans. A. Stoekl. Manchester University Press, Manchester.
Bataille, G. (1988) *The Inner Experience*. SUNY Press, Albany, NY.
Bataille, G. (1997) *Literature and Evil*. Marion Boyers, London.
Bataille, G. (2001) *Eroticism*. Intro. C. MacCabe. Penguin, London.
Nietzsche, F. (1974) *The Gay Society*. Vintage, New York.

Bateson, Gregory (1904–80)

William K. Rawlins

Gregory Bateson was a Cambridge-educated anthropologist whose life's work spanned and influenced many academic fields, including anthropology, communication, education, psychotherapy, and sociology. Using cybernetic concepts to theorize human–environmental interaction in holistic and recursive ways, Bateson developed sophisticated and continually evolving accounts of reflexive relationships among culture, consciousness, communication, levels of messages, social and biological contexts, epistemology, and learning.

Bateson's early fieldwork with the Iatmul in New Guinea resulted in *Naven* (1936), a book that presaged three enduring concerns of his scholarship. First, he endeavored to describe and analyze the culture holistically, involving inextricable interconnections among all aspects of their life (e.g. food production and consumption, emotional expression, cosmology and religious beliefs, performances of gender, social organization, etc.). Second, he introduced the concept schismogenesis, which formulated cultural activities as dynamic patterns of interaction occurring across time. Two such patterns of progressive differentiation were termed *symmetrical* – the exchange of similar behaviors, like boasting, commercial rivalry, threats, or warlike posturing and arms development, which can escalate until the interacting system breaks down; and *complementary* – the exchange of different behaviors, like assertiveness and submissiveness, exhibitionism and admiration, each behavior tending to promote its complement, which can distort the respective parties' comportment and their treatment of each other until the system breaks down. Importantly, Bateson did not view these patterns as linear occurrences with one party their undisputed originator; rather, all participants' behaviors were considered reactions to reactions. Attributing causes for behaviors derives from one's point of view. Third, Bateson reflected in depth on the value and validity of his own interpenetrated activities of participating in and thinking and writing about the Iatmul's culture, thereby anticipating contemporary concerns in social studies with the politics of representation. Bateson pursued further fieldwork in New Guinea with his wife Margaret Mead, and they co-authored *Balinese Character: A Photographic Analysis* (1942), the pioneering use of extensive photography in anthropological study.

Bateson participated actively after World War II in the Macy Conferences on cybernetics, ideas that captivated his intellectual imagination and further informed his tendencies to think about human interaction in terms of self-regulating patterns between persons as well as social groupings and their environments. His work researching alcoholism with psychiatrist

Jurgen Ruesch resulted in *Communication: The Social Matrix of Psychiatry* (1951), a landmark volume explicitly formulating psychiatry as communicative activity. The book presents groundbreaking discussions of several staples of contemporary communication theory. First, it explores hierarchical levels of communication and metacommunication, that is, communication about communication, which comprises all the nonverbal cues and verbal propositions exchanged between communicators concerning how their actions and words will be interpreted, as well as the nature of their relationship. In addition, three types of codification are introduced: *digital* codification involves input (e.g., the word "sadness") that is significantly different from the external events it stands for; *analogic* codification involves processing recognizable models of external events (e.g., dejected posture modeling sadness); and *gestalt* codification allows people to summarize experience and recognize similarities in events despite differences in their particulars (e.g., identifying both a funeral and someone's loss of a job as sad occurrences). The book also discusses interrelationships among codification, social action, and values; all meaning-making simultaneously combines selective interpretation and behavioral performance as it necessarily instantiates and reinforces cultural values.

In characterizing the multiple levels of abstraction shaping human interaction, Bateson developed the concept of framing. He conceived frames (or contexts) as communicated premises for delimiting a set of meaningful actions. For example, a play frame stipulates that another's shoves or aggressive remarks are not to be taken seriously. Frames are negotiated through exchanging metacommunicative messages that classify and evaluate behaviors and messages occurring within the frame (or context). The fluidity of frames derives from the reflexive nature of the messages that simultaneously constitute and label them. Consider: when is a shove too hard or a remark too hurtful to maintain a perception of the interaction as play? Bateson suggested that other messages or cues at a higher level of abstraction function metacommunicatively to preserve the play frame, but he also observed that every message or cue has the metacommunicative potential to constitute or define a frame. The

reflexive quandary rendering human communication so vulnerable to misinterpretation is how communicators distinguish between the framing metacommunicative messages and those that are framed. Bateson believed that paradox was prevalent in human communication because of this self-reflexivity as the simultaneous vehicle for and referent of classifying messages. Context persisted as a critical watchword for Bateson's theorizing, and his conceptual nuances of framing inspired Erving Goffman's important book, *Frame Analysis* (1974).

Arguably Bateson's most prominent theoretical contribution to social theory, the double bind theory of schizophrenia, emerged from his funded research with Don Jackson, Jay Haley, and John Weakland in further investigating "the paradoxes of abstraction in communication." A double bind situation involves two or more persons with repeated experiences of their communicative relationship. In this ongoing relationship threats are made by a powerful person on a primary level (often verbally) that are contradicted by messages (e.g., "Do not view this as a threat") occurring at another level of abstraction (often nonverbally). All this interaction transpires in a situation from which the person being threatened cannot escape or comment upon. When persons have learned to perceive their social world in this conflicted and incapacitating way, experiencing any feature of the double bind interaction is likely to create considerable anxiety, anger, and/or a confused inability to understand how others are framing their messages (e.g., as playful, sarcastic, loving, or threatening).

This theoretical work with its emphasis on troubling social contexts interactively created through stifling and incongruent communicative practices significantly undermined reductive explanations analytically isolating psychopathologies within individual persons. It inspired and informed R. D. Laing and other proponents of the anti-psychiatry movement and provided considerable theoretical impetus for establishing the discipline of family therapy. The term double bind appears frequently in popular parlance and has been invoked heuristically in multiple ways, for example, to describe perceptions of political impotence among broad social constituencies in contemporary life. Although the theory has been largely discredited as a causal explanation for schizophrenia, it remains a compelling description of conditions surrounding disturbed communication practices and corrupted potential for mutually beneficial dialogue.

Bateson viewed all communicators as embedded in a ceaseless stream of contexts of learning about the premises of communication emerging from and regulating their interaction. For Bateson, learning transpires on multiple levels. In Learning I, persons learn to adapt their behaviors to pertinent cues within a specific context; for example, acquiring basic ways to greet other persons. But persons also must learn how to distinguish among contexts; for example, greeting family members on a typical morning, versus greeting strangers, or family members who have long been absent or are angry about something. This latter knowledge, termed Learning II or learning to learn, allows people to revise their set of behavioral choices depending upon the appropriate recognition of context. For Bateson, character refers to a person's resulting habits of punctuating interactional sequences (i.e., demarcating their beginning and end) and identifying contexts. This learned basis for recognizing how interactive situations are evolving and the proper behaviors called for by self was considered self-validating by Bateson. It is therefore difficult for individuals to change significantly their basic worldviews as they tend to seek out and define contexts in ways that justify their behaviors, and they will behave in ways that interactively create sensible contexts for their actions. While Learning III conceivably involves changing one's self-validating habits for discriminating among contextual possibilities, Bateson deemed it rare and necessitating a profound reorganization of character. A comprehensive effort to systematize Bateson's conceptions of communication theory underpinned Watzlavick, Beavin, and Jackson's *Pragmatics of Human Communication* (1967), which attracted worldwide attention to Bateson's ideas.

Bateson was concerned about the nature and limits of linear thinking and simplistic notions of individuals' intentions. He distrusted the conscious purposes of human beings in trying to exert unilateral control over the co-evolution of human and natural ecologies. First, he considered persons' conscious control over

interaction limited because persons are only conscious of the products of their perceptual activities. They remain unaware of the culturally patterned processes (e.g., conventional understandings of reality and linguistic structures) through which perception occurs. Second, persons conceive means–end relationships in narrow and self-serving ways. They typically do not understand how the arcs of their conscious activities are embedded in, affect, and in turn are affected by enveloping circuits of message pathways and consequences for living ecological systems. Bateson was deeply troubled by what he viewed as the toxic potentials of reductionistic explanations separating mind and body, conscious and unconscious purposes, reasons of the heart and reasons of the mind, art and science, selves and societies, organisms and their environments, ideas and their contexts. His masterwork, *Steps to an Ecology of Mind* (1972, reissued 2000), is an indispensable resource assembling his published essays addressing all of his diverse interests up to 1972.

Convinced that our ways of understanding and describing the world have practical, aesthetic, and moral consequences, Bateson devoted much of his later life to developing an epistemology suitable for understanding co-evolving living systems. He emphasized that we are part of the contexts we study and that arbitrarily separating the knower from the known is an epistemological error. How and what we know about our human and natural environments will influence how we interact as part of those environments, which in turn will alter them and recursively present constraints and possibilities for further knowledge creation and understanding. Harries-Jones (1995: 8) terms this Bateson's "ecological epistemology," which involves a compelling pronouncement: "Our own survival depends on understanding that not only are we coupled to our own conceptualization of ecosystems and ecological order, but also to embodiments of our own ways of thinking about them and acting on them." If we cannot recognize the errors in our own ways of thinking about and living as parts of interconnected human and biological orders, we may create the conditions for our own demise. Bateson urged holistic ways of thinking to grapple responsively and responsibly with the predicaments of our own making. He recommended both rigor and imagination in confronting living questions, as well as humility and respect for the larger circuits of causation patterning our possibilities.

SEE ALSO: Goffman, Erving; Human–Non-Human Interaction; Interaction; Pragmatism

REFERENCES AND SUGGESTED
READINGS

Bateson, G. (1979) *Mind and Nature: A Necessary Unity*. E. P. Dutton, New York.

Bateson, G. (1991) *Sacred Unity: Further Steps to an Ecology of Mind*. Harper Collins, New York.

Bateson, G. & Bateson, M. C. (1987) *Angels Fear: Toward an Epistemology of the Sacred*. Macmillan, New York.

Bateson, M. C. (1984) *With a Daughter's Eye: A Memoir of Margaret Mead and Gregory Bateson*. William Morrow, New York.

Berger, M. M. (1978) *Beyond the Double Bind*. Brunner/Mazel Publishers, New York.

Bochner, A. P. (1981) Forming Warm Ideas. In: Wilder-Mott, C. & Weakland, J. H. (Eds.), *Rigor and Imagination: Essays from the Legacy of Gregory Bateson*. Praeger, New York, pp. 65–81.

Harries-Jones, P. (1995) *A Recursive Vision: Ecological Understanding and Gregory Bateson*. University of Toronto Press, Toronto.

Lipset, D. (1980) *Gregory Bateson: The Legacy of a Scientist*. Prentice-Hall, Englewood Cliffs, NJ.

Rawlins, W. K. (1987) Gregory Bateson and the Composition of Human Communication. *Research on Language and Social Interaction* 20: 53–77.

Sluzki, C. E. & Ransom, D. C. (1976) *Double Bind: The Foundation of the Communication Approach to the Family*. Grune & Stratton, New York.

Beard, Mary Ritter (1876–1958)

John P. Bartkowski

Mary Ritter Beard was a historian, social critic, and first-wave feminist. She was also a proponent of women's suffrage in the US during the early decades of the twentieth century. Beard's work highlighted women's contributions to American society and cultures across the world. She was also a social reformer who fought for women's rights and organized working women in early twentieth-century America.

Mary Beard was born and raised in Indiana. She and Charles Beard (a noted historian) met at DePauw University in the 1890s and married in 1900, fittingly a date that many consider to be the dawn of the Progressive Era to which the Beards notably contributed. Mary Beard's own work, both social reform and scholarship, was beholden to a critical intellectual orientation. During the second decade of the twentieth century, Mary Beard promoted women's suffrage and the empowerment of women workers. Following the passage of women's right to vote, the suffragist movement broke into competing factions. Beard allied herself with suffragists who, while supporting women's political enfranchisement, were opposed to the Equal Rights Amendment. Beard and her compatriots feared that the Equal Rights Amendment would be used to undermine protective legislation for women, including union-sponsored laws that regulated women's wages, work hours, and work conditions.

Beard is considered by many to be one of the founders of women's studies. She strongly promoted women's access to education and was among the first to propose university courses about women. She created the World Center for Women's Archives, which collected documents related to women's historical contributions. Beard's vision for this archive placed a particular emphasis on representing women's diversity by race and class, a focus that was unusual for the time during which she lived. In *Woman as Force in History* (1946), widely considered her most important and influential work, Beard argued against conventional feminist thinking of the time, later popularized in Simone de Beauvoir's *The Second Sex*. Feminist convention during that period held that women were a wholly subjugated group or "second-class" sex. Beard called the idea of women's complete historical subjection to men a "fantastic myth." If women's subjugation had been complete, she contended, then there would be no compelling reason for historians – most of whom were men – to take seriously women's impact on history. Arguing that women's influence was ignored by historians rather than empirically absent from history, Beard urged historians to refocus their analytical range of vision to account for women's critical social contributions. Her later work focused on women in Japan, a highly patriarchal society.

Beard viewed women's most vital social role as that of civilizing men and society at large. In her view, the life of men initially resembled that of "beasts," and women "lifted" men out of their uncivilized existence. Civilization itself, Beard surmised, was largely the accomplishment of women, and historians' shortsightedness and patriarchal bias led them to neglect this fact. Her work can be read as an effort to correct for this gender bias. Early in her career, Beard took to task the *Encyclopedia Britannica* for its failure to recount women's influence in American history, including their civilizing role on the frontier and their facilitation of urban social reform.

Beard's brand of feminist historical analysis would seem to imply that women were morally different from – and even superior to – men. This idea remains popular among some "difference feminists" today, who emphasize the distinctiveness of women's moral reasoning. However, claims about women's civilizing influence are also quite controversial because they render what some charge is an essentialist, homogenizing portrayal of "uncivilized" men counterposed to "civilizing" women. However, a careful reading of Beard's work reveals that it does not essentialize women but instead highlights women's diversity.

Although one of the primary motifs in Beard's work focused on women's civilizing influence in history, there were also many subplots winding through her historiographies. Years before feminist scholars began theorizing women's resistance against patriarchy, Beard was examining such oppositional tactics in fine-grained detail. She called attention to the ways in which economically disadvantaged women's subjection was influenced by a combination of their social class position and gender. Consequently, Beard's historiographies examined intersecting inequalities such as race, class, and gender many decades before this approach was to become common practice in

women's studies, gender studies, history, and the social sciences.

SEE ALSO: Feminism; Feminism, First, Second, and Third Waves

REFERENCES AND SUGGESTED READINGS

Beard, M. R. (1946) *Woman as Force in History: A Study in Traditions and Realities*. Macmillan, New York.

Cott, N. F. (1992) *A Woman Making History: Mary Ritter Beard through Her Letters*. Yale University Press, New Haven.

Lane, A. J. (Ed.) (2001) *Making Women's History: The Essential Mary Ritter Beard*. Feminist Press at CUNY, New York.

Trigg, M. (1995) "To Work Together for Ends Larger than Self": The Feminist Struggles of Mary Beard and Doris Stevens in the 1930s. *Journal of Women's History* 7: 52–85.

Beauvoir, Simone de (1908–86)

Vicky M. MacLean and Patricia Parker

The French existentialist philosopher, writer, and social essayist Simone de Beauvoir is most widely known for her pioneering work *Le Deuxième Sexe* (1949), published in English as *The Second Sex* (1953). Her exposé of woman as "Other" and her calling attention to the feminine condition of oppression as historically linked to motherhood are considered her major contributions to modern feminist thought. While not generally acknowledged as a sociologist, Beauvoir nevertheless contributed to sociology in *The Second Sex, The Coming of Age* (*La Vieillesse*, 1970), a study of old age, and, to a lesser extent, her writings on the media (Deegan 1991) and death and dying (Marks 1973). Simone de Beauvoir is also internationally read and widely known for her novels, autobiographies, and travelogues. In

1954 her novel *Les Mandarins* was awarded the Prix Goncourt, clearly placing Beauvoir among the most highly acclaimed French literary writers of her time. Beauvoir's theorizing corrects androcentric biases found in earlier gender-neutral theoretical frameworks, particularly in her use of social categories to inform individually oriented philosophical theories of self-determination and freedom (Walsh 2000). She systematically examined the historically situated or lived experiences of women relative to men. Deeply influenced by the existential philosophy of her lifelong companion Jean-Paul Sartre, Simone de Beauvoir extended Sartrean existential philosophy to encompass social and cultural determinants of the human condition. She used existential philosophy, as a guide for understanding herself as a woman and as a framework for understanding the condition of women more generally.

The first of two daughters, Simone de Beauvoir was born in Paris January 9, 1908 to a devout, aristocratic, middle-class Catholic family. Her father, a lawyer and amateur actor, having no money for a sufficient dowry, urged Simone to pursue higher education. As early as age 11, the young Beauvoir disavowed marriage and motherhood and shortly thereafter, she disavowed her belief in God. Unlike most women of the time, Beauvoir began a lifelong pursuit of educational advancement, excelling in various disciplines. In 1924, she earned her first baccalaureate in Latin and literature. She earned a second degree one year later in mathematics and philosophy. In the course of earning two baccalaureates in 1925, she attended the Institut Sainte-Marie to take courses in Latin and literature, the Institut Catholique for courses in mathematics, and the Sorbonne for philosophy and literature. In 1926, she passed her exams for certificates in Latin, literature, and mathematics, and in the following year she earned her certificate in philosophy. In 1928, Beauvoir became friends with fellow teaching trainees Maurice Merleau-Ponty and Claude Lévi-Strauss, and in 1929 she began her lifelong relationship with Sartre. The two met while preparing for major examinations in philosophy, in which Beauvoir, the youngest of the group, was placed second. Sartre was placed first, but only after having failed his first attempt the previous year. Some of the reviewers of the exam argued for a reversal of the rankings, however, thus suggesting a gender bias in the final placement (Bieber 1979; Brosman 1991).

In 1929, Beauvoir began her teaching career, holding various positions in the French lycée system at Marseilles (1929–33), Rouen (1933–7), and Paris (until 1944). Beauvoir moved around for a number of years while Sartre served in the military. In 1931, the two discussed the prospect of marriage, since married couples were generally assigned to teach at the same universities (Bieber 1979; Brosman 1991). However, Beauvoir declined Sartre's offer, refusing to sacrifice their autonomy to the bourgeois convention of marriage. In 1933, Sartre met Olga Kosakiewicz, a student of Beauvoir's, and for a time the couple expanded to become an ill-fated trio, an experience reflected in Beauvoir's first novel, *She Came to Stay* (1943). Through the years, both Sartre and Beauvoir took on various lovers, while maintaining their own unique relationship. In 1944, Beauvoir was suspended from her teaching position at the Lycée Victor Duruy after a parent complained of Beauvoir's undue influence on her daughter (Brosman 1991). Although Beauvoir's position was subsequently reinstated, she nonetheless resigned from the university, retiring from teaching to travel and to pursue her career as a writer. Beauvoir met Nelson Algren, another of her prominent lovers, while visiting the United States in 1947. Beauvoir's now internationally renowned essay on existential morality, *The Ethics of Ambiguity*, was published in that year, followed by her publication *America Day by Day*, a travelogue providing a view of American culture and social life. In 1949, after three years of research and writing, Beauvoir released the highly controversial *Second Sex*. Twenty thousand copies were sold in France in its first week of distribution and the 700-page book was later translated into 26 languages (Bair 1989).

True to her existentialist philosophy, Beauvoir's writings avoid any attempt to discover a single universal "truth" as prescriptive for intellectual or personal freedom for all women. Her efforts to understand women's historical oppression, contemporary situation, and future prospects drew from fiction and literary criticism, as well as from biology, historical anthropology, political economy, and psychoanalysis. However, Beauvoir found extant writings either erroneous or incomplete and developed her own distinctively sociological argument, noting that "one is not born, but rather becomes, a woman" (1953 [1949]: 267). Consistent with existentialist philosophy, Beauvoir saw the human condition as defined foremost by the freedom to choose, as humans are born with no fixed essence or nature. Despite this freedom, however, it is *external social forces* that undeniably shape transcendent possibilities for self-creation. Thus for a woman to be defined as Other is to be defined as second to man, less than man, and for man's pleasure. Beauvoir explored this idea further, addressing the condition of lesbian women who choose other women as sexual partners as a means of transcending societal restrictions on women. Critiquing the ambiguities of psychoanalysts who accepted socially defined categories of masculine and feminine, she stated that labeling women as "masculine" for choosing to be themselves is to deny women authenticity.

> To define the "masculine" lesbian by her will to "imitate the male" is to stamp her as inauthentic. ... The truth is that man today represents the positive and the neutral – that is to say, the male and the human being – whereas woman is only the negative, the female. Whenever she behaves as a human being, she is declared to be identifying herself with the male. ... Her activities in sports, politics, and intellectual matters, her sexual desire for other women, are all interpreted as "masculine protest"; the common refusal to take account of the values toward which she aims, or transcends herself, evidently leads to the conclusion that she is, as subject, making an inauthentic choice. (p. 408)

Beauvoir's theorizing took a distinctively sociological dimension in *The Second Sex*, contributing to the social basis for the study of gender. Similarly, the scope of her research methodology contributed to revisionist history, as she theorized from sources and documentation from women themselves, including letters, diaries, autobiographies, case histories, political and social essays, and novels (Bair 1990).

In *The Second Sex* Beauvoir began by asking "what is woman?" evaluating societal institutions and their influences and definitions of women and femininity. She dispelled the idea that womanhood is a natural existing phenomenon and maintained that the concept of Other is a duality that has existed as long as consciousness itself. Always present in religion and mythology, Otherness is a concept upon which humans base their realities. For example, we have day and night, good and evil, and, at the heart of *The Second Sex*, male and female. In the context of the sexes, male, historically defined as the sovereign of the sexes, is the Self by which we judge, and female is the Other, the alter and opposite of male. Throughout history, women's value as procreator has been viewed as secondary to men's more prominent contribution to society as warrior (p. 64). Beauvoir's analysis further demolished historical myths and images of women and she identified moments throughout history when women made significant progress toward emancipation. In particular, Beauvoir believed that socialism, to the extent that it removes sole responsibility for the family and childrearing from women, is necessary for women's liberation. Although Beauvoir placed most of the blame for women's oppression on the actions of men, she did not exonerate women for their complacencies. She noted that declining to be the "Other" would require women to forsake the benefits they received from their alliances with men (p. xxvii). Ultimately conceding that women will never fully achieve a complete independence from men as in a socialist class revolution, Simone de Beauvoir advocated solidarity between women and men in the struggle for freedom.

In *The Coming of Age* and *The Second Sex*, Beauvoir used a similar approach, drawing from history and literary criticism as well as from first-hand observation to address the indignities suffered by the aged in contemporary societies. Boldly, Beauvoir proclaimed her intent to "break the conspiracy of silence" that hides from public view and discussion the material and social impoverishment forced upon older persons. Beauvoir systematically reviewed the historical circumstances of the aged in various times and cultures. She called to task the failure of society to admit to its own impending old age by pointing out that we deny ourselves by refusing to see ourselves in the faces of the old (pp. 13–14). In comparing conditions of older persons in primitive societies with those in modern technocratic societies, she drew attention to housing, employment, retirement earnings, and hospital and institutional settings. All were examined and found lacking. She also addressed the subjective understandings and experiences of older individuals: loss of occupation, of privacy, of sexual relations, of health, of personal relationships, and even of death. Prior to the development of the field of gerontology, Beauvoir told us what it means to grow old in contemporary society. She beseeched her readers to break the conspiracy of silence reflecting the failure of modern civilization to admit what the state of the aged really is and, when understood, to call for radical systemic changes.

In yet another sociological dimension of her work, Beauvoir examined images of women's sexuality as portrayed by the media. Her sympathetic portrait *Brigitte Bardot and the Lolita Syndrome* (1959) can be viewed as a liberated or transcendent expression of woman's sexuality. In the French actress Bardot, Beauvoir found the image of a "sex kitten" embodying the ambiguities of seductress with childhood innocence, the desired with the forbidden, and the accessible with the inaccessible (Deegan 1991). Examining pictures of Bardot from media snapshots, Beauvoir argued that Bardot reflected a "spontaneous dignity" in her ability to turn up her nose at artificial jewels, perfumes, and glamorous clothing, while tempting even the most virtuous saint with her lascivious walk and dance. Beauvoir's early analysis represents a genre of media research that would later surface in numerous sociological and popular culture studies.

Throughout Beauvoir's writings, particularly her autobiographies and novels, there is a central preoccupation with death (Marks 1973; Bieber 1979). In *Memoirs of a Dutiful Daughter*, realization of her own mortality as a girl, and as a young woman she describes the loss experienced upon the death of her childhood friend "Zaza." One whole volume, *A Very Easy Death* (1964), was written on the topic of death after her mother became ill and died of cancer. The

book deals with the profound personal impact of her mother's death, as well as the more general conditions of dying, euthanasia, and the functional preparation for one's own death, through the "dress rehearsals" of burying loved ones. In *Adieux: A Farewell to Sartre* (1981), Beauvoir said her public goodbye to the man who was her lasting companion, reflecting on her years with him and on the connections between death and aloneness, and admitting no regrets. There is significant discussion among Beauvoir's critics and supporters surrounding the nature of her relationship with Sartre and his influence on her work. The two were companions and scholarly critics of each other's writings from the time of their first acquaintance in 1929 until Sartre's death in 1980. Although Sartre's existentialist framework significantly shaped Beauvoir's work, her writings contributed unique theory and gave voice to both existential and feminist thought, particularly in her defense of the victims of prejudice and social injustice. Indeed, the originality and merits of her many writings are indisputable. Through fiction and non-fiction she identified dilemmas of the human condition, particularly those embodied in situational and societal restrictions on freedom (Deegan 1991).

Though Beauvoir regarded herself as a writer and novelist first and foremost (Bair 1990), her contributions to the field of sociology are significant. Her emphases on the social construction of femininity and of woman as Other, a similar emphasis on the social construction of old age by institutions that deny the humanity of the older person, her attention to the role of the media in portraying images of women, and her profound honesty in creating a greater social awareness of death and dying are notable examples of her contributions. As a social philosopher, Beauvoir was not only a scholar but also an activist. She traveled extensively, taking more than 200 trips abroad including visits to Italy, Germany, Austria, Czechoslovakia, Morocco, Spain, Soviet Russia, Cuba, the United States, Sweden, Norway, Turkey, Greece, Japan, China, Egypt, Israel, and northern Africa. She supported independence for both Algeria and North Vietnam. In addition, she actively supported social and political causes, participating in marches and vigils for abortion on demand, workers' emancipation, students' rights, the impoverished, and for women's liberation (Bieber 1979; Brosman 1991).

SEE ALSO: Aging and the Life Course, Theories of; Cultural Feminism; Culture, Gender and; Existential Sociology; Gender, Aging and; Inequality/Stratification, Gender; Sex and Gender

REFERENCES AND SUGGESTED READINGS

Bair, D. (1989) Introduction to the Vintage Edition of *The Second Sex*. Vintage, New York.
Bair, D. (1990) *Simone de Beauvoir: A Biography*. Touchstone, New York.
Beauvoir, S. de 1947 [1948]) *The Ethics of Ambiguity*. Trans. B. Fretchman. Citadel, Secaucus, NJ.
Beauvoir, S. de (1949 [1943]) *She Came to Stay*. Trans. Y. Moyse & R. Senhouse. Secker & Warburg, London.
Beauvoir, S. de (1953 [1948]) *America Day by Day*. Trans. P. Dudley. Grove Press, New York.
Beauvoir, S. de (1953 [1949]) *The Second Sex*. Trans. and Ed. H. M. Parshley. Alfred A. Knopf, New York.
Beauvoir, S. de (1956 [1954]) *The Mandarins: A Novel*. Trans. L. M. Friedman. World, Cleveland.
Beauvoir, S. de (1960 [1959]) *Brigitte Bardot and the Lolita Syndrome*. Trans. B. Fretchman. Reynal, New York.
Beauvoir, S. de (1962 [1960]) *The Prime of Life*. Trans. P. Green. World, Cleveland.
Beauvoir, S. de (1966 [1964]) *A Very Easy Death*. Trans. P. O'Brian. Putnam, New York.
Beauvoir, S. de (1972 [1970]) *The Coming of Age*. Trans. P. O'Brian. Putnam, New York.
Beauvoir, S. de (1984 [1981]) *Adieux: A Farewell to Sartre*. Trans. P. O'Brian. Pantheon, New York.
Bieber, K. (1979) *Simone de Beauvoir*. Twayne, Boston.
Brosman, C. (1991) *Simone de Beauvoir Revisited*. Twayne, Boston.
Deegan, M. J. (1991) Simone de Beauvoir. In: Deegan, M. J. (Ed.), *Women in Sociology: A Bio-Bibliographical Sourcebook*. Greenwood Press, New York.
Marks, E. (1973) *Simone de Beauvoir: Encounters with Death*. Rutgers University Press, New Brunswick.
Walsh, M. (2000) Beauvoir, Feminisms, and Ambiguities. *Hecate* 26 (May).

Beccaria, Cesare (1738–94)

Marilyn D. McShane and Frank P. Williams III

Cesare Beccaria was born Cesare Bonesana, Marchese di Beccaria, in 1738 in Milan, Italy. His writings became associated with the classical school of thought on crime and punishment. Many of his ideas laid the groundwork for the reform of courts and laws throughout the world as well as the enactment of constitutions and proclamations of individual freedoms in emerging nations like the United States.

The eighteenth century was a time of massive social change. The industrial revolution, the rise of the middle class, colonization, and urbanization around the world brought new cultural ideas and shifts in conceptions of government responsibility. The courts of this era were often said to be barbarous and cruel. Accusations were made in secret and torture was inflicted particularly on the poor. There were comparatively few written laws and judges ruled politically to suppress anyone who threatened the aristocracy or the Church.

The son of noble parents, Beccaria studied at a Jesuit school in Parma and then at the University of Pavia, earning a doctorate in law, before returning home to marry the daughter of a military officer. With a background in law, math, and economics the young scholar spent a great deal of time conversing with his colleagues about the applications of utilitarian theory to public policy. His discussion group, led by the brothers Alessandro and Pietro Verri, published a journal, *Il Caffe*, where topics such as taxes and tariffs, supply and demand, and labor force issues were argued. Emphasizing the logical, rational thought that was popular during this period of enlightenment, Beccaria penned *Dei Deliti e Delle Pene* (On Crimes and Punishment) outlining his thoughts on a model penal system. Fear of recrimination, however, forced him to publish the work anonymously in 1764 and it was not until the work received popular acclaim that he stepped forward in 1768 to acknowledge authorship. That same year he took the chair in political economy and commerce at the Palatine School in Milan, but he left the position within two years. In 1771, he received an appointment to the Supreme Economic Council of Milan and remained a public official for the rest of his life.

In his treatise, Beccaria covered many aspects of the criminal justice system – from the construction of laws through the processing of the suspect and the punishment of the convicted. He posited that vague or obscure laws would be corrupted and that defendants must be given time and the means to prepare a defense, one of the cornerstones of our due process tradition. He argued that torture should never be used and that capital punishment was an indefensible act. To him, the evil of punishment should be only a slight bit greater than the benefits of the crime it seeks to prevent. As a rational being, man would choose the least painful path, and the principle of deterrence would prevail.

Like other philosophers of this time, Beccaria espoused the idea that free will was the basis of our behavior and that, under the terms of the social contract, each person gave up hedonistic liberty for the benefit of the greater needs of society. He acknowledged that it was incumbent upon society to devise and enforce just laws but, having seen first hand how such laws could be corrupted, he cautioned the citizenry to watch over the process to ensure that justice was available to all regardless of birthright or means.

Although there was much demand for him to make public appearances and to travel for speaking engagements, he was so shy that his first such invitation, to Paris, ended in his flight home and afterward he declined all invitations and retired quietly. While some critics argue that Beccaria's ideas were neither unique nor groundbreaking, and some have even said that Pietro Verri was responsible for them, most will agree his succinct treatise summarizes the ideas that were popular at this time. Moreover, it clearly outlines the judicial reforms many believed were necessary in an evolving civilized society.

Even today, thousands of college students each year are assigned his work to read. His writing endures no doubt because it is very readable and direct. For example, when considering courtroom procedures he argues that: "Every judge can be my witness that no oath ever made any criminal tell the truth." His focus on preventing crime still rings true today: "[S]ee to it that the laws are clear and simple and that the entire force of a nation is united in their defense, and that no part of it is employed to destroy them. See to it that the laws favor not so much classes of men, as men themselves. See to it that men fear the laws and fear nothing else."

Beccaria worked most of his life as a lecturer and as a public official. Beset with a number of family and health problems in later life, he died in November of 1794.

SEE ALSO: Crime; Criminal Justice System; Deterrence Theory

REFERENCES AND SUGGESTED READINGS

Beccaria, C. (1963 [1764]) *On Crimes and Punishments*. Trans. H. Paolucci. Bobbs-Merrill, Indianapolis.

Beirne, P. (1991) Inventing Criminology: The "Science Of Man" in Cesare Beccaria's *Dei Delitti e Delle Pene*. *Criminology* 29: 777–820.

Bellamy, R. (Ed.) (1995) *Beccaria: On Crimes and Punishments and Other Writings*. Cambridge University Press, Cambridge.

Maestro, M. T. (1973) *Cesare Beccaria and the Origins of Penal Reform*. Temple University Press, Philadelphia.

Monachesi, E. (1955) Cesare Beccaria. *Journal of Criminal Law, Criminology, and Police Science* 46: 439–49.

Williams, F. & McShane, M. (2004) *Criminological Theory*, 4th edn. Pearson Education, Upper Saddle River, NJ.

behaviorism

Evans Mandes

Behaviorism was a dominant school of American psychological thought from the 1930s through the 1960s. Its principal founder, John B. Watson, clearly defined behaviorism as follows: "Psychology, as the behaviorist views it, is a purely objective branch of natural science. Its theoretical goal is the prediction and control of behavior. The behaviorist recognizes no dividing line between man and brute" (Watson 1914: 158). Other behaviorists following in Watson's footsteps included Clark Hull (drive reduction theory), Edward Chace Tolman (purposive behaviorism), and B. F. Skinner (radical behaviorism). The most successful of these was Skinner, who developed the dominant theory of behaviorism for 30 years, working on a more or less non-theoretical basis, using only objective measures of behavior. He was squarely on the nurture side of the nature–nurture controversy and on the deterministic side of the free will–determinism issue. He disavowed favorite psychological constructs such as consciousness, freedom, indwelling agents, dignity, and creativity. In each case Skinner argued that these examples either represent constructs from one's own biological/environmental histories or are behaviors in which the antecedents (controlling agents) are not clearly understood (Skinner 1971).

Unlike classical sociological theory, which is often defined by the work of major sociologists of the times (e.g., Du Bois, Weber), classical psychological theory is often defined by schools of thought (e.g., Gestalt, functionalism, structuralism) championed by several individuals who espouse variations on the acceptable truth. Skinner worked through the 1940s, 1950s, and 1960s, when other important behaviorists challenged the acceptable orthodoxy in interesting ways. Hull, for instance, argued that the dominant *cause célèbre* for behaviorism was drive reduction. Any action associated with the satisfaction of a biological or social drive state became learned, and learning could only happen under drive reduction states. Hull then quantified this process in a theory he called mathematico-reductive, his attempt to provide post hoc curve-fitting equations to specific drive reduction states (Hull 1943). Although influential, his work diminished in importance as other types of learning where the clear drive reduction antecedents were not known came into vogue. These included social modeling, latent learning, and exposure learning.

A leader in this latter form of behaviorism, called purposive behaviorism, was Tolman (1959). His research was aimed at isolating learning situations where the clear drive reduction antecedents could not be easily specified and where certain mentalistic concepts – anathema to radical behaviorism – were used to help explain latent learning phenomena. Tolman's favorite term, "cognitive map," was an example. He used this term to clarify how animals and humans are influenced by latent cues in their everyday lives, cues which may not be observable in a behavioral sense, but which still operate in a coercive and deterministic stimulus-response fashion as determiner of behavior. Tolman, with seeming prescience, predicted the coming of the cognitive revolution in the 1970s, which surpassed behaviorism as a major theory. The cognitive revolution allowed the return of mentalistic concepts such as mind and consciousness into the vocabulary of cognitive behaviorism and ushered in a new look for theoretical psychology.

Although Skinner's radical behaviorism is no longer a major player in psychological theory, the applications that his research fostered are very much a part of the contemporary scene. These applications span many areas in contemporary psychology, including clinical psychology and therapy. He gave us a strong hint of his application of learning called operant conditioning in his one and only novel, *Walden Two*, a book first published in 1948 and still in print. The novel represented Skinner's attempt to engineer a utopian society based upon Skinnerian operant principles. Sometimes called social engineering, Skinner's novel was his solution to the horrors of World War II. He hoped to engineer out of the human repertoire all negative emotions, leaving only the positive ones. This is an example of behavioral modification, and many of its elements (positive reinforcement, successive approximations, gradual change in behavior through desensitization) have been incorporated successfully in therapy today. The removal of unwanted behaviors such as phobias, tics, etc. can be successfully treated using behavior modification techniques; these are accomplished through the non-reinforcement of unwanted behaviors. Behavior modification techniques, which are part of a larger classification of therapies called behavior therapy, have been successful in reducing the amount of self-destructive behaviors among children suffering from infantile autism.

The principal set of events that led to the demise of behaviorism as a compelling theory was the growth of connectionism and the cognitive revolution of the 1970s, which was theoretically friendlier to the biological causes of behavior. More specifically, the Chomsky (1971)–Skinner (1957) debates of the 1960s concerning the origins and development of native languages sealed the fate of radical behaviorism, since Skinner was never able to deal with the irrepressible novelty of human speech. Young children usually speak grammatically and in novel form with each new utterance, a fact that is anathema to any learning paradigm of language acquisition.

The legacy of behaviorism for modern psychology was its insistence upon measurable behavior, thus transforming psychology from its introspective and subjective past into the world of scientific inquiry. This process allowed psychology to embrace new disciplines such as statistics and measurement theory in attempts to add legitimacy to its new endeavors at the expense of more humanistic approaches to psychology.

SEE ALSO: Social Learning Theory; Theory

REFERENCES AND SUGGESTED READINGS

Chomsky, N. (1971) The Case Against B. F. Skinner. *New York Review of Books* (December 30): 18–24.

Hull, C. (1943) *Principles of Behavior.* Appleton-Century-Crofts, New York.

Skinner, B. F. (1948) *Walden Two.* Macmillan, New York.

Skinner, B. F. (1957) *Verbal Behavior.* Appleton-Century-Crofts, New York.

Skinner, B. F. (1971) *Beyond Freedom and Dignity.* Alfred A. Knopf, New York.

Tolman, E. C. (1959) Principles of Behavior. In S. Koch (Ed.), *Psychology: A Study of a Science*, Vol. 2. McGraw-Hill, New York.

Watson, J. (1914) *Behavior: An Introduction to Comparative Psychology.* Holt, Rinehart, Winston, New York.

belief

Carlo Prandi

Popular dictionaries define the term belief in the following general terms: (1) a feeling of certainty that something exists or is good; (2) an opinion about which one feels sure. While the concept of belief is not, therefore, immediately associated with a religious context, it does not exclude it. When the "certainty that something exists" refers to a transcendent entity, then it is close to the idea of faith understood as a religious belief in a particular God. The semantic dichotomy between faith and belief originates and is developed especially in the historical context of western Christianity, when, beginning with the "confession of faith" established by the Council of Chalcedon (451 CE), the concept of faith assumes an undoubtedly confessional character.

From the time of the Protestant Reformation, the conflict between Luther and the church in Rome derived, among other things, from the claim that each possessed the "true faith." The traditions of the Roman Church were, for Luther, *traditiones humanae*, beliefs that were not legitimated by the revealed writings. For the founder of the Reformation, what did not come from God, through the Revelation, came from the Devil. As a consequence the reformers abrogated traditions which, for the Roman Church, were an integral part of the Catholic faith: some of the sacraments, purgatory, the cult of both the Madonna and the saints, religious holidays, fasting, and monastic vows.

The faith–belief duality is very important within the churches, as it is the basis for their theological and institutional identity. From the standpoint of sociological research, however, a clear distinction between faith and belief does not exist except in the sense that the former has an essentially religious content. In fact, while there may be a difference in extension and depth between the two terms, from a sociological point of view the common substantial nucleus of both is constituted by the adhesion of a subject or group to realities that, by their nature, are not verifiable from an empirical or scientific standpoint.

The definitions proposed above do not cover the whole spectrum of human beliefs. There are some behaviors which, although making no reference to unverifiable reality, confirm Durkheim's thesis that opinion is an eminently social fact and, as such, is a source of authority (Durkheim 1965 [1912]). Religious belief, according to Durkheim, is the fruit of social pressure that produces a constellation of symbolic figures in which society represents its own values by identifying them with divine figures. Durkheim's scheme is also useful for interpreting the type of manipulation practiced by an authoritarian political power over the masses in order to reach determined objectives. This is the case of the cult of personality, a belief shared by a group in the charismatic qualities of a leader who is recognized as having the ability not only to interpret the present world, together with its history, but also to elaborate revolutionary projects.

Belief is, therefore, a cognitive approach to reality that ignores, without necessarily excluding, the experimental method that western culture, from Galileo on, has set as an essential condition of scientific knowledge. Both Enlightenment thinking and positivism have traced a structure of human thought that refers to a world of reason, logic, and positive science, in which the demands of the mythical conscience (which is founded to a large extent on belief) find no place. In reality, in belief one can see the persistence of that primitive structure of the human mind that Lévy-Bruhl described as "participation." For him, the advent of conceptual representation and of scientific explanation did not necessarily lead to the cancelation of that mystical and mythical residue that is at the root of belief. Even if it had succeeded in eliminating the mystical and mythical residue, which was the great conceptual effort undertaken by positivism and Marxism (in turn creating new mythologies), the fact remains that the concept does not constitute the only form of thought even where the scientific method presides over the great transformations of the modern world. Belief is located in that sphere of human thought where the emotional, extra-logical, and non-critically filtered aspects persist. Beliefs do not constitute simple extraneous fragments, erratic masses, or past residues but are a functional part of that complex relationship with reality that does not exhaust the structure, historically achieved in modern western society, of scientific laws and conceptual abstraction.

The Weberian definition of charisma, considered an extraordinary quality endowed with strengths and supernatural or superhuman characteristics (Weber 1968 [1922]), has the structure of belief. In fact, Weber writes that decisions are made through the spontaneous recognition of charisma by those who are dominated, and this is granted through proof that begins to grow from faith in the revelation, from veneration of the hero, and from trust in the leader. Charisma, therefore, relies on a collective belief that reduces, or annuls, any distance between the subject (the community that lives the charismatic experience) and the object (the charismatic leader). The subject does not follow the route that is offered to him or her by modern rationality, but lives the situation and directly participates in it without critical mediation.

Charismatic leadership, of which the great ideologies of the nineteenth century have provided abundant examples, is realized, therefore, by activating collective representations (beliefs) that testify to both an intensely lived participation (often multidirected) and the persistence of extra-logical elements in the cultural, political, and religious life of a society. In the symbolic elements of belief, rational and "irrational" (better: extra-rational) blend together and constitute, as Lévy-Bruhl writes, a "participating" form of thought. It is a question, to some degree, of a constant of human culture, including that which is a protagonist of modern scientific-technical development. The frontiers between the two different formalities of human thought are not canceled even in a regime of advanced modernity, but they maintain a relative mobility.

Among the complex forms of belief, there is also the collective perception of "difference" and the reactions that it provokes. The social construction of this process is evident: individuals have a tendency to follow the models of behavior suggested by the culture to which they belong. This is due to the fact that a culture strengthens cohesion and facilitates communication among its members, while the adherence of these individuals to the socially shared cultural scheme allows them to collectively identify themselves as "us," in opposition to "others." The product of the process by which identity is constructed is that particular and inevitable belief we call "ethnocentrism." This, in specific sociohistorical conditions, is defined as the negative perception of human groups that are socially, culturally, and religiously different from our own. Ethnocentrism and prejudice are tightly connected sources of belief, and can manifest themselves in different fields: racial, social, religious, generational, and ethnic.

At the origin of more or less dogmatic certainties or dogmatically approved beliefs are motivations that can be traced to support or defend both personal and group affairs. The serenity that originates from the certainty of acting correctly whenever we behave in accordance with the culture to which we belong may be considered as the social construction of beliefs that appear to be convenient. In this case the picture of beliefs approaches that of ideology; worldviews tend to be reduced to a dualistic scheme in which what is "usual" for a determined social group appears normal, correct, and valid, in opposition to what is "different," which appears anxiety-provoking, risky, unfair, negative, and thus an object of beliefs that are only partially controllable. A typical case is represented by the "blood-charge," the expression used for around a millennium to designate the legend that Jews used the blood of Christians as an ingredient in food and drinks prescribed for Easter holidays. An ancestral fear of the unknown, sometimes connected to a specific desire for power, can lead to feelings of deep threat from "others," against which defensive positions are assumed that are legitimated by beliefs made up of a collective elaboration of fear, and the desire to marginalize, if not eliminate completely, that which is "different." These mechanisms of construction of socially shared beliefs are manifested in the following instances: (1) when the social structure is heterogeneous, or when it is losing its original homogeneity: the individuals that compose it differ in skin color, language, ways of living and dress, and in religious faith; (2) when rapid social and cultural change is in progress in a society: feelings of rivalry and hostility develop among heterogeneous groups, with the consequent construction of uncontrolled

beliefs; (3) when a minority group tends to increase in size and is perceived as a threat to the majority; (4) when exploitation of a minority group favors the community: in the United States, blacks were long thought to be intellectually and morally inferior, and Genesis 9:20–7 was often cited to justify beliefs regarding blacks' racial inferiority; (5) when a society exalts ethnocentrism, and racial and cultural assimilation is not favored. Among the factors that promote prejudice and the social production of uncontrolled beliefs are habit, a tendency to conform, uncritical attachment to one's own original culture, and blind acceptance of current ideas in the in-group.

Ernest Renan, historian of both ancient civilizations and Christianity and an intellectual educated in rational and positive thinking, was convinced that the inferior races of the earth were represented by the blacks of Africa, Australian Aborigines, and Native Americans. He maintained that at the origin of humankind the whole earth was populated by members of these races, which were progressively eliminated by other races. According to Renan, wherever the Aryans and Semites established themselves in a country and found uncivilized races, they proceeded to exterminate them. The inferior races were not merely primitive and uncivilized, in Renan's view, they were incapable of being civilized. He talks of their "absolute inability to achieve organization and progress," of the "eternal infancy of these non-perfectible races," of "people vowed to immobility." Obviously, faith in reason and beliefs without scientific basis can coexist even in those individuals who are considered to be among the protagonists of the rationalist turning point of the contemporary age.

Modernity, together with the advent of scientific-technical rationality and the "disenchantment of the world" (Weber), has cleared the field of many beliefs whose groundlessness became evident: the scientific method has its own internal logic founded upon the inductive method, the repetition of the experiment, and the aid of the mathematical tool. Science, already conceptualized by Francis Bacon as free of various "idola," i.e., beliefs with no rational base, has abandoned the ground of uncontrolled individual ingenuity, chance, the arbitrary, and hasty synthesis. Instead, science proceeds methodically, according to experimentation built not *ex analogia homini* (from the variability of human feelings) but *ex analogia universi* (on the constancy of universal laws) and is founded upon an awareness of the instrumental nature of cognitive faculties.

Modern thought has learned from the scientific method to avoid magic, emotional and religious elements connected with a social symbolism that is not strictly functional and rational. Yet modernity appears as the producer of new beliefs, as well as intent upon preserving ancient and "pre-logical" beliefs. To give just one example, astrology has spread through the most technologically advanced societies, while maintaining its ancient traditions, which attributed personal or divine intelligence to the stars and believed in a direct relationship between the action of the stars and natural events, and, above all, human life. It was believed possible to establish, using criteria elaborated by ancient civilizations, a more or less close relationship between the celestial and human orders. Astrology believes in a universe that is alive, made up of hidden but real correspondences (even if not scientifically proven), in which astral combinations influence and regulate the destiny of every human, from the moment of conception or birth.

The examination of certain forms of belief which technologically advanced societies have not been able to expel sets up the problem of the *operation* of the collective mentality. Different questions arise. Has modernity totally eliminated mythological production, or is it the producer of its own myths (and therefore beliefs)? Does there exist between primitive thought (participant and mythical, emotional and symbolic) and modern thought (trained to use rational and scientific categories) an unbridgeable separation and a radical heterogeneity, or is there instead a sort of gangway that allows a continuous transit from one to the other? Is primitive thought extraneous to the mentality of modern humans or is it, within certain limits and in specified forms, able to find a place in humanism, which has matured over centuries of reason and science? Modern humans are not without myths, nor devoid of values, archetypes, norms, and models that can be globally termed beliefs.

It is possible that mythical activity is a necessary and spontaneous function of the intelligence, an activity elicited in the human mind by the emotions that accompany intelligent deductions. It is congenital and common to all humans, it belongs not only to all peoples, but also to every person, at any age, and it belongs to all cultures and to any level of awareness reached by a society. Cassirer evoked the Mesopotamian myth of Marduk who kills the monster Tiamat, and with the quartered parts of his body gives form and order to the world up to the creation of humanity. According to Cassirer, the world of human culture can be described in the words of the Babylonian legend. It could not have originated until the obscurity of the myth had been fought and defeated. But the mythical monsters were not entirely destroyed. They were used in the creation of a new universe and even today they survive in it. The strengths of the myth were being opposed and subjugated by superior strengths. While these intellectual, ethical, and artistic strengths are in full vigor, the myth is tamed and subdued, but as soon as they start to lose their vigor, chaos returns. Then mythical thought starts reaffirming itself and pervades the entire human cultural and social life (Cassirer 1983 [1946]). The fear and distrust that Cassirer shows toward the mythical monsters are partly justified: the twentieth century has given ample demonstration of the devastation produced in the web of civilization by the myths of the hero, race, state, political party, war, and blood.

Both technology and science are powerful bulwarks against the return of beliefs and old-fashioned myths, but they leave open the mystery of existence, the problem of the meaning of life, birth, and death. Science and technology have freed humans from the ancient seduction of mythology and magic and have established the regime of critical conscience; however, the eternal quest for meaning is insistent and goes beyond positive science, which is research into second causes. The data of the mythical conscience, the producer of beliefs, thus have a radical ambivalence: irrelevant and negative if observed from the perspective of scientific thought, they can be positive when they are not polluted by tendencies that are rigidly ethnocentric. Modern humans can be subject to two possible alienations: the alienation of myth, of uncontrolled belief, which is entirely subject to emotion and prejudice, and the alienation of abstract rationality. Both result in two forms of unfaithfulness to the human condition. Gusdorf (1953), with the intention of recovering the existential value of religion, utopia, feeling, fable, and legend, maintains that scientific knowledge interprets nature according to its own measure, which nevertheless is shown to be insufficient when an existential thematic arises that requires a different type of category. His conviction is that those who claim to eliminate myth (and therefore every form of belief) are covertly forced to reintroduce it when they want to deal with problems of the meaning of existence.

To recognize the meaning and function of myths and legends, understood as socially shared beliefs, is not the same as admitting that critical conscience loses its supremacy over mythical conscience. The world composed of emotional and imaginative connections that Cassirer called "mythical thought" and Lévy-Bruhl called "participation" seems to be, therefore, an anthropological structure that logic cannot dethrone. Between the two there is no competition: each answers a different purpose. The two factors are undoubtedly able to react to each other, but it is impossible for them to eliminate each other. A structural analysis of the different ways to interpret the world replaces the evolutionary scheme, so dear to positivists, of two successive ages of the human conscience. Logic and myth, rationality and belief, are two superimposed layers and not two mutually replaceable types of interpretation placed at the same level, such that logic and scientific rationality are necessarily destined to replace myth and belief.

If it is true, therefore, that the birth of the sciences of nature and sociology expels myth as conclusive *Weltanschauung* and desecrates the universe by introducing the category of the "profane," it is also true that the technical and profane dominion of nature leaves behind it an emptiness and nostalgia, a kind of demand for sacredness remaining as a potential state surviving from the Weberian "disenchantment." Ancient and new beliefs are where modernity does not resolve, but, on the contrary, reopens, the questions of meaning.

SEE ALSO: Anti-Semitism (Religion); Atheism; Charisma; Civil Religion; Culture; Eurocentrism; Fundamentalism; Ideology; Magic; Millenarianism; Myth; Orientalism; Popular Religiosity; Sacred; Sacred/Profane; Satanism; Televangelism

REFERENCES AND SUGGESTED READINGS

Berger, P. & Luckmann, T. (1966) *The Social Construction of Reality*. Doubleday, New York.
Cassirer, E. (1946) *Language and Myth*. Trans. S. Langer. Harper & Brothers, New York and London.
Cassirer, E. (1983 [1946]) *The Myth of the State*. Greenwood Press, Westport, CT.
Cassirer, E. (1992 [1944]) *An Essay on Man: An Introduction to a Philosophy of Human Culture*. Yale University Press, New Haven.
Durkheim, É. (1965 [1912]) *The Elementary Forms of Religious Life*. Free Press, New York.
Gusdorf, G. (1953) *Mythe et métaphysique (Myth and Metaphysics)*. Flammarion, Paris.
Lévy-Bruhl, L. (1985 [1926]) *How Natives Think*. Trans. L. Clare. Princeton University Press, Princeton.
Renan, E. (1947–61 [1848]) *Histoire générale et système des langues sémitiques (General History and System of the Semitic Languages)*. *Œuvres complètes (Complete Works)*, Vol. 8. Calmann-Lévy, Paris.
Todorov, T. (1989) *Nous et les autres: La réflexion française sur la diversité (We and the Others: The French Reflection on Diversity)*. Éditions du Seuil, Paris.
Weber, M. (1968 [1922]) *Economy and Society: An Outline of Interpretive Sociology*, 3 vols. Bedminster Press, New York.

bell curve

Alex Bierman

The bell curve, also known as the normal distribution, provides a foundation for the majority of statistical procedures currently used in sociology. It can be thought of as a histogram of a continuous variable, but with such fine distinctions between outcomes that it is not possible to differentiate individual bars, so that the histogram appears to be a smooth line in the shape of a bell. Beneath this line is 100 percent of the possible outcomes, with the x-axis describing the range of possible outcomes and the y-axis describing the proportion or probability for each outcome.

The shape of the distribution is symmetrical, so that if it is divided in two, one half is the mirror image of the other. It is also unimodal, meaning that there is only one mode (most frequent value in the distribution). Because the bell curve is unimodal and symmetrical, the distribution's mean, median, and mode are identical and in the exact center of the distribution. Additionally, the "tails" of the curve extend indefinitely, without ever actually reaching the x-axis.

The bell curve has a specific distribution of scores. One standard deviation from the mean will always take up 34.13 percent of the area under the curve, or 34.13 percent of scores for the variable. Two standard deviations from the mean will always take up 47.72 percent of the area under the curve. Three standard deviations will always take up 49.87 percent of the area under the curve. Since the distribution is symmetrical, the distance from the mean will be the same regardless of whether the standard deviations are above or below the mean. Each additional standard deviation from the mean adds progressively less area under the curve because scores are less likely the farther they are from the mean.

The bell curve is especially useful for hypothesis testing because of the central limit theorem. This theorem states that, *even when individual scores are not normally distributed*, in random samples of a sufficient size, the distribution of sample means will be approximately normally distributed around the population mean. This facilitates hypothesis testing by allowing a sociologist to examine the probability of producing a specific sample mean, based on a hypothesized population mean. If this sample mean is unlikely to occur simply through chance, the sociologist can reject the hypothesized population mean. Similarly, relationships between variables can be tested by measuring their relationship in a sample, and studying how likely it would be to find this relationship if there was no relationship in the population.

SEE ALSO: Confidence Intervals; Hypotheses; Measures of Centrality; Random Sample; Standardization; Variables; Variance

REFERENCES AND SUGGESTED READINGS

Agresti, A. & Finlay, B. (1997) *Statistical Methods for the Social Sciences*. Prentice-Hall, Upper Saddle River, NJ.

Healey, J. F. (2005) *Statistics: A Tool for Social Research*. Thomson Wadsworth, Belmont, CA.

Ritchey, F. (2000) *The Statistical Imagination: Elementary Statistics for the Social Sciences*. McGraw-Hill College, Boston.

Bell Curve, The (Herrnstein and Murray)

Stephen K. Sanderson

Herrnstein and Murray's *The Bell Curve* (1994) is one of the most controversial and widely debated works of social science in the second half of the twentieth century. Almost instantly upon publication, the book set off a firestorm that took years to die down. What were the authors saying that was so incendiary? Their main arguments can be summarized approximately as follows. The US has increasingly evolved into a society stratified along the lines of intelligence. At the top of this stratification system is a cognitive elite of highly educated professionals, business managers, government officials, and the like who are increasingly set off from the rest of the population by their very high levels of intelligence. The cognitive elite has become increasingly separated from the rest of society by their attendance at elite universities, where they meet other highly intelligent individuals and intermarry, thus producing highly intelligent children who are likely to remain members of the elite intergenerationally. These consequences have resulted substantially from the fact that intelligence is highly genetically heritable, on the order of 40–80 percent. Intelligence is of great social importance. High intelligence is necessary for high levels of educational attainment, social status, and income. By contrast, low intelligence is associated with low levels of these outcomes, and also with a variety of social pathologies, such as higher rates of illegitimacy, poverty, welfare dependency, and crime. There are significant differences among racial and ethnic groups in intelligence, and these differences are largely genetic in origin. Such differences go far in explaining why blacks are overrepresented in the categories of social pathology mentioned above. The situation seems to be worsening, and thus the gap between the cognitive elite and the underclass growing, because of the tendency of poorer individuals of lower intelligence to out-reproduce the more wealthy and more highly intelligent. Moreover, "Unchecked, these trends will lead the US toward something resembling a caste system, with the underclass mired ever more firmly at the bottom and the cognitive elite ever more firmly anchored at the top" (p. 509).

Although *The Bell Curve* is not primarily about race, most of the controversy focused on the chapters that claimed that racial and ethnic differences in IQ scores have a large genetic component. Data presented by the authors show that the group that scores the highest on IQ tests is Jews, especially Ashkenazi Jews of Eastern European origin, and almost all American Jews are so descended. The authors report that Ashkenazi Jews score, on average, about a half to a full standard deviation above the mean for whites, which translates into roughly 7–15 IQ points. Next in line are East Asians and Americans of East Asian descent, who tend to score an overall average of about 106 (with about 110 on the spatial-mathematical component and 97 on the verbal component). American whites and Western European whites average about 100. American blacks average about 85, or a full standard deviation below whites. Actually, Herrnstein and Murray compile the results from 156 studies to show that the average black–white difference is 1.08 standard deviations, or about 16 IQ points.

Although a standard objection to IQ tests is that they are culturally biased, the authors show that on those test items deemed the most culturally biased, blacks actually score higher than on the so-called culturally neutral items. The other major standard objection to such findings is that IQ is highly correlated with social environment, especially socioeconomic level. Indeed, this is so, and both whites and blacks of higher socioeconomic status have higher reported IQ scores. However, the black–white gap does not diminish when socioeconomic status is controlled. Indeed, it widens.

Herrnstein and Murray show that cognitive test scores are excellent predictors of economic success, and, moreover, that the gap in earnings between American whites and blacks virtually disappears when cognitive test scores are controlled. When these scores are factored out of the equation, black income is 98 percent of white income. This finding leads the authors to conclude that the black–white income gap has very little to do with racism or racial discrimination and mostly to do with differences in cognitive abilities.

In the years immediately following the publication of *The Bell Curve* there appeared a "mountain of essays and books purporting to refute that work and its conclusions" (Chabris 1998). As of 1998 at least five major critical books had appeared. Two of these are works by serious social scientists: Devlin et al. (1997) and Fischer et al. (1996). Devlin et al. (1997) contend that the heritability of IQ is much lower than the .40–.80 claimed by Herrnstein and Murray. They also point to adoption studies that they claim show that IQ is largely determined by environment. Fischer et al. (1996) contend that intelligence is a poor explanation of social inequalities because the abilities of individuals are much more complex and changeable than can be captured by old-fashioned notions of intelligence. Social inequalities, they claim, are determined more by patterns of education, jobs, and taxation. As for race differences, they claim that ethnic minorities score low on intelligence tests because they are of low status, not that they are of low status because they score low on intelligence tests.

In defense of *The Bell Curve*, Bouchard (1995) claimed that, in fact, the evidence shows that low IQ is an important risk factor for poor social and economic outcomes and that high IQ is an important protective factor. The effect of

IQ is much greater than parental socioeconomic status. Moreover, because of the enormous controversy the book engendered, the American Psychological Association created a task force on intelligence, which gave its report in 1996 (Nessier et al. 1996). The task force concluded that the size of the black–white IQ difference is indeed approximately one standard deviation; that cultural biases in IQ tests cannot explain this difference; and that IQ tests are equally predictive of social, economic, and educational outcomes for both blacks and whites (cf. Murray, 2005).

In terms of policy recommendations, Herrnstein and Murray oppose Affirmative Action and other compensatory programs on the grounds that they either have not worked, or have actually worsened the situation for minorities. The authors favor a society in which everyone has a valued place commensurate with their abilities. They do not favor wholesale income redistribution, but they do favor augmenting the incomes of the poorest segments of the population so that an income floor is established. They also favor policies that would strengthen marriage, since single parenting is a serious risk factor for low social outcomes.

SEE ALSO: Class and Crime; Educational Inequality; Income Inequality and Income Mobility; Intelligence Tests; Race; Race (Racism); Stratification, Race/Ethnicity and

REFERENCES AND SUGGESTED READINGS

Bouchard, T. J. Jr. (1995) Breaking the Last Taboo. *Contemporary Psychology* 40.

Chabris, C. F. (1998) IQ Since "The Bell Curve." *Commentary* 106(2): 33–40.

Devlin, B., Fienberg, S. E., Resnick, D. P., & Roeder, K. (Eds.) (1997) *Intelligence, Genes, and Success: Scientists Respond to The Bell Curve.* Springer, New York.

Fischer, C. S., Hout, M., Jankowski, M. S., Lucas, S. R., Swidler, A., & Voss, K. (1996) *Inequality by Design: Cracking the Bell Curve Myth.* Princeton University Press, Princeton.

Herrnstein, R. J. & Murray, C. (1994) *The Bell Curve: Intelligence and Class Structure in American Life.* Free Press, New York.

Murray, C. (2005) The Inequality Taboo. *Commentary* 120(2): 13–22.

Nessier, U. et al. (1996) Intelligence: Knowns and Unknowns. *American Psychologist* 51: 77–101.

benefit and victimized zones

Harutoshi Funabashi

The concept of a benefit zone refers to a social zone or space in which residents in the zone possess a unique opportunity to consume and enjoy various goods that are refused to those living outside of the zone. In direct contrast, in the victimized zone those inside are deprived of opportunities to satisfy their needs. In other words, a victimized zone is defined by the imposition of various external negatives (e.g., pollution and industrial diseases). Whereas the entry to a benefit zone has a barrier to keep others from getting in, a victimized zone is surrounded by a barrier to prevent victims from getting out. In this way, "the handicapped" become "the deprived" when they are refused entry to a benefit zone or they cannot escape from a victimized zone.

Empirical studies that use this theoretical perspective comprise one of the origins of Japanese environmental sociology. According to the group that developed these concepts, the theory of benefit and victimized zones belongs, in Merton's sense, to the "sociological theory of the middle range." This methodological orientation has contributed to the creation of these new concepts through case studies in contemporary Japanese society.

The concept of benefit and victimized zones provides a useful theoretical framework for analyzing characteristics of various social problems, the process of social conflict, and the possibility and difficulty of social consensus. By adding supplementary viewpoints we can distinguish various types of benefit zones, victimized zones, and combinations of the two.

Firstly, the size and shape of theses zones vary. There is a pinpoint zone, a linear zone, a circle zone, and a plane zone. On the one hand, there are widespread and large zones, on the other, dense and narrow zones. Some zones have a clear-cut border, whereas others have vague, indistinct boundaries.

Secondly, the relation between benefit zones and victimized zones that are produced by the same factor or activity is very important. The two basic types of interrelation between the zones are the overlapping type and the separate type. The overlapping type refers to cases where the benefit zone and the victimized zone overlap completely. By contrast, with the separate type the two zones are entirely separate from each other. Between these two basic types there is an intermediate type, namely, a differently overlapping type, which refers to an overlapping-type relationship in which there is a different degree of benefit and victim within a zone.

These concepts enable us to analyze why social consensus is so difficult today and to discern the type of structural injustices that occur in various regional conflicts, especially those involving environmental issues. The most prominent feature of many regional conflicts today is the separation of the benefit zone and the victimized zone. For example, those that benefit from the construction of a bullet train are a totally separate group of people from those that suffer from the environmental destruction caused by such a construction (Funabashi et al. 1985). Separation of the two zones occurs not only in the context of space but also in time. For example, the generations that have created the greenhouse effects caused by CO_2 or radioactive waste might not suffer from their long-term effects. Generally speaking, it is more difficult to find social consensus in conflicts that result in spatially or temporally separate zones than it is in conflicts that involve overlapping zones.

Similarly, the localization of a victimized zone into a narrow sphere and the wide reach of a benefit zone reduce the chances of achieving social consensus. For example, the noise pollution and the vibrations caused by the bullet train affect victims in a linear and relatively narrow zone along the railway. They are minorities that possess little political power, whereas the beneficiaries of this high-speed form of transportation are the majority in Japanese society and therefore have far greater political power.

Using this theoretical perspective we can analyze the changing meaning of the idea of

"public interest" in contemporary society. Why has the notion of public interest lost the power to create social consensus in many conflicts today? Benefit and victimized zones theory can provide a clear answer to this question. When the benefit zone and victimized zone are completely separate, the idea of public interest is not persuasive.

The notion of benefit and victimized zones has led to the creation of other theoretical concepts that enable us to analyze environmental problems in terms of more macroscopic social structures. The notion of the external imposition of the environmental burden was developed by generalizing the concepts of the benefit zone and the victimized zone and by clarifying the relation between the two. This indicates that some social units do not bear the environmental burdens they create. Rather, these burdens are imposed on others.

Geographically, the external imposition of the environmental burden occurs frequently between the center and the periphery within various spatial scales: in a town, in a prefecture, in a country, and in the world. The external imposition of the environmental burden is today an essential tool in the measurement of environmental degradation. Frequently, the flow of the environmental burden from the center, the benefit zone, to the periphery, the victimized zone, is followed by enormous sums of money. Such money flows produce overwhelming political power and a domination structure. For example, in Japan, all kinds of radioactive wastes are imposed on a peripheral village (Rokkasho) in a peripheral prefecture (Aomori) and this is followed by an enormous flow of money in the name of compensation. The periphery, in this case the village and prefecture, is obliged to accept the external environmental burden because it is politically weak and economically poor.

Another way of developing the concept of the benefit and victimized zones is to combine them with the theory of social dilemmas. The prototype of the social dilemma model for analyzing environmental problems is the "tragedy of the commons" as presented by Hardin (1968). Theoretically, a social dilemma is a paradox of rationality concerning collective goods. It is defined as follows: an individual actor's rational actions pursued in his short-term private interests have the long-term, cumulative effect of destroying the environment, the collective good, and injuring the actor as well as others. Combining the idea of social dilemma with the theory of the benefit and victimized zones, Funabashi (1992) presented different types of social dilemmas, namely the self-harming type and the others-harming type. Hardin's tragedy of the commons model considers only the self-harming type, in which the benefit and victimized zones overlap completely. However, the social dilemma of the others-harming type occurs when the benefit and the victimized zones are separate, as is often the case in contemporary environmental disputes. Resolving the others-harming type of social dilemma is more difficult than the self-harming type.

The concept of benefit and victimized zones enables us to be sensitive to environmental justice, to highlight an unjust situation in various social contexts. At the same time, these concepts stimulate the quest for normative principles and a valid general policy orientation. Representative normative principles based on these concepts can be summed as follows.

Firstly, when a victimized zone is produced by a project, in order to bring about social justice, it is necessary to cut-off the benefit in the benefit zone and to compensate the suffering in the victimized zone by transferring the cut-off benefit. Secondly, promoters of any project must respect the voice of the victimized zone in order to achieve social consensus. And thirdly, in order to attain social consensus more easily, the separation of the benefit and victimized zones should be avoided. Similarly, in order to resolve today's environmental problems, an overlapping of the benefit and the victimized zones should be an essential precondition of any proposed project.

One theoretical task is to enlarge the range and relevance of this theoretical perspective by developing supplementary concepts based on various case studies and combining them with the notion of the benefit and victimized zones. For example, faced with various risk problems, we need supplementary concepts such as "latent" and "explicit" victimized zones to describe complicated situations more precisely.

Another theoretical issue to be further discussed concerns the method of identifying the benefit and the victimized zones. As to social conflicts raised by risk problems, subjective factors inevitably intervene in the definition of the benefit and the victimized zones. How is it possible to identify objectively the benefit and the victimized zones? Or is the definition of these zones always subjective and a result of social construction?

These questions may not be easily resolved. However, if we try to enrich such supplementary concepts and viewpoints through empirical research of various social problems, sociological studies using the concept of benefit and victimized zones can continue to produce fruitful insights in both descriptive research and in the normative sphere.

SEE ALSO: Distributive Justice; Environmental Movements; High-Speed Transportation Pollution; Pollution Zones, Linear and Planar; Social Justice, Theories of; Social Structure of Victims

REFERENCES AND SUGGESTED READINGS

Funabashi, H. (1992) Social Mechanisms of Environmental Destruction: Social Dilemmas and the Separate-Dependent Ecosystem. In: Krupp, H. et al. (Eds.), *Energy Politics and Schumpeter Dynamics*. Springer, New York.

Funabashi, H., Hasegawa, K., Hatanaka, S., & Katsuta, H. (1985) *Shinkansen Kogai: Kosoku Bunmei no Shakai Mondai* (Environmental Destruction Caused by Bullet Train: Social Problems of a High Speed Civilization). Yuhikaku, Tokyo.

Hardin, G. (1968) The Tragedy of the Commons. *Science* 162: 1243–8.

Benjamin, Walter (1892–1940)

Margaret E. Farrar

German literary critic and philosopher Walter Benjamin was born into an upper-middle-class Jewish family in Berlin. In 1912 he began attending the University of Freiburg and graduated *summa cum laude*. However, his Habilitation, *The Origin of German Tragic Drama*, was ultimately rejected by the University of Frankfurt in 1925, and thereafter Benjamin was unable to secure steady academic employment. (*The Origin of German Tragic Drama* would later be regarded as a classic of twentieth-century literary criticism.) In 1917 Benjamin married Dora Pollak, and a year later had a son, Stefan. For many years, Benjamin supported himself and his family through his work as a critic for *Frankfurter Zeitung* and *Literarische Welt*.

Over his lifetime Benjamin developed and maintained deep, intellectual friendships that profoundly influenced his writing. In 1915 Benjamin met Gershom Scholem, a scholar of Kabbalah and the first Professor of Jewish Mysticism at Hebrew University. Scholem and Benjamin corresponded for years, and Benjamin often considered moving to Jerusalem to join his friend there. In the 1920s Benjamin met both Theodore Adorno and Bertolt Brecht, and became intensely interested in dialectical materialism and the role of the proletariat in shaping history. This interest was strengthened by his affair with Asja Lacis, a Latvian actress and journalist who lived in Moscow.

In 1930 Benjamin divorced Dora. Benjamin's financial and personal situation worsened with the ascendance of fascism in Germany; in 1933, he was forced to emigrate to Paris, where he became affiliated with the Institute for Social Research. When the Institute moved from Paris to New York, Benjamin made an attempt to leave Paris as well. Persuaded by Adorno and with a visa negotiated by Max Horkheimer, Benjamin planned to leave Paris for the US via Spain in 1940. Upon trying to cross the Franco-Spanish border on September 25, however, a local official refused his group entry and threatened to turn them over to the French authorities. Rather than face the Gestapo, Benjamin took his own life that night. The next day, the rest of his party was permitted to cross the border. Benjamin is buried in Port Bou, Spain.

WORK AND INFLUENCE

In the introduction to a volume of Walter Benjamin's collected writings, Hannah Arendt describes Benjamin as one of "the unclassifiable ones." His work, she writes, "neither fits the existing order nor introduces a new genre that lends itself to future classification" (Benjamin 1968: 3). Benjamin is indeed "unclassifiable." His work blends historical materialism, Jewish mysticism, and poetic nostalgia to chronicle the experience and contradictions of modernity.

In large part because of its idiosyncrasies, Benjamin's work received scant attention in the decades immediately following his death. In 1968 came the first publication of his work in book form with Arendt's edited *Illuminations*; since that time there has been tremendous interest in his oeuvre, especially in the fields of art criticism, literary studies, and philosophy. Benjamin's most important works include the essays "Goethe's Elective Affinities," "One-Way Street," "The Work of Art in the Age of Mechanical Reproduction," and "Berlin Childhood in 1900." Reflecting his diverse intellectual influences, mysticism and Marxism are intertwined in Benjamin's writing, where both incisive critique and messianic hope can be found in equal measure.

Perhaps Benjamin's most famous essay, "The Work of Art in the Age of Mechanical Reproduction," has become a standard text for scholars trying to make sense of the political implications of the technological developments in art under modern capitalism. In it, Benjamin argues that our ability to reproduce art inaugurates a new moment in history where the realm of authenticity is made increasingly meaningless through art's reproducibility; the "aura" of a work of art, he states, "withers in an age of mechanical reproduction" (Benjamin 1968: 221). Film in particular irrevocably transforms the masses' sensual and intellectual experiences of art, rendering contemplation and judgment impossible in the face of a constant stream of moving images. When politics becomes aestheticized, Benjamin concludes, the results are fascism and war.

The second aspect of Benjamin's work that is especially relevant for sociologists is the figure of the flâneur. Found in his essay "Paris, Capital of the Nineteenth Century," and developed in reference to Benjamin's study of poet Charles Baudelaire, the flâneur represents a particularly modern sensibility: a detached observer of urban life who is connected to and yet not part of the bourgeoisie. The flâneur moves through the city's crowded streets and its arcades, simultaneously part of and yet not an active participant in urban life.

Benjamin's other writings on cities employ a similar method: reflection, recollection, and a kind of self-conscious urban archeology: "[One] must not be afraid to return again and again to the same matter," Benjamin (1978: 26) writes, "to scatter it as one scatters earth, to turn it over as one turns over soil." While this approach might be seen by some as a search for fixed objects or a static past, Benjamin's writings problematize this interpretation, because the objects he uncovers are never constant or found in a pure, unchanged state. In "Berlin Chronicle," a piece written as he is about to be exiled from the city by the Nazis, Benjamin painstakingly details elements of a city that no longer exists, or a city on the verge of disappearing. Benjamin's text drifts (as a flâneur might stroll through the streets of a town) to the cafés and parks, avenues and back alleys that constitute the topography of his past. Thus the Berlin encountered in the "Chronicle" is not Berlin at the time of Benjamin's writing, nor is it precisely Berlin in 1900; instead, it is what Benjamin (1968: 5) calls "lived Berlin"; it is a Berlin thoroughly imbued with and mapped by memory. In this and his other city essays (for example, "Moscow," "Marseilles," and "Naples") Benjamin artfully weaves together strands of time, place, and loss.

Apart from *The Origin of German Tragic Drama*, Benjamin never completed a book-length work. In 1927, however, he began work on a newspaper article on the Parisian arcades, which he considered the most significant architectural forms of the nineteenth century. The arcades, for Benjamin, represented both the infrastructure and the ruins of capitalism, a rich archeological site littered with literary, psychological, economic, and technological fragments to be excavated and examined.

This newspaper article became the foundation for *Das Passagenarbeit*, an exhaustive study of the arcades that would become Benjamin's life work. For 13 years he took extensive notes on countless aspects of the arcades, trying to recreate the dreamscape, or in his words "phantasmagoria," of modern urban life.

Eventually, he organized these fragments into 36 sections, or "Convolutes," on topics that included fashion, iron construction, advertising, photography, and prostitution. Each convolute includes juxtaposed observations, quotations, aphorisms, and references; together, they comprise a multi-layered picture of bourgeois Parisian life that Susan Buck-Morss famously described as Benjamin's "dialectics of seeing." As such, the Arcades Project is perhaps the best example of Benjamin's methodology: a cultural history that resists and subverts historical narrative, replacing it with a montage of images that could be combined to form constellations of ideas.

Das Passagenarbeit remained a work in progress until Benjamin's death in 1940. Benjamin never completed the book, and burned his copy of the manuscript before he committed suicide at the Spanish border. A copy of the work survived, however; it was published in German in 1982 as *Das Passagen-Werk*, and was translated into English in 1999.

SEE ALSO: Adorno, Theodor W.; Arcades; Commodities, Commodity Fetishism, and Commodification; Consumption, Mass Consumption, and Consumer Culture; Critical Theory/Frankfurt School; Film; Flânerie; Mass Culture and Mass Society; Media and Consumer Culture

REFERENCES AND SUGGESTED READINGS

Adorno, T. W. (1973) Letters to Walter Benjamin. Trans. H. Zohn. *New Left Review* 81: 46–80.

Benjamin, W. (1968) *Illuminations: Essays and Reflections*. Ed. H. Arendt. Trans. H. Zohn. Schocken Books, New York.

Benjamin, W. (1978) *Reflections: Essays, Aphorisms, Autobiographical Writings*. Ed. P. Demetz. Trans. E. Jephcott. Schocken Books, New York.

Benjamin, W. (2002) *The Arcades Project*. Ed. H. Eiland. Trans. K. McLaughlin & R. Tiedemann. Belknap Press, Cambridge, MA.

Buck-Morss, S. (1989) *The Dialectics of Seeing: Walter Benjamin and the Arcades Project*. MIT Press, Cambridge, MA.

Eagleton, T. (1981) *Walter Benjamin or Towards a Revolutionary Criticism*. New Left Books, London.

Gilloch, G. (1997) *Myth and Metropolis: Walter Benjamin and the City*. Polity Press, Cambridge.

Jameson, F. (1972) *Walter Benjamin, or Nostalgia*. In: Boyers, R. (Ed.), *The Legacy of the German Refugee Intellectuals*. Schocken Books, New York.

Bernard, Jessie (1903–96)

Joyce E. Williams and Vicky M. MacLean

Dubbed the "reasonable rebel" by many of her supporters, Jessie Bernard is internationally recognized for her contributions to sociology and to feminist thought (Lipman-Blumen 1988). She was one of the most productive of female sociologists although her career developed during a time considered by many as hostile to women in the profession (Deegan 1991). She authored over a dozen books, and co-authored almost that many, as well as over a hundred articles, book chapters, encyclopedia entries, and essays. Her impact on sociology spans more than six decades and includes the areas of marriage and family, gender and sex roles, community studies, the history of the discipline, sociology of knowledge, and social problems and public policy. Her greatest legacy emerged in the last 30 years of her life as reflected in the contributions made to the development of feminist thought and gender scholarship. Trained as a traditional sociologist, Bernard's intellectual journey progressed through social positivism, functionalism, and finally to feminism (Lipman-Blumen 1979). Over time Bernard became a strong critic of the discipline, its dominant paradigms and masculine biases, and of broader public policies and practices. Bernard helped to found the Society for the Study of Social Problems (SSSP) in 1951, an act of rebellion against the American Sociological Association (ASA) and its timidity in leadership in such issues as poverty, inequality, racism, sexism, McCarthyism, and academic freedom (Bernard 1973). She served as president of SSSP in 1963. Her professional associations, activities, awards, and honors are many. The Jessie Bernard Award for outstanding scholarship in gender studies was established in 1976 and is presented at the annual ASA meetings. It is a living reminder of the debt the field owes to Bernard (Cantor 1988).

Jessie Sarah (later changed to Shirley) Ravitch was born in Minneapolis to Eastern European immigrant parents Rebecca (Bessie) Kantar and David Revici, the father's name later anglicized to Ravitch and finally to Ravage (Bannister 1991: 18). The name changes were not unusual for that day, often to accommodate Anglo pronunciations and sometimes to obscure a foreign identity. Jessie was the third of four children and by the time of her birth her father had risen from a Transylvania candlemaker to become a real estate broker. Her parents settled in a middle-class Jewish community, largely of Romanian origin, on the South Side of Minneapolis, but soon after Jessie was born they moved to the suburbs where they were the only Jewish family. There are varying and conflicting accounts (some from Bernard herself) as to how much her Jewish heritage influenced her life. On the one hand, she reported being "only vaguely conscious of myself as a Jew." On the other hand, she remembered her grandmother as setting "the Jewish stamp on our home." Her biographer represented her childhood as one of "ever-present tension between Jewish and Gentile culture" (Bannister 1991: 26). Some of Bernard's professional writings are about Jews as a minority group in the United States (1925, 1942a, 1942b) and also about the tensions within the Jewish community in social class and religious differences (Bannister 1991). She expressed these contradictions in two early writings on Jewish culture, one published anonymously, and the other, largely autobiographical, describing the biculturality of Jews as "social schizophrenia" (Graeber & Britt 1942: 243–93).

In 1920, at age 16, Jessie entered the University of Minnesota where she earned both bachelors and masters degrees in sociology. There she met sociology professor and well-published author Luther L. Bernard (LLB), a Chicago PhD (1910), who became her mentor and collaborator. In 1925, although 21 years her senior, and non-Jewish, Luther married Jessie and, in the custom of the day, she took his name. Marriage to LLB, a well-known but contentious sociologist who in 1932 served as president of the ASA, in many ways defined Jessie's life and work. The two moved frequently and along the way Jessie took graduate work at Chicago, at Tulane, and at Washington University (St. Louis) where she remained long enough to secure her doctorate in 1935 and later to teach at nearby Lindenwood College (1940–7). She was profoundly influenced by Chicago and her graduate study with Ellsworth Faris, Robert Park, and George Herbert Mead.

According to Jessie's biographer, the marriage was conflictual as LLB was controlling and dogmatic in both personal and professional matters (Bannister 1991). Between completion of work on her doctorate and the Lindenwood job, Jessie lived apart from LLB and worked for the Bureau of Labor Statistics in Washington, DC. In those years she also did research for what was to become a major, definitive history of sociology, *Origins of American Sociology* (1943). During her Washington years, Jessie actually filed for divorce but the two reconciled, apparently with LLB finally agreeing to her having children. Three children were subsequently born to the Bernards: Dorothy (1941), Claude (1945), and David (1950), born shortly before LLB died in 1951.

The Bernards left Washington University in 1947 for Pennsylvania State University. This time it was Jessie who secured the job and LLB moved with her. She was hired as an assistant professor and he as a lecturer. Jessie remained at Pennsylvania until 1964 when she gave up full-time teaching and university affiliation for life in Washington, DC, writing and, from time to time, accepting visiting professorships and research appointments. Her location in Washington gave her access to governmental projects, with varying results. For example, she was one of several well-known social scientists who participated in Project Camelot sponsored by the Department of Defense, ostensibly to develop a general social systems model to predict social change in developing countries. The project was canceled, however, when it became known that the Defense Department had a covert agenda for the governance of Chili (Horowitz 1967). From her Washington vantage point, Bernard also had opportunity to influence social policy and public opinion, particularly with regard to the family and roles

of women. *Marriage and Family Among Negroes* (1966) grew out of work with the Children's Bureau and efforts to address the issue of unwed mothers. Her book *Women and the Public Interest* (1971) began as a position paper for the Democratic campaign of 1968, laying out an agenda and conceptual framework for addressing issues relating women to public policy.

Bernard's work is not easily classified as it is among the most eclectic of any sociologist of comparable reputation. One explanation is provided by Bernard herself as she defined her life's work as reflecting "four revolutions" (1973) in the discipline of sociology: the quantification of sociology in the 1920s; the expansion of sociology from the defining influence of the Chicago School in the 1930s, a change in which her husband played an important role; her participation in the founding of SSSP as an alternative to ASA in the 1950s; and, finally, the feminist revolution of the 1960s. According to Bannister, Bernard's work on the historical development of American sociology was to have been her doctoral thesis, but, influenced by the quantification revolution in sociology, she opted instead to present a more empirical study on patterns of neighborhood settlement (Bannister 1991: 57). Her early effort to comply with the push for quantification in sociology is particularly evident in her efforts to quantify "success" in marriage in some of her earliest publications.

While her involvement in SSSP followed the death of her husband who had served as an early president of ASA, it was in many ways reflective of his influence as he had led an internal revolution at ASA in the early 1930s, helping to remove it from the influence of the University of Chicago, a move that she supported even though her own experience with the University of Chicago had been a positive one.

The final phase of Bernard's "life calendar" reflects her "conversion" to feminism, beginning with her involvement in Sociologists for Women in Society, which grew out of the Women's Caucus of the ASA (1973). Bernard, considered an "expert" on marriage and the family, came to feminism late in life and lent her name and support to the cause. Her feminist transformation is clearly traceable in her works on women: *Academic Women* (1964), *The Sex Game* (1968), *Women and the Public Interest* (1971), *The Future of Marriage* (1972, 1982), *Women, Wives, and Mothers* (1975), *The Female World* (1981), and *The Female World from a Global Perspective* (1987). The first of these books, *Academic Women*, addresses the careers of women in academe and undoubtedly reflects an important intellectual and personal turning point for Bernard, even though she said the book was met with "a great big yawn" among her peers (Lipman-Blumen 1988: 272). In it she raised the question as to why women were less productive than men given that women in the academy were a select group with higher intelligence and abilities than the average man. She concluded that much of the work done in the academy took place in a single-sex, male-privileged arena (the "stag effect"), giving men greater positional advantage in the communication system. *The Sex Game* is a somewhat humorous survival guide to help women negotiate their roles in the midst of rapid social change, much of which they were responsible for unleashing. In *Women and the Public Interest*, Bernard set forth what is essentially a position paper on the changing roles of women with a focus on the necessity of maximizing these roles for the public good. It is written primarily as an explanation of the "movement women" of the 1960s and early 1970s. *The Future of Marriage* won critical acclaim for Bernard even though it began as simply a review of the body of knowledge relevant to marriage in order to provide some predictions for the future. The work evolved as a reconceptualization of marriage as "his marriage" and "her marriage," substantively and qualitatively different because of the "structural strain" built into the wife's marriage. All data pointed to the fact that marriage was a more positive experience for the husband than for the wife. According to Bernard, she did not begin this work with the idea that marriage was bad for wives. Indeed, she acknowledged that the facts had been known for a long time, and that she had reported many of them herself. This time, however, she saw them differently, no doubt from a more feminist perspective. In *Women, Wives, and Mothers* Bernard provides an important synthesis and critique of the state of research on sex differences and the misuse of this body of

knowledge to promote a gender ideology that perpetuates sex inequality. In this work Bernard comes into her own in her explicit development of feminist consciousness through her examination of women's socialization and motherhood over the life course.

Bernard wrote two final books that took her feminist theorizing to a new level. *The Female World* (1981), considered by most as her best work, is a conceptualization of the female world as existing *sui generis* and parallel to the presumptive, normative world of males. She characterized this female world structurally as *gemeinschaft* and culturally as an ethos of love and/or duty. The title of Bernard's final book, *The Female World from a Global Perspective* (1987), suggests that it is only a modification of the earlier title. However, it is far more. Her discussion of "feminist enlightenment" warns that in the context of an increasingly global world, and particularly against the backdrop of the third world, feminist scholarship could descend into another form of colonialism. Bernard returned to philosophy of science issues that concerned her early in her career when her work was paradigmatically functionalist, assuming the universality of western science. She had written intermittently about such issues (1949, 1950, 1960) and in this final work came back to questions about scholarship and scientific values with warnings that feminist scholarship should not slide into romantic idealism or angry polemics.

Most of Bernard's books were written after she retired from full-time teaching but while she was still the single parent of three children. In addition to the above, her contributions to sociology include works on the community, on methodology, on game theory, on the sociology of conflict, and on philosophy of science and the development of sociology. In her autobiographical history of sociology, "My Four Revolutions," Bernard concluded that "practically all sociology to date has been a sociology of the male world" (1973: 782). Indeed, she knew the history of sociology to be a male history for she, along with husband Luther, had helped to write it. Their massive, 860-page volume *Origins of American Sociology* (1943) is still the definitive history of the discipline, but it is one lacking in female contributions. Using inductive methodology, exhaustive publications on American social thought, and the vast resources of the Library of Congress, the Bernards traced the development of American sociology from its European influences. They construct, more conceptually than empirically, a Social Science Movement with roots in English and French social thought, social reform, and Comtean positivism. Despite the emergence of American sociology from social reform and social problems, there is no mention of women such as Jane Addams whose settlement house activities played such a vital role in early descriptive and empirical sociology. Some 30 women are indexed in the book but most as authors of pre-sociological, historical works. The only woman to receive multiple citations is Harriet Martineau and she is cited only in relation to her translation of Auguste Comte. While her husband was the first author on this publication, Jessie subsequently acknowledged having done all of the research for the volume and in a footnote more than 30 years later stated that she contributed 33 chapters to the work and Luther 27 (1978: 341). He at the time was, of course, a well-known and well-published sociologist. Some of Bernard's work for the book was published as a chapter in a volume on *Trends in American Sociology* (Lundberg et al. 1929: 1–71).

Despite Bernard's early efforts to become a quantitative sociologist, she tended to favor an inductive form of writing, and most of her work is qualitative. Whether writing on the family, the community, or marriage, she tended toward exhaustive and critical literature reviews as well as analysis of relevant theoretical frameworks. She always looked at where we have been and where we are going. Her strength was in synthesizing, and in reconceptualizing a body of empirical work. Above all, she ferreted out fresh ideas from the works of others and inspired new areas of scholarship for those who followed. On October 6, 1996, at age 93, when she considered her feminist revolution still a work in progress, Jessie Bernard died in a nursing home in Washington, DC.

SEE ALSO: American Sociological Association; Family Conflict; Gender, Work, and Family; Inequality/Stratification, Gender; Marriage; Sex and Gender

REFERENCES AND SUGGESTED READINGS

Bannister, R. C. (1991) *Jessie Bernard: The Making of a Feminist*. Rutgers University Press, New Brunswick, NJ.
Bernard, J. S. (1925) Relative Rate of Change in Custom and Beliefs of Modern Jews. *Proceedings of the American Sociological Society* 19: 171–6.
Bernard, J. S. (1942a) An Analysis of Jewish Culture. In: Graeber, J. & Britt, S. H. (Eds.), *Jews in a Gentile World: The Problem of Antisemitism*. Macmillan, New York.
Bernard, J. S. (1942b) Biculturality: A Study in Social Schizophrenia. In: Graeber, J. & Britt, S. H. (Eds.), *Jews in a Gentile World: The Problem of Antisemitism*. Macmillan, New York.
Bernard, J. S. (1949) The Power of Science and the Science of Power. *American Sociological Review* 14: 575–85.
Bernard, J. S. (1950) Can Science Transcend Culture? *Scientific Monthly* 71: 268–73.
Bernard, J. S. (1960) Citizenship Bias in Scholarly and Scientific Work. *Sociological Inquiry* 30: 7–13.
Bernard, J. S. (1966) *Marriage and Family Among Negroes*. Prentice-Hall, Englewood Cliffs, NJ.
Bernard, J. S. (1973) My Four Revolutions: An Autobiographical History of the ASA. *American Journal of Sociology* 78: 773–91.
Bernard, J. S. (1976) The Family and Stress. *Journal of Home Economics* (Fall).
Bernard, J. S. (1978) *Self-Portrait of a Family*. Beacon Press, Boston.
Bernard, L. L. & Bernard, J. S. (1943) *Origins of American Sociology*. Crowell, New York. Reprint Russell & Russell, 1965.
Cantor, M. G. (1988) Jessie Bernard: An Appreciation. *Gender and Society* 2 (September): 264–70.
Deegan, M. J. (1991) Jessie Bernard. In: Deegan, M. J. (Ed.), *Women in Sociology: A Bio-Bibliographical Sourcebook*. Greenwood Press, Westport, CT, pp. 71–80.
Graeber, J. & Britt, S. H. (Eds.) (1942) *Jews in a Gentile World: The Problem of Antisemitism*. Macmillan, New York.
Horowitz, I. L. (1967) *The Rise and Fall of Project Camelot*. MIT Press, Cambridge, MA.
Lipman-Blumen, J. (1979) Bernard, Jessie. In: Sills, D. (Ed.), *The Encyclopedia of the Social Sciences*. Free Press, New York, pp. 49–56.
Lipman-Blumen, J. (1988) Jessie Bernard: A "Reasonable Rebel" Speaks to the World. *Gender and Society* 2 (September): 271–3.
Lundberg, G., Bain, R., & Anderson, N. (1929) *Trends in American Sociology*. Harper & Brothers, New York.

bifurcated consciousness, line of fault

Marjorie L. DeVault

Dorothy Smith's influential feminist essay, "A Sociology for Women," begins by calling attention to a "line of fault": "a point of rupture in my/our experience as woman/women within the social forms of consciousness – the culture or ideology of our society – in relation to the world known otherwise, the world directly felt, sensed, responded to, prior to its social expression" (1987: 49). Insisting on the anchorage of consciousness in located bodily experience, Smith was pointing to the shift away from embodied experience into a governing conceptual, ideological mode of consciousness associated with the "ruling relations" of industrial capitalism (1999). She saw in most women's lives in that period a distinctive subjectivity, a "bifurcated consciousness" organized by women's household or reproductive labor and the supporting and applied tasks assigned to them, historically, in the occupational division of labor. As mothers, wives, community volunteers, nurses, secretaries, and so on, Smith argued, women engage with people where and as they actually live, "working up" individuals so as to fit them to the more abstract frameworks that organize institutional activity. Located thus, at the juncture of embodied specificity and ideological abstraction, women in such positions hold in their consciousness both ways of seeing and thinking. Typically, their movement from one to the other framework is achieved without conscious thought as an expert practice of everyday action. However, when attention is directed to this dual formation, the disjuncture can be seen as a "line of fault" which opens this organization of social life to analytic scrutiny, as an earthquake opens the earth's crust.

Smith's early sociological work dealt with the sociology of mental illness, family and class, and the social organization of knowledge. She was an immigrant from Britain to the US and then Canada, a single mother, and an activist.

The new scholarly networks and constituencies that grew out of the women's movement of the 1970s provided a context in which she developed her influential approach to investigating the social world, which she views as neither method nor theory but "an alternative sociology." She first wrote of women's bifurcated consciousness in the early 1970s (Smith 1974). Like other feminist thinkers of that time, she was considering how to conceptualize a state of consciousness women were discovering in the feminist activity of consciousness-raising – a distinctive but only indistinctly articulated sense of alienation from dominant modes of subjectivity. In addition to its sources in feminism, Smith's account drew from the materialist method of Marx, the social psychology of George Herbert Mead, and the phenomenology of Alfred Schutz. In later writings, she and her students developed an "institutional ethnography" (IE) approach (Campbell & Manicom 1995; Campbell & Gregor 2002), which sketches out methods designed to explore the disjunctures of life within textually mediated societies.

The injunction to "begin with women's experience," which is central to Smith's feminist writing, parallels in various ways the writings of other socialist feminists of the time, such as Sheila Rowbotham, Sandra Harding, and Donna Haraway, as well as Patricia Hill Collins's account of a "black feminist thought" tied to a position as "outsider within." Smith is often categorized, with Harding, Haraway, and Collins, as a "standpoint feminist." Smith has resisted the label and its flattening of differences among these feminist thinkers (Smith 2005). For Smith, the notion of a "standpoint" is not a specific perspective whose content can be defined or achieved, but only a pointer toward the disjunctures that may serve as productive starting points for social inquiry; it produces a "subject position" or "site for the knower" who is committed to an inquiry that retains the sensual, embodied experience of particular places. One might also see parallels with formulations developed around other kinds of oppression, such as the idea of home and school languages of working-class children, W. E. B. Du Bois's account of African

Americans' "double consciousness," or Franz Fanon's writing of the "masks" worn by the colonized, and Smith was likely influenced by these kinds of writing. However, she would want to insist on the specificities of consciousness associated with distinctive positions in social formations, and the ways in which subjugated and dominant consciousnesses are fostered, nurtured, and inhibited in each situation; therefore, her theoretical and epistemological writing should be read alongside her historically grounded accounts of transformations in the relations of ruling (Smith 1985; Smith 1999: ch. 5; Griffith & Smith 2005: ch. 1).

SEE ALSO: Black Feminist Thought; Consciousness Raising; Double Consciousness; Feminism and Science, Feminist Epistemology; Feminist Methodology; Feminist Standpoint Theory; Matrix of Domination; Strong Objectivity

REFERENCES AND SUGGESTED READINGS

Campbell, M. & Gregor, F. (2002) *Mapping Social Relations: A Primer in Doing Institutional Ethnography*. Garamond, Aurora, ON.
Campbell, M. & Manicom, A. (1995) *Knowledge, Experience, and Ruling Relations*. University of Toronto Press, Toronto.
Griffith, A. I. & Smith, D. E. (2005) *Mothering for Schooling*. Routledge Falmer, New York.
Smith, D. E. (1974) Women's Perspective as a Radical Critique of Sociology. *Sociological Inquiry* 44: 7–13.
Smith, D. E. (1985) Women, Class, and Family. In: Burstyn, V. & Smith, D. E. (Eds.), *Women, Class, Family, and the State*. Garamond, Toronto, pp. 1–44.
Smith, D. E. (1987) *The Everyday World as Problematic: A Feminist Sociology*. Northeastern University Press, Boston.
Smith, D. E. (1999) *Writing the Social: Critique, Theory, and Investigations*. University of Toronto Press, Toronto.
Smith, D. E. (2005) *Institutional Ethnography: A Sociology for People*. AltaMira, Lanham, MD.

Big Science and collective research

Brian Woods

Although Big Science is a rather nebulous term, most commentators have used it to describe an array of perceived changes in science and scientific practice during and after World War II. Following Alvin Weinberg's *Reflections on Big Science*, the term has often been associated with the rise of a military-industrial-government-academic complex, the use/production of huge machines, the investment of massive resources, and the growth of large techno-scientific organizations. As such, Big Science is often compared against a pre-war Little Science, usually characterized by lone or heroic scientists (typically, a Thomas Edison or Albert Einstein-type figure) working in their makeshift laboratory. Yet large-scale science is not a twentieth-century phenomenon. Astronomy, for example, modeled itself on the factory system during the nineteenth century, with an increase in the hierarchical division of labor and a focus on large-scale, mission-oriented projects. These developments coincided with increased funding (mainly philanthropic) and the construction of ever-larger telescopes, upon which the field of inquiry came to depend.

Nonetheless, the Manhattan Project, which brought together resources and labor power on an unprecedented scale to produce the first atomic bomb, often serves as the symbol for the beginnings of Big Science. Because of this, many commentators have seen technology as the driving force behind Big Science. The use of big machines, huge scientific instruments, and/or complicated technological systems have necessitated large systems of organization and control, which in turn have required industrial-scale inputs of labor and capital: a pattern that led some observers to claim Big Science as the industrialization of research, or what Paul Zilsel called the emergence of "think factories." In *Scientific Knowledge and Its Social Problems* (1972), Jerome Ravetz argued that the industrialization of science has meant that pure science now involved increasing capitalization, which necessitated a structural division of labor between scientists and their industrial managers.

Because of the huge resources needed to fund it and because of its size, many commentators have viewed Big Science as an inherently political activity (as opposed to a supposedly apolitical Little Science), which is embroiled in bureaucratic and national politics. The growth and growing influence of government laboratories (particularly after the Manhattan Project) on science development, the creation of the idea of science as a "public good," and the coming together of government and private capital to serve sociopolitical ambitions and goals of national importance led many to question the autonomy of Big Science. Like Ravetz, Weinberg had witnessed the rise of the science administrator with some trepidation and argued that Big Science's requirement for both state and industrial support was skewing science away from the "quest for truth" towards a market-conscious, product-oriented, capital-intensive activity that has taken on the impersonal nature of industrial enterprise. From this perspective, the trend towards technological goals rather than scientific understanding is a corruption of science by government and corporate interests.

The entanglement of science and politics, while evident in all industrialized countries, was especially so in the old Soviet Union. Soviet science was distributed into what Graham (1992) termed three gigantic pyramids: the university system, the academy of sciences system, and the industrial and defense ministry system. After the 1917 revolution the Soviets organized science into large centralized institutes, with the Academy of Sciences as the leading center of basic/fundamental research. While the State Planning Commission of the Council of Ministers determined the budgets for each of the three pyramids, they all had relative autonomy, though very powerful leaders dominated each. After World War II, Big Science took on a whole different character when the Soviet Union began construction of large "science cities" that housed thousands of scientists and researchers all working in close proximity on large state-oriented projects, such as space and nuclear weapons.

The most renowned analysis on Big Science is probably Derek de Solla Price's *Little Science, Big Science* (1963). Price was less concerned with the condition of science than he was with charting its historical growth. Using statistical data on increasing numbers of scientists and scientific papers, Price demonstrated the "first law" of scientific growth: that science had maintained a general exponential growth for 300 years, doubling in size every 15 years. For Price, Big Science was a stage in the historical development of science: a point between Little Science and the start of an epoch of New Science. Although Price did not define the detailed nature of this change, he did state that the exponential growth of science could not continue indefinitely, that it must reach saturation. With saturation and an exhausting of resources came the onset of new conditions, where centuries of tradition would break down, giving rise to new escalations, redefinitions of basic terms, and beginning to operate with new ground rules. According to Price, Big Science showed "all the familiar syndromes of saturation."

Other observers have noted that the ever-increasing dimensions of science have brought with it new sets of problems. Scientific credibility becomes harder to earn, not because scientists today are any less competent, but simply because there are more of them. Research under Little Science (so the argument goes) was more open to critical scrutiny because of a smaller audience, but under Big Science it is more likely that the research will go unread once it enters the deluge of information overload. Coupled with this is the problem that fewer people are eligible to dispute a given knowledge claim (both because of specialization and because of the high expense of reproducing experiments), while simultaneously these claims are playing a greater role in legitimating policies, actions, and events. In addition, the increased government reliance on science to underwrite its activities is also leading to the long-term tendency for Big Science to become a more acute instrument of political power as its sphere of accountability diminishes.

SEE ALSO: Citations and Scientific Indexing; Military Research and Science and War; Science and Public Participation: The Democratization of Science; Scientific Literacy and Public Understandings of Science; State; State and Economy; War

REFERENCES AND SUGGESTED READINGS

Capshew, J. & Rader, K. (1992) Big Science: Price to the Present. *Osiris* 2(7): 2–25.
Fuller, S. (2000) *The Governance of Science: Ideology and the Future of the Open Society.* Open University Press, Buckingham.
Graham, L. (1992) Big Science in the Last Years of the Big Soviet Union. *Osiris* 2(7): 49–71.

bilingual, multicultural education

Amy Lutz

The term bilingual education is used to refer to a variety of different language programs in schools with different goals and methods. These programs range from those that transition minority-language students to the majority language as quickly as possible, to programs that build or maintain high-level proficiency in a second language through teaching content area in that language. One of the ways of distinguishing different types of bilingual education programs by their goals and methods is to classify them as strong or weak forms of bilingual education (for more on forms of bilingual education, see Baker 1996). Weak forms of bilingual education are programs where the goal is monolingualism or limited bilingualism, whereas strong forms of bilingual education are programs where the goal is bilingualism and biliteracy. Weak forms of bilingual education include submersion or structured immersion programs in the majority language, programs that transition students into the majority language, mainstream education programs with foreign language teaching, and segregationist language programs. Strong forms of bilingual education – those programs emphasizing fluency in two languages – include immersion in a

minority language, maintenance/heritage language programs, two-way/dual language programs, and bilingual education in two majority languages in populations with two majority languages. Some bilingual education programs include or are a part of multicultural education. Multicultural education acknowledges the ethnic and cultural differences of a diverse student population and seeks to provide equal access to education for all students. While some have equated multiculturalism to cultural pluralism, the former differs in that it not only recognizes differences among groups, but also aims to provide equal access to institutions for all groups (for more on multiculturalism, see Goldberg 1994; Hollinger 1995; Mahajan 2002).

In the US, weak forms of bilingual education, such as programs emphasizing a transition to English rather than augmenting the language skills in the mother tongue with English language skills, have generally been utilized in educational systems, although forms of bilingual education have varied over time and by state (for more on bilingual education in the US, see Fishman & García 2002). From the eighteenth century to World War I, there was an atmosphere of general tolerance with regard to the use of languages other than English in public and even as the medium for instruction in schools (Baker 1996). During the two world wars, public suspicion of foreign languages extended to their use in the classroom. Classes were generally taught in English and the use of other languages in schools was forbidden in some places. However, by the 1960s and 1970s, bilingual education became part of a wider multicultural education movement that emerged from civil rights and desegregation efforts with the goal of making the educational system more equitable for ethnic minorities. For linguistic minorities, the provision of equal access to education may include some form of bilingual education. The Bilingual Education Act of 1968 provided federal funding to schools in support of coursework taught in the students' native language and was the first federal legislation in the US focused on enhancing educational opportunities for Mexican, Puerto Rican, and Native American students (Ricento & Burnaby 1998). In 1974, in the case of *Lau v. Nichols*, the US Supreme Court ruled that, in accordance with the Civil Rights Act, language minority students have the right to receive education in their mother tongue. In order to comply with the 1974 Supreme Court ruling, the Office of Civil Rights developed a set of procedures, programs, and regulations on the provision of bilingual education, often referred to as the Lau Remedies (Ricento & Burnaby 1998).

The demand for programs to address the educational needs of language minority students has created conflicts in the school systems in three general areas: the cost of the programs, the shortage of bilingual teachers (particularly in certain subject areas), and the capacity of the language programs to integrate students into the general student bodies in schools (Cervantes-Rodríguez & Lutz 2003; see also Johnson et al. 1997). In the 1980s and 1990s, the "English Only" movement sought to limit the use of languages other than English in US public institutions, including as a medium of instruction in schools. The early 1980s marked a shift away from the Lau Remedies due to decreases in funding of strong bilingual education programs, legislative efforts that limited enforcement of the Lau Remedies, and policies that allowed states and districts to determine whether their policies and programs complied with the Civil Rights Act (Ricento & Burnaby 1998). Some states, such as California, have since passed ballot initiatives to eliminate bilingual education from the states' public school systems. Passed in 2002, the No Child Left Behind Act continues the trend away from strong forms of bilingual education; it sets a 3-year limit on instruction in children's mother tongues and directs federal funds toward programs that promote a transition to English rather than bilingualism.

Much of the past research on bilingual education in the US has focused on the acquisition of English and educational outcomes of students with limited English abilities (for more recent sociological research on bilingual education, see Roscigno et al. 2001). More recent sociological research has focused on the educational outcomes associated with proficiency in an immigrant mother tongue in addition to English (e.g., Fernandez & Nielson 1986). Authors in the segmented assimilation perspective, in particular, have argued that maintenance of an ethnic mother tongue is associated with enhanced educational outcomes (Portes &

Schauffler 1994; Zhou & Bankston 1998; Portes & Rumbaut 2001).

In Latin America, indigenous languages have become part of bilingual/bicultural education in some countries and school curricula throughout the region are increasingly including a variety of programs to promote English-language skills. Bilingual education has been ongoing in Mexico since about the 1930s, but was implemented more widely in the 1970s, often as a means to transition indigenous students to Spanish (Mar-Molinero 2000). By the 1980s the use of indigenous mother tongues in school curricula was more accepted, but Mexico's participation in NAFTA with the US and Canada led to increased pressures to focus on English language acquisition by the 1990s. Support for bilingual education in Peru also increased in the 1970s after Quechua gained status as an official language. The Puno bilingual education project in Peru, which used the students' mother tongue (either Aymara or Quechua) as the main medium of instruction and Spanish as a second language, has been influential throughout Latin America (Mar-Molinero 2000; for more on the Puno project, see Hornberger 1988). Despite the program's success in enhancing students' knowledge of academic content, the experimental bilingual education program in Puno was discontinued in 1990, although efforts at similar programs have emerged since that time (Hornberger and López 1998). Bolivia's educational reform efforts in the 1990s entailed a program to include indigenous languages as both a subject and a means of instruction (Mar-Molinero 2000). Unlike bilingual education programs in much of Latin America (and much of the rest of the world), the Bolivian program is aimed at promoting proficiency in indigenous languages (in addition to Spanish) for *both* majority and minority language speakers (for more on bilingual education programs in Mexico, Bolivia, and Peru, see Mar-Molinero 2000).

Bilingual education in Canada includes heritage language programs intended to promote and maintain fluency in immigrant languages and French immersion programs. Heritage language bilingual education is available in some provinces, meaning that children receive academic instruction in an immigrant mother tongue or ancestral language for about half the school day (Baker 1996). In other provinces, heritage language classes are offered to teach children a heritage language outside of the school day. In the 1960s, Canada began experimental programs in French language immersion. These programs were innovative in that they used the target language as the medium rather than the subject of academic instruction (Genesee 1998). The Canadian immersion programs provide an educational experience in which majority English-language speakers are immersed in French at school, thereby allowing them to have proficiency in both of Canada's official languages (Genesee 1998).

The success and popularity of the French immersion programs in Canada has led to the creation of similar programs in Australia, Spain, the UK, Finland, and Switzerland (Baker 1996). Other bilingual education programs throughout the world offer bilingual education in two majority languages. These programs utilize two (or more) majority languages as the medium of instruction of content area. Often, they feature a national and international language, with the goal that students become fluent in both. Such programs can be found in Luxembourg, Taiwan, Singapore, Germany, and Nigeria (Baker 1996). In Luxembourg, for example, the language that is used as a medium of instruction shifts from Luxembourgish, to German, and then French as the students progress through the school system; students also learn additional foreign languages such as English and Latin as a subject in the secondary level, with the option of additional languages if they select the language stream in the curriculum (Hoffmann 1998). Private international schools (such as those found in Asia and the Middle East) often utilize bilingual education programs in two majority languages or teach content predominantly in English or another European language with the goal of bilingualism and preparation for continuing study in European or US university systems (Baker 1996).

In the European Union, decisions related to linguistic rights, bilingual planning, and educational programs are generally left to national governments. A variety of bilingual education programs and philosophies exist and programs are targeted at building bilingual proficiency among regional and immigrant language minority children, as well as programs targeted at bi- or multilingualism among majority-language speakers. Member states are encouraged to promote fluency in at least two "foreign" languages, one of which should be an official language of a European Union member state (Extra & Yağmur 2004). Exchange programs for teachers and students such as LINGUA, ERASMUS, and SOCRATES are also aimed at building bilingual skills in the various languages that exist throughout the member countries. The European Union indirectly promotes bilingual education for language minorities through directives and recommendations on language minority rights such as the 1977 directive recommending that children of immigrants be taught in their own mother tongue, and more recent charters on rights of regional language minorities and through funding for research, publications, and conferences on issues related to regional language minorities. However, support for bilingualism tends to focus more on the promotion and preservation of the European Union's official languages and European minority languages than on the preservation of mother-tongue skills among immigrant minorities (Extra & Yağmur 2004).

In this sense, there is a distinction between the bilingual programs for regional language minorities and immigrant minorities. Regional languages lost institutional support and speakers through processes of consolidation of European nation-states in the nineteenth century that included the selection of official languages for communication, business, and educational purposes within nation-states. In recent years, many bilingual education programs have had a goal of rebuilding skills in European regional languages and promoting cultural diversity within nation-states. For example, in Spain the democratic transition following the end of the Franco regime created a opening for greater use of regional minority languages (prohibited during much of the Franco era), including as a medium of instruction in schools. In areas where there is strong support for and use of a regional language some academic subjects are taught in local languages such as Galician or Basque, while other academic subjects are taught in Castilian (Cenoz 1998; Mar-Molinero 2000). In Cataluña, Catalan is now the principal language of the school system.

In addition to regional language minorities created by nation-building processes in the nineteenth century, changes in national borders as a result of the world wars and the fall of the Soviet Union have also resulted in language minorities, particularly in Central and Eastern Europe (in both EU and non-EU European countries). In some cases language minority students take a substantial part of their coursework in their mother tongue. For example, Hungarian ethnic students in Slovakia and Romania receive content area instruction in both the majority language and Hungarian (Fitzgerald-Gersten 2001). Guestworker programs and immigration have also resulted in non-European language minorities (with Turkish and Arabic being the largest such language groups) as well as European language minorities (such as Finns in Sweden). There are also important refugee populations residing in European countries from Latin America, Africa, Asia, and the Middle East. There is not a standard bilingual education curriculum or program for children of immigrants, refugees, and guestworkers in the European Union. Germany, for example, with the largest immigrant population in Europe, has a variety of different types of bilingual education programs both within and across cities with large immigrant populations. Language programs for children of immigrants, guestworkers, and refugees range from weak bilingual education programs that focus on the primary acquisition of majority language skills, to strong bilingual language programs that intend to promote fluency in both the language of the country of origin as well as the majority language, to segregationist programs that utilize the curricula and language of the country of origin (Skutnabb-Kangas 1984; Romaine 1995; Extra & Yağmur 2004).

Internationally, sociological research on bilingual and multicultural education addresses the often overlapping issues of language minority rights (such as speakers of indigenous languages in Latin America, guestworkers and immigrants in Europe, and Spanish speakers in the US), issues related to colonial and postcolonial language policies and linguistic practices (particularly with respect to curricula in India, Latin America, Africa, and the Middle East), language maintenance and shift, and the impact of bilingual and multilingual skills on academic outcomes. Methodologically, the greatest obstacle to sociological research on the impact of language on educational outcomes is a lack of national and international survey data that include measures of proficiency in majority and minority languages as well as specific demographic and educational data.

SEE ALSO: Acculturation; Bilingualism; Culture; Diversity; Ethnic Groups; Ethnicity; Globalization, Culture and; Globalization, Education and; Immigrant Families; Immigration; Immigration and Language; Language; Migration, Ethnic Conflicts, and Racism; Multiculturalism; Race and Schools

REFERENCES AND SUGGESTED READINGS

Baker, C. (1996) *Foundations of Bilingual Education and Bilingualism*. Multilingual Matters, Clevedon.

Cenoz, J. (1998) Multilingual Education in the Basque Country. In: Cenoz, J. & Genesee, F. (Eds.), *Beyond Bilingualism: Multilingualism and Multilingual Education*. Multilingual Matters, Clevedon.

Cervantes-Rodríguez, A. M. & Lutz, A. (2003) Coloniality of Power, Immigration, and the English–Spanish Asymmetry in the United States. *Nepantla: Views from South* 4: 523–60.

Extra, G. & Yağmur, K. (2004) *Urban Multilingualism in Europe*. Multilingual Matters, Clevedon.

Fernandez, R. & Nielson, F. (1986) Bilingualism and Hispanic Scholastic Achievement: Some Baseline Results. *Social Science Research* 15: 43–70.

Fishman, J. A. (1972) *The Sociology of Language: An Interdisciplinary Social Science Approach to Language in Society*. Newbury House Publishers, Rowley, MA.

Fishman, J. A. & García, E. E. (2002) *Bilingualism and Schooling in the United States*. Mouton de Gruyter, Berlin.

Fitzgerald-Gersten, B. (2001) A Bilingual Hungarian/Slovak School in the Slovak Republic. In: Christian, D. & Genesee, F. (Eds.), *Bilingual Education*. Teachers of English to Speakers of Other Languages (TESOL), Alexandria.

Genesee, F. (1998) A Case of Multilingual Education in Canada. In: Cenoz, J. & Genesee, F. (Eds.), *Beyond Bilingualism: Multilingualism and Multilingual Education*. Multilingual Matters, Clevedon.

Goldberg, D. T. (1994) *Multiculturalism: A Critical Reader*. Blackwell, Oxford.

Hoffmann, C. (1998) Luxembourg and the European Schools. In: Cenoz, J. & Genesee, F. (Eds.),

Beyond Bilingualism: Multilingualism and Multilingual Education. Multilingual Matters, Clevedon.

Hollinger, D. A. (1995) *Postethnic America: Beyond Multiculturalism*. Basic Books, New York.

Hornberger, N. (1988) *Bilingual Education and Language Maintenance: A Southern Peruvian Quechua Case*. Foris Publications, Dordrecht.

Hornberger, N. & López, L. E. (1998) Policy, Possibility and Paradox: Indigenous Multilingualism and Education in Peru and Bolivia. In: Cenoz, J. & Genesee, F. (Eds.), *Beyond Bilingualism: Multilingualism and Multilingual Education*. Multilingual Matters, Clevedon.

Johnson, J. H., Jr., Farrell, W. C., Jr., & Guinn, C. (1997) Immigration Reform and the Browning of America: Tensions, Conflicts and Community Instability in Metropolitan Los Angeles. *International Migration Review* 31: 1055–95.

Mahajan, G. (2002) *The Multicultural Path: Issues of Diversity and Discrimination in Democracy*. Sage, New Delhi.

Mar-Molinero, C. (2000) *The Politics of Language in the Spanish-Speaking World*. Routledge, New York.

Portes, A. & Rumbaut, R. G. (2001) *Legacies: The Story of the Immigrant Second Generation*. University of California Press/Russell Sage Foundation, Berkeley.

Portes, A. & Schauffler, R. (1994) Language and the Second Generation: Bilingualism Yesterday and Today. *International Migration Review* 28: 640–61.

Ricento, T. & Burnaby, B. (1998) *Language and Politics in the United States and Canada: Myths and Realities*. Lawrence Erlbaum Associates, Mahwah, NJ.

Romaine, S. (1995) *Bilingualism*, 2nd edn. Blackwell, Oxford.

Roscigno, V., Vélez, M. B., & Ainsworth-Darnell, J. W. (2001) Language Minority Achievement, Family Inequality, and the Impact of Bilingual Education. *Race and Society* 4: 69–88.

Rumbaut, R. G. & Portes, A. (2001) *Ethnicities: Children of Immigrants in America*. University of California Press/Russell Sage Foundation, Berkeley.

Skutnabb-Kangas, T. (1984) *Bilingualism or Not: The Education of Minorities*. Multilingual Matters, Clevedon.

US Department of Education, Office for Civil Rights (1998) *The Provision of an Equal Education Opportunity to Limited-English Proficient Students*. US Government Printing Office, Washington, DC.

Veltman, C. (1988) Modeling the Language Shift Process of Hispanic Immigrants. *International Migration Review* 22: 545–62.

Zhou, M. & Bankston, C. L. (1998) *Growing up American: How Vietnamese Children Adapt to Life in the United States*. Russell Sage Foundation, New York.

bilingualism

Lilia I. Bartolomé

Bilingualism is succinctly defined by Uriel Weinreich in his book *Languages in Contact* (1953) as the ability to alternatively use two languages. He defined the person involved in using two languages as bilingual. Bilingualism is common throughout the world and results from various language contact situations including: (1) colonization – colonizer imposition of a language different from the native language; (2) residing in officially bilingual countries (e.g., Canada, where English and French are official languages, and Finland, where Finnish and Swedish are official languages); (3) growing up in a bilingual household where caretakers use two different languages; and (4) migrating to a new society where immigrants often continue to use their native language at home while learning the host country's dominant language and using it in official institutions. Bilingualism can occur at either the individual or societal level and can be examined using a variety of disciplinary lenses. For example, individual bilingualism is examined via disciplines such as neuropsychology, cognitive psychology, developmental psychology, and psycholinguistics. Societal bilingualism is studied by researchers representing various disciplines such as sociology, the sociology of language, sociolinguistics, and anthropology.

At the individual level, how learners acquire a second language and become bilingual is the focus of study. A speaker can, at various ages and developmental stages, acquire two languages in diverse learning contexts such as the home, school, or work. Factors that influence second-language acquisition include learner (1) age, (2) ability or intelligence, (3) previous school and literacy experiences, (4) attitudes, and (5) personality. In addition, since second-language acquisition represents an acculturation process, access to second-language speakers and culture determines, to some degree, successful second-language acquisition. Second-language acquisition can be adversely affected when learners experience social distance (lack of opportunity to authentically interact with native speakers) or feel psychological distance from the second-language speakers and their culture (Schumann 1978). The process by which learners acquire a second language also varies. For example, learners can acquire two languages concurrently or sequentially: the former begins at the inception of language acquisition and the latter begins at approximately age 5, when the essential elements of the first language have been acquired (McLaughlin 1984).

Few bilinguals are balanced bilinguals, that is, equally proficient in both languages, since each language is typically used in different contexts for differing purposes and functions. In addition, individuals' language use and skill do not necessarily remain constant over time. Furthermore, the term *bilingualism* is somewhat ambiguous in that it does not specify a level of proficiency required for a speaker to be labeled "bilingual." Levels of proficiency range from fully, balanced bilingual to "semilingual," a pejorative term used to signal the lack of native-like proficiency in either language. The notion of "semilingualism" is regarded as linguistically inaccurate since notions of language proficiency typically reflect social biases and preferences for standard academic language registers as used by dominant culture speakers. (For an example of this literature, see Bartolomé 1998.) Moreover, a comprehensive view of proficiency exceeds the mere ability to understand and speak and also includes reading and writing abilities as well as mastery of phonology, lexicon, syntax, and semantics across the four language modes. In sum, there are numerous linguistic dimensions along which the learner's language skill can vary from complete fluency to minimal command.

Bilingualism is also used to describe the use of two languages at a societal level. Sociolinguistics is one major discipline that has studied societal bilingualism. This disciplinary perspective points out the inadequacy of utilizing solely physiological and psychological perspectives to understand the phenomenon of bilingualism and emphasizes the importance of studying the interaction between language use and social organization. Although a recent field of study, developing only since the beginning of the 1960s, sociolinguistics specifically examines phenomena such as bilingualism, ethnic/

linguistic conflict, language planning efforts, and language standardization movements.

In any society, it is highly improbable that two languages are used for identical functions; a language community is more likely to use each language in certain contexts and for specific purposes. Charles Ferguson (1959) initially coined the term *diglossia* to describe a specific type of societal bilingualism where two varieties of the same language exist side by side. In this linguistic situation, a "low" or colloquial variety is used for everyday affairs in informal institutions (e.g., family) and the "high" or "classical" form is used for formal affairs in official institutions (e.g., church). One example of diglossia is in Arab nations where there is a clear separation in the use of classical and colloquial Arabic. Later, Joshua Fishman (1972) extended the meaning of the term *diglossia* to refer to the use of two separate languages in one society. Societal bilingualism can be either stable or unstable. In stable bilingual societies, languages tend to be reserved for different domains with clearly differentiated functions and uses. In transitory or unstable bilingual societies, the domain–language separations are not as clear cut and, ultimately, allow for the use of the two languages across various domains and functions.

Another dimension of bilingualism has to do with the social status of speakers. For example, there is a distinction between "elite" bilingualism and "folk" bilingualism (Fishman et al. 1966). The former refers to high-status groups who speak the society's dominant language and who further enhance their status by learning a second socially prestigious language. The latter, "folk" bilingualism, refers to languages spoken by groups such as immigrants and linguistic minority groups who reside in a society where the dominant language is not their own and where they occupy sociopolitical and economic positions of low status.

The concepts of "additive" and "subtractive" bilingualism also reflect speaker social-status issues (Lambert 1975). An additive bilingual situation is where the addition of a second language and culture does not require that students lose their first language and culture. In fact, in an additive bilingual context, the first language and culture are maintained and supported. In a subtractive bilingual situation, the opposite is true – the second language and culture are expected to replace the learners' first language and culture. Typically, learners from groups that are considered low status (e. g., Mexican Americans in the US) are schooled under subtractive conditions while high-status learners (English speakers in Canada) are expected to maintain their first language while acquiring French as a second language.

Where linguistic minorities possess significant political power, they are often able to require state-provided bilingual education. Bilingual education programs vary widely in orientation, purpose, implementation, and results and reflect either additive or subtractive philosophies. Some programs strive to teach learners a second language while maintaining their first (e.g., maintenance and two-way bilingual programs), while others focus on teaching the second language and only utilize the students' first language as a way of accessing the second (e.g., transitional bilingual education). (For examples of bilingual education programs and the orientations that inform them, see Crawford 2004.)

Currently, critical sociolinguists urge greater recognition of the political and ideological dimensions of bilingualism in order to develop more comprehensive linguistic theories that explore the complex relationship between language, ideology, and social organization and their implications for solving urgent educational problems of linguistic minorities and oppressed groups of people. (For an example of this literature, see Macedo et al. 2004.) They propose that bilingualism cannot be understood fully outside a power relations framework that can shed light on the constant tensions and contradictions between linguistic hegemonic tendencies (i.e., the present attack on bilingual education in the United States where laws are being promulgated to prohibit instruction in languages other than English) and the increasing cultural and ethnic self-affirmation of linguistic minority groups that look at the native language as a point of reference for identity formation.

SEE ALSO: Bilingual, Multicultural Education; Biracialism; Immigration and Language; Language; Literacy/Illiteracy; Multiculturalism

REFERENCES AND SUGGESTED READINGS

Bartolomé, L. (1998) *The Misteaching of Academic Discourses: The Politics of Language in the Classroom.* Westview Press, Boulder, CO.
Crawford, J. (2004) *Educating English Learners: Language Diversity in the Classroom,* 5th edn. Bilingual Educational Services, Los Angeles.
Ferguson, C. (1959) Diglossia. *Word* 15: 325–40.
Fishman, J. A. (1972) *The Sociology of Language: An Interdisciplinary Social Science Approach to Language in Society.* Newbury Press, Rowley, MA.
Fishman, J. A., Nahirny, V., Hofman, J., & Hayden, R. (1966) *Language Loyalty in the United States: The Maintenance and Perpetuation of Non-English Mother Tongues by American Ethnic and Religious Groups.* Mouton, The Hague.
Hakuta, K. (1986) *Mirror of Language: The Debate on Bilingualism.* Basic Books, New York.
Lambert, W. E. (1975) Culture and Language as Factors in Learning and Education. In: Wolfgang, A. (Ed.), *Education of Immigrant Students.* Ontario Institute for Studies in Education, Toronto, pp. 55–83.
Macedo, D., Dendrinos, B., & Gounari, P. (2004) *The Hegemony of English.* Paradigm Press, Boulder, CO.
McLaughlin, B. (1984) *Second-Language Acquisition in Childhood.* Vol. 1: *Preschool Children.* Erlbaum, Hillsdale, NJ.
Schumann, J. (1978) *The Pidginization Process: A Model for Second Language Acquisition.* Newbury Press, Rowley, MA.

biodemography

James R. Carey

Although still a modest subfield within demography, biodemography is arguably the fastest growing part of demography and one of the most innovative and stimulating. The two main branches today involve: (1) biological-demographic research directly related to human health, with emphasis on health surveys, a field of research that might be called biomedical demography (or "epidemography" because it is a cross between demography and epidemiology), and (2) research at the intersection of demography and biology (as opposed to biomedicine), an endeavor that will be referred to as biological demography. The first branch is characterized by demographers engaging in collaborative research with epidemiologists. This is very important, for both fields and for deeper understanding of human health. Researchers in the second branch face an even bigger challenge. Demographic and epidemiological concepts and methods are fairly similar, whereas the underlying paradigms of demography and biology are less related.

Both of the two main branches of biodemography have many smaller branches. As in any innovative, rapidly growing interdisciplinary field, these smaller branches form tangles and thickets. Consequently, it is difficult to present a coherent structure for the evolving research in biodemography. One way to proceed is to make use of the hierarchical ordering of knowledge within biology. This provides a basis for ordering the research subdivisions that range from the molecular and cellular to the ecological and evolutionary. This ordering of biodemography by levels is useful because, as the eminent physiologist George Bartholomew noted over four decades ago, the significance of every level of biological organization can be found above and explanations of the mechanism in the level below. For example, the results of studies on different APOE gene alleles shed important light on molecular mechanisms for different risks of ischemic heart disease, Alzheimer's disease, and other chronic conditions, thus providing information on a person's individual risk of these chronic diseases and, in turn, informing the design of population surveys and model construction for epidemiological forecasting.

BIOLOGICAL DEMOGRAPHY

Biological demography is an emerging interdisciplinary science concerned with identifying a universal set of population principles, integrating biological concepts into demographic approaches, and bringing demographic methods to bear on population problems in different biological disciplines. Whereas biomedical demography brings survey techniques, biomedical information, modeling strategies, and statistical methods to bear on questions about the health of different *human populations*, biological demography brings experimental paradigms, model systems, evolutionary perspectives, and comparative techniques to bear on questions about the demographic characteristics of different *species*. Biomedical demographers might ask questions about the shape of the trajectory of human mortality at advanced ages. In contrast, biological demographers will ask the more general question of whether the slowing of mortality at advanced ages is a universal life-table characteristic of species as diverse as nematodes, fruit flies, mice, and humans. Biological demography not only situates the population traits of humans within the broader demographic characteristics of all living organisms, but it also provides a scientific framework for asking basic questions that differ from, but are complementary to, conventional demography.

Because of the range of the subdisciplines within biology and of the subspecialties within demography, the term "biological demography" does not fully reflect the diversity of its main intellectual lineages including gerontology, population biology, and demography, the complexity of its deep historical roots, or the scope of the questions that are commonly addressed by biological demographers themselves. Although biological-demographic researchers use mathematical and statistical modeling techniques similar to those used in classical demography, they also use experimental methods to address questions about the nature of mortality and fertility, development, and aging in such model organisms as fruit flies and rodents. Thus, unlike most research in classical demography, biological-demographic research exploits the hierarchical ordering of knowledge that unites and drives the biological sciences.

Biological demography embraces all the research at the intersection of demography and biology. It hence includes studies of fertility, migration, and mortality. To date, however, the main emphasis has been on studies of survival and longevity, with some emerging research on fertility and on the links between fertility and mortality. Whereas the traditional paradigm around which biological gerontology is framed is concerned with questions at molecular, cellular, and/or physiological levels, the biological-demographic paradigm of aging integrates research at the organismal level – the quintessence of biological relevance because all discoveries at lower levels of biological organization concerning aging must ultimately be tested at the level of the whole organism. And unlike traditional research in both classical demography and the biology of aging, biological demography draws from population biology and thus emphasizes evolutionary and ecological concepts, life history theory, and comparative methods. This multidisciplinary synthesis represents a unique research paradigm that is concerned with both proximate questions (e.g., those concerned with the *mechanisms* of aging) and ultimate ones (e.g., those concerned with the evolutionary and ecological *function* of a particular life span). Thus biological-demographic research embraces many questions about both aging and life span that do not fall within the bounds of either traditional demography or gerontology.

AN EMERGING BIOLOGICAL-DEMOGRAPHIC PARADIGM

The view of many demographers toward biology is similar to the view of many sociologists who believe that "biology" and the "social" are locked in an explanatory zero-sum game in which any ground ceded to the former diminishes the value of the latter. But even if sociologists (and, by extension, demographers) did banish "biological" explanations of social behavior from their own forums, swelling interest in the topic would still exist elsewhere in the academy, as would a flourishing of curiosity among the general public. What separates biological perspectives in sociology (sociobiology) and demography (biodemography) from their more conventional alternatives is not whether biological perspectives on sociological or demographic questions are correct, but how useful specifically biologically minded thinking and experimental methods are for understanding human demography.

In the perennial struggle of all disciplines, including demography, to define and renew themselves and to ensure their relevance in an ever changing world, each discipline is always faced with decisions regarding whether to move in new directions. Demography, like other social sciences, is slowly coming to terms with important truths that the biological sciences have proved beyond doubt – that both the human mind and human behaviors are as much products of biological evolution as is the human body. Human beings may be unique in their degree of behavioral plasticity and in their possession of language and self-awareness, but all of the known human systems – biological and social – taken together form only a small subset of those displayed by the thousands of living species.

Inasmuch as demography is concerned with whole-animal phenomena (birth, death), model systems (e.g., nematode worms, fruit flies, laboratory rodents) can be brought to bear on fundamental questions concerning the nature of fertility and mortality. However, a stumbling block in mainstream demography for the serious use of these model systems in studying aging has been the mistaken belief that, because causes of death in humans are unrelated to causes of death in non-human species (particularly in invertebrates such as nematodes and fruit flies), little can be learned from detailed knowledge of age-specific mortality in these model species. This perspective is based on a theory familiar to most demographers – the "theory of the underlying cause" in public health and medicine which states that if the starting point of a train of events leading to death is known (e.g., cancer), death can be averted by preventing the initiating cause from operating. For aging research the problem with this perspective is that death is seen as a single force – the skeleton with the scythe. A more apt characterization that applies to deaths in all species is where deaths are viewed as the outcome of a crowd of "little devils": individual potential or probabilistic causes of death, sometimes hunting in packs and reinforcing each other's efforts, at other times independent. Inasmuch as underlying causes of death are frequently context-specific, difficult to distinguish from immediate causes, and their post-mortem identification in humans is often arbitrary (in invertebrates virtually impossible), studying the causes of death often provides little insight into the nature of aging. If aging is considered as a varying pattern of vulnerability to genetic and environmental insults, then the most important use of model species in both teaching and research on the demography of aging is to interpret their age patterns of mortality as proxy indicators of frailty. That is, different model systems can be used to address questions at different levels of demographic generality.

The demographic profiles of humans have characteristics typical of a wide variety of organisms due to similarity in evolutionary selection pressures. For example, the characteristic of higher male than female mortality during prime reproductive ages is typical in sexually reproducing animals of a large number of vertebrate and invertebrate species. The pattern is an evolutionary result of sexual selection on males and, as such, is a *general characteristic* of a large number of species. Other observed general characteristics include the variable rate of change in mortality with age (rates that decline after earliest stage and then increase with age) and a slowing of mortality at the most advanced ages. Given such generalities, there are also characteristics of mortality profiles that pertain more specifically to a particular species (or other taxonomic group). Such species-level characteristics are imposed on some general pattern.

The mortality experience for humans can thus be considered at two levels. The *general level* exhibits a decline after infancy, increases through the reproductive life span (the overall U-shaped trajectory), and a sex differential. The *specific level* pertains to details of the mortality experience unique to humans including the actual probabilities of death by age, inflection points of age-specific mortality, the cause-specific probabilities of death, and the age-specific pattern of the sex differential. The observed mortality pattern is a combination of the evolutionary components of the trajectory (which will be common to a large number of species with overlapping life history characteristics) and the proximate age and sex-specific factors contributing to mortality under certain conditions. For example, under contemporary conditions male reproductive competition selects for riskier behavior and results in deaths due to accidents and homicides during early adulthood. The general and specific components of any population's mortality schedule can only be determined through studies using model systems; that is, the use of experimental demography and comparative biology.

BIOMEDICAL DEMOGRAPHY

Demographers over the past half century have increasingly become involved with the design of surveys and the analysis of survey data, especially pertaining to fertility or morbidity and mortality. Recently various kinds of physical measurements (such as height and weight), physiological measurements (of blood pressure, cholesterol levels, etc.), nutritional status (assessed by analysis of blood or urine and other methods), physical performance (e.g., handgrip strength or ability to pick a coin up from the floor), and genetic makeup (as determined by analysis of DNA) have been added to surveys. Such biological measurements can be used as covariates in demographic analyses in much the same way that social and economic information is used: developing such analysis is an important activity of biomedical demographers.

In particular, there has been rapid growth of interest in using genetic information in medical-demographic research. Particularly exciting is the use of information from DNA about specific genes. Information from DNA about genetic polymorphisms (i.e., mutations) can be used to determine the genetic structure of a population and to make inferences about the influence of migration and inbreeding on the population. A central goal of such "molecular demography" is to identify genetic polymorphisms that affect mortality, morbidity, functioning, fecundity, and other sources of demographic change. Much of this research to date has focused on finding genetic variants that influence longevity. This relationship can be studied by analyzing changes with age in the proportion of survivors who have some specific allele (i.e., version of a gene). If in a given cohort the allele becomes more frequent with age, that allele may be associated with lower mortality.

It should not be forgotten, however, that much can be learned about genetics even if DNA is unavailable. The genetic and common environment components of these variations — in life spans, fertility, and other demographic characteristics – can be analyzed in humans using demographic data on twins, siblings, cousins, and other relatives of various degree. These data are available in genealogies and in twin, household, parish, and other population's registries. What is necessary is to have information about the proportion of genes shared by two individuals and about shared non-genetic influences. Analysis of variance methods, correlated frailty approaches, and nested event-history models have been applied by demographers.

In sum, both the biomedical-demography branch of biodemography and the biological-demography branch are vibrant areas of demographic research that are rapidly growing and that have great potential to enrich and enlarge the domain of demography in particular, and sociology in general.

SEE ALSO: Aging, Demography of; Aging and the Life Course, Theories of; Demographic Techniques: Epidemiology; Life-Table Methods; Ecological Problems; Gender, Aging and; Healthy Life Expectancy; Mortality: Social Epidemiology; Transitions and Measures

REFERENCES AND SUGGESTED READINGS

Carey, J. R. (2003) *Longevity: The Biology and Demography of Life Span*. Princeton University Press, Princeton.

Carey, J. R. & Tuljapurkar, S. (Eds.) (2003) Life Span: Evolutionary, Ecological, and Demographic Perspectives. *Population and Development Review* 29: 1–320.

Carey, J. R. & Vaupel, J. W. (2005) Biodemography. In: Poston, D. & Micklin, M. (Eds.), *Handbook of Population*. Kluwer Academic/Plenum, New York.

Ewbank, D. (2000) Demography in the Age of Genomics: A First Look at the Prospects. In: Finch, C. E., Vaupel, J. W., & Kinsella, K. (Eds.), *Cells and Surveys: Should Biological Measures Be Included in Social Science Research?* National Academy Press, Washington, DC, pp. 64–109.

Freese, J., Li, J. C. A., & Wade, L. D. (2003) The Potential Relevance of Biology to Social Inquiry. *Annual Review of Sociology* 29: 233–56.

Hauser, P. M. & Duncan, O. D. (1959) The Nature of Demography. In: Hauser, P. M. & Duncan, O. D. (Eds.), The Study of Population. University of Chicago Press, Chicago, pp. 29–44.

Kohler, H. & Rodgers, J. L. (2003) Education, Fertility, and Heritability: Explaining a Paradox. In: Wachter, K. W. & Bulatao, R. A. (Eds.), *Offspring: Human Fertility Behavior in Biodemographic Perspective*. National Academy Press, Washington, DC, pp. 46–90.

Vaupel, J. W., Carey, J. R., Christensen, K., Johnson, T. E., Yashin, A. I., Holm, N. V., Iachine, I. A., Kannisto, V., Khazaeli, A. A., Liedo, P., Longo, V. D., Zeng, Y., Manton, K. G., & Curtsinger, J. W. (1998) Biodemographic Trajectories of Longevity. *Science* 280: 855–60.

Wachter, K. W. & Bulatao, R. A. (Eds.) (2003) *Offspring: Human Fertility Behavior in Biodemographic Perspective*. National Academy Press, Washington, DC.

Wachter, K. W. & Finch, C. E. (1997) *Between Zeus and the Salmon: The Biodemography of Longevity*. National Academy Press, Washington, DC.

Wilson, E. O. (1998) *Consilience: The Unity of Knowledge*. Alfred A. Knopf, New York.

Yashin, A. I., De Benedictis, G., Vaupel, J. W., Tan, Q., Andreev, K. F., Iachine, I. A., Bonafe, M., Valensin, S., De Luca, M., Carotenuto, L., & Frenceschi, C. (2000) Genes and Longevity: Lessons from Studies of Centenarians. *Journal of Gerontology: Biological Sciences* 55A: B319–B328.

biography

Janet Hoskins and Gelya Frank

The use of biography in the social sciences has come to new prominence in recent decades because of disciplinary shifts towards narrative analysis, reflexivity, phenomenology and hermeneutics, psychoanalysis, and postmodernism, as well as the persistence of Marxist and feminist thought. The longer history of biography goes back to humanistic portraits of "great men" enshrined in literary biographies and historical studies. Still earlier models in the Christian West embrace the lives of saints and religious exemplars.

Around 1900, social scientists began to modify that heritage by focusing on the lives of persons in places and social classes unrepresented, or represented inaccurately, in the mainstream. Like journalists, novelists, and missionaries of the same era, they began to describe the lives of individuals in non-literate societies, ethnic and racial minorities, rural poor and urban working classes, in gendered roles under patriarchy, and situations of cultural dissidence. The social scientist's unique contribution was twofold: (1) employing analytic schemata to dig beneath the surface of easy assumptions or stereotypes; and (2) including narratives or at least a paraphrase of the subject's self-expressed perspectives. Most biographies in the social sciences since then have "studied down" by focusing on disadvantaged people at the margins of society. Massive adoption of qualitative methods by scholars in practice disciplines once ancillary to the social sciences, however, has produced an avalanche of biographical studies recently in fields such as education, social work, counseling, psychology, occupational therapy, nursing, and even medicine to identify and comprehend treatable problems among mainstream and elite populations. As a result, almost no category, group, or class of people in the US and Europe today escapes social science representation through biographical methods.

Biography has long been a part of the social sciences, having been introduced in different disciplines as "case histories" (psychiatry), "life histories" (anthropology), "personal documents" (sociology, psychology) and, more recently, "life stories" (linguistics, oral history), each focused on understanding individuals as the unit of analysis. Recent years have seen more interdisciplinary dialogue seeking to redefine the importance of individual lives to broader social and cultural phenomena. Anthropology, which made the recording of individual lives in an interview setting a cornerstone of ethnographic methodology, is but one of many disciplinary sources for narrative and biographical approaches in the social sciences today. But it remains a pivotal and innovative site for working through issues of representation through the modernist period and the period of postmodernist critique (Kluckhohn 1945; Langness & Frank 1981; Frank 2000). Most of the pioneering research focused on American Indians in an effort to salvage evidence of cultures undergoing rapid and destructive colonization. A more sophisticated reading of such documents was outlined by Ruth Benedict (1959), who defined the unique value of life histories as showing "the repercussions

the experiences of a man's life – either shared or idiosyncratic – have upon him as a human being molded in that environment." She stressed the value of subjectivity and an insider's perspective, not just cultural inventories; she also saw the usefulness of these documents for studying individual variation within a larger social whole. Benedict's turn to the humanities, and particularly philosophy and literary criticism, sought more adequate models for interpreting human lives than was then usual for the social sciences, in an early and perhaps prescient articulation of what would later be called the "interpretive turn."

Benedict's humanistic impulse was carried out most fully by Oscar Lewis, who in 1961 published *The Children of Sanchez*, a novelistic compilation about urban slum dwellers which reached a wide audience with stories that emphasized a shared humanity and emotional identification. Lewis's work was severely criticized, however, for suggesting that the urban working classes were mired in a "culture of poverty," an analytic lens that softened a more sweeping political and economic analysis of oppression by the ruling classes in Mexico by focusing microscopically on beliefs and behaviors of the oppressed. Sidney Mintz's (1960) life of a Puerto Rican peasant was received more favorably for maintaining a materialist analysis of worker oppression. Generally, sociologists have made immigration and labor history their focus, from Znaniecki and Thomas's *The Polish Peasant* (1927) to Willis's *Learning to Labour* (1977).

Anthropology in the late twentieth century through the present has focused explicitly on what formerly were background issues in the study of culture: diasporic identities, communities at the margins of nation-states, contested beliefs and practices, hybridity and borders. Alfred Gell (1998) has argued that the biographical approach is particularly suited to anthropology, since the view it takes of social agents tends to replicate the time perspective of these agents themselves. (In contrast, the temporal scope of history or sociology could be described as "supra-biographical" and that of social and cognitive psychology as "infra-biographical.") Because anthropology tends to concentrate on social action in the context of particular lives – or a particular stage of these lives – it is necessarily preoccupied with the life cycle and the individual agent. The specifically biographical depth of focus defines a methodology that works best in the spaces traversed by agents in the course of their biographies. Many of these spaces are now transnational and multicultural; some are even transgendered. At the same time, we have also experienced what has been called the narrative turn, in which scholars have attempted to distinguish self-narrated life stories from scholarly-authored biographies, cutting loose from naturalistic, materialistic moorings.

Inspired by European philosophical traditions of phenomenology and hermeneutics, Bertaux (1981), a sociologist, argued that biographical self-reports should not try to create the illusion of a naturalistic unfolding of an individual's development, but should instead be treated as "life stories." By this he refers to discrete speech acts elicited under particular circumstances and illuminating particular needs of the subject's lived experience. He highlighted the methodological issues of the sociology of knowledge, in which biographic statements can be used to understand the lived experience of others and analyze how these experiences are constructed textually into personal narratives. Life-story approaches have been greatly accelerated with innovative methodological and substantive contributions by linguists (Linde 1993), sociologists (Denzin 1989), psychologists (Rosenwald & Ochberg 1992), feminist social critics (Personal Narratives Group 1989), and many others. Seen also in anthropology, this life-story impulse turns away from totalizing life histories constructed to correspond to a specific research agenda and toward the incorporation of partial self-narratives or life stories within more open texts (Ginsburg 1989; Kondo 1990). Crapanzano's *Tuhami* (1980) followed the model of a psychoanalytic case history to include the dreams, fantasies, and imagined encounters of a tailor involved in a spirit possession movement, looking at his own private psychological world and not only the factual events of his life. More attention has also been paid to reflecting on the elicitation frame or context, including analyses of the power relations between the biographer and the biography subject, with the goal of producing not only texts but also analyses in a more collaborative way than before.

When the subject of a biography is alive, then there is clearly a process of exchange in which certain documents and confidences are offered in response to certain questions, and the accounts of the biographical subject and the writer come to construct each other. These new "collaborative biographies" mark a shift away from viewing the observer/observed relationship as "a scaffolding separate from content, to the view that the relationship is inseparable from content" (Freeman 1989: 432). Rather than referring to "informants," persons seen as a means to an end, "informing" on their culture, Freeman speaks of "narrators" who construct new selves in dialogue with an investigator, thus co-creating the data that will later be analyzed. As part of the process of experimenting with the genre of ethnographic writing more generally, there is a new playfulness in the writing of biographical accounts that often involves co-authorship and analysis of the shaping factors of the anthropologist's relevant life concerns, described as the "biography in the shadow" (Frank 1979, 2000; Behar 1993). The increasing popularity of mass market autobiographies and memoirs, often written as testimonies to the newly crafted identities of members of ethno-racial minorities, GLBT communities, or grassroots political activists, has brought a new vitality and particularity to anthropological writings as well.

Abu-Lughod (1993) argued that biographies of ordinary Bedouin women can be used to "write against culture," resisting and destabilizing anthropological generalizations about the structural features of certain types of society (in this case, Arab or Middle Eastern societies), which she fears have a tendency to congeal into too reified an idea of "cultures" as self-contained entities. Chapter headings that stand for classic anthropological categories of analysis (patrilineality, polygyny, honor and shame) label collections of stories that serve to unsettle assumptions about those categories. The question that concerns her is: What is it like to *live* those institutions, those ideologies? The particularities of individual experiences and family disputes conveyed in the narratives serve to qualify, or even dissolve, the notion of "Bedouin culture"; they shed a more nuanced and sensitive light on women's opinions, and their efforts to achieve their own goals and maintain their own honor within the constraints of the structures within which they must operate.

In this way, Abu-Lughod turns around the central problem about life narratives from the point of view of the anthropologist, sociologist, or historian, which has been the question of representativeness. What in the way of insights into generalities can be extracted from their uniqueness? The issue of subjectivity has been endlessly debated in the social sciences. The recent interpretive turn emphasizes the fact that life stories are consciously staged and directed, as both narrator and investigator look for moral lessons and a sense of coherence. The "self" that is presented will vary on both an individual and a cultural level, but its representativeness rests not so much in what materially happens to people as in what people imagine or know might happen, and also how they interpret what does happen, how they make sense of it. Biographical narratives allow researchers to capture the point of view of the subject, and to explain how in spite of particular idiosyncrasies, each person is also a product of his or her culture, place, and time.

The intersection of history with personal experience and the individual life with the collective heritage makes biography a particularly significant locus for the analysis of historical memory. The microcosm of one person's biography does not disqualify each unique narrative from any hope of generalization, but can be seen precisely as part of its value. Each narrative enlarges our sense of human possibilities, and enriches our understandings of what it has meant to live in a particular society and culture.

More than that, giving a cultural dimension to the study of biography develops the possibility of a knowledge that is itself more fully intersubjective. The investigator who tries to capture a narrator's particular ways of telling a story, the idiom and emotional tone of speech, constructs a self for the subject of each biographical study. Preserving traces of that dialogical encounter allows readers to glimpse the dynamics of that collaborative process, and to participate in the translation of culture that occurs as each life is narrated. Ethnographic research has expanded beyond the study of small societies to larger global contexts and connections, but the emphasis on the individual agent and stages of the life cycle remains important, and is perhaps a trademark of even multi-sited fieldwork. The agentive turn which has become prominent in various forms of practice theory requires attention to biographical frames of meaning and individual relations established through things with other persons.

There have also been moves to innovate by developing new genres, including cultural biographies (Frank 2000), biographies of things (Appadurai & Kopytoff 1986; Hoskins 1998), biographies of popular movements (Passerini & Erdberg 1996), and biographies of scientific objects (Dalton 2000). For example, the notion of biography has provided new perspectives on the study of material culture, and prompted new questions about how people are involved with the things they make and consume (Appadurai & Kopytoff 1986; Hoskins 1998). To what extent is our notion of biography culturally bounded? Do other cultures operate with a notion of the life cycle that extends beyond the grave to include reincarnation or the continued involvement of the ancestors in the lives of their descendants? The extension of the term "biography" to entities other than persons is often linked to the idea of a life cycle of birth, youth, maturity and old age which can be applied to groups, institutions, and concepts.

In summary, three key "moments" can be observed in the use of biography in the social sciences. First, a period when life histories were "collected" as data which would then be subjected to criteria of cultural typicality or, in other disciplines than anthropology, analyzed through schemata designed to destabilize conventional biographical assumptions while establishing diverse disciplinary imperatives. Second, a period when concerns of representing the humanity of the oppressed or the exotic took center stage, in what has retrospectively come to be seen as a kind of "tactical humanism." Third, what could be called the narrative turn, in which the primary concern has been how lived worlds have been constructed by language and made to mask certain unspoken relations of power, often articulated as part of a Foucauldian linkage of knowledge and power.

SEE ALSO: Autoethnography; Ethnography; Life History; Methods; Phenomenology; Psychoanalysis

REFERENCES AND SUGGESTED READINGS

Abu-Lughod, L. (1993) *Writing Women's Worlds: Bedouin Stories*. University of California Press, Berkeley.

Appadurai, A. & Kopytoff, I. (1986) *The Social Lives of Things: Commodities in Cross Cultural Perspective*. Cambridge University Press, Cambridge.

Behar, R. (1993) *Translated Woman: Crossing the Border with Esperanza's Story*. Beacon Press, Boston.

Benedict, R. (1959) Anthropology and the Humanities. In: Mead, M. (Ed.), *An Anthropologist at Work: Writings of Ruth Benedict*. Houghton Mifflin, Boston.

Bertaux, D. (1981) *Biography and Society: The Life History Approach in the Social Sciences*. Sage, London.

Crapanzano, V. (1980) *Tuhami: Portrait of a Moroccan*. University of Chicago Press, Chicago.

Dalton, L. (Ed.) (2000) *Biographies of Scientific Objects*. University of Chicago Press, Chicago.

Denzin, N. K. (1989) *Interpretive Biography*. Qualitative Research Methods Series 17. Sage, London.

Frank, G. (1979) Finding the Common Denominator: A Phenomenological Critique of Life History Method. *Ethos* 7(1): 68–74.

Frank, G. (2000) *Venus on Wheels: Two Decades of Dialogue on Disability, Feminism and Cultural Biography*. University of California Press, Berkeley.

Freeman, J. (1989) *Hearts of Sorrow: Vietnamese-American Lives*. Stanford University Press, Stanford.

Gell, A. (1998) *Art and Agency: A New Anthropological Theory*. Oxford University Press, Oxford.

Ginsburg, F. (1989) *Contested Lives*. University of California Press, Berkeley.

Hoskins, J. (1998) *Biographical Objects: How Things Tell the Stories of People's Lives*. Routledge, New York.

Keesing, R. (1985) Kwaio Women Speak: The Micropolitics of Autobiography in a Solomon Island Society. *American Anthropologist* 87: 27–39.

Kluckhohn, C. (1945) The Personal Document in Anthropological Science. In: Gottschalk, L. et al. (Eds.), *The Use of Personal Documents in History, Anthropology, Sociology*. Social Science Research Council Bulletin 53.

Kondo, D. (1990) *Crafting Selves: Power, Gender and Discourses of Identity in a Japanese Workplace*. University of Chicago Press, Chicago.

Langness, L. & Frank, G. (1981) *Lives: An Anthropological Approach to Biography*. Chandler & Sharp, Novato, CA.

Lewis, O. (1961) *The Children of Sanchez: Autobiography of a Mexican Family*. Vintage, New York.

Linde, C. (1993) *Life Stories: The Creation of Coherence*. Oxford University Press, New York.

Mintz, S. (1960) *Worker in the Cane*. Yale University Press, New Haven.

Passerini, L. & Erdberg, L. (1996) *Autobiography of a Generation: Italy, 1968*. Wesleyan University Press, Middletown.

Personal Narratives Group (1989) *Interpreting Women's Lives: Feminist Theory and Personal Narratives*. Indiana University Press, Bloomington.

Radin, P. (Ed.) (1926) *Crashing Thunder: The Autobiography of an American Indian*. Appleton, New York.

Rosenwald, G. & Ochberg, R. (Eds.) (1992) *Storied Lives: The Cultural Politics of Self-Understanding*. Yale University Press, New Haven.

Simmons, L. W. (1942) *Sun Chief: The Autobiography of a Hopi Indian*. Yale University Press, New Haven.

Watson, L. & Watson-Franke, M.-B. (1985) *Interpreting Life Histories: An Anthropological Inquiry*. Rutgers University Press, New Brunswick, NJ.

Willis, P. (1977) *Learning to Labour*. Saxon House, Farnborough.

Znaniecki, F. & Thomas, W. (1927) *The Polish Peasant in Europe and America*. Knopf, New York.

biosociological theories

Richard Machalek

Biosociological theories integrate biology into sociological explanations of human social behavior. They do so by incorporating theoretical ideas and empirical discoveries from various branches of biology including evolutionary biology (especially *sociobiology* and *behavioral ecology*), ecology, ethology, neurobiology, endocrinology, and population genetics. In sociology, most biosociological theories are emerging in a new specialty area known as *evolutionary sociology*.

Not to be confused with the pseudoscience of "Social Darwinism," the new evolutionary sociology is grounded in and guided by well-established explanatory principles, models, research methods, and rules of evidence developed and used by contemporary biologists. Increasingly, the traditional disciplinary boundaries that once clearly separated biologists from social and behavioral scientists, and social and behavioral scientists among themselves, are being eroded by those working within the framework of *neo-Darwinian* evolutionary theory – the integration of Darwinian evolutionary theory with Mendelian genetics.

The emergence of the new evolutionary sociology was made possible by several important theoretical developments in twentieth-century evolutionary theory. In 1964, W. D. Hamilton introduced the ideas of *kin selection* and *inclusive fitness*, concepts now central to biological explanations of social behavior, in his seminal theoretical formulation on the genetic basis of social behavior. Kin selection is a form of natural selection by which individuals influence the survival and reproductive success of genetic relatives other than offspring. Inclusive fitness is defined as the sum of an individual's reproductive success plus that individual's influence on the reproductive success of its genetic relatives, other than direct descendants. These two ideas are important in biosociological theory because they help explain how cooperative social behavior can favor the replication and transmission of genes, the driving force of organic evolution. Shortly thereafter, G. C. Williams in his classic book *Adaptation and Natural Selection* (1966) clarified and sharpened the concept of *adaptation*: a heritable morphological, physiological, or behavioral trait that increases an individual's chances of survival and reproductive success. This led to a better understanding of social behavior as a product of natural selection.

Before long, R. L. Trivers formulated the theoretical notion of *reciprocal altruism* to explain the evolution of cooperation among individuals lacking common genetic interests (1971). In 1975, E. O. Wilson synthesized these and other theoretical and empirical developments in his landmark book, *Sociobiology: The New Synthesis*, thereby laying the foundation for the emergence of neo-Darwinian social theory.

The controversy surrounding sociobiology and its applicability to human social behavior gradually subsided. During this time, systematic research and theory building by an expanding community of scholars and scientists led to the rise of neo-Darwinian enterprises such as Darwinian anthropology, evolutionary psychology, evolutionary economics, and most recently, evolutionary sociology. Neo-Darwinian social

theory is unified by shared, fundamental concepts and theoretical principles derived from contemporary evolutionary biology, especially sociobiology and behavioral ecology. Among the most important of such ideas is the *maximization principle*, which states that organisms tend to behave in a manner that maximizes their inclusive fitness, i.e., their overall influence on the perpetuation of their genes in subsequent generations (Lopreato & Crippen 1999).

Biosociological theorists view social behavior as the product of two types of causes: *proximate* causes, such as neural or hormonal activity or environmental stimuli that trigger physiological activity, and *ultimate* causes, which refer to evolved adaptations that generate behaviors. If behaviors feature a heritable component, then they are subject to natural selection and can become established in a phylogenetic line. For example, the chain of proximate causes that influences a female's preference for one male over another as a potential mate may include an unconscious perception of and preference for bilateral (left/right) symmetry in males. The adaptive value of this perception and preference in mate choice appears to be based in the fact that bilateral symmetry often signifies developmental stability in heritable traits, such as a robust immune system, a quality from which offspring would benefit significantly. Thus, behaviors pertaining to mate choice entail both proximate and ultimate causation. Evolutionary theorists often say that proximate causes account for *how* a behavior is produced (its generative mechanisms), and ultimate causes explain *why* the behavior occurs (its adaptive benefits).

Although a few biosociological theorists attempt to explain social behaviors at both proximate and ultimate levels, it is more common for them to focus on either one or the other. Consequently, most biosociological theories can be grouped loosely into three categories: those that focus primarily on (1) proximate physiological or morphological causes of behavior, (2) proximate ecological causes of behavior, or (3) evolved adaptations as ultimate causes of behavior.

Recently, biosociologists have theorized about patterns of hormonal activity as proximate causes of phenomena such as gender differences in behavior, variation in emotional states, or variation in the development of patterns of aggression and violence. Similarly, biosociological theorists also have attempted to explain the origins of human sociality as the product of a complex history of neurological, hormonal, social organizational, and environmental interactions, the roots of which extend far back into primate evolutionary history.

Other biosociological theorists focus on ecological factors as proximate causes of patterns of human social behavior. At the micro-level of social analysis, for example, some theorists use *evolutionary game theory* to explain how the strategy ecology within which individuals interact influences the development of patterns of cooperation or conflict among actors. At the macro-level of analysis, other theorists use evolutionary and ecological principles to analyze entire social systems and changes therein. Occasionally, biosociologists use organic evolutionary theory as a source of analogies for describing and analyzing processes of social organization and change. For example, analogues to genetic processes such as mutation, recombination, or genetic drift are said to be found in cultural processes such as innovation, invention, or diffusion. Sometimes called "stage theories of evolution," these theories typically characterize societies as complex systems of behavioral adaptations by which populations cope with the material conditions and demands of human life. It is common for such theories to feature taxonomic schemes developed for comparative and historical analysis of human societies. For example, such theories often distinguish among major societal types such as foraging (or hunting-gathering), horticultural, agrarian, industrial, and post-industrial societies, each of which is understood as a distinct complex of adaptations to those societies' environments. Some theories posit close parallels between organic and socio-cultural evolution, while others reject such parallels and describe societies as complex systems of organization that develop (versus evolve) in response to ecological challenges such as extracting resources from environments and reducing mortality rates in human populations. However, all such theories, both evolutionary and ecological, place primary explanatory emphasis on proximate causes of human social behavior, such as material, demographic, technological, or social organizational factors.

Recently, biosociological theorists have begun to express increasing dissatisfaction with the tabula rasa ("blank slate") view of human nature. Many have abandoned the longstanding view of the human brain as a general, all-purpose learning machine lacking specific, innate algorithms that give rise to the development of complex social behaviors. Instead, like neo-Darwinians in general, biosociologists increasingly subscribe to a new understanding of the human brain as densely populated by a rich and extensive array of *cognitive algorithms*, or innate mental mechanisms, that help generate complex patterns of social behavior. These mechanisms are believed to have evolved in the ancestral human environment commonly called the *environment of evolutionary adaptedness*, or *EEA*. Also described as *behavioral predispositions*, these mechanisms are conceptualized as species-typical, domain-specific adaptations which, in archaic human environments, enabled ancestral humans to cope with specific survival and/or reproductive challenges such as threat detection, foraging, mating, coalition formation, and parenting. The manner and extent to which such mechanisms may continue to be adaptive in *contemporary* societies, however, remains a point of debate among biosociologists and other neo-Darwinian social scientists.

One example of a highly influential biosocial theory that attributes patterns of complex social behavior in contemporary societies to evolved adaptations for group life is a theory of homicide (Daly & Wilson 1988). Guided by Hamilton's analysis of cooperation based on kin selection, evolutionary reasoning suggests that the intensity of conflict among individuals, such as family members, will be mediated by the degree of biological kinship among them. Family members are much less likely to be killed by consanguine kin (with whom they share common descent) than they are by affines (those to whom they are related only by marriage). As predicted by the principles of *kin selection* and *inclusive fitness*, genetic relatedness appears to suppress the expression of lethal violence among individuals engaged in conflicts of interest. Many evolutionary theorists interpret these differences as evidence of evolved, fitness-enhancing psychological adaptations that operate in both ancestral and contemporary social environments.

It is common among biosociological theorists to devote considerable attention to the evolutionary origins of male–female behavioral differences, many of which are attributed to *sexual selection*. This theoretical interest derives from evolutionary biology's explanation that, in sexually reproducing species like humans, the genetic interests of reproductive partners overlap but do not coincide. Accordingly, a strategy adopted by males for maximizing their reproductive output may not maximize the reproductive success of their female reproductive partners, and vice versa. Consequently, a surprising degree of conflict between males and females can be expected even when they are reproductive partners. According to Trivers (1972), mates compete for *parental investment*, the limiting resource in reproductive effort. As a result, significant male–female conflict, even among humans, may be expected when one reproductive partner attempts to secure maximal parental investment at the other's expense. Following this and related lines of biological reasoning, biosociological theorists have explored gender relations among humans with regard to behaviors such as marriage, divorce, remarriage, parental care, the household division of labor, sexual coercion, and gender stratification (Lopreato & Crippen 1999).

Another topic that has been subjected to biosociological theorizing using the concept of *kin selection* is how cooperation evolves among members of groups consisting of genetically unrelated individuals (non-kin). For example, ethnic group membership extends to large populations of individuals, often dispersed globally, who are not close kin. Yet, members of such groups often share a strong sense of collective identity and exhibit stable patterns of cooperation and even altruism toward each other, despite the fact that they are no more related to each other than they are to other members of their societies' populations. Biosociologists explain the development of strong social ties among members of these groups as based on kin-selected psychological adaptations acquired by ancestral humans in the EEA. Ethnic identity, for example, is explained as a human trait built upon a platform of evolved mechanisms such as *kin recognition*. Similarly, some biosociologists regard the intense social ties that unite members of some contemporary religious groups as manifestations of the same evolved psychological architecture that generated high levels of solidarity and cohesion among members of small groups of ancestral humans who were unified by the dual forces of kin selection and reciprocity.

Another topic engaging the energies of biosociologists is *gene–culture coevolution*, a phenomenon identified by Wilson (1975) and other sociobiologists. Evolutionary theorists view genes, cognition, and culture as aspects of the natural world that are conjoined in complex systems of interaction and mutual causal influence. They regard culture as the product of human cognition and learning, which themselves are the indirect products of genes and direct products of the brains they construct. Central to the theory of gene–culture coevolution is what psychologists call *prepared* (also called *biased* or *directed*) *learning*. The phenomenon of prepared learning demonstrates that, as in many other species, humans possess innate mental algorithms that predispose them to learn and retain some types of behavior more easily than others. One such socially relevant learning bias for which experimental evidence has been adduced is a "cheating detection mechanism" that appears to enable individuals to recognize with considerable ease the incidence of non-reciprocity in a social contract.

In gene–culture coevolution theory, culture is conceptualized not only as a product of natural selection, but as a selection force as well. As an information system that organizes and regulates patterns of social organization, if culture influences the expression of behaviors that have heritable components, it can alter gene frequencies across generations, thereby affecting the course of organic as well as sociocultural evolution.

SEE ALSO: Biodemography; Complexity and Emergence; Game Theory; Social Exchange Theory

REFERENCES AND SUGGESTED READINGS

Daly, M. & Wilson, M. (1988) *Homicide*. Aldine de Gruyter, Hawthorne, NY.

Freese, L. (1997) *Evolutionary Connections*. JAI Press, Greenwich, CT.

Hamilton, W. D. (1964) The Genetical Evolution of Social Behavior, I & II. *Journal of Theoretical Biology* 7: 1–52.

Kemper, T. (1990) *Social Structure and Testosterone.* Rutgers University Press, New Brunswick, NJ.

Lopreato, J. & Crippen, T. (1999) *Crisis in Sociology: The Need for Darwin.* Transaction, London.

Sanderson, S. (1999) *Social Transformations: A General Theory of Historical Development.* Rowman & Littlefield, Lanham, MD.

Trivers, R. L. (1971) The Evolution of Reciprocal Altruism. *Quarterly Review of Biology* 46: 35–57.

Trivers, R. L. (1972) Parental Investment and Sexual Selection. In: Campbell, B. (Ed.), *Sexual Selection and the Descent of Man, 1871–1971.* Aldine, Chicago, pp. 136–79.

Turner, J. H. (2000) *On the Origins of Human Emotions: A Sociological Inquiry into the Evolution of Human Affect.* Stanford University Press, Stanford, CA.

Van den Berghe, P. (1981) *The Ethnic Phenomenon.* Elsevier, New York.

Wilson, E. O. (1975) *Sociobiology: The New Synthesis.* Belknap Press, Cambridge, MA.

biracialism

Alison Roberts

Biracialism is used to indicate a racial ancestry comprised of two "races." The term generally refers to first-generation persons of "mixed race" heritage, i.e., individuals who have parents of *socially defined*, distinct racial groups. Biracialism is sometimes used interchangeably with multiraciality or "mixed race." Social scientists are concerned with the myriad meanings of biracialism in private and public spheres. Micro-level analyses delve into the process of racial identity development and how biracial persons construct their racial identities in social interaction. Macro-level analyses examine how race is measured and its role in demographic statistics, government policies, and state politics.

"Mixed race" ancestry, steeped in the legacy of colonialism and slavery, is not a new social phenomenon, but biracialism is a relatively young concept. The emergence of "biracialism" reflects a growing acceptance – or at least,

recognition – of "mixed race" populations, and illustrates the successful lobbying of biracial persons and interracial families to dismiss single-race classification schemes as inadequate for identifying or categorizing people of "mixed race" heritage. An increasingly diverse global society is characterized by growing rates of immigration and interracial unions. Coupled with shifting racial boundaries, a new cultural space has opened up for biracial individuals to define themselves and claim racial identities previously unavailable to them – insofar as these identity options exist within the social structure.

Ifekwunigwe's (2004) organization of "mixed race" scholarship into three distinct stages provides a useful conceptual framework for understanding the development of biracialism: pathology, celebration, and critique. Pseudoscience was the reigning influence of the "age of pathology," resulting in the stratification of socially defined racial categories. This racial hierarchy positioned the "white" race at the top; the dominating myth of white racial purity defined miscegenation as a threat to white supremacy and a pollutant of the white race. Offspring of interracial unions were considered genetically inferior to those of the white race. Sound science prevailed eventually, demanding a departure from treating race as biologically determined.

With academic roots in counseling and developmental psychology, early studies on biracialism relied primarily on psychoanalytic perspectives of identity formation as a theoretical framework. These studies advanced our knowledge by proposing different models of biracial identity development, but also drew heavily from clinical samples – contributing in part to the continued stigmatization of biracialism. The groundbreaking anthology of both popular and scholarly writing, *Racially Mixed People in America* (Root 1992), was important because many of the authors were themselves biracial, and they treated biracial people as an independent population rather than as a subset or subculture of a racial minority parent group. The "age of celebration" was ushered in with personal memoirs of biracialism and theoretical exploration of "mixed race" identity, and was distinguished by a "mixed race"-centric perspective. Studies remained small in scope, however, and relied more on theory than on empirical data.

With this foundation in place, the field of biracialism and "mixed race" theory flourished throughout the 1990s, became increasingly interdisciplinary, and invited more critical approaches. The current "age of critique" is marked by unresolved matters including the development of a comprehensive model for understanding biracial identity in all its forms; reconciliation of personal identity with racial categorization; and the limitations of a "multiracial movement" within the larger struggle for racial justice. Sociological analyses of biracialism have pushed the field forward with empirical research focusing on the personal and political aspects of multiraciality.

Sociologists have contributed by employing symbolic interaction as a theoretical framework. Rockquemore and Brunsma's (2002) pioneering study showed that biracial individuals develop their racial identities from a constellation of interacting factors including phenotypic appearance, socialization via family and school, age and life course stage, neighborhood community, social networks, and geographical location. Building on earlier conceptions of biracial identity, their research yielded four typologies to characterize biracialism: border identity (based on neither single race but an integration of the two); singular identity (based exclusively on one race); protean identity (based on situational context); and transcendent identity (based on the absence of race as a factor). Although their national, representative sample was limited to black and white biracial Americans, the results illustrated that there is no single, universal conception of biracial identity – a biracial individual's racial identity can be dynamic, changing according to time, place, and circumstance.

The meaning of race is also fluid, and racial designations are inevitably associated with economic, political, and social struggles. Racial identity is a paramount construction, with racial classification closely linked to government-prescribed policies and programs. The politics of biracialism are part of a broader discourse on racial justice. Important issues include the likely consequences of a multiracial designation in racial democracies; conservatives' co-optation of the "multiracial movement" to advocate for a color-blind society (in which racial inequalities are ignored); and how biracialism is situated in the global society – currently within a white/non-white dichotomy and potentially within a black/non-black paradigm in the future – and what that means for biracial people and other racial minorities.

Conducting research on biracialism merits special attention to methodological challenges. Perhaps the most obvious and shared concern is finding an honest way to write about race without reifying it. Studying biracialism involves an inevitable confrontation with the limitations of word usage and its underlying connotation – that race does have a biological or genetic reality. Identifying and recruiting biracial people can be taxing for a number of reasons: the population is small, complicated to define, and difficult to locate. Self-identification remains the most clear-cut approach for identifying a particular biracial population, but the presumption of a static identity is limiting. Researchers are still in the midst of determining the best methodological practices for defining a biracial population and ensuring representative sampling.

As researchers continue to be more critical in their approach, future directions must incorporate a diasporic approach to theoretical frameworks; just as states and nations have different racial structures, so too do they have different conceptualizations of biracialism and "mixed race." Scholars must extend their expertise beyond the polarizing black/white paradigm that dominates North American and European literature. Theoretical approaches and empirical studies should be developed to examine the diversity within "mixed race" populations, inclusive of all permutations of "mixed race" – especially those which do not include "white" as part of the equation. The question of how class intersects biracial identity remains largely unanswered, as does the role of gender in the experiences of biracial individuals. The study of biracialism, multiraciality, and "mixed race" theory will be ever evolving so long as "race" continues to be a powerful force in shaping people's life chances and experiences.

SEE ALSO: Color Line; Hybridity; Interracial Unions; Polyethnicity; Race; Race (Racism); Racial Hierarchy

REFERENCES AND SUGGESTED READINGS

Dalmage, H. M. (2000) *Tripping on the Color Line: Black–White Multiracial Families in a Racially Diverse World.* Rutgers University Press, New Brunswick, NJ.

Ifekwunigwe, J. O. (Ed.) (2004) *"Mixed Race" Studies: A Reader.* Routledge, London.

Parker, D. & Song, M. (Eds.) (2001) *Rethinking "Mixed Race."* Pluto Press, London and Sterling, VA.

Rockquemore, K. A. & Brunsma, D. L. (2002) *Beyond Black: Biracial Identity in America.* Sage, Thousand Oaks, CA.

Root, M. P. P. (1992) *Racially Mixed People in America.* Sage, Newbury Park, CA.

Root, M. P. P. (1996) *The Multiracial Experience: Racial Borders of the New Frontier.* Sage, Thousand Oaks, CA.

Storrs, D. (1999) Whiteness as Stigma: Essentialist Identity Work by Mixed-Race Women. *Symbolic Interaction* 22(3): 187–212.

Zack, N. (Ed.) (1995) *American Mixed Race.* Rowman & Littlefield, London.

Birmingham School

Chris Barker

Birmingham School refers to the work of the Centre for Contemporary Cultural Studies (CCCS), which operated as a research center at the University of Birmingham (UK) between 1964 and 1988. The Birmingham School represents a decisive moment in the creation of the intellectual and institutional project of cultural studies, as well as a "cultural turn" in sociology. The substantive focus of the Birmingham School was popular culture as explored through the concepts of ideology and hegemony. Indeed, the work of CCCS contributed to the legitimization of popular culture as a field of academic inquiry. Among the substantive topics of research undertaken by CCCS were the mass media, youth subcultures, education, gender, race, and the authoritarian state. The media were of special significance insofar as the texts of popular culture in the contemporary world are forged within their framework.

CCCS was founded in 1964 as a postgraduate center by Richard Hoggart and developed further under the leadership of Stuart Hall. It is during the period of Hall's directorship (1968–79) that one can first speak of the formation of an identifiable and distinct domain called cultural studies. A West Indian-born British thinker initially associated with the New Left of the late 1960s, Hall was interested in the regeneration of western Marxism while critical of its reductionist tendencies. Sociology (along with English literature, psychoanalysis, feminism, and continental philosophy) was one of a number of intellectual influences on the thinkers of the Birmingham School. However, cultural studies can now be considered as an academic domain in its own right, so that neither CCCS nor cultural studies is best described as a subcategory of the discipline of sociology per se. Rather, sociology and cultural studies are cousins with "family resemblances."

CULTURAL STUDIES AS A POLITICAL PROJECT

Within the English literary tradition that formed a backdrop to the early work of CCCS, popular culture was commonly regarded as inferior to the elevated cultures of "high" art. However, CCCS sought to challenge the criteria used to police the boundaries of "good works," arguing that they are not universal but rather are derived from an institutionalized and class-based hierarchy of cultural tastes. More importantly still, the Birmingham School understood popular culture to be the decisive arena in which consent and resistance to the ascendant meanings of a social formation were won and lost. This is a political conception of popular culture as a site where cultural hegemony is secured or challenged. For CCCS, then, evaluations of popular culture were not made on the basis of cultural or aesthetic value per se, but are concerned with issues of power, politics, and ideology.

In that context, members of the Birmingham School generally regarded their work as a political project of an intellectual character rather than as an abstract academic discipline. Indeed, cultural studies writers of this period had aspirations to forge links with political movements outside of the academy. In particular, the

Birmingham School's Gramscian thinking located cultural analysis and ideological struggle at the heart of western politics. It placed a special premium on "organic" intellectuals and their relations with other participants in social struggle. Organic intellectuals are thinkers who form a constitutive part of working-class (and later feminist, postcolonial, African American, etc.) struggle, acting as the theorists and organizers of the counter-hegemonic class and its allies.

Thus, the Birmingham School conceived of cultural studies as an intellectual project that aimed to provide wider social and political forces with intellectual resources in the "ideological struggle." CCCS intellectuals sought to play a "demystifying role" by pointing to the constructed character of cultural texts. They aimed to highlight the myths and ideologies embedded in texts in the hope of producing political opposition to subordination. However, it is open to doubt whether cultural studies has been connected with political movements in any "organic" way. Rather, as Hall (1992) has wryly commented, cultural studies intellectuals acted "as if" they were organic intellectuals or in the hope that one day they could be.

BIRMINGHAM'S THEORETICAL PERSPECTIVES

Culturalism and Structuralism

The initial focus of CCCS was on "lived" class culture, a focus that chimed with the work of Richard Hoggart and Raymond Williams. This has been described by Hall (1992) as the moment of "culturalism" and is associated with the adoption of a broadly anthropological definition of culture that takes it to be an everyday lived process. Culturalism stressed the "ordinariness" of culture and the active, creative capacity of people to construct shared meaningful practices. Methodologically, culturalism has favored concrete empirical research and ethnography. Paul Willis in particular was a proponent of ethnographic research into culture as sensual lived experience. In his most famous work, *Learning to Labour* (1977), Willis describes his ethnographic study of a group of working-class boys and the way that they reproduced their subordinate class position.

However, culturalism was surpassed within CCCS by the influence of structuralism, particularly as it was articulated with Marxism. Structuralism is concerned with social and cultural structures or predictable regularities, so that a structuralist understanding of culture is concerned with the "systems of relations" of an underlying structure (usually language) and the grammar that makes meaning possible. Structuralism extends its reach from "words" to the language of cultural signs in general, so that human relations, material objects, and images are all analyzed through the structures of signs making culture analogous to (or structured like) a language. Thus, members of CCCS began to explore culture with the tools of semiotics (or the study of signs).

Dick Hebdige's *Subculture: The Meaning of Style* (1979) illustrates the structuralist influence within the Birmingham School. Hebdige explores subcultures in terms of the autonomous play of signifiers and in doing so asserts the specificity of the semiotic and cultural. For Hebdige, style is a signifying practice of spectacular subcultures that displays obviously fabricated codes of meaning. Through the signification of difference, style constitutes a group identity that is achieved by transforming the signs of commodities into a bricolage that acts as a form of semiotic resistance to the hegemonic order. British Punk of the late 1970s, an especially dislocated, self-aware, and ironic mode of signification, was Hebdige's favored exemplar.

Neo-Gramscian Marxism

Despite the influence of structuralism, it was arguably Marxism that formed the most important theoretical paradigm within the Birmingham School. At the height of its activities CCCS sought to fuse aspects of Marxism, with its stress on history, materialism, capitalism, and class, with the more synchronic approach of structuralism.

In developing its particular version of a structuralist Marxism oriented to the study of culture, the Birmingham School mined the intellectual resources of Barthes, Althusser, and (most crucially) Gramsci. The key conceptual tools were those of text, ideology, and hegemony as explored through the notion of popular culture as a site of both social control and resistance.

The significance of both Althusser and Gramsci to the Birmingham School was that they offered a way to explore culture on its own terms while remaining within a Marxist problematic. Classic Marxism had argued that the cultural "superstructure" is shaped by the economic "base" or mode of production. By contrast, Althusser proposed a model in which ideology, politics, and the economy were grasped as discrete levels or practices of a social formation that worked relatively autonomously from each other. Gramsci's work stressed the importance of meaning, common sense, and ideology in the cultural domain. Althusser and Gramsci helped the Birmingham School move away from the economic reductionism of the base and superstructure model. They argued that although the analysis of economic determinants may be necessary to any understanding of culture, it is not – and cannot be – self-sufficient because cultural phenomena work within their own rules and logics (as structuralism argued).

For the Birmingham School, the concept of ideology referred to discourses that "bind" social groups and "justify" their actions. Ideologies, while purporting to be universal truths, are understood by Marxism to be historically specific understandings that obscure and maintain the power of social groups (e.g., class, gender, race). The concept of hegemony was developed largely from the work of Gramsci, for whom it describes a situation where a "historical bloc" of ruling-class factions exercises social authority and leadership over the subordinate classes through a combination of force and, more importantly, consent. Hegemony involves a temporary closure of meaning supportive of the powerful and describes the process of making, maintaining, and reproducing the governing sets of meanings of a given culture.

One of the seminal texts of cultural studies, *Resistance through Rituals* (1976) edited by Hall and Jefferson, encapsulates the Gramscian thrust of the Birmingham School in its title. Here, British youth subcultures are explored as stylized forms of resistance to the hegemonic culture. It was argued that, in reaction to the decline of traditional working-class values, spaces, and places, youth subcultures sought to reinvent through stylization the lost community and values of the working class. For example, skinheads were held to be recapturing in an imaginary way the tradition of working-class male "hardness" through their cropped hair, boots, jeans, and braces.

Gramscian themes of ideology, hegemony, resistance, and containment are also apparent in Hall and colleagues' *Policing the Crisis* (1978), a book that explores the 1970s moral panic in the British press surrounding street robbery. The authors explore the articulation of mugging with race and the alleged black threat to law, order, and the British way of life. Specifically, the text sets out to give an account of the political, economic, ideological, and racial crisis of Britain that formed the context of the moral panic about mugging and to dispute its association with a black British presence. In doing so, Hall and his colleagues sought to demonstrate the ideological work done by the media in constructing mugging and connecting it with concerns about racial disorder. In particular, *Policing the Crisis* explores the popularization of hegemonic ideology through the professional working practices of the media.

Texts and Audiences

The Gramscian influence within the Birmingham School was also evident in a series of textual analyses that explored the operations of ideology in news and current affairs, soap opera, advertising, and popular film. Here the concept of a text is a metaphor for the construction of meaning through the organization of signs into representations. A text is constituted not simply by the written word, but includes all forms of signification so that dress, television programs, advertising images, sporting events, pop stars, etc. can all be read as texts. Textual analysis for the Birmingham School usually involved deconstructing the practices of cultural coding to show us how the apparent transparency of meaning is an outcome of cultural habituation.

The power of textual representation lies in its enabling of some kinds of knowledge to exist while excluding others in what may be called a "politics of representation." For example, members of the Birmingham School developed a hegemonic model of news production in which the ideological character of news is understood to be an outcome of the routine attitudes and working practices of staff. News journalists are said to learn the conventions and codes of "how things should be done," thereby reproducing ideology as common sense. It particular, their reliance on "authoritative sources" leads the media to reproduce primary definers' (e.g., politicians, judges, industrialists, the police, and other official agencies) accounts of the news.

Similarly, CCCS's analysis of advertising stressed the selling not just of commodities but also of ways of looking at the world. Acquiring a brand is not simply about purchasing a product, but rather is concerned with buying into lifestyles and values. Thus, objects in advertisements are signifiers of meaning that we decode in the context of known cultural systems associating products in adverts with other cultural "goods." While an image of a particular product may denote only beans or a car, it is made to connote "nature" or "family." In buying commodities we emotionally invest in the associated image and so contribute to the construction of our identities through consumption.

However, while textual analysis founded on semiotic theory and framed by the problematic of ideology and hegemony was a core concern of the Birmingham School, key participants also explored the relationship of audiences to texts. In particular, they moved away from the idea that texts fixed the meanings for readers in order to investigate the way that audiences produced a variety of meanings. This was theorized by Hall through his "encoding-decoding" model and researched empirically by David Morley.

Hall conceived of the process of encoding-decoding as an articulation of the linked but distinct moments of production, circulation, distribution, and reproduction, each of which has its specific practices which are necessary to the circuit but which do not guarantee the next moment. In particular, the production of

meaning does not ensure consumption of that meaning as the encoders might have intended because television texts are polysemic and can be interpreted in different ways. That is not to say that all the meanings are equal among themselves; rather, the text will be *structured in dominance* leading to a *preferred meaning*.

Hall proposed a model of three hypothetical decoding positions: (1) the dominant-hegemonic decoding which accepts the preferred meanings of the text; (2) a negotiated code which acknowledges the legitimacy of the preferred meanings in the abstract but makes its own rules and adaptations under particular circumstances; and (3) an oppositional code where people understand the preferred encoding but reject it and decode in contrary ways. David Morley's research into the audience for a British news "magazine" program, *The Nationwide Audience* (1980), was based on Hall's encoding-decoding model and gave empirical backing to it. It was argued that dominant, negotiated, and oppositional decodings had been made by different groups of viewers according to their social class.

RACE AND GENDER: THE POLITICS OF DIFFERENCE

At its inception a good deal of the work of the CCCS was focused on class as the central dimension of cultural power and struggle. Yet the Birmingham School was formed at a moment in British history when race was a significant issue in the political arena. There could be few British cities that exemplified this more than Birmingham, with its large Caribbean, Indian, and Pakistani diaspora populations. The Handsworth region of Birmingham is the largest "black" residential area in Europe. And yet a key figure within CCCS, Paul Gilroy, argued that the legacy of Raymond Williams had endowed cultural studies with too nationalistic an orientation to culture that had sidelined important issues of race and migration within Britain. The 1984 CCCS collective book *The Empire Strikes Back* and Gilroy's book *There Ain't No Black in the Union Jack* (1987) set out to address these issues. Further, as has been noted, *Policing the Crisis* was concerned with law and order, the media, and race in Britain, while a sub-theme of Hebdidge's work on subculture was the engagement of white youth cultures with the post-war black presence in Britain.

Just as Gilroy argued that race was being sidelined within CCCS, so a number of women writers began to argue that the Birmingham School was reproducing male hegemony in its work. For example, the early discussions of subcultures appeared to be centered on boys and men to the detriment of girls and women. However, the emergence of feminism within CCCS began to challenge this gendered perspective. Indeed, Hall once famously described feminism at CCCS as a "thief in the night": feminism broke into the cosy male world of CCCS and shook it up. For example, Angela McRobbie began to explore girls' magazine and female subcultures with a feminist eye allied to the overall project of CCCS. Although feminism had to shout to be heard, it does share with the Birmingham School a desire to produce "knowledges" of and by "marginalized" and oppressed groups with the avowed intention of making a political intervention. Certainly, feminism has emerged as a major strand of subsequent work within cultural studies.

ENDGAME

In 1988 CCCS ceased being a postgraduate research center and become a university department that included undergraduate teaching before it too was closed in the 1990s. Indeed, one might see the Birmingham School as a distinct institutional and intellectual project as coming to an end in the mid-1980s, after the departure of Stuart Hall a few years earlier. However, cultural studies as a project continued to grow. For example, one CCCS graduate, Lawrence Grossberg, was influential in the growth of cultural studies in the US. Today, cultural studies as an intellectual project has practitioners across the world, while poststructuralism has arguably eclipsed both structuralism and neo-Gramscian Marxism as the decisive theoretical paradigm. It would thus be wrong to equate the Birmingham School with cultural studies as a whole. However, it would be equally mistaken to displace the decisive influence of the Birmingham moment in its formation.

SEE ALSO: Althusser, Louis; Cultural Critique; Cultural Studies; Cultural Studies, British; Encoding/Decoding; Gramsci, Antonio; Hegemony and the Media; Ideological Hegemony; Ideology; Marxism and Sociology; Popular Culture; Structuralism; Subculture

REFERENCES AND SUGGESTED READINGS

Barker, C. (2003) *Cultural Studies: Theory and Practice*. Sage, London.

Bennett, T., Martin, G., Mercer, C., & Woollacott, J. (Eds.) (1981) *Popular Television and Film*. British Film Institute, London.

Fiske, J. (1992) British Cultural Studies. In: Allen, R. (Ed.), *Channels of Discourse, Reassembled*. Routledge, London.

Hall, S. (1977) Culture, the Media and the Ideological Effect. In: Curran, J. et al. (Eds.), *Mass Communications and Society*. Edward Arnold, London.

Hall, S. (1992) Cultural Studies and its Theoretical Legacies. In: Grossberg, L., Nelson, C., & Treichler, P. (Eds.), *Cultural Studies*. Routledge, London.

Hall, S. Hobson, D., Lowe, P., & Willis, P. (Eds.) (1980) *Culture, Media, Language*. Hutchinson, London.

McGuigan, J. (1992) *Cultural Populism*. Routledge, London.

McRobbie, A. (1991) *Feminism and Youth Culture*. Macmillan, London.

Morley, D. (1992) *Television, Audiences and Cultural Studies*. Routledge, London.

Turner, G. (1990) *British Cultural Studies: An Introduction*. Unwin Hyman, London.

bisexuality

Christian Klesse

Definitions of bisexuality are manifold and heterogeneous. There are at least four seemingly contradictory meanings associated with the term. Firstly, in early sexology bisexuality was conceived of as a primordial state of hermaphroditism prior to sexual differentiation. Secondly, bisexuality has been invoked to describe the co-presence of "feminine" and "masculine" psychological traits in a human being. The idea of androgyny has impinged to a certain degree on popular ideas about bisexuality. Thirdly, bisexuality has provided the concept to account for people's propensity to be sexually attracted to both men and women. This is currently the most common understanding of bisexuality. Fourthly, bisexuality is frequently seen as a pervasive "middle ground" (of merged gender, sex, or sexuality). This representation of bisexuality includes the notion that "we're all bisexual, really," which may imply either an essential androgyny or a universal "latent bisexuality" in the sense of an abstracted potential to love people of both genders (or irrespective of gender) (Hemmings 2002).

Bisexuality plays a rather paradoxical role in the history of sexuality. Although it has been integral, if not central, to most modern theories of sexuality, it has rarely been acknowledged or taken seriously in or for itself. Thus, Angelides (2000) shows that bisexuality has been a central concept in the establishment of an *economy of (hetero) sexuality* in the spreading discourses of (evolutionary) biology and medical sexology in the second half of the nineteenth century. The Russian embryologist Aleksandr Kovalevsky was the first to use the category of bisexuality in his 1866 discussion of hermaphroditic ascidians. Charles Darwin appropriated these findings in *The Descent of Man* (1871) in order to bolster up his theory of evolution. He declared primordial hermaphroditism to be the missing link in his theory of the descent of man from invertebrate organisms. This theory was linked with an insight from within comparative anatomy, according to which the sexual organs of even higher vertebrates went through stages of hermaphroditism in their early development. Darwin drew upon both theories when he speculated about the possibility that "some remote progenitor of the whole vertebrate kingdom appears to have been hermaphrodite or androgynous" (Darwin, quoted by Angelides 2000: 32). This model further rested on Ernst Haeckel's extremely influential recapitulation theory, according to which "ontogeny recapitulates phylogeny." This principle established the conviction that in the development from fetus to adulthood each human would recapitulate the complete life history of the entire species. Recapitulation theory proved a powerful tool to back up the sexist and racist claims so pervasive in nineteenth-century scientific thought that

black people and women would be closer to the state of primitive hermaphroditism. It attests to the thoroughly racialized character of western conceptualizations of sexuality. Bisexuality both marked the original intersexed character of the human embryo and an ambiguous sexual character of uncivilized and primitive systems of sexual social organization (Storr 1997). Evolutionist theories of primordial bisexuality further provided key theoretical elements to the shift in the understanding of homosexuality from a theory of sex role inversion to one of object choice at the turn of the century. Richard Krafft-Ebing saw homosexuality as an archaic residue of primordial bisexuality and Havelock Ellis conceptualized it as "a psychic and somatic development on the basis of latent bisexuality" or better as a result of its unsuccessful repudiation.

Freudian psychoanalysis, too, the most significant (non-biological) theory on sexuality at the beginning of the twentieth century, located a theory of essential bisexuality at the core of its explanation of sexual orientation via the resolution of the Oedipus complex. However, due to the linear narrative structure of this theory and its perception as a standard route to an unequivocal adult sexual orientation, Freud did at the same time face inevitable difficulties to account for modes of desire that did not repudiate one or the other gendered object-choice. Post-Freudian developments of psychoanalytic theory were frequently even more reluctant to consider the validity of bisexual object-choices (Angelides 2000). A counter-tendency may consist in Cixous's (1981) critique of Freudian and Lacanian accounts of bisexuality. Although the notion of bisexuality has been epistemologically instrumental and necessary for most modern conceptualizations of homosexuality and heterosexuality, bisexuality has generally been written "out of the present" in theories that evolve around a hetero/homo dichotomy (Angelides 2000).

Alfred Kinsey and his colleagues challenged the dominant dichotic or binary understanding of sexuality that divides the human population into heterosexuals (the majority) and homosexuals (a few deviants) in their influential sex surveys *Human Sexual Behavior in the Male* (1948) and *Human Sexual Behavior in the Female* (1952). These controversial publications revealed that the majority of the respondents recollected both sexual activities with men and with women as part of the lifetime sexual experience. Rather than clearly belonging to one camp or the other, the authors suggested, most people would consequently fall somewhere in the middle ground of a continuum ranging from exclusively heterosexual to exclusive homosexual. In order to define individual sexual orientation they invented a heterosexual-homosexual rating scale. The so-called Kinsey scale encourages people to place themselves on a 7-point scale ranging from 0 (exclusively heterosexual) to 6 (exclusively homosexual). Points 1 to 5 stand for varying combinations of homosexual and heterosexual experience. A range of researchers have since modified the Kinsey scale, adding further dimensions such as sexual or romantic feelings, fantasy, relationship history, etc. The best-known of the models is probably the Klein Sexual Orientation Grid (KSOG) which tries to provide a "dynamic and multi-variable framework" for understanding sexual orientation. The KSOG evolves around the variables sexual attraction, sexual behavior, sexual fantasies, emotional preference, social preference, self-identification, and lifestyle. It further adds a time dimension by asking people to reflect about each of these issues regarding their past, present, and anticipated (wished for) experiences (Klein and Wolf 1985; Rodríguez 2000). Despite this concern for complexity and contingency, such attempts at refined measurement appear futile in the face of the inherent ambiguity of (bi)sexual desire.

In sociology the interest has nowadays largely shifted from "sexual orientation" to the more flexible concept of "sexual identity." The consideration of bisexuality has contributed novel insights to the understanding of sexual identity development. Research has suggested that for most bisexuals identity formation is not a linear process with a fixed outcome, but an ongoing process of self-location and renegotiation (Firestein 1996). The specificities of bisexual identification (such as a comparatively late coming-out process and frequent identity changes) are often read to signify a lack of authenticity. In contradistinction, Rust (1996) has argued that bisexual identification processes reveal the insufficiency of linear coming-out models. Rust suggests

replacing the linear model with a social constructionist perspective that conceives of "identity as a description of the location of the self in relation to other individuals, groups, and institutions." According to this perspective, sexual identities appear as "landmarks on a sexual landscape" which is historical, socially constructed, and shaped by multiple power relations. In order to understand identity change we consequently would have to consider changes in the social context and the language available for self-description, too. The focus consequently moves away from "coming-out" to broader questions of identity formation and maintenance. The study of lesbian and gay coming-out narratives has shown that individuals tend to rewrite their past and construct a certain future in order to legitimate their current sexual identities (and lifestyles) as a consequence of their deep personality structures. Although it is questionable that the temporality at the heart of "traditional" coming-out narratives can fully represent experiences of bisexual desire, most coming-out stories of self-identified bisexuals are also structured around the logic of a "before" and "after" (Hemmings 2002).

The emergence of self-conscious and assertive bisexual social movement networks and organizations in many countries since the late 1970s has resulted in the consolidation of a bisexual identity. Bisexuals have been active in a range of social movements around gender and sexuality since their inception, in particular the feminist, lesbian and gay, S/M, polyamory, and queer movements. The marginalization of bisexuality in many political environments has led many self-identified bisexuals to campaign around this aspect of their identity. Historically, it has been in particular the contestation of bisexuality in the gay male and (even more so) the lesbian feminist movements that has fed into the motivation to set up an autonomous social movement (Rust 1995). The emergence of affirmative bisexual identity politics has led many bisexual activists and theorists to clearly define bisexual identities in sharp distinction to other sexualities. Some have used the term "monosexual" to refer to both heterosexuals and homosexuals as a set of people who would only desire one gender and take for granted the sexual dualism of the hetero/homo binary. Within the juxtaposition of bisexuality and monosexuality, bisexual identity thus is accredited an enlightened reflexivity and a progressive transformative potential.

However, some writers have cautioned that it is in particular the attempt to create a closed and clear-cut definition of bisexual identity that would undermine the potential of bisexuality to exceed the constrictive binary logic of western models of sexuality (Rodríguez 2000). Drawing on the theory of monosexuality, bisexual oppression has been framed as an effect of "monosexism" (i.e., the normative belief that one should only be attracted to one gender). This model can be said to lack specifity in that it fails to explore the differences in the ways bisexuals tend to be stigmatized in heterosexual, lesbian, or gay spaces and does not pay attention to the unequal power relations between distinctly positioned groups (Hemmings 2002). The concept biphobia has proven to be more flexible in explaining the specific forms of discrimination faced by bisexuals in different social contexts. Biphobia entails prejudiced behavior, stereotypical representation, and strategies of discrimination and marginalization. Biphobia entails a range of stereotypes, such as the beliefs that bisexuals would be shallow, narcissistic, untrustworthy, morally bankrupt, promiscuous, incapable of monogamy, HIV carriers, fence sitters, etc. Biphobic representation intersects with other discriminatory discourses, in particular the ones around sexism, racism, and classism. It is marked by a certain overlap with homophobia or heteronormativity, but cannot be fully subsumed by either of these concepts.

Bisexual movement politics have transformed bisexual identities and given rise to specific bisexual theories. They have also provided the basis for the growth of literature that directly addresses bisexuality. Apart from a handful of publications in the second half of the 1970s there had been an absolute silence in the anglophone scientific literature on bisexuality after the publication of the Kinsey studies. Only since the late 1980s, when bisexual organizing gained momentum, has a range of books concerned with social and political activism been edited (Tucker et al. 1995; Off Pink Collective 1996; BiAcademic Intervention 1997). Bisexual feminists started to explore the interrelation between feminism and bisexuality (Weise 1992;

George 1993; Rust 1995). Until the 1990s most of these publications assumed the form of first-person narratives and committed themselves to a bisexual visibility politics. Academic research was still scarce and remained limited to very specific topics, such as mixed-orientation marriages. Only worries about the HIV/AIDS epidemic triggered some largely epidemiological research into (behavioral) bisexuality. From the 1990s onwards it is possible, according to Hemmings (2002), to identify a shift within the writing on bisexuality. Many authors abandoned their concern with positive images and started to explore issues regarding epistemology. This work is primarily concerned with the potential gains and losses of discourses around bisexuality (Hall & Pramaggiore 1996; Angelides 2000; cf. Storr 1999). Debates within this kind of (post)bisexual theory have centered on the questions why queer theory has been reluctant to engage actively with bisexuality and what the effects of a bisexual perspective could be for a deconstructive theory of sexuality. At the same time, historians have embarked on the task of writing a critical genealogy of (bi)sexuality in order to uncover the largely hidden role of bisexuality in modern discourses on sexuality. This work suggests that social scientific research into sexuality and gender needs to draw on an integrated focus on "bisexuality" in order to comprehend fully the complex web of meanings around sexuality. This is the more urgent, because most aspects of bisexuality (whether as identity, behavior, desire, or discourse) are still vastly under-researched.

SEE ALSO: Coming Out/Closets; Feminist Activism in Latin America; Gay and Lesbian Movement; Heterosexuality; Homophobia and Heterosexism; Homosexuality; Lesbianism; Psychoanalysis; Queer Theory; Sexuality Research: History

REFERENCES AND SUGGESTED READINGS

Angelides, S. (2000) *A History of Bisexuality*. University of Chicago Press, Chicago.
Bi Academic Intervention (Ed.) (1997) *The Bisexual Imaginary: Representation, Identity and Desire*. Cassell, London.

Cixous, H. (1981) The Laugh of the Medusa. In: Marks, E. & Courtrivon, I., de (Eds.), *New French Feminisms: An Anthology*. Schocken Books, New York, pp. 245–64.

Firestein, B. A. (Ed.) (1996) *Bisexuality: The Psychology and Politics of an Invisible Minority*. Sage, London.

George, S. (1993) *Women and Bisexuality*. Scarlet Press, London.

Hall, D. E. & Pramaggiore, M. (Eds.) (1996) *Re-Presenting Bisexualities: Subjects and Cultures of Fluid Desire*. New York University Press, London.

Hemmings, C. (2002) *Bisexual Spaces: A Geography of Sexuality and Gender*. Routledge, London.

Klein, F. & Wolf, T. (Eds.) (1985) *Bisexualities: Theory and Research*. Haworth Press, London.

Off Pink Collective (Ed.) (1996) *Bisexual Horizons: Politics, Histories, Lives*. Lawrence & Wishart, London.

Rodríguez, R. (Ed.) (2000) *Bisexuality in the United States: A Social Science Reader*. Columbia University Press, New York.

Rust, P. C. (1995) *Bisexuality and the Challenge to Lesbian Politics: Sex, Loyalty and Revolution*. New York University Press, London.

Rust, P. C. (1996) Sexual Identities: The Struggle for Self-Description in a Changing Sexual Landscape. In: Beemyn, B. & Eliason, M. (Eds.), *Queer Studies: A Lesbian, Gay, Bisexual and Transgender Anthology*. New York University Press, London.

Storr, M. (1997) The Sexual Reproduction of "Race": Bisexuality, History and Racialization. In: Bi Academic Intervention (Ed.), *The Bisexual Imaginary*. Cassel, London, pp. 73–88.

Storr, M. (1999) *Bisexuality: A Critical Reader*. Routledge, London.

Tucker, N. et al. (Eds.) (1995) *Bisexual Politics: Theories, Queries and Visions*. Harrington Park Press, London.

Weise, E. H. (1992) *Closer to Home: Bisexuality and Feminism*. Seal Press, Seattle.

black feminist thought

April L. Few

Black feminist thought is a collection of ideas, writings, and art that articulates a standpoint of and for black women of the African Diaspora. Black feminist thought describes black women as a unique group that exists in a "place" in US social relations where intersectional processes of race, ethnicity, gender, class, and sexual orientation shape black women's individual and collective consciousness, self-definitions, and actions (Collins 1991, 1998). As a standpoint theory, black feminist thought conceptualizes identities as organic, fluid, interdependent, multiple, and dynamic socially constructed "locations" within historical context (hooks 1984; Collins 1998; Smith 1998; James & Sharply-Whiting 2000). Black feminist thought is grounded in black women's historical experience with enslavement, anti-lynching movements, segregation, Civil Rights and Black Power movements, sexual politics, capitalism, and patriarchy.

DEFINING BLACK FEMINIST FRAMEWORKS

Distinctive tenets of contemporary black feminist thought include: (1) the belief that self-authorship and the legitimatization of partial, subjugated knowledges represents a unique and diverse standpoint of and by black women; (2) black women's experiences with multiple oppressions result in needs, expectations, ideologies, and problems that are different than those of black men and white women; and (3) black feminist consciousness is an ever-evolving process of self-conscious struggle (i.e., emancipatory historiography) for the liberation of black women, black men, and black communities through activism. In the landmark book *Black Feminist Thought* (1991), Patricia Hill Collins delineated a similar list to describe elements of black feminist thought. For instance, Collins posited that black feminists (1) acknowledged black women's historical struggle against multiple oppressions; (2) examined how black women and their families negotiate the intersections of race, ethnicity, gender, sexual orientation, and class; (3) eradicated malignant images of black womanhood; and (4) incorporated an activist perspective into their research through the co-creation of knowledge with informants, consciousness-raising, and empowerment within the context of black women's lives.

The cornerstone of black feminist thought is the significance of black women defining and validating their own relationships to self and others while eradicating and replacing deleterious images of black womanhood. Black feminist thought is standpoint theory about black women's radical subjectivity. bell hooks described radical subjectivity as a process that emerges as a person comes to understand how interlocking structures of domination influence choices made in her life. This awareness incites emancipatory historiography and resistance against grand narratives of being and social relationality. Black radical subjectivity is created using fluid terms, parameters, and locations specified, validated, and lived by black women and the communities of which they are a part. In *Yearning* (1990), bell hooks discussed the importance of language in defining self. She saw language as a place of struggle and resistance for black women. Language is the conduit to define identity and validate experience. In *Learning from the Outsider Within: The Sociological Significance of Black Feminist Thought* (1991), Collins argued that black women's insistence on self-definition, self-valuation, and black female-centered analysis was significant for two reasons. First, valuing one's own self-defined standpoint is a means of resisting racist and sexist ideologies and other dehumanizing processes endemic to systems of domination. Second, black female self-definition allows black women to reject internalized, psychological oppression. Alice Walker's *The Color Purple* (1982) and Ntozake Shange's *For Colored Girls Who Have Considered Suicide/When the Rainbow is Enuf* (1976) are two literary examples of the necessity for black female self-definition.

Attention to the interlocking nature of race, ethnicity, gender, class, and sexual orientation over the course of time, generation, and geography is a recurrent theme in the writings of black feminists (Beale 1970; Davis 1981; Lorde 1984; Walker 1984; King 1988; Collins 1991; Guy-Sheftall 1995; Springer 2002). Black feminists assert that all black women have the common experience of negotiating oppression(s) despite occupying different social locations and possessing variable privileges. The strategies through which black women claim, reframe, and politicize their specific situatedness in respect of unjust hierarchical social relationality is the politics of location. Black women

"do" identity politics out of necessity for survival and exist in the politics of location by default as a result of imposed marginalization. Identity politics is in effect an individual and a group process of consciously and subconsciously negotiating intersectionality. In *Yearning*, hooks argued that even in the margins of discourse one can actively and consciously engage the politics of location on an individual or group basis in liberating ways. Black feminists recognize that although black women and black men are tied inextricably by the experience of racism and classism, sexism is a domain that remains to be contended in private and public relationships. The complexity of black and white women's relationship has been shaped by historical sexual politics, first in the private domain during the period of enslavement in the United States, and second in the public domain in workplace relations, activism (e.g., exclusion by white feminists/activists in the suffrage and birth control movements and women's political organizations), and in academia (e.g., women's studies programs and in the articulation of feminist and critical theory).

BLACK FEMINISM AND ACTIVIST ROOTS

Black feminist thought has been expressed historically through collective social and political activism. Linking thought with action is a defining characteristic of black feminist consciousness. The contributions and deliberate acts of nineteenth-century and early twentieth-century black women and activists such as Anna Julia Cooper, Harriet Tubman, Sojourner Truth, Harriet Jacobs, Mary Church Terrell, Amy Jacques Garvey, Pauli Murray, and Ida B. Wells Barnett could be described as the first steps in the development of black feminist thought. Although none of these women would describe themselves as purveyors of black feminist thought, their visionary activism and commitment to social justice reflect a keen awareness of the impact of multiple oppressions on the physical, economic, and psychological well-being of black women, black families, and black communities. Black women leaders sought to redefine the images of black womanhood and address racism through organizing national black women's clubs and organizations. For instance, Mary Church Terrell founded the National Association of Colored Women (NACW) in 1896. The NACW became the intellectual and political umbrella organization for black women's clubs in the country. Black women's clubs focused on disseminating positive images and models of respectable black womanhood for public consumption. Ida B. Wells Barnett was a founder of the National Association for the Advancement of Colored People (NAACP) and is remembered best for her eloquent analysis of the intersections of race, gender, and sexuality in her anti-lynching work. She documented over 700 lynchings occurring in the late 1800s. She confronted racism and sexism by highlighting the incessant sexual assaults on black women by unpunished white men and the simultaneous racist and erroneous projection of white male lascivious behavior onto black men as rapists of white women. Mary McLeod Bethune was the founder of both the Bethune Cookman Institute and National Council of Negro Women (NCNW) and president of the NACW. In 1936, she was appointed director of the Division of Negro Affairs in the National Youth Administration. At this post, Bethune arranged a historic meeting between Eleanor Roosevelt and a group of black female activists to discuss progressive policies for social change. A fervent civil rights activist, attorney, and poet, Pauli Murray provided her legal thesis to be used as foundational material to try the *Topeka Board of Education* case. Among her many accomplishments, Murray was a co-founder of the National Organization of Women (NOW) and co-wrote the mission statement of NOW. She also became the first black female Episcopalian priest in the United States. Frances Beale, founder and leader of the Student Non-Violent Coordinating Committee (SNCC) Black Liberation Committee, argued in her groundbreaking article "Double Jeopardy: To Be Black and Female" (1970) that black women experienced racism and sexism simultaneously and that there were opportunities available to black women beyond reproduction. At the time, some black nationalists believed that black women could best help the struggle for racial

liberation by remaining home and having babies. Beale wanted to broaden the political and economic roles of black women by making motherhood compatible with employment and political activism.

In the 1970s, black feminist activists would birth two explicitly black feminist activist organizations – the National Black Feminist Organization and the Combahee River Collective. In 1973, Margaret Sloan, Eleanor Holmes Norton, and Florence Kennedy founded the National Black Feminist Organization (NBFO), the first explicitly black feminist organization in the United States. The NBFO resulted from black women's frustration with racism experienced in the women's movement and a grassroots desire to raise the consciousness of all black women and to connect to black women from all social stations in life. The first NBFO regional conference was held in New York City in 1973 with the promise of continuing much of the liberatory, self-defining work started by earlier black women's organizations. The Boston Chapter of the NBFO became the Combahee River Collective, an anti-capitalist, socialist revolutionary organization of intellectuals and grassroots activists. Barbara Smith, Beverly Smith, and Demita Frazier wrote the seminal "A Black Feminist Statement" (1977) on behalf of the Combahee River Collective. In this statement, the authors delineated the genesis of contemporary black feminism and their understanding of the impact of multiple oppressions; identified the legacy and divisiveness of sexual politics in black communities; rejected black lesbian separatism in the black feminist movement; documented problems in organizing black feminists; and indicated black feminist issues and future policies. In addition, the statement revealed criticisms against the black liberation and mainstream white women's liberation movements for their blatant inattention to the ways in which various aspects of identity – race, class, gender, and sexuality – are inseparable for black women. The black liberation movement of the 1970s was largely conceived as a black male movement. Michelle Wallace's *Black Macho and the Myth of the Superwoman* (1978) was a stinging analysis of black male sexism and misogyny in the black liberation movement.

BLACK FEMINISTS' BREAK FROM MAINSTREAM FEMINISM

Given that black feminists broke with mainstream feminism in the 1970s, black feminist thought reflects a provocative, sophisticated critique of the mainstream white women's movement and theorizations. In her classic work, Frances Beale (1970) argued that the praxis of white feminist groups was grounded in a privileged, middle-class experience and was not cognizant of an anti-racist, anti-capitalist ideology. Beale, and later Michelle Wallace in *A Black Feminist's Search for Sisterhood* (1975), contended that black and white women could not unite around common grievances or discuss these issues in a serious manner if white feminist groups failed to acknowledge their complicity in and the impact of racism and capitalism on black women's lives. In *Age, Race, Class, and Sex: Women Redefining Difference* (1995), black lesbian feminist Audre Lorde explained the processes in which black women are "Othered" by white feminists. Paula Giddings (1984) argued that the alliances between black and white women were strained because white feminist organizations did not address the issues of poor and working-class black women. Black feminists documented several ways in which black and white women experienced sexism differently. For instance, historically, stereotypes of black and white womanhood differ and traditional housewife models of womanhood are not applicable to most black women (hooks 1984). In addition, historically, black women have been more likely to be heads of household than white women and their labor contribution to the marketplace has always exceeded that of white women (Guy-Sheftall 1995). It should be noted that black feminist writings do not advocate wholly a separatist movement from mainstream feminism but do call for a recognition and the deliberate inclusion of the diversity of all women's experiences in scientific inquiry.

BLACK FEMINIST LITERATURE

The actions of black female activists paved the way for an inspiring plethora of black feminist creative writing and scholarship in the 1970s to the present day. Toni Cade Bambara's *The Black Woman: An Anthology* (1970) was a groundbreaking anthology of poetry, essays, and short stories by and of black women. This anthology includes works by novelist Alice Walker, poets Audre Lorde and Nikki Giovanni, writer Paule Marshall, activists Grace Lee Boggs and Frances Beale, and musician Abbey Lincoln. In their own way, the authors candidly discuss how issues of race, gender, sexuality, body image, the economy, politics, and labor impact the lives of black women. In "The Dialectics of Black Womanhood" (1979), Bonnie T. Dill explored the contradictions of being a member of a group (e.g., based on racial identity) yet simultaneously being set apart from it by virtue of another identity or consciousness (e.g., gender). Barbara Smith's essay "Toward a Black Feminist Criticism" (1977) is often cited as a major catalyst in opening the field of black women's literature. This essay also presented the first serious discussion of black lesbian writing. In the 1970s, the literature of black feminists concentrated on examining primarily the relationship of race, gender, sexuality, and class.

The 1980s saw black women scholars building a bridge of theory and practice between the ivory tower and the community. Scholars wrote about their pedagogical experiences in such works as Gloria Hull, Patricia Bell-Scott, and Barbara Smith's *All the Women are White, All the Men are Black, But Some of Us are Brave: Black Women's Studies* (1982) and bell hooks's *Talking Back: Thinking Feminist, Talking Black* (1989). Black feminist scholars continued to explore the daily negotiation of multiple identities or intersectionality. For instance, radical black feminist warrior/poet Audre Lorde penned the incomparable *Sister Outsider* (1984), a collection of personal reflections on facing cancer, being part of an interracial lesbian couple raising a son, sex, poetry, rage, and restraint. Other examples include Kimberle Crenshaw's "Demarginalizing the Interaction of Race and Sex: A Black Feminist Critique of Antidiscrimination Doctrine, Feminist Theory, and Anti-Racist Politics" (1983) and Deborah King's "Multiple Jeopardy, Multiple Consciousnesses: The Context of a Black Feminist Ideology" (1988). In the 1980s, black feminist literature illuminated the historical and courageous contributions of black women in American civil rights and women's movements. Paula Gidding's *When and Where I Enter: The Impact of Black Women on Race and Sex in America* (1984) and Angela Davis's *Women, Race, and Class* (1981) are seminal works that carefully contextualized black women's agency in American social movements. In addition, black women scholars critiqued their place in mainstream feminism and pushed themselves to define feminisms (see hooks 1984).

In the 1990s and early twenty-first century, black women scholars focused efforts to articulate the tenets or characteristics of black feminist thought, an Afrocentric standpoint theoretical framework. Patricia Hill Collins published her landmark manifesto, *Black Feminist Thought: Knowledge, Consciousness, and the Politics of Empowerment* (1991), and addressed critiques of this work in *Fighting Words: Black Women and the Search for Justice* (1998). Authors such as Henry Louis Gates, Stanlie James and Abena Busia, Beverly Guy Sheftall, and Joy James and T. Denean Sharpley-Whiting compiled significant anthologies to capture the dynamic, multifaceted pulse of black feminist thought. During this time, black feminists also spotlighted black women's experiences of intimate violence and resistance to center concerns of sexism over racism in the context of violence. Melba Wilson wrote about black women healing and surviving incest. Nellie McKay examined the high-profile sexual harassment case of Anita Hill and Clarence Thomas, and the works of Beth Richie, Traci West, and Carolyn West brought sophisticated theory into a multifaceted analysis of the interlocking roles of racism, classism, and sexism, not only in abusive intimate relationships but also in how those "isms" are perpetrated against abused black women in institutions such as the criminal justice system.

CONTEMPORARY BLACK FEMINISM AND RESEARCH

Black feminist scholars and activists who are currently in their twenties and thirties sometimes are referred to as third-wave black feminists. As Generation X and millennials, third-wave feminists may tap into popular culture (e.g., hip-hop, neo-soul) and art (e.g., performance, photography, dance) to conduct their analyses of black women's lives, activism, and the development of black female radical subjectivity. There are, however, black feminists such as Kimberly Springer who reject the label of "waver" on the basis that "wave ideology" or models may perpetuate the exclusion of multi-ethnic feminists' contributions to the women's movement history and feminist theorizing. In 1995, Kristal Brent Zook published a highly important article that questioned the existence of black feminist activism at the organizational level. Zook chastised black women of the previous generation for failing to organize on behalf of black women and for surrendering leadership roles to serve black male-oriented causes such as the Million Man March. In 2000 Barbara Ransby critiqued Zook, stating that she failed to recognize the positive effects of grassroots, decentralized black feminist organizations on black women and communities.

Methodologically, black feminist thought frameworks are conducive to qualitative, quantitative, or mixed-method designs. Black feminists incorporate traditional data (e.g., interviews, narratives, case studies, oral histories) and non-traditional and non-literal data (e.g., poetry, storytelling, diaries, photographs, creative art) to document the personal experiences of participants. Methodological critiques of the utility of black feminist thought in scientific inquiry have included the difficulty of operationalizing black feminist concepts and the lack of predictive power in regard to behavioral outcomes. Black feminist scholars have attempted to address these critiques in their empirical research. Using survey data from the 1994 National Black Politics Study, political scientists Simien and Clawson conducted a confirmatory factor analysis to examine the structure of black feminist consciousness and its relationship to race consciousness and policy attitudes. Family scholars Few, Stephens, and Rouse Arnett shared their own experiences incorporating black feminist frameworks into their research designs, data collection methods, and representation choices for the resulting metanarratives. Future research directions should include additional attempts to demonstrate the utility of black feminist thought in empirical research and to explore generational change and direction among identified second- and third-wave black feminists.

SEE ALSO: Feminism; Feminism, First, Second, and Third Waves; Feminist Standpoint Theory; Multiracial Feminism; Outsider-Within; Third World and Postcolonial Feminisms/Subaltern; Transnational and Global Feminisms; Womanism

REFERENCES AND SUGGESTED READINGS

Beale, F. M. (1970) Double Jeopardy: To Be Black and Female. In: Bambara, T. C. (Ed.), *The Black Woman: An Anthology*. Signet, New York, pp. 90–100.
Christian, B. (1985) *Black Feminist Criticism: Perspectives on Black Women Writers*. Pergamon, New York.
Collins, P. H. (1991) *Black Feminist Thought: Knowledge, Consciousness, and the Politics of Empowerment*. Routledge, New York.
Collins, P. H. (1998) *Fighting Words: Black Women and the Search for Justice*. University of Minnesota Press, Minneapolis.
Crenshaw, K. (1983) Demarginalizing the Interaction of Race and Sex: A Black Feminist Critique of Antidiscrimination Doctrine, Feminist Theory, and Anti-Racist Politics. In: Weisberg, D. (Ed.), *Feminist Legal Theory: Foundations*. Temple University Press, Philadelphia, pp. 383–411.
Davis, A. (1981) *Women, Race, and Class*. Women's Press, London.
Few, A., Stephens, D., & Rouse-Arnette, M. (2003) Sister-to-Sister Talk: Transcending Boundaries in Qualitative Research with Black Women. *Family Relations* 52: 205–15.
Giddings, P. (1984) *When and Where I Enter: The Impact of Black Women on Race and Sex in America*. William Morrow, New York.
Guy-Sheftall, B. (Ed.) (1995) *Words of Fire: An Anthology of African American Feminist Thought*. New Press, New York.
hooks, b. (1984) *Feminist Theory: From Margin to Center*. South End Press, Boston.
Hull, G., Bell-Scott, P., & Smith, B. (Eds.) (1982) *All the Women are White, All the Men are Black, But Some of Us are Brave: Black Women's Studies*. Feminist Press, New York.
James, J. & Sharply-Whiting, T. D. (Eds.) (2000) *The Black Feminist Reader*. Blackwell, Cambridge, MA.
King, D. (1988) Multiple Jeopardy, Multiple Consciousnesses: The Context of a Black Feminist Ideology. *Signs* 14: 42–72.
Lorde, A. (1984) *Sister Outsider: Essays and Speeches*. Crossing Press, Trumansburg, NY.
Smith, B. (1998) *Writings on Race, Gender, and Freedom: The Truth That Never Hurts*. Rutgers University Press, Piscataway, NJ.
Springer, K. (2002) Third Wave Black Feminism? *Signs* 27: 1060–82.
Walker, A. (1984) *In Search of Our Mother's Garden: Womanist Prose*. Harcourt Brace Jovanovich, San Diego.
Wallace, M. (1978) *Black Macho and the Myth of the Superwoman*. Verso, London.

black urban regime

John Arena

Black urban regime refers to large, majority or near-majority black cities in the United States governed by black mayors. The first examples of a black urban regime were Carl Stokes's and Richard Hatcher's election in Cleveland and Gary, respectively, in the late 1960s. The majority of black urban regimes arose in the 1970s and later. In the late 1980s, 13 US cities were defined as black urban regimes, while in 2001 the number had risen to 19 (Bositis 2002: 11, 26; Reed 1999: 254).

Black urban regime theory addresses the origins, structural constraints, and sociopolitical conflicts faced by black urban regimes. Three key questions guide research on the black urban regime: Why does the regime leadership pursue policies that hurt the material interests of its predominantly black poor and working-class electoral base? How does the regime gain the consent of the black community to a pro-corporate development model? How would a progressive, pro-working-class regime arise in the context of a majority black city?

Analyzing the historical origins of black urban regimes is important for understanding the pro-corporate character they have taken. Although many post-war US cities faced employment losses due to deindustrialization, exodus of affluent, mostly white, residents, and a decimated tax base, majority black cities tend to be the hardest hit by these trends (Horan 2002: 28). In fact, these negative trends are what, in many ways, allow for the ascension of a predominantly black political leadership at the municipal level. Furthermore, by the late 1970s, as several black mayors were coming to power, the federal government began to drastically reduce funding to cities. Thus, there were – and are – strong structural factors that encourage black urban political leaders to pursue a business-oriented "pro-growth" development model. A pro-corporate urban economic development model appears as the only viable strategy to lure investment and jobs back to cities.

Although the structural constraints are important, they are not sufficient to explain the pro-corporate character of the black political leadership. Reed (1988) points to the social origins of the black political class to explain the regressive development model they support. Black political leaders -- even those with a civil rights background – have tended to come from a professional-managerial stratum. Furthermore, many were groomed for political office in federal government and private foundation-funded poverty programs (Reed 1999: 88–9). Thus, their class background, past political formation, and attendant ideological worldview predisposed them to a pro-business agenda.

Further solidifying black middle-class support for the pro-corporate model are the material benefits that accrue. The opening of high-level positions in the public sector, and the awarding of public contracts to African Americans that had previously been limited to whites, has tended to benefit the black middle class. Thus, similar to urban regime theory as developed by Stone (1989), black urban regime theory identifies a dominant *governing coalition*, composed of a black-led public sector and a white-dominated corporate sector. This alliance represents the power structure in majority black cities. Its members cooperate to carry out urban economic regeneration projects.

The governing elite alliance is not without conflict. A major point of contention has been over affirmative action programs in the awarding of contracts. Nonetheless, there tends to be agreement on the overall pro-corporate orientation of the regime.

The focus of *urban regime theory* is to analyze the process of cooperation and conflict between the public and private sector segments of the governing elite. To examine the content of this relationship the major, pro-growth corporate organization is normally studied. For example, in his classic urban regime theory-informed study Stone (1989) analyzed the Central Atlanta Progress (CAP), which was that southern city's most powerful corporate planning organization. In contrast to this research agenda, a distinguishing feature of *black urban regime theory*-informed studies is their focus on the impact of the pro-corporate agenda on black working-class communities and how regime elites legitimate inequality. For example, Oden (1999) found that Oakland's black urban regime delivered only symbolic, rather than substantive, redistributive benefits to poor and black working-class communities. Reed (1987) pointed to the discursive powers of black mayors – in this case, Atlanta's Maynard Jackson – as key to obfuscating the material, class-based distributive stakes embedded in the pro-growth agenda.

There are several theoretical, methodological, and political issues that must be addressed to extend and develop this research agenda. Theoretically, future studies need to draw connections between the meso, or middle-range, level that black urban regime theory operates within and the macro, extra-local-level changes and forces. Lauria (1997) recommends employing regulation theory as one way to make the macro–micro connection. Methodologically, researchers must refine their data-gathering techniques to highlight the key unit of analysis of black urban regime theory-informed studies – the class relationship between the governing elite and the overwhelming black working-class popular base of the regime. To obtain rich data, researchers must develop meaningful relationships of trust with black working-class communities.

The methodological challenges are tied to implementing the political agenda of black urban regime theory. Like all theories, black urban regime theory has a normative or political component. The political goal is to use theory and research to strengthen the capacity of working-class communities to challenge the regressive pro-corporate agenda of the governing elite. Researchers face three challenges to realizing this normative agenda. The first is to allow black working-class communities to define issues that need to be studied. The second is to include workers as participants in research. The third is to develop ways for workers to draw on research findings to improve the political practice of the working-class movement. Arena (2006, forthcoming) has drawn from the political action research model to articulate and implement the embedded political goals of black urban regime theory.

SEE ALSO: Inequality and the City; Metropolis; Race; Social Exclusion; Urban Policy; Urban Renewal and Redevelopment; Urbanization

REFERENCES AND SUGGESTED READINGS

Arena, J. (2006) Repression, Racism and Resistance: The New Orleans Black Urban Regime and a Challenge to Racist Neoliberalism. In: Coates, R. (Ed.), *Race and Ethnicity: Across Time, Space and Discipline*. Brill, Lydon, forthcoming.

Bositis, D. A. (2002) *Latest Report of Black Elected Officials: A Statistical Summary*. Joint Center for Political and Economic Studies, Washington, DC.

Horan, C. (2002) Racializing Regime Politics. *Journal of Urban Affairs* 24(1): 19–33.

Lauria, M. (1997) *Reconstructing Urban Regime Theory*. Sage, London.

Oden, R. S. (1999) Power Shift: A Sociological Study of the Political Incorporation of People of Color in Oakland, California, 1966–1996. University of California, Santa Cruz.

Reed, A. (1987) A Critique of Neo-Progressivism in Theorizing about Local Development Policy: A Case from Atlanta. In: Stone, C. N. & Sanders, H. T. (Eds.), *The Politics of Urban Development*. University of Kansas Press, Lawrence.

Reed, A. (1988) The Black Urban Regime: Structural Origins and Constraints. In: Smith, M. P. (Ed.), *Power, Community, and the City*. Transaction Press, New Brunswick, NJ.

Reed, A. (1999) *Stirrings in the Jug: Black Politics in the Post-Segregation Era*. University of Minnesota Press, London.

Smith, M. P. (2001) *Transnational Urbanism: Locating Globalization*. Blackwell, Oxford.

Stone, C. (1989) *Regime Politics: Governing Atlanta, 1946–1988*. University Press of Kansas, Lawrence.

blasé/neurasthenic personalities

Chris Rojek

The concept of blasé/neurasthenic personalities was coined by the German sociologist Georg Simmel to refer to distinctive psychological responses to modern, metropolitan life. In his masterpiece, *The Philosophy of Money* (1907), Simmel analyzed modern, metropolitan existence in relation to a variety of ubiquitous social effects. Among the most prominent are the fragmentation of relations; the increasing preponderance of technology in everyday life; the leveling effect of monetary exchange transactions; the separation of subjectivity from culture; and the recession of tradition. In these circumstances, Simmel argued, there are strong tendencies for men and women to adopt blasé or neurasthenic characteristics in their personality and interpersonal behavior. The blasé personality is punch-drunk by the ephemerality and instability of modern conditions. They become indifferent to suffering and injustice. They retreat into a cocoon of purely subjective considerations and initiatives. The neurasthenic personality is wired by the impermanence and prolific possibilities offered by modernity. Their behavior is characterized by ceaseless anxiety and nervousness, which prevents them from fully committing to transcendent goals.

Simmel's analysis of the psychology of modernity influenced David Riesman and Christopher Lasch in the 1950s and 1970s, but it only became prominent in sociology and cultural studies during postmodernism and the so-called collapse of grand narratives. Simmel's categories of psychological types captured the romantic uncertainty of living without guarantees and with globalization and disembeddedness. However, as with much in Simmel's work, it offered no politics of social reconstruction.

SEE ALSO: Alienation; Metropolis; Modernity; Simmel, Georg

REFERENCES AND SUGGESTED READINGS

Fribsy, D. (1985) *Fragments of Modernity*. Polity Press, Cambridge.

Frisby, D. (1989) Simmel and Leisure. In: Rojek, C. (Ed.), *Leisure for Leisure*. Macmillan, Basingstoke, pp. 75–91.

Simmel, G. (1907) *The Philosophy of Money*. Routledge, London.

Simmel, G. (1965) *Essays on Sociology, Philosophy and Aesthetics*. Harper & Row, New York.

Simmel, G. (1971) *Individuality and Social Forms*. University of Chicago Press, Chicago.

Blau, Peter (1918–2002)

Omar Lizardo

Peter Blau is one of the most influential figures in post-war American sociology. His long career and range of substantive interests span the range from small-groups and social exchange theory to organizational theory, the analysis of status attainment, and finally general sociological theory. One significant legacy is his macrostructural theory, or as he referred to it in his landmark book *Inequality and Heterogeneity* (1977), his "primitive theory of social structure."

Blau began his sociological training with a Parsonian interest in broad theoretical systems. However, his orientation toward theory was significantly transformed during the course of his training at Columbia University under the tutelage of Paul Lazarsfeld and Robert Merton. From Merton and Lazarsfeld he developed a concern with the measurement of abstract concepts and their connection to theory. Blau is sometimes considered the last great "grand theorist" of twentieth-century American sociology. His notion of grand theoretical sociology as primarily a general, explanatory, and empirical form of doing science continues to form the core of mainstream sociological theory and research into the twenty-first century.

In spite of its apparent "heterogeneity," it can be argued that a single strand runs through Blau's diverse body of work. For Blau, the study of the structural limits posed by large-scale distributions of actors, positions, and resources on the opportunities and choices of individuals constituted the central subject matter of sociology. Nevertheless Blau made seminal contributions to many sociological fields. His life's work can be divided into four major components: status attainment, his work on organizations, his exchange theory, and his macrostructural theory.

STATUS ATTAINMENT AND MOBILITY

Blau and Duncan's classic monograph *The American Occupational Structure* (1967) introduced to a sociological audience multiple regression and path analysis, which is today the bread and butter of quantitative sociology. Blau himself seems to have considered this focus to be only a peripheral afterthought in the context of his other work. In a later recollection he noted that he was urged to undertake a large-scale study of mobility in the American occupational structure since in 1950 none yet existed. He enlisted the help of the legendary Otis Dudley Duncan because he considered his own experience with quantitative analysis inadequate. The book remains a landmark mainly because of its quantitative innovations. Most of its admittedly overly optimistic substantive conclusions regarding a future of increasing mobility and decline of ascription have since then come under criticism.

ORGANIZATIONAL THEORY

Blau's first major contributions to sociology were in the field of organizations. His first major publication – an elaboration of his dissertation research – was *Dynamics of Bureaucracy* (1955), which at the time formed part of a rising post-Weberian wave of organizational studies. This research consisted in exploring how far the received image of the Weberian bureaucracy as an efficient, mechanical system of roles, positions, and duties held up under close scrutiny in the empirical study of social interaction within organizations. Blau (1955) contributed to this strand of research by highlighting the ways in which the real life of the organization was structured along informal channels of interaction and socio-emotional exchange, and how the incipient status systems formed through these back-channels were as important to the continued functioning of these organizations as the formal status structure. Thus, Blau was primarily concerned with the interplay between formal structure, informal practices, and bureaucratic pressures and how these processes affect organizational change.

Blau's second major contribution to organizational analysis centered on the study of the determinants of the "bureaucratic components" of organizations. He collected data on 53 Employment Security Agencies in the US and 1,201 local offices. The major outcome of this work was Blau's (1970) general theory of differentiation in organizations. This article had an immediate impact in the field of organizations in particular and in American sociology in general. It featured for the first time what would become Blau's characteristic style of deductive theorizing. Blau derived several useful generalizations, the most important of which are (1) increasing size results in an increase in the number of distinct positions (differentiation) in an organization at a decreasing rate, and (2) as size increases the administrative component (personnel not directly engaged in production but in coordination) decreases. This article generated a flurry of research attempts to further formalize, test, and qualify the theory. Most of these studies (primarily by Bruce Mayhew and his students) supported Blau's generalizations.

Because organizational theory in sociology moved away from nomothetic generalizations about determinants of intra-organizational structure and to the study of organizational environments, Blau's article only had a brief influence on organizational research. However, as an exemplar of how to do research and how to build theory, and as a way of showing that general and fruitful deductive theory was possible in sociology, Blau's article (and his later macrostructural theory) deeply influenced a generation of researchers. Because Blau's formal style of theorizing was naturally compatible with attempts at mathematical formalization (and both his organizational and later his macrostructural theory were indeed formalized

by mathematical sociologists such as Norman Hummon, Thomas Fararo, and John Skvoretz), it can be said that Blau's work at this stage constituted an important impetus for the development of mathematical sociology as a coherent and productive subfield in American sociology.

EXCHANGE THEORY AND SMALL GROUP BEHAVIOR

From his original study of social activity in bureaucracies, Blau developed a "microstructural" theory of exchange and social integration in small groups (Blau 1960b). His work on this type of non-economic exchange and its interaction with the status and power structure of the group (flows of advice, esteem, and reputation) would later become important in the influential formalization of exchange theory in the hands of Richard Emerson. To this day Blau is seen in social psychology (along with George Homans) as one of the intellectual progenitors of modern exchange theory in structural social psychology.

While this strand of Blau's work may appear anomalous from the point of view of his later focus on macrostructure, it is important not to be misled by the issue of scale (micro versus macro). Even at this early stage Blau showed a predilection for a distinctive style of Durkheimian explanation, in which individual-level outcomes in small groups (competitiveness, cooperativeness, orientation toward peers and clients, etc.) were seen as at least partly derivable from "structural effects" (Blau 1960a) associated with the overall distribution of these qualities in the group, and with the position of the individual in the network of relations of the group.

MACROSTRUCTURAL THEORY

For Blau (1977), social structure consisted of the networks of social relations that organize patterns of interaction across different social positions. This view of social structure was faithful to Radcliffe-Brown's definition of social structure as the network of actually existing relations that connects human beings in a society. Blau broke with Radcliffe-Brown on how he conceptualized the components of social structure. For Blau, the basic components of social structure where not natural persons, but instead social positions. Thus, the "parts" of social structure are classes of people like men and women, rich and poor, etc. The relations between these components are none other than the actual network connections that may (or may not) obtain between members of different positions.

Blau thought that the genesis of social structure can be found whenever an undifferentiated group begins to array itself along some socially relevant distinction. In Blau's view, to speak of social structure is to speak of differentiation among people. By a socially relevant distinction, Blau means a social distinction along some distinguishable social characteristic (age, race, sex, religion, ethnicity, etc.) which comes to determine who interacts with whom. Blau used the term parameter of social structure to refer to socially relevant positions along which people could be classified. For Blau, a particular criterion of classification was not a parameter if it did not actually affect the real social relations of individuals "on the ground."

In Blau's (1974) view, two major classes of parameters could be distinguished: graduated and nominal. Modern society was characterized, following an insight of Simmel's, by the fact that they were composed of (1) a multiplicity of socially relevant positions and (2) that these positions were connected to one another in complex and sometimes mutually contradictory ways, resulting in cross-cutting social circles. Two positions are connected in a mutually contradictory manner if increasing interaction along one distinction leads to decreasing interaction on another. Positions may also be connected in a mutually reinforcing way, whenever interaction along one distinction increases the chances of connecting along some other distinction.

For Blau, one important consequence for rates of intergroup interaction follows from the distribution of people across social positions. The heterogeneity theorem states that increasing heterogeneity across any given dimension of association (more even distribution of people along the "slots" that define a given parameter, such as years of education) increases the probability of intergroup relations.

Thus, in a hypothetical society in which 90 percent of the population has 20 years of education and the other 10 percent has 6 years of education, we should expect less intergroup relations along the education dimension in a society in which people are evenly distributed across this dimension even when holding constant the individual preferences to associate with people of the same educational level. Thus, the lower or higher levels of intergroup contact caused by the distribution of people across positions is a "structural effect" (Blau 1960a) separable from individual-level attributes.

The theory was put to empirical test by Blau and Schwartz (1984), where many of the propositions of the theory found verification with data on rates of intermarriage among different groups in SMSAs in the US. The theory was refined and restated one last time by Blau (1994). At the later stages of his career, Blau attempted partially to reformulate some of the areas of research that he had touched on earlier (such as social exchange, mobility, and organization processes) in terms of his later macrostructural framework. This effort, however, remained partial at best, and met with some empirical disconfirmation. Therefore, a complete macrostructural theory remained outside Blau's grasp.

However, Blau's legacy lives on: his idea of social structure as the distribution of individuals along a multidimensional space (Blau 1977; Blau & Schwartz 1984) has become the central element of McPherson's "structural-ecological" general theory of affiliation, where this multidimensional social space has been rebaptized as Blau Space in his honor. Fararo and Skvoretz have been able to formalize Blau's ideas regarding different interaction probabilities given different distributions of people across social positions and different levels of in-group and out-group preferences, showing it to be formally compatible with Granovetter's strength of weak-ties principle. In this and many other ways, Blau's foundational ideas continue to be the impetus for theoretical development and innovation in contemporary social science.

SEE ALSO: Exchange Network Theory; Merton, Robert K.; Organization Theory; Organizations as Social Structures; Simmel, Georg; Social Exchange Theory; Social Structure

REFERENCES AND SUGGESTED READINGS

Blau, P. M. (1955) *Dynamics of Bureaucracy*. University of Chicago Press, Chicago.

Blau, P. M. (1960a) Structural Effects. *American Sociological Review* 25: 178–93.

Blau, P. M. (1960b) A Theory of Social Integration. *American Journal of Sociology* 65: 545–56.

Blau, P. M. (1965) The Flow of Occupational Supply and Recruitment. *American Sociological Review* 30: 475–90.

Blau, P. M. (1970) A Formal Theory of Differentiation in Organizations. *American Sociological Review* 35: 201–18.

Blau, P. M. (1974) Presidential Address: Parameters of Social Structure. *American Sociological Review* 39: 615–35.

Blau, P. M. (1977) *Inequality and Heterogeneity*. Free Press, New York.

Blau, P. M. (1994) *Structural Contexts of Opportunities*. University of Chicago Press, Chicago.

Blau, P. M. (1995) A Circuitous Path to Macrostructural Theory. *Annual Review of Sociology* 21: 1–19.

Blau, P. M. & Duncan, O. D. (1967) *The American Occupational Structure*. Wiley, New York.

Blau, P. M. & Schwartz, J. E. (1984) *Crosscutting Social Circles: Testing a Macrostructural Theory of Intergroup Relations*. Academic Press, New York.

blockbusting

W. Edward Orser

Real estate blockbusting, pervasive in many American cities in the post-World War II period, is the intentional action of a real estate broker to place an African American resident in a previously all-white neighborhood for the express purpose of the excessive profit to be made by panicking whites into selling low, then in turn charging marked-up prices to incoming minority residents (Helper 1969). The Civil Rights Act (Fair Housing Act) of 1968 declared it an illegal practice "for profit, to induce or attempt to induce" sales and rentals "by representations regarding the entry or prospective entry into the neighborhood of [a] person or persons of a particular race, color, religion, etc." (Section 804 [e]). The 1968 Act, which declared discrimination in residential sales, rentals, or loans illegal, specifically outlawed blockbusting and indirectly barred other discriminatory real estate practices, including steering and redlining.

Rigid adherence to residential segregation designed to maintain a racially separated (dual) housing market paradoxically enabled blockbusting to flourish under certain circumstances. Typically, blockbusters preyed upon the racial prejudices and fears of white residents in segregated neighborhoods by selling or renting to African Americans – or even by spreading rumors of black settlement – to panic property owners unwilling to accept residential integration. Such actions, sometimes referred to as "panic selling" or "panic peddling," severely depressed housing values, enabling the operators to purchase houses well below prior market value. As whites succumbed to blockbusters' tactics, "white flight" often ensued, further depressing the prices they were willing to accept. In turn, blockbusters sold the properties to African American home-seekers, previously denied such residential options within the rigid confines of housing segregation, at markups considerably in excess of normal business margins. The profit from such transactions, which could be considerable, was sometimes referred to as "the color tax" or "black tax," the price African Americans had to pay to gain new housing opportunity. Since prospective African American home buyers often lacked access to conventional financing due to discrimination from mainstream financial organizations, blockbusters also often profited from loan arrangements, including second mortgages and land contracts, which protected their investment but left purchasers exposed to considerable risk.

In the first decades of the twentieth century the growth of African American populations in urban centers as part of the First Great Migration led to early variations by real estate agents dubbed "white blockbusters." Focusing their activities on the margins of formative urban ghettos, these operators recognized the profit to be made in tenement districts like New York's Harlem or Chicago's South Side, where housing values were depressed, of introducing African American tenants, who had little choice historically but to pay substantially higher rents than whites (Osofsky 1963; Philpott 1978).

Blockbusting reached its peak in the United States in the post-World War decades of the 1950s and 1960s, however. During the first half of the twentieth century, the formal and informal mechanisms undergirding residential segregation had hardened, even as African American populations in urban areas increased substantially. Early efforts to assure housing segregation by discriminatory zoning failed court tests, but restrictive covenants on the basis of race or religion were introduced widely into single-family housing neighborhoods and subject to enforcement by community improvement associations. Not until 1948 in *Shelly* v. *Kramer* did the US Supreme Court rule that restrictive covenants were unenforceable. Federal mortgage loan programs, introduced in the 1930s as part of the New Deal effort to stimulate the housing industry and encourage homeownership, not only sanctioned but also encouraged residential segregation. Policies intended to protect the risk of lenders "redlined" neighborhoods where racial mixing occurred, considering them likely to become unstable and therefore poor investments, and prevented African Americans from gaining access to conventional financing in such areas (Jackson 1985; Massey & Denton 1993). The mainstream real estate industry, members of the National Association of Real Estate Brokers (claiming the title "Realtors"), was equally committed to preserving residential segregation. Its "Code of Ethics," adopted in 1924 and continued in much the same form into the 1950s, contained a section which committed its members to an anti-blockbusting standard, but left a backdoor opportunity to small firms, white and black, which did not – or could not – belong to the organization and therefore were not bound by such guidelines. Finally, violence and the threat of violence often played a role in preventing African American settlement in white neighborhoods.

The mechanisms of segregation held remarkably firm in cities across the nation, even as African American urban populations swelled during and after World War II in the era of the Second Great Migration. Equally remarkable, however, was how rapidly they crumbled during the post-war decades. While blockbusting likely accelerated rather than caused the episodes of rapid racial transition that ultimately led to an expanded but still racially segregated ghetto, it played a critical role in a process which unfolded with extraordinary similarity in city after city – New York, Chicago, Cleveland, Detroit, Boston, Baltimore, St. Louis, Kansas City, Dallas-Ft. Worth. With the mainstream real estate and finance industry focused on new suburban housing, underwritten by favorable federal policies and generally available only to whites, blockbusters and real estate speculators reaped profits from the exceptional convergence of white prejudice and African American need. Especially vulnerable to blockbuster tactics were single-family neighborhoods adjacent to the traditional ghetto; however, blockbusting triggered racial change at such a rapid rate in some instances that areas well beyond the earlier informal boundaries soon experienced its effects. While African Americans gained improved housing opportunities, neighborhood amenities, and living space, the instability of neighborhood turnover, the cost of inflated prices and risky financing, and the commercial disinvestment which often accompanied racial change frequently produced resegregation and subsequent socioeconomic decline.

Localities sometimes attempted to curb or prevent blockbusting practices, adopting ordinances intended to quell panic by limiting "for sale" signs or various forms of solicitation. African American real estate agents and others sometimes challenged local restrictions as unreasonable restraints on their legitimate business and the interests of their clients. In some cities, firms accused of blockbusting were sued for unethical business practices and exploitative transactions. Fair housing organizations in localities like Cleveland and Chicago sought to combat real estate practices which adversely affected prospects for residential segregation, including blockbusting, with affirmative programs aimed at achieving stable levels of racial diversity.

Following adoption of the Fair Housing Act, flagrant instances of blockbusting have declined, though steering continues to be more pervasive. The anti-blockbusting provisions of the law were upheld by federal court decisions in 1971 (*United States* v. *Mitchell* and *United States* v. *Bob Lawrence Realty*) and again in 1975 (*Zuch* v. *Hussey*) (Metcalf 1988). The weak enforcement mechanisms of the original law were strengthened by the 1988 Fair Housing Act.

SEE ALSO: Race (Racism); Redlining; Restrictive Covenants; Steering, Racial Real Estate; Urban Policy; Urbanization

REFERENCES AND SUGGESTED READINGS

Helper, R. (1969) *Racial Policies and Practices of Real Estate Brokers*. University of Minnesota Press, Minneapolis.

Jackson, K. T. (1985) *Crabgrass Frontier: The Suburbanization of the United States*. Oxford University Press, New York.

Massey, D. S. & Denton, N. A. (1993) *American Apartheid: Segregation and the Making of the Underclass*. Harvard University Press, Cambridge, MA.

Metcalf, G. R. (1988) *Fair Housing Comes of Age*. Greenwood Press, New York.

Osofsky, G. (1963) *Harlem: The Making of a Ghetto*. Harper & Row, New York.

Philpott, T. L. (1978) *The Slum and the Ghetto: Immigrants, Blacks, and Reformers in Chicago, 1880–1930*. Oxford University Press, New York.

Blumer, Herbert George (1900–87)

Thomas J. Morrione

Herbert George Blumer, tutored by his parents to be keenly observant of society, was early on a serious scholar of history and philosophy. He emerged from rural Missouri to study at Chicago under George Herbert Mead already enamored of the prospects for examining and explaining the interactions among human beings and the world. He was fortunate as an undergraduate at the University of Missouri to be able to work with Charles Ellwood, a sociologist, and Max Meyer, a psychologist, both of whom nurtured his progress toward Phi Beta Kappa recognition.

Blumer was always grounded in the real world of labor and economics. He had to drop out of high school to help in his father's woodworking shop and worked summers as a roustabout to pay for his college education at the University of Missouri (BA 1921, MA 1922). He later taught part-time and played professional football (1925–33) with the Chicago Cardinals while he worked toward his PhD at Chicago. He then taught at Chicago from 1928 until 1951 when he was appointed the first chair of the Department of Sociology at the University of California at Berkeley, a post he held until he retired in 1967. With Emeritus Professor status until 1986, he remained actively engaged in writing and research until shortly before his death. Throughout his long career Blumer combined research and theory with practical involvements in the public and private sectors: with the Department of State's Office of War Information (1943–5), as a charter member of the US Board of Arbitration, and as chair of the Board of Arbitration for the US Steel Corporation and the United Steel Workers of America (1945–7). He headed various professional organizations including the American Sociological Association (1956), UC Berkeley's Institute of Social Sciences (1959–65), and the Pacific Sociological Association (1971–2) and was regularly recognized for his achievements, including the Career of Distinguished Scholarship Award from the American Sociological Association in 1983. In each role, he strived to foster and focus scholarly debates on topics that combined theoretical relevance with practical significance (see Morrione 1999 and Blumer 2004 for additional biographical information).

Blumer's (1969) preeminent contribution to sociology and social psychology is his formulation of a distinctive theoretical and methodological perspective known as "symbolic interactionism." Based on the philosophy and social psychology of both George Herbert Mead and John Dewey, it is firmly grounded in pragmatists' assumptions about human action and the nature of the self. The theory underlies his lifelong critique of mainstream, deductively formulated, positivistic, and structural-functional sociology.

In building this theoretical perspective and its associated methodological position, Blumer (2004) drew heavily from the work of Mead to present social action and social structure as ongoing processes of individual and collective action predicated on the uniquely human capacity for self-indication. Symbolic interactionism articulates Blumer's rationale for rejecting theoretical stances not based on close examination of individual and collective human experience. He particularly disdained theories that ignore or belittle the role individuals play in creating, sustaining, and changing the social world through the ubiquitous processes of self-indication, interpretation, and action. His wide-ranging macro- and micro-oriented research emphasized the empirical focus of symbolic interactionism (Prus 1996), its anti-positivist, anti-behaviorist perspective, and its utility as an all-encompassing theory of human action (Maines 1988; Morrione 1988).

Blumer (1969) sets out the perspective's three basic premises in *Symbolic Interactionism: Perspective and Method*: (1) people act individually and collectively on the basis of the meanings of "objects" in their world; (2) the meanings of these material (an automobile, a pencil, a statue), abstract (justice, truth, love), or social (a friend, soldiers, a parent) objects are constructed in encounters people have with one another; and (3) during interaction people use interpretive processes to change these meanings. He then discusses the "root images" of the perspective: human group life, interactions, objects, actors, actions, and interconnections among individual and group acts or lines of action.

Blumer always sees human group life, including social structures, in terms of action that occurs as people endeavor to manage situations. As individuals construct acts they define the situations they confront and create definitions of reality to guide action. When the meaning of a gesture is shared between or among people it becomes, as Mead says, "significant," enabling communication, concerted action, and ultimately, the formation of social organization.

For Blumer, like Mead and Dewey, neither action nor interactions are, as behaviorists may argue, mere responses to stimuli; they are outcomes of processes of indication and interpretation that mediate between stimulus and response. These processes result in the creation of symbols or stimuli to which meanings are attached. All Blumer's sociology rests on this pivotal detail. The fact that people point out or indicate things to themselves, attach meanings to them, and thereby create objects, would be of little significance without the understanding that people act on the basis of the meanings of the objects in their life experience. Without self-indication and symbolic interaction, there would be no social world.

Methodologically, the indication–definition–action link is key because it means that in order to understand why individuals or groups do whatever they do, one has to grasp the meaning of the objects in their world, as they define them and as they bring them to bear on action. For Blumer, this means that careful examination of processes of collective definition is central to any work that investigates macro structural phenomena, including social change, industrialization, social problems, or social movements.

The idea that one must strive to see the world from the point of view of those experiencing it lies at the heart of contemporary ethnographic research and attends to Robert E. Park's warning about problems created by substituting the views of the researcher for the views of the participants. Blumer similarly valued Charles H. Cooley and W. I. Thomas's understanding of action-related interpretive and definitional processes, and crafted a pragmatist's version of Cooley's "sympathetic introspection." Blumer's view defines social reality as more than a mental phenomenon and serves as a basic element in ethnographic research.

Blumer contends that action is formed and guided through processes of role-taking based on indication, self-interaction, and object and situation definition. To create or "build up" an act an actor must, wittingly or not, point things out to him/herself and anticipate what the other(s) might do in turn as they regard the projected act. Being able to be an object to oneself, possessing a self, allows this to occur. Acts are, according to Blumer, formed through a process of ongoing definition and interpretation and have infinitely variable careers. Some acts are linked together as people "fit" their lines of action together. These "joint acts," as he calls them, are the essence of social organization and social structures such as marriage, a corporate board meeting, a Senate hearing, a protest march, or a multinational disaster relief effort. Joint acts, made up of acts predicated on individual and collective definitions, also present "obdurate" realities that exist in their own right, apart from the ways people confronting them may wish to see them.

Blumer espouses a distinctly non-reified definition of social structures as processes involving action and a recursive model of society conceived of as a "network of interaction." He depicts society, not as a system with innate needs striving to maintain equilibrium as functionalists do, but rather as a dynamic "framework" comprised of "acting units" (individuals, interest groups, organizations, communities) "interlinked" through symbolic interaction and "joint activity" meeting and handling a never-ending stream of situations within which individual and collective acts of all sizes and durations occur. This view facilitates analyses of macro social phenomena (Lyman 1988). Although Blumer (1969: 57) argues that sociology should concern itself with "molar parts or aspects" of society like "institutions, stratification arrangements, class systems, divisions of labor, [and] large-scale corporate units" lodged within it, he employs these conventional terms in an unconventional way, rejecting the notion that they are abstract forces or variables capable of *causing* individual or collective acts.

Blumer believed that the self, through interpreting and defining whatever is encountered in situations, allows people to *construct* action and that all structures, including culture, norms, or biological and psychological conditions, affect, but do not determine, action. In *Industrialization as an Agent of Social Change* (1990), he says that industrialization plays a "neutral role" in shaping human behavior; it does not determine it. Industrialization impacts society as people who confront its aspects imagine the potential impact and assess the consequences according to their own world of meaning.

Using this fundamental premise Blumer crafted major and often discipline-defining analyses of a host of subjects that included collective behavior, social movements, fashion, race relations, industrial and labor relations, social problems, morale, public opinion, social attitudes, social change, public sector social science research, and social psychology. Consistent with his perspective, he assigned social interaction the central role in creating, maintaining, and changing social reality. Blumer's

(1939) analysis of collective behavior and social movements, for instance, foreshadows major themes in "resource mobilization" and "new movement" theory while directing inquiry into processes of individual and social definition and group conflicts revolving around cultural, ethnic, and economic bases of power, any of which might spur individuals and groups to contest the status quo.

Race relations was a hot topic at the University of Chicago; Robert Park, Louis Wirth, Robert Redfield, Everett C. Hughes, as well as Blumer, studied it. He saw race prejudice as motivated by a "sense of group position" and reflected in a "color line" embodying socially constructed images of group dominance and subordination. These images, Blumer (1958) observed, emerge from a collective process of definition and comparison, framing acts that eventuate in social structural arrangements supporting racism. His analysis challenges psychological and psychoanalytic models of race prejudice that locate its origins in psychological phenomena such as personality traits or attitudes. Blumer, instead, emphasized the value of a macro-structural (Lyman 1984) historical sociological perspective sensitive to processes of social interaction and individual and collective definition.

Although symbolic interactionism seems likely to continue to draw criticism from positivists, structuralists, and others who espouse methodologies that are more removed from the actualities of human activity, reflection, and interaction, its assumptions and central concepts inform a wide range of empirically grounded ethnographic depictions of "structure-as-action" as well as specific considerations of the self, human activity, and interchanges as meaningful, adjustive processes.

Building on the conceptual and methodological emphases in Herbert Blumer's work, Patricia and Peter Adler, Howard S. Becker, Gary Allen Fine, John Lofland, Lyn H. Lofland, Stanford M. Lyman, David R. Maines, Thomas J. Morrione, Robert Prus, Clinton Sanders, Tamotsu Shibutani, Anselm Strauss, and Jacqueline Wiseman, among others, have contributed notably to the interactionist perspective. Readers may refer to their works for a fuller sense of what has become known as Blumerian or Chicago-style symbolic interaction.

Attending to individual and collective action, regardless of the subject matters or interactional features at hand, Herbert Blumer not only emphasizes the importance of comprehending and examining social reality as it is developed within the emergent flow of situations experienced and adjustively handled by people in ever shifting arenas in which they find themselves, but he also stresses the need for developing a set of trans-situational or generic social processes each of which is to be informed by examining human group life in the instances in which it takes place.

SEE ALSO: Cooley, Charles Horton; Dewey, John; Mead, George Herbert; Park, Robert E. and Burgess, Ernest W.; Pragmatism; Symbolic Interaction

REFERENCES AND SUGGESTED READINGS

Blumer, H. (1939) Collective Behavior. In: Park, R. E. (Ed.), *An Outline of the Principles of Sociology*. Barnes and Noble, New York, pp. 219–80.

Blumer, H. (1958) Race Prejudice as a Sense of Group Position. *Pacific Sociological Review* 1: 3–7.

Blumer, H. (1969) *Symbolic Interactionism: Perspective and Method*. Prentice-Hall, Englewood Cliffs, NJ.

Blumer, H. (1990) *Industrialization as an Agent of Social Change*. Ed. D. R. Maines & T. J. Morrione. Aldine de Gruyter, Hawthorne, NY.

Blumer, H. (2004) *George Herbert Mead and Human Conduct*. Ed. T. J. Morrione. AltaMira Press, Walnut Creek, CA.

Lyman, S. (1984) Interactionism and the Study of Race Relations at the Macro-Sociological Level: The Contribution of Herbert Blumer. *Symbolic Interaction* 7(4): 107–20.

Lyman, S. (1988) Symbolic Interactionism and Macrosociology. *Sociological Forum* 3(2): 295–301.

Maines, D. R. (1988) Myth, Text, and Interactionist Complicity in the Neglect of Blumer's Macro Sociology. *Symbolic Interaction* 11: 43–57.

Morrione, T. J. (1988) Herbert G. Blumer (1900–1987): A Legacy of Concepts, Criticisms, and Contributions. *Symbolic Interaction* 11: 1–12.

Morrione, T. J. (1999) Blumer, Herbert George. In: Garraty, J. & Carnes, M. (Eds.), *American National Biography*, 24 vols. Oxford University Press, New York, pp. 73–6.

Prus, R. (1996) *Symbolic Interaction and Ethnographic Research*. SUNY Press, Albany, NY.

Boas, Franz (1858–1942)

Bernd Weiler

Franz Boas, born in Minden, Westphalia, is commonly regarded as the most influential figure of American anthropology in the first third of the twentieth century. Raised in an assimilated Jewish family, which had strong sympathies for the liberal ideals of the revolution of 1848, Boas studied natural sciences and mathematics at the universities of Heidelberg, Bonn, and Kiel, graduating in 1881. In a complex intellectual "odyssey" he abandoned his materialistic *Weltanschauung* and, under the influence of neo-Kantianism, shifted his attention from the field of physics to Fechnerian psychophysics to Ratzel's anthropogeography, and finally, several years after graduating from university, to ethnology (Stocking 1982: 133–60). In 1883–4 he spent a year among the Inuit of Baffinland to examine the influence of the natural environment on the life of the people. Upon his return to Germany Boas published the results of his first fieldwork, obtained the docentship for geography at the University of Berlin, intensified his relationship with the leading German physical anthropologist, pathologist, and liberal politician R. Virchow, and worked as an assistant of A. Bastian at the *Royal Ethnographical Museum* at Berlin. Fascinated by the museum's collection of North Pacific Coast culture, Boas went to do fieldwork in British Columbia in 1886. The culture of the Native Americans of the Northwest Coast was to remain at the center of Boas's ethnographic research throughout his life. Returning to New York in 1887, Boas accepted the position as an assistant editor of the journal *Science* and, for political, professional, and personal reasons, decided to settle in the New World. From 1889 to 1892 he taught anthropology at Clark University, supervising the first American PhD in anthropology. From 1892 to 1894 he worked as an anthropologist at the *World's Columbian Exposition* at Chicago. While serving as a curator of the American Museum of Natural History (1896–1905) Boas organized the famous Jesup North Pacific Expedition, which set out to study the historical relationships between Asian and North American peoples. In 1896 he became a lecturer of physical anthropology and in 1899 was appointed the first full professor of anthropology at Columbia University, a post he held until his retirement in 1936–7.

As a key figure in the professionalization of anthropology Boas helped to establish the American Anthropological Association as well as other anthropological organizations, founded and edited various anthropological journals, helped to organize the International School of American Archaeology and Ethnology in Mexico, and taught the first generations of academic anthropologists in the US, many of whom went on to establish and hold posts at prestigious anthropological departments and institutions. Apart from his numerous scientific writings, Boas was also a well-known public intellectual who spoke and wrote on a variety of socially contested issues such as racism, nationalism, and immigration. His name has remained closely associated with the doctrine of cultural determinism and the anti-racist movement.

Though few would deny the importance of Boas's role in the history of anthropology, opinions diverge when it comes to judging his scientific accomplishments. Those viewing his legacy in a positive light argue that his rigorous criticism of social evolutionism (the dominant paradigm in anthropology around 1900), his rejection of racial explanations of cultural differences, his emphasis on the fundamental sameness of the human mind the world over, his idea that race, language, and culture were distinct categories which had to be studied independently of each other, and the prominence given to diffusion and to the historicity of so-called "primitive" societies contributed decisively to the modern relativistic and pluralistic concept of culture (Stocking 1982). Because of his insistence on grasping the Native's point of view and uncovering the subconscious categories underlying the Native's language, Boas is also credited with laying the foundations for the hermeneutic method in anthropology. As a physical anthropologist Boas is said to have proven the instability of the human type in general and of the cephalic index in particular. Finally, it is argued that by his continuous warning against "premature" theories and by calling for extensive fieldwork

and "painstaking" data collection, Boas set new standards of proof, put an end to "armchair anthropology," and became a leader of the scientific revolution in anthropology in the early twentieth century.

Critics of the Boasian tradition argue that as an ethnographer Boas was unable to synthesize his vast collection of data and to present a coherent picture of the cultures he studied (White 1963). Furthermore, his overall idiographic orientation, his deep-seated belief that facts will eventually speak for themselves, and his tendency to take one negative instance to discard established theories are said to have hampered theory building in anthropology. In recent years doubts have also been raised about the accuracy of Boas's data in his famous study on the changes of immigrants' head shapes. These doubts have reinforced the criticism that Boas's cultural determinist stance, which was most fully developed by his students Benedict and Mead, suffers from a severe ideological bias, namely from the neglect of biology and the strong preference of nurture over nature.

SEE ALSO: Anthropology, Cultural and Social: Early History; Biosociological Theories; Cultural Relativism; Culture; Mead, Margaret; Race; Race (Racism); Scientific Racism

REFERENCES AND SUGGESTED READINGS

Andrews, H. A. et al. (1943) Bibliography of Franz Boas. In: Kroeber, A. L. (Ed.), Franz Boas, 1858–1942. *American Anthropological Association*, Memoir 61, Vol. 45, Nr. 3, Part 2, pp. 67–109.

Boas, F. (1938 [1911]) *The Mind of Primitive Man.* Macmillan, New York.

Boas, F. (1945) *Race and Democratic Society.* Augustin, New York.

Boas, F. (1982 [1940]) *Race, Language, and Culture.* University of Chicago Press, Chicago.

Cole, D. (1999) *Franz Boas: The Early Years, 1858–1906.* University of Washington Press, Seattle.

Hyatt, M. (1990) *Franz Boas, Social Activist: The Dynamics of Ethnicity.* Greenwood Press, New York.

Stocking, G. W. (1982 [1968]) *Race, Culture, and Evolution: Essays in the History of Anthropology.* University of Chicago Press, Chicago.

Stocking, G. W. (Ed.) (1989 [1974]) *A Franz Boas Reader: The Shaping of American Anthropology,*

1883–1911. University of Chicago Press (Midway Reprint), Chicago.

Stocking, G. W. (ed.) (1996) *Volksgeist as Method and Ethic. Essays on Boasian Ethnography and the German Anthropological Tradition*. University of Wisconsin Press, Madison.

White, L. A. (1963) *The Ethnography and Ethnology of Franz Boas*. Texas Memorial Museum, Austin.

body, abominations of the

Debra Gimlin

Erving Goffman (1963) describes three types of "stigma," or attributes that are socially discrediting: violations of accepted behavior or belief, membership in a despised national, religious, or racial group, and abominations of the body. The final category involves physical characteristics that compromise bodily appearance or functioning. Whether voluntarily or involuntarily acquired, abominations of the body can be regarded as a form of deviance. Like the other types of stigma, undesirable physical characteristics isolate some individuals, disqualifying them from "full social acceptance" (p. 1). Everything about the stigmatized person is interpreted in light of the negative trait, so that interaction with the non-stigmatized is often awkward and uncertain. Tension is manifest in people's tendency to avoid eye contact, make guarded references to the stigma, or avoid everyday words that suddenly become taboo; it leads both parties to consider avoiding or withdrawing from encounters.

Two main types of bodily abomination are *violations of aesthetic norms* and *physical disability*. Aesthetic norms are standards for appearance, including height, weight, and the absence of disfigurement. Individuals whose body deviates from the norms of their society are often treated as less than fully human. Examples include uncircumcised females in many African countries and hermaphrodites (who are born with both male and female sexual characteristics) in the West. Conversely, societies reward persons who conform to aesthetic standards. The tendency to link physical attractiveness with positive characteristics and life outcomes

has been documented since the 1970s (Dion et al. 1972). In particular, physical attractiveness increases perceived sociability and popularity (Eagley et al. 1991). There are concrete benefits as well; attractive people earn higher salaries (Frieze et al. 1991) and report having more sexual partners (Berscheid & Walster 1974).

The second category of bodily stigma, physical disability, refers to the difficulties that impaired persons face in engaging with their environment and their exclusion from full social participation (Oliver 1996). Whether impairment becomes disability depends largely on societal context – not only structural and environmental factors, but also imagery and attitudes about impairment. In some countries, injury and illness prevention campaigns may actually foster the notion that physical impairment is intolerable (Wang 1992). In addition, research indicates that "able-bodied" Americans prefer to avoid impaired people, as evidenced by their stated preference to work with, live next door to, and socialize with other "able-bodied" individuals (Katz 1981).

Some bodily abominations are more discrediting than others. For example, paralysis may be more stigmatizing than shortness due to its greater visibility, obtrusiveness, and perceived consequences for functioning. Beliefs about the bearer's culpability – be they accurate or not – also influence reactions to stigma. Obesity is often attributed to self-indulgence and laziness, even though researchers are unsure about what makes some people fatter than others (Grogan 1999). At the same time, the stigmatized are not always held responsible for bodily abominations that are the unintended consequences of voluntary acts. The amputated limb of a professional mountaineer, for instance, is readily seen as evidence of courage and competitive spirit. Ultimately, whether one attaches blame to stigma is largely a matter of cultural context.

Individuals respond differently to the social consequences of their bodily abomination. Some internalize the negative attitudes of others, believing that they deserve to be stigmatized. Many obese people, for instance, develop feelings of self-loathing. Like the majority, they too come to see themselves as slothful and undisciplined (Cahnman 1968). Other individuals respond by forming collectivities or engaging in political action. In recent decades, racial minorities, homosexuals, and the disabled have all fought for equal access to material and cultural resources, claiming that their perceived stigma is an illegitimate basis for social exclusion. Finally, some groups consciously adopt stigmatizing physical markers as a form of political protest. The tattooing, facial piercing, and Native American "Mohawk" hairstyles worn by 1970s British "punks," for example, have been described as expressions of social disaffection and rebellion (Hebdige 1979). Similarly, some contemporary body modifiers use "tribal style" scarification, branding, tongue-splitting, and genital piercing to convey solidarity with indigenous peoples and establish membership in a subcultural community (Pitts 2003). Such activities are becoming increasingly mainstream, however, and questions have been raised about their efficacy as a form of political resistance (Kleese 1999). Nonetheless, given that many body modifiers understand their abominations as a means of valorizing physical difference and conveying cultural dissent, the significance of these practices remains open to interpretation, at least for the time being.

SEE ALSO: Body and Cultural Sociology; Body Modification; Body and Society; Deviance; Goffman, Erving; Identity, Deviant; Labeling; Stigma

REFERENCES AND SUGGESTED READINGS

Berscheid, E. & Walster, E. H. (1974) Physical Attractiveness. In: Berkowitz, L. (Ed.), *Advances in Experimental Social Psychology*, 7th edn. Academic Press, New York, pp. 158–215.
Cahnman, W. J. (1968) The Stigma of Obesity. *Sociological Quarterly* 9(3): 283–99.
Dion, K., Berscheid, E., & Walster, E. (1972) What is Beautiful is Good. *Journal of Personality and Social Psychology* 24: 285–90.
Eagley, A., Ashmore, R., Makhijani, M., et al. (1991) What is Beautiful is Good But. . .: A Meta-Analytic Review of Research on the Physical Attractiveness Stereotype. *Psychological Bulletin* 110: 109–28.
Frieze, I. F., Olson, J. E., & Russell, J. (1991) Attractiveness and Income for Men and Women in Management. *Journal of Applied Social Psychology* 21: 1039–57.

Goffman, E. (1963) *Stigma: Notes on the Management of Spoiled Identity*. Prentice-Hall, Englewood Cliffs, NJ.
Grogan, S. (1999) *Body Image: Body Dissatisfaction in Men, Women and Children*. Routledge, London.
Hebdige, D. (1979) *Subculture: The Meaning of Style*. Routledge, London.
Katz, I. (1981) *Stigma: A Social Psychological Analysis*. Lawrence Erlbaum, Hillsdale, NJ.
Kleese, C. (1999) "Modern Primitivism": Non-Mainstream Body Modification and Racialized Representation. *Body and Society* 5(2–3): 15–38.
Oliver, M. (1996) *Understanding Disability*. Macmillan, London.
Pitts, V. (2003) *In the Flesh: The Cultural Politics of Body Modification*. Palgrave Macmillan, New York.
Wang, C. (1992) Culture, Meaning and Disability: Injury Prevention Campaigns and the Production of Stigma. *Social Science and Medicine* 35: 1093–102.

body and cultural sociology

Bryan S. Turner

Diverse theoretical traditions have been influential in the development of the contemporary sociology of the body, such as philosophical anthropology, Marxist humanism, and phenomenology. However, Michel Foucault (1926–84) has been a dominant influence in late twentieth-century historical and sociological approaches. His research on sexuality, medicine, and discipline gave rise to a general theory of the government of the body. The distinction between the discipline of the individual body ("the anatomo-politics of the body") and regulatory controls ("a bio-politics of the population") in *The History of Sexuality* (1978) stimulated a general sociological investigation of "governmentality" (Burchell et al. 1991). Systematic sociological interest in the body began in the 1980s with *The Body and Society* Turner 1984) and *Five Bodies* (O'Neill 1985). The journal *Body and Society* was launched in 1995 to cater for this expanding academic market.

Taking a wider perspective, there has been a persistent but erratic and uncertain interest from symbolic interactionism in body, identity, self, and interaction. Erving Goffman in *The Presentation of Self in Everyday Life* (1959) demonstrated the importance of the body for identity in disruptions to interaction. Recognition of the need to manage bodily functions to avoid embarrassment was an important consequence of Goffman's approach. While the body began to appear in the study of micro-interactions, it also had major implications for the historical sociology of the norms of civilized behavior undertaken by Norbert Elias in *The Civilizing Process* (1978). The training of the body, especially in relation to martial arts, dance, and general comportment, was studied by Elias in the transformation of court society. Domestic utensils, such as the fork or spittoon, were important features of the regulation of manners through the training of the body. By the 1990s, the history of the body had become a major academic development in research on sexuality, culture, and the representation of the human body.

Academic interest in the body was a response to significant changes in post-war society, namely, the rise of consumerism and the growth of leisure industries. In the nineteenth century, the body was an implicit problem of economic theory in relation to labor as a factor of production. The issue was to make the body productive by increasing its efficiency through training, regulation, and management. Diet was a government of the body, and the efficiency of the human body was increased by correct rationing, exercise, and dietary control (Turner 1992). Taylorism in the management of labor in factory conditions would be another example, and domestic science for girls in schools was recognized as a method of making the working-class body more healthy and efficient. In the 1920s, the eugenic management of the body became an important part of government policy in societies such as Turkey, Sweden, and Germany. Fascism in Italy also sponsored mass sport and gymnastics as a method of disciplining populations and of incorporating the working class into fascist aesthetics.

In the late twentieth century, there was increasing social and economic emphasis on leisure and consumption rather than production. The growth of a new hedonistic culture was identified by Daniel Bell in *The Cultural Contradictions of Capitalism* (1976). Bell described new contradictions in a society that still required a disciplined labor force, but also encouraged and promoted hedonism through advertising, credit, and consumerism. In a neglected article on the "expressive revolution," Talcott Parsons (1974) noted a shift away from the cognitive-rational components of culture to the affective-expressive elements. He suggested that countercultural religious movements would articulate the new quest for self-enjoyment, gratification, glorification of the self, and "pure love." Leisure industries, mass consumption, and extended credit have developed in tandem with the emphasis on youthfulness, activism, and the body beautiful. The body became a major conduit for the commodification of the everyday world and a symbol of the youth cultures of post-war society. In addition, aging, disease, and death no longer appear to be immutable facts about the human condition but contingent possibilities that are constantly transformed by medical science. Cosmetic surgery has become a growth industry in western societies through which the body can be constructed. These cosmetic practices have become the target of the ironic surgical drama of the French artist Orlan, whose facial reconstruction is filmed as an artistic performance.

The post-war baby boomers became the social carriers of a popular culture that focused on the athletic, groomed, and sexual body as an icon of liberalism and the do-it-yourself culture that followed the Events of 1968. There are two salient social phenomena that illustrate these developments in consumerism – the global growth of mass sport, especially international football, and popular dance. Football stars, such as David Beckham, are the new celebrities whose bodies are an essential marketing device for major football teams. The creation of dance fashions from disco to "storm rave" and the transformation of venues from the dance halls of the 1950s to the club experience of the 1990s created social spaces for the expressive and erotic body. Popular dance forms have become a global "dancescape" in which the body is sexually charged as part of the gay scene. Finally, the playful body, the body as a personal project of self-development, the eroticism of bodily experience, and the erosion of a sharp division between straight and gay bodies have been associated with the postmodernization of society. The postmodern body is one that can be endlessly recreated and reshaped.

FOUR PERSPECTIVES ON THE BODY: CONSTRUCTION, REPRESENTATION, EXPERIENCE, AND BODY TECHNIQUES

We can usefully identify four theoretical perspectives in the sociology of the body. The first shows that the body is not a natural phenomenon but is socially constructed. The second considers how the body is a representation of social relations of power. The third examines the phenomenology of the lived body, or the experience of embodiment in the everyday world. The final perspective, which has been significantly influenced by anthropology, looks at the body as a collection of practices or techniques.

Firstly, feminist theory in particular examined the social construction of the body. For example, Simone de Beauvoir in *The Second Sex* (1972) argued that women are not born but become women through social and psychological processes that construct them as essentially female. Her work inaugurated a research tradition concentrating on the social production of differences in gender and sexuality. The basic contribution of feminist theories of the body has been to social constructionism, that is, the differences between male and female bodies that we take for granted as if they were facts of nature are socially produced. Feminism in the 1970s was important in establishing the difference between biologically determined sex and the social construction of gender roles and sexual identities. Empirical research has subsequently explored how the social and political subordination of women is expressed in psychological depression and physical illness. Creative research examined anorexia nervosa, obesity, and eating disorders such as Susan Bordo's *Unbearable Weight* (1993). There have also been important historical studies of anorexia, but the popular literature was influenced by Susan Orbach's *Fat is a Feminist Issue* (1985). Research on the body in popular culture has explored how women's bodies are literally constructed as consumer objects. For example, Lolo Ferrari had her breasts enlarged by silicon implants and appeared as a comical character on Channel 4's "Eurotrash" show. With her massive breasts, Lolo had herself become, partly ironically and partly tragically, consumer trash. Although feminism has been critical of the commercialization of the female body, postmodern irony often makes the classification of the body as a consumer object problematic and uncertain. Madonna is simultaneously religious icon, social critic, and consumer success.

Secondly, the body is often discussed as a cultural representation of social organization. For example, the head is employed as a metaphor of government and the word "corporation" to describe the modern company has its etymological origins in bodily metaphors. In the anthropological tradition, the divisions of the body are used to make moral distinctions between good and bad. For example, left-handedness represents things that are sinister. Research on tattooing shows how the skin is both a physical and cultural boundary in which tattoos are markers of inclusion and exclusion. Sociologists have studied how the body enters into political discourse as a representation of power, and how power is exercised over the body. Following Foucault, historical research has shown how representations of the body are the result of relations of power, particularly between men and women. One classic illustration is the historical argument that anatomical maps of the human body vary between societies in terms of the dominant discourse of gender.

Thirdly, the concept of the "lived body" was developed by the French philosopher Maurice Merleau-Ponty in his *Phenomenology of Perception* (1982). In developing the phenomenology of the everyday world, he was concerned to understand human consciousness, perception, and intentionality. His work was original in applying Edmund Husserl's phenomenology to intentional consciousness but from the perspective of corporeal existence. He wanted to describe the lived world without the use of the conventional dualism between subject and object. Hence, Merleau-Ponty was critical of the legacy of René Descartes's *cogito ergo sum* ("I think, therefore I am") that became the foundation of the dualism between mind and body. Merleau-Ponty developed the idea of the "body-subject" that is always situated in a social reality. Rejecting behavioral and mechanistic approaches, he argued that the body is central to our being in the world. Perception cannot be treated as a disembodied consciousness. Research inspired by this idea of the lived body and lived experience has been important in demonstrating the intimate connections between body, experience, and identity. Studies of traumatic experiences relating to disease or accident have shown how damage to the body transforms the self and how sharing narratives can be important in sustaining an adequate sense of self-worth.

Finally, we can also examine how human beings are embodied and how people learn corporeal practices that are necessary for walking, dancing, shaking hands, and so forth. Social anthropologists have been influenced in particular by Marcel Mauss (1979), who invented the concept of "body techniques" to describe how people learn to manage their bodies according to social norms. Children, for instance, have to learn how to sit properly at table and boys learn how to throw in ways that differentiate them from girls. This anthropological legacy suggests that we think about the body as an ensemble of performances. These assumptions have been developed by Pierre Bourdieu in terms of two influential concepts. "Hexis" refers to deportment (gait, gesture, or posture) by which people carry themselves. "Habitus" refers to the dispositions through which taste is expressed. It is the habitual way of doing things. Bourdieu has employed these terms to study the everyday habitus of social classes in *Distinction: A Social Critique of the Judgment of Taste* (1984). The body is invested with symbolic capital whereby it is a corporeal expression of the hierarchies of social power. The body is permanently cultivated and represented by the aesthetic preferences of different social classes whereby, in French culture, mountaineering and tennis require the flexible, slim, and pliant bodies of the middle and upper classes, whereas the working-class sports of wrestling produce an entirely different body and habitus. Bourdieu's work has been influential in studies of habitus in a range of human activities from boxing to classical ballet.

We can simplify these complex theoretical traditions by suggesting that research on the body is confronted by two distinctive options. There is either the cultural decoding of the body as a system of meaning that has a definite structure existing separately from the intentions and conceptions of individuals, or there is the phenomenological study of embodiment that attempts to understand human practices that are organized around the life course (of birth, maturation, reproduction, and death). The work of Bourdieu offers a possible solution to this persistent tension between meaning and experience or between representation and practice. Bourdieu's development of the notions of habitus and practice in *Outline of a Theory of Practice* (1977) provides research strategies for looking simultaneously at how status difference is inscribed on the body and how we experience the world through our bodies, which are ranked in terms of their cultural capital. This reconciliation of these traditions can be assisted by distinguishing between the idea of the body as representation and embodiment as practice and experience.

BODY, EMBODIMENT, AND PERFORMANCE

In considering the future of the sociology of the body, two issues are important. There is a general view that, while there has been an extensive theoretical debate about the body, there is an insufficient and inadequate empirical research tradition. In this respect, the ethnographic work of anthropologists has been a useful corrective. Secondly, there is a growing research interest in embodied performance, which may also offer further empirical grounding for the study of the body. For example, to study ballet as performance rather than as representation, sociologists need to pay attention to the performing body. Richard Shusterman in *Performing Live* (2000), drawing on the work of Bourdieu and developing a pragmatist aesthetics, has argued that an aesthetic understanding of performance such as hip-hop cannot neglect the embodied features of artistic activity. The need for an understanding of embodiment and lived experience is crucial in understanding performing arts, but also for the study of the body in sport. While choreography is in one sense the text of the dance, performance takes place outside the strict directions of the choreographic work. Dance has an immediacy, which cannot be captured by discourse analysis. It is important to recapture the intellectual contribution of the phenomenology of human embodiment in order to avoid the reduction of bodies to cultural texts.

Over the last two decades, a variety of perspectives on the body have emerged. It is unlikely and possibly undesirable that any single theoretical synthesis will finally emerge. The creative tension between seeing the body as cultural representation and experience will continue to produce innovative and creative research. There are, of course, new issues on the horizon which sociologists will need to examine: the posthuman body, cybernetics, genetic modification, and the genetic mapping of the body are obvious issues. The wealth and quality of this research suggest that the sociology of the body is not a passing fashion but an aspect of mainstream sociology.

SEE ALSO: Beauvoir, Simone de; Body Modification; Body and Sexuality; Body and Society; Civilizing Process; Consumption and the Body; Elias, Norbert; Emotion Work; Foucault, Michel; Gender, Consumption and; Posthumanism; Sport and the Body

REFERENCES AND SUGGESTED READINGS

Beauvoir, S. de (1972) *The Second Sex*. Penguin, Harmondsworth.
Bell, D. (1976) *The Cultural Contradictions of Capitalism*. Basic Books, New York.
Bordo, S. (1993) *Unbearable Weight: Feminism, Western Culture, and the Body*. University of California Press, Berkeley.
Bourdieu, P. (1977) *Outline of a Theory of Practice*. Cambridge University Press, Cambridge.
Bourdieu, P. (1984) *Distinction: A Social Critique of the Judgment of Taste*. Routledge & Kegan Paul, London.
Burchell, G., Gordon, C., & Miller, P. (Eds.) (1991) *The Foucault Effect: Studies in Governmentality*. Harvester Wheatsheaf, London.
Elias, N. (1978) *The Civilizing Process*. Blackwell, Oxford.
Featherstone, M. (Ed.) (1999) *Body Modification*. Special issue of *Body and Society* 5(2/3). Sage, London.
Foucault, M. (1977) *The History of Sexuality*. Tavistock, London.
Goffman, E. (1959) *The Presentation of Self in Everyday Life*. Doubleday Anchor, Garden City, NY.
Mauss, M. (1979) Body Techniques. In: *Sociology and Psychology: Essays*. Routledge, London, pp. 95–123.
Merleau-Ponty, M. (1982) *Phenomenology of Perception*. Routledge & Kegan Paul, London.
O'Neill, J. (1985) *Five Bodies: The Human Shape of Modern Society*. Cornell University Press, Ithaca, NY.
Orbach, S. (1985) *Fat is a Feminist Issue*. Faber, London.
Parsons, T. (1974) Religion in Postindustrial America: The Problem of Secularization. *Social Research* 41(2): 193–225.
Shusterman, R. (2000) *Performing Live: Aesthetic Alternatives for the Ends of Art*. Cornell University Press, Ithaca, NY.
Turner, B. S. (1984) *The Body and Society: Explorations in Social Theory*. Blackwell, Oxford.
Turner, B. S. (1992) *Regulating Bodies: Essays in Medical Sociology*. Routledge, London.

body modification

D. Angus Vail

Body modification practices have proved fertile ground for sociologists interested in deviance, social control, and the social construction of problematic behavior. Most of this literature fits within the symbolic interactionist tradition, focusing specifically on the ways that people negotiate definitions of body art such that it becomes scary or beautiful, dangerous or alluring, rebellious or inclusive, and so on. The vast majority of this work is framed in discussions of labeling and differential association orientations which explain social definitions and the processes through which body modifiers learn how to be successful in changing the ways their bodies look to themselves and those with whom they come in contact.

Considering the fact that humans have practiced body modification of one form or another (the most common permanent practices of which are tattooing, cicatrization [a.k.a. scarification], and infibulation [a.k.a. piercing]) in virtually every civilization, it is interesting that so many find these practices disturbing. Tattooing, especially, has a long and not so illustrious connection with seedier elements in society, most saliently with outlaw bikers, convicts and gang members in prison, enlisted members of the military carousing on leave, prostitutes, and other "deviants." While these affiliations are longstanding and still quite common, the social meanings that make them what they are have begun to change as more affluent and less threatening people have become increasingly visibly tattooed, pierced, scarred, and/or branded. Many of these changes have developed in homologous fashion with the "tattoo renaissance."

In the late 1960s and early 1970s a two-pronged "renaissance" began in tattooing. Spearheading the cultural facet of the renaissance, San Francisco tattooist Lyle Tuttle tattooed Janis Joplin and other popular music stars who made tattoos visible to their middle-class fans. Spearheading the artistic movement, San Francisco tattoo artist Don Ed Hardy and Chicago tattoo artist Cliff Raven combined formal training in art with Japanese full-body aesthetics and American popular iconography to introduce "fine art tattooing" in America. Soon, middle-class Americans realized that tattoos could be aesthetically sophisticated and their popularity and visibility began spreading across class, gender, and racial lines. It would not be unreasonable to claim that, since it has become so widely accepted and practiced among such diverse segments of the population, tattooing is no longer deviant when practiced with restraint.

As greater diversity and availability have come to characterize tattooing practices, people's decisions to become tattooed have become more subtle and more complex. People no longer have merely to consider whether they should get a tattoo; they now have to consider which kind of tattoo best suits them, and whether it should be visible. Among those who get tattoos, some are quite explicitly oriented toward artistic merit, creativity, and uniqueness of design, while others tend to focus more directly on getting "classic Americana" designs (e.g., panthers, roses, vow tattoos, unicorns, and the like).

The ascendance of tattoo-oriented magazines has made tattooing more visible as an artistic expression to a greater segment of the population. With this greater exposure, the tattoo world has become divided among different *taste publics*, each of which tends to emphasize different kinds of tattoos and different purposes for collecting and/or applying them. Gang members tend to value the autobiographical functions of their iconography; bikers tend to value a tattoo's relative value in "showing class" (i.e., frightening "citizens" with outlandish behavior); soldiers and sailors tend to value classic military designs that connect them with a broader historical tradition; artistic collectors tend to value custom designs, worked out especially for them. Within each of these taste publics, different kinds of tattoos will garner different degrees of status, as will the extent of coverage. In artistic circles, for example, the full back tattoo, or "backpiece," garners significant status, whereas it is not visible enough to frighten "citizens" and therefore is less important among bikers; among navy personnel, bluebirds at the collar (a tattoo signifying the sailor's trip across the equator while on duty) will earn respect that those unfamiliar with navy iconography will not acknowledge; "classic" tattoo designs garner higher status among Americana collectors, especially as they age, whereas those less intimately connected to the tattoo world may consider them ugly. However, some of these aesthetic orientations are more likely than others to be accepted outside of the taste public under consideration. Current evidence seems to suggest, for example, that middle-class parents are less concerned by their offspring's choices to get tattooed as long as the designs are aesthetically pleasing and easily concealed.

While artistic merit is clearly an important factor in the relative shock value of any tattoo, its placement may be even more important. Tattoos on "public skin" (i.e., hands, neck, face, and/or head) tend to have greater shock value, almost irrespective of the nature of the design, which is one reason that tattoo artists are often reluctant to tattoo public skin on anyone other than a known and committed tattoo collector. The aversion to tattoos on public skin is most likely a byproduct of the tattooee's apparent unwillingness to conceal what many consider a mark of stigma. Facial tattoos have not always held this status, however.

Tattooing came to the West by way of Captain Cook, who brought the practice back to the British aristocracy. While early western exposure to tattooing tended to take the form of exhibitions of tattooed "natives" brought back from the South Sea Isles, women in the aristocracy soon began requesting and receiving cosmetic tattoos that took the form of permanent eyeliner, rouge, and lipstick. British Prime Minister Winston Churchill's mother was among those adorned with permanent makeup.

As tattoos became more visible and more acceptable, punks and "modern primitives" began looking for other permanent forms of body modification that would express their alienation from contemporary, developed western culture. The more common of these practices is piercing. While tongue and eyebrow piercing are certainly less shocking than they once were, more "radical" forms of piercing such as genital piercing, stretching earlobes, and piercings located in other uncommon sites on the body (usually measured by quantity as much as quality) are still unsettling to many. Piercing, more than other forms of permanent body modification, is often associated directly with intense sensation and "body play" which make it widely practiced among B&D/S&M (bondage and discipline/sadomasochism) cultures and other segments of the population interested in exploring the connections between pain and pleasure.

Most sociological analysis of body modification practices has been ethnographic with fairly explicit connections to symbolic interactionist discussions of the social construction of art, culture, deviance, and/or reality more broadly construed. Current interest among those practicing postmodernist and/or poststructuralist cultural text analysis of the body has also yielded a sizeable literature. Within this latter tradition, *metatheorists* tend to view the body as a site for inscription of cultural meanings, thereby *queering* not only their bodies but also the nature of the interactions they are likely to have with other people. In queering their

bodies and interactions, they regain control over their bodies in an age when body image is dominated by mediated constructions of beauty that have little to do with realistic and/or lived corporal experience of reality.

SEE ALSO: Body, Abominations of; Body and Cultural Sociology; Culture; Deviance; Labeling; Subculture

REFERENCES AND SUGGESTED READINGS

Atkinson, M. (2003) *Tattooed: The Sociogenesis of a Body Art*. University of Toronto Press, Toronto.

Caplan, J. (2000) *Written on the Body: The Tattoo in European and American History*. Princeton University Press, Princeton.

De Mello, M. (2000) *Bodies of Inscription: A Cultural History of the Modern Tattoo Community*. Duke University Press, Durham, NC.

Gell, A. (1993) *Wrapping in Images: Tattooing in Polynesia*. Oxford University Press, New York.

Pitts, V. (2003) *In the Flesh: The Cultural Politics of Body Modification*. Palgrave Macmillan, New York.

Vail, D. A. (1999) Tattoos are like Potato Chips... You Can't Have Just One: The Process of Becoming and Being a Collector. *Deviant Behavior* 20: 253–73.

Vail, D. A. (2000a) The Commodification of Time in Two Art Worlds. *Symbolic Interaction* 22: 325–44.

Vail, D. A. (2000b) Slingin' Ink or Scratching Skin? Producing Culture and Claiming Legitimacy Among Fine Art Tattooists. In: Lopata, H. Z. & Henson, K. D. (Eds.), *Current Research on Occupations and Professions*. Vol. 11: *Unusual Occupations*. JAI, Stamford, CT, pp. 55–73.

body and sexuality

Beverley Chaplin

All cultures have mechanisms which serve to organize and regulate sexuality. This is affected through a range of social institutions with the (gendered) body integral to this organization. In terms of social sanction, the variety of human sexual practices comprise a hierarchy which runs in a continuum from those conforming to the dominant heterosexual model to practices which constitute areas of contestation. Sociological analysis of the body and sexuality thus constitutes something of a materialist–discursive divide, with the former focusing on the physical, innate aspects of the body and sexuality, while discursive or representational analysis focuses on the cultural and communicative aspects of the body, a body as an "object" constructed within cultural discourses and practices. Feminist and poststructuralist challenges to materialist explanations point to the (particularly female) body as a "sign" or "symbol" within discourse. Consequently, materialist/discursive explanations of the body and sexuality roughly equate to a "masculinist"/"feminist" divide. There has, however, been little research conducted into the *experience* of embodiment per se – the body as "vehicle in being" (Merleau-Ponty) and the relation of this to sexuality.

"Naturalistic" accounts of the body and sexuality view the biological body as fundamental to society and social relations and the creator of social meanings. Until the eighteenth century the male body was viewed as a superior "norm," with the female body conceived as simply an inverted, inferior version: Lacqueur's "one sex/one flesh," genderless model. Eighteenth-century scientific inquiry saw the elaboration of gender onto the body, which affected the conception of men and women as possessing "oppositional" bodies. The embellishment of gender derived from Enlightenment egalitarian ideals at odds with the material reality of female subjugation to men. Thus, the emphasis on *difference* became socially inscribed. Together with the development of the view of sexuality as integral to individual self-identity, "naturalistic" accounts of the body provided the biological legitimation of the supposed "inferiority" of female corporeality, and thus female subordination: the public/private divide. This gendered view of the body was further elaborated upon by the increasing medicalization of the female body in the nineteenth century, when women's bodies were viewed as rooted within their reproductive capabilities and their behavior deemed as governed by reproductive "pathologies": the nature/culture divide. In addition, as late as the 1970s, sociobiological explanations attempted both to explain and to justify social inequalities and difference which, it was claimed, could be located within the structure of genes. Such explanations were not confined merely to gender inequalities however, but encompassed homosexuality, which was defined as deriving from the presence of a "homosexual gene." The assignment of sex difference to sex hormones in turn led to a questioning of the legitimacy of both feminist and homosexual demands for equality and the conception of both women and homosexuals as the "Other."

The sexologist Richard von Krafft-Ebbing's conception of homosexuality as "primitive" and degenerate in *Psychopathia Sexualis* (1965) was challenged to an extent by the publication of Havelock Ellis's *Sexual Inversion* in 1908, wherein he posited that cultural factors, as well as a congenital predisposition to same-sex love, contributed to the incidence of homosexuality. Ellis also argued that women's increasing liberation and education in the early twentieth century was responsible for the "masculinization" of middle-class women, resulting in lesbian "sexual inversion," a view which has been celebrated by those women who choose to "perform" what Judith Halberstam terms "female masculinity." Magnus Hirschfeld, who, in 1928, became the founder of the World League for Sexual Reform, challenged the notion of sexual polarity, calling for cultural and legal sexual reform, wherein homosexuals could embrace and celebrate their homosexuality and wherein women should be treated fairly and without discrimination. Edward Carpenter's *The Intermediate Sex* (1908) suggested that homosexuals were, in some senses, superior to their heterosexual counterparts with regard to their finer sensitivity, and, in the case of female homosexuals, their "masculine" strength and independence. Nevertheless, the idea of lesbians as "masculine" women simply contributed further to prevailing conceptions of the supposed superiority of the male intellect and the male body as the privileged body and heterosexuality as the dominant (and thus socially acceptable) sexuality. The empirical findings of the Kinsey Report in 1948 and 1953 pointed to the widespread occurrence and regularity of homosexual sex, and thus in some senses facilitated the subsequent legalization of homosexuality in the West. Nevertheless, homosexuality remains illegal in some countries, often due to religious beliefs, and heterosexuality remains the dominant sexual practice. Queer theory itself often defies definition, with some arguing that it refers not merely to lesbian and gay sex, but to any sexual practices which are outside of dominant "normative" practices.

Some "naturalist" feminists, notably during the late 1970s, but also within later ecofeminist theorizing, have celebrated women's biological difference to men, arguing that women's bodies and in particular their reproductive abilities should be regarded as a particular source of knowledge and thus recognized as having social parity with male knowledge and experience. Contemporary naturalistic accounts of reproduction tend to stress the appropriation of offspring by fathers, via marriage and fatherhood, resulting from men's separateness from women's experience of, and access to, creative continuity. Thus, it is argued that this deprivation forms the basis of male control over social institutions and the separation of public from private spheres of social life. Others criticize this stance, concerned that the conception of a specific female "essence" does little to combat oppressive cultural ideologies.

Naturalistic/materialist views of the body and sexuality have therefore been regarded by many sociologists as reductionist in the sense that their reliance upon biological *difference* results in a too simplistic analysis which fails to account for social change and cultural disparity, and a stress upon the *natural* basis of social inequality.

Discursive approaches to the body and sexuality emphasize the manner in which the individual "becomes" a particular being, examining how the body and sexuality are socially *constructed* and the power relations inherent to that construction. There is then, within social constructionist theories, a basic distinction which is formulated between the material body and its social and cultural representations. However, beneath the broad umbrella of "social constructionist" views there exists a number of disparate and often contradictory explanations of the relationship between bodies, sexualities, and the social. Foucault's genealogical approach demonstrates how bodies increasingly became constituted as the objects of discourses

which have had profound effects on the social construction of sexuality and the body, so that sex becomes a "regulatory ideal." This is constitutive of a shift during the eighteenth and nineteenth centuries from a religious concern with the *subject's* sexual "body as flesh," to an emphasis on the body as *object*, achieved via a shift from the regulation of individual bodies to a panoptic concern with the social body. This in turn affected the construction of normative heterosexuality and the classification of variations from this "norm" as "deviant." Therefore, there occurred a shift from overt sexual repression to the incitement of desire, resulting in more widespread discriminatory forms of control and systems of representation. Foucault's analysis of sexuality, in particular his conception of the "hysterization" of the female body has, in turn, facilitated the questioning by feminists of naturalistic conceptions of gendered social inequalities predicated upon biology towards a recognition that these conceptions are themselves socially constructed (Shilling 2003). The effect upon the female body of what Foucault terms the disciplining and surveillance of the body within modern society has, many feminists argue, resulted in the pathologizing of women's reproductive capabilities.

The relation of the social construction of gender to the female body and sexuality has been explored by feminists and has (certainly, in the early years of second wave feminism) taken the form of a denunciation of "naturalistic" conceptions of the female body as reducible to its biology. Thus, the goal of much feminist thought has been to liberate female sexuality from its reproductive confines. The conception of women as sexually passive and the female body as the (unwilling) receptor of male sexual advances has historically rendered women as conceptualized by uninterest in sex. The key feminist text in the 1970s was Simone de Beauvoir's *The Second Sex* (1947), in which she depicted the female body as a tabula rasa upon which is inscribed "masculinist" sexual ideologies pertaining to female sexual expression. Feminists have tackled the issues of rape and pornography, arguing that rape is a direct result of the unequal relations between men and women within the sexual domain, an inequity which sees men as the dominant partner and women as the submissive "other." Feminists disagree, however, on the issue of pornography, with some, such as MacKinnon (1987), arguing that it is a major site of female oppression, constitutive of male power and control, and reflective of women as the object of male heterosexual desire and conquest. Others argue that the anti-porn stance is to deny women access to their own brand of erotica, which serves to deflect attention from other important sources of female oppression.

Feminists have also argued that the specificity of female biology and the association of childbirth and childrearing, which sees women relegated to the private sphere, must be overcome if women are to attain embodied equality with men. Within such conceptions, motherhood is therefore regarded as the site of patriarchal rule. However, the psychoanalytic feminist Julia Kristeva argues for a discourse on pregnancy which empowers women. Similarly, Donna Haraway in her *Simians, Cyborgs and Women: The Reinvention of Nature* (1991), asserts that modern technologies of surveillance have diminished the power of the pregnant woman to the extent that this has altered her relationship with her unborn fetus and, indeed, with her own body (Brook 1999).

Gayle Rubin's argument that the cultural fusion of gender with sexuality has resulted in the feminist essentializing of the relation of sexual intercourse to sexuality provides evidence of the disparities which exist within feminist thought regarding the relation of female sexuality to the female body. The work of Judith Butler utilizes the discursive approach of Foucault and posits gender as a continuing performance wherein bodies become embroiled within a heteronormative discourse, such that the performance itself becomes "normalized" and "natural." Her later work poses the problem that if gender is the social elaboration of sex within a given culture, the body simply *becomes* its regulatory social meanings. If, however, these regulatory norms require reiteration, this implies that bodies do not ever quite conform to the materiality of sex.

Mary Douglas's anthropological approach in *Purity and Danger: An Analysis of Pollution and Taboo* (1966) considers that, since blood and

other body fluids are "naturally" contained, female menstruation is viewed as a *liminal* state of being. This culminates in the conception of the female body as a site of abjection. Julia Kristeva questions why menstrual blood is viewed as "polluting" in the same manner as excrement, for example, arguing that the female body as the site of abjection can be positively utilized by women, particularly as it transforms during pregnancy, as this change signifies the total "otherness" of the female body. Essentially, both theorists argue that the emission of essentially "female" body fluids effects the rendering of the female body as a site of pollution, although they differ in their ideas of the usefulness or otherwise of the concept of abjection. Conceptions of the "purity" of sexual exchange have also been examined in the context of AIDS/HIV by Grosz (1994), wherein she cites contemporary AIDS discourse as specifically aimed at women, who are ironically held to be socially responsible for the containment of the spread of this "polluting" virus. The panic surrounding AIDS/HIV is also part of a wider "risk discourse" in late modernity, which is, as Williams and Bendelow claim in *The Lived Body* (1998), reinforcing of a "moralizing discourse" separating the "good" body from the "bad." In addition, there appears to be some incongruence between the growth of such a discourse and the representation of sexualized bodies within the media and within consumer culture. In terms of gender, the media representation of the sexualized and thus objectified female body is one which reinforces it as "other," despite the fact that there has occurred an increase within consumer culture of representations of the sexualized male body. Representations within advertisements, film, and literature, along with the institutional structuring of sexuality, give rise to gendered patterns of male and female sexual behavior, in a type of scripted role-play. Thus, much feminist thought attempts to counter or challenge such gendered stereotypes. The potential *disembodiment* which may be experienced within cybersex has been variously theorized as enabling the development of a "second self," wherein an individual is freed from the embodied boundaries of gender or race, as in the work of Turkle (1984) or as reflective of the continued existence of gen-dered boundaries, particularly in terms of the discursive construction of science and technol-ogy as masculine and rational (Sophia 1992).

Feminists in particular have examined the relation to women's self-identity of the hetero-sexual "male gaze," citing the representation of women's bodies as the site of male sexual desire as a causal factor in women's often problematic relationship with size and body image. How-ever, the increasing objectification of and repre-sentation within advertising media of both male and female bodies has led to an increase in eating disorders and in the use by both sexes of cos-metic surgery. Alongside the more traditional types of female surgery, such as breast implants and the newer trend for vaginal "tightening," men too are now attempting to enhance their sexual attractiveness via the use of pectoral and chest implants and penis enlargement. Thus, in late modernity, the (sexualized) body becomes a *disciplined* body, a body subject to *self-surveillance*, itself reflective of prevailing concepts of smallness in women and largeness in men, concepts themselves metaphorically related to inequities of power relations and, some argue, to capitalist relations themselves.

There does appear to be a lack of a more phenomenological approach to the body and sexuality, an approach which views the body as a "lived" body, with all its attendant secre-tions, messiness, and corp*oreality*. Plummer (2003) refers to this as a "stunning omission (such that) the living and breathing, sweating and pumping, sensuous and feeling world of the emotional, fleshy body is hardly to be found" within the literature on the body and sexualities. Exceptions to this are to be found in the work of Deborah Lupton. Such theorizing may be all the more important in late moder-nity as sexuality becomes, according to Gid-dens, the property of the individual, freed from the bonds of reproduction and intimately bound up with the project of "self." This, he argues, points to a "decentered" form of sex within "late" modernity and the conception of a type of "plastic sexuality," a kind of "pure relationship," which refers to the development of relationships which are contingent, rather than bound within institutionalized forms. Nevertheless, despite legal increases in the

rights of minority groups to define and practice their own particular brand of sexuality, there continues to be a New Right political backlash against these advancements which is currently manifest within varying issues centering on the body and sexuality. Such indictments are accompanied by the propounding of a return to more traditional values via the retention of virginity among young people and the rein-statement of traditional institutions such as marriage and "compulsory" heterosexuality.

SEE ALSO: Body and Society; Ellis, Havelock; Gender, the Body and; Hirschfeld, Magnus; Kinsey, Alfred; Krafft-Ebing, Richard von; New Reproductive Technologies; Pornography and Erotica; Sexual Citizenship; Sexual Politics; Transgender, Transvestism, and Transsexualism

REFERENCES AND SUGGESTED READINGS

Brook, B. (1999) *Feminist Perspectives on the Body*. Longman, London.
Butler, J. (1990) *Gender Trouble: Feminism and the Subversion of Identity*. Routledge, New York.
Grosz, E. (1994) *Volatile Bodies: Toward a Corporeal Feminism*. Allen & Unwin, St. Leonards.
Halberstam, J. (1998) *Female Masculinity*. Duke Uni-versity Press, Durham, NC.
Kristeva, J. (1982) *Powers of Horror: An Essay on Abjection*. Columbia University Press, New York.
Laqueur, T. W. (1990) *Making Sex: Body and Gen-der from the Greeks to Freud*. Harvard University Press, Cambridge, MA.
Mackinnon, C. A. (1987) *Feminism Unmodified: Dis-courses on Life and Law*. Harvard University Press, Cambridge, MA.
Plummer, K. (2003) Queers, Bodies and Postmodern Sexualities: A Note On Revisiting the Sexual in Symbolic Interactionism. *Qualitative Sociology* 26 (4): 525.
Rubin, G. (1984) Thinking Sex: Notes For a Radical Theory of the Politics of Sexuality. In: Vance, C. S. (Ed.), *Pleasure and Danger: Exploring Female Sexuality*. Routledge & Kegan Paul, New York.
Shilling, C. (2003) *The Body and Social Theory*, 2nd edn. Sage, Thousand Oaks, CA.
Sophia, Z. (1992) Virtual Corporeality: A Feminist View. *Australian Feminist Studies* 15 (Autumn): 11–24.
Turkle, S. (1984) *The Second Self: Computers and the Human Spirit*. Simon & Schuster, New York.

body and society

Bryan S. Turner

Over the last two decades there has been growing interest in the sociology of the body, as illustrated by the publication of *The Body* (Featherstone et al. 1991), *The Woman in the Body* (Martin 1989), *Five Bodies* (O'Neill 1985), *The Body and Social Theory* (Shilling 1993), and *The Body and Society* (Turner 1984). Three philosophical works were particularly important in initially stimulating sociological analysis of the human body. First, *The Absent Body* (Leder 1990) was critical of Cartesian dualism that separates mind and body. Employing a phenomenological perspective, Leder studied the absence of the "lived body" in everyday life, and showed how disruptions of illness bring the body into focus. Second, *The Body in Pain* (Scarry 1985) explored the problem of physical pain in torture and war, and demonstrated the centrality of the body to contemporary moral issues. Third, Michel Foucault's historical studies of medicine in *The Birth of the Clinic* (1973) and sexuality in *The History of Sexuality* (1978) generated interest in the interaction between the body, medical practice, and systems of belief. Foucault opened up new ways of thinking about how bodies are imagined, constructed, and represented. Georges Canguilhem's important work on *The Normal and the Pathological* (1994) influenced Foucault's approach to the history of systems of thought, including our knowledge of the human body. Foucault has remained central to research on power and the body as a representation of society. For example, Thomas Laqueur's *Making Sex* (1990) demonstrated major historical changes in the anatomical representation of the sexual organs, reflecting different theories of gender. This general interest in the sociology of the body has seeped into medical sociology by suggesting innovative theoretical frameworks and new topics of empirical inquiry (Turner 2004).

TWO THEORIES OF THE BODY

The sociology of the body has been divided analytically into two distinctive, often contradictory, approaches. These two traditions represent alternative answers to the question: is the human body socially constructed? In social constructionist approaches, the body is treated as a system of cultural representations. In the phenomenological tradition, the "lived body" is studied in the everyday world of social interaction.

The body is often studied as a cultural representation of social life. For example, in medieval art, there was considerable fascination, especially in the fifteenth century, with the spiritual significance of the bare-breasted Virgin Mary and the child Jesus. In the theological tradition of the *virgo lactans*, the Virgin was a figure of spiritual salvation whose milk acquired a status similar to Christ's blood. The female breast is a representation of divine care. In this sociological and anthropological tradition, research considers the ways in which the body enters into political discourse as a representation of power, and how power is exercised over the body. This approach to the body, which has been dominated by the legacy of Foucault, is concerned with questions of representation and control in which diet is for example a regulation or government of the body. The Foucauldian perspective is not concerned to understand our experiences of embodiment; it does not aim to grasp the lived experience of the body from a phenomenology of the body.

The principal starting point for an analysis of the lived body has been the research of the French philosopher Maurice Merleau-Ponty. In the *Phenomenology of Perception* (1982) he examined how perception of reality occurs from the specific location of our body, and hence he showed how cognition is always an embodied perception of the world. Phenomenology is a critique of the dualism of the mind and body, in which body is seen to be passive and inert. Research inspired by the phenomenological tradition has been important in showing the intimate connections between body, experience, and identity. For example, traumatic experiences of disease have a major impact on self-perception and identity, and hence loss of a body part can have devastating consequences for self-identity. This division between the body as representation and as experience has dominated the sociological debate about the body, and there have been many attempts to reconcile this difference.

While there is therefore a sociological and anthropological tradition which examines the body as a symbolic system, we can also examine how human beings are embodied and how human beings learn a variety of cultural practices that are necessary for walking, sitting, dancing, and so forth. The study of embodiment has been the particular concern of anthropologists who have been influenced by the concept of "body techniques" (Mauss 1973). These anthropological assumptions have in turn been developed by Pierre Bourdieu through the concepts of hexis and habitus in which our dispositions and tastes are organized. For example, within the habitus of social classes, Bourdieu showed in *Distinction* (1984) that the body is invested with symbolic capital in which the body is a living expression of the hierarchies of social power. The body is permanently cultivated and represented by the aesthetic preferences of different social classes. The different sports that are supported by different social classes illustrate this form of distinction. Weight lifting is part of the habitus of the working class; mountaineering, of upper social strata.

If the body is understood exclusively as a system of cultural representation, it becomes very difficult to develop an adequate sociology of the body as lived experience. Sociologists have therefore become interested in bodily performances, which cannot be grasped simply as static representations. Richard Shusterman in *Pragmatist Aesthetics* (1992), drawing on the work of Bourdieu, has argued that an aesthetic understanding of performance cannot neglect the embodied features of artistic activity. The need for an understanding of embodiment and lived experience is crucial in understanding performing arts, but also for the study of the body in sport. Research on the body from the perspective of Bourdieu creates innovative approaches for understanding the relationship between injury, careers, identity, and embodiment. The study of injury and accident in ballet performances provides general sociological insights into the relationships between trauma, embodiment, and identity.

The work of Bourdieu offers one possible solution to this division between the meaning and experience of embodiment or the cultural representation of the body. Bourdieu's development of the notions of habitus and practice in *Logic of Practice* (1990) creates research strategies for examining how, for example, status differences are inscribed on the body and how we experience the social world through our bodies that are ranked in terms of their cultural capital. This analytical reconciliation can be supported by clearly distinguishing between the idea of the body as cultural representation and embodiment as practice and experience.

FEMINISM, GENDER, AND THE STARVING BODY

The contemporary anthropology and sociology of the body has been continuously influenced by feminist social theory. Simone de Beauvoir's *The Second Sex* (1972) was a major contribution to the study of the patriarchal regulation of the female body. She argued that women are not born but become women through social and psychological processes that construct them as essentially female. Her work inaugurated a tradition of research on the social production of differences in gender and sexuality. Feminist theories of the body have employed social constructionism to show how the differences between male and female bodies, that we take for granted as if they were facts of nature, are socially produced. Germaine Greer's *The Female Eunuch* (1970) and Kate Millet's *Sexual Politics* (1969) were important in establishing the difference between biologically determined sex and the social construction of gender roles and sexual identities. More recently, there has been increasing interest in the question of men's bodies, health, and masculinity in, for example, R. W. Connell's *Masculinities* (1995).

The underlying theory of gender inequalities was the idea of patriarchy and much empirical research in sociology has subsequently explored how the social and political subordination of women is expressed somatically in psychological depression and physical illness. Creative scholarship went into historical research on body image, diet, obesity, and eating disorders. The sociological analysis of anorexia nervosa and bulimia has occupied a critical place in the evolution of feminist theories of the body. Anorexia charts the contradiction between increasing body weight and the aesthetic ideal of the slim body.

AGING, DISABILITY, AND IMPAIRMENT

The sociological analysis of the body has played an important role in the development of the "social model" in disability studies, especially in establishing a distinction between disability, impairment, and handicap. By focusing on the notion that the human body is socially constructed, activists rejected the medical model of disability, arguing that the disability label results in a loss of social rights. While "the disabled body" is socially constructed, researchers have also emphasized the importance of examining the lived experience of impairment. Empirical work has contributed significantly to our understanding of the complex connections between rehabilitation, embodiment, and self.

Phenomenological studies of impairment and disability question the legacy of mind/body dualism, and promote analysis of the embodied self and the disruptions of everyday life. Chronic illness and impairment pose interesting questions about the continuity of the self and the discontinuity of embodiment. Disability, while socially produced by systems of classification and professional labels, has profound significance for the self, because our identity is necessarily constituted by our embodiment. Since our biographical narratives are embodied, disability is an existential challenge in terms of its contested meaning for the self. The problems of mobility and autonomy are fundamental to the life world of the elderly, the chronically sick, and the disabled. These traumatic experiences shape selfhood by transforming the relationships between the self, body image, and social world.

Research on the aging body has also been associated with new perspectives on gerontology as a system of social regulation and representation of senile bodies. Other studies emphasize the lived experience of aging.

CONCLUSION: MICHEL FOUCAULT AND BIO-POLITICS

The human body, or more specifically its genetic code, is now central to economic growth in a wide range of biotech industries. In a paradoxical manner, the pathology of the human body is itself a productive factor in the new economy. Body parts have become essential commodities within a consumer society and with globalization the exchange of organs has become an aspect of international trade. Disease is no longer regarded as simply a constraint on the productivity of labor, but as an actual factor of production. The body is increasingly regarded as a code or system of information from which economic profits can be extracted through patents rather than merely a natural organism, and the body as a topic of medical science is being radically transformed by the Human Genome Project. In terms of media debate, the new reproductive technologies, cloning, and genetic screening are important illustrations of public concern about the social consequences of the new genetics. Improvements in scientific understanding of genetics have already had major consequences for the circumstances under which people reproduce, and genetic surveillance and forensic genetics may also transform criminal investigation and the policing of societies. The human body lies at the center of legal concerns about human rights, especially the rights of ownership of the body and its code. The major political question of modern times concerns the possibility of what Francis Fukuyama (2002) has called *Our Posthuman Future*. The cultural dominance of the body in late modernity is not difficult to document, but its very complexity has raised intractable analytical and political problems about how to understand and how to manage the body.

These changes in biomedicine illustrate the distinction made by Foucault (1978: 139) between the study of the individual body and the study of populations. In the "anatomo-politics of the human body," Foucault examined how various forms of discipline of the body have regulated individuals. In the "bio-politics of the population," he studied the regulatory controls over populations. Anatomo-politics is concerned with the micro-politics of identity and concentrated on the sexuality, reproduction, and life histories of individuals. The clinical examination of individuals is part of the anatomo-politics of society. The bio-politics of populations used demography, epidemiology, and public health sciences to examine and manage whole populations. Foucault's study of the body was thus organized around the notions of discipline and regulatory controls. The new genetics have created enhanced opportunities for governmentality as a strategy of political surveillance and economic production (Foucault 1991). The government of the body as a consequence remains a critical issue in the management and regulation of individuals and populations in contemporary society.

In conclusion, the sociology of the body has been important for medical sociology because it has propelled the analysis of medical institutions into the mainstream of modern sociological research. Whereas the study of medicine as well as health and illness was strangely absent from classical sociology, in contemporary social theory the medicalized body has become part of the core concern of theoretical sociology, because the body is now recognized as central to the debate about agency and structure. The cutting edge of sociological research is now concentrated on questions relating to the possibility of the social as nature is being radically transformed. Medicine and the body raise questions that are critical for the future of human society, and these questions are reformulating sociological theory.

SEE ALSO: Beauvoir, Simone de; Body and Cultural Sociology; Body Modification; Body and Sexuality; Bourdieu, Pierre; Disability as a Social Problem; Foucault, Michel; Gender, Aging and; Illness Experience; Sex and Gender

REFERENCES AND SUGGESTED READINGS

Beauvoir, S. de (1972) *The Second Sex*. Penguin, Harmondsworth.

Bourdieu, P. (1984) *Distinction: A Social Critique of the Judgement of Taste*. Routledge & Kegan Paul, London.

Bourdieu, P. (1990) *The Logic of Practice*. Polity Press, Cambridge.

Canguilhem, G. (1994) The Normal and the Pathological. In: Delaporte, F. (Ed.), *A Vital Rationalist: Selected Writings from Georges Canguilhem*. Zone Books, New York, pp. 321–50.

Connell, R. W. (1995) *Masculinities*. Polity Press, Cambridge.

Featherstone, M., Hepworth, M., & Turner, B. S. (Eds.) (1991) *The Body: Social Processes and Cultural Theory*. Sage, London.

Featherstone, M. (Ed.) (1999) *Body Modification*. Sage, London.

Foucault, M. (1973) *The Birth of the Clinic: The Archaeology of Medical Perception*. Tavistock, London.

Foucault, M. (1978) *The History of Sexuality*, Vol. 1. Penguin, New York.

Foucault, M. (1991) Governmentality. In: Burchell, G., Gordon, C., & Miller, P. (Eds.), *The Foucault Effect: Studies in Governmentality*. Harvester Wheatsheaf, London, pp. 87–104.

Frank, A. (1991) *At the Will of the Body*. Houghton Mifflin, Boston.

Fukuyama, F. (2002) *Our Posthuman Future: Consequences of the Biotechnology Revolution*. Farrar, Straus, & Giroux, New York.

Greer, G. (1970) *The Female Eunuch*. MacGibbon & Kee, London.

Laqueur, T. (1990) *Making Sex: Body and Gender from the Greeks to Freud*. Harvard University Press, Cambridge, MA.

Leder, D. (1990) *The Absent Body*. University of Chicago Press, Chicago.

Martin, E. (1989) *The Woman in the Body: A Cultural Analysis of Reproduction*. Open University Press, Milton Keynes.

Mauss, M. (1973) Techniques of the Body. *Economy and Society* 2: 70–88.

Merleau-Ponty, M. (1982) *Phenomenology of Perception*. Routledge & Kegan Paul, London.

Millet, K. (1969) *Sexual Politics*. Abacus, London.

O'Neill, J. (1985) *Five Bodies: The Human Shape of Modern Society*. Cornell University Press, Ithaca, NY.

Scarry, E. (1985) *The Body in Pain: The Making and Unmaking of the World*. Oxford University Press, New York.

Shilling, C. (1993) *The Body and Social Theory*. Sage, London.

Shusterman, R. (1992) *Pragmatist Aesthetics: Living Beauty, Rethinking Art*. Blackwell, Oxford.

Turner, B. S. (1984) *The Body and Society: Explorations in Social Theory*. Blackwell, Oxford.

Turner, B. S. (2004) *The New Medical Sociology: Social Forms of Health and Illness*. W. W. Norton, New York.

Bonfil Batalla, Guillermo (1935–91)

Luis Méndez y Berrueta

Guillermo Bonfil Batalla was a Mexican ethnologist who studied at the National School of Anthropology and History (*Escuela Nacional de Antropología e Historia*, ENAH) and received his doctorate in anthropology at Mexico's National Autonomous University (*Universidad Nacional Autónoma de México*, UNAM). He is one of the most important representatives of the new generation of Mexican anthropologists who began to dominate the academic panorama after 1968. This generation was characterized by its strong criticism of the state's official *indigenismo*, which is understood as the set of state policies, institutions, and laws in relation to indigenous people. In light of both his theoretical reflections and his political work, Guillermo Bonfil Batalla is frequently considered one of the precursors in Latin America of the theoretical and ideological emergence of the autonomies of autochthonous peoples and of academic reflections on the consolidation of pluricultural states.

Throughout his life, Bonfil Batalla held various political positions, such as director of the National Institute of Anthropology and History (*Instituto Nacional de Antropología e Historia*, INAH) in 1972, director of INAH's Center for Research and Higher Studies (*Centro de Investigaciones y Estudios Superiores del INAH*, CISINAH) in 1976, and director of the National Museum of Popular Cultures (*Museo Nacional de Culturas Populares*) in 1981. From 1989 to 1991, the year of his death, he was first Director of Popular Cultures, and then in charge of the Cultural Studies Seminar of the National Council for Culture and the Arts (*Consejo Nacional para la Cultura y las Artes*, CONACULTA). He was also president of the Latin American Association of Anthropology (*Asociación Latinoamericana de Antropología*) and was named a National Researcher, having received the *Presea Manuel Gamio al Mérito Indigenista* award in 1988. He also participated actively in the First (1971) and Second (1979) Declarations of Barbados.

Guillermo Bonfil Batalla's anthropological works, spanning three important decades in Mexico's history (from the early 1960s until 1991), can be read as a theoretical synthesis of a twofold political crisis: on one hand, the crisis of the institutional *indigenista* model, consolidated during the General Lázaro Cárdenas government (1936–40), soon after the Mexican Revolution, and, on the other, the crisis within Mexican anthropology. The latter crisis was historically and ideologically dependent on the *indigenista* model, while at the same time being affected by the reality in Latin America, which pointed toward a forced entry into modernity on unequal terms but which also translated into resistance to that path, opting for the socialist model(s), revolution, and guerrillas.

As a student at ENAH, an institution which was at that time dedicated to educating professionals for official *indigenismo*, Bonfil Batalla generated his work in a context which was increasingly replete with diverse, contradictory theoretical and political positions and which had begun to criticize that model. Mexican official *indigenismo* had been the result of a long process of legitimization of revolutionary values. One of those fundamental values was the construction of a national identity in which, at least ideologically, it was imperative to recuperate the indigenous past of this colonized country. At the same time, it was equally important to generate a political praxis for integrating the *historic* native Mexican with the *real* native Mexican, and to develop a certain coherence between them. In other words, in the homogenizing framework of a national culture that brandished its indigenous past as only one of the values of *mestizaje*, the presence of a *real* indigenous population was acknowledged for the first time. This was viewed as important not only because of the indigenous population's statistical density or the extent to which it was marginalized, but also – and perhaps above all – because of its *difference*. In order to carry out programs in favor of native Mexicans, it was necessary to know who they were. Manuel Gamio and Alfonso Caso ideologically created this *indigenismo*, which attempted to articulate the concept of national culture and indigenous culture through the word "integration," which, at least as understood by Gamio, consisted of exchanging values between the indigenous community and the national community. In short, the indigenous population should not assimilate into the *mestizo* culture but should, rather, integrate itself into an exchange of values.

Nevertheless, that term assumed other nuances when, in the hands of Caso, the need to establish an *indigenista* policy was confronted. Caso was to provide *indigenista* institutions, specifically the *Instituto Nacional Indigenista* (INI), founded in 1948, with the bureaucratic structure and ideological guidelines that it retained until its recent closure. This policy was understood fundamentally as a government decision designed to protect indigenous communities and integrate them into the nation's economic, social, and political life. It was explained above all by the right of those communities to equality, in the unequal framework of poverty and marginalization in which they lived. Thus official *indigenismo* ended up as a policy defined as integrationist and protection-oriented.

Meanwhile, academic work in this area was shifting toward the idea of applied anthropology, which aimed to find solutions to communities' concrete problems. Nevertheless, it was Gonzalo Aguirre Beltrán who had offered a theoretical explanation of *indigenismo*. This theoretical defense of integrationist policies was guided by two key points: a theory of the acculturation process, and the notion of regions for taking refuge (these were areas of the country where it was possible to preserve the structure inherited from the colonial period and an archaic pre-industrial culture, to protect people from the onslaught of civilization). Integration was thus viewed as part of a process of acculturation. Consequently, from 1940 to 1964, extending after the Cardenist period, indigenous policy shifted from the notion of the dissolution of the Mexican native to that of regional development, more in line with Aguirre Beltrán's theory. The goals of INI during this period identified literacy as their central concern, as an element that would promote changes in the region. By the 1960s, however, and especially within the academic community, dissident voices began to express their disagreement with this model.

In 1962, Bonfil Batalla published one of his first articles, "Diagnóstico del hambre en Sudzal, Yucatán: un ensayo de antropología aplicada" (Diagnostic assessment of hunger in Sudzal, Yucatán: an attempt at applied anthropology), in which he criticized the notion of applied anthropology within official *indigenismo*. er as subjectivism based on psychologism, as a product of the metaphysical denial of the social structure, while anthropology ignored the genuine cultural structure of communities and attempted to change subjective elements that were erroneously considered to be the reasons behind the communities' negative situation. At the end of the 1960s, the controversy within academic circles in relation to official *indigenismo* lar repercussions in Mexican anthropology in 1968–70. Specifically, the severe criticism of colonialism and imperialism in economic and cultural terms had a strong influence on social science in general, and on social anthropology in particular, in direct relation to anthropological practice, consequently interpreted as cultural penetration. The triumph of the Cuban Revolution and of the decolonization process in Africa, the emergence of the theory of the third world, struggles for liberation, the proliferation of guerrillas and social movements, the Vietnam War, and particularly the Mexican student movement of 1968 all left their mark, above all in the formulation of an emerging debate on the social role of the scientist. This debate led to an interpretation of the anthropologist as an active agent of imperialism. A number of students and professors at ENAH were actively involved in the student movement of 1968. In 1969, Bonfil Batalla's contract was canceled and he left the school, together with a number of other professors, who resigned in protest.

By 1970, the diversity of currents of thought within ENAH was already considerable (at that time ENAH was the primary center for dissemination of anthropology and for educating professionals in the field). In addition to official *indigenismo*, there were also Marxist positions and a critical tendency, represented by Bonfil Batalla and other members of his generation (Margarita Nolasco, Arturo Warman, Salomón Nahmad, Mercedes Olivera, Enrique Valencia, Rodolfo Stavenhagen), who in the same year published *De eso que llaman antropología mexicana* (*On What is Referred to as Mexican Anthropology*). From that time on, Bonfil Batalla became one of the main representatives of a new form of *indigenismo* which, in Latin America, anticipated future reflections on the autonomy of indigenous communities and on the vital nature of the ethnic issue. Bonfil Batalla's contribution to that book (Bonfil Batalla 1970) could be described as a review of the theoretical-political position that he would maintain during the rest of his life, and which would reach its definitive form in the work entitled *México profundo*, published a decade later.

Bonfil Batalla's first proposal was that Mexican *indigenismo* had originated in the ideals of the Mexican Revolution, and in what he called the need to confront those ideals with the nation's cultural reality. In his terms, official *indigenismo* had proposed the disappearance of Mexican natives as its goal, even though the "conservation of values" was used in its discourse. Anthropologists criticized the notion of the integration of native Mexicans, which, according to this set of ideas, did not imply the establishment of relations between native Mexicans and the nation (which already existed, for good or ill), but rather the complete assimilation of what was indigenous, resulting from their total loss of identity. They were also critical of the concept of a national culture, in which social and cultural differences were diluted into a *mestizo* sector ideologically constructed and declared official, leading to the erroneous conclusion that there was something that could be referred to as a common culture for all Mexicans.

These ideas were theoretically within the current of thought that had been inaugurated by the French anthropology of 1968 (by Jaulin, Debray, Perrot, and Condominas, among others) and which, as a result of anthropological projects in Vietnam and the Camelot project in Latin America, had begun to criticize the political role played by anthropological practice. Bonfil Batalla owed a particular theoretical debt to Jaulin, who was one of the first authors to define the notion of ethnic diversity as opposed to the notion of integration. He identified the latter as a form of ethnocide, understood as the cultural extermination of ethnic groups through integration as a process promoted by any form of capitalist domination. Similarly, Bonfil Batalla analyzed the "native Mexican" voice, which essentially referred to the colonized status of a group of subjects, in direct

opposition to a fact that, no matter how fundamental, was ignored: Mexico's ethnic and cultural plurality. This coincided with the need to reformulate anthropological practice as "science with commitment," reducing the anthropologist's field of action to serving as an adviser and promoter of the needs of the communities under study. It is important to add that this idea was not exclusive to Bonfil Batalla's work, but was common among anthropologists with a Marxist leaning. Together they called for support of anthropology that was committed to the causes for which the people and ethnic minorities were struggling.

This position of so-called "anthropology with commitment" was immediately criticized by official *indigenismo*, fundamentally through Aguirre Beltrán, and also by Marxist anthropologists in academic circles. The criticism intensified in 1972 when Bonfil Batalla accepted the position of director of INAH. This criticism can be read as the development of a crisis, clearly theoretical in nature, at the very heart of the country's *indigenistas* policies. Just as the academic sector had become polarized into political factions, and official *indigenismo* was obliged to defend itself against increasingly harsh criticism (such as the accusation that it attacked national sovereignty by allowing the work of the Summer Linguistic Institute, whose aims were clearly religious, and that it had facilitated the work of US linguists and anthropologists in the Camelot project), the two primary institutions charged with addressing the indigenous problem in Mexico during the government of Luis Echeverría Álvarez (1970–6) were headed by two adversaries (Bonfil Batalla and Aguirre Beltrán, respectively). In short, the crisis had become institutionalized.

In the theoretical arena, Aguirre Beltrán's primary criticism of Bonfil Batalla consisted of an absolute rejection of what he referred to as the constitution of "native Mexican power." He argued that this would end up becoming consolidated, as in the United States, in a "reservation economy" that would lead to an ethnic consciousness, not a class consciousness, necessary for the development of communities, thus eliminating the possibility of a class struggle and transforming the conflict between national society and indigenous communities into a conflict of castes. Thus, unlike Bonfil Batalla, who focused the problem of *indigenismo* on the difficulties surrounding the nation's cultural diversity and on the problem of the cultural and political autonomy of indigenous communities, Aguirre Beltrán viewed it as fundamentally important to accelerate the transformation from a caste consciousness (inherited from Mexico's colonial past) to a class consciousness. His theoretical position on this point was very similar to the positions maintained by Marxist anthropologists, who viewed the indigenous as part of the social class of peasants and whose intention was to "integrate" native Mexicans into the social revolutionary class. There were, however, more critical positions in this regard, such as that of Ángel Palerm, who, in contrast to Aguirre Beltrán, proposed that the state and the nation were different phenomena and that, at least in theory, a nation-state might accept cultural plurality without jeopardizing its internal structure. This implied that the *indigenistas* policy of a nation-state would not necessarily have to be one of assimilation and destruction of identity.

In 1971, one year before Bonfil Batalla assumed the directorship of INAH, he participated, along with a group of distinguished Latin American anthropologists (including Darcy Ribeiro and Stefano Varese), in the Declaration of Barbados. The anthropological proposal from the 1970s was synthesized in this declaration, and it outlined the ideological tendency of indigenous movements in Latin America that can still be observed today. The Declaration of Barbados analyzed the role of the state, religious organizations, and anthropologists in relation to autochthonous peoples. The state, according to this Declaration, should guarantee that indigenous peoples maintain rights over their territory as a collectively owned, extensive, and inalienable property, based on the assumption that the rights of indigenous societies come before those of the national society. The problem of autonomy was once again addressed, emphasizing the need for the state to recognize the right of indigenous peoples to organize and govern themselves according to their own specific cultural characteristics. It was suggested that religious missions should discontinue all types of activities,

and that the purpose and responsibility of anthropologists consisted in contributing knowledge to communities and serving as intermediaries between these communities and society.

From that time on, Bonfil Batalla's theoretical works turned toward responding to the question of whether autochthonous cultures could be understood as "class cultures"; in other words, he focused on the role of indigenous cultures within the state and in the nation's cultural reality. This in turn made it necessary to first define the nation's cultural reality. His arguments, developed in his earlier works, are synthesized in *México profundo*, in which he maintained that Mexican society was composed of a multiplicity of subcultures that had never been harmonious; in fact, they existed amidst constant tension and were contradictory, antagonistic, and encompassed a complex set of class cultures. The traditional anthropological concept of culture highlighted the homogeneous, harmonious aspects of the cultures studied. The concept of class cultures, referring to the culture of oppressed groups within a larger dominant system, was introduced with the objective of eliminating asymmetrical relationships, and thus leading to the possibility of constructing a pluricultural state.

In the political arena, Bonfil Batalla's central idea was to contribute toward consolidating an indigenous movement and anthropological reflections emerging from the point of view of autochthonous peoples themselves. This effort led to partial results in the Second Barbados meeting of 1977. Unlike the first meeting, the entire body of the declaration was elaborated by indigenous representatives from native Mexican movements and organizations. According to Bonfil Batalla, this was because, during 1975, the Mexican government began to sponsor the formation of indigenous organizations, in parallel to the historic events taking place at that time, specifically the international rise in ethnic movements, with Vietnam's triumph and the advances in China as particularly representative of this tendency. In this panorama, Bonfil Batalla pointed to notable differences in indigenous discourses, with some "rationalizing" official *indigenismo* in their own terms, others maintaining self-management and autonomy-oriented discourses, and yet others advocating millennium-inspired ideas with utopian tendencies. At the institutional level, by 1979 Bonfil Batalla had managed to develop a training program for ethnolinguists, with the idea of educating members of the communities to serve as anthropological professionals who would then initiate direct dialogue with anthropologists and even with institutions.

This turbulent period of contradictions around the role of the native Mexican in the Mexican nation exploded a decade later. Mexico's neoliberal adventure and its forced insertion in the globalized world rendered futile any proposal on official indigenous policy. It is not by accident that, by 2004, the INI was closed down, after an accelerated process of dismantling. Nor is it surprising that INAH changed its traditional orientation toward the indigenous world, focusing instead on other global projects more oriented toward tourist consumption. In short, the struggle of the 1960s and 1970s between different positions on the ethnicity issue continues unresolved. The integrationist position defended by Aguirre Beltrán still exists, although outside the framework of the exhausted nationalist-revolutionary order. The pluriculturalist position defended by Bonfil Batalla, as well as by many other anthropologists, is now outside the institutional context, although it has not disappeared and has instead taken on the form of social movements that resist the globalized world.

SEE ALSO: Culture; Ethnic Groups; Ethnicity; Indigenous Movements; Indigenous Peoples; Multiculturalism; Revolutions

REFERENCES AND SUGGESTED READINGS

Aguirre Beltrán, G. (1973 [1953]) *Teoría y práctica de la educación indígena*. FCE, Mexico.
Barabas, A. (1987) *Utopías indias. Movimientos socio-religiosos en México*. Grijalbo, Mexico.
Barbados, Grupo de (1979) *Indianidad y descolonización en América Latina. Documentos de la Segunda Reunión de Barbados*. Nueva Imagen, Mexico.
Bonfil Batalla, G. (1969) Reflexiones sobre la política indigenista y el centralismo gubernamental en México. *Work presented at the Sociedad de Antropología Aplicada*, Mexico.
Bonfil Batalla, G. (1970) Del indigenismo de la Revolución a la antropología crítica. In: Warman, A. et al. (Eds.), *De eso que llaman antropología mexicana*. Nuestro Tiempo, Mexico.
Bonfil Batalla, G. (1972) El concepto de indio en América Latina. *Anales de antropología*, Vol. 9. Mexico.
Bonfil Batalla, G. (1978) Los pueblos indios: viejos problemas, nuevas demandas en México. In: Valencia, E. et al., *Campesinado e indigenismo en América Latina*. Celats, Lima.
Bonfil Batalla, G. (Selection, Notes, Introduction) (1981) *Utopía y revolución: el pensamiento político contemporáneo de los indios en América Latina*. Nueva Imagen, Mexico.
Bonfil Batalla, G. (1986) La teoría del control cultural en el estudio de los procesos étnicos. *Anuario Antropológico*. Brasilia.
Bonfil Batalla, G. (1987) *México profundo: una civilización negada*. SEP, Mexico.
Bonfil Batalla, G. (Comp.) (1992) *Identidad y pluralismo cultural en América Latina*. Centro de Estudios Antropológicos y Sociológicos Sudamericanos, Buenos Aires.
Bonfil Batalla, G. (Coordinator) (1993) *Nuevas identidades culturales de México*. CONACULTA, Mexico.
Bonfil Batalla, G. (1995 [1962]) Diagnóstico del hambre en Sudzal, Yucatán: un ensayo de antropología aplicada. In: Güemes, L. Ó. (Selection), *Obras escogidas de Guillermo Bonfil*, Vol. 1. INI-DGCP, Mexico.
Colombres, A. (Ed.) (1975) *Por la liberación indígena: documentos y testimonios*. Ediciones del Sol, Buenos Aires.
Colombres, A. (Ed.) (1977) *Hacia la autogestión indígena: documentos y testimonios*. Ediciones del Sol, Quito.
García Mora, C. (Coordinator) (1987) *La antropología en México. Los hechos y los dichos (1880–1986)*, Vol. 15. INAH, Mexico.
García Mora, C. & Medina, A. (Comps.) (1986) *La quiebra política de la antropología social en México*, 2 vols. UNAM, Mexico.
Instituto Nacional Indigenista (1957) *Regiones de refugio*. UNAM, Mexico.
Instituto Nacional Indigenista (1988) *Instituto Nacional Indigenista: 40 años*. INI, Mexico.
Palerm, Á. (Comp.) (1976) *Aguirre Beltrán: obra polémica*. FCE, Mexico.
Villoro, L. (1950) *Los grandes momentos del indigenismo mexicano*. El Colegio de México, Mexico.
Warman, A. et al. (Eds.) (1970) *De eso que llaman antropología mexicana*. Nuestro Tiempo, Mexico.

Bottomore, T. B. (1920–92)

William Outhwaite

Tom Bottomore brought to British sociology a concern with social theory, especially (but by no means entirely) Marxist theory, with social movements, and with what came to be called the third world. He was one of the leading members of the generation of British sociologists who passed through the London School of Economics just after World War II. After a year's research in Paris on Marx and on the French civil service, he returned to LSE, where he taught from 1952 to 1965. Following two years at Simon Fraser University in Vancouver he took up a Chair at the University of Sussex, which he held until his retirement in 1985. He put into practice his thoroughly international approach in many years of patient work developing the International Sociological Association, of which he was president from 1974 to 1978; he was also president of the British Sociological Association from 1969 to 1971.

Bottomore's publishing career began with an edited collection of Marx's writings, and he continued to write and edit books on Marx and Marxism (including Austro-Marxism and the Frankfurt School) throughout his life. He also began a translation of Georg Simmel's *Philosophy of Money*, completed by David Frisby, and retranslated Rudolf Hilferding's *Finanzkapita* (1991) and Karl Löwith's essay of 1932 on *Max Weber and Karl Marx*. He also wrote substantially on classes and elites, on political sociology, and increasingly on economic sociology. At the time of his death he was working on two books, one on the concept of planning and another on socialist democracy. A six-month trip to India meant that his magisterial textbook *Sociology* (1962) was substantially oriented to that country, as well as displaying a sensitivity to issues of global development otherwise rare in British sociology at the time. His many books remain a major reference point for contemporary work across a wide range of fields.

Bottomore was anything but an orthodox Marxist; he had no time, for example, for the concept of dialectic. For him, Marxism was a sociological theory *and* a political project, but the efficacy of each was to be judged on the ground, in practice. Most unorthodox, perhaps, though anticipated in the neo-Kantian Marxism of the Austro-Marxists, was his insistence on the fact/value distinction. He was in many ways an honorary Austro-Marxist, attracted by their combination of economic rigor, political sensitivity, and theoretical openness and flexibility.

But the diffusion and revival of Marxist social theory, which was perhaps Bottomore's principal achievement in Britain, was part of a broader impulse to deprovincialize British sociology in both its theoretical resources and its substantive concerns. He was probably happiest working outside Britain, and his intellectual and practical internationalism and wanderlust gave him a strategic place along with the great immigrants who substantially shaped British sociology in the second half of the twentieth century – such figures as Norbert Elias, Ralf Dahrendorf, Ernst Gellner, John Rex, Ilya Neustadt, Stuart Hall, and Zygmunt Bauman.

He did not predict the sudden collapse of the European state socialist regimes, though he noted their serious economic and political problems and the possible restoration of capitalism. He envisaged and hoped for a more moderate transformation, involving political democratization and the decentralization of economic decision-making. As he had noted earlier, the possibility of the restoration of capitalism undermines the original Marxist notion of a one-way irreversible movement to socialism. "But ... Marx's ... analysis still needs to be pursued in new conditions" (Bottomore 1991: 98).

SEE ALSO: Capitalism; Class; Communism; Critical Theory/Frankfurt School; Marx, Karl; Marxism and Sociology; Neo-Marxism; Socialism; Theory

REFERENCES AND SUGGESTED READINGS

Bottomore, T. (1975) *Marxist Sociology*. Macmillan, London.

Bottomore, T. (1987 [1962]) *Sociology: A Guide to Problems and Literature*. Allen & Unwin, London.

Bottomore, T. (1991 [1965]) *Classes in Modern Society*. Harper Collins, London.

Bottomore, T. (1993 [1964]) *Elites and Society*. Penguin, London.

Bottomore, T. (1993 [1979]) *Political Sociology*. Hutchinson, London.

Halsey, A. H. (2005) *A History of Sociology in Britain: Science, Literature, and Society*. Oxford University Press, Oxford.

Outhwaite, W. & Mulkay, M. (Ed.) (1987) *Social Theory and Social Criticism: Essays for Tom Bottomore*. Blackwell, Oxford.

Taylor, B. & Outhwaite, W. (1989) Interview with Tom Bottomore. *Theory, Culture and Society* 6(3): 385–402.

boundaries (racial/ethnic)

Andreas Wimmer

The study of ethnic and racial boundaries is intimately connected to the constructivist view on race and ethnicity. Rather than individual ethnic or racial "groups," their history, culture, and social organization, the boundaries between such groups and the mechanisms of their production and transformation move to the foreground. This implies a shift away from concerns with the given culture, identity, and social cohesion of ethnic groups toward strategies of boundary *creation* and transformation as they relate to the strategies of other individuals and groups. Perceived cultural or racial similarity or historical continuity thus are now seen as *consequences* rather than *causes* of the making of ethnic and racial boundaries. Such boundaries form a central dimension of the social organization of complex societies and their stratification systems.

The literature goes back to Frederik Barth's introduction to an edited volume (Barth 1969) in which he laid out the constructivist agenda for coming decades of research. Studying ethnic boundaries has since then become a major preoccupation of mainstream anthropology and of the sociology of race and ethnicity. Special attention has been given to the mechanisms of boundary *maintenance*, for example through selection of diacritical elements, linguistic markers, enforcement of endogamy, or more broadly the policing of sexual boundaries.

The constructivist perspective later spilled over into the field of nationalism studies. It has become a commonplace – with the notable exception of Anthony Smith (1986) – to see the boundaries of a national community as resulting from a reversible political process of inclusion and exclusion rather than as a consequence of cultural homogeneity and historical continuity (Wimmer 2002: ch. 3). Spinning off from this nationalism literature, the territorial aspect of the boundary-making process has received some attention. A growing literature subsumed under the banner of "border studies" has emerged from this.

In the study of race relations the constructivist stance has also gained ground over the past two decades. While earlier scholarship, especially in the US, took the existence of racial groups for granted, a newer strand has looked at the role of the state in *creating* and sustaining racial boundaries through strategies of "racialization" (Miles 1993). The focus on boundary making has greatly been enhanced by the emergence of a literature that compares different countries from a macro (e.g., Marx et al. 1999) or a micro perspective (e.g., Lamont 2000) because it helped to denaturalize racial distinctions and highlight the varying nature and salience of racial boundaries in different contexts. Historical research has uncovered that the characteristics of racial divides may change considerably over time and that individuals and entire ethnic groups may have crossed the racial lines over the past generations, thus supporting a broadly constructivist perspective.

Three major limitations of the Barthian paradigm have been discussed over the past decades. First, the importance of power relationships in the making and unmaking of ethnic and racial boundaries was greatly underestimated in the original formulation. Recent scholarship emphasizes the role of the powerful apparatus of the modern state in drawing and enforcing ethnic and racial boundaries through policies of nation building, assimilation, "minority" incorporation, and so on. Others, especially those studying individual ethnic political movements, have emphasized "resistance" of individuals or groups against such policies or the everyday "making" of ethnic boundaries in social networking and moral discourses. The exact relationship between dominant and subordinate strategies of boundary making remains to be determined by future research.

A second problem associated with the earlier literature is the lack of attention given to individual variability. Most fully fledged analyses of boundary making have developed from a "groupist" perspective, to cite Jenkins's (1997) term, which takes ethnic groups as actors with a unified purpose and strategy, assumed to be one of boundary maintenance and policing rather than of dissolution and assimilation. This does not fit well with the ethnographic record, which shows that various, sometimes contradicting, claims to groupness are put forward by persons that share an ethnic background (Brubaker 2004). However, an equally diverse sample of examples could be cited as support for the *opposite* proposition: that ethnic boundaries are drawn unambiguously and are agreed upon by a vast majority of individuals. We know that ethnic conflict and violence tend to enhance such unity and produce clear-cut boundaries. Beyond such rather general observations, no systematic literature has yet developed which would try to explain the variation in the degree of variability.

The last and most widely discussed problematic refers to the limits to the malleability, transformability, and strategic adaptability of ethnic boundaries. Recently, a number of insightful critiques against the more exaggeratedly constructivist interpretations of Barth's essay have appeared. This new literature acknowledges that it is a matter of *degree*, not of *principle*, whether or not ethnic boundaries can be reconstructed and reorganized, following Katherine Verdery's advice to "situate the situationalisms" of Barth (Verdery 1994). A number of mechanisms have been identified that lead to a "hardening" of ethnic boundaries, less strategic malleability, and thus more stability over time.

Contrary to Barth's famed assertion that it is the boundary that matters in ethnic relations, not the "cultural stuff" they enclose, a number of authors have emphasized that this stuff may indeed make a difference. In the continuous landscape of cultural variations we may find discontinuities or ruptures, such as brought about by migration or conquest, along which ethnic boundaries will follow with a high likelihood. Various authors have used different language to make this point.

Bentley and Wimmer have used Bourdieu's habitus theory (Bentley 1987). Cornell (1996) distinguishes between ethnic groups that are held together by shared culture or shared interest, the latter being more prone to boundary manipulation and change. Hale (2004) takes a cognitive perspective and argues that communication barriers or embodied, visible differences will make it more likely that an ethnic or racial boundary emerges and stabilizes. Finally, the precise way boundaries are constructed may have consequences regarding their stability and manipulability through strategic action. Systematic comparative research will have to establish the validity of these various new approaches in a more precise and empirically solid way.

SEE ALSO: Assimilation; Ethnic Groups; Ethnic and Racial Division of Labor; Ethnicity; Race; Race (Racism); Racial Hierarchy; Separatism; Stratification, Race/Ethnicity and

REFERENCES AND SUGGESTED READINGS

Barth, F. (1969) Introduction. In: Barth, F., *Ethnic Groups and Boundaries: The Social Organization of Culture Difference*. Allen & Unwin, London.

Bentley, C. (1987) Ethnicity and Practice. *Comparative Studies in Society and History* 29(1): 24–55.

Brubaker, R. (2004) *Ethnicity Without Groups*. Harvard University Press, Cambridge, MA.

Cornell, S. (1996) The Variable Ties that Bind: Content and Circumstance in Ethnic Processes. *Ethnic and Racial Studies* 19(2): 265–89.

Hale, H. E. (2004) Explaining Ethnicity. *Comparative Political Studies* 37(4): 458–85.

Jenkins, R. (1997) *Rethinking Ethnicity: Arguments and Explorations*. Sage, London.

Lamont, M. (2000) *The Dignity of Working Man: Morality and the Boundaries of Race, Class, and Immigration*. Harvard University Press, Harvard.

Marx, A. W. et al. (1999) *Making Race and Nation: A Comparison of the United States, South Africa, and Brazil*. Cambridge University Press, Cambridge.

Miles, R. (1993) *Racism After "Race Relations."* Routledge & Kegan Paul, London.

Smith, A. D. (1986) *The Ethnic Origins of Nations.* Blackwell, Oxford.

Verdery, K. (1994) Ethnicity, Nationalism, and State-Making. In: Vermeulen, H. & Govers, C. (Eds.), *The Anthropology of Ethnicity: Beyond "Ethnic Groups and Boundaries."* Het Spinhuis, Amsterdam.

Wimmer, A. (2002) *Nationalist Exclusion and Ethnic Conflict: Shadows of Modernity.* Cambridge University Press, Cambridge.

Bourdieu, Pierre (1930–2002)

Christine A. Monnier

Pierre Bourdieu was born in rural southern France and pursued an educational career that led to his enrolment at the École Normale Supérieure as a philosophy major. He spent his military service in Algeria, at the time a French colony, and engaged in anthropological work on Kabylia. There he examined for the first time the effects of power and stratification in the context of colonialism as it interacted with native cultural practices. From then on, his sociological work on the nature and dimensions of power in culture made him one of the most influential contemporary sociologists. For Bourdieu, *culture* is a symbolic order that provides the components of social domination and unconscious mechanisms of reproduction of such domination between social classes. Bourdieu was also a sociologist of practices, that is, how symbolic structures are incarnated in the actions of social agents. Whatever topics he engaged – education, cultural practices, or artistic productions – Bourdieu always considered how both culture and practices sustain forms of social domination. This approach was designed to resolve the traditional dilemmas of sociology: objectivism versus subjectivism, structure versus agency, determination versus freedom. For Bourdieu, those dilemmas could only be transcended by taking into account the existence of invisible objective structures and agents' subjective interpretations of their circumstances.

Drawing from structuralism, Bourdieu conceptualized social and institutional settings as fields or markets. A field is a structured space of positions, a hierarchy (dominant/dominated) based on the unequal distributions in the domains of economics (wealth), social relationships, symbols (prestige), or culture (educational credentials). The amounts and types of capital with which agents are endowed determine their relative positions in the field. In the educational field, upper-class students are endowed with different forms of capital that place them in a more valued position than lower-class students. As a result, fields are characterized by struggles to improve one's position and to define what counts as legitimate production. For instance, in the artistic field, avant-garde artists may struggle to challenge the definition of what is considered "art" against what may be defined as commercialization. Fields also compete with one another for dominance. Religious and political actors may want to influence what counts as legitimate art. According to Bourdieu, any sociological analysis should start by examining the field under study to determine the different positions, what kind of capital is most valued, how legitimacy is defined and by whom, and the struggles and strategies actors engage in. Such structural analysis provides the structural framework of social action.

For Bourdieu, the major determinant of practices is *habitus*: the set of dispositions actors acquire in their social milieu that generate and organize practices and representations. Habitus is the source of many types of ordinary behaviors, shaping artistic tastes (*distinction*), table manners, speech patterns (*language and symbolic power*), body language (*masculine domination*), writing styles, food and drink preferences, educational success (*reproduction in education, the state nobility*), etc. In all these practices are embodied a social hierarchy. For instance, not all artistic tastes are equally valued in the field of cultural production, and not just any writing style is valued in the educational field. To prefer Hollywood blockbusters to avant-garde cinema is to display a lower-class habitus; to be at ease in select restaurants and know how to choose the right wine reveals a high-class habitus. In all cultural practices and fields, habitus is what distinguishes and divides social classes and determines dominant and dominated positions. In this sense, an agent's subjectivity is itself structured through the inculcation of habitus and reveals the social conditions in which it was acquired as well as the capital (or lack thereof) with which the agent was endowed.

If field and capital are what determine action from the outside, habitus is what determines action from the inside. Therefore, any complete sociological analysis should include agents' representations and attitudes as they shape their experience in any given field. By combining analysis of both field and habitus, Bourdieu is able to transcend the structure/agency dilemma by integrating them (Swartz 1997: 141).

For Bourdieu, if habitus, capital, and field determine practice, then the academic world and the sociologist herself should not be exempt from sociological analysis. All sociology should involve reflexivity: the sociological analysis of the conditions of production of sociological work. After all, the academic world is a field of power, as any other field, and the sociologist is an agent vying for recognition (capital). How sociologists study the social world, the topics and methodologies they select, etc., therefore should be analyzed as products of a specific field and strategies to improve their producer's position. Also, agents operating in the academic world develop an academic habitus, a topic that Bourdieu studied in *Homo Academicus*.

In the last part of his life, Bourdieu entered the public sphere to engage major political issues, something he had always been reluctant to do as he was wary of being co-opted by social movements. However, he saw economic, political, social, and cultural developments as justifying his intervention in the public debate. Nevertheless, Bourdieu's position remained uncompromising and reflexive. He believed that entering the public debate should be done carefully, and intellectuals thus risking manipulation by political organizations or by the media should offer not merely signatures on petitions, but also their expertise in building an informed political agenda. For his part, Bourdieu used his carefully developed concepts and research to illuminate social issues.

In his work on television, Bourdieu examined the impact and influence of the logic of the market on the journalistic field. This influence generates a tension between "pure" and commercial poles. At the pure pole, the journalistic field is organized autonomously according to its own internal ethical codes and principles. At the commercial pole, demand imposed on actors in the field mostly comes from external constraints, advertising revenues, polls, and ratings. Bourdieu's concern is that the commercial pole is becoming dominant and this implies consequences not only for the journalistic field but for other fields as well, as the journalistic field, heteronomous by definition, has the capacity to influence other fields – culture, science, academia, and so on.

One important consequence of the domination of the market over the journalistic field is the depoliticization of news through a focus on anecdotes, human interest stories, and scandals at the expense of socially and politically significant news. At the same time, journalists may themselves be turned into celebrities, their power deriving from popularity rather than from credibility based on their field's standards. This is significant because journalists are dominated agents among the dominants; they are subjected to the authority of network/newspaper owners (mostly corporate groups), editors, and the logic of market revenues in general. As a result, they might develop a self-censoring habitus, drifting toward the commercial pole of the field without being directly coerced to do so. Correlatively, the media become a place of choice for actors from other fields, where they may have been failures, but now can find celebrity and fame in the media field. This is particularly visible in science where failed scientific agents – those who failed according to the mechanisms of the scientific field, such as professional research and publications – may find new credibility and power, their lack of professional credibility ignored if they fit the journalistic field.

As a result of such depoliticization, newsworthy items – especially from non-western countries – tend to be downplayed unless they provide some temporary sensational stories. Many US 24-hour news cable channels tend to summarize foreign news through segments with such titles as "The World in 60 Seconds." When such networks do address the news, it is usually depoliticized and uncritical, using simplistic dichotomies (democrats versus republican, pro versus con) which mask complex issues.

In his final writing, Bourdieu takes on the social uses of the concept of "globalization" that has become an obligatory reference in all sociopolitical and economic debates. He argues that globalization is both a descriptive concept that refers to the worldwide expansion of financial speculation and market capitalism and a normative concept conveying the idea that global capitalism and the dominance of the market are *faits accomplis*, an inescapable reality to which societies and social agents must adapt. Globalization is thus presented as a new utopia: the "natural" next evolutionary stage in socioeconomic structure. For Bourdieu, this view is a carefully constructed myth whose "naturalistic" touch hides its social production mechanisms and power relations.

For Bourdieu, in the social reality masked by the myth of globalization, representatives of the states are liquidating the progressive welfare systems established in western democracies. State agents are thereby eliminating one of the most important roles of the nation-state: the social protection of its citizens. Under the new doxa (neoliberal ideology), or dominant discourse, such protection has to be eliminated in the name of flexibility, budgetary constraints imposed from outside, and global competition. This decline in power of the nation-state correlates with the rise in power of global institutions, such as the World Bank, the International Monetary Fund, and the World Trade Organization, all of which lack accountability.

This structural reconfiguration of institutions, misleadingly presented as necessitated by the times, is actually the product of social and ideological strategies by actors in the economic field to increase their symbolic capital. One such strategy has been the successful imposition of the new neoliberal doxa that presents globalization as an economic necessity. Bourdieu demonstrates that the creation and imposition of this new doxa is actually a deliberate social product.

The idea of globalization as the next step in the evolution of economic systems was promoted by think-tank economists as part of a large-scale lobbying effort to promote this new doxa. Economic issues were addressed in the media as an objective domain in their own

right, completely independent from political and social considerations and to be dealt with by economic experts. This economic discourse was then presented as objective, scientific, and rational, disqualifying it from critique by its rivals which ostensibly lacked such qualities. Additionally, globalization of market mechanisms, as part of the new doxa, becomes the new revolution toward progress and democracy. Therefore, any opponent could be labeled as anti-democratic, archaic, or selfishly reactionary. Finally, to paraphrase Bourdieu, the new doxa tends to universalize the particular, i.e., to impose worldwide a mode of thinking and an economic system specific to the United States while presenting them as natural universals.

The result of this strategy was to increase the symbolic and social capital of economists as globalization experts in the academic and media fields. Such an increase in capital was also accomplished by turning economics into an entirely abstract and mathematical discipline, churning out models by which economic reality and policies were to be measured. In cases of disjunctions between models and reality, the models can never be wrong and the blame would be placed on politicians or citizens, too ignorant or undisciplined to make the right economic choices. The difficult reality that results from neoliberal policies would be left to other social scientists with less symbolic capital to examine.

For Bourdieu, to substitute abstract mathematical models for economic and social reality produces two types of effects. First, it amounts to mistaking the things of logic for the logic of things. In other words, the model always prevails and reality becomes irrelevant. Second, mathematical skills become a new tool of social selection and reproduction in the educational and academic fields.

The real consequences of such policies were explored at length in empirical work by Bourdieu and his team in *The Weight of the World*. For Bourdieu, these consequences are disastrous for democracy as they include depoliticization, that is, a growing political apathy and crisis of legitimacy of the political class. This depoliticization is directly the result of the takeover of economic matters by global institutions with no accountability to any constituencies. As a result, social agents understand that no matter which group of politicians they elect, the economic policies will not change. Another social consequence hidden by the new doxa is the destruction of everything collective – unions, collective contracts, and wage scales. The social agent is left to fend for herself in an individualized labor market, whose main characteristic is the casualization of work, insecurity, and flexibility.

SEE ALSO: Capital: Economic, Cultural, and Social; Habitus/Field; Poststructuralism; Structuralism; Structure and Agency

REFERENCES AND SUGGESTED READINGS

Bourdieu, P. (1977) *Outline of a Theory of Practice.* Cambridge University Press, Cambridge.
Bourdieu, P. (1984) *Distinction: A Social Critique of the Judgment of Taste.* Harvard University Press, Cambridge, MA.
Bourdieu, P. (1990) *The Logic of Practice.* Stanford University Press, Stanford, CA.
Bourdieu, P. (1991) *Language and Symbolic Power.* Harvard University Press, Cambridge, MA.
Bourdieu, P. (1993) *The Field of Cultural Production.* Columbia University Press, New York.
Bourdieu, P. (1998a) *On Television.* New Press, New York.
Bourdieu, P. (1998b) *Acts of Resistance: Against the Tyranny of the Market.* New Press, New York.
Bourdieu, P. (2003) *Firing Back: Against the Tyranny of the Market 2.* New Press, New York.
Jenkins, R. (1992) *Pierre Bourdieu.* Routledge, London.
Swartz, D. (1997) *Culture and Power: The Sociology of Pierre Bourdieu.* University of Chicago Press, Chicago.
Webb, J., Schirato, T., & Danaher, G. (2002) *Understanding Bourdieu.* Sage, London.

bourgeoisie and proletariat

Wout Ultee

Engels and Marx are regarded as the founders of a theoretical tradition in sociology called historical materialism. This perspective takes economic power as the prime dimension of social stratification and holds that the history of all hitherto-existing societies is the history of class struggles. The main classes in the societies Engels and Marx studied most intensively were the bourgeoisie and the proletariat. More particularly, classical historical materialism postulated several trends supposedly characteristic of any society with private ownership of the means of production, such as machines and factories (capital goods) and free markets for capital, labor, and consumption goods. According to the "general law of capitalist accumulation," the longer the capitalist mode of production prevails, the more capital will have accumulated, leading to both higher profits for capital owners (the bourgeoisie) and to worsening living conditions for the people who live by their labor (the proletariat). Although recognizing in the early phases of the capitalist mode of production the presence of small and large proprietors as well as skilled and unskilled workers, the persistence of the capitalist mode of production would lead to a disappearance of the middle classes. Small proprietors would become less common, as they lose out in the fierce competition from large proprietors. Workers skilled in using their hand tools would also become less common as proprietors replace them with cheaper unskilled workers operating machines. In addition, since the persistence of the capitalist mode of production is accompanied by ever deeper economic downturns, wages tend to fall while the percentage of unemployed workers rises.

Engels charted the condition of the working class in England in the early 1840s by adducing personal observations and authentic sources. He also pointed towards proletarian violence during economic downturns, and maintained that each new economic crisis would be accompanied by more violence. Two decades later Marx sought to "illustrate" the general law of capitalist accumulation by way of governmental statistics for the UK. Production of coal and iron had increased, more railway tracks were in use, and exports had boomed. At the same time profits grew, and the numbers on the official lists of paupers increased. Of course, the proletariat never violently overthrew the bourgeoisie.

Around 1900, Eduard Bernstein, of the revisionist wing of historical materialism, pointed out that wages had increased. He invoked the rise of better-paid skilled labor, necessary for the operation and construction of machines. He also predicted that labor unionism, the introduction of general suffrage, and the increasing vote for social democratic parties would lead to a gradual reform of capitalism. After World War II the revisionist prediction was that rising standards of living would result in the embourgeoisement of the working class.

Within orthodox historical materialism the old hypothesis that under capitalism the bourgeoisie gets richer and the proletariat poorer cropped up in different guises. Before World War I, Rosa Luxemburg held that the rise of wages in the mother countries of colonial empires was offset by a decline in the living conditions of colonial workers. In the 1970s, after the political independence of most colonies, Immanuel Wallerstein's world-system theory postulated a trend towards more absolute poverty in the periphery of the world economy (the old colonies) as a consequence of the increasing power of multinational companies (with their head offices in the old imperial centers) extracting raw materials in the periphery to be processed in the center. Of late, in connection with the elimination of import barriers in rich countries against manufactured goods from poorer countries, it has been argued that globalization fosters unhealthy working conditions and child labor in the periphery of the world economy.

These orthodox hypotheses have led to systematic quantitative research, and the results suggest that they contain at least some truth. In addition, the issue of whether income inequalities and extreme poverty are rising on a world scale is hotly debated and frequently researched in contemporary sociology. Also, although mass unemployment during the 1930s gave way to several decades of almost full employment after World War II, double-digit unemployment levels in several Western European countries beginning in the 1980s have brought old questions about the developmental tendencies of market economies to the fore again.

SEE ALSO: Capitalism; Class Consciousness; Employment Status Changes; Engels, Friedrich; Income Inequality, Global; Marx, Karl; Marxism and Sociology

REFERENCES AND SUGGESTED READINGS

Chase-Dunn, C. & Grimes, P. (1995) World-Systems Analysis. *Annual Review of Sociology* 21: 387–417.
Engels, F (1969 [1845]) *The Condition of the Working Class in England.* Panther, London.
Goldthorpe, J. H., Lockwood, D., Bechhofer, F., & Platt, J. (1969) *The Affluent Worker in the Class Structure.* Cambridge University Press, Cambridge.
Klein, N. (2000) *No Logo.* Picador, New York.
Wallerstein, E. (1983) *Historical Capitalism.* Verso, London.

brand culture

Jonathan E. Schroeder

Brand culture places brands firmly within culture to look at the complex underpinnings of branding processes. Much brand research emerged from the allied fields of management, marketing, and strategy, which generally hew toward positivistic models of brand "effects" driven by quantitative analysis. Recently, sociologists, anthropologists, and cultural studies researchers have looked at brands from historical, critical, and ideological perspectives, acknowledging the growing importance of brands in society (Koehn 2001; Lury 2004). An emphasis on brand culture forms part of a larger call for inclusion of sociological issues within the management and marketing research canon, joining in the contention that culture and history can provide a necessary contextualizing counterpoint to managerial and information processing views of branding's interaction with consumers and society.

Brand culture refers to the cultural influences and implications of brands in two ways. First, we live in a branded world: brands infuse culture with meaning, and brand management exerts a profound influence on contemporary society. Second, brand culture constitutes a third dimension for brand research – in conjunction with traditional research areas of *brand identity* and *brand image*, brand culture provides the necessary cultural, historical, and political grounding to understand brands in context. The brand culture concept occupies the theoretical space between strategic concepts of brand identity and consumer interpretations of brand image, shedding light on the gap often seen between managerial intention and market response.

Recent research has shown that brands are interpreted or read in multiple ways, prompting an important and illuminating reconsideration of how branding "works," and shifting attention from brand producers toward *consumer response* to understand how branding creates meaning (Holt 2004; Schroeder & Salzer-Mörling 2005). Cultural codes, ideological discourse, consumers' background knowledge, and rhetorical processes have been cited as influences in branding and consumers' relationships to advertising, brands, and mass media. Consumers are seen to construct and perform identities and self-concepts, trying out new roles and creating their identity within and in collaboration with brand culture.

If brands exist as cultural, ideological, and sociological objects, then brand researchers require tools developed to understand culture, ideology, and society, in conjunction with more typical branding concepts such as *brand equity*, *strategy*, and *value*. Thus, brand culture implies an awareness of basic cultural processes that affect contemporary brands, including historical context, ethical concerns, and consumer response. In other words, neither managers nor consumers completely control branding processes – cultural codes constrain how brands work to produce meaning. In this way, research on brands and branding has opened up to include cultural, sociological, and philosophical inquiry that both complements and complicates economic and managerial analysis (Lury 2004; Arvidsson 2005).

How do brands interact with culture? From a cultural perspective, brands can be understood as communicative objects. The brand manager wants consumers to buy into a symbolic universe as defined by, in part, the brand identity. In theory, brand management is about communicating a message interpreted in line with the brand owner's intention (Kapferer 2004). This

perspective fails to take into account consumers' active negotiation of brand meaning, contextual effects such as time, space, and personal history, and cultural processes such as the No Logo and anti-globalization movements. At one level, consumer choice is critical to understand why certain brands become more successful than others. However, the meanings consumers ascribe to brands are not only the result of a projected brand identity – a process of negotiation also takes place in and between a marketing environment, a cultural environment, and a social environment. Managing brands successfully mandates managing the brand's meaning in the marketplace – the brand image. Yet the brand meaning is not wholly derived from the market. Culture, aesthetics, and history interact to inject brands into the global flow of images.

Brands are not only strong mediators of cultural meaning – brands themselves have become strong ideological referents that shape cultural rituals, economic activities, and social norms among consumers and producers. In this way, brands and branding can be seen as a central historical and cultural force with profound impacts on the perception of the marketplace and of the consumer. Furthermore, brands may preempt cultural spheres which used to be the privilege of religion or politics. Brands promote an ideology closely related to theological and political models that equate consumption with happiness – a classic advertising proposition. Strong brands constantly develop prescriptive models for the way we talk, the way we think, and the way we behave.

Brands have become a contested managerial, academic, and cultural arena. Many of the world's biggest companies – and most highly valued brands – are seen as *corporate brands* rather than corporate entities – such as McDonald's, Nike, BMW, and Coca-Cola – each valued more for their intangible brand attributes than for any other assets (Interbrand 2005). These corporate brands are an increasingly important, powerful, and visible part of culture and demand distinctive research approaches. Scholars from different disciplines squabble over who owns the brand literature, with marketing, management, corporate identity, and advertising academics squaring off for dominance.

The cultural landscape has been profoundly transformed into a commercial brandscape in which the production and consumption of brands rival the production and consumption of physical products (Baudrillard 1981). This shift has been called an attention economy, an experience economy, an information society, and an image economy. Future research questions include: What does this transformation imply for branding and consumer culture? How do brands command so much value? What roles do brands play in cultural and social institutions, rituals, and trends?

SEE ALSO: Branding and Organizational Identity; Brands and Branding; Consumption, Spectacles of; Consumption, Visual; Mass Media and Socialization; Media and Consumer Culture

REFERENCES AND SUGGESTED READINGS

Arvidsson, A. (2005) *Brands: Meaning and Value in Postmodern Media Culture*. Routledge, London.
Baudrillard, J. (1981) *For a Critique of the Political Economy of the Sign*. Telos, St. Louis, MO.
Hackley, C. (2004) *Advertising and Promotion: Communicating Brands*. Sage, London.
Holt, D. B. (2004) *How Brands Become Icons: The Principles of Cultural Branding*. Harvard Business School Press, Boston.
Interbrand (2005) The 100 Best Global Brands by Value. Online. www.interbrand.com.
Kapferer, J.-N. (2004) *Strategic Brand Management: Creating and Sustaining Brand Equity Long Term*. Kogan Page, London:.
Klein, N. (1999) *No Logo: Taking Aim at the Brand Bullies*. Picador, New York.
Koehn, N. F. (2001) *Brand New: How Entrepreneurs Earned Consumers' Trust from Wedgewood to Dell*. Harvard Business School Press, Boston.
Lury, C. (2004) *Brands: The Logos of the Global Economy*. Routledge, London.
Muñiz, A. M., Jr. & O'Guinn, T. C. (2001) Brand Community. *Journal of Consumer Research* 27: 412–32.
Schroeder, J. E. & Salzer-Mörling, M. (Eds.) (2005) *Brand Culture*. Routledge, London.

branding and organizational identity

Matthew Higgins

Branding and organizational identity refer to a process through which a pattern or a structure is ascribed to a group of individuals and recognized as unique, autonomous, and relatively stable in space and time. There are two components to this: the organizational identity, which is a concern with *what and who* the organization is, and branding, which is primarily concerned with how the organization is represented to key stakeholders. In part, the development of the body of work relating to branding and organizational identity can be summarized as the story of how writers and practitioners have sought to clarify the relationship between these components and increasingly of late to see how branding and identity can be treated holistically through multidisciplinary perspectives.

Organizational identity is conventionally concerned with how an organization's members conceptualize who "we" are and what "we" stand for. A relatively recent field of study, it is largely informed by social identity theory, examining how identity is formed through social interaction and how individuals identify with the organization. Within the literature, organizational identity is often contrasted with corporate identity, the latter being a concern with how the organization expresses itself, or brands itself. Issues of branding and organizational identity have traditionally straddled the business disciplines and have received increasing attention since World War II. Scholars in strategy, organizational studies, accounting, and marketing have adopted approaches to the subject that reflect the primary interests and motivations of their respective disciplines. This is evidenced with the myriad of differing terms through which to explore branding and organizational identity. Thus, we see contributions on corporate image, corporate reputation, corporate branding, corporate communication, corporate personality, and corporate identity.

Each of these terms draws from a particular intellectual and cultural background and provides a distinct focus on the subject. The term of preference is largely at the whim of fashion, each term's popularity ebbing and flowing as preferences change.

Each perspective usually privileges certain aspects of branding and organizational identity, whether it be examining who the organization is and what the organization stands for, or how, what, and to whom the organization communicates. For example, strategists employ the term organizational identity to refer to a concern with an organization's competitive position and reputation within the marketplace. This provokes a perspective that incorporates representations of the internal and external environment, with a focus upon what the organization is and how it is presently positioned and how it would ideally be positioned. The audience for the output of this examination is primarily internal (e.g., managers within the organization). These themes are developed with a marketing perspective that is often focused on the interconnections between image and product propositions, stretching this idea to emphasize the need for coherence in the image between the producer and the produced. Accordingly, strategic marketers have offered a view of organizational identity that is seen as both an analytical tool for examining strategic positioning within the environment, while also being a means of defining parameters of the organization and establishing distinctiveness within a competitive marketplace. This is often complemented by marketing communication that is concerned with the manner through which the organization communicates to the external stakeholders and the content and design of that message. In contrast, accountants have sought to measure the financial value accrued through the organization's identity by examining the strength of the identity across key stakeholders, appreciating the distinctive qualities of that identity within a given context, and using this information to attach a financial value to the organization's brand – more commonly referred to as brand equity. The significance of a financial value being attached to the strength of brand identity has encouraged many organizations to strengthen their image and to move away from representing themselves as

simply "producers" to organizations with a sense of "being" or personality. Thus, accountants are primarily concerned with how the organization is presented to an external audience and how that presentation is perceived.

These externally focused perspectives have often received the label *corporate identity*, while studies that looked inward at the way in which identity was formed have employed the term *organizational identity*. This latter term is often the preferred expression for scholars in organizational studies, who explore perspectives on organizational structure, and examine the interaction between culture, the self, identity, and image within an organization. Within organizational studies, organizational identity is a field of study that traces its origins to Albert and Whetton's (1985) influential article on the organization's central character, distinctiveness, and temporal continuity aspects. This approach argues that an organization may possess multiple personalities and that these may be at both the individual level and the level of the organization. Of particular interest is the temporal and evolving nature of identity, with issues of identity having particular congruence at particular stages of the organization's development. Albert and Whetton's ideas have been subject to critique for their proposition that an organization's identity is enduring. Writers in the last decade have sought to question how enduring an organization's identity is, viewing organizational identity as dynamic and suggesting that identity is increasingly fluid and transient to enable it to respond to environmental change.

The central role of communication in the processes of identity formation is also relevant to this discussion. Burke's (1966) "rhetoric of identification" links identity with issues of persuasion and processes of organizing. Burke argues that identification is a necessity due to the estrangement experienced by the individual through the division of labor. The individual responds to the division by acting to identify with others, seeking personal meaning through corporate identities. These identities may be manifested through labels and names, enhancing the self through status and prestige. For example, by identifying with a particular group within an organization, any praise directed at the unit is also directly or indirectly praise for the individual. While Burke's identification is usually associated with the individual act of identifying, the organization can provide assistance in this process through symbolic processes that associate and disassociate the individual with specified groups. Within organization communications the use of "we" and "they" is important to induce cooperation. The managers within an organization may seek to encourage the individual employee that they and the organization are like them, that they share similar values and beliefs, or that the individual shares with the manager and the organization a common enemy against which the parties should unite.

However, these differing perspectives to the body of thought have highlighted the multifaceted nature of branding within the organizational context. In the process they have offered new ways of conceptualizing organizations, with a particular focus on the presentation of the identity within and of the organization. Increasingly, the differing perspectives from organizational studies, marketing, accountancy, and human resource management are being drawn together. The outwards directed communications and identity presentation has been supplemented with identity formation and internal communications to employees, shareholders, suppliers, and distributors. The idea of what constitutes the corporate image has also broadened. The corporate brand has moved away from a monologue through advertising and press releases, to an interactive "experience" (Schmitt 1999). Increasingly, organizational branding is seen as a means for the specialist functions of an organization (e.g., marketing, accounting, and human resource management) to work together in support of a cohesive entity. Issues of distinctiveness encompass not merely the differentiation from other organizations, but also the ability of the organization to demonstrate who they are and what they stand for. This is epitomized by Schultz et al. (2000), who bring together the differing perspectives to suggest that a holistic approach to organizational branding is necessary.

This extension of branding to organizations has been driven by a number of factors, most notably deregulation of industries, mergers, acquisitions, and the internationalization of business. The growth of the service sector and the development of electronic exchanges have required organizations to rely increasingly upon the development of familiar visual cues and symbols to attract and reassure the customers in the absence of more tangible evidence. With the renewal of debates surrounding corporate social responsibility in the 1990s, the need for an organization to demonstrate what it stands for has seen a focus upon activities that enhance the organization's reputation and realize its responsibility as a "corporate citizen." In a period of shortened product life cycles and difficulty in recruiting and retaining quality staff, a strong corporate identity can provide a degree of protection from competitors. In the building of an identity, particular attention is paid to the structures, actions, communications, products, and services associated with the organization.

Perhaps significantly, the push to develop a coherent identity for the organization coexists with the problematization of the boundaries of the organization. The processes within a value chain are often spread across organizations, requiring the cooperation of a number of organizations in the fulfillment of the desired outcome. Strategic alliances, secondment, the outsourcing of supply, and subcontracting of production thus provide examples of where divisions between organizations become blurred. The distinction between the customer and selling organization is also problematized. The means by which organizations communicate is transforming this relationship as digital media enable an increasing number of communication channels and promote an approach to relations that emphasizes the need for interactivity.

Due to the relative youth of the area, researchers approach organizational identity through a multitude of differing perspectives and there has been a concentration on conceptual issues rather than methodological approaches. Methods used to research organizational identity and branding include functionalist approaches which view corporate identity as a social fact. This is exemplified by market research attitude surveys, and psychometric tests that seek to establish the feelings and perceptions of individuals (e.g., customers and other key external stakeholders to the brand) are frequently used tools. In contrast, more interpretive perspectives are beginning to draw linkages between identity, image, and culture, examining how symbols, rites, and infrastructure are used to construct meaning. Such approaches have also problematized the identity of the stakeholders and defining whether stakeholders are external or internal to the organization. A more relational approach is being adopted that seeks to undertake a more longitudinal perspective on how an individual relates to the organization. Discourse analysis offers a particularly intriguing method for exploring how myths and stories help to formulate the organization's identity. Such an approach also exposes the probability of there being a number of storytelling narratives that are not necessarily coherent and quite likely to be contradictory. The manner in which the employee is constructed within such narratives and how the employee seeks to live up to the story being told becomes an area of interest. This moves us into the way in which the employee uses branding to exhibit a particular form of self to the organization that is enterprising and simulates the values expressed through the organization. With the convergence of perspectives and the emphasis on developing a multidisciplinary perspective on organizational identity and branding, a number of research tools that seek to fulfill this approach are being promoted. Of particular recent managerial interest is the AC^{2}ID Test developed by Balmer and Greyser (2002). The authors are seeking to develop a holistic perspective on organizational identity and branding, drawing from functionalist and interpretive perspectives. Rather than assume a monolithic organizational identity, Balmer and Greyser propose that any organization comprises a number of identities and these identities are pertinent to different groups both within and beyond the organization. The AC^{2}ID Test provides a framework within which these identities can be explored, the aim being to manage these identities and to ensure alignment.

Over the last decade, the sociopolitical aspects of branding and organizational identity have been explored and work in this area has enjoyed a broad audience. Popular texts have employed the ideas of branding and organizational identity to illuminate broader social problems. Texts such as Naomi Klein's *No Logo* (2000), Douglas Coupland's *MicroSerfs* (1995), and Morgan Spurlock's documentary film *Supersize Me* (2004) have made significant contributions to the debate. These, and similar texts, position branding and organizational identity as an integral aspect of what could be referred to as marketing culture. This is the acknowledgment that the consumer sign-based structure of society is incorporated within the discourse of civil society and is integral to the structuring of social relations. The distinction between consumption and production is blunted as the act of working itself becomes an act of consumption, employment becoming an integral part of identity formation. Who you work for and the way in which you work are increasingly as important as the clothes worn, places seen, and the labels displayed in the presentation of the self. With the convergence of the shopper and the worker, the debates on organizational identity and branding are central to discussions of the construction of the individual within contemporary society.

SEE ALSO: Brands and Branding; Consumption, Spectacles of; Consumption, Mass Consumption, and Consumer Culture; Globalization, Consumption and; Identity Theory; Management Consultants; Organizations and the Theory of the Firm

REFERENCES AND SUGGESTED READINGS

Albert, S. & Whetton, D. (1985) Organizational Identity. *Research in Organizational Behaviour* 7: 263–95.

Balmer, J. M. T. & Greyser, S. A. (2002) Managing the Multiple Identities of the Corporation. *California Management Review* 44(3): 72–86.

Balmer, J. M. T. & Greyser, S. A. (2003) *Revealing the Corporation: Perspectives on Identity, Image, Reputation and Corporate Branding*. Routledge, New York.

Burke, K. (1966) *Language and Symbolic Action: Essays on Life, Literature and Method*. Cambridge University Press, Cambridge.

Coupland, D. (1995) *Microserfs*. Flamingo, London.

Klein, N. (2000) *No Logo: No Space, No Choice, No Jobs, Taking Aim at the Brand Bullies*. Flamingo, London.

Schmitt, B. (1999) *Experiential Marketing: How to Get Customers to Sense, Feel, Think, Act, and Relate to Your Company and Brands*. Free Press, New York.

Schultz, M., Hatch, M. J., & Larsen, M. H. (2000)
The Expressive Organization: Linking Identity, Reputation, and the Corporate Brand. Oxford University Press, Oxford.

brands and branding

Albert M. Muñiz, Jr.

According to the American Marketing Association, a brand is any name, sign, or symbol designed to identify and differentiate the goods or services of one producer from those of competing producers. Brands can be distinguished from the more generic constructs of products and services, which can be defined as anything offered for sale to a market to satisfy a need or a want. At a deeper level, a brand is the total constellation of meanings, feelings, perceptions, beliefs, and goodwill attributed to any market offering displaying a particular sign. Unbranded products and services are commodities (flour, soap, beer). Brands allow for the differentiation of generic products and services by associating them with particular meanings and qualities. Branding refers to the advertising, marketing, and managerial practices designed to develop, build, and sustain the characteristics, properties, relationships, and signifiers of a particular brand.

Brands and branding have greatly facilitated competitive market economies by allowing producers a way to differentiate similar offerings. Hence, market capitalism is intimately linked with the concepts of brands and branding. Brands have also changed the ways in which consumers make consumption decisions, relate to the market, define themselves, and interact with others. By virtue of their pervasiveness and the sophistication with which they are produced and managed, brands can now be considered one of the chief sources of meaning in modern consumer culture. Brands and branding have become much accepted hallmarks of contemporary society and consumer culture by both their proponents and their critics (Schudson 1984; Twitchell 1999).

Today, brands are applied to everything including political parties, universities, and

religions. Even water and dirt are branded. Despite its current prevalence, the practice of branding is a relatively recent development. While there are precedents that go back much further (stonemasons and other artisans have marked the goods they produced with watermarks and other symbols in order to identify their source for centuries [Hine 1995]), what we would recognize today as true branding did not begin until the second half of the nineteenth century. As recently as 1875, most products were still sold as unmarked and unbranded commodities. Producers sold their goods to distributors and retailers who then dispensed them in a largely generic fashion. Consumers simply purchased what was available. Soap was sold by weight from an unbranded cake, flour was dispensed from unmarked sacks, and beer was drawn from an unnamed keg. These practices changed as the first national manufacturers' brands emerged in the latter decades of the nineteenth century.

Several convergent forces made the emergence of brands possible. Advances in manufacturing and packaging fostered the efficient production and standardization necessary for successful product differentiation, while improvements in transportation made national distribution possible. Changes in trademark and patent laws allowed manufacturers the ability to protect their brands, trademarks, and innovations. A growing and increasingly literate population created consumers that could read and understand the claims different brands were making, while the emergence of national media enabled these claims to be easily disseminated to a national audience (Keller 1998). However, the most important precursor to the emergence of brands was the rise of the modern advertising industry. Modern advertising, using national media, allowed marketers an increasingly sophisticated way to reach the population in order to create, elaborate, and project their brands onto the national consciousness (Fox 1984; Marchand 1985).

The first products to be branded were patent medicines and tobacco. During the 1850s tobacco producers first began to engage in truly modern branding efforts, including creating colorful brand names and distinctive packaging. Advertising and branding quickly caught on and the practice spread rapidly, particularly among packaged goods manufacturers. By the early twentieth century, national mass-marketed brands began to dominate and then replace unmarked (and often local) commodities sold from bulk containers. Brands soon became prominent and respected.

During the twentieth century, branding evolved considerably. Following the development of the first national brands, the practice of branding became far more specialized and scientific. Experts emerged in the many different aspects of branding, such as trademark design, marketing research, and advertising. The role of advertising in promoting brands also increased as advertising agencies developed more professional copy and slogans. Shortly before World War II, packaged goods manufacturer Procter and Gamble introduced the brand management system (Low & Fullerton 1994). Rather than leaving responsibility for a brand spread among experts in several different functional areas, the brand management system assigned a single manager to be responsible for the performance of that brand. This fostered greater consistency in the strategy and tactics applied to these brands and served to make them even more powerful.

The brand management system became standard practice during the national brand and economic boom following World War II. As this approach became more sophisticated, marketing and branding efforts began to focus on segmenting, targeting, and positioning, creating increasingly specific meanings that were aimed at increasingly smaller and better-defined markets. In the 1980s, branding became focused on the concept of brand equity, the value (particularly financial) added to a functional product or service by associating it with a brand name. The emphasis on brand equity focused attention on defining, measuring, valuing, and controlling strong brands. This was when the concepts of family branding and brand extension became particularly powerful, resulting in a multiplicity of brand variations, such as the several varieties of Coke now available: Coke Classic, Coke II, Coca-Cola C2, Cherry Coke, Vanilla Coke, Diet Coke, Caffeine Free Coke, and Caffeine Free Diet Coke. New challenges include the rapid proliferation of brands and products, the fragmentation and saturation of media and markets, threats to intellectual brand

property and logos, and an increasingly vocal anti-branding movement.

Brands have greatly impacted the practice of business. Branding allows marketers to charge a premium for their offerings. Manufacturers are able to impart different, additional, and particular meaning to their generic commodities, resulting in far fewer acceptable substitutes at a given price. This increases profits and provides protection against price competition. Brands provide the manufacturer with leverage in distribution channels. Distributors and retailers prefer strong brands because they are less risky. This results in wider distribution and ample and prominent shelf space. Brands also lower marketing and advertising costs by making consumer awareness and loyalty more efficient to maintain.

Brands have also changed the lives of consumers. Brands simplify purchase decision-making by fostering predictability and accountability. Consumers who have tried a particular brand understand what that brand offers and believe that they can expect the same experience every time they consume it. Consumers also know who they can hold responsible if a branded product does not live up to its expectations. Brands are a powerful source of meaning. Some have suggested that the meaning of a brand is its most important characteristic (O'Guinn & Muñiz 2005). Others have gone further and argued that brands (and the advertising and marketing efforts on which they are predicated) are the chief vessels of meaning in contemporary consumer culture and are important cultural resources for individual identity projects (Holt 2002). By consuming different brands, consumers are able to construct a social self and communicate their identity to others.

Just as the practice of branding has evolved, so too has the way in which brands are understood and researched. For decades, brands were approached almost exclusively from psychological and economic perspectives which stressed individual, passive, and rational consumers. Brands were treated as a set of weighted attributes, which were conveyed to consumers who largely accepted them in toto. Though broadening in focus and complexity, these models have kept their focus on the passive, rational individual. Recently, the fields of marketing and consumer behavior have begun to embrace sociological and anthropological perspectives, focusing attention on what consumers do with brands rather than what brands do to consumers (Brown et al. 2003; Thompson 2004). These perspectives treat brands as social creations and view consumers and their various social aggregations as active interpreters and co-creators of brands (Firat & Venkatesh 1995; Fournier 1998; Kates 2004).

The Internet and the World Wide Web allow consumers an unprecedented ability to talk to like-minded others about their brand beliefs and experiences and have created new opportunities and challenges for branding. These media allow marketers a chance to observe consumer conversations in order to learn what consumers really think about their brands. They have provided an opportunity for marketers to affect these conversations via peer to peer, grassroots, and viral branding efforts. These media have also created challenges by fostering consumer interaction and aggregation that is beyond the control of marketers. Consumers can now share their thoughts and feelings in online forums and consumption communities.

One particularly relevant form of consumption community, and one becoming increasingly pervasive due to the Internet and World Wide Web, is the brand community (Muñiz & O'Guinn 2001). Brand communities are specialized, non-geographically bound communities that form among users of brands. They share characteristics with more traditional conceptualizations of community, being marked by a shared consciousness, rituals, and traditions and a sense of moral responsibility, though these qualities have a particular expression owing to the commercial and mass-mediated ethos of brands. Brand communities are important participants in the brand's larger social construction and play a vital role in the brand's ultimate legacy. They have also been the site of transformative and emancipatory consumer experiences, allowing consumers to transcend and resist the market (Muñiz & Schau 2005). By sometimes accepting and amplifying marketer actions while other times rejecting them, brand communities make the brand a contested space between the marketer and the consumer. Given the brand's prominent place in modern capitalism and the assumed complicity of

modernity in the loss of community, brand communities represent an intriguing and ironic adaptation of a fundamental form of human aggregation.

Large brands, particularly global, multinational brands, have become the target of a great deal of criticism and opposition, often seen as being emblematic of and responsible for the contemporary consumer society and its impact on global and local cultures, media, the environment, and human rights. Books such as Naomi Klein's *No Logo: Taking Aim at the Brand Bullies* (1999), Kalle Lasn's *Culture Jam: The Uncooling of America* (1999), or Alissa Quart's *Branded: The Buying and Selling of Teenagers* (2003) have fostered a growing anti-branding movement that is reflected in the guerila anti-marketing actions of groups like AdBusters, the Billboard Liberation Front, and the Church of Stop Shopping. By some accounts, this opposition to brands is becoming larger and more organized. Others suggest opposition is easily co-opted by corporate brand strategy (Frank 1997).

Brands are not just names and signs. They are increasingly important cultural resources and centers of social organization. Future research on brands should continue to examine the role of consumers and their collectives in the creation of the brand experience, particularly with regard to resisting markets and marketers. More research should examine the role of the brand as a cultural resource. An emerging perspective on brands suggests that brands will be unable to continue to draw from other cultural texts (such as movies, music, celebrities, and art) as a source of brand content. Instead, this perspective asserts that brands will have to develop their own contribution as a cultural resource by providing original and relevant cultural materials with which consumers can construct their identity (Holt 2002). Future research can examine if this transformation takes place and how it impacts consumers in their personal identity projects.

SEE ALSO: Advertising; Brand Culture; Branding and Organizational Identity; Conspicuous Consumption; Consumption and the Internet; Consumption, Mass Consumption, and Consumer Culture; Culture Jamming

REFERENCES AND SUGGESTED
READINGS

Brown, S., Kozinets, R. V., & Sherry, J. F., Jr.
(2003) Teaching Old Brands New Tricks: Retro
Branding and the Revival of Brand Meaning. *Journal of Marketing* 67 (July): 19–33.
Firat, A. F. & Venkatesh, A. (1995) Liberatory Postmodernism and the Reenchantment of Consumption. *Journal of Consumer Research* 22(3):
239–67.
Fournier, S. (1998) Customers and Their Brands:
Developing Relationship Theory in Consumer
Research. *Journal of Consumer Research* 24
(March): 343–73.
Fox, S. (1984) *The Mirror Makers: A History of American Advertising and Its Creators.* Vintage, New York.
Frank, T. (1997) *The Conquest of Cool: Business Culture, Counterculture, and the Rise of Hip Consumerism.* University of Chicago Press, Chicago.
Hine, T. (1995) *The Total Package.* Back Bay Books,
Boston.
Holt, D. B. (2002) Why Do Brands Cause Trouble?
A Dialectical Theory of Consumer Culture and
Branding. *Journal of Consumer Research* 29 (June):
70–90.
Kates, S. M. (2004) The Dynamics of Brand Legitimacy: An Interpretive Study in the Gay Men's
Community. *Journal of Consumer Research* 31, 2
(September).
Keller, K. L. (1998) *Strategic Brand Management:
Building, Measuring, and Managing Brand Equity.*
Prentice-Hall, Upper Saddle River, NJ.
Low, G. S. & Fullerton, R. A. (1994) Brands, Brand
Management and the Brand Manager System.
Journal of Marketing Research 31 (May): 173–90.
Marchand, R. (1985) *Advertising: The American
Dream.* University of California Press, Berkeley.
Muñiz, A. M., Jr. & O'Guinn, T. C. (2001) Brand
Community. *Journal of Consumer Research* 27
(March): 412–32.
Muñiz, A. M., Jr. & Schau, H. J. (2005) Religiosity
in the Abandoned Apple Newton Brand Community. *Journal of Consumer Research.*
O'Guinn, T. C. & Muñiz, A. M., Jr. (2005) Communal Consumption and the Brand. In: Mick, D.
G. & Ratneshwar, S. (Eds.), *Inside Consumption:
Frontiers of Research on Consumer Motives, Goals,
and Desires.* Routledge, New York.
Schudson, M. (1984) *Advertising, The Uneasy
Persuasion.* Basic Books, New York, pp. 129–46.
Thompson, C. J. (2004) Marketplace Mythologies
and Discourses of Power. *Journal of Consumer
Research.*
Twitchell, J. B. (1999). *Lead Us Into Temptation.*
Columbia University Press, New York.

Braudel, Fernand (1902–85)

Immanuel Wallerstein

Fernand Braudel was the leading figure of the
so-called second generation of the Annales
School of historiographic tradition, a tradition
that distinguished itself from the outset by its
emphasis on what it called "total history."
Within this tradition, Braudel's work is noted
for four major emphases: (1) concern with the
unit of analysis, and in particular with a construct he called a "world-economy" (*économie-monde*); (2) analysis of social temporalities,
which he asserted to be multiple, and in particular that of the *longue durée*; (3) his insistence
on interscience, which refers to his concern
with breaking down the barriers between history and the other social sciences (sociology,
geography, political science, and economics);
and (4) an interpretation of economic life that
drew a sharp and unusual distinction between
the market and capitalism.

Braudel was a prolific author. He is known
especially for three major works, each multivolume: *The Mediterranean and the Mediterranean World in the Age of Philip II* (1972; in
French 1966); *Capitalism and Civilization,
15th–18th Centuries* (1981–4; in French 1979);
and the unfinished *Identity of France* (1988–90;
in French 1986). The exposition of his epistemological views is, however, primarily to be
found in his essays, which exist in various
collected versions.

His concept of a world-economy (*économie-monde*) is different in crucial ways from the
standard economist's term of world economy
(*économie mondiale*). A world-economy (hyphenated in English to make the distinction, which
is easier to make clear in French) is not "the
economy of the world" (seen as a collection of
nation-states) but "an economy that is a
world," that is, an integrated economic structure, involving a division of labor. Hence a
world-economy can be, and usually has been,
a geographical entity smaller than the globe.
Braudel himself sought to demonstrate this
idea in his work on the sixteenth-century

Mediterranean. By shifting the focus to a world-economy as opposed to the various political units that are located within it, Braudel was analyzing what he considered to be the effective social unit within which economic life was lived and social institutions were constructed. It was a radical shift of standpoint from which to do social science, and it has proved to be very fruitful.

In the same book on the Mediterranean in which he elaborated and used the concept of the world-economy, Braudel also introduced his notion of the multiple social temporalities. He organized the book in three parts, each viewing the Mediterranean from a different temporal standpoint, what he called in French *structure, conjoncture, événement,* or structure, cycle (not conjuncture in English), and event. Structures existed, he said, in the *longue durée.* They persisted over long periods of time and formed the frameworks within which social action occurred. In his famous epistemological manifesto, "Histoire et la longue durée" (*Annales E.S.C.,* 1958), he specifically distinguished the *longue durée* from the *très longue durée* (or eternal time), which, he said, "if it exists, must be the time of the sages." The latter is the time he associated with nomothetic social science. Structural time, by contrast, is longlasting and constraining, but it is not at all eternal (or universal, in some language conventions). Rather, it is specific to particular historical entities.

The cyclical processes which he described (*conjonctures*) were cycles *within* structures, middle term in length. Braudel thus was not endorsing the ancient and familiar idea that history is nothing but a series of cyclical processes (e.g., Vico, Toynbee, Sorokin). Rather, he was arguing that the life of historical structures was made up of continuous fluctuations or cycles (such as expansions and contractions of economic processes or demographic movements). Therefore, he insisted, in order to understand the sociopolitical happenings of a particular period within the life of a historical structure, one had to ascertain within which swing of a cycle the structure was located at that specific point of time.

And finally, of course, there were innumerable events, which were short term and idiographic. Constructing the sequence of events had traditionally been the principal grist of most historians' writings. But for Braudel, in a famous quip that he meant to be taken quite seriously, "events are dust." If we concentrate upon them, they will tell us very little because we would have missed the structures and cycles that embody the meaningful historical narrative. Events are dust in two senses: they are ephemeral (dust is easily blown away), and they distract us from the real story (dust in our eyes).

It follows from his rejection of the *very* long term (the eternal) on the one hand, and of the ephemeral short term (events) on the other, that we are pushed to being both historical (the *longue durée* but not the *très longue durée*) and systemic (structures and cycles) at the same time. This is the heart of the idea of interscience. The distinction between history on the one hand and the other social sciences on the other was, for Braudel, not only false but also deadly. It keeps us from practicing the necessary skills of combining the historic and the systematic into a single exercise. This was of course an intellectual position, and Braudel was well aware of the organizational obstacles to its realization. This is why he tried to create a Faculty of Social Sciences at the Sorbonne, in which historians as well as other social scientists would be located. This is why he constructed the faculty of the VIe Section of the École Pratique des Hautes Études out of a combination of those historians, anthropologists, sociologists, and economists who would be ready to work together. And this was the central objective of the program of the Maison des Sciences de l'Homme, of which he was the administrator.

The work, however, that has had the most impact on the world of social science was *Capitalism and Civilization.* As he organized *The Mediterranean* in three parts around three social times, he organized *Capitalism and Civilization* around the metaphor of three stories in a house. The bottom story was that of material, everyday life, the life everyone leads in all historical systems – what we eat, where we live, our kin systems, our religious practices, our modes of working and of entertaining ourselves. Above this bottom floor stands the market – a persistent, natural effort of exchanges, small and large, that enable us to maximize the consumptions of everyday life. Markets, he said, were so natural that, whenever anyone tried to suppress them, they reemerged covertly, even clandestinely, but always vigorously.

The top floor was capitalism, a floor that, unlike the market, was not inevitable and in point of fact had not always been in existence. Far from capitalism being those structures in which a (free) market existed, he insisted that capitalism was quite the opposite – the anti-market. Capitalism was the effort to monopolize economic life in order to maximize profit. Capitalism functioned by constraining the markets for the benefit of those who controlled capitalist institutions. In many ways, he saw much of history as a contest between the forces of the market and the forces of capitalism, which he envisaged as a contest between libertarian and oppressive structures.

His conception of capitalism was an upside-down one, contrasting sharply with the prevailing views of Adam Smith (and his successors) and Karl Marx (and his successors), both of whom saw competitive capitalism for the most part as the modal form of modern life, from which monopolistic tendencies were a deviation and represented either an anachronism or a distortion. Braudel, on the contrary, saw monopolistic tendencies as the defining central feature of capitalism, living on the top floor of the economic world and oppressing both the market and everyday life beneath it.

Braudel was a very active academic organizer. He succeeded Lucien Febvre as the president of the VIe Section of the École Pratique des Hautes Études in Paris, which became the principal locus of work in social science in France, and has been since renamed the École des Hautes Études en Sciences Sociales. He was the editor for almost two decades of *Annales E. S.C.* He was the founding administrator of the Maison des Sciences de l'Homme (MSH) in Paris from its beginning to his death. The MSH is a structure that combines affiliated research centers, a major social science library, and programs of international collaboration among and across the social sciences. He was the co-founder of the International Association of Economic History, and its president

(1962–5). He served for some 15 years as president of the scientific committee of the very influential *Settimana di Studi di Storia Economica*, an international structure located in Prato, Italy. He taught at the Collège de France, and he was a member of the Académie Française. In the 1960s, he sought, valiantly but unsuccessfully, to establish a faculty of social science (separate from that of Letters) at the Sorbonne.

The combination of his intellectual production (translated into over 20 languages) and his organizational work meant that his influence rippled outward throughout his life and afterwards in two senses: from France and the French-speaking intellectual world to all of Europe and the Americas, and latterly to Asia; and from the narrow disciplinary niche of economic history to other kinds of history, and to the other social sciences – sociology, anthropology, and geography in particular.

His initial links with sociology were in his long and continuous dialogue (private and public) with Georges Gurvitch. But it was with the rise of historical sociology as a major subdiscipline, particularly in the United States and Great Britain, that Braudel began to be read and appreciated extensively among sociologists. Furthermore, the last 15 years of his life coincided with both the publication of *Capitalism and Civilization* and the onset of a Kondratiev B-phase, or major cyclical downturn, in the world-economy. Suddenly, both the media and political economists began to notice the relevance of Braudel's approach to the understanding of capitalism and current happenings in the world-system. He began to be extensively interviewed by journalists about the post-1970 world. He became a living exemplar of what he had been preaching – the breaking down of the barriers between the archival work that historians traditionally have done and the work on the contemporary world of sociologists and political scientists, and latterly anthropologists as well.

Braudel felt misunderstood and disavowed, even betrayed, by his students. He often wondered about how lasting was his influence, how long his works would be read. But, like most important thinkers, it is less in the number of citations of his work by future authors that his influence is being felt than in the slow anchoring of his mode of analysis and his epistemological assumptions in the assumptions of future historical social scientists. The details of historical research are quite regularly superseded by later work. The mode with which we do our work and the spirit in which we analyze is seldom spelled out by the authors of scholarly works. It is in the tacit acceptance by many of his key concepts – the world-economy as the unit of analysis, the importance of the *longue durée*, the dubiousness of the traditional boundaries that created walls between the social sciences, and the centrality of monopoly to the analysis of capitalism – that we can measure his lasting contribution. These concepts are not yet the consensus views of the historical social sciences. But they are all on the table, and for that we must thank Braudel.

SEE ALSO: Capitalism; Gurvitch, Georges: Social Change; Kondratieff Cycles; Marx, Karl; Smith, Adam; Sorokin, Pitirim A.

REFERENCES AND SUGGESTED READINGS

Aguirre Rojas, C. A. (1992) Between Marx and Braudel: Making History, Knowing History. *Review* 15, 2 (Spring): 175–219.

Aymard, M. (1987) Fernand Braudel, the Mediterranean, and Europe. *Mediterranean Historical Review* 2, 1 (June): 102–14.

Braudel, F. (1972a) History and the Social Sciences. In: Burke, P. (Ed.), *Economy and Society in Early Modern Europe*. Routledge & Kegan Paul, London.

Braudel, F. (1972b) *The Mediterranean and the Mediterranean World in the Age of Philip II*, 2 vols. Harper & Row, New York.

Braudel, F. (1981, 1982, 1984) *Capitalism and Civilization, 15th–18th Centuries*, 3 vols. Harper & Row, New York.

Hexter, J. H. (1972) Fernand Braudel and the *Monde Braudélien* ... *Journal of Modern History* 44, 4 (December): 480–539.

Makkai, L. (1983) Ars Historica: On Braudel. *Review* 6, 4 (Spring): 435–53.

Review (1978) The Impact of the Annales School on the Social Sciences. *Review* 1, 3/4 (Winter/Spring).

Wallerstein, I. (2001) Revisiting Braudel. In: *Unthinking Social Science: The Limits of Nineteenth-Century Paradigms*, 2nd edn. Temple University Press, Philadelphia, pp. 185–226.

Braverman, Harry (1922–76)

Stephen Wood

Harry Braverman, journalist, publisher, and a director of Monthly Review Press (1967–76), is best known for his book *Labor and Monopoly Capital*, published in 1974. This helped to continue the Marxist tradition within class theory at a time when it was being debated out of sociology by a mixture of alternative theories and empirical analysis centered on the rise of the middle class and the increasingly diamond-shaped nature of the class structure, as well as by the emerging emphasis on subjectivity in sociology. It also refueled a Marxian current that had never been very strong in work sociology, which C. Wright Mills (in the late 1940s) had famously termed "cow sociology" for its instrumental, managerial emphasis on ways of improving employee performance.

The core of *Labor and Monopoly Capital* is a Marxist theory of the capitalist labor process. Marx had outlined how the development of the labor process was a key defining feature of capitalism. It was geared to profitable production, through generating more value from workers than is returned in the form of wages. The factory system had brought the worker and the labor process under the direct control of the capitalist and facilitated an ever more rapid accumulation of capital, through harnessing the detailed division of labor and the systematic, scientific study of work. This entailed a deskilling of both jobs and individuals.

In the twentieth century, assembly line work, as pioneered by Henry Ford, came to represent the paradigm case of deskilled jobs, with very short job cycles (often well under a minute) and training times. Deskilling had thus long been recognized, but with the advent of new forms of more advanced technologies (e.g., in process industries) and the increasing size of employment in service jobs (e.g., in finance and health), a belief began to emerge in the 1950s and 1960s that the number of deskilled jobs would decline. Research by Blauner in the United States (published in 1964), for example, suggested that, at higher levels of automation, higher levels of skills would be demanded. Also jobs in the expanding service sector were widely thought to require higher levels of skills and education than the average factory job.

Within this context Braverman sought to reinstate the primacy of Marx's theory of the labor process. First, he stressed the centrality of Taylor's scientific management to the development of the United States in the twentieth century. Technology is of secondary importance, as Taylorism is concerned with the control of labor at any level of technological development. Taylorism is central because it represents the rationality of capitalism: it is "the explicit verbalization of the capitalist mode of production." Second, he reinforced the connections between Taylorism, deskilling, and the demise of the craft worker. Thus he interpreted Taylor's dictat that the conception of tasks should be divorced from their execution, and management should have sole responsibility for conception, as meaning that workers would be deskilled and have no control over their work. Third, he viewed the new computerized technologies (e.g., computer numerically controlled machines) that were emerging in the 1970s as being designed to embody Taylorist principles, and hence as building the control of the worker into the machine and eliminating any remaining skills that Taylorism had failed to remove through organizational means. Fourth, he highlighted how Taylorism was being applied in the service sector and to white-collar and even administrative managerial work.

The main implication that Braverman drew out from his account of "the degradation of work in the twentieth century" (the subtitle of his book) is that deskilling remains inherent to capitalism. It has guaranteed the capitalist's control over the labor process and wage rates that maximize profits, and has meant that the working class has become homogeneous and the class structure polarized. Consequently, discussion and measures of class based on

occupational categories are wrong and accept "tailored appearances as a substitute for reality" (p. 426). In addition, attempts to supersede Taylorism, founded for example on the human relations movement's emphasis on participative management through group processes, or psychology's job redesign aimed at increasing workers' discretion, did not reverse the central tendency of capitalism. Rather than reversing Taylorism they reinforced it, as they provided the tools for managers to maintain "the human machinery" of production and habituate the worker to the dictates of capitalism.

It is hard to reconcile Braverman's thesis of a long-term trend for the degradation of the worker with the changing overall skill levels of workers over the past century and a half, not least because the majority of workers in the nineteenth century lacked basic skills such as literacy which are now (perhaps mistakenly) taken for granted. In the twentieth century the numbers of craft-type workers did not, in fact, decline to the extent implied by Braverman, and the main consequence of mass production was a whole new set of semi-skilled occupations, not the substitution of craftwork by routinized labor. Variations in the nature and extent of Taylorism between different countries highlighted by historical and comparative empirical studies also show how deskilling is not a consistent trend. For example, the relatively high skill levels in a country such as Germany may enable capitalists to develop high-quality products or services that they could not produce in other countries.

The most fundamental criticism that has been made of the deskilling thesis is that control of labor need not become an end in itself for management and the achievement of its prime objective – profitability – may not always be furthered by deskilling work. For example, the number of workers may be reduced by increasing the discretion of a smaller core workforce; and the more refined is the division of labor and the more limited the range of aptitudes possessed by individual workers, the greater are the coordination costs and problems for the organization of adjusting to fluctuating product market conditions and new technological opportunities.

Nevertheless, a key legacy of Braverman was to ensure that scientific management and its effects on workers were not increasingly treated as simply a benchmark of the first era of mass production. Much work in the twenty-first century, as in the twentieth century, remains low skilled: there have been clear cases where technology has reduced the skill level required in particular jobs and the discretion given to individuals, e.g., in engineering; and many of the jobs created in the past 20 years with the great growth in the service sector are low skilled, e.g., work in fast-food chains, though not necessarily routinized. Hochschild's conception of emotional labor also implies that the capitalist's quest for control can extend to regulating the interpersonal relations at the heart of many transactions in the service sector. Current concern for deskilled jobs particularly has focused on call centers, which are often presented, with some justification, as modern sweatshops where customer service representatives have calls automatically fed to them, deal with customers through menu-driven instructions and pre-set scripted replies, and have little or no discretion over working arrangements.

SEE ALSO: Capitalism; Class, Status, and Power; Division of Labor; Emotion Work; Fordism/Post-Fordism; Labor–Management Relations; Labor Process; Marx, Karl; Mass Production; Taylorism; Work, Sociology of

REFERENCES AND SUGGESTED READINGS

Attewell, P. (1987) The Deskilling Controversy. *Work and Occupations* 14: 323–46.

Braverman, H. (1984) *Labor and Monopoly Capital: The Degradation of Work in the Twentieth Century.* Monthly Review Press, New York.

Braverman, H. (1994) The Making of the US Working Class. *Monthly Review* (November): 14–35.

Hochschild, A. R. (1983) *The Managed Heart: Commercialization of Human Feeling.* University of California Press, Berkeley.

Thompson, P. (1999) *The Nature of Work: An Introduction to Debates on the Labour Process*, 2nd edn. Macmillan, London.

Wood, S. (Ed.) (1982) *The Degradation of Work?* Hutchinson, London.

Zimbalest, A. (Ed.) (1979) *Case Studies on the Labor Process.* Monthly Review Press, New York.

bricolage

Andrew Milner

Bricolage is a French word, with no direct equivalent in British, North American, or Australasian English. In everyday usage, it describes the work done by a bricoleur – very roughly, but not quite, a cross between an odd job man and a handyman. In the 1950s and 1960s, though less so today, its meaning carried the sense of proceeding in an apparently disorganized and non-rational fashion, but nonetheless producing effective results. It connoted the process of finding out how to make things work, not from first principles but from messing around with whatever materials were to hand. The term was introduced into the social sciences by the distinguished French anthropologist Claude Lévi-Strauss to explain the "science of the concrete" developed in neolithic times and still present in some tribal cultures. It was taken up by the philosopher Jacques Derrida, who argued that all discourse is bricolage, and by the sociologist Michel de Certeau, who saw everyday reading as a form of bricolage. In each case, it actually functions as an analogy rather than a concept. More recently, postmodern cultural studies has tended toward the view that there is something distinctively contemporary and distinctively valuable about bricolage as method.

Lévi-Strauss's *La Pensée sauvage*, first published in 1962 and later translated into English as *The Savage Mind*, is one of the classic works of structuralist anthropology. It sought to explain how "primitive" mythical thought was able to produce an impressive body of reliable knowledge about matters such as pottery, weaving, agriculture, and the domestication of animals. Lévi-Strauss insisted that this "science of the concrete" was very different from modern science, but nonetheless no less scientific in its procedures and results. Explicitly likening it to the work of the modern bricoleur, he argued that, whereas modern science uses "concepts," which aim to be wholly transparent vis-à-vis reality, bricolage and myth use "signs," which require the interposition of culture into that reality. The science of the modern engineer therefore aims in principle to go beyond the constraints imposed by culture, whilst bricolage and myth remain confined within them (Lévi-Strauss 1966: 16–20). The characteristic feature of myth and bricolage is thus that they build up structured sets "not directly with other structured sets but by using the remains and debris of events" (p. 22). Art, Lévi-Strauss continued, lies midway between modern science and myth/bricolage, for if the scientist creates events by means of structures, and the bricoleur creates structures by means of events, then the artist unifies events by revealing a common structure within them (pp. 22–6).

Derrida's famous essay "Structure, Sign and Play in the Discourse of the Human Sciences" was first published in English in 1966, but included the following year in *L'Écriture et la différence* and later in its English translation, *Writing and Difference*. He sought to deconstruct Lévi-Strauss's binary opposition between engineer and bricoleur by arguing that all discourse borrows concepts from the "text of a heritage." The notion that the engineer breaks with bricolage is thus "theological," he concluded. But if scientists and engineers are themselves also bricoleurs, then, as Derrida recognizes, "the idea of bricolage is menaced and the difference in which it took on its meaning breaks down" (Derrida 1978: 285). This characteristically poststructuralist move reduces Lévi-Strauss's own sense of "neolithic" difference to sameness, paradoxically enough in the name of difference. Moreover, not only is engineering bricolage, but so too, according to Derrida, is Lévi-Strauss's own method (p. 286). Here, the philosopher is on firmer ground, since Lévi-Strauss had indeed noted the "mythopoetical" nature of bricolage and would indeed later argue that his own studies of myth were themselves a kind of myth (Lévi-Strauss 1966: 17; Lévi-Strauss 1969: 6). This is an early example of what would later become the postmodern valorization of bricolage as method.

In the first volume of *L'Invention du quotidien*, first published in 1980 and subsequently translated into English as *The Practice of Everyday Life*, de Certeau also borrowed analogically from the art of the bricoleur. He did so at two levels. Firstly, he distinguishes between the strategies and tactics of everyday consumption in general, arguing that, whilst strategy proceeds in terms of rational means–ends relations, tactics often work by way of bricolage: combining heterogeneous elements in the manner of a decision where an opportunity is seized, as distinct from that of a rational discourse (de Certeau 1984: xviii–xix). Secondly, and more specifically, he argues that reading can be considered a form of bricolage, in which the reader "poaches" from writing. Readers are travelers, he writes: "they move across lands belonging to someone else, like nomads poaching their way across fields they did not write" (p. 174). This notion has been further explored, with special reference to television audiences, in Henry Jenkins's *Textual Poachers* (1992).

SEE ALSO: Certeau, Michel de; Deconstruction; Poststructuralism; Structuralism

REFERENCES AND SUGGESTED READINGS

Certeau, M. de (1980) *L'Invention du quotidien*. Vol. 1: *Arts de faire*. Union Générale Éditions, Paris.

Certeau, M. de (1984) *The Practice of Everyday Life*. Trans. S. Rendall. University of California Press, Berkeley.

Derrida, J. (1967) *L'Écriture et la différence*. Éditions du Seuil, Paris.

Derrida, J. (1978) *Writing and Difference*. Trans. A. Bass. University of Chicago Press, Chicago.

Lévi-Strauss, C. (1962) *La Pensée sauvage*. Plon, Paris.

Lévi-Strauss, C. (1966) *The Savage Mind*. University of Chicago Press, Chicago.

Lévi-Strauss, C. (1969) *The Raw and the Cooked*. Trans. J. & D. Wightman. Harper & Row, New York.

British Sociological Association

Jennifer Platt

The British Sociological Association (BSA), founded in 1951, is the national learned society for sociology, affiliated as such with the International Sociological Association. Starting when sociology was hardly a distinct discipline, or institutionalized within British universities, it expanded rapidly as sociology expanded, and has developed a wide range of functions. (These do not, however, as in some professional associations, include the certification of sociologists or their qualifications.) It both organizes activities for sociologists and represents them in the wider society (see the BSA website, www.britsoc.co.uk).

Initially based at, and subsidized by, the London School of Economics, then home of the only university sociology department, it now has an independent administrative office in Durham, and is funded by subscriptions and the profits from publications and conferences. Subscription rates have been related to income, reflecting egalitarian principles also shown in the strong influence of the women's movement on many aspects of its organization. Membership is open to all sociologists, and to other interested individuals in academia and elsewhere, though most members are higher education staff or students. Levels fluctuate as a proportion of Britain's academic sociologists; since 1999, total membership, including some overseas members, has been around 2,200.

The BSA's earliest activities included running study groups on specialist fields, such as sociology of education, and holding conferences; there are now over 30 study groups and an annual conference, where several hundred participants attend papers given in many parallel sessions. Its first journal, *Sociology*, started in 1967; this was followed by *Work, Employment, and Society* in 1987, and in 1996 the electronic journal *Sociological Research OnLine*; these are all intellectually and financially successful. Edited volumes of papers from most annual conferences have also been published. Since 2000, Sociology Press, supported by the BSA, publishes at low prices research monographs and edited collections chosen on academic rather than commercial grounds. A members' newsletter has appeared three times a year from 1975.

Codes of practice, on subjects such as the ethics of research practice, guidelines on non-sexist language, and postgraduate research supervision, have also been promulgated. Other activities have arisen from the felt need to respond to external situations. Initially, data were collected on employment for sociology graduates. During the growth in degree courses of the late 1960s, advice was given on syllabuses and teaching was discussed; a summer school for graduate students, especially helpful for smaller departments and part-time students, has run since 1965. When many sociology students were active in student unrest, the BSA attempted to resolve conflicts and maintain a favorable public image for sociology. When in the 1980s university funding was heavily cut, and sociology was out of favor with the government, it fought against cuts and, with other learned societies, opposed attempts to close the Social Science Research Council, the major governmental research funding body (later the Economic and Social Research Council). Over its history the BSA has liaised with that body, attempted to influence its policy, and made nominations for its committees, as it has also for other national policy initiatives such as the University Research Assessment Exercises held since 1992.

SEE ALSO: American Sociological Association; Professions, Organized

REFERENCES AND SUGGESTED READINGS

Platt, J. (2000) *The British Sociological Association: A Sociological History*. Sociology Press, Durham.

Brown v. Board of Education

David B. Bills and Erin Kaufman

The 1954 *Brown* v. *Board of Education of Topeka, Kansas* stands as the most significant Supreme Court decision in the history of American education, as well as one of the most important statements on racial equality and the relationship between various levels of American government. A half century later, the impacts and implications of *Brown* are still emerging.

Prior to *Brown*, American education followed the edict of "separate but equal," first established in the 1896 Supreme Court decision *Plessy* v. *Ferguson*. According to the Court's ruling, the denial of access to public railway accommodations did not violate the plaintiff's rights, as long as "separate but equal" accommodations were available. The Supreme Court subsequently affirmed the "separate but equal" doctrine for postsecondary education in *Berea College* v. *Kentucky* (1908). This ruling upheld the criminal conviction of officials of Berea (a private college) for allowing African American students to be educated with white students. Two decades later the Supreme Court extended the "separate but equal" doctrine to K–12 education in *Gong Lum* v. *Rice* (1927). This ruling permitted a Mississippi school to exclude a student of Chinese descent from a white school.

In the mid-1950s the practice of Jim Crow was firmly established in the Southern US. Under Jim Crow (a term believed to have originated in 1830s minstrel shows, in which whites performed racially demeaning impersonations of blacks), virtually all public spaces were rigidly and legally segregated across racial lines. The practice of Jim Crow was stringently enforced through both legal and extra-legal means, no less in public schools than in transportation, hotel accommodations, eating and drinking establishments, and the voting booth.

In the decades prior to the *Brown* decision in 1954, the National Association for the Advancement of Colored People (NAACP) supported the filing of three claims involving issues of equality in higher education. Importantly, these Supreme Court decisions served as precedent for dismantling the system of "separate but equal" that shaped the American public school system. First, *Missouri ex rel. Gaines* v. *Canada* (1938) required that states either establish separate graduate schools for African Americans or integrate them into existing ones. Lloyd Gaines, an African American man, was refused admission to the Law School at the University of Missouri. Instead of admission, the state offered to pay Gaines's tuition for law school in a neighboring state; this offer complied with Missouri state law. Gaines brought action on the grounds that the denial violated the equal protection clause of the 14th

Amendment. The Court agreed, claiming that the state's system of legal education provided white students with a privilege denied to their African American counterparts.

Second, *McLaurin* v. *Oklahoma State Regents* (1950) challenged the provision of "separate but equal" accommodations in higher education. McLaurin, an African American resident of Oklahoma, was admitted to the Graduate School of the University of Oklahoma as a doctoral candidate in education. In light of a state law requiring segregation at institutions of higher education, the University assigned McLaurin to a seat in a row designated for African American students, restricted him to a special table at the library, and, although allowed to eat in the cafeteria at the same time as other students, limited him to a special table there. The Court ruled that such conditions violated the equal protection clause of the 14th Amendment. The Court noted that the segregated conditions set McLaurin apart from his colleagues, inhibited his ability to study, and generally impaired his pursuit of a graduate degree.

Finally, *Sweatt* v. *Painter* (1950) involved equality in both the formal and the more informal elements of equality in graduate education. Petitioner Sweatt was denied admission to the University of Texas Law School, solely because the state law prohibited the admission of African Americans to the law school. Sweatt was instead offered admission to a law school that the state had established for African Americans. Sweatt filed suit on grounds that the policy violated the Equal Protection Clause of the 14th Amendment. The Court agreed, citing disparities between the two schools in terms of course offerings, opportunities for specialization, student body size, library holdings, and the availability of law review and other activities. The Court also recognized disparities in the more informal elements of legal education such as faculty reputation, the experience of the administration, influential alumni, community standings, tradition, and prestige.

Brown v. *Board of Education* was not the first legal challenge to racially segregated public schools in the US, a distinction that goes back to the 1849 case *Roberts* v. *City of Boston, Massachusetts*. It was rather the culmination of a long and concerted history of judicial challenges

(Kluger 1976). The case itself was initiated and organized by the NAACP under the leadership of Charles Hamilton Houston and later by future Supreme Court Justice Thurgood Marshall. The NAACP recruited African American parents in Topeka, Kansas for a class action suit against the local school board. African American children in Topeka were only allowed to attend designated public schools, which were strictly based on race. The case is named for plaintiff Oliver L. Brown, the father of Topeka student Linda Brown.

The Supreme Court's unanimous decision in *Brown* v. *Board of Education* overturned the "separate but equal" doctrine that had previously structured public schooling throughout the country. Chief Justice Earl Warren showed significant consensus-building skills through his ability to ensure a unanimous decision from the Court; this unanimity in turn reinforced the importance of the Court's decision. Consolidating claims from Delaware, Kansas, South Carolina, Virginia, and Washington, DC, *Brown* ruled that, even though physical facilities and other tangible elements in public schools might be equal, laws permitting or requiring racial segregation in public schools violate the equal protection clause of the 14th Amendment. According to the Court, the segregation of children in public schools on the basis of race deprives minority students of equal educational opportunities. The Court also cited the work of social scientists Kenneth and Mamie Clark as evidence that segregation on the basis of race generates in minority students an enduring feeling of inferiority about their social status. In the "doll test," for example, the Clarks used four dolls, identical except for color, to determine self-perception and racial preference among 3- to 7-year-olds. When asked which doll they preferred, the majority of the minority children chose the white doll, and they assigned positive characteristics to it. The Clarks interpreted these findings to mean that "prejudice, discrimination, and segregation" caused children to develop a sense of inferiority. Based on these findings, the Court ruled that the doctrine of "separate but equal" has no place in public education and that separate facilities are by definition unequal.

Although ordering the positive step of integration lay beyond the jurisdiction of the Court, the Court could provide direction for dismantling the system of segregation it had prohibited. *Brown* v. *Board of Education* (1955), known as *Brown II*, provided these guidelines. Stopping short of mandating a specific implementation timeline, *Brown II* ordered that communities desegregate schools "with all deliberate speed." The Court placed the primary responsibility for this process on school authorities, and it called on the lower courts to assess whether schools were making good faith efforts to desegregate.

Legal challenges to racial segregation in public schooling did not end with *Brown*, but rather continued consistently in the years following the 1954 decision (Russo 2004). In *Griffin* v. *County School Board of Prince Edward County* (1964) the Supreme Court prohibited the state of Virginia from undermining desegregation initiatives by establishing a "freedom of choice" program. Furthering this reasoning, *Green* v. *County School Board of New Kent County* (1968) provided "Green" factors for determining successful desegregation efforts, including the desegregation of facilities, faculty, and staff, extra-curricular activities, and transportation. In 1971 the influential *Swann* v. *Charlotte-Mecklenburg Board of Education* ruled that schools could use numerical ratios and quotas as starting points in their efforts to desegregate. Notably, Swann brought the issue of busing into the desegregation debate, and the decision was the last unanimous Court ruling in a major school desegregation case. In *Keyes* v. *School District No. 1, Denver, Colorado* (1973), the Court extended its focus from de jure to de facto segregation, claiming as unconstitutional not only legal segregation, but also any school board action that resulted in segregating schools.

The Court's 1974 decision in *Milliken* v. *Bradley* (*Milliken I*) contrasted its earlier, more proactive desegregation rulings. In this case, the Court ruled unconstitutional a multi-district desegregation plan in Detroit, Michigan on the grounds that it compromised the autonomy of local districts. Since this decision, the Court has shown relatively little interest in continuing to pursue cases of educational desegregation, and federal presence from local remedies has fallen considerably from its 1970s levels.

Despite waning judicial interest in an active desegregation agenda, the legacy of *Brown* v. *Board of Education* shaped later civil rights legislation (as was intended by the NAACP in bringing the case). The *Brown* decision was a critical event in the Civil Rights Movement that eventually led to the 1964 Civil Rights Act, a landmark piece of legislation that made discrimination on the basis of race, religion, sex, and other categories illegal in the US. Further, *Brown* was instrumental in laying the foundation for the 1965 Voting Rights Act, which granted African Americans the right to vote. More recently, the elimination of the "separate but equal" doctrine established by *Brown* has been important in the extension of educational opportunity to students in special education programs and to Hispanic students.

While it is difficult to overestimate the significance of *Brown*, its implementation has often been slow and uncertain. In the years after the Court handed down its decision, many opponents of desegregation responded with both open and subtle tactics of resistance. Elected politicians at all levels – congressional, gubernatorial, and mayoral – often openly defied the *Brown* decision under the doctrine of "states' rights." Resistance to the *Brown* decision was especially severe in such Southern cities as Little Rock, Arkansas, and Farmville, Virginia, although busing efforts in Northern cities, notably Boston, also met with opposition.

Along with resistance to the *Brown* decision and the Court's position on desegregation have come challenges associated with de facto segregation, which results from segregated neighborhoods and racialized housing patterns. Although some neighborhoods have become less segregated over the past decade, concentrations of African American and Latino students in metro areas help to account for the continued existence of highly segregated public schools. For example, the country's 27 largest urban school districts have lost the majority of their white students and now serve one-fourth of the country's African American and Latino students. Although white students are the most segregated group of students in the country, attending on average schools that are at least 80 percent white, Latino students are the most segregated minority group in terms of both race and poverty; many times, linguistic

segregation exacerbates this latter situation. De facto segregation also helps to explain the development of what Frankenberg et al. (2003) call apartheid schools, which enroll almost all minority students and often deal with problems of widespread poverty and limited resources.

SEE ALSO: Civil Rights Movement; Race; Race (Racism); Race and Schools; School Segregation, Desegregation; Segregation

REFERENCES AND SUGGESTED READINGS

Frankenberg, E., Lee, C., & Orfield, G. (2003) *A Multiracial Society with Segregated Schools: Are We Losing the Dream? The Civil Rights Project*. Harvard University Press, Cambridge, MA.

Kluger, R. (1976) *Simple Justice: The History of Brown v. Board of Education and Black America's Struggle for Equality*. Alfred A. Knopf, New York.

Orfield, G., Eaton, S. E., & the Harvard Project on School Desegregation (1996) *Dismantling Desegregation: The Quiet Reversal of Brown v. Board of Education*. New Press, New York.

Russo, C. J. (2004) Brown v. Board of Education at 50: An Update on School Desegregation in the US. *Education and the Law* 16: 183–9.

Buddhism

Massimiliano A. Polichetti

Buddhism is a neologism, created in Europe in the middle of the nineteenth century CE, from the Sanskrit word buddha, literally the awakened one. It is derived from an epithet attributed to Siddharta Gautama, born in Northern India – one of the dates accepted by scholars for his life being 563–483 – the bodhi, or awakening. Far from designating a man or preexisting godhead, the term buddha defines all those beings who, starting from the same conditions of common beings, succeed through their own spiritual merits in being released from worldly pains to gain eternal bliss and omniscience.

During its history, which spans at least 25 centuries, Buddhadharma – the spiritual law of the Buddha, a term which is certainly to be preferred to the western term Buddhism – has differentiated into schools which western scholars used to call the Southern school, because of its enduring presence today in Sri Lanka and Southeast Asia, and the Northern school, the Himalayan regions, Tibet, China, Mongolia, Korea, Japan, and in other parts of Asia. More appropriate denotations of these two traditions, to use Northern school terminology, are mahayana and hinayana, i.e., the great vehicle and the lesser vehicle. The word vehicle is very apt in expressing the idea of a method – religion – which becomes unnecessary once the goal of awakening is attained, but which until that moment is an indispensable tool in transcending samsara, the world of rebirths. The school which mahayana defines, in derogatory fashion, as hinayana uses other terms to describe itself, such as theravada, the followers of the elders. For the mahayana school, the ideal of holiness is embodied in the figure of the bodhisattva – the hero of awakening motivated by the ideal of bodhicitta, the altruistic thought of awakening – who continues to be reincarnated until all other beings have been saved. The theravada school urges its followers to emulate and devote themselves to the ideal of the arhat – the venerable destroyer of the enemy – who strives to attain awakening by progressively annulling the dissonant emotions (klesha) which force beings to be reborn without any possibility of choice.

Even though this is not the place to undertake an in-depth analysis of the difficult issue of the relationship between western and eastern philosophical terminologies, it should be at least pointed out that, while Buddhist philosophy in the East and Christian philosophy in the West both place the doctrine that seeks to define causes as the main foundation of their gnoseological methods, the outcomes of these pursuits differ. Christian philosophy requires an uncaused cause – a concept which originated with Greek philosophers and was given a final formalization by Aristotelian Thomism. Buddhist thought does not attempt to define a beginning in the endless chain of causes. Causes are thus considered as being generated in turn by other causes since a time with no beginning. The effects generated by any cause subsequently become causes of further effects. If it were admissible to slot Buddhist thought into the categories of the history of western philosophy, it would be classified as one of the immanentistic solutions to the gnoseological problem. In its cosmological outlook this all feeds into the consideration that no one phenomenon or event in the existential order is absolutum, independent, or self-generated, and that all are composed and produced, and thus depend on causes, parts, and conditions; in a word, they are interdependent. Furthermore, in most cases – with few exceptions, such as space – they are subject to becoming and are thus impermanent. When applied to the ought-to-be of human beings, this vision means that every behavior matters greatly: every act and every thought is destined to last forever because of the law of cause and effect (karma) and will be reproduced on an exponential scale. Karma is increased by the frequency and the regularity with which a given action is performed. Once a karmic imprint is fixed within the mental continuum (santana) of an individual, it is difficult to mitigate its results. The Buddhist goal, nirvana, is the ceasing of the uncontrolled and compelled embodiment of the mental principles. A life, this life, is just a link in the chain of samsara. Far from being a sweet hope of eternal life, samsara is the context which needs to be transcended since it holds no place for freedom, simply because of the compulsion it involves to continue to take on new forms of life as a result of the karma produced on the basis of disturbing mental factors. The reason given to explain the need to avoid rebirth is extremely straightforward and well reflects the eminently pragmatic method of Buddhadharma: even the higher types of rebirth – including humans and worldly divinities – involve discomfort. The Buddhist spiritual path has never developed a justification of a moral type for pain: it is only an alarming symptom of the perils of relying on limited concepts and realities.

In presenting himself as a model, the Buddha provides the disciple with all the indications needed to emulate him completely. This is something which occurs more through the seduction of conviction than through a process of persuasion based solely on his inscrutable superiority. The community of the emulator-disciples is called sangha, and together with the Buddha and his dharma forms, the so-called triple gem (triratna) are the foremost elements of this tradition.

Anyone who seriously undertakes to travel the path leading to nirvana realizes from the very first steps that no one else can travel this demanding path in his or her stead. All of the Buddha's teaching hinges on this premise and, as a result, the emphasis returns time and time again to the central position of individual responsibility; for the Buddha is first and foremost the master (guru) who expounds the theoretical and practical means that can be used to achieve liberation. He does not assert he is able to take upon himself the burden of the negative actions of beings, he does not take upon himself the weight of the imperfections of the world. The Buddha only points the way to be traveled by those individuals who are capable of fathoming the depths of such an acceptance of responsibility. Buddhist salvation -- to be understood, it should be recalled, as emancipation from samsara -- is mainly expressed and achieved through the teaching and the application of the Buddhadharma. The substance of the Buddha's sermon, delivered at the Deer Park in Sarnath near Varanasi in Northern India to his first five disciples, concerned the four noble truths (chatvari arya satya) which mark the real beginning of his formal preaching. These truths are defined as noble (arya) both because they were taught by the Buddha, who is noble and superior to common beings, and because they are capable of making those beings who are currently subjected to the contingencies of a conditioned existence noble and superior themselves.

The first of these truths is that of true sufferings, which are the physical and mental aggregates which arise as the result of actions defiled by disturbing mental afflictions. True suffering also includes all the activities of the mind, the speech, and the body of each ordinary being, except for the actions generated through pure spiritual aspiration and meditations. They can also be considered in positive terms as the effective understanding of the fact that all physical and mental phenomena are subject to change, birth, old age, and death and that all conditions of worldly life are unstable and devoid of the causes of lasting bliss.

The second truth is that of true origin. Origin stands for the source of suffering located in mental afflictions and the compulsive actions they cause. This truth expresses the understanding that suffering is first and foremost a condition of the mind, which unceasingly creates expectations and cravings that are regularly disappointed by the actual reality of the world. In addition, physical discomfort and pain do not correspond to the full dimension of suffering for our suffering minds, which produce all the unstable existential conditions – which as such are incapable of quenching the boundless thirst for bliss inside all beings -- and which cause future opportunities for experiencing pain.

The third truth is that of true ceasing, which teaches that two previous truths – suffering and, especially, the cause of suffering – can be eliminated. This is achieved essentially by understanding that suffering begins in the mind and then returns to the mind.

The fourth truth is that of true path or the means whereby the truth of ceasing can be attained. These means are the practice of virtue by conducting one's life intelligently and bravely, taking great care not to damage other beings, and being able to have insight into how the importance of each present moment can be usefully seized.

It is worth here considering the first of the practical effects of the Buddhist philosophical construction on human morality. The first path comprises right understanding, which translates into a realistic assessment of suffering, its origin, and the path leading to its elimination; the understanding of what is to be pursued and what is to be abandoned; the understanding of the lack of a permanent self in the person; the understanding of the mechanisms leading to rebirth, and so on. This is followed by right intentions: being able to turn the mind to positive content, such as benevolence and kindness, and to draw it away from grasping, preconceived, and mistaken opinions. Right speech: shunning lies, slander, and harsh or meaningless speech. Right conduct: refraining from taking lives, stealing, and improper sexual behavior. Right livelihood: ensuring the right standard of living for oneself and one's loved ones, without damaging others directly or indirectly. Right effort: committing oneself to being aware and detached in all circumstances. Right mindfulness: remembering to be mindful of everything done in thought, speech, and act. Right concentration: freeing oneself from all the conditions which interfere with the naturally clear state of the mind, attaining the various levels of meditational absorption, and thus achieving higher levels of knowledge such as clairvoyance.

Not only is the analysis of the link existing between form and mind the first step toward every gnoseological definition of reality as an ontological unity, but also the possibility of this analysis in itself indicates that when human beings produce works of art they are substantially shaping the subtle matter forming the plane sustaining the universal field of interaction, hence the opportunity here for some thoughts on Buddhist art. Buddhist sacred art, through whatever physical medium it is expressed, refers back to a main determining reason. The paintings, sculptures, illuminations, and many specific elements of the architecture – mainly the stupa, an impenetrable monument around which the devotee practices a circumambulating clockwise interaction – are conceived in order to be utilized as perceptible supports for a practice informed, in relation with the body–mind compound, by a non-dualistic spiritual attitude, whose complex symbolic codes, in the absence of a specific initiation to those liturgies, remain difficult to access and understand. The specific function of a Buddhist painting or sculpture is thus the one favoring concentration of mind of a contemplator on the image of a divinity, at least during the initial stages of meditation. Gradually the devotee progresses toward various levels of awareness at the end of which the necessity of considerable material support is surpassed. Buddhist sacred art thus expresses the attempt to impress in the image a vigorous mystical valency, evoked by a practitioner for effective transmission – with minimum possible variants – to another practitioner, using complex symbologies, iconogrammetric structures, and iconological codes, giving ground to the representation of extremely complex concepts. For example, the bhavachakra, the cosmological chart illustrating the six worlds of

rebirth (hell, famished spirits, animals, men, titans, worldly divinities), and the mandala, the psychocosmogram – to use the, by now, classic definition formulated by Tucci – that illustrates the subtle relations between the individual microcosmos and the universal macrocosmos.

Some fundamental ideas regarding, in different cultural environments, the transformation of something – a food, a metal – into something else draw their symbolic meaning from the process of transmutation of a human into a divinity (theosis). It would be useful in using terms like theosis to understand the description of some inner processes made by the vajrayana (the diamond-vehicle, i.e., the esoteric aspect of Buddhadharma) schools, but only when it is made clear that these terms are rooted in traditions formally, historically, and theoretically external to the esoteric aspect of Buddhadharma, a lore in which the ontological gap between a god-creator and the creatures simply does not exist. In the Buddhist Indo-Tibetan tradition, the mahayana–vajrayana lineages preserve till today some systems – called tantra – promising shortcuts toward awakening with an altruistic aim. In some rites related to those systems, the performers, in order to assure the correct execution of the rite itself, are requested to divinize themselves from the beginning of the liturgy. The human body in this context is considered akin to the chrysalis from which one day the angelic butterfly will be released. This is certainly not a marginal idea within the culture it has occurred in over the course of time, but rather an instrumental notion, a thirst for improvement to be made use of on the path of transformation which humans travel over time in order to attain the full achievement of their natural potential. This can be done by actualizing the so-called divine pride (devamana), in the periodic training of remembering the divinity (devanusmrtianupurvaprayoga) admitted by the formal practice (sadhana) of the esoteric resultant vehicle (phalayana), or tantrayana, opposed to the exoteric causal vehicle (hetuyana), also called vehicle of perfections (paramitayana) or sutrayana. In the Indo-Tibetan vajrayana the various psychic essences constitute indeed a sort of synapsis between the physiological and visible part of the person and the intellectual, invisible one. These essences are described according to different functional valences. Also the fluids and the tissues, like blood, are not only simple objects to be mentally analyzed but sacramental substances. The concept of the transformation of blood into the nectar of immortality (Sanskrit: *amrta*; Greek: *ambrotos*) draws its symbolic validity from the process of transmutation of a human into a divinity. Eventually, this process will lead to the actual divinization of the practitioner (sadhaka) himself. The transformation of the ordinary human being into a blissful and omniscient divinity is an idea not condivisible by the Semitic theological frame shared by Jews, Christians, and Muslims. Also if some particular details inside the Abrahamic revelations seem to point toward the divinization of creatures – *diis estis* (you'll be gods) in the Old Testament – these aspects remain nevertheless mainly marginal by referring to the most orthodox connotation. The ritual transformation of the time and space context is widely used in Indo-Tibetan vajrayana, the structure of which thought hinges both on sympathetic compassion (karuna) and on intuitive understanding (prajna) of the ultimate mode of existing (shunyata). Karuna and prajna enable the adept to make full use of the workings of the liberated mind, so as to be able to overcome the cycle of unconscious rebirths and become an awakened one, a buddha released from any conditioning, free from failing to identify himself with the unmeasurable order of consciousness, and thus finally able to effectively do the welfare of all transmigrating beings. It is always useful to interpret these psycho-experimental systems in light of the dual focus of sympathetic compassion and vision of the truth, in considering the effect of tantric systems both on metaphysics and on morality.

Since its historical beginning, the Buddhadharma has been a doctrine that assumes a lifestyle characterized by challenging social renunciations. But the need to spread the practice of virtue to everyone led to the definition of a lay path, which does not require the integral renunciation of social activities. Furthermore, in the vajrayana some daily ceremonies are recommended or compulsory for everyone, not only for monks. These ceremonies or rites are today taught also in western countries. On one hand, the greed for tangible goods pushed modern contemporary western humanity to strive hard for the satisfaction of material needs. On the other hand, the reminiscence of a blissful homeland, set in some afterlife, persists as a background sound in urbanized reality. The novelty is that the Christian churches, even in the areas where they are deep-rooted, are not considered any longer as holders of all paths to wisdom. The adaptation and rooting of Buddhist esoteric lore in the western cultural milieu are still in progress, thus their practical results are still unforeseeable.

SEE ALSO: Religion; Religion, Sociology of

REFERENCES AND SUGGESTED READINGS

Davidson, R. M. (2002) *Indian Esoteric Buddhism: A Social History of the Tantric Movement*. Columbia University Press, New York.

Hopkins, J. (1983) *Meditation on Emptiness*. Wisdom Publications, London.

Huntington, S. L. (1985) *The Art of Ancient India: Buddhist, Hindu, Jain*. Weather-Hill, New York and Tokyo.

Phra Prayuth, Paytto (1995) *Buddhadharma: Natural Laws and Values for Life*. SUNY Press, Albany, NY.

Polichetti, M. A. (1993) The Spread of Tibetan Buddhism in the West. *Tibet Journal* 18(3): 65–7.

Schumann, H. W. (1982) *Der historische Buddha*. Diederichs, Cologne.

Tenzin, Gyatso (XIV Dalai, Lama) (1995) *The World of Tibetan Buddhism: An Overview of its Philosophy and Practice*. Wisdom Publications, Boston.

Williams, P. (1998) *Mahayana Buddhism: The Doctrinal Foundations*. Routledge, London.

built environment

Joel A. Devine

At its most basic level, the built environment refers to all elements of the human-made physical environment, i.e., it is defined in contrast to the natural environment. Dunlap and Catton's (1983) distinction between the "built," the "modified," and the "natural" environments is heuristically useful inasmuch as it more readily acknowledges the intermediate, mediative, and continuous possibilities of inter-action and reciprocal relations between and among these divisions. Given its essentially con-trast-dependent definition, it is not surprising that the term has become increasingly in vogue in the era of environmental consciousness.

Usage varies widely and not always consis-tently across disciplines depending on the con-creteness (pun intended) of the application, chosen placement along a micro–macro conti-nuum, and over time. Within the engineering professions the phrase typically references infrastructural elements, components, support activities, technology, and/or systems as in, for example, the vast network of roads, rails, bridges, depots, and support facilities that enable the circulation of persons and/or things, i.e., the transportation infrastructure. Similarly, the "built environment" is used to capture the complex of activities, technologies, practices, and structures implicated in the generation, transmission, and delivery of energy and other utilities (e.g., water, sewerage, sanitation, com-munication, and information).

Among the building trade professions and many applied architects and designers, usage also is often somewhat narrowly focused on site planning, design, and materials as well as the properties, mix, and juxtapositions thereof. Aesthetic and functional considerations are sali-ent as well. Alternatively, numerous architects, planners, urban designers, and developers, as well as members of allied professions, employ the phrase with a more inclusive, extensive, and often more macro orientation. While not neces-sarily eschewing the aforementioned foci, this usage necessarily entails a somewhat larger, more aggregate, and decidedly urban perspec-tive and is necessarily relational inasmuch as it includes consideration of how the intended development of structures, utilities, services, functions, space (in its undeveloped, partially developed, and/or wholly developed forms), and the attendant ambience and aesthetics inter-face with either extant design and usage or among a plurality of objects. In practice, this contextualization may range from a single site and its immediate environment to far larger aggregations such as a housing tract, industrial park, mixed development, neighborhood, city, region, or even national policy. Inasmuch as this

is a developmental process, temporal as well as spatial considerations may figure prominently.

The above-mentioned sensibilities continue to be highly relevant and have been institutio-nalized in the United Kingdom in the Centre for Education in the Built Environment (CEBE), one of 24 subject centers forming the Higher Education Academy, and the Commis-sion for Architecture and Built Environment (CABE). At the same time, the term "built environment" has also evolved in a more expansive, holistic, integrative direction that extends well beyond the traditional applications and disciplinary boundaries. The latter argu-ably owes to an increasing appreciation of the complexities, interactions, and interdependen-cies characterizing urbanism amidst the back-drop of globalism, but also has resulted from extensive cross-fertilization with the social sciences (including the so-called "new geogra-phy"). Over the past 20 years, much of this newer sensibility has been recast by the dis-course of postmodernism.

While ultimately interconnected and often explicitly recognized as such, two broad sets of analytically distinguishable themes are espe-cially prominent within this emergent multidis-ciplinary sensibility. The first may be thought of as the environmental imperative. It concerns issues of urban development, livability, and sustainability and addresses effects and conse-quences of the built environment (*qua* urbani-zation) on the natural environment (or aspects thereof). Within this genre, substantial subli-teratures focus on the implications of a variety of developmental practices on the health of the natural environment writ large as well as the consequences for particular flora and fauna (e.g., sprawl vis-à-vis habitat destruction; auto emissions and climate change; population den-sity and air, water, and ground contamina-tion; green space and quality of life).

The second thematic set concerns the influ-ence of the built environment in shaping human behavior and vice versa. Hence, it is not surprising that it is in this realm that the linkage between sociology and the built environment is manifest most dramatically. Lynch's pioneering work on mapping and meaning in 1960 represents a critical early watershed in this emerging behavioral orienta-tion, one subsequently superseded by an increasingly subtle and dynamic sensitivity regarding the behavioral, cognitive, and social relational aspects of the built environment. Within this broad framework, the built environment and the attendant concepts of space and spatial practices have shifted from (epiphenomenal) status as marker of location to one of central theoretical concern now understood as both a reflection (consequence) and conditioner (determinant) of social relations.

Often exhibiting substantial interdisciplinarity as well as formidable diversity with respect to theoretical orientation and methodological practices, a considerable array of subgenres flourish under this broad rubric. Among these, a focus on the built environment as: interactional constraint and enabler; as place, heritage, historical and cultural identifier; as non-verbal (semiotic) communications; and as a source and resource of contention and conflict.

SEE ALSO: City Planning/Urban Design; Environment and Urbanization; Lefebvre, Henri; Urban Political Economy; Urban Space

REFERENCES AND SUGGESTED READINGS

Crysler, C. G. (2003) *Writing Spaces: Discourses of Architecture, Urbanism, and the Built Environment, 1960-2000.* Routledge, New York.

Dear, M. (1986) Postmodernism and Planning. *Environment and Planning D: Society and Space* 4: 367–84.

Dunlap, R. E. & Catton, W. R. (1983) What Environmental Sociologists Have in Common (Whether Concerned with "Built" or "Natural Environments"). *Sociological Inquiry* 53(2/3): 113–35.

Giddens, A. (1985) Time, Space and Regionalism. In: Gregory, D. & Urry, J. (Eds.), *Social Relations and Spatial Structures.* St. Martin's Press, New York, pp. 265–95.

Goss, J. (1988) The Built Environment and Social Theory: Towards an Architectural Geography. *Professional Geographer* 40(4): 392–403.

Hinkle, L. E., Jr. & Loring, W. C. (1977) *Effect of the Man-Made Environment On Health and Behavior: A Report of the Inter-University Board of Collaborators.* CDC, Atlanta.

Lefebvre, H. (1991) *Critique of Everyday Life.* Verso, New York.

Schultz, M. S. & Kasen, V. L. (1984) *Encyclopedia of Community Planning and Environmental Management.* Facts on File, New York.

Urry, J. (2001) The Sociology of Space and Place. In: Blau, J. R. (Eds.), *The Blackwell Companion to Sociology.* Blackwell, Malden, MA, pp. 3–15.

bureaucracy and public sector governmentality

Stewart Clegg

While bureaucracy stretches back into antiquity, especially the Confucian bureaucracy of the Han dynasty, the modern rational legal conception of bureaucracy emerged in France in the eighteenth century. Indeed, the word is French in origin: it compounds the French word for an office – *bureau* – with the Greek word for rule. In the nineteenth century, Germany provided the clearest examples of its success because of the development of a disciplined bureaucracy and standing army, inventions that became the envy of Europe.

Bureaucratic organization depends above all on the application of "rational" means for the achievement of specific ends. Techniques would be most rational where they were designed purely from the point of view of fitness for purpose. Max Weber, the famous German \sociologist, defined bureaucracy in terms of 15 major characteristics: (1) power belongs to an office and not the office holder; (2) authority is specified by the rules of the organization; (3) organizational action is impersonal, involving the execution of official policies; (4) disciplinary systems of knowledge frame organizational action; (5) rules are formally codified; (6) precedent and abstract rule serve as standards for organizational action; (7) there is a tendency toward specialization; (8) a sharp boundary between bureaucratic and particularistic action defines the limits of legitimacy; (9) the functional separation of tasks is accompanied by a formal authority structure; (10) powers are precisely delegated in a hierarchy; (11) the delegation of powers is expressed in terms of duties, rights, obligations, and responsibilities specified in contracts; (12) qualities required for organization positions are increasingly measured in terms of formal credentials; (13) there is a career structure with promotion either by seniority or merit; (14) different positions in the hierarchy are differentially paid and otherwise stratified; (15) communication, coordination, and control are centralized in the organization.

Weber identified authority, based on rational legal precepts, as the heart of bureaucratic organizations. Members of rational bureaucracies obey the rules as general principles that can be applied to particular cases, and which apply to those exercising authority as much as to those who must obey the rules. People obey not the person but the office holder.

Weber saw modern bureaucratic organizations as resting on a number of "rational" foundations. These include the existence of a "formally free" labor force; the appropriation and concentration of the physical means of production as disposable private property; the representation of share rights in organizations and property ownership; and the "rationalization" of various institutional areas such as the market, technology, and the law. The outcome of processes of rationalization was the production of a new type of person: the specialist or technical expert. Such experts master reality by means of increasingly precise and abstract concepts. Statistics, for example, began in the nineteenth century as a form of expert codified knowledge of everyday life and death, which could inform public policy. The statistician became a paradigm of the new kind of expert, dealing with everyday things but in a way that was far removed from everyday understandings. Weber sometimes referred to the results of this process as disenchantment, meaning the process whereby all forms of magical, mystical, traditional explanation are stripped from the world, open and amenable to the calculations of technical reason.

Bureaucracy is an organizational form consisting of differentiated knowledge and many different forms of expertise, with their rules and disciplines arranged not only hierarchically in regard to each other, but also in parallel. If you moved through one track, in theory, you need not know anything about how things were done in the other tracks. Whether the bureaucracy was a public or private sector organization would be largely immaterial. Private ownership might enable you to control the revenue stream, but day-to-day control would be done through the intermediation of experts. And expertise is always fragmented. This enables the bureaucracy to be captured by expert administrators, however democratic its mandate might be, as Michels's studies of trade union bureaucracy established. Bureaucracy in the nineteenth century was largely identified with public sector management, yet as private enterprises grew in size they adopted the classical traits of bureaucracy as well as innovating some new elements.

Weber constituted an idea of bureaucracy conceived in terms of liberal ideals of governance. Hence, the characterization of bureaucracy as rule without regard for persons premised on a democratic ideal against blandishments of power and privilege was both a moral and abstractedly ideal empirical description, which, for much of the twentieth century, stood as a proximate model of what public sector responsibility was founded upon. Nonetheless, criticisms of bureaucracy have been legion, perhaps best captured in the exquisite command of the rules of the bureaucratic game shown by the participants in the British television comedy series *Yes, Prime Minister*.

The criticisms of bureaucracy suggested that it was not so much rational as incremental; it enabled exploitation of uncertainty for sectional benefit; it generated both individual and organizational pathology; and it suffered from segmentalism, where many employees in strictly formal bureaucracies displayed a relative disinterest in the broader conduct of organizational life. The process of reform of bureaucracy seeks to ascribe new norms of authority in the governmental relation between members in the hierarchy. Chief among its methods has been the application of new design principles to the classical bureaucracies whose qualities Weber captured in his model; they have been reengineered to achieve greater efficiencies. A major mechanism is the removal of a bureaucratic ethos and its replacement with a cost-cutting mentality – in the guise of efficiency – which elevates one dimension of public sector management above all other considerations. Outputs increasingly come to be defined and measured and performance-based orientations developed toward them. These changes are often associated with the widespread development of contracting out in the public sector, as market-testing principles are introduced: what was previously internal work organized according to hierarchy increasingly has to be contracted out to the cheapest provider. The main contemporary mechanisms for reforming public sector bureaucracy have been privatization of government-owned assets and the outsourcing of specific activities. The specialist skills brought by the outsourcing service provider take elements of government's back office into the front office of the service provider. By moving some elements from intraorganizational to contractual control, increased efficiency occurs. The modern tendency is for markets increasingly to replace bureaucratic hierarchies. These "new organizational forms" are attracting considerable contemporary attention as changed paradigms for management.

As the designs of bureaucracy were changing, so too were the mentalities of those who occupied them. If the Weberian bureaucrat valued ethos, character, and vocation, the contemporary bureaucrat is expected to be enterprising. To capture the sense of new forms of government and mentality, the French theorist Michel Foucault came up with a neologism, governmentality, based on the semantic merger of government with "mentality." He was pointing to a fusion of new *technologies* of government with a new political *rationality*. "Governmentality" refers both to the new institutions of governance in bureaucracies and to their effects. These effects are to make problematic whole areas of government that used to be accomplished through the public sector, seamlessly regulated by bureaucratic rules; now they are moved into calculations surrounding markets. Foucault defines government as a specific combination of governing techniques and rationalities, typical of the modern, neoliberal period. Bureaucracies, rather than regulating conduct, now enable individuals in civil society to act freely through markets to get things done, in normatively institutionalized ways governed increasingly by standards, charters, and other codes, and public administrators to recreate themselves as entrepreneurial actors.

SEE ALSO: Bureaucratic Personality; Governmentality and Control; Rational Legal Authority; Weber, Max

REFERENCES AND SUGGESTED READINGS

Du Gay, P. (2000) *In Praise of Bureaucracy: Weber, Organization, Ethics.* Sage, London.
Foucault, M. (1977) *Discipline and Punish: The Birth of the Prison.* Allen & Lane, London.
Weber, M. (1978) *Economy and Society: An Outline of Interpretive Sociology.* University of California Press, Berkeley.

bureaucratic personality

Christopher W. Allinson

An important factor in the development of human personality during adulthood is the influence of the work organization. A long-standing concern among social scientists in this respect has been the impact of bureaucracy. Max Weber, in his classic description of bureaucracy, observed that the individual may become little more than a cog in the bureaucratic machinery, a process explained by Karl Mannheim in terms of *functional rationalization*: the idea that a sequence of actions is organized in such a way that it leads to a previously determined goal with every action in the sequence receiving a functional role. This has important outcomes for the individual, as it eventually induces *self-rationalization* or training to a specific psychological disposition. In extreme cases, this may amount to cognitive restructuring.

The seminal account of this process was that of Robert Merton. He suggested that the values and attitudes necessary for the bureaucratic official to make a useful contribution are embraced to such a degree that the needs of the organization become secondary to the workings of the bureaucracy itself. This is explained to some extent by Veblen's concept of *trained incapacity*: actions based on skills that have proved effective previously continue to be applied even though they lead to unsuitable responses in altered circumstances. This is similar to Dewey's idea of *occupational psychosis*: as a result of the demands of the organization of their occupational roles, people develop particular predilections, biases, and priorities that may hamper the effective execution of their work. Merton contended that attention switches from the goals of the organization to the details of the control system. Rules become ends in themselves rather than means to ends, and are applied in a ritualistic manner regardless of circumstances. Rigid compliance with formal procedures, and a punctilious insistence on observing regulations, may cause the bureaucrat to lose sight of what really needs to be done. Behavior becomes so rule oriented that it is impossible to satisfy clients, thus giving rise to the pejorative connotations of impersonality and petty officialdom so commonly associated with bureaucracy. Although Victor Thompson denied that this kind of behavior (which he described as *bureaupathic*) is associated with any one type of person, Merton, like Mannheim, saw the bureaucrat as having internalized an externally rationalized order that yields a relatively stable pattern of stimulus–response connections. This pattern is widely regarded as constituting personality.

Merton observed that the sentiments associated with the bureaucratic personality emanate from several sources. One is the bureaucrat's career structure. Rewards resulting from conformity, such as regular salary increases and pension benefits, cause the individual to overreact to formal requirements. Moreover, fixed progression keeps competition between colleagues to a minimum, and encourages an esprit de corps that often takes on a higher priority than work objectives. Another is the tendency for bureaucratic procedures to become "sanctified," the official performing them in an impersonal manner according to the demands of the training manual rather than the requirements of individual cases. Additionally, administrators are so mindful of their organizational status that they often fail to discard it when dealing with clients, thus giving the impression of a domineering attitude.

It is frequently argued that the behavior associated with the bureaucratic personality derives from personal insecurity. Several sources of insecurity in the work context have been identified in the literature. An important factor is fear of superiors. Afraid of being blamed for violation of rules, bureaucrats often apply them to the letter, even when discretion is needed. Similarly, there may be fear of specialists. They have to be trusted to employ their skills properly, and the anxieties emerging from possible mistrust may lead to an inflated tendency on the part of the bureaucrat to control and ritualize. There may also be fear of inadequacy. This can be ameliorated by the ritual performance of quite simple activities, with officials finding comfort in familiar routines. A further problem is fear of uncertainty. A typical response is conformity to the demands of the system by following rules, and documenting that they have been followed, and offloading ambiguous responsibilities. Finally, there is fear of failure. Doubt over whether or not one is destined for career success may lead to exaggerated attempts to appear conscientious and conformist.

The traditional stereotype is that the bureaucratic personality is most prevalent among those employed in government agencies and other public sector organizations. This may be due to a perception that higher accountability and goal ambiguity in the public sector prompt more formal, rule-based controls than are necessary in private organizations. Empirical evidence, however, suggests otherwise. Several recent studies found that private sector managers (mostly in business firms) expressed greater commitment to rules and procedures than did their public sector counterparts. A possible explanation for this may be that private companies more closely resemble the structured, decentralized bureaucracies characteristic of Weber's classic description than do those in the public sector.

SEE ALSO: Bureaucracy and Public Sector Governmentality; Mannheim, Karl; Merton, Robert K.; Rational Choice Theories; Weber, Max

REFERENCES AND SUGGESTED READINGS

Allinson, C. W. (1984) *Bureaucratic Personality and Organization Structure*. Gower, Aldershot.

Mannheim, K. (1940) *Man and Society in an Age of Reconstruction*. Harcourt, Brace, & World, New York.

Merton, R. K. (1940) Bureaucratic Structure and Personality. *Social Forces* 18: 560–8.

Thompson, V. A. (1961) *Modern Organization*. Alfred A. Knopf, New York.

Weber, M. (1947) *The Theory of Economic and Social Organization*. Ed. A. M. Henderson & T. Parsons. Free Press, Glencoe, IL.

Burundi and Rwanda (Hutu, Tutsi)

René Lemarchand

There is more to Rwanda and Burundi than the arcane histories of two overpopulated (7 million each), poverty-stricken micro-states in the heart of the African continent: their minute size belies the magnitude of the tragedies they have suffered. The first will go down in history as the site of one of the biggest genocides of the last century, resulting in the systematic killing of an estimated 800,000 people, mostly Tutsi, in a hundred days from April to July 1994. The second lives on in the collective memory of the survivors as a forgotten genocide: who today remembers that in 1972, between 200,000 and 300,000 Hutu were massacred at the hands of a predominantly Tutsi army?

Behind these horror stories lies a sociological puzzle: although Rwanda and Burundi have more in common than any other two states in the continent, in terms of size, traditional institutions, ethnic maps, language, and culture, they have followed radically different trajectories, one (Rwanda) ending up as a republic under Hutu control at the time of independence (1962), the other (Burundi) as a constitutional monarchy under Tutsi rule. Not until 1965 did the army abolish the monarchy. And while both experienced genocide, the victims in each state belonged to different communities – predominantly Tutsi in Rwanda and overwhelmingly Hutu in Burundi. Today Rwanda has emerged as a thinly disguised Tutsi dictatorship, while Burundi is painstakingly charting a new course toward a multiparty democracy.

The key to the puzzle lies in history. Sometimes referred to as "the false twins" of the continent, traditional Burundi was far from being a carbon copy of Rwanda. In neither state is ethnic conflict reducible to age-old enmities, yet the Hutu–Tutsi split was far more pronounced and therefore potentially menacing in Rwanda than in Burundi. In contrast with the rigid pattern of stratification found in Rwanda, where the "premise of inequality" formed the axis around which Hutu–Tutsi relations revolved, Burundi society was more complicated and hence more flexible. The monarchy was conspicuously weak compared to its Rwanda counterpart, and real holders of power were the princes of the blood (ganwa) rather than centrally appointed chiefs and subchiefs. Although both states crossed the threshold of independence at the same time (July 1962), they did so under very different circumstances: while Rwanda had already gone through the throes of a violent Hutu-led, Belgian-abetted revolution (1959–62), Burundi was relatively free of ethnic tension. The focus of conflict had little to do with Hutu and Tutsi, involving instead political rivalries between the two principal ganwa-led factions, Bezi and Batare.

The years immediately following independence saw a drastic transformation of the parameters of conflict, where the Rwanda model took on the quality of a self-fulfilling prophecy in Burundi. As many Hutu elites in Burundi increasingly came to look to Rwanda as the exemplary polity, growing fears spread among the Tutsi population of an impending Rwanda-like revolution. Unless Hutu claims to power were resisted, they would share the fate of their Rwandan kinsmen. This meant a more or less systematic exclusion of Hutu elements from positions of authority. Exclusion led to insurrection, and insurrection to repression. The first act of insurrection came in 1965, shortly after Hutu candidates were denied the fruit of their electoral victory. An abortive Hutu-led coup by gendarmerie officers led to the arrest and execution of scores of Hutu leaders, and the flight to Europe of the panic-stricken king Mwambutsa, leaving the throne vacant. Another major purge of Hutu leaders occurred in 1969, after rumors spread of an impending Hutu plot against the government. The crunch came in April 1972 in the wake of a localized

Hutu insurrection. The government responded by the wholesale slaughter of all educated Hutu elites, and potential elites, including secondary school children. An estimated 200,000 Hutu – some Tutsi analysts claim 300,000 – died in the course of what must be seen as the first recorded genocide in independent Africa. From 1972 to 1993, when the first multiparty legislative and presidential elections were held since independence, the state and the army remained firmly in Tutsi hands.

There are obvious differences between the Rwanda genocide and the Burundi bloodbath, in terms of scale, target group, and circumstances. The killings in Rwanda came about in the wake of a long and bitter civil war (1990–4), triggered by the invasion of Tutsi exiles from Uganda on October 1, 1990. There was nothing in Burundi comparable to the virulent anti-Tutsi media campaign organized by Hutu extremists, and the central role played by Hutu youth groups, the infamous *interahamwe*, in planning and organizing the killings. Most importantly, in Rwanda the killers were eventually defeated by the Tutsi-dominated Rwandan Patriotic Front (FPR); in Burundi, by contrast, they came out on top, in full control of the army and the government. Yet there are parallels as well, in that both were retributive genocides, occurring in response to perceived threats; in each case the army and the *jeunesses* were the driving force behind the killings; and in Rwanda as in Burundi the post-genocide state emerged stronger than before, and ethnically homogeneous.

A critical turning point in post-genocide Burundi came with the 1993 elections, and the short-lived tenure in office of Melchior Ndadaye, the first popularly elected Hutu president of Burundi. His assassination by a group of army officers on October 21, 1993, unleashed a violent civil war, from which the country is only barely recovering. An estimated 300,000 people died in the course of what some referred to as a genocide in slow motion. The power-sharing agreement negotiated at the Arusha conference (1998–2000) did not bring an end to ethnic and factional violence – to this day, a small, militant Hutu-dominated faction, the Forces Nationales de Libération (FNL), continues to engage in sporadic attacks against civilians – but it did pave the way for a major

political turnaround, by substantially reducing the scale of violence, putting in place a three-year transitional government consisting of an equal number of Hutu and Tutsi, and by taking the constitutional, legislative, and administrative steps required for holding multiparty legislative and presidential elections in April 2005. Not the least significant of such measures is the allocation to Hutu and Tutsi candidates of respectively 60 and 40 percent of the seats in the legislature and the government to Hutu candidates, and the restructuring of the army on a 50/50 share of officers' positions.

The contrast with post-genocide Rwanda could not be more striking. The recognition of ethnic identities is central to an understanding of the pluralistic character of the emergent Burundi polity; in Rwanda, the elimination of such identities by decree is no less important to appreciate the extent of the transformations enforced by the Kagame regime. There are no Hutu or Tutsi in today's Rwanda, only Rwandans, or Banyarwanda. Yet at no time in its violent history has Rwanda been more thoroughly dominated by Tutsi elements, or, more specifically, Tutsi from Uganda. Tutsi survivors, the so-called *rescapés*, are systematically excluded from positions of authority. The Hutu are at the bottom of the heap, not just politically but socially and economically. The depth of inequality between Hutu and Tutsi is without precedent in colonial or precolonial history. To hold the regime responsible for ethnic discrimination makes no sense, however, since Hutu and Tutsi no longer exist, officially at least, as separate ethnic categories.

By the criteria normally used by political scientists to define a regime as totalitarian (an official ideology, a single political party, a centrally directed economy, governmental control of mass communications, party control of the military, and a secret police), Rwanda qualifies as one of the few totalitarian states in existence in Africa, and the only one in which an ethnic minority representing 15 percent of the population holds unfettered control over the state, the media, the economy, and the armed forces. It is also one of the largest recipients of foreign assistance per capita, and thanks to the generosity of the international community it boasts one of the largest armies in the continent (approximately 75,000 men). Last but not least, it is the only country on the continent that has invaded a neighboring state – the Congo – on three different occasions, looted its mineral wealth, and used its influence to manipulate client factions – all of the above without incurring effective sanctions from the international community.

Rwanda's claim that its security is threatened by the presence in the Congo of former *génocidaires*, though not unfounded, is greatly exaggerated. But it serves as a convenient pretext to carve out a major sphere of influence in a vitally important swath of territory in its neighbor to the west. In the past the histories of Rwanda and Burundi were closely interconnected. Today, the destinies of the three states that once formed Belgian Africa are more closely intertwined than at any time in history, past or present.

SEE ALSO: Ethnic Cleansing; Genocide; Holocaust; Tribalism; Truth and Reconciliation Commissions

REFERENCES AND SUGGESTED READINGS

Eltringham, N. (2004) *Accounting for Horror: Post-Genocide Debates in Rwanda*. Pluto, London.
Jones, B. (2001) *Peacemaking in Rwanda: The Dynamics of Failure*. Lynne Rienner, Boulder, CO.
Kuper, L. (1985) *The Prevention of Genocide*. Yale University Press, New Haven.
Lemarchand, R. (1994) *Burundi: Ethnic Conflict and Genocide*. Cambridge University Press, Cambridge.
Prunier, G. (1998) *The Rwanda Crisis: History of a Genocide*. Columbia University Press, New York.